MW00780693

The German Army
in the
Spring Offensives
1917

Respectfully dedicated by gracious permission to
HRH The Duke of Kent KG
who at Sandhurst, many years ago,
guided my first footsteps as a soldier.

By the same author:

The German Army on the Somme 1914 – 1916
The German Army at Passchendaele
The German Army on Vimy Ridge 1914 -1917
The German Army at Cambrai
The German Army at Ypres 1914
The German Army on the Western Front 1915
The Germans at Beaumont Hamel
The Germans at Thiepval

With Nigel Cave:

The Battle for Vimy Ridge 1917
Le Cateau
Ypres 1914: Langemarck
Ypres 1914: Messines
Ypres 1914: Menin Road

The German Army in the Spring Offensives 1917

Arras, Aisne and Champagne

by

Jack Sheldon

Pen & Sword
MILITARY

First published in Great Britain in 2015
PEN AND SWORD MILITARY
An imprint of
Pen & Sword Books Ltd
47 Church Street
Barnsley
South Yorkshire, S70 2AS

ISBN 978 1 78346 345 9

A CIP catalogue record for this book is
available from the British Library.

Printed and bound in England by
CPI Group (UK) Ltd, Croydon, CR0 4YY

Typeset in Times by CHIC GRAPHICS

Pen & Sword Books Ltd incorporates the imprints of Aviation, Atlas,
Family History, Fiction, Maritime, Military, Discovery, Politics,
History, Archaeology, Select, Wharncliffe Local History, Wharncliffe
True Crime, Military Classics, Wharncliffe Transport, Leo Cooper,
The Praetorian Press, Remember When, Seaforth Publishing and
Frontline Publishing.

For a complete list of Pen & Sword titles please contact
PEN & SWORD BOOKS LIMITED
47 Church Street, Barnsley, South Yorkshire, S70 2AS, England
E-mail: enquiries@pen-and-sword.co.uk
Website: www.pen-and-sword.co.uk

Contents

Introduction

A t the turn of the year 1916/17, the Allies had good reason to be confident about the future course of the war. They had inflicted huge casualties on the German army at Verdun and on the Somme; and although their own losses had been heavy and they had come nowhere near to breaking the German army, nevertheless, their greater manpower reserves meant that it was far easier for them than for the Central Powers to replenish worn down formations and create new ones. On the industrial front, despite the fact that the Hindenburg Plan (which was also making great demands on German male manpower) was beginning to get into its stride, the Allies were also pulling ahead in the battle to produce larger and larger quantities of guns, aircraft and munitions. None of the Allied leaders or military commanders was under any illusion about the size and complexity of the task which lay before them, but they were unanimous in their agreement forged at Chantilly in November 1916 to launch a major combined offensive aimed at the shoulders of the giant German salient between the Somme and the Oise. This was intended to be mounted in irresistible force, to break through the German defences swiftly and to eject that army from all the territory it had captured in the west.

For the Germans it was a time of intensive operational analysis and a switch of emphasis towards the Western Front. The situation in the east was still far from decided, but it was clear that the intensity of campaigning had slackened, so that the necessity to maintain co-located headquarters with the Austro-Hungarian high command was less pressing. Kaiser Karl moved his headquarters to Baden bei Wien, between Vienna and Wiener Neustadt, whilst the Germans, retaining the possibility of using Pleß at some future date, physically moved westwards, so as to be nearer the main threat. It was assessed that further attacks were likely in all theatres of operations, including the Isonzo front in Italy, and that the Allies enjoyed a superiority in manpower and materiel of at least sixty percent overall. Importantly, the British, who up until then had lagged well behind the French in heavy artillery, had increased the numbers available at the front from 761 in July 1916 to 1,157 by the turn of the year and would have nearer to 1,500 heavy guns and howitzers available by the end of March 1917. Impressive though this increase was and hard the pounding of the German troops around Arras in early April would be, the French army still had a great many more - some 5,000, which made it possible to allocate an average of approximately forty to every divisional front and a great many more where they were concentrated opposite potential breakthrough points.

At the start of 1917 it was still difficult for German intelligence staffs to be certain where the blows would fall, though every effort was made to collate agents' reports and to monitor railway usage and placement of reserves in order to pick up early indications. There was also increasing concern that the very layout of the German front line almost invited attack – that the sheer size of the salient to be defended would stretch manpower to the limit and beyond. These considerations were what drove the decision, taken at Cambrai on 5 September 1916, to begin the construction of massive new defensive lines to the rear. Even though at that time there was no immediate pressing need to move to such positions, the very fact of their planned construction along the lines Arras - St Quentin - La Fère - Condé, near Soissons (*Siegfriedstellung* = Hindenburg Line) and Pont à Mousson - Verdun (*Michelstellung*), together with lesser works along other stretches of the front, indicated that sooner or later they would have to be occupied. Priority went to the *Siegfriedstellung* so, while the autumn battles continued to rage along the Western Front, work directed by Army Group Crown Prince Rupprecht went ahead from October that year at high speed on a truly colossal building site, which stretched for over 140 kilometres and absorbed the labour of a 65,000 man workforce and immense quantities of raw materials.

It seems clear that at the turn of the year, OHL [Supreme Army Headquarters] still hoped to be able to carry out some offensive of its own and thus avoid adopting a policy of strategic defence in 1917, but staff studies soon indicated that even if four more divisions could be transported west from the Eastern Front, by March 1917 only a total of seventeen divisions could be made available. That effectively ruled out any sort of significant German attack and, as evidence of Allied intentions continued to mount, there was additional concern that with a total of only 129 divisions in the west to counter the 168 at the disposal of the Allies - and those somewhat weaker in manpower - the only feasible solution was to go on the defensive and hope to hold until the recently launched unrestricted submarine warfare, together with the increased production of war materiel under the Hindenburg Plan, began to bear fruit.

Other reasons were adduced at the time to justify the withdrawal, which involved voluntarily yielding more ground than had ever been captured up that point in the war: a carefully timed move would disrupt Allied plans; the forward positions on the Somme were in an appalling state and there would be little or no possibility of improving them before the Allied offensive broke; it would be easier to extract valuable equipment and stores if this was done without enemy pressure; and a scorched earth policy would make it hard for the Allies to close up rapidly on the new German positions. Naturally, there was some truth in all of this, though the deliberate wrecking of the Somme rear areas came close to bringing Crown Prince Rupprecht to the point of resignation, so disgusted was he at what was planned. All that aside, ultimately it was manpower, the overall lack of it and the need to shorten the line in order to thicken up forward defences and create operational reserves, that finally led to the implementation of *Alberich*, the withdrawal to the Hindenburg Line. Significantly, as will be described later, most of the divisions so released by the shortening of the line were rushed south to help counter the anticipated French attacks.

In the meantime Allied plans were beginning to firm up, though there was considerable negotiation, right up to and including the notorious Calais Conference of

26/27 February 1917, which finally led to an agreement that the British army would be placed under the operational control of the new French Commander in Chief, General Nivelle, for the duration of the joint offensive. Then came *Alberich*, which threw the original Allied planning into confusion. Not only that, but the unmistakable preparations for the offensive and appalling French operational security, meant that there was no strategic and hardly any tactical surprise. The German defenders knew more or less precisely what was going to happen before the preliminary bombardments for the British thrusts either side of Arras even began. As a result, when the British army attacked on 9 April 1917, it was certainly not lack of foreknowledge that led to the initial Allied successes astride the Scarpe.

In the wake of *Alberich* it was soon obvious that the French had no intention of attacking near St Quentin, but the build up opposite the Aisne and east of Reims grew visibly week by week. In response, during the days leading up to 16 April 1917 there was decisive and timely German reinforcement on a huge scale. Headquarters First Army, for example, was withdrawn entirely from Army Group Crown Prince Rupprecht and moved south, ready to be inserted between Seventh and Third Armies when the precise locations of the French thrusts were identified. A combination of this imaginative command and control of the Aisne/Champagne area and the resolute defence mounted by the ground holding divisions meant in turn that, despite the assembly of an unprecedented weight of men and materiel, the French offensive ran into major difficulties from the outset.

Not only did the French army fail to break through as planned and explicitly, if foolishly, promised, the utter disillusionment and dislocation of expectations this caused led directly to the abrupt sacking of Nivelle, a crisis in morale and widespread mutiny. Indirectly, it forced the British army to go on attacking east of Arras, long after its offensive had run its natural course and suffering in consequence, all the time it lasted, the highest daily rate of casualties of the entire war. Rarely in military history has a campaign mounted with such high expectation of success crashed and burned so swiftly; rarely has a commander's star faded so rapidly. The story of these tumultuous weeks is at root one of overconfidence and underestimation of an opponent. Tens of thousands of soldiers paid an appalling price in death and wounds as a result.

Jack Sheldon
Vercors, France, April 2015.

Acknowledgements

As ever, I am grateful to a number of people who have assisted me with the writing of Volume 7 of my continuing series about the old German army in the Great War. Dr Robert Dunlop examined the literature concerning the effects of phosgene gas on its victims and helped me to understand what the German doctors were trying to achieve with their experimental treatment of some of the casualties. Chris Roberts, a leading Australian military historian and expert on the Battle of Bullecourt, kindly read and commented most helpfully on that chapter, though naturally I am fully responsible for the final outcome. Dr Alex Fasse, a good friend in Germany, was once again able to explain one or two obscure passages to me. My friend, co-author and editor, Nigel Cave, was his usual painstaking and helpful self throughout and I am grateful too, for the enthusiastic assistance I received from the team at Pen and Sword Books. I reserve my greatest and most special thanks to my wife, Laurie, who has taken enormous care with the maps and has provided me with strong and loving support throughout the lengthy period of research and preparation of the book.

Author's Note

This book, like the others in the series, draws extensively on work published in Germany during the 1920s and 30s. The loss of the Prussian archives in 1945 makes this inevitable; their authors had full access to material we shall never be able to consult. Of course sources such as regimental histories have to be used with caution and corroborated wherever possible, so as to ensure that the narrative is as close to the truth as is possible one hundred years after the events they describe. With experience it is usually possible to determine if the author is sticking close to the facts or not and to caveat as appropriate.

The battles around Arras involved formations from Canada and Australia, as well as smaller contingents from elsewhere in the British Empire, so on this occasion it is not only Scots, Irishmen and Welshmen whom German authors referred to collectively as *Engländer*, the same applies to all others who fought as part of the British army of 1917.

German time, one hour ahead of Allied time, is used throughout the book.

Every effort has been made to avoid infringing copyright. Should this have occurred inadvertently, I should be grateful if the holder would contact me via the publisher.

Maps

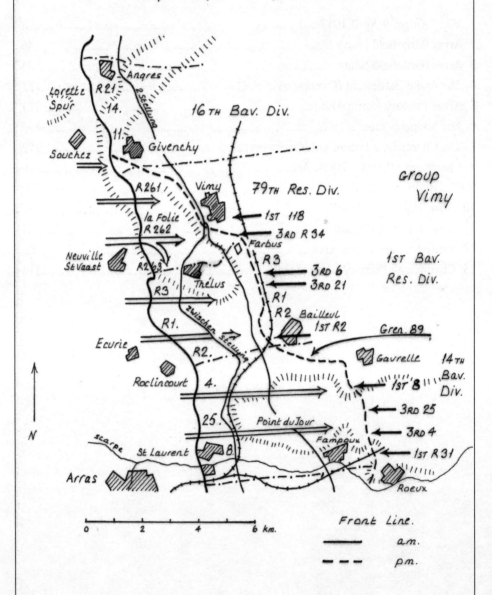

Vimy Ridge   9 April 1917.

Lorette Spur · R21 · 14. · 11. · Souchez · Angres · 2.Stellung · Givenchy · 16TH BAV. DIV.

R261 · Vimy · 79TH RES. DIV. · Group Vimy

la Folie · R262 · 1ST 118 · 3RD R34

Neuville St Vaast · R2 03 · Farbus · R3 · 3RD 6 · 3RD 21 · 1ST BAV. RES. DIV.

R3 · Thélus · R1

R1 · Zwischen Stellung · R2 · Bailleul · 1ST R2 · Gren. 89

Ecurie · R2. · Gavrelle · 14TH

Roclincourt · 4. · 1ST 8 · BAV. DIV.

25. · Point du Jour · 3RD 25 · 3RD 4

Scarpe · St Laurent · 8. · Fampoux · 1ST R31

Arras · Roeux

0   2   4   6 km.

Front Line.
———— a.m.
- - - - p.m.

N

CHAPTER 1

Vimy Ridge

In the wake of the unexpected German withdrawal to the Hindenburg Line, the British army had to recalibrate its participation in the forthcoming joint offensive. So, as March turned to April, the British began to mass the formations of their First (initially involving only a much reinforced Canadian Corps) and Third Armies, north and south of Arras, ready to assault the German Sixth Army. The main effort was to be on the left flank of a front running from Souchez in the north to Quéant in the south, with particular emphasis on the capture of Vimy Ridge (which was entrusted to the Canadian Corps) and operations astride of the Scarpe in the direction of Cambrai. In parallel, a bombardment of hitherto unheard of intensity began to come down all along the attack frontage. In the skies above the battlefields, British and German aircraft fought hard for air superiority and, despite the ensuing heavy cost to the Royal Flying Corps during so-called 'Bloody April', when between 4 and 8 April 1917 alone the British lost no fewer than seventy five aircraft shot down and a further fifty six aircraft in accidents,[1] the effect of the gunfire was considerably enhanced by aerial observation of the fall of shot.

In all the destructive bombardment lasted for the best part of two weeks and it was calculated later that the weight of explosive delivered during the first week was twice that fired the previous year prior to the battle of the Somme. Bearing in mind that the front was much shorter than had been the case in 1916 and that the fire brought down during the final week before the assault was about six times greater, it is easy to see why the German defenders suffered so much and their ability to defend was so drastically reduced when the blow fell. Long before 9 April, all the forward positions were wrecked and all the identified German batteries were either destroyed or continually drenched with gas. In support of the operational priorities, a huge weight of fire came down along Vimy Ridge between Givenchy and Farbus.

During the early stages of the bombardment it was still possible for reasonably accurate estimates of the shelling to be maintained. 79th Reserve Division, manning the highest part of the ridge, counted between 12,000 and 15,000 shells per day landing in its area. As the bombardment ground on, coming down ever more heavily, it became impossible even to guess at the number of shells involved. Approach routes and depth targets were also included in the overall fire plan so, following the deaths of numerous French inhabitants in the affected area, the entire civil population was evacuated. Once it was clear that the British had begun to prepare the battlefield, Commander I Bavarian

Reserve Corps [Group Vimy], General der Infanterie Karl Ritter von Fasbender, issued his corps concept for battle to his subordinate formations: 79th Reserve Division, 1st Bavarian Reserve Division and 14th Bavarian Infantry Division. This interesting directive provides a clear insight into the way he intended to prepare for and meet the forthcoming offensive.[2]

"Subject: Preparations for the Defensive Battle

1. In view of the extent of the work necessary on the positions, it is especially important that, within the context of an all-embracing plan, efforts are concentrated on those places that will be tactically the most important in the defensive battle. All other [work] is ruthlessly to be set aside in favour of priority places. The divisions have the necessary oversight. They must ensure that they exert decisive influence on the type and extent of the work on the positions. This must be done on the basis of a division-wide work plan which covers all the individual sectors and lays down precise tasks. The necessary materiel and manpower is then to be provided at the relevant times and places. [The plans must be drawn up] so as to ensure that regimental and divisional boundaries are not treated as dividing walls against tactical cooperation. It is essential that care is taken through the placement of machine guns, so that their mutually supporting fire can be brought to bear from a flank.

2. It is anticipated that, with the exception of the *Siegfried-Ecke* [Siegfried Corner] to the south of the Scarpe, the British attack will be directed all along the front from the Souchez River to the Scarpe. Within this front the enemy is likely to launch particularly heavy attacks against particular localities. Points will be selected for major break-ins where the enemy considers that they offer the best chances for the continuation of the attack in order to achieve the overall aim. The places which the enemy has singled out for damage by means of artillery and mortar fire or raids provide a starting point in this respect. At Verdun and on the Somme the enemy concentrated their attacks against sector boundaries. In view of this, particular attention would seem to be appropriate in the following places:

• The divisional boundary to the right [north] of 79th Reserve Division.
• The positions in the Second Line either side of the junction of *Fischergang* and *Staubwasserweg* [Fischer Alley and Staubwasser Way].
• The positions in the Second Line either side of the junction of *Prinz Arnulf Tunnel* and *Prinz Arnulf Weg*.
• The positions in the Second Line either side of the junction of *Grenadierweg* [Grenadier Way] and the *Völkertunnel*.
• The positions either side of the road Neuville St Vaast – Thélus (Divisional boundary).
• The positions in the First line either side of the forward limit of *Grävenitzweg*.

• Positions either side of the track between Roclincourt and Thélus.

3. In addition every effort is to be made, by means of the closest possible observation of enemy digging operations and the placement of their destructive fire, to clarify further the assessment of probable enemy main break-in points.

4. Special measures are to be taken at the probable enemy main break-in points to ensure that any enemy attack can be beaten off or nipped in the bud, or that any enemy who have managed to break in can be prevented from expanding their foothold and can be rapidly ejected by means of a counter-stroke. This can be achieved by:

• Prepared defences. (Constant improvement of the smashed trenches and obstacles; placement of stop lines and obstacles at right angles to the front; company dumps of wire obstacles that can be laid rapidly.)

• Deployment of the garrison. (Distribution of machine guns, light mortars and grenade launchers.)

• Increases in destructive and defensive fire. (Due consideration having been given to the [risk of] loss of our guns.)

• Artillery preparations. (Designed to engage enemy forces and armoured vehicles which have broken in.) The guns of the close support battery are in themselves insufficient for this purpose.

5. *These passive preparatory measures alone are insufficient.*[3] Enemy batteries should already be being engaged systematically whenever suitable opportunities present themselves. The necessary ammunition for this is ready and available. All necessary steps are to be taken in order to ensure that the means are available to fire gas as soon as the enemy preparations for the attack commence. We must adapt our response to the gradual transition to battle. This means that we must make it difficult for the enemy to prepare for battle by engaging with planned, heavy, destructive fire their observation points, mortar base plates and approach routes.

In both respects we must do considerably more than has been done so far. More precisely, we must ensure that the medium mortars and, wherever they can be deployed successfully, the heavy howitzers are better exploited and so deliver destructive fire.

6. There is to be:

• sharpest attention to detail, in order to ensure that enemy attack plans are discovered in good time.

• carefully planned and controlled, but ceaseless, digging efforts, in order to maintain and improve the tactically most important parts of our positions.

• systematic engagement of the enemy artillery and destruction of all installations that are particularly valuable to the enemy as they complete their attack preparations.

Signed: von Fasbender

Upon receipt of this directive, the divisions which made up Group Vimy were quick to issue their own complementary orders, because at this local level all the commanders were sure that the opening of the attack was drawing close. The army group commander was not entirely convinced.

Crown Prince Rupprecht of Bavaria: Diary Entry 26 March 1917 [4]

"Sixth Army has written in its weekly report for 24 March, 'The reinforcement of the enemy artillery, which has been observed since the end of February, has been confirmed further ... ' The reason for the massing of enemy forces either side of Arras is still not completely clear. Possibly the enemy fears an attack and, therefore, has only deployed some of the available divisions in the front line. Whatever the explanation, the deployment is not normal for a major offensive. Because the possession of Vimy Ridge would be of far greater significance than the gaining of ground around Arras, it would seem, despite the greater concentration of force near the latter, that an attack on Vimy Ridge is the more probable. Nevertheless, both possibilities must be borne in mind."

For several weeks, the Canadians had pursued a policy of aggressive raiding and patrolling against Vimy Ridge. Sometimes these enjoyed success, on other occasions they failed in their aim. Late on 29 March, for example, Reserve Infantry Regiment 263, 79 Reserve Division, captured four men of the Canadian 31st Battalion, 6 Brigade, 2nd Canadian Division during a raid launched astride the Neuville-Thélus road in sector *Arnulf 3*. The objective of the operation had been to capture German prisoners but, the tables turned, subsequent interrogation of these Canadian soldiers yielded very useful intelligence for the defence. On 31 March, an initial report, signed off by Major Lenz, Chief of Staff I Bavarian Reserve Division, was widely distributed:[5]

"From statements by prisoners belonging to 2nd Canadian Division the following points have arisen:
• The mission of the 2nd Canadian Division is to attack to the south of the road Neuville – Thélus – Farbus.
• To its south it appears that 1st Canadian Division has been inserted between it and 51st (Highland) Division
• To the north are located 3rd and 4th Canadian Divisions in that order. 5th Canadian Division *may* be a designated reserve.[6]
• The Arras – Souchez front is to be rolled up from south to north. If that succeeds, the cavalry will be released onto the [Douai] Plain ...

"The statements sound probable and fit well with the picture built up by the Corps concerning the direction of the [forthcoming] attack and the main break-in points. Divisional Infantry and Artillery counter-measures would seem to be indicated."

Interrogation of these prisoners continued the following day. A second report, dated 1 April,[7] was issued and an additional one on 2 April.[8] In the 1 April document the interrogators reported:

"Units of [6 Canadian] Brigade conducted attack exercises between 13 and 23 March to the north of Grand Servin. Each day between 8.00 am and 1.00 pm drills were rehearsed and attacks were practised on a training area adapted to resemble the actual terrain of the attack. The target of the attack, which was intended to be launched some time between 26 March and 6 April, was declared to be Thélus and Farbus Wood [modern Bois de Berthonval]. The German trenches were marked out with white tapes and the communication trenches were represented by red flags. The roads Arras - Lille and Neuville – Thélus were marked with yellow flags. Blue flags were used to show the village of Thélus and the wire obstacle was indicated with two wires.

"A small wood near the training area was used for Farbus Wood. Each exercise began with the troops advancing in 'diamond artillery formation', then the attack was conducted by the individual companies in three waves against Thélus and Farbus Wood. 27th Battalion had been designated to capture Thélus, whilst the 31st Battalion was intended to move through it and thrust towards Farbus Wood..."[9]

Additional information included in the 2 April report included confirmation that the attack was to be launched between Lens and Arras and that the bombardment was scheduled to last six to ten days. As a further illustration of the value of careful prisoner interrogation, a great deal of information concerning the whereabouts of supply dumps and gun positions was extracted, whilst the precise weight of and methods to be used in the attack on the Thélus - Farbus front were also obtained. The whereabouts of large stacks of ammunition and numerous gun pits was described, as was the fact that that twelve out of sixteen companies of 6 Brigade would participate in the attack on Thélus/Farbus, whilst the remainder would be in reserve. The exact tactics to be deployed and the reason behind them were volunteered in detail, as were numerous minor points of general interest. This of course was only one report of many but, in combination, they left the defenders in no doubt at all about what would happen along Vimy Ridge when the barrage lifted. Meanwhile the shelling, interspersed with raiding and patrolling, continued to take a huge toll in casualties. It became increasingly difficult to repair the trench systems, withstand the incessant Canadian operations, or even to keep an accurate account of the shelling. The intensity of the bombardment was simply beyond anything previously experienced.

Despite all these problems, the German defence tried everything possible to prepare and launch a limited assault, code named Operation Munich, in late March or early April. Originally a proposal in mid March by Headquarters VI Reserve Corps and designed to disrupt Allied preparations and improve the German positions in the Givenchy area by capturing the northern end of Zouave Valley, it went through several amendments, was repeatedly postponed and in the end was never launched. Ironically, in its final form it was to have been mounted on 10 April, though the army group commander, having been convinced of its necessity, certainly hoped that it could have taken place earlier.

Crown Prince Rupprecht of Bavaria:
Diary Entry 3 April 1917 [10]

"Because the enemy have driven numerous galleries under the *Gießler Höhe*, clearly with the intention of preceding the attack there with major mine explosions and because we are somewhat behind with our counter-measures (the enemy are able to drive their mine galleries forward horizontally from the foot of the hill, whereas we have to dig down deep to be able to counter their work), it seems to me to be highly desirable that 16th [Bavarian] Division's Operation Munich be launched as soon as possible. That way, capture of the enemy's trenches means that we shall be able to destroy the entrances to their galleries. So far it has been postponed because the rain has saturated the ground and made it impassable…"

Diary Entry 5 April 1917 [11]

"Because a major enemy offensive against Sixth Army and more particularly against the front from Souchez to Tilloy, is to be launched in only a few days time, it would be a very good thing if Operation Munich could be conducted earlier. That would certainly get the ball rolling."

Whilst work on this continued, staffs in the different headquarters were fully committed preparing to ensure that the forthcoming defensive operations could be conducted effectively. I Bavarian Reserve Corps, for example, issued a typical order on 3 April explaining the changed command arrangements and laying down how the newly arrived minor artillery reinforcements were to be deployed.[12]

"From midday 3 April 1917 the southern Corps of the Army are to be known as 'Groups'. The various designations are as follows:

VI (VIII) Reserve Corps	Group Souchez
I Bavarian Reserve Corps	Group Vimy
IX Reserve Corps	Group Arras

"…Additional artillery has been placed at the disposal of Group Vimy:

• Field Artillery Regiment 25 (six batteries of field guns). Together with a regimental staff and one artillery battalion of 79th Reserve Division, these guns will be subordinated to 1st Bavarian Reserve Division.

• From Field Artillery Regiment 600 (six batteries of light field howitzers) the regimental staff and one artillery battalion will deploy to 1st Bavarian Reserve Division. One battalion will deploy to 14th Bavarian Infantry Division.
• Once the newly subordinated battalion from Field Artillery Regiment 600 is in position, 1st Bavarian Reserve Division is to release 2nd Battalion Field Artillery Regiment 9 to Group Arras.
• The batteries of these regiments are to be emplaced where they can superimpose their fire on the [most probable] break in points.

"From Foot Artillery Battalion 68 (100 mm guns), the regimental staff and two batteries are allocated to 14th Bavarian Infantry Division and one battery to 1st Bavarian Reserve Division. The 100 mm batteries of the two divisions must exploit their long range and be employed to fire gas shells at the enemy batteries that are outside the range of the howitzers.

"The heavy, low trajectory artillery of 1st Bavarian Reserve Division must be placed so as to be in a position to bring down flanking fire on a possible break in to the east of Souchez; and that of 14th Bavarian Infantry Division to be able both to counter thrusts to the east of Neuville and to bring down harassing fire along the roads leading to Arras.

Signed: von Fasbender

Whilst the higher headquarters were at full stretch adapting deployments, procedures and tactics so as to be ready when the attacks began, the forward troops clung on in their front line positions, attempting to withstand shelling more intense than anything they had previously experienced. One by one the dugouts were smashed, whilst the wet weather, in combination with the sheer scale of the bombardment, rendered all attempts to repair the trenches completely hopeless. The entire forward area was soon reduced to a sea of mud, which made resupply of trench stores, food, drink and even ammunition virtually impossible. Somehow artillery ammunition resupply was maintained, though it took an immense effort by men and horses to achieve it and to ensure that there were sufficient shells dumped on the gun lines in preparation for the forthcoming attacks.

Some idea of the prevailing conditions may be obtained from reports sent to his brigade commander, Generalmajor Lamprecht, on 6 and 8 April by Major Anton Maier, commander Bavarian Reserve Infantry Regiment 3, 1st Bavarian Reserve Division, which was deployed on the Thélus-Farbus Front.

"Bavarian Reserve Infantry Regiment 3, 6 April 1917, 5.30 pm

"The enemy artillery fire and its effects have increased day after day. In none of the First, the Third, the Stop Lines or the *Zwischenstellung* [Intermediate

Position] is it possible to speak of continuous lines of defence. For the most part the trench lines have been flattened, to such an extent that they are simply crater fields. The same is true of the approach routes. Due to crushing and burying of the dugouts, there has been an extraordinary reduction in the ability to provide protected accommodation for the troops.

"Enemy activity has the entire garrison on edge. Raids, both large and small, keep coming in; sometimes with artillery preparation; sometimes without; sometimes here; sometimes there. The usual artillery and mortar fire is often interrupted by repeated, violent and sudden concentrations, often in the strength of drum fire and lasting up to twenty minutes at a time. These concentrations appear to be lifted (by day) when white flares are fired.

"Deploying the battalions on the positions for eight days continuously, as has been the case up to now, cannot be continued in the present circumstances. But a rotation of two days in the front line and two days in support means that the reserve battalion can only have a rest period of two days at a time. This routine cannot be maintained for more than a few weeks. The allocation of a fourth battalion for each sector, as already requested, is urgently sought: [at the latest] at the time of the next relief."[13]

"Bavarian Reserve Infantry Regiment 3
Subject: Battleworthiness of the Troops

"Following on from my report of 6 April, 5.30 pm, I regard it as my duty to forward the enclosed report by the Regimental Medical Officer, concerning the current state of health, which he prepared for me on his own initiative. The trigger for this was my request for an explanation as to why thirty one men from 12th Company reported sick simultaneously and to make it clear to him that all men, except the most pressing medical cases, were to be directed back to their companies.

"Currently the troops in the sector are deployed as follows:
"Ten companies are manning the position: four companies in *Loën North*, four companies in *Loën South* and two companies in Bois Carré and the Second Position respectively (on high alert). Only two companies are resting. Each battalion has spent eight days manning the sub-sectors. Each company has spent four days in the Forward Position (First and Second Lines) and four days in support (North: Third Line and Stop Line; South: Third Line only). In this context, deployment in support is to be equated with service in the front line, because the Third Line, the Stop Line and the *Zwischenstellung* [Intermediate Position] are constantly under almost the same weight of fire as the First and Second Lines. There is no mortar fire, but this is replaced by large calibre shells from the enemy artillery.

"To this must be added the fact that the companies in support have already sent several sections to the forward companies, because their average strength (which has sunk to eighty men) is insufficient for the manning of company sub-sectors 350 metres wide.[14] When a battalion is relieved after eight days on the position, two companies move to the dugouts in Bois Carré and the Second Position, both of which are under constant fire. Only two companies are able to move into billets in Fresnoy.

"As a result, each company spends ten days on the positions; under constant fire and without a break. When this is coupled to the need to counter the daily enemy raids, both large and small, by day and night, it amounts to a commitment which leaves anything on the Somme or at Verdun in the shade; not, perhaps, in terms of casualties, but certainly in the demands it makes on the battleworthiness of the troops."

It is the wording of official reports such as these that brings home the reality of expressions such as 'softening up the enemy' or '*sturmreif*', which applied absolutely to the situation in Group Vimy. When the assault was launched the fighting troops of the three regiments of 1st Bavarian Reserve Division had been reduced to an extraordinary degree: Bavarian Reserve Infantry Regiment 1 – 1,360; Bavarian Reserve Infantry Regiment 2 (which had suffered particularly from the effect of raids) – 850 and Bavarian Reserve Infantry Regiment 3 – 1,000.[15]

In the 79th Reserve Division sector, which ran along the highest part of the ridge, the situation was similar. In most cases the regiments maintained one or two companies in the front line. One or two companies were placed in support and the remainder were kept back in reserve role. A pre-Easter check revealed that infantry company strengths were down to between fifty and ninety riflemen and there were additional casualties during the final forty eight hours of the bombardment. Because of this, Reserve Infantry Regiment 262 had to deploy elements of its assault pioneer company in a reinforcing role as early as 5 April, its 2nd Battalion having suffered sixty five casualties during the previous two days.[16] In a further attempt to alleviate the problems, all the divisional machine guns, including the six of Machine Gun Sharp Shooter Troop 20, which arrived at the end of March, were arranged in depth positions amongst the craters, forming the backbone of the defence in the absence of sufficient riflemen.[17]

The British army was by now present in overwhelming strength. The defenders calculated that up to 140 guns and 50 mortars of various calibres were in action along each kilometre of frontage north of the Scarpe. A Sixth Army report, dated 7 April, stated that, 'During the past two weeks, fire has been observed coming from 679 different positions'.[18] In effect this meant that more than 400 guns and 150 mortars could bring fire down against 79th Reserve Division, which could only reply with eighty nine guns and a few mortars, some of which were destroyed later in the bombardment. It is clear to see why morale sagged and men felt that they had been abandoned to their fate. Hungry, thirsty and worried about the risk of mine explosions, it can be seen clearly that the offensive when it opened would be launched against a defence well under strength, comprising men whose nerves were on edge, who were physically exhausted, mentally drained and so sick that the majority of them should have been in bed under medical supervision.

Further proof of the strain of the past few days appears in a report dated 5 April and forwarded to the commander of Group Souchez [VIII Reserve Corps] by Generalmajor Ritter von Möhl, commander 16th Bavarian Infantry Division, in which he described the dire state of the positions between Hill 145 and the *Gießler Höhe* and illustrated its effect by a disciplinary problem which had occurred.[19]

"The bombardment, in combination with the weather conditions, has greatly reduced the defensive value of the position. Currently there is no continuity within the First or Second Lines because, in places, the trenches have been flattened. On the left flank of *Döberitz,* forward of the Third Line, [the defences] are reduced to sentry posts in craters. Large numbers of the dugouts have been buried and the approach routes are unusable in places.

"The constant heavy bombardment, the ceaseless high state of alert in a severely shot-up position, protected by only fragments of an obstacle, coupled with the endless work each night on positions which are generally destroyed again the following day, has naturally had a negative effect on the morale of the troops and has led to some isolated incidents...My oral report yesterday was somewhat limited, because I had just been informed about examples of gross insubordination within a regiment, in whose fighting ability I had previously had the highest trust."

From Möhl's words, it can be seen that in some cases his men had been driven to the limit of endurance by the bombardment – small wonder, because during each twenty four hour period the 79th Reserve Division divisional sector, for example, was engaged with at least 12,000 shells. On some days the total must have been a good deal higher; then, finally, from 7 April there were no more attempts to keep an accurate tally. 'The number of enemy shells fired cannot be determined...Mortar fire was broadly comparable to the previous few days', they reported that day.[20] One of the battalion commanders of Bavarian Reserve Infantry Regiment 2, deployed in Sector *Wittelsbach.* later described what this weight of fire meant in practice for the forward defenders.

Major von Dittelsbach 1st Battalion Bavarian Reserve Infantry Regiment 2[21]

"The enemy had divided up the battlefield like a chessboard. Strip after strip was ploughed and torn up. The entire defensive works were to be demolished and the nerves of the defenders shredded. As it unfolded it made for dreadful scenes. The explosion of the massive shells ripped great craters out of the earth, sent their contents skywards then, as they fell to ground, once more repeated the process in chaotic confusion. The earth rocked, the air rushed like gusts of wind past the ears: thunderclap after thunderclap.

"In between were the light and medium calibre shells, fired from the front and the flanks to carry out their work all along the line, or to come down as harassing fire on the cold, wrecked slopes where the clouds of gas clung. New monsters crashed down on the front line: torpedo mines, 138 pounders, landing with massive effect; whilst, along the approach routes, the long-barrelled guns brought down hails of fire and claimed victims in the villages."

It was just the same in Sector *Zollern*, where Reserve Infantry Regiment 262 was deployed in the centre of the 79th Reserve Division front. An unnamed company commander, defending the La Folie area, later produced an extremely graphic account from his perspective.[22]

"I exercise command over a crater field more than one kilometre in extent. At my disposal are: four platoons of infantry; one reserve platoon; six machine guns; three light mortars; one telegraph station and five telephone points. To that must be added assault groups, the artillery forward observation officer, reporting points, messengers and flare relay stations to pass on signals and so alert the artillery. We can only move in this crater field during the hours of darkness. During the day my time in my dugout is so full of the need to produce reports and returns, sketches and defence plans that my head is buzzing. If everything goes perfectly, it takes me three hours to tour the sentry posts; if I add in the need to link up with the neighbouring sectors, this rises to six hours.

"I have created five independent mixed defensive teams. The men are magnificent. Every day half of them are buried [by the fire]. Sentry duty is an immense burden. The food is cold; even fetching it involves extraordinary exertion. The men are working until they are nearly dropping from exhaustion. But none of these brave young men are grumbling or complaining. Covered in clay and mud, they can only snatch rests on the freezing cold ground, but their eyes light up at the thought of being able to give the Tommies what for. Mindful of our joint responsibility, they stick it out through the heaviest concentrations of fire. The demands they make are the minimum to sustain life – a shining example to the greedy drones back home. They have just gone thirty six hours with no food, but nobody is cursing about it. The wounded are stoical and are simply grateful for a cigarette that we place in their helpless lips.

"We have now been subjected to ceaseless drum fire for eight days and our casualties are severe. Yesterday the company lost nine men. All we could do was to drag them unconscious out of the trenches under the constant clatter of British [*sic*] machine gun fire. The British [*sic*] pressurise us indefatigably. Yesterday we had two men stabbed to death in their trench at 2.00 pm. Then there is the ceaseless fire: 600 mortar bombs and one hundred shells on the company sector in only twelve hours. We are enduring a second Battle of the Somme here. The battalion is already in an awful state. There has been no warm food for forty eight hours. The men are in a state of collapse. The British major offensive is about to begin. Here in the Second Line, I am down to only one section of men. I have been waiting since 9.00 pm for warm food for the company.

"The British are simply miles ahead of us in their superiority in mortars, artillery and technology, so we infantry just have to soldier on with no artillery support. But our men are truly outstanding. Because more and more dugouts are being collapsed every day, we shall all soon be forced to move out into the open. My dugout is full of the wounded; the trench outside of the dead. Nobody has come for them. My best men are either dead or wounded...

"My men are beyond all praise! The company commander expressly ordered the occupation of an essential sentry position that was in such a dangerous place that anybody manning it was certain to be more or less seriously wounded within a very short space of time. Not a man flinched and, sure enough, the dugout adjacent to that of the men waiting to go on duty has gradually filled up with seriously wounded men..."

The artillery fire reduced considerably on 7 April, but it was a temporary lull and it increased again in the face of German counter-battery fire. During the afternoon and evening of Easter Day rates increased to drum fire, which was maintained throughout the following night. It was now obvious that the waiting was over and Vimy Ridge was about to be attacked. In anticipation, the corps commander issued a final rallying call to his men, though how many actually saw it or were motivated by it is a moot point.

"Group Vimy: Corps Order of the Day, Easter Sunday 1917[23]

Soldiers!

For days the enemy has been trying to wear you down through an immense weight of artillery fire. The enemy has succeeded in smashing our trenches and obstacles, but has made no impression on the steadfastness of our courageous infantry. Each time raids have been launched against our positions they have been repulsed bloodily and prisoners have been taken.

"Our excellent, strong, artillery has supported the infantry admirably. Each gunner understands that it is his duty and a matter of honour to come self-sacrificially to the aid of the infantry in its hour of need.

"Our airmen and anti-aircraft gunners have all performed brilliantly. During the past week twenty five enemy aircraft have fallen to the guns of the Richthofen Squadron and the anti-aircraft guns have brought down two more. The achievement and maintenance of air superiority is an essential pre-requisite for success.

"In battle and at the cost of huge labour, the engineers, mortar men and pioneer battalions have all played their part in supporting the infantry.

"Soldiers! The day of the decisive assault draws near! It will demand nothing less than a supreme performance from all ranks. Be ready at all times to begin the defence! The British must not be allowed to gain one single foot of ground. Wherever they succeed in breaking in they must ejected without delay.

"Do not forget that here we are facing *the* enemy which actually caused this dreadful war; who alone bears the guilt that it is still continuing.

"You all know what is at stake: Victory and Peace.

Signed: von Fasbender"

The following day, in the wet and cold of an April dawn, with snow flurries in the wind, an extraordinary hurricane of fire broke over the forward positions the length of Vimy Ridge The earth itself shook. The front line trenches were mainly engaged by field guns and mortars, supported by large numbers of machine guns, but depth targets were hit by medium, heavy and super-heavy guns, and all known battery positions were gassed. The German were soon totally cloaked by dense clouds of smoke and fountains of mud and earth were thrown up everywhere. Yellow flares went up all along the front line as the trench garrisons called for defensive fire; but before there could be a response from those few German guns still able to fire the bombardment suddenly lifted and there was a whole series of explosions as the entrance to the many subways prepared in advance were blown to provide the attacking troops with easy covered access to the German lines.

At once huge masses of Canadian infantry, well fed, equipped and rested, surged forward. Many of the leading wave were lightly equipped with just side arms and grenades, so as to produce an immediate shock effect, then came the follow up waves hard on their heels. Wherever the shelling had snuffed out resistance the front line trenches were quickly overrun. Elsewhere the surviving German infantry began to take a heavy toll of the attackers then, as the fighting became hand to hand, there were desperate struggles with knives and bayonets. South of Thélus there had been close support from tanks moving forward along the roads leading from Arras and the German First and Second Positions were taken rapidly. Although, as will be described later, the longest Allied advance of the day by far was made by the British 34th Division in the sector of 14th Bavarian Infantry Division, the fate of 1st Bavarian Reserve Division, deployed just to the south of 79th Reserve Division in Sectors *Loën, Wittelsbach* and *Rupprecht*, was of much greater significance as far as the battle for Vimy Ridge was concerned.

Deployed just to the south of Reserve Infantry Regiment 263, on the northern flank of 1st Bavarian Reserve Division, was Bavarian Reserve Infantry Regiment 3, commanded by Major Anton Maier from a dugout known as *Leipziger Hütte* [Leipzig Cottage], located just south of the present day Bois Carré Cemetery. By the end of the first day of battle, Major Meier was posted missing, so it was Major von Poschinger who later described what happened when the regiment was attacked by 1st Canadian Division.[24]

"9.4.1917. …Of the battalions deployed on the position, the 1st Battalion had relieved the 3rd Battalion during the night 7/8 April, whilst 2nd Battalion had already been located forward on the position from 4 April. The uncommitted companies (11th and 12th) were back at Fresnoy in reserve. After extremely heavy artillery and mortar fire came down on the sector during the night 8/9April, just as it had been for the past few days, destroying almost all of the dugouts of the First Position, at 5.30 am 9 April drum fire started coming down all along the divisional sector.

"From this moment onwards all contact was lost with the front line. After the heaviest imaginable drum fire by artillery and mortars, lasting a quarter of an hour, the enemy infantry began its attack in great waves. Opposite Sub-Sectors L[oën] 3 and L4 the enemy used flamethrowers and, at the moment of the attack, two enemy aircraft were in the air above the position.

"Despite constant demands for defensive fire, the response of our artillery was extremely weak. As a result, the tiny garrison of the First and Second Lines (the companies averaged only a bayonet strength of sixty men) was simply overrun. The main enemy break in point was along the road Neuville – Thélus. It appears that the enemy broke straight through here to the Third Line in the first rush; at least no more reports were received by the regiment from 5th Company, which was deployed there - none of the runners despatched there ever returned.

"In L[oën] South the enemy was checked for a considerable time by small arms fire, but gradually they made progress here too, breaking down the resistance of the weakened companies of 1st Battalion once they had advanced in the neighbouring sectors. At 5.45 am the two companies of 3rd Battalion located in Fresnoy, which had only just been relieved at 2.00 am in Bois Carré and the Second Position by 9th and 10th Companies, were alerted and ordered to move forward with two machine guns to Bois Carré…

"In the meantime the garrison of the *Riegel-Stellung* [Stop Line] (8th Company assisted by survivors from the first three lines) maintained an obstinate resistance, holding up the enemy for approximately three hours. About 10.00 am, after the *Riegel-Stellung* had been completely smashed, the British [*sic*] succeeded in penetrating its northern part, from the Neuville-Thélus road. At the same time the enemy managed to force a way into the centre of Thélus, whose western edge was still being held by elements of 79th Reserve Division.

"Whilst artillery fire came down on the trenches around Bois Carré, at about 10.30 dense skirmishing lines of British [*sic*] soldiers advanced on Thélus East and Bois Carré. Here 9th Company, with about forty riflemen and two machine guns and led by the Regimental Commander, was still holding out. The staff of 2nd Battalion Reserve Infantry Regiment 3 was also here, having been forced to withdraw once the enemy had advanced over the *Riegel-Stellung* towards *Augsburger-Weg* [Augsburg Way].

"Despite suffering heavy casualties from rifle and machine gun fire, the enemy worked their way forward to Bois Carré, [helped by the fact] that resistance had ceased north of the Thélus – Bailleul road. Once the enemy had begun advancing along *Preussen-Weg* [Prussian Way] and were threatening the rear of 9th Company, located between Bois Carré and *Leipziger-Haus* [*sic - Hütte*], it was ordered at 11.30 am to withdraw along *Loën-Weg* to the Second Position, in order to avoid being cut off. Once *Leipziger-Haus* had been destroyed by fire, the regimental staff moved their command post to the dugout of an aid post at the southwest corner of Farbus Wood.[25] Throughout the morning the Second Position, which was manned by 11th and 12th Companies, was under extremely heavy artillery fire.

"At about 12.45 pm the British [*sic*] launched forward in dense masses from *Preussen-Weg* against the Second Position. Despite obstinate resistance they succeeded in penetrating the left flank of the regiment from *Weisses Haus* [White House] and simultaneously to outflank, then to encircle the right flank of the regiment from the northwest, once Infantry Regiment 261 [*sic – Reserve Infantry Regiment 263*] had withdrawn to the railway embankment east of Vimy/Farbus. Those elements of 3rd Battalion (which by now incorporated survivors of the other two battalions) who managed to break clean of the enemy – nobody returned from 10th Company – moved after 1.30 pm to occupy the railway embankment east of Farbus, in extension of the line of Infantry Regiment 261 [*sic*].

Once the Second Position had fallen, the British [*sic*] pushed forward initially only to the eastern edge of Farbus Wood. About 4.00 pm they attempted, using cavalry, to break through to the east. Of a twelve man patrol which rode forward along the road Farbus – Willerval, six were shot by rifle and machine gun fire and two men were captured in Willerval. The remainder escaped. Of another which pushed along the line of the railway embankment towards Bailleul, all, bar two, were shot down.

"Once the full weight of enemy artillery fire began coming down on the railway embankment, this was simply held by security outposts. The line was pulled back seventy metres and everyone began to dig in. Here the remnants of the companies were relieved at 7.30 pm by elements of Infantry Regiments 6 and 21…"

Such were the losses of territory by 1st Bavarian Reserve Division that not only was Major Maier declared missing, Oberstleutnant Brunner of Bavarian Reserve Infantry Regiment 2 was captured.[26] Despite all the difficulties, German command and control was reasonably effective throughout the day. The main problem for the defence was the speed of events, which meant that the Canadians remained inside the German decision cycle all day long, making it impossible for them to react before orders were overtaken by events on the ground. In the event, Generalmajor Freiherr von Pechmann, the divisional commander, issued at least six operation orders during the day (at 8.00 am, 9.00 am, 11.00 am, 11.45 am, 12.00 pm, 3.00 pm and 10.50 pm),[27] but nothing effective could be achieved by the defence until after the Canadian attacks, with their limited objectives, had run their course and there was a pause in the fighting.

The 79th Reserve Division deployed north of Thélus had a very similar experience. On the divisional left flank adjoining 1st Bavarian Reserve Division were the battalions of Reserve Infantry Regiment 263, commanded by Oberstleutnant von Behr. Their trenches were all smashed, as were most of their dugouts. The companies had been badly worn down by the shelling, so only relatively few men were able to man the defences. As a result, despite doing their best to withstand the Canadian pressure with hand grenades, they were overwhelmed quite quickly. One of the company commanders, deployed in the Third Line of the First Position in Sector Arnulf North, stood waiting for dawn to break.

Reserve Leutnant Bittkau Reserve Infantry Regiment 263[28]

"Gradually the first streaks of dawn began to light up the darkness. Light squalls of snow blew across the cratered landscape. There was a striking stillness. Suddenly, between Arras and Lens, came great flashes and wild arcs of light in the sky: signal flares? Mine explosions? All of a sudden, as though at a single word of command, down came drum fire from thousands of large and small calibre muzzles. Shell fire rose to crazy heights. It was impossible to distinguish the firing signatures from the shell bursts. It was just one mass of fire amidst an extraordinary racket.

"It was like the final intake of breath before a race. Nerves were stretched to breaking point as we took in these scenes, which were like a painting of terrible beauty. Standing there for just a few seconds, a shell landed just to my left and a fragment hit my left side at chest height. My nerves took another knock! My heart was like lead, the gorge rose in my throat; blood ran into my mouth, taking my breath away. I was at the end of my strength; ready to faint. Suddenly came a thin shout, seemingly from far off, 'The British [*sic*]! Get out! Get out!'

"They were coming from the left, through the hollow, heading directly for Bonval Wood. Battle was joined: rifle shots – shouts – hand grenades. Hans Voigt, the drummer, came running up, carrying ammunition and information, whilst down below secret documents were being burned. 'They are coming from the left – here they are!' A man was pulled down inside moaning...stomach wound. He lay there completely still. More bawling and shouting. 'They are right above us!' Then it was quieter – completely quiet until a strange voice called down [in English], 'Come out!'

"The light flickered...thoughts ran through my numbed head: what were they going to do? Throw down hand grenades? Smash my skull? No, better to shoot myself. But the revolver was lying on the table and I could not move. Should I wait for a counter-attack? …A Tommy came through the tunnel, looked carefully round the corner, a large revolver in his hand. 'Officer?' he asked, then left to fetch his comrades."

From his command post in rear of his forward companies, the commanding officer of its 1st Battalion later described how the attack unfolded in his sector.

Major Meyer 1ˢᵗ Battalion Reserve Infantry Regiment 263[29]

"At 5.30 am on 9 April enemy drum fire, supplemented by machine gun fire, came down. It was impossible to make out the position and in fact it was almost impossible to make out signal flares amidst the clouds of smoke and dirt thrown up by the shells. At 6.30 am heavy small arms fire could be heard and, at that moment, a message was sent by light signal to the rear, 'Heavy enemy attack'. About half an hour later the wounded Musketier Hagemann happened to pass Battalion Headquarters, reporting that the British [sic] had broken into the battalion position from the right and were already occupying the Third Line. According to members of 9th Company Reserve Infantry Regiment 263, the British [sic] had overrun the right flank of 1st Bavarian Reserve Division and had then attacked our battalion in great strength from the left and rear.

"Unfortunately Musketier Hagemann's statements were soon confirmed when the battalion staff spotted that British [sic] infantry were already closing in and were mounting a machine gun in the remains of a ruined house. Because there were no reserves of any sort available for a counter-attack, the officers and men of the battalion staff left the indefensible command post and pulled back to the Intermediate Position in order to conduct the subsequent defence as far as possible from there. On the way there two officers and all the other ranks, bar two runners and three signallers, were killed or wounded."

Although the front line was quickly overrun, determined defence by 12th Company and elements of the 10th Company brought the Canadian attack to a temporary halt then, rushing forward from the *Felsenkeller* [a mined dugout and command post of *KTK South* of Sector *Arnulf*], Vizefeldwebel Borcherding led the reserve platoon of 10th Company over the open, cratered landscape to come to the assistance of their heavily pressed comrades. However, despite every effort, the serious thrust by the 1st Canadian Division south of Les Tilleuls began to have an effect on Sector *Arnulf*. Following up, large numbers of Canadian reinforcements advanced from the Arras-Lens road, forced their way against the flanks and rear of the 263rd, rolled them up from the south and then encircled them completely. It soon proved to be impossible to defend the First Position any longer. As a result, the Intermediate Position running from Thélus to Vimy fell as well.

In the nick of time Major Meyer, commanding officer 1st Battalion, together with his staff, succeeded in withdrawing as far as the railway embankment; whilst the regimental commander, Oberstleutnant von Behr, personally led 8th Company and what remained of the assault pioneer company to a blocking position south of Vimy. Here they managed to conduct a successful defence for several hours before Leutnant von Rohrscheidt, commanding 8th Company, was killed along with many of his men. When no more could be achieved, a handful of defenders led by an offizierstellvertreter pulled back and linked up with reinforcements who had arrived at the railway embankment south of the Vimy-Acheville underpass. Summarising the day later, Meyer, whose command post in the *Schwabentunnel* in Sector *Arnulf North* was outflanked early from the south, wrote:

Major Meyer Commanding Officer 1st Battalion Reserve Infantry Regiment 263[30]

"The regimental commander [Oberstleutnant von Behr] was briefed in person by the battalion commander. Major Meyer then received orders, together with Oberleutnant Heinicke, to take 6th Company Reserve Infantry Regiment 261, ten machine guns of Reserve Infantry Regiment 263, three companies of 2nd Battalion Reserve Infantry Regiment 263 and approximately fifty men of 1st Battalion Reserve Infantry Regiment 263 (who were back with the heavy baggage) and move to defend the line of the railway embankment to the east of Vimy. The vulnerable point of this position was at Farbus Wood, where the Canadians could close up to the embankment using covered routes. If they were to succeed in crossing the embankment the danger was that its entire length could be enfiladed by machine gun fire and therefore become untenable.

"Temporarily there was a similar danger for the right flank at Vimy Station, but this was removed through the deployment of 'Detachment von Block' (1st Battalion Infantry Regiment 118 and elements of Reserve Infantry Regiment 262), which subsequently succeeded in counter-attacking as far as the slopes of the so-called Telegraph Hill. During the afternoon of 9 April, large masses of Canadian soldiers were observed assembling in Farbus village, apparently in order to conduct an assault on the railway embankment. At that the battalion commander directed two machine guns into action at the southern underpass where they could bring enfilade fire down on Farbus Wood. In addition, the deployment of 6th Company Reserve Infantry Regiment 261 and a platoon from 2nd Battalion Reserve Infantry Regiment 263, which had thus far been held back, meant that the left flank could be extended to a point to the south of Farbus Wood. The regimental commander was also requested to make forces available to reinforce and thus improve the security of the threatened left flank.

"A little while later enemy cavalry was observed in the area of Willerval. At approximately the same time two companies (10th and 12th Companies Reserve Infantry Regiment 34) arrived. One company was deployed to strengthen the left flank, whilst the other company remained concentrated behind the right flank in case the enemy succeeded in breaking through at Vimy. In the meantime the enemy kept the railway embankment and the two flanks in particular under fire by heavy shells and shrapnel. Towards evening Oberstleutnant von Behr arrived once more at the railway embankment in order to direct a counter-attack. This was to sweep round the flank of Detachment von Block, roughly in the area of Petit Vimy, then was to be directed against Telegraph Hill. The troops that had been subordinated to Major Meyer were initially to support his attack by means of machine gun fire, then to undertake a frontal attack. This action was begun, but had to be halted when information arrived that the Bavarians had not succeeded in recapturing Farbus; that it was still in Canadian hands, which meant that the left flank of the attack would have been in acute danger.

"During the night the companies were withdrawn to the railway embankment. They were reinforced by, amongst other units, elements of Reserve Infantry Regiment 224, which had been placed at the disposal of 1st Bavarian Reserve Division, but which had strayed rather too far to the right as they advanced and so had become mixed up with the battle line of Detachment Meyer. To the left, 12th Company Reserve Infantry Regiment 34 was now deployed, with its left flank resting on the road Willerval – Farbus Station. To its south there was a gap of 800 metres for which no troops were available to fill. Also that same night two machine guns were deployed in the area of the windmill at the southwestern exit of Vimy. Their role was to secure the left flank of Detachment von Block, which was located around the Vimy crossroads. During the morning of 10 April, Oberstleutnant von Beyr, to whom Detachment von Block was also subordinated, withdrew on order of brigade to the cross roads about 1,200 metres further to the east. Two newly-arrived companies of Infantry Regiment 64 were deployed in the second line to the east of Farbus in order to improve the security of the railway embankment.

"A short time later 9th Company Reserve Infantry Regiment 34 arrived at the railway embankment. Two of its platoons were used to occupy the southern edge of Vimy and so improve the security of the left flank of Detachment von Block and one platoon was deployed to the north of Vimy Station to secure up to the right. Towards the afternoon a weak enemy force attacked the left flank near to Farbus Wood, but was easily repulsed. During the evening Hauptmann Lüters, commander of 1st Battalion Infantry Regiment 118, who was in telephone contact with Major Meyer but not Hauptmann von Block, told the former that he had been attacked by strong forces and had been forced back into the Second Position. He had suffered about 30% casualties and required reinforcements, small arms ammunition and grenades. Because links to regiment were destroyed, Major Meyer allocated to Hauptmann Lüters 1st Battalion Reserve Infantry Regiment 262, 10th and 12th Companies Reserve Infantry

Regiment 34 and 3rd Platoon 9th Company Reserve Infantry Regiment 34. This information was passed immediately to brigade and later, when communications were restored, to the regiment. Patrols launched by 3rd Battalion Reserve Infantry Regiment 34 established that the enemy was digging in along the wood edge to the south of Vimy. Weak sallies from this location were beaten off easily. The ground between the villages of Farbus and Vimy was free of enemy troops."

In Sector *Zollern* Reserve Infantry Regiment 262 was attacked by 3rd Canadian Division. This particular assault was initiated by several massive mine explosions that killed or neutralised many of the front line defenders. Those not directly caught in this way were few in number and could not provide much in the way of organised resistance. As a result the Canadian troops pushed right up to the third line. At that point they were held up by the well aimed fire of the supports, but this phase did not last long. Very soon the attackers were probing forward on either flank and the survivors had to withdraw to the depth positions, bringing with them the information that the First Position was been lost almost in its entirety. At that the commanding officers of 2nd and 3rd Battalions assembled their meagre reserves (7th and 10th Companies) and despatched them forward in a counter-stroke. Shortly afterwards, Major Reschke, commanding the 3rd [Fusilier] Battalion, was himself captured after a hand to hand battle and command devolved on Oberleutnant Freiherr von Richthofen.

Further south, men of 7th and 10th Companies managed to push the attackers back about a hundred metres and then held off several renewed attacks, though Hauptmann Kröber, commander of the 2nd Battalion and his adjutant, Leutnant Uhlhorn, were seriously wounded, Kröber dying a few days later in a field hospital. Having been ordered forward from Drocourt by the regimental commander, Major Freiherr von Richthofen, 9th Company, and the machine gun reserves arrived at about 8.00 am. With their aid and by dint of hard fighting it proved possible to hold the eastern edge of the ridge for the time being. Further assistance arrived when Leutnant Kopka and 2nd Machine Gun Company, Reserve Infantry Regiment 261, having force marched forward from Vimy, were put at the disposal of Reserve Infantry Regiment 262. Kopka, however, was killed later that day, shot through the head.[31] Throughout the day, the left flank of the regiment was in the air and under constant threat. However, Reserve Infantry Regiment 262 fought hard to retain the position and it was held for a considerable period against everything that the Canadians could throw at it.

To the north of the Reserve Infantry Regiment 262 front was Sector *Fischer*, which was defended that day by Reserve Infantry Regiment 261.

Feldwebel and Offizierstellvertreter Paul Radschun 3rd Company Reserve Infantry Regiment 261[32]

"Foggy, grey and dull, Easter Monday dawned to an icy wind and squalls of snow. Relief was due to take place that night. Suddenly, in the early dawn, thousands of British guns opened up as one, pouring their thunderous hail of iron on our positions. For the regiment a bombardment of such violence was totally unprecedented. In all directions an endless, dense series of fountains of clay shot upwards. Rocks were reduced to dark dust and tiles into red dust clouds. There was a constant terrible banging and crashing and, now and again, enormous thunderclaps, which could be heard above everything else, as ammunition dumps blew up. Impassively, but tense, von Goerne's regiment stuck it out in its trenches, completely surrounded by dreadful circles of roaring, blood-red fire, but with hands clutching the butts of the weapons tightly, determined to defend every last foot of ground to the last, in accordance with Prussian tradition.

"Then the British [*sic.*] came. As the fire which had been coming down intensely for hours lifted to the rear, the sentries of Reserve Infantry Regiment 261, peering through the dark blanket of mist and mud, caught sight of dense columns trudging forward through the clinging clay of No Man's Land with their rifles slung around them. At long last! Now it was going to be a matter of a battle with the same weapons; shot for shot, throw for throw. As the enemy came up to the barbed wire, there was a sudden burst of fire as Goerne's Grenadiers opened up on them, strengthened by their tough, firm and knightly soldierly spirit. The machine guns and rifles of the grenadiers crashed constantly. The dense British [*sic.*] columns were broken up and scattered by this determined defensive front. Heaps of khaki-clad bodies began to pile up in front of the trenches. Unfortunately, on the left flank the heavy enemy fire had destroyed almost all the machine guns. Only here did the enemy have it easy. Favoured by the bumps and dips of the craters, they succeeded in breaking through along the boundary with our neighbouring unit and were able to threaten our left flank and rear.

"Hand grenades fell in dreadful numbers among the brown-clad enemy. Finding themselves embroiled in the toughest of defensive battles, the flanking companies began to bleed to death. Only a few men succeeded in breaking out and some survivors fell into the hands of the enemy. But the British [*sic.*] also succeeded in breaking through on the right boundary. Once again there was bitterly hard fighting everywhere. The cracks of the infantry small arms were mixed with the drum beats of the hand grenades and, roaring above it all, was the thunder of the guns. Heroism and faithful duty escalated to titanic heights. Heavily outnumbered, the German grenadiers fought on. The weather conditions, namely the damp and the cold, caused stoppages in the feed mechanisms of the machine guns. Sometimes it was possible to clear them quickly but at other times no amount of blows, shaking or rattling would free the damp belts of these precious weapons and they remained silent, to be replaced by the use of grenades and the bayonet. In the meantime the enemy losses rose steeply, but again and again new brown masses surged forward, threatening to encircle the regiment, which fought on in a superhuman way. Everywhere the battle had broken down into a dreadful close-quarter battle, man against man."

It is an extraordinary fact but here in Sector *Fischer* the front line trenches that guarded the direct approaches to Hill 145 were very weakly held. In position in the front line were only 3rd Company (Balla), 1st Company (Wittkop), 11th Company (Wagner) and 9th Company (Neumann) but, despite their lack of numbers, they managed to halt the Canadian attack immediately to their front in No Man's Land. However there was greater Canadian success in the adjoining Sectors *Zollern* and *Döberitz*. Here thrusts had reached as far as the third line of the First Position and attempts were already being made to neutralise from the rear pockets of defenders who were still in action. Hauptmann Zickner, *KTK* of the northern sub-sector, known as 'Island Fischer'[33], immediately gave orders for a counter-stroke by 2nd Company (Hoppe) and 4th Company (Ketzlick) from the *Potsdamer Riegel* [Postdam Stop Line]. This was reasonably successful. Other uncommitted subunits, frequently acting on their initiative, rushed to assist more hard pressed elements of the regiment so, despite hard, close range fighting, the overall situation remained essentially the same for most of the day.

Reserve Infantry Regiment 261, an especially tough formation, was proving to be a hard proposition for the attacking 4th Canadian Division; the relative handful of machine gunners and riflemen who had not been caught by the bombardment maintained a torrent of fire, aided by well stocked dumps of ammunition. They fought with total desperation and determination, repeatedly bringing attacks to a bloody standstill out to their front. In fact, as the day wore on, the greatest danger was attack from one or other flank. At one point a determined Canadian effort was launched out of Sector *Zollern*. This threatened the integrity of the 3rd [Fusilier] Battalion, but the problem was spotted in time and *KTK* South, Major von Knobelsdorff, ordered an immediate counter-stroke by his reserves (10th and elements of the 12th Company) Reserve Infantry Regiment 261. There were serious casualties but, for the time being, the enemy thrust from the south was neutralised. Post war one of the participants left this account.

Feldwebel and Offizierstellvertreter Paul Radschun 3rd Company Reserve Infantry Regiment 261[34]

"In the meantime the enemy losses rose steeply, but again new brown masses surged forward, threatening to encircle the regiment, which fought on in a superhuman way. Everywhere the battle had broken down into a dreadful close-quarter battle, man against man. Without being able to help, my company commander, Leutnant Balla, had to look on, whilst his company was reduced to a tiny handful of men. Smoke, noise, wild shouts gradually died away in the evil, muddy battlefield. It was all over! Honour these heroes, who hoped to cheat death! Through the iron curtain, the fusiliers of the regiment, together with elements of 5th Company and the Infantry Engineer Company, continued to fight on and before this fresh defensive wall, which was inspired by the same spirit as the remainder, the last waves of the British [sic.] burnt out and the dreadful storm of steel ebbed away. A circling infantry cooperation pilot was able to make out the message of the signalling panels: 'We are holding the line'. During the morning of the following day came the moment of relief. The regiment lost twenty officers and 860 NCOs and men during this tough battle. It had not yielded. It had defended its appointed place to the last drop of blood; worthy of its fathers; worthy of its parent formation, the Prussian Guard; worthy of the heroic spirit of its beloved commander, who had always taught it to stand firm against the odds in all circumstances.

Leutnant Koschmieder, one of the last of the regimental officers unwounded at that point, was killed during this action as he manned a machine gun; and with him too were numerous other members of the counter-stroke force. The survivors fought on grimly, making use of captured Lews guns in many cases. If the situation on this flank could be described as 'precariously stable', other threats built up from Sector *Döberitz*, to the north. As a result, elements of 1st Battalion were at full stretch for hours on end, as they attempted with some success to fend off repeated Canadian attacks. Leutnant Klabisch was killed during these battles, but a counter-stroke conducted on Hauptmann Zickner's orders by 2nd and 4th Companies managed to throw the Canadians back. The cost was high. Leutnant Ketzlick, commander 4th Company, was killed, together with one of his platoon commanders, Leutnant Lehmann, as well as numerous other ranks.

Hauptmann Behrmann Reserve Infantry Regiment 261[35]

"While the soldierly fate of the right flank companies was being determined, great masses of British [sic] soldiers broke in along the boundary between Reserve Infantry Regiment 261 and Bavarian Infantry Regiment 11 (16th Bavarian Infantry Division). This caused an immediate break in the desperate defence. Whilst the main thrust continued to the east, strong forces swung south, falling against the flank of the 1st Company (Reserve Leutnant Wittkop) and 3rd Company (Reserve Leutnant Balla). In this area, too, all the machine guns were out of order. The first serious resistance did not come until the enemy hit the *Berliner-Riegel* [Berlin Stop Line], where the weapon of Gefreiter Neumann was still in full working order.

"Of the first three British [sic] waves, almost nothing remained, but then there was a stoppage which could not be cleared. Frantic efforts, shaking and pulling could achieve nothing. Having soaked up dirt and moisture for days, the belt was jammed and could not be freed. Shot through the head, Gefreiter

Neumann fell, as did the rest of his crew, together with a large group manning the trench. Some brave lads rescued the machine gun and carried it into an adjacent post. To the front the enemy, who had been pressing strongly, were pinned down in the muddy craters by the fire of the remaining infantrymen."

The Canadian 4th Division had also suffered considerably, so further attacks were suspended until night fell. However, a further major effort was directed at Sector *Döberitz*. When battle was joined there, the ensuing confused action gained ground. Leutnant Hoppe was wounded and evacuated. Leutnants Ketzlich and Lehmann were killed, so command in this vital sector passed to Reserve Leutnant Fladt, who had himself been wounded in the head. He eventually had no choice but to pull back towards the *Potsdamer Riegel* [Potsdam Stop Line] and the Intermediate Position (North). Elsewhere, Reserve Infantry Regiment 261 was still holding right forward in the centre of the position. Extraordinary though it sounds, what was left of 3rd, 1st, 11th and 9th Companies was still holding on there, despite increasing exhaustion and casualties that went on mounting.

As an example of the physical strain involved, Leutnant Balla, commanding 3rd Company, noted that during one hand grenade battle when the Canadians were throwing Mills bombs up to thirty metres, his worn out men, each having thrown dozens of grenades, could only achieve half that distance. Despite this, the fight went on. One cool rifleman of his company, benefitting from the protection of an infantry shield, fought off one large group of Canadians single handed for several hours. The company also enjoyed the occasional stroke of luck. When a British aircraft appeared overhead to engage the company in its crater position, the defenders fired white flares at it. Apparently this was a British recognition signal and the aircraft flew away again.

Hauptmann Behrmann Reserve Infantry Regiment 261[36]

"Bringing down concentrated fire against the forces pushing down from the east were the machine guns, echeloned back towards the rear, and the remainder of the garrison under Leutnant Balla. British [sic] losses were heavy, but ever more groups kept streaming forward through the gap that existed between our left hand neighbouring division and us. Forward, elements of 3rd Company under Leutnant Klabisch hung on grimly, regardless of their casualties. They fought with the desperation of the heroes of yesteryear, but without being able fully to beat back the troops who were able to take cover in the numerous shell holes. Firing from the rim of a crater, Gefreiter Siefert shot at every worthwhile target, whilst the British [sic] threw grenades from a range of thirty to thirty five metres. One by one these throwers were picked off. 'Yet another', the courageous [Siefert] would shout after each shot.

"Unteroffizier Becker was despatched to Battalion Headquarters with a report on the situation, upon which piece of paper each of their valuable lives depended. Becker was never seen again and, minute by minute, the daring little band that was 3rd Company reduced in numbers. A few more shots, a last grenade then, in one final desperate effort, Leutnant Klabisch and his grenadiers fixed bayonets and charged the enemy. Wild shouts were drowned in the noise of British [*sic*] grenades exploding, there was a final flurry of hand to hand fighting and the flickering shadows disappeared into the mud like ghosts. It was all over. Honour the memory of these men who, staring certain death in the face, nevertheless hoped to cheat it."

By mid afternoon, when things were becoming desperate for the defence, some assistance arrived when the regimental commander, Oberstleutnant von Goerne, sent forward the last of his reserves, namely two platoons of 5th Company, to the Fusilier [3rd] Battalion. Their numbers boosted, what was left of the battalion was able to re-establish the link to Reserve Infantry Regiment 262 and maintain it. The broader question, however, was if it would prove possible to launch a large scale counter-attack before the ground holding troops were worn down completely. The omens were not good. The comprehensive Canadian Corps fire plan had destroyed or neutralised a high proportion of the German guns and means of communication were almost totally wrecked. This meant in turn complete reliance on runners, who had to negotiate the cratered area under constant heavy fire. One runner, despatched from the summit of Hill 145 to the regimental command post of Reserve Infantry Regiment 261 near Vimy village, for example, took three and a half hours just to cover the two and a half kilometre distance involved.

In addition, mistakes in staff work meant that operational reserves were held too far to the rear that day. Nevertheless, it was essential to arrange some sort of counter action, using whatever troops were to hand. One of the company commanders involved in an attempted counter-attack in the 16th Bavarian Infantry Division sector described his experiences later in a manner that leaves no room for doubt concerning the obstacles he had faced.

Reserve Oberleutnant Trummert 4th Company Bavarian Infantry Regiment 14[37]

"We were rudely awakened from our sleep during the early hours of Easter Monday. An unimaginable increase in enemy fire to the densest drum fire, coupled with the noise of several mine explosions and the roar of our own defensive fire, set in so swiftly that no more effective alarm system to wake us could possibly be devised. Within a few moments, more or less equipped for battle, we were assembled in our companies and ready to move on the road in front of the miners' cottages at Méricourt. There we stood, whilst every man wondered why our services had not been called on. There was a simple explanation why the Divison did not make use of us or 3rd Battalion Bavarian Reserve Infantry Regiment 11, located in Hénin Liétard, which formed the other part of the reserve. It was because the first information concerning the attack, which had occurred at 5.00 am, did not arrive at Divisional Headquarters until 8.00 am and, when it did, unfortunately it did not make the situation clear.

"As a result, initially we had several hours at our disposal to prepare ourselves for what was to come, distribute coffee, then issue ammunition, hand grenades and rations. Towards 10.00 am the Battalion received orders to move forward as brigade reserve. Because the roads were packed with ammunition wagons, transport for the wounded etc., we advanced along previously reconnoitred trackways. We soon found that even these routes were swept with artillery fire, which forced us to make numerous time-consuming detours, but had no other effect. Nevertheless, by about midday, we arrived at La Coulotte. We spent the first part of the afternoon there whilst the battalion Commander went to find out what the situation was. It transpired that the morning attack had been limited to Vimy Ridge, but that a large part of the First Position had been lost.

"Bavarian Infantry Regiment 14 had maintained its positions on the *Gießler Höhe,* however, which meant that there was a dangerous gap to its left which had to be closed. Towards 6.00 pm the expected order arrived from Brigade. The Battalion was to launch a counter-attack in Sector *Döberitz*, which would enable Bavarian Infantry Regiment 14 to hold on to its positions. The battalion ordered the following dispositions: 3rd Company *Sandgrube* [Sand Pit] 3; 4th Company *Sandgrube* 2; 2nd Company Givenchy north of the track to Souchez and 1st Company to the south of the same track. From these assembly areas, the further advance was to begin at 8.00 pm and, because the companies were not able to set off until 6.30 pm, timings were tight.

"In addition a number of other circumstances made matters even more difficult: the difficult going underfoot; the snow squalls, which meant that darkness fell early; lack of knowledge of the route and the terrain; and last, but by no means least, the considerable amount of enemy fire. As a result, it was not until 11.00 pm that it could be reported that all companies were in position. This in turn meant that the advance could not begin until midnight: the line to be achieved was defined as one linking Bavarian Infantry Regiment 14 with weak elements of Bavarian Infantry Regiment 11, who were holding out near the *Sachsen Lager.*

"For my 4th Company the objective was in the former Third Line in the area *Souchez Weg – Koch Weg* [Souchez – and Cook Ways]. Between my start line, the *Hamburgergraben* [Hamburg Trench] and *Souchez Weg* lay the 500 metre wide *Givenchy Mulde* [Givenchy Hollow], which was always wet and, as a result of the winter weather and years of shelling, had become a bottomless crater field. Founded mostly on Jurassic chalk, the entire re-entrant was as good as impassable. As a result not one single communications track led forward from Givenchy in the direction of Souchez across it. Now, across this terrain, which was completely unknown to them, 3rd and 4th Companies had to advance, through snow squalls and the pitch black night.

"From *Hamburgergraben* the ground dropped away sharply to the base of the hollow, which was located much closer to this trench than to *Souchezweg*. I set off with two platoons leading and one following up, right rear, with the task of maintaining contact with 3rd Company. To begin with the formation was maintained quite well, but the closer we got to the base of the hollow the swampier the ground became. With each step we sank up to our knees. We were no longer advancing; this was mere staggering forward. Anybody who had chosen to wear jackboots rather than the more practical lace-up boots with puttees was extremely lucky not to lose them. Many were in this predicament and unable to continue. The remainder waded gallantly on, some moving faster; some slower, encumbered as they were by the heavy weight of ammunition, hand grenades, rations and other items.

"As a result the company was soon strung out. Flares that helped us to maintain direction and cohesion were only fired occasionally, but there were continuous salvoes of enemy artillery fire in the Hollow, interspersed with bursts of enemy machine gun fire. I was in the lead with my so-called company staff (two runners and my brave Sanitäts-Unteroffizier Schönberger). Because there was no sign of the enemy, we made our way forward as quickly as possible, reasoning that the platoons would be following close behind. After what seemed to be a very long time, we arrived, dog-tired and pouring with sweat, at a collapsed trench, which from its direction and dimensions could only be *Souchezweg*. Here we realised for the first time that we had lost all contact with our platoons.

"We lurked there for some time, our eyes straining to pierce the darkness. We seemed to be entirely alone. Certainly there was not a trace of the enemy, our company or any other. I despatched my runners to find the platoons and remained there with Unteroffizier Schönberger. More time passed without us seeing another person, so we moved further on, in order to reach the Third Line. Suddenly we saw steel helmets sticking up out of the mud very close. It was impossible to tell if they were the flat British helmets or the coal-scuttle shaped German ones. The wearers were not moving any more than we were, so I attempted to contact them in a neutral manner, by giving a quiet whistle. Now there was some movement. The whistles were returned and to my joy I realised that we had German helmets in front of us.

"It was the commander of 1st Company who, together with some of his men, had moved to find us. Oberleutnant Völk was in a similar situation to me, He too had pressed on with a few men in advance of his company. Soon we were joined by some sections of 2nd Company Bavarian Infantry Regiment 14 under Reserve Leutnant Türk. Before the remainder of the Battalion arrived we came across a few men of Bavarian Infantry Regiment 11 in an almost totally collapsed dugout; but of the enemy there was no sign. Soon, moving along either side of the communication trench, came 1st and 2nd Companies, more or less complete, then a platoon of my 4th Company under Vizefeldwebel Rupp turned up. To our left 3rd Battalion Bavarian Infantry Regiment 11 had moved strong forces forward into the Third Line, which now seemed to be held in sufficient strength.

"In the circumstances my platoon and I could be spared, so after a discussion with Oberleutnant Völk I headed back to the start point, collecting the other two platoons of my company on the way. They had got lost in the hollow and were stuck. Back at the assembly area I met up with 3rd Company, which had swung round so much during its advance that it ended up in Sector *Burg* [i.e. on the right flank of the divisional frontage, rather than the left!]. I went to Command Post *Augsburg* in Givenchy, which was occupied by the commanding officers of our battalion and that of 3rd Battalion Bavarian Infantry Regiment 11, where I made a written report concerning the results of the night's operation and the current situation in the Third Line. Both commanders were of the opinion that as much had been achieved with the forces available as had been expected."

Further south, once Brigade Commander 79 Reserve Infantry Brigade, Generalleutnant Dieterich, received information about enemy penetrations into the 1st Bavarian Reserve Division sector, together with news that there had been break in on both flanks of 79th Reserve Division, he ordered his immediate reserves, 2nd Battalion Reserve Infantry Regiment 261 (Hauptmann von Goerne) and 2nd Battalion Reserve Infantry Regiment 263 (Oberleutnant Heinicke), to move to the railway embankment south of Vimy and to get their machine gun companies there by the fastest possible means. Simultaneously, 2nd Battalion Reserve Infantry Regiment 262 (Hauptmann von Block) was called forward to the cross tracks at La Gueule d'Ours, east of Vimy, as a final reserve. Once these forces were in position the immediate threat of a breakthrough in the Reserve Infantry Regiment 262 sector had been countered, but the troops in place were still far too weak to contemplate launching an attack at that time.

However, about midday, 79th Reserve Division was ordered by Group Vimy to recapture the Third Line and the commander learned that 1st Battalion Infantry Regiment 118, 56th Division and 3rd Battalion Reserve Infantry Regiment 34, 80th Reserve Division, had been sent to reinforce him. Orders had reached these troops in Billy Montigny a few minutes earlier. They were to move at once and their midday meals had to be abandoned uneaten in the field kitchens. This was not the best preparation for battle but, nevertheless, they force marched forward, trying to avoid constant shrapnel fire.[38] General von Bacmeister, commander 79th Reserve Division, decided to use his reinforcements to close the gap which had opened up between his southern regiment and 1st Bavarian Reserve Division and to launch a counter-attack against Telegraph Hill [Hill 135, north of Thélus]. For this task he allocated 1st Battalion

Infantry Regiment 118 and one company of Machine Gun Sharpshooter Detachment 20 to Generalleutnant Dieterich.

This was part of a broader operation to attempt to restore the situation along the ridge. Action was urgently required, but such were the problems that it was 6.00 pm before the troops were in position and able to cross their start lines.

Sergeant Dorrmann 6th Company, Reserve Infantry Regiment 261[39]

"During the early hours of Easter Monday a dull rumbling from the front woke us. Soon we received the order, 'Get your assault order on. Everything else must stay here!' Each man was to take a piece of bread with him. The most senior of the NCOs were placed in charge of sections of soldiers and then the company set off, leading the battalion. The field artillery was going into positions to the left and right, with British shells landing in amongst us. Nevertheless we reached the railway embankment near Vimy unscathed. The 210 mm howitzers of a Saxon foot artillery regiment were in position here. My group took up position near some of these monsters. With each shot I thought that my eardrums would burst. In addition, shell fragments and pieces of ballast from the embankment were flying everywhere and hitting our helmets. Later the Tommies lifted their fire more to the rear areas, where I could observe the approach of our ammunition columns. A gunner standing jacketless by one of the guns stopped a wagon and swiftly unloaded it. Then, just like a baker placing loaves of bread in the oven, he loaded one shell after the other into his gun, which was readjusted right and left after each shell. If I had been allowed to leave my post I would have run over to this comrade to express my appreciation.

"As things became a little calmer we left sentries up on the embankment and took cover in the dugouts of the artillery. Towards 9.00 pm, we were ordered forward. I went with Leutnant Rahlfs at the head of our platoon. The artillery fire of both sides hindered our movement. Wearing our gas masks, we leapt from one crater to another, dodging the falling gas and phosphorous shells. In the meantime the sky had darkened so much that it was impossible to see the next man, even if it was possible to touch him. There was then a shower of hail which, even though it was thoroughly unpleasant, saved us. We were not far off from the howitzer position, which had once been German, when we came under fire from there. Because our flanks were hanging in the air, we were later ordered back to our jumping off point. Unfortunately two men were missing and we never heard anything of them again. Towards 4.00 am we were meant to be launching another assault, but this was cancelled later.

"Gradually we began to feel hungry, because we had each only brought a piece of bread forward with us. The gunners and our sister regiment 263, to whom we had been allocated, gave us something to eat; the number of casualties meant that not all the rations had been consumed. During the morning [presumably 10 April], heavy fire continued to fall on the rear areas and during the afternoon on our position too. A shell wounded the sentry in front of our dugout and we took him to the medical dugout at the railway underpass. I then went and checked on the sentries, noticing that Grenadier W., who was always very fearful when he had not had a drink, was flinching whenever a shell landed. I moved him ten metres to the left and said, 'Keep your chin up, they're not shooting at the place where you are standing now'.

"The sentry who had been relieved and I continued on, when suddenly a shell exploded, we flew through the air like dolls and found ourselves lying on our stomachs with wounds to the shoulder and arm. We moved to the medical dugout, where we were bandaged and had the well-known labels attached to us. I reported to the company commander and requested to be allowed to stay with the company, but he said, 'My dear Dorrmann, you are the father of a family and wounded. Even though your wound may not be very severe, go where you are sent. Nobody knows what is going to happen here, or even if anyone will come out of it alive!' We parted with a powerful handshake and, with his good wishes ringing in my ears, I made my way to the medical company."

Even once the attack began, the problems continued to mount. Visibility was very bad due to the darkness and repeated snow squalls, so maintaining direction was difficult. Canadian advanced groups were pushed out of Vimy village itself, but it proved to be impossible to advance beyond the Second Position. Furthermore, contact was not established with the left flank of Reserve Infantry Regiment 262, nor was it possible to consolidate at La Compte Wood [the northwest extension of Goulot Wood], until much later in the evening. The 1st Bavarian Reserve Division counter-attack force had enormous difficulty getting forward and this in turn affected the ability of the troops to advance effectively from the railway embankment. As a result, this attack was held along the track Vimy-Farbus, mainly because of heavy artillery fire. Knowing that this force was isolated and effectively out of contact, Oberstleutnant von Goerne ordered it to drop back to the railway.

In response, Generalleutnant Dieterich allocated half of 3rd Battalion Reserve Infantry Regiment 34 and some machine guns to Reserve Infantry Regiment 263, This enabled Oberstleutnant von Behr to order the consolidation of the southern edge of Vimy and establish contact with elements of Reserve Infantry Regiment 261. Given that Vimy village and the surrounding area were being shelled constantly with high explosive and gas, it took the whole night to achieve this and, as dawn broke, there was still a wide gap to 1st Bavarian Reserve Division. Again Dieterich reacted to the situation, by sending one company of Reserve Infantry Regiment 34 and two engineer mining companies to Reserve Infantry Regiment 263 so as to thicken up its left flank defences.

Nightfall was also the signal for the Canadians to attack those members of Reserve Infantry Regiment 261 who were still holding out on Vimy Ridge, well forward of the remainder of 79th Reserve Division. It had proved impossible to reinforce this isolated group and mortar and machine gun fire had continued to take a heavy toll on the defenders. With their ammunition running out, pressed on three sides by greatly superior numbers, they were forced, post by post, to surrender. Leutnants Balla, Wittkop and Osthold (severely wounded) were taken prisoner, as were those who were left of 1st and 3rd Companies. Offizierstellvertreter Stracke (1st Company), Leutnant Klabisch (3rd Company), Leutnants Lehman and Ketzlich (4th Company) had all been killed, as had many other NCOs and men. Their three machine guns had broken down already, but were finally destroyed with hand grenades. The light mortars and grenade launchers, out of ammunition, were buried, though their crews fought on for a time.

In the end, with the Canadians closing in the last pockets of resistance, with all grenades thrown and rifle ammunition fired, a desperate attempt was made by a party under Leutnant Balla to pull back to the depth positions. Unluckily, just as they set off to dash to the rear, a heavy artillery concentration came down, killing some and scattering the remainder, very few of whom made it to the rear. Balla had a very lucky escape from death when he fell into a water filled shell hole and only just managed, by using his last reserves of strength, to avoid drowning. Stuck fast in the mud, he could only lie there exhausted until help came. Unfortunately for him he was found by a party of Canadians, who pulled him out, so that he, too, went into captivity.

Further to the rear, a maximum effort by Reserve Infantry Regiment 261 produced sufficient defenders to hold on to Intermediate Position, which ran along the eastern edge of the ridge; the deployment during the night 9/10 April of 3rd Company Engineer Battalion 18 made the situation even more secure. The same could not be said to the south, where Reserve Infantry Regiment 262 clashed throughout the night with units of the Canadian 3rd Division and where there was a risk of outflanking or even encirclement until 1st Battalion Infantry Regiment 118, under Hauptmann von Block, managed to advance, link up and close the gap. Then, during the morning of 10 April the arrival of a company of Reserve Infantry Regiment 34 eased the manpower situation further.

Despite the fact that ground had been lost, as dawn broke on 10 April the German chain of command felt that hard fighting by the forward troops had bought sufficient time for the immediate crisis to be over. The previous evening two battalions from 111th Infantry Division had already arrived followed, on 10 April, by the remainder of the division. Placed at the disposal of Group Vimy, two units – 2nd Battalion Infantry Regiment 73 and 3rd (composite) Battalion Infantry Regiment 164 – were at once allocated to 79th Reserve Division, which sent them forward to Generalleutnant Dieterich. Their march to the front, first in a snow storm and then later, when the skies cleared, under direct enemy observation from Vimy Ridge, was anything but straightforward. Having arrived at La Gueule d'Ours about 10.00 am, two companies and some machine guns were sent at once to assist the regiments fighting further forward. Dieterich kept the remaining two companies of 3rd Battalion Infantry Regiment 164 in reserve, together with a total of eight machine guns. The primary task of this group was to be prepared to move to defend the divisional left flank if required.

Reserve Hauptmann Mierzinsky 3rd Battalion Infantry Regiment 164[40]

"The next objective was a small rise in the ground about three kilometres away. There I ordered a halt and the preparation of hasty defences whilst I went to the Brigade Command Post, which was located further forward in a deep chalk pit. I wished to report in so that I could be given further orders and be briefed on the situation. After we had covered another kilometre the snow stopped, the skies cleared and it was a bright, sunny day. The enemy must have been able to see us clearly from Vimy Ridge, but apparently the observers must have had bad communications with their guns. There was absolutely no cover and we just had to go on hurrying forward because the situation to the front was known to be grave.

"We were still about 1,000 metres from our destination when very heavy enemy shrapnel fire came down. It would have accounted for all of us had it not been directed too far to our rear. We were also lucky again because a thick snow squall came down before the enemy guns could home in on us. In the meantime the companies were able to dig in for protection behind a fold in the ground. The ground was one morass, but soft clay and chalk were accepted as the price to pay and there were no casualties. Together with Leutnant Reinhardt and six runners I reached the chalk pit where the Brigade staff was located and reported our arrival.

"I experienced a great feeling of relief because three quarters of an hour previously, when we left Rouvroy and moved into the open ground, I had not believed that it would be possible to move the Battalion forward so easily and with no casualties…The Brigade Commander, General Dieterich, whose headquarters was situated in a weakly constructed dugout in the chalk pit, was highly delighted at our arrival. There was still a further 1,500 metres to the front line, but this was only weakly held. The enemy could very easily have overrun us and captured the brigade staff. However, everybody who was still occupying holes in and around the chalk pit was under clear orders from the Brigade Commander and was determined to defend it to the last.

"The general himself gave the briefing and the orders, not leaving it to his adjutant or orderly officer. The orders were very specific. 1st and 3rd Companies were to take over protection of the left flank from the weak forces currently manning the railway embankment there and were to be echeloned in depth. 11th and 12th Companies were to act as divisional reserve: 12th Company providing further protection on the left flank and 11th Company remaining in the area of the chalk pit. It was recommended that I used one of the dugouts in the chalk pit for my own command post because, in the event of an attack from the endangered left flank, I should be able personally to observe the ground from there.

"Together with the company commanders I reconnoitred the ground, which was under shrapnel fire. Two hours later, split into small groups to avoid casualties and taking advantage of the snow squalls, the companies could be led forward to their appointed locations. Because the field kitchen would not be arriving until the following morning, I authorised the consumption of the iron rations."

In the event no attack occurred but this standby duty was nevertheless thoroughly unpleasant. Unteroffizier Schwarze of 3rd Company wrote later, 'From 9.00 am until the evening we lay there in the snow and dug in. We then pulled our groundsheets around us. Freezing and numb with cold we crouched down in our holes. During the night we dug in again, further forward on the left flank, near a sunken road.'

The front in the area where the break in had occurred now ran as follows: western edge of the village of Givenchy – eastern edge of Vimy Ridge – south of Vimy to the railway embankment – from there south of Bailleul eastwards, bending backwards along the western edges of the villages of Gavrelle, Monchy and Wancourt. This was clearly a serious setback but, as always, the German reaction had been swift and decisive. Already the defence had been strengthened and an attempt by British troops, reinforced with tanks, to attack the rear of 79th Reserve Division from the Farbus direction was brought to a swift halt by massed gunfire. There was, however, further intense fighting on Vimy Ridge itself. Its eastern edge had been lost temporarily, but was recaptured in a determined counter-stroke. However, the situation of 1st Battalion Reserve Infantry Regiment 261 soon became virtually untenable, as Canadian troops continued to press heavily on either flank.

Having fought so hard to retain its part of the Ridge, the battalion was very reluctant to withdraw to the Second Position. It carried on defending *Potsdamer Graben* [Potsdam Trench] and the Intermediate Position (North), while the Canadians dug in to its front. 3rd Company Pionier Regiment 18 arrived to reinforce it that afternoon, and 6th Company Fusilier Regiment 73, under Leutnant Gipkens, also appeared forward the following morning. There followed an intense battle for possession of the Intermediate Position, by now the front line. It was now almost over for the defence as it was forced back to the *Sachsenlager* after heavy shelling and further Canadian attacks. A stand in *Sachsenweg* [Saxon Way] prevented any more progress for the time being. However, by that evening, it became clear that the battalion was outflanked left and right. All the remainder of Vimy Ridge was by now controlled by the Canadians and British divisions to its north and there was no chance of further reinforcement. The realisation grew that they had done all they could to hold the ridge, so the commanding officer decided to use the discretion granted to him a day earlier and to withdraw to the Second Position. In a final skilful operation, covered by a rearguard, what was left of 1st Battalion and its attached engineers pulled back, taking with them their wounded, their telephones and reserve rations.

By this time the men of 79th Reserve Division had spent an extended period at the front, enduring dreadful conditions. As a formation they were fought out, so Group Vimy decided to relieve them during the early hours of 11 April with units of 111th

Infantry Division. The process began as soon as 2nd Battalion Infantry Regiment 76, along with its regimental staff, and 2nd Battalion Infantry Regiment 164 arrived. It was indicative of the trial through which Reserve Infantry Regiment 261 had passed that Infantry Regiment 76 only had to deploy 7th and 8th Companies forward in the Second Position to relieve all of the survivors. 5th and 6th Companies and 2nd Machine Gun Company went into reserve east of the railway embankment. They then spent several unpleasant hours here, exposed under heavy fire in smashed, mud-filled trenches which lacked dugouts.[41]

It had of course been the intention of the higher commanders to arrange for reinforcements to be on the scene far quicker and soon enough to intervene decisively during the early stages of the battle. As it was, delays and indecision cost the defence dearly. One good example is the experience of 1st Battalion Fusilier Regiment 73. It was meant to have been called forward as early as 8 April, but twelve hours after the start of the battle it was still back in its holding area. Its commanding officer, Rittmeister Böckelmann, was absent at the time, so the move was organised by one of the company commanders.

Reserve Leutnant Schmidt 1st Battalion Fusilier Regiment 73[42]

"At 5.00 pm on Easter Monday we were stood to in response to a telephone call from the regiment then, at 6.30 pm, came the order to be ready, less our heavy equipment, to board a train at Seclin at 7.00 pm. That was impossible because it was nine kilometres away, so I managed to get the order changed to 'as soon as possible'. Our spirits were dampened by the weather; it began to snow hard and through it the battalion marched via Attiches to Seclin, prior to waiting a solid two hours at the station before we could be loaded.

"We then sat for four hours in freezing cold carriages and it was not until 3.00 am 10 April that we alighted in Beaumont. After reporting in to 79th Reserve Division, we then began to look for billets, which were already full to overflowing with other troops. The company commanders raced around searching and, about an hour later, somewhere had been found for everybody. At 7.00 am we departed for Drocourt. Here I handed over command to Rittmeister Böckelmann, who had by now arrived and, a little later, the battalion headed off to Fresnoy."

By dawn on 11 April the Vimy Ridge sector had been reorganised and the exhausted troops of 79th Reserve Division largely withdrawn. Still in position in the part of Sector *Zollern* near the eastern edge of Vimy Ridge, a few men of Reserve Infantry Regiment 262 hung on grimly in muddy craters covered in a fall of fresh snow. Despite all efforts it had proved to be impossible to get reliefs forward the previous night, so they had to endure a further twenty four hours in the line until they were finally withdrawn the following night.[43]

The German battle line now ran along the Second Position, bending back from the south western corner of Vimy to the railway embankment. For a short period and for the sake of continuity, 79th Reserve divisional, brigade and sector commanders remained in command of the troops of 111th Infantry Division, even after their own infantry had been relieved. Simultaneously, when Vimy Ridge was evacuated during the night 10/11 April, the last of the batteries which still deployed west of the railway embankment were withdrawn to less vulnerable places. Some went into action at La Gueule d'Ours; others right back behind the Third Position. A British attack directed at Vimy on 11 April was shot to a standstill by the German defensive fire. Ominously for the British army, the number of serviceable guns was already increasing markedly. Only two days after the offensive opened, this sector of the front was being defended by twenty two field guns and twelve heavy guns forward of the Third Position.

At this time the main British effort was concentrated along the line of the Arras-Cambrai road. Taking advantage of the relative calm on the Vimy front and given that the Second Position here was effectively untenable with the Canadians established on the ridge, Army Group Crown Prince Rupprecht decided to break clean, pulling back to the Third Position along the line Lens-Avion-Méricourt-Acheville-Arleux-Oppy-Gavrelle. Most of the artillery was pulled out during the night 11/12 April, then the following night everything else, less a few rearguards left behind for deception purposes, was also withdrawn. By dawn on 13 April, all the German Positions from Liévin via Vimy to Gavrelle had been evacuated. Command then passed to 111th Infantry Division and, on 14 April, the surviving batteries of Reserve Field Artillery Regiment 63 were also withdrawn to rest and re-equip.

The withdrawal itself was planned well and executed smoothly. Although the staffs at various levels were stretched dealing with the contact battle, care was taken to produce clear orders and to distribute them in good time to those involved. The war diary of 2nd Battalion Fusilier Regiment 73 recorded how the operation unfolded at unit level.[44]

"The front line was to be evacuated at 3.00 am and the railway embankment by 4.00 am. At 4.30 am, following the blowing of charges, the last of the patrols commanded by officers was to withdraw. The use of roads was to be avoided during the withdrawal. During the night we had an unpleasant surprise when our artillery began bringing down fire at 2.15 am on the embankment, which was to have been denied until 4.00 am. The telephone system failed and it was some time before they could be stopped. Later, stage by stage, all the companies arrived safely in Rouvroy."

The definitive withdrawal to the Third Position marked the end of the fighting for the main battle for Vimy Ridge. However, there had been hard fighting around The Pimple, west of Givenchy, on 12 April. Both Bavarian Infantry Regiments 11 and 14, 16th Bavarian Infantry Division had taken severe casualties during the days leading up to

9 April and then subsequently once the offensive opened. Because of the confused situation the decision was taken not to relieve the Bavarians, but instead to introduce reinforcements from 4th Guards Division to reinforce initially, then to complete the relief later. As a result, Fusilier [3rd] Battalion Grenadier Guard Regiment 5 and 1st Battalion Reserve Infantry Regiment 93, having arrived in the early hours of 11 April, were the units defending the Pimple and the surrounding area on 12 April when 46th, 50th and 44th Battalions of 10th Canadian Brigade attacked it in strength. A composite 2nd Battalion Bavarian Infantry Regiment 14 was retained in reserve and the defence was commanded from a Grenadier Guard Regiment 5 *KTK* at *Angres-Kreuz*.

The overall situation for the defence was extremely worrying. What was left of the network of trenches had been smashed by the shelling and every crater or portion of trench was full of mud and freezing cold water. To makes matters worse, incessant British artillery fire continued to take a toll of the defenders. This was not the end of the problems. Despite reinforcement, there were simply too few troops on the position to be able to conduct a continuous defence. As a result there were several gaps in the front line ranging up to three hundred metres wide. It was quite clear that a determined attack would be unstoppable. No more reinforcements could be made available, all the telephone lines were cut and it was impossible to arrange light signalling. No more troops could be made available, so the companies had to make the best of the situation. Reduced to reliance on runners and messenger dogs for the passage of information, the defence clung on in the vile conditions and awaited their fate. Strangely there does not seem to have been any suggestion that a voluntary withdrawal should be arranged, despite the fact that anyone could see how vulnerable the position was.

During the early hours of 12 April British artillery fire crashed down all over the positions, hammering the half starved and chilled defenders. Casualties mounted, evacuation was extremely difficult then, at about 4.00 am, the attacks started to come in. For a time these were blunted by small arms fire and large scale use of hand grenades but, within an hour, with visibility reduced severely by a snow squall, heavy calibre fire began pounding depth positions and a mass of Canadian infantry advanced close up behind a rolling shrapnel barrage. In the circumstances it is remarkable that there was any defensive fire from the German guns. However, even when it arrived, somewhat late, it was too weak to cause the Canadians any problems.

Exploiting the wide gaps, the Canadian infantry thrust deep into the *Givenchy Mulde* with relative ease. Despite the hopeless position, numerous small groups of defenders hung on, using their rifles and grenades, until one by one they were overrun. The remnants of 9th Company, commanded by Vizefeldwebel Bröker, for example, clung on in their shell holes until only four men were still fit to fight. At that, seeing that it was hopeless, Bröker ordered them to pull back, but he remained where he was to provide covering fire. Bröker was killed at this time and of the entire 9th Company, only Fusiliers Heinrichs, Koog and Palubitski made it back to join their comrades in rear. It was the same throughout the *Gießlerhöhe*, *Givenchy Mulde* and Givenchy Wood, where only a handful of men managed to fight their way back to relative safety in Givenchy village.[45]

One of the company commanders of 3rd Battalion Bavarian Infantry Regiment 14 later described the fighting; though it uses a certain amount of purple prose, it provides a reasonably accurate overview of the desperate struggle fought out on 12 April.

Hauptmann G Marsching Bavarian Infantry Regiment 14[46]

"[On 12 April] it was hard to obtain a clear view forward. The sentries huddled deep into their coats. Suddenly the sound of hand grenades could be heard, together with rifle and machine gun fire. Then it was quiet once more for a time, before the noise increased again... Up went the flare signals, which brought down destructive fire from hundreds of guns. A few moments passed then a curtain of shell splinters, smoke and dust came down in front of our forward positions. A runner rushed past, 'They have been beaten off'.

"...*Sandgrube* [Sand Pit] 4 was actually located well back as the fourth line of defence. To our front, forming the third line, was another sand pit. There and in the two forward trenches, fought a battalion of the Fusilier Guards.[47] To the south the ground fell away into the bottomless muddy morass of the *Givenchy Mulde* [Hollow]. A few deep mined dugouts in the side of the sand pit had been crushed. In the centre of the workings were two shell holes, six metres wide and full of water and mud. In a corner to the left was a machine gun in an improvised firing position. Our machine guns gave us our best chance of holding on in the event of an attack. The second machine gun was still down in a dugout.

"Had all hell broken loose? An ear-splitting racket began and great crashes filled the air, continuing as the first of the 150 mm shells began landing in the pit. A dugout was crushed, but there was no time to dwell on it. Everybody stood to. Sleet and snowflakes whirled about until showers of shell splinters merged with them, ripping apart anything they touched. Our nerves were on edge. What was happening forward? The first of the wounded stumbled past. 'The Tommies have broken through!' We were enraged – impossible! But it was true. The fire slackened. Like a whirlwind the brave lads of 12th Company made their way forward through mud knee deep towards the shell-torn firing line.

"Two machine guns were swiftly mounted on the damaged stands. Come on then, Canadians! Two hundred metres from us and not a step further! Suddenly, lunging forward from Sand Pit 2, came the Canadian assault troops, disdaining to take cover. They assumed that their hellish fire had killed or buried us all. Suddenly fire was opened! Who gave the order? In no time the first Canadian wave was swept away. Had they just gone to ground? Fresh masses of troops launched forward. Our machine guns hammered away angrily and the second line sank bloodily into the deep mud. The ground to our front was clear of enemy. Some tens of wounded were dragged into the dugouts and we buried one dead man carefully by the entrance to one of them.

"Two runners rushed towards the command post. One of them got stuck in the mud and lost his boots, but the other delivered a short, sharp message to Major Utz [Commanding Officer 3rd Battalion Bavarian Infantry Regiment 14], 'Sand Pit 4 is firmly in our hands!' But they never gave up. Heavy flanking fire, rising to drum fire, started coming down from the Loos salient. We stood in this hellish rain for a whole hour, nerves stretched to breaking point. Suddenly the enemy fire was lifted. At a shout our gallant little band rushed to man their positions and fired until their barrels glowed. The enemy were unable to start their attack. The morale of our men under their outstanding leader, Leutnant Link, was sky high. The price the enemy paid in blood was heavy. We watched as they attempted to dig in in the marshy ground, which had been ploughed up by shells. German fire had forced them to seek cover.

"Another message winged its way back to the *KTK*, 'Beaten off again!' It went on snowing, but our hearts were rejoicing. It was a day of honour for the Bavarian 3rd Battalion from Central Franken. They had been under drum fire for nine days, six of them with hardly anything to eat, taking cover far away from day light in their deep dugouts. It was a day of honour, too, for the entire regiment. None of its positions had been lost, not a foot of ground had been conceded to the enemy."

For 3rd Battalion Grenadier Guard Regiment 5, which had so recently arrived in the area, it was a day of serious casualties. Its commander, Major Roosen, was killed by a direct hit on his command post, which also claimed the lives of his dog handler and one of the two messenger dogs. Three of the company commanders, those of 9th, 10th and 11th Companies (Leutnants Kurt Bronsch, Erich Riemke and Kurt Hühnerbein) were also killed, together with Leutnant Paul Schmidt, Roosen's orderly officer. [48] In common with the situation throughout the mid April battlefield, not one of them has a known grave. 1st Battalion Reserve Infantry Regiment 93, which had arrived at the same time as the men of Grenadier Guard Regiment 5 and was deployed more to the south, also had a hard time on 12 April but, luckily for them, they were not on the receiving end of the main Canadian effort. After the war a surviving company commander published an interesting account of his tour of duty near Givenchy.

Reserve Leutnant Ueckert 2nd Company Reserve Infantry Regiment 93 [49]

"It was immediately obvious when we arrived at the appointed position that it had been the scene of heavy fighting. Those companies of the Bavarians that had not been completely wiped out were down to a strength of about ten men and they were completely intermingled along the main defensive line. The relief was extremely difficult to carry out because the front line trace varied throughout its length. Dawn was already appearing on the eastern horizon by the time the companies of the 1st Battalion had occupied their designated sector.

The Givenchy salient was very like Thiepval. On the right flank, marked by the *Souchez-Gang* [Souchez Way], the Third Line was occupied by 1st Company, whilst the left flank was held by the 3rd Company, with sentry positions distributed from *Kaisergang* [Emperor's Way] down to the lower *Sachsenlager* [Saxon Dugouts].

"Forward at the most prominent part of the salient there was a large gap between the companies. This was because this point was already occupied by the enemy. To the 2nd Company fell the task of closing the gap. I made use of part of the existing *Koch-Gang* [Cook's Way], and caused a new line to be extended right through the crater field to the right flank of the 3rd Company. Fortunately this re-grouping went very well and was completed swiftly. As a result, by the time it was fully daylight the company was dug in all along the new line. Despite the extremely difficult situation in which we found ourselves, everyone was alert and ready for the coming operations. Most of 11 April was taken up with the exchange of considerable quantities of artillery fire on both the forward positions and routes to the rear.

"My main concern was the left flank of the company and the battalion, which was hanging in the air, because I expected an outflanking enemy attack from the south from La Folie Wood. [In 1917 the remains of this wood extended all the way into Sector *Fischer.*] In the event completely the opposite happened. It went dark early, because the skies were full of threatening snow clouds; and an icy wind blew across the battlefield. Reinforced night sentries went on duty. The need for reliefs meant that there was little opportunity for rest in the dugouts. Those off duty had to lie there with their equipment on, helmets pushed back on their heads, rifles to hand; ready at any moment to be torn out of their slumbers by the shouts of alarm of the sentries in the trenches.

"In the enemy trenches all was quiet. There was no sign that any operation was to be undertaken that night. Suddenly, in the early hours of 12 April, the sentries raised the alarm. Within a minute the company was out of the dugouts and stood-to along the parapet. Squally snow showers blotted out the dawn and it was impossible to see more than five metres. Insanely violent drum fire came down on our trenches and the village of Givenchy. Under the protection of the driving snow, the enemy had attacked and had gained a lodgement in the sector of the Grenadier Guards. Suddenly the enemy appeared in *Koch-Gang* as well and began to roll up the company position, taking some prisoners. Everyone was taken by surprise by this sudden appearance of the Tommies in the trench. Nobody could explain it. Had the 1st Company been surprised?

"I immediately launched a counter-stroke. The Canadians left the trench rapidly, pulling back to the *Souchez-Graben*. In an instant the entire trench garrison of the *Koch-Graben* launched forward charging after the enemy. Within a few moments, Vizefeldwebel Beutel and his platoon had caught up with them, capturing two officers and nine men. The remainder of the enemy were scattered and the prisoners they had taken were freed. Other remnants of the enemy were captured by 1st Company. Meanwhile 2nd Company had returned to *Koch-Gang*. The snow squalls eased off and the drum fire died away gradually. The whole business had only lasted a few minutes. The entire company was elated. One thing was clear: the Tommies had been given a bloody nose by 2nd Company.

"The same fate had befallen the enemy in front of 1st Company which, under the command of Leutnant Roland Müller, had energetically beaten them off. The 3rd Company was not involved in this attack. At the end of it the 1st Battalion was in complete control of the sector that it had taken over on 10 April. The situation was a good deal worse in the area of our right hand neighbours, the Grenadier Guards. Despite a vigorous defence, the enemy had broken into the trench system and were working their way forward along *Souchez-Graben*. The enemy break-in had occurred to the north of *Fünf-Wege-Kreuz* [Five Way Junction]. We realised that the prisoners were very drunk. Later there was unanimous agreement that the enemy assault troops were completely drunk.[50] The situation became serious for us once more. Enemy parties had worked their way forward about 300 metres along the *Souchez-Graben*. I ordered the company to occupy the whole of *Koch-Gang* and to block off *Souchez-Gang*, to avoid the risk of being cut off from Givenchy.

"This meant that the company was occupying a narrow wedge-shaped position, which meant that, gradually, it was having to defend two fronts. To our front there was the eerily silent, but ever present, threat from the salient further forward. Luckily the enemy did not seem to appreciate exactly where our positions lay and we were left alone from that direction. The entire attention of the company was directed towards the *Souchez-Gang* and the hollow to its rear. We could watch large scale enemy movements there and the sentries engaged them. Enemy patrols were constantly pushing forward in order to determine the size and shape of our positions.

"For the most part, these patrols were shot up by our grenadiers. This provided an important lesson to the infantryman, who in this way learnt once more to appreciate the value of their own weapons. Trench warfare had meant that the hand grenade had become the principal weapon, with the rifle playing only a subordinate role, but rifle fire could have a devastating effect on the enemy – even at short range. The whip-like crack of the shots, coupled with their sharp sound through the air, had a much greater demoralising effect on the enemy than the dull thuds of the hand grenades and so it was near Givenchy. Our well aimed rifle fire held the Tommies completely in check, forcing them to bring forward fresh troops in order to be able to continue the advance.

"By now the sky had cleared and the afternoon brought spring-like warmth from the sun. Our situation became ever more threatening as the arrival of enemy reinforcements increased the pressure on us. Towards 5.00 pm strong enemy columns were seen forming up, front facing southeast, behind the wire and level with *Fünf-Wege-Kreuz* [Five Way Junction]. Similar enemy detachments could be seen massing in the salient to our front and further to the south. In view of this perilous situation I immediately discussed fresh defensive measures with Leutnant Roland Müller. Then, at 5.30 pm, we were surprised to receive an order from the battalion, ordering a withdrawal by 1st and 3rd Companies to Givenchy then on to Avion. 2nd Company was to remain in position as rearguard.

"It would be no easy task to hold the position until 3.00 am, because a major enemy attack from north and south could be launched against Givenchy at any moment. The grenadiers, who had been absolutely staunch up until this point, began to get somewhat uneasy in view of the changed situation, but were nevertheless all prepared to defend themselves and their position to the utmost. Shortly before 7.00 pm, 1st and 3rd Companies withdrew from their positions and pulled back to Givenchy, where they occupied positions in the *Souchez-Gang* left and right of Battalion Headquarters.[51] My grenadiers suddenly felt an oppressive feeling of being isolated. I had to take immediate measures because the enemy, who had spotted the withdrawal of 1st Company, immediately began to tighten the noose around us by occupying the abandoned trenches south of *Souchez-Gang*.

"2nd Company, every man of which was stood-to, brought the groups of enemy under fire. I had stops erected in the trenches to block off the trench to the north and south. In *Souchez-Gang* things remained lively, with the grenadiers bringing down rapid rifle fire whenever they detected the flat helmets of the Tommies. It was absolutely vital that our blocks were not overrun, otherwise the line of our withdrawal to the village would have been cut. The enemy columns were assembled like gathering thunder clouds on the heights to the east of *Fünf-Wege-Kreuz*, ready to launch an attack on Givenchy. The masses increased in size before our eyes and we waited tensely for the moment when they would launch forward. Then, about 6.30 pm, a runner arrived from the battalion bearing the following order: '2nd Company is to pull back to Command Post Augsburg. Only the rearguard will remain in *Koch-Graben*. (Enemy about to launch an attack.)' Everybody heaved a sigh of relief as I directed the company to prepare to move out. Leaving one platoon behind as a rearguard in *Koch-Graben*, the other two pulled back to Givenchy. The withdrawal was spotted by the enemy, but although we came under heavy fire we had no casualties. It now fell to the 1st Battalion to hold the village of Givenchy until 9.00 pm.

"Shortly after 7.00 pm the enemy columns attacked with the evening sun behind them from their positions east of *Fünf-Wege-Kreuz*. At that the final rearguard pulled back from *Koch-Gang*. Firing from a small heap of rubbish near the command post, four machine guns from the 1st Machine Gun Company, under Leutnant Jeibmann, and supported by some rifle sections from 1st and 2nd

Companies, brought down a torrent of rapid fire on the unsuspecting enemy. There was complete confusion. The attackers all went to ground and stretcher bearers came forward to carry back the wounded. The attack was beaten off without the aid of a single German gun, but the British artillery lost no time in bringing down revenge fire.

"Heavy shells crashed down around the firing positions and they had to be abandoned. It was now 9.00 pm and high time to depart if the battalion was not to be surrounded; the enemy was already in Givenchy and in rear of the 93rd. Finally the companies began to fall back. First to go was 3rd Company, followed at fifteen minute intervals by the 2nd, 1st and 4th. Enemy artillery fire increased minute by minute to drum fire. The enemy seemed to be preparing for another attack. At the double we pulled back along *Souchez-Gang* to the *Kronprinzen-Lager* [Crown Prince Dugouts], straight through a hail of British shells. An intense box barrage sealed off the rear of the village. Near the church everything was in flames. We were witnessing the funeral pyre of Leutnant Jaap of 4th Company, who met his end at that time.

"He had intended to blow up his dugout and, to facilitate that, had carried sacks of powder and mortar bombs into it. When it was time to go he ordered everyone out, placed several packets of flares on the charge and lit the fuse. As he raced up the stairs, he saw that the entrance was blocked by his men who were unwilling to brave the move into the open and the hell of the British drum fire. A heavy shell suddenly crashed down into the entrance of the dugout collapsing the timber framework of the entrance and hurling several of the men at the top of the stairs (including Leutnant Jaap) back down. Simultaneously the charge went off with a dreadful crash. Flames, metres long, roared up, engulfing both the men and their commander. All attempts at rescue were in vain."[52]

The evacuation of Givenchy by Reserve Infantry Regiment 93 was a model of its kind. Good leadership and discipline ensured that, as the last of the battles for Vimy Ridge died away, at least one unit would emerge with relatively light casualties. The total of only nine killed, sixty eight wounded and twelve missing was also a reflection of the fact that the Canadian main effort had been targeted at the grenadier guards. Overall, however, losses among the regiments that had been in action since 9 April were high. Once a complete check had been made, a I Bavarian Reserve Corps report to Sixth Army and Army Group Crown Prince Rupprecht stated that Group Vimy had suffered the following casualties:[53] '79th Reserve Division: forty five officers, 4,000 other ranks, twenty machine guns, thirty mortars and thirteen guns, one of which was heavy; 1st Bavarian Reserve Division: forty five officers, 3,000 other ranks, twenty eight machine guns, thirty five mortars and thirty eight guns, of which twelve were heavy; 14th Bavarian Infantry Division: seventy officers, 3,500 other ranks, twenty four machine guns, twelve mortars and sixty nine guns, of which thirty were heavy.' Once all stragglers, walking wounded and similar personnel had been accounted for correctly, these figures were subject to amendment. The corrected figures of killed, wounded and missing for 1st Bavarian Reserve Division, for example, were later computed to be: Officers ninety three, other ranks, 2,679 – which amounted to a large underestimate of officer casualties and an overestimate for other ranks of eleven percent.[54] However they are calculated these were serious casualties and not dissimilar to those of the attacking Canadian formations.

Numerous honours and awards were made to those who fought on Vimy Ridge that April. One well deserved award was the *Pour le Mérite* presented to the commander of Reserve Infantry Regiment 261, Oberstleutnant Wilhelm von Goerne, whose regiment had fought with such determination and courage. His citation is a reflection of the fact that his men had held 4th Canadian Division at bay for two full days with only four weak companies in the line and a further four in support. It reads:

"For outstanding leadership, distinguished military planning and successful operations during the 1917 British offensive. The award was also given in recognition of distinction in action during the Battle of Arras and especially the fierce fighting at Vimy Ridge when Reserve Infantry Regiment 261 prevented a British [*sic*] breakthrough between 9 and 13 April 1917."[55]

The dates quoted in the citation are significant. The fighting here may have been heavy and the casualties on both sides high, but it produced a decisive result. Never again, not even at the height of their 1918 offensives, would the German army set foot on Vimy Ridge, a dominating feature which they had held for thirty months. It played no future part in the battles around Arras. Instead, for the next few weeks, the focus of the fighting moved firmly to the east.

Notes

[1] Jones *The War in the Air Vol III* pp 334-335.
[2] Kriegsarchiv München 1 R. Korps *Betreff: Vorbereitungen für die Abwehrschlacht* General Kommando I. Bayer. Res. Korps Abteilung Ia No. 13 720 K.H.Qu., 21.3.1917.
[3] Original emphasis.
[4] Kronprinz Rupprecht *Mein Kriegstagebuch Zweiter Band* p 124.
[5] Kriegsarchiv München 1 R.I.B. Bd 37 General-Kommando I. Bayer.Res.Korps Abteilung Chef No. 14 326 K.H.Qu., 31.3.1917.
[6] Original emphasis. The Germans constantly asked questions of prisoners concerning the whereabouts of a 5th Canadian Division. In fact it remained in the United Kingdom until it was disbanded in 1918. Quite why it is mentioned in this report is a mystery, although confusion may have been caused by the fact that the 5th British Division was used in the Corps' assault, its 13 Brigade being assigned to the Canadian 2nd Division to take part in the second phase of the opening attack.
[7] Kriegsarchiv München A.O.K. 6 Bd 433 A.O.K. 6. B. Nr. 8950 1.4.17
[8] Kriegsarchiv München A.O.K. 6 Bd 433 A.O.K. 6. B. Nr. 8961 2.4.17
[9] In fact once Les Tilleuls had been taken on 9 April, 31st Battalion advanced to capture Thélus and

27th Battalion subsequently took Farbus Wood. Nevertheless the Germans fully understood the mechanics of the attack in advance.

[10] Kronprinz Rupprecht *Mein Kriegstagebuch Zweiter Band* pp 128-129

[11] *ibid.*

[12] Kriegsarchiv München Pi. Btl. 17 Bd 7 Gruppe Vimy Abt I a /Art No. 14 553 K.H.Qu., den 3.4.17

[13] Kriegsarchiv München R.I.R. 3 Bd. 3 Nr 5154 Bayer.Res.Inf.Regt. Nr. 3 6.4.1917 5.30 abds.

[14] When it is remembered that the overall manning situation was unchanged and that there would have been additional casualties in the interim, it is easy to see why the attackers were able to advance swiftly across an area defended by fewer than one man every five metres.

[15] Kriegsarchiv München OP 38887 1 Res.Inf.Brigade Nr. 9340 *Gefechtsbericht über die Ereignisse am 9., 10. und 11. April 1917* Brig.St.Qu., 6.6.17.

[16] Fischer History Reserve Infantry Regiment 262 p 109

[17] Dieterich *Die 79. Reserve Division* p 10

[18] Kriegsarchiv München HGr Rupprecht Bd 122 *AOK 6 No 239 7/4 Beurteilung der Lage.*

[19] Kriegsarchiv München 16. Inf. Div. Bd. 4 Bayer 16. Infanterie-Division Ia,. No. 1767 *Wochenbericht für die Zeit vom 29. März 1917 – 5. April 1917* Division.St.Qu., den 5. April 17.

[20] Kriegsarchiv München 1 Res Division Bd 20 79. RESERVE-DIVISION *Nachrichtenblatt vom 6.4.1917* D.St.Qu., den 7.4.1917.

[21] Behrmann: *Die Osterschlacht bei Arras 1917 I.Teil* pp 30-31.

[22] Fischer: *op. cit.* pp 109-110.

[23] Kriegsarchiv München: R.Pi.Kp. 1 Bd. 5 Gruppe Vimy Korpstagesbefehl H.Qu., Ostersonntag 1917

[24] Kriegsarchiv München 1 R.I.B. Bd 30: Bayer.Res.Inf.Regt. Nr. 3 *Gefechtsbericht über die Kämpfe am 9. und 10. April 1917.*

[25] This place was a point very close to the Commandant's House on the extreme right of the Canadian Corps sector.

[26] After the war the precise circumstances of Brunner's capture were the subject of a comprehensive Board of Enquiry, which found that he was in no way to blame for what had occurred. Kriegsarchiv München OP 38887.

[27] Kriegsarchiv München 1. Res. Div. Bd 21 *Divisionsbefehle 9.4.17.*

[28] Behrmann *Die Osterschlacht bei Arras 1917 I.Teil* p 37.

[29] Heinicke History Reserve Infantry Regiment 263 pp 116-117.

[30] *ibid.* pp 117-119

[31] Leutnant Peter Kapka is buried in the *Kamradengrab* of the German cemetery at Neuville St Vaast/Maison Blanche. he is one of only a handful of German casualties of the battle who has a known grave.

[32] Reserve Infantry Regiment 261 *Nachrichtenblatt Nr. 49* pp 3-4

[33] For unknown reasons the terms *'Island Fischer'* and *'Falkland Fischer'* were used (at least by Reserve Infantry Regiment 261 and possibly more generally) to describe Sub-Sectors *Fischer North* and *Fischer South* respectively. Although it is a fact that *Island* [Iceland] is in the North Atlantic and *Falkland* [The Falkland Islands] are located in the South Atlantic, it is difficult to make a connection. It is additionally problematic because on most maps *Fischer* was split officially into three sub-sectors.

[34] Reserve Infantry Regiment 261 *Nachrichtenblatt Nr. 49* pp 3-4

[35] Reserve Infantry Regiment 261 *Nachrichtenblatt Nr. 45* pp 5-7

[36] *ibid.* pp 5-7

[37] History Bavarian Infantry Regiment 14 pp 226 - 230

[38] Freund *History Infantry Regiment 118* pp 178 - 180

[39] Reserve *Infantry Regiment 261 Nachrichtenblatt Nr. 41* pp 3-4

[40] *History Infantry Regiment 164* pp 361-362

[41] Sydow *History Infantry Regiment 76* p 128

[42] Voigt *History Fusilier Regiment 73* pp 480-481

[43] Fischer *History Reserve Infantry Regiment 262* pp 122

[44] Voigt *op. cit* p 483

[45] Stosch *History Grenadier Guard Regiment 5* pp 367-369

[46] Delmensingen *Das Bayernbuch vom Weltkriege* pp 408 - 409

[47] Marsching is incorrect. The unit involved was 3rd Battalion Grenadier Guard Regiment 5. The Fusilier Guards did not become involved in the Battle of Arras until later, when they served south of the Scarpe. It is probable that he was confused by the fact the 3rd Battalion, in common with other Guard and Reserve Guard Regiments, was known as the Fusilier Battalion.

[48] Stosch *op. cit.* p 370

[49] Sievers *History Reserve Infantry Regiment 93* pp 182 - 188

[50] This accusation appears regularly in German accounts. It is impossible to comment on its probability here.

[51] The actual timings given here cannot be correct, but the sequence of events is clear.

[52] Leutnant Alfred Jaap is buried in the *Kamaradengrab* of the German cemetery at Neuville St Vaast/Maison Blanche. In view of the circumstances of his death and the rarity of named German burials from April 1917, this is quite remarkable.

[53] Kriegsarchiv München HGr. Rupprecht Bd. 93 *A.O.K. 6 541 11/4 gruppe vimy meldet an heeresgruppe kr Rupprecht – voraussichtliche verluste in den kaempfen vom 9/4 17*

[54] Kriegsarchiv München OP 38887 Nr. 9340 1.Res.Inf.Brigade *Gefechtsbericht über die Ereignisse am 9., 10. und 11 April 1917* Brig.St.Qu., 6.6.1917.

[55] Quoted by Godefroy Andrew, *The German Army at Vimy Ridge* in Hayes (Ed.) *Vimy Ridge: A Canadian Reassessment* p 233

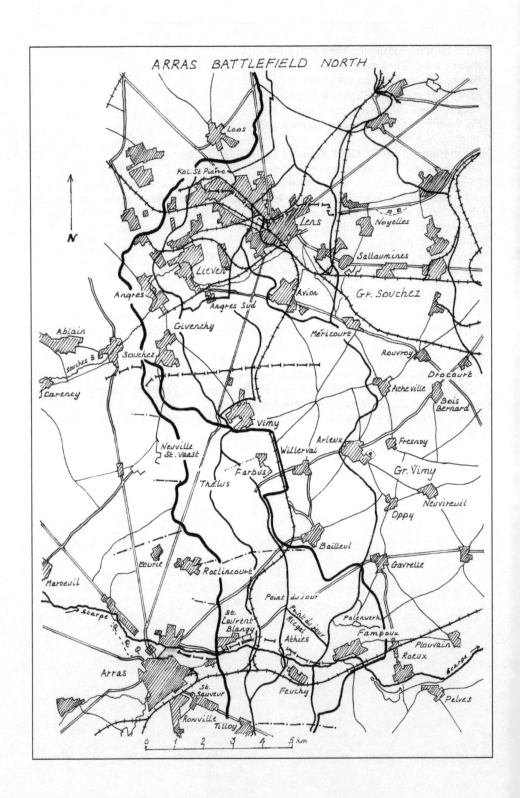

ARRAS BATTLEFIELD NORTH

N

Loos
Kol. St Pierre
Lens
Noyelles
Sallaumines
Lieven
Avion
Gr. Souchez
Angres
Angres Sud
Givenchy
Méricourt
Ablain
Rouvroy
Souchez B
Souchez
Dracourt
Acheville
Bois
Carency
Bernard
Vimy
Arleux
Fresnoy
Neuville
St. Vaast
Willerval
Gr. Vimy
Farbus
Thélus
Neuvireuil
Oppy
Bailleul
Ecurie
Gavrelle
Maroeuil
Roclincourt
Point du jour
Scarpe
Point du jour
St.
Riegel
Polenwerk
Laurent
Fampoux
Blangy
Athies
Plouvain
Roeux
Scarpe
Arras
St.
Feuchy
Sauveur
Pelves
Ronville
Tilloy

0   1   2   3   4   5 km

CHAPTER 2

The British Assault North of the Scarpe

T he 14th Bavarian Infantry Division occupied the sector of the front to the south of 1st Bavarian Reserve Division from opposite Roclincourt to the River Scarpe. Its frontage was subdivided into Sectors *Eberhard*, *Schwaben* and *Habsburg*, manned by Bavarian Infantry Regiments 4, 25 and 8 respectively. This part of the battlefield was the objective of the British XVII Corps and there was to be a serious attempt at breakthrough just north of the Scarpe, where 9th (Scottish) Division, attacking with three brigades in line, each on a 500 metre front, had the task of smashing through to the German Second Position between Le Point du Jour and Athies.[1] Exploitation as far as Fampoux was to be entrusted to follow up waves from 4th Division. Ambitious use of smoke shells on a large scale by the supporting artillery, both mixed in with the rolling barrage and employed further forward to blind German batteries, which had already been subject to intense bombardment and drenched with gas, was to prove a strikingly successful innovation when the attack was launched against the weakened and disorientated Bavarians.

The division had only assumed responsibility for this sector towards the end of March from the Saxon 24th Reserve Division. Although the division had officially moved from 'rest', in actual fact the personnel were worn down and near exhaustion from the demands placed on them the previous winter on the Somme and during the days leading up to their deployment. In a later official report to 14th Bavarian Infantry Division, the commander of 8 Bavarian Infantry Brigade painted a bleak picture of this period.

Generalmajor Karl von Reck 8 Bavarian Infantry Brigade[2]

"During the tour of duty of the three regiments near Serre, north of the River Ancre, from the end of November 1916 to the beginning of February 1917, it proved impossible because of the great width of the sector – over four kilometres – and the constant tense situation, to maintain the usual three-way split of trench duty, support and rest. Many companies spent more than forty days on trench duty or in support without a break or, at the most, a two to three day pause. This type of deployment during the Somme winter in the wet and the mud, frequently under heavy enemy fire, not to mention numerous limited British attacks, very quickly wore down the strength of the troops. The 'rest' in February was dominated, as far as the Infantry Regiments 4 and 8 were concerned, by the most strenuous, if necessary, work to make essential improvements to the *Siegfried-Stellung* [Hindenburg Line]. Then, instead of the brigade being at long last granted the hoped for rest after their final duties near Le Transloy were complete, during the *Alberich* period[3] the order was received to go into the line near Arras."

It was not just a problem of manpower. The temporary commander of the divisional Mortar Company 14, Leutnant Henigst, later noted that, 'providing horses to pull the vehicles and mortars presented us with great difficulties. The bad winter weather near Gommecourt on the Somme front helped spread pneumonia and mange, which reduced our stock of horses drastically. There were simply insufficient replacements and what we did receive were mostly unusable or, suffering also from these illnesses, had to be sent back to the veterinary hospital a few days later.'[4] On top of these problems the handover/takeover itself was far from smooth. 1st Battalion Field Artillery Regiment 76, which had been moved in to come under command of Bavarian Field Artillery Regiment 23, whose commander had overall responsibility for defensive fire here north of the Scarpe, remarked later that, 'There had been no preparation. Neither maps, nor defensive fire plans were available, not even sketch maps of the battery positions. The telephone connections were in complete chaos and the batteries had to move by sections to occupy gun lines that were at best only partially complete and frequently completely unprepared.'[5]

Despite all the difficulties, Oberstleutnant Theodor Ritter von Herrmann of Bavarian Field Artillery Regiment 23, who was in overall command of the divisional artillery at the time, moved rapidly to create a coherent structure, forming three groupings to correspond to the regimental sectors. Group *Habsburg*, covering the critical St Laurent Blangy area, comprised the staffs of 1st Battalion Field Artillery Regiment 76 and 2nd Battalion Field Artillery Regiment 600, with the guns of Field Artillery Regiment 6 being reinforced by 6th Battery Field Artillery Regiment 600 and 6th Battery Bavarian Field Artillery Regiment 23. Group *Schwaben*, headed by the staffs of 2nd and 3rd Battalions Bavarian Field Artillery Regiment 23, had under command 2nd, 5th, 7th and 8th Batteries Bavarian Field Artillery Regiment 23, together with 4th and 5th Batteries Field Artillery Regiment 600. Finally, to the north and adjoining 1st Bavarian Reserve Division, was Group *Eberhard*, led by the staff of 1st Battalion Bavarian Field Artillery Regiment 23, with 1st, 3rd, 4th and 9th Batteries Bavarian Field Artillery Regiment 23 under command, together with 3rd Battery Landwehr Field Artillery Regiment 11.[6] It was little enough, but the best that could be made available in the circumstances.

The British artillery preparations in this sector were every bit as thorough and persistent as those experienced elsewhere, making the daily existence of the defenders extremely problematic and rendering significant improvement to the state of the defences a near impossibility, as this account makes clear.

Oberleutnant Scheer 1st Battalion Field Artillery Regiment 76 [7]

"From 3rd April 1917 the [artillery] battle, which had been gaining momentum for several days, increased yet again in intensity. It was striking that on this day there was heavy bombardment by guns of all calibres throughout the rear area, special attention being devoted to approach routes, built up areas, trenches, batteries, observation posts and the depression by the railway line which housed the *Hapsburg* artillery command post. Only through total commitment of all ranks was it possible, sometimes by telephone, mostly by runners, to maintain links between the batteries and the Group and contact from the Group to the Regiment. Even the deeply buried cables were unequal to the weight of fire. Their repair was just as impossible as the attempts to lay fresh line. From 6 April onwards all communication had broken down; it was now completely out of the question to maintain telephone contacts and runners very rarely made it through to the Group command post. Orders only ever arrived after a delay of several hours.

"On 8 April, the rate of fire increased even more. Throughout the day the *Habsburg* command post and all the batteries were permanently under the heaviest possible fire and gas attack. Not one single order or situation report reached the Group that day. The same applied to the infantry commander [Oberst von Rücker, Bavarian Infantry Regiment 8], whose command post was adjacent. He did not receive any information from his battalions, whereas as late as the previous day he had had situation reports from his front line positions. By now the only means of communicating with the batteries was by signal flare, calling for defensive or destructive fire. The Group used these means whenever there was a demand from the infantry, but it was necessary to be sparing because in the current conditions forward resupply [of cartridges] was impossible.

"During the night 8/9 April the artillery fire increased constantly in weight then, around 5.30 am, drumfire of an intensity we had never experienced on the Somme came down suddenly throughout the area from the front line to the railway. Use of the last of our signal flares brought down swift defensive fire. This had some effect on the initial assault, but could do nothing to stop the immense masses of British infantry following up."

It was natural for the gunners to maintain that they responded to calls for help; in fact their ability to do so was strictly limited. In the twenty four hours leading up to the opening of the assault, 14th Bavarian Infantry Division estimated – how it is impossible to say, given the problems with communications – that '*Eberhard* had been hit by 5,500 shells, *Schwaben* by 6,000 and *Habsburg* by 7,600. In reply the divisional artillery had fired only 2,650 rounds.'[8] Essentially, the forward infantrymen were on their own. Some of the practical difficulties caused by the combination of high explosive and gas were described later by an officer of the divisional mortar company.

Leutnant F Henigst Bavarian Mortar Company 14[9]

"There was no longer any doubt; we were facing a serious situation. During the night 5/6 [April] the unpleasant harassing fire was suddenly accompanied by heavy enemy gas shoots, the effects of which were enhanced by an almost complete absence of wind. Very soon the entire area reaching back well beyond the gun lines was cloaked in a thick fog. Both men and animals could only move masked up, which made the supply of rations and other stores extremely difficult. In some parts of the position it was necessary to make use of the iron rations, because nothing could be got forward. In the front line there was an increased number of direct hits on trenches and dugouts and we were shocked to discover how well the enemy had unobtrusively ranged in. Our mortars fired as best they could during these days, receiving the 'thanks' of the enemy in return. In consequence, as was frequently the case elsewhere, the neighbouring infantry asked us to cease fire."

Manning the remnants of the wrecked front line and support trenches in the critical *Habsburg* sector from north to south were Oberleutnant Bickel's 6th Company then 8th, 7th and 5th Companies commanded by Leutnants Telthörster, Bröcker and Heikaus respectively. Back in the third line were elements of 12th Company under Reserve Leutnant Behr (north) and 11th Company, commanded by Oberleutnant Schwemmer (south). The *KTK* was Hauptmann Schmidt, commanding officer 2nd Battalion, whose command post was located immediately north of St Laurent Blangy. During the bombardment, the regimental commander, Oberst von Rücker, had had to be medically evacuated, so command on the fateful day of 9 April devolved to Major Felser, commanding officer 3rd Battalion. The importance of resisting strongly just north of the Scarpe was fully appreciated, so the defensive plan envisaged holding firm, exploiting to the full the potential of the available strong points, bunkers and pill boxes. Orders were issued directing the troops to resist at all cost and, ignoring potential enemy thrusts on the flanks, to hold on until relieved by immediate counter-stroke action.

So much for the plan; in the event it was soon overtaken by events. During the night 8/9 April, the positions were shelled and gassed for five hours continuously, forcing the garrison to mask up and exhausting the protective potential of their gas masks. From about 3.00 am the shelling reduced in intensity then, between 3.15 and 5.00 am, ceased altogether. The reason was unclear, because fire came down with undiminished intensity on neighbouring divisions, but the pause was extremely welcome. It enabled the large number of wounded and gas poisoning cases to be evacuated, food, drink and ammunition to be brought up and collapsed dugout entrances to be cleared out. However, at 5.30 am a massive infantry attack, supported by tanks and flamethrowers, was launched. In the half light, with visibility reduced to almost nil by smoke shells and clouds of dust and preceded by a creeping barrage, an attack of extreme violence hit the centre of Bavarian Infantry Regiment 8 before the defenders had time to get organised or even begin to react.

7th and 8th Companies were simply overwhelmed, the desperate efforts of the survivors notwithstanding, so a gap 400 metres wide opened up. Initially 6th Company was able to offer reasonably effective resistance, but a thrust through the Bavarian Infantry Regiment 25 in Sector *Schwaben* was followed by a great build up in pressure against its right flank and rear. 5th Company, benefitting from swampy going in the strip of ground by the Scarpe, was able to bring down intense small arms fire and temporarily hold up the advance. This meant that St Laurent Blangy was still being held as a firm shoulder of the forward defence but, just to the north, British flamethrower crews were able to expand the break in, the piercing screams of men hit by great jets of burning oil clearly audible above the racket of explosions and firing. Even in the built up area resistance was short lived. Wave after wave of attackers pressed on into it, not only from the west, but also from the southern edge of the village, where the attackers clashed violently with an 11th Company platoon which had been moved forward simultaneously with the start of the offensive at 5.30 am. Within an hour, despite the best efforts of the courageous Leutnant Heikaus, the fighting was over here and 5th Company had suffered a considerable number of all ranks killed, showing just how bitter the struggle against the odds had been.

Any intention of making a stand around the *KTK* also came to nothing. Because of the restricted availability of suitable accommodation, it had had to be placed well forward. As a result, even before the barrage had fully lifted, it was virtually surrounded. Torrents of fire from the attacking troops also made it impossible for its personnel to move at all. With all routes to the rear cut off, the entire staff, including Hauptmann Schmidt, his adjutant Leutnant Schüsler and his artillery liaison officer, Leutnant Ettwein from Field Artillery Regiment 76, were captured, as was every single officer of the forward companies, less those who were killed outright. Within one and a half hours the entire First Position was lost and only a mere handful of survivors succeeded in escaping to join 12th Company back in the Third Line. Subsequently the regiment highlighted two reasons for this setback. The divisional reserve (three battalions held at readiness) could not deploy quickly enough, due to the weight of enemy artillery fire and the fact that their own guns, either neutralised or destroyed, were unable to fire the necessary defensive fire missions.

The story was similar on the divisional right flank in Sector *Eberhard*, where two battalions of Bavarian Infantry Regiment 4 manned the forward positions. As the attacks came in flares calling for artillery fire went up all along the front and were faithfully re-transmitted by other signalling positions all the way to the gun lines, but it was no use; flare after flare was fired, hung in the sky and fell to the ground. The

German artillery had simply been utterly crushed and, which was also extremely serious, because the Allied fire plan included curtains of shells continuously raking forwards and backwards, many of the defenders' machine guns were also out of action. Very quickly after the attack began, 1st and 4th Companies, deployed forward left and centre, were driven back out of their first and second line trenches whilst, slightly further to the north, the use of tanks to spearhead the attack meant that the resistance of 3rd Company was also swiftly broken. It proved to be impossible to hold along the line of the second trench and such was the speed of advance that large numbers of defenders were captured, some of them still sheltering in dugouts and tunnels as the attack swept over and around them.

There was brief resistance along the line of the third trench, where the survivors of the front line joined forces with 2nd and 6th Companies and launched an immediate counter-stroke. Despite the fact that German grenades and small arms fire tore gaps in the British ranks, reinforcements constantly pressed forward to fill up the ranks once more. As German casualties mounted, the British continued to press forward and by 7.00 am this line had also been lost. A few members of Bavarian Infantry Regiment 4 got away but, overwhelmingly, the defenders were killed, wounded or captured. It was the same story to the north in Sector *Rupprecht*, where Bavarian Reserve Infantry Regiment 2 of 1st Bavarian Reserve Division was more or less simultaneously driven back to their third trench. All along the front, command and control had effectively broken down. Reports were not arriving at command posts, the artillery was unable to respond to calls for help and all the time relentless British artillery fire was taking a toll on the defenders and their remaining positions. Already by 6.30 am, fire was coming down on the Intermediate Position, which more or less coincided with the line of the Arras – Bailleul railway in Sectors *Schwaben* and *Hapsburg*.

At his regimental command post, located at a cross tracks about 1,000 metres west of Bailleul, Major Hoderlein, commanding Bavarian Infantry Regiment 4, was in a complete quandary about what to do next. He had no clear idea how far the British had advanced, he was receiving no information from his forward battalions and he had only a few sections under Reserve Leutnant Riel at his immediate disposal. His own 5th Company, which had been held back in Brigade reserve, had been released as soon as the final pre-attack drum fire began but, starting from positions near Gavrelle, it would be some time before it arrived, especially because it would have to negotiate a route forward through the British barrage. His 3rd Battalion, located back in Douai, was simply too far in rear to be able to play any immediate role in the battle. Meanwhile, the British troops were pressing forward against the Intermediate Position and the railway [The British 'Blue Line'] itself, where what was left of 7th and 8th Companies, led by Leutnants Wackenreuder and Hiller, were attempting to spread their thin resources and hold as best they could.

Despite all their heroics, however, there was no realistic chance of stemming the tide of British attackers that began inexorably to probe the weaknesses of the thinly held positions. Hiller, supported by only about two sections of infantry who were almost choked to death by the lyddite fumes of exploding shells, could barely see twenty metres from his position up on the railway embankment. At about 7.00 am, he managed to send a report back to the *BTK* [*Bereitschaftstruppenkommandeur* = commander of the supports], warning him that the situation forward on the Intermediate Position was becoming critical, but it is far from clear that the message went any further because within thirty minutes Hauptmann Fasel, the *KTK*, was in danger himself of being swamped by the oncoming masses of British infantry. With the sound of the close quarter battle for the railway embankment clearly audible, Fasel and his men fought on, despite realising that there was no possibility of relief. They were swiftly outflanked and ultimately mopped up by follow up forces.

The British barrage ground on, pausing for a significant period in the low ground just west of the railway and on the boundary between *Schwaben* and *Eberhard*. Despite this, rapid fire from the defenders bought a certain amount of time, but the lack of effective defensive artillery fire meant that there was little to prevent the British from pressing further forward and by 8.30 am they were threatening to overrun both the Intermediate Position and the railway in the Bavarian Infantry Regiment 4 sector. This was a real crisis. Once through at this point the way to Bailleul would be wide open. Very gallantly, despite being under pressure themselves, a reinforced platoon of Bavarian Infantry Regiment 25 launched a hasty counter-attack into the flank of this thrust from a start line near Maison Blanche Wood. This had some effect, but some panicking defenders were already beginning to stream to the rear.

Fortunately stouter individuals were still managing to stand their ground and intervene to assist the more hard pressed places. Leutnant Schramm led the last of the immediate regimental reserves – 5th Company Bavarian Infantry Regiment 4 – forward to the Second Position [The British 'Brown Line'] south southwest of Bailleul, arriving about 8.30 am. At that Reserve Leutnant Riel gathered together about thirty men and, supported by a machine gun, launched an attack along the line of the railway towards the regimental *BTK*.

Shelled by the British barrage, under fire from low flying aircraft, nevertheless progress was made, but only slowly. As a result British pressure continued to mount, the remaining men of 7th and 8th Companies were pushed back and a determined assault was launched by the attackers. In the very nick of time Riel's men reached a position from which they could pour fire into the British flank. Taken by surprise, this had a disproportionate effect on the advance; it held up the move towards the German Second Position for some time; but here, too, effective resistance ended as the day wore on. One kilometre west of Bailleul, around the cross tracks which housed the headquarters of Bavarian Infantry Regiment 4, the shelling and gassing had become so extreme that the wooden supports of the dugout were actually ablaze. At that, Major Hoderlein decided around 9.30 am to move to join Landwehr Hauptmann Otto, the artillery group commander, at his command post by the railway junction just southwest of Bailleul. On arrival he found the situation equally chaotic. It was quite impossible to exercise control and yet the risk of a British breakthrough was very high. Hoderlein decided that the only feasible action was to pull right back to the incomplete Third Position, here just west of Gavrelle; there to attempt to reorganise the defence as reserves were fed forward from Douai. This timely move made tactical sense and probably spared him and his staff the capture that was the fate of so many others that day.

The elements of Bavarian 14th Mortar Company that had been deployed forward were also destroyed or captured with almost all the other front line infantrymen. Its acting commander, who had been attempting to arrange for the relief of the forward crews after the hammering they had received during the past few days, had also to make a swift decision if any of his men were to be able to contribute to the defence.

Leutnant F Henigst Bavarian 14th Mortar Company [10]

"In this situation those elements of the company that were located in the rear and which were to have conducted the relief had no realistic option but to make themselves available to the division as a reserve. Led by me (Oberleutnant Barth, the company commander, had been sent away on sick leave a week earlier) and strengthened with a few infantry orderlies, altogether about sixty men, were despatched to Gavrelle where Brigade [8 Bavarian Infantry Brigade – Generalmajor Karl von Reck] Headquarters was supposed to be located. The march was fraught with difficulty. Some of those who set off with us that morning must have felt that they were unlikely to live until evening. Men caught in the hell of the forward positions have no time for introspection but, when you are without notice moved out of a safe, secure place and are suddenly faced with the near certainty of death, it becomes a severe test of nerve. The further forward our little band came the heavier the fire, which was coming down along the Cambrai – Arras road. As we approached Fresnes, which we knew well, we simply had to leave the road. By chance we discovered that the brigade staff was there. Taking advantage of a pause in the fire, we marched up to the house by the exit to the village where the staff was located. To my amazement I came across the brigade commander in a ground floor room, despite the fact that heavy shells kept detonating nearby. Virtually alone in front of his maps, I shall never forget the calming sight of the general standing in front of his desk, just as though he was on exercise and giving me my briefing.

"The impression of an exercise was further intensified when I rushed across the road to get my hands on belts of ammunition. A field gun ammunition column raced through the village, one wagon after the other, the poor horses frightened to death, but thundering on in a mad scramble along the beautiful avenue towards Gavrelle. I thought to myself that if ammunition could be brought that far forward, things could not be too bad. I soon realised, however, that the actual situation was quite different when I, having collected ammunition, left the village by the same road. The column which had driven forward so boldly had run into heavy shrapnel and shell fire and had become an appalling tangled mess, which could neither move forward nor back. Meanwhile enemy artillery fire continued to crash down madly in its midst. I later discovered that the ammunition was very unlikely to have found a user.

"My mission was to report to the regimental staff of [Bavarian] Infantry Regiment 4 (Major Hoderlein) in Gavrelle but, as I later found out, this staff had already moved to *Pionier Wäldchen* [Engineer Copse] by Fresnes, where we had been previously deployed. In view of the warning example of the fate of the ammunition column, it seemed inadvisable to continue on along the road so instead I moved cross country over open ground to the south of the road, without shaking out as a group of infantrymen (which overtook us somewhat disdainfully) had done. The enemy seemed to spot our advance and brought down shrapnel fire, which came down rather too near the road itself and did no damage. The shelling had no effect either; the ground was so boggy that the [rounds] were either duds or smothered."

On the left flank of the division, down near St Laurent Blangy, events took a slightly different course. Major Felser, normally commanding officer 3rd Battalion Bavarian Infantry Regiment 8, had taken over command of the entire regiment on 1 April 1917 when Oberst von Rücker was medically evacuated. On the morning of 9 April he was located well forward in his command post, dug into the railway embankment about one thousand metres north of the Railway Triangle. From there he tried desperately to maintain contact with his battalion commanders and to build up a picture of what was happening out to the front. Unfortunately for him, such was the concentration of gas, smoke and high explosive on his forward positions when the attack opened that it was impossible to move or pass messages in this area. Finally the fire began to slacken and lifted to the east somewhat towards 7.00 am. It was then possible to gain an impression of the desperate fighting in the forward positions. Red flares fired by the infantry and guiding the British artillery were going up all along the front so as to indicate progress; whilst the defenders, those who had survived the bombardment, brought their remaining machine guns to bear and managed briefly to hold the advance up and cause the British to fire yet another preparatory bombardment.

As shells landed all around the railway, Major Felser attempted to summon assistance from the German guns, but the artillery group commander's nearby command post had already been smashed and abandoned. The British were expected to close right up to this area at any moment but Felser, weighing up his options, decided to stay where he was and fight it out, setting a good example to his men and counteracting a growing tendency to drift to the rear.

Major Felser Commander Bavarian Infantry Regiment 8 [11]

"What purpose would it have served to redeploy the regimental command post to the rear, where there were no reinforcements – especially because the tactical situation would have ruled out the withdrawal of the troops towards the rear. There could be no thought of yielding the position. Instead it had to be fought for. The enemy strength could not be determined; only that they were deploying beyond the trenches of the forward position. I was also unaware of the situation in the neighbouring sectors. The amount of enemy gun fire indicated that it was an offensive on a grand scale; nevertheless it was possible that the attack on our neighbours would enjoy less success. That said, even unfavourable news from that source would not have budged me from my determination not to give up the Intermediate Position. There were no infantry units worth the name between there and the gun lines. In any case I did not view the defence of the Intermediate Position as a battle in a lost cause. It was much more a matter of gaining time while those elements of the division which were located in the rear could be got forward to intervene. Thus far I hoped that I should be able to hold the line of the railway with artillery support; I felt that it was out of the question that the artillery would be quite unable to provide necessary support. However, only about four or five shells came down."

About 7.30 am Major Felser was appraised of the situation forward when an unteroffizier, accompanied by a small group of men, succeeded in making his way to the command post. His was the one and only report to get through and it told a sorry story of the total destruction of 2nd Battalion. There was still no news from the flanks or rear, though Leutnant Zimmerman, who was holding the Second Position with 10th Company, did set off with two of his platoons to reinforce. On the way heavy fire caused numerous casualties and the group to splinter so that when he arrived, bleeding from a neck wound, he had only twenty five men with him. He himself was killed less than an hour later but, in the meantime, he placed his men in position along the railway embankment, adding their fire to what was left 9th and 12th Companies. Their concentrated small arms fire succeeded in causing a great many casualties and holding the attack on this front 300 metres short of the railway line – but only briefly. In a repetition of a situation played out repeatedly that day, a thrust into the German positions to the north meant that they were outflanked and subject to an attack designed to roll up their positions.

The fighting degenerated into a wild hand to hand struggle, but once again numbers told. Leutnant Heckel, Offizierstellvertreter Winter and Viefeldwebel Sulbacher of 9th Company were all killed and, despite every effort by the defenders, the situation north of the St Laurent – Athies road soon deteriorated. In places some of the attackers had been forced into cover; elsewhere, supported by fresh artillery concentrations and the direct intervention of a tank, the defence began to crumble. Around Felser's command post resistance was still reasonably effective but, suddenly, the attackers were through just where the St Laurent – Athies road crossed the railway line. Fired at from three sides, ammunition running out, the defenders were in serious trouble. Leutnant Zimmermann, still encouraging his men, was mortally wounded, shot twice through the chest and collapsed, still clinging on to his rifle. Casualties went on mounting until a 350 metre front was being held by only the survivors of the regimental staff and the remnants of 10th Company – four officers, fifty men and one machine gun, which was soon put out of action by a grenade.

Amazing to relate, this battle with 8th Battalion Black Watch went on for another hour. There was no sign of reinforcement or relief, no information from the flanks and the German artillery was completely silent. Nevertheless, buoyed up by Major Felser's decision to stand and fight, everything possible was done to hold on. The regimental orderly officer, Leutnant Krembs, rushed around carrying orders and redistributing the small amount of ammunition still available, but he too fell victim to a shot through the head, dying instantly.[12] It was by now almost 9.00 am and obvious to all concerned that the few remaining riflemen could not contend with pressure from three sides. Finally, grenades were thrown into the dugouts. More or less simultaneously the last of the ammunition was fired. Major Felser decided that it was pointless to order a final bayonet charge and, at approximately 9.15 am, he ordered the few survivors to surrender.[13] By then the defenders were reduced to Felser himself, his adjutant, Oberleutnant Mayer, and his signals officer, Reserve Leutnant Friedensburg, together with a handful of unwounded men. The regimental historian later summed up this heroic, but brief and ultimately hopeless, stand in this way:

"The enemy pushed tanks through St Laurent and along the road to Athies in the direction of the railway bridge and, supported by heavy artillery fire, set foot in overwhelming force in the Intermediate Position on our right flank. Repeatedly our fire held them back until, exploiting a gap in the neighbouring sector to our right, a surprise enemy attack from our right flank and rear was launched, forcing a way into our position along the railway, despite an obstinate defence, especially around the road bridge over the railway on the Gavrelle- St Laurent road. The longingly awaited divisional reserve – three battalions – did not arrive on time. Our artillery, itself severely pressed and suffering from lack of ammunition, could not support the infantry. Only when, bit by bit, close quarter fighting died away in various places was the defence, including that to the south of the road bridge, exhausted and the Intermediate Position was lost about 9.15 am. Only very few men of 2nd and 3rd Battalions were able to escape and battle their way back towards Athies and the Second Position, where they consolidated under artillery fire."[14]

So much for the situation on the divisional flanks. In the centre, manning Sector *Schwaben*, Bavarian Infantry Regiment 25 had made the final preparations to meet the forthcoming attack by reinforcing the front line garrison. There had been much patrol and raid activity against it and the bombardment had taken its toll on 1st Battalion and 5th Company. As a result, elements of 7th Company were moved forward to strengthen the line. Behind in support was Headquarters 2nd Battalion, 8th Company and the remainder of 7th Company along the line of the Arras – Lens railway. The guns of 1st and 2nd Machine Gun Companies were deployed at tactical points throughout the forward battle area, 6th Company was back in depth near regimental headquarters just west of Gavrelle, with a forward post at Point du Jour and 3rd Battalion in divisional reserve was located as far back as Brebières.[15] This deployment was judged about as optimal as could be arranged in the circumstances but, as in so many other points along the front, a combination of the weight of the bombardment and the mass attack simply overwhelmed the forward defenders, many of whom were trapped in their dugouts and must have been overrun before they had a chance to react.

This at least is the assumption. Sounds of the battle could be heard, as could the noise of the machine guns, but in fact not one report from any of the forward companies or the *KTK*, Landwehr Hauptmann Sailer, ever reached either the *BTK* or Oberstleutnant Seemüller, the regimental commander. Later, a handful of survivors of the loss of the third line of the First Position were able to throw some light on the subsequent developments. By 7.00 am the battle was in full swing for this trench. Pinned by frontal attacks, especially in the centre of the sector, the line was ultimately rolled up by British troops advancing south from the Bavarian Infantry Regiment 4 sector and pushing north from Sector *Habsburg*. Neither Reserve Leutnant Nabholz, nor Reserve Leutnant Martin, commanding 7th and 8th Companies respectively, survived the fighting,[16] but one of the NCOs later noted down his impressions of the morning.

Unteroffizier Sohmer 7th Company Bavarian Infantry Regiment 25[17]

"After the loss of the Third Line, we saw a striking sight. Standing bolt upright, about five metres in front of the trench, was a long line of figures, looking as though they were rooted to the spot. Because of the stormy weather it was impossible to say if they were German or British. This lasted for a solid half hour, so the thought gradually crystallised that German prisoners had been placed there, lacking any cover, in order to prevent our artillery from firing. Then the greater part of the British who had broken in gathered together, stepped out of the trench and formed section columns. One strange sight was the deployment of two lines of soldiers, formed up right and left of the columns. Eventually a sector 500 – 600 metres wide was marked with black, white and red flags and the columns prepared to move.

"During the thirty to forty minutes devoted to this preparation, the odd British solder continued to emerge from the captured forward lines. It was almost beyond comprehension that this all occurred without being disturbed in any way, or indeed with any consideration that there might be German interference. To us, occupying the Railway Position in the midst of heavy fire by high explosive and gas shells, it seemed a total mystery why our artillery did not break up this parade square manoeuvre and bring down defensive fire to protect our position. Finally the section columns began to advance, shaking out during the movement into dense skirmish lines, which slowly but surely bore down on the Railway Position. I then heard from all sides the sound of rapid fire from our machine guns."

In fact the lack of artillery fire, which has already been discussed in part, was due to attrition in the gun lines, gassing of battery positions, failure of communications and battlefield obscuration. Elements of the Silesian Field Artillery Regiment 42, which was actually subordinated to 11th Infantry Division to the south, were deployed north of the Scarpe near Athies and some observation posts had been pushed forward as far as the Third Line trenches, which of course were soon under enemy pressure that morning. One of the battery commanders, far from being able to bring effective fire down, was soon scrambling to save his own life and to get information back to where it was needed.

Leutnant Deloch 3rd Battery Field Artillery Regiment 42[18]

"Not until I had emerged from the mousetrap with my telephonists and unteroffizier – and that was far from easy – could I attempt to get an enemy situation report through. We waited until the British drew level with us then destroyed our observation equipment and took off our coats and caps. We then pretended to be a section of advancing British troops but in the end were spotted and came under fire. However the presence of overlapping shell holes provided excellent cover where we could get our breath back before haring off once more. In this way I made my way back to my battery. Of the two remaining guns, one was smashed by a direct hit. Despite having to repair the last one frequently, it fired another 1,000 rounds."

The *BTK* in Sector *Schwaben* was Hauptmann Grau, commanding officer 2nd Battalion Bavarian Infantry Regiment 25. He and his men had been on immediate standby ever since the drumfire heralding the offensive had opened up at 5.30 am. Now, with very little warning, they found themselves engaged in an unequal fire fight with the advancing British troops. Reserve Leutnant Weil, his orderly officer, took charge of assorted runners, signallers and other soldiers who had pulled back from the forward positions and attempted to defend the immediate area and maintain contact with two platoons of 7th Company under Leutnant Zapf, which were dug in either side of the bridge carrying the Bailleul – St Laurent Blangy road over the railway.[19] An intense, close quarter battle rapidly developed, ebbing and flowing as hand grenades, thrown by a party under Leutnant Weil and Unteroffiziers Rosenberg and Göschel, succeeded in pinning the attackers down in a line of shell holes just west of the railway, thanks partly to rapid fire from a machine gun in a position just to the south. Suddenly the weapon fell silent. Men were sent to investigate and recover the machine gun if possible, but none of them was seen again.

The situation was extremely tense as the minutes ticked by then, about twenty minutes later, a fresh British artillery concentration began landing all around the railway line. Because the range was known to a metre, casualties began to rise rapidly in 7th Company and a gap appeared between it and the *BTK*. This coincided with the arrival of further British reinforcements, the gap was exploited during a renewed assault and, suddenly, the railway line was teeming with British soldiers. There were clashes at close range, a great many defenders fell then, gripped with panic, many of the survivors turned tail and raced towards the Second Position, though such was the weight of fire directed at them that relatively few got through unscathed. This was not just a matter of infantry action. Once more British aircraft, flying at an extremely low level, machine gunned anything in *Feldgrau* which moved. The situation around the *BTK* was rapidly becoming totally untenable. Attackers were closing in on all sides and machine gun fire was being poured down at the last of the defenders, so Hauptmann Grau took the decision to attempt to break through the near total encirclement and fall back on Point du Jour. It was a nightmare of a move. Men were hit constantly, neither Hauptmann Grau or his medical officer, Feldunteroffizier Lurch, made it; both were killed,[20] whilst Reserve Leutnant Weil was very seriously wounded and later captured.

The prolonged heavy bombardment had caused a large number of casualties. In addition, the dreadful weather led to the medical evacuation of a good many other individuals. The result was that once the front line trenches had been fully manned, there were relatively few sub units left to provide essential depth to the defences. As far as 14th Bavarian Infantry Division was concerned, this meant that when the offensive opened the Second Position was only manned as follows: Behind Sector *Habsburg* (Bavarian Infantry Regiment 8) 10th Company; behind Sector *Schwaben* (Bavarian Infantry Regiment 25) 6th Company and behind Sector *Eberhard* (Bavarian Infantry Regiment 4) 5th Company. In addition to this, elements of Machine Gun Sharp Shooter Detachment 22 and the three engineer companies were deployed forward and the divisional Recruit Company was later moved into the Third Position. In normal circumstances this weak defence would not have mattered unduly but, on 9 April, the circumstances were far from normal; the British were threatening to break through on a large scale.

The field recruit depots were maintained by all the divisions behind the lines on both the Eastern and Western Fronts. These were men who had carried out basic training and were then transported forward to complete their advanced training in theatre, where the instructors could tailor what was taught to reflect the latest battle experience and gradually introduce the new arrivals to front line duties. In an emergency such as this, they could be used as normal reinforcing troops. Not everybody was entirely impressed with their potential, especially when on occasions such as this they had not been in France for long.

Leutnant F Henigst Bavarian 14th Mortar Company [21]

> "We soon had contact to our right. There on our right flank, covering up to the Gavrelle – St Laurent road, were the youthful men of the Field Recruit Depot, who had only arrived the previous day from the Homeland. They were unloaded, marched forward for over ten hours and were thrown on arrival straight into the yawning gap. Now unprotected from weather and fire, they lay wedged in like sardines in the narrow and weak trenches. Had it come to a fight I think that these men would have been nothing more than a hindrance, because none of them had fired anything other than blank ammunition and they were not up to the physical demands."

Adding to the difficulties, in an error repeated elsewhere along the Arras front that day, the immediate divisional reserves – 1st Battalion Bavarian Infantry Regiment 8, 3rd Battalion Bavarian Infantry Regiment 25 and 3rd Battalion Bavarian Infantry Regiment 4, were held back in Lambres, Brebières and Douai respectively. This certainly kept them clear of the risk of being hit by long range artillery, but it meant that they were simply too far in the rear to be able to intervene in the contact battle in a timely manner. Nevertheless there was a reaction as soon as the forward positions came under seriously heavy bombardment. 3rd Company Engineer Battalion 29 moved to occupy the Second Position north of the Gavrelle – St Laurent road, 5th Company Engineer Battalion 18 did the same to the south of the road, whilst Reserve Engineer Company 11 held on for a time at Point du Jour. Approximately one platoon of rear details were attached to each company, but the situation was far from reassuring. During the early morning of 9 April, for example, a one kilometre stretch of the Second Position in Sector *Habsburg* running north from Athies was manned by one unteroffizier and twelve men; all that were left of 10th Company Bavarian Infantry Regiment 8 after most of its manpower was sent forward by Major Felser to assist in the fight at the railway embankment.

Despite the presence of a number of machine guns, there were many gaps and the whole situation was extremely precarious. Further north, 6th Company Bavarian Infantry Regiment 25 under Reserve Leutnant Küffner and 5th Company Bavarian Infantry Regiment 4, commanded by Leutnant Schramm, were in position in Sectors *Schwaben* and *Eberhard* but, given the widths to be defended, these were little more than token forces. Returning wounded provided the first clues concerning the British attack but, as elsewhere, their statements, which always had to be treated sceptically, were not backed up with any tangible information. There was still no sign of the enemy advance despite a good lookout being maintained, but an intensification of gunfire as the British barrage moved forward indicated that it would not be long before the British attack, one they were ill equipped to face, would reach them. Suddenly, towards 8.00 am, came the noise of battle through clouds of smoke and gas that were hanging around all over the battlefield. Spotting the danger, a machine gun, commanded by

Unteroffizier Schober, opened up at 900 metres on the attackers from a position by the St Laurent – Gavrelle road.

Amidst the racket of shells exploding came the muffled thuds of hand grenades and the sound of machine guns as the enemy began to push forward east of the railway line, systematically clearing or wrecking dugouts as they came. Suddenly, an entire British infantry company, closed up in column, began to advance towards Athies. It came immediately under rapid machine gun fire and those not hit were scattered. Such successes were, however, few and far between, though the handful of guns of 2nd Company Machine Gun Sharp Shooter Battalion 22 stuck manfully to their task in order to provide cover for an artillery battery firing from a re-entrant just east of Athies. By the time the battery had exhausted its ammunition, harnessed up and pulled back, one gun team led by Unteroffizier Meyer had fired 8,000 rounds in keeping the attackers at a range of 400 metres and another a further 3,000 before it was knocked out by a shell burst.

It was soon time for the machine gun teams located up on Hill 100, northeast of Athies, to withdraw as well. British troops, exploiting dead ground in the area, threatened to outflank and encircle them too so, having remained in position until about 10.30 am, they then pulled back to the Fampoux area through heavy British shellfire that wounded several of them. Further north other machine guns disrupted the British advance; but by mid-morning all concerned realised that unless counter-stroke forces arrived soon they, too, would be manoeuvred out of their positions and have to yield more ground, because the men of 6th Company Bavarian Infantry Regiment 25 and 5th Company Bavarian Infantry Regiment 4, their numbers dwindling as a result of shelling, would not long be able to hold their overextended frontages. Already a scratch force of echelon troops located at Point du Jour was beginning to splinter and lose cohesion as individuals began to pull back in the face of relentless pressure.

Leutnant Stricker, commanding the sharpshooter company, sized up the situation and decided that he needed to pull back with all the surviving machine guns to the Third Position, just west of Gavrelle; there to make a firm stand together with any survivors from the small infantry forces in the Second Position. Reserve Leutnant Tannen, who had taken over command of 6th Company Bavarian Infantry Regiment 25 when Leutnant Küffner was wounded,[22] tried in vain to communicate from his positions around Point du Jour with his battalion commander, Hauptmann Grau, but Grau was already dead and Tannen had no choice but to withdraw as best he could. As the attack gained ever more ground, the defending gunners were drawn into close quarter action themselves. Unable to extract their guns, most of which had long since been destroyed, there were numerous incidents of the remaining guns being served until the ammunition ran out then, having destroyed or at least rendered them inoperable, the crews pulled back.

One such battery of Field Artillery Regiment 29 from Württemberg stayed in action near Athies, firing gas shells into Arras until all were expended; then the guns were put out of action. This was a wrench. Up until this point the regiment had never been in such a position. Now all the guns that remained were those in the rear area being repaired. The regimental historian later described the desperate final moments before the withdrawal:

"So far the regiment had never lost a gun; now all those deployed forward were gone. The few back in the workshops were all that were left. Both officers and men had held on until the last. So, for example, Vizefeldwebel Dittus and Gefreiter Hafner of 5th Battery calmly fired the only serviceable gun in the battery until the last shell had been used. Until the enemy broke in, Unteroffizier Scheerle devoted himself totally to the maintenance of links within the battery, providing a shining example to his men. Unteroffizier Müller of 3rd Battery daringly hung on in his observation post and succeeded in directing the fire of 2nd and 3rd Battery at the main break in point. Leutnant Kösler, whose battery had no serviceable guns left, kept carrying ammunition under heavy fire to an adjacent battery until he was wounded and fell into enemy hands. Some idea of the weight of the enemy fire experienced may be obtained from this description:
" 'The main observation post of 1st Battalion was near Athies. The batteries were located in and around houses and barns which were [originally] in good condition. The drum fire began to come down. Within minutes nothing could be seen but dust and smoke. When after a while this moved on, you could look in vain for a building. These had, without exception, disappeared. There was great concern for the batteries, because it seemed impossible that anything could have survived. Tense minutes passed, enemy fire increased in intensity once more. Suddenly runners arrived from the batteries, their steel helmets, faces and clothes caked with red brick dust. They reported huge losses of materiel, but if new guns could be brought up the batteries could fire on. Casualties had not been high. However, despite all efforts, no guns could be got forward.' "[23]

This pattern was repeated up in Sector *Schwaben*, where Bavarian Field Artillery Regiment 23 was in action, firing with what guns and ammunition were available to the last minute. In order to try to prevent the British from pushing on past Point du Jour, the commander of 2nd Battery, Reserve Oberleutnant Ebert, heroically stuck to his observation post, which was under constant heavy shell fire, directing fire onto the advancing masses until he was forced by their immediate proximity to race back to the battery position. One after the other his guns were knocked out or their crew killed or wounded. Eventually, together with Reserve Leutnant Hörauf and Reserve Vizefeldwebel Steinburger, he served the last remaining gun until there was no ammunition left. In recognition of his outstanding courage and the example he set that day, he was later awarded the Knight's Cross of the Military Max Josef Order.[24]

Despite their unfavourable location a long way to the rear, already by about 6.30 am 14th Bavarian Infantry Division was issuing orders to its reserves to begin moving forward and a few minutes later the chief of staff, Major Ritter von Jahreiß, informed

Generalmajor von Reck, commander 8 Bavarian Infantry Brigade, that the three battalions would be placed at his disposal, together with other nearby reserves, for the purpose of delivering a counter-stroke. Speed was of the essence, it was clear that time of arrival of these forces would vary considerably, but Reck did not have the luxury of waiting until all were in position before launching them forward. Unfortunately, this compromised the chances of success from the outset. Nevertheless, the best had to be made of a bad job. The first unit to arrive in Fresnes les Montauban was 3rd Battalion Bavarian Infantry Regiment 4, commanded by Hauptman Weigel. His unit had force marched forward and was given orders by Reck to form up in the high ground north of Fampoux then, with his left flank passing just north of Athies, he was to thrust forward to the railway embankment, seize it and push the enemy back. The idea was to send the second battalion to arrive forward to extend his frontage to the north, but Weigel was also directed, because of the urgency of the situation, not to wait for these reinforcements, but to press on.

To state that this plan was ambitious is barely to hint at the problem. The British were constantly reinforcing their advance, the assault was to take place over unreconnoitred ground and without any promise of artillery support. Only the extreme danger of a breakthrough could have justified it. Regardless of this, Weigel did his best to give substance to the order. Making use of the line of the Third Position, he placed 9th Company under Reserve Leutnant Dowe on the left on the northern edge of Fampoux, with Reserve Leutnant Jobmann's 10th Company on its right and 11th Company, commanded by Oberleutnant Hartmann, beyond that again. 12th Company was directed to a standby position in the sunken road leading from Fampoux up to the *Polenwerk* [Hyderabad Redoubt] and on to Gavrelle. Bit by bit, the companies got into position, though there was a delay with the arrival of 9th Company, which mistook an abandoned trench leading north from Fampoux for the start line and did not eventually arrive on the Third Position until 11.00 am, by which time the others had been there for at least half an hour.

In the event the holdup was not crucial because Hauptman Weigel, having had to wait for information concerning fire support, was not in a position to give out his final orders until midday. At first glance his plan seems reasonably sound:

"9th, 10th and 11th are to attack. The left flank of 9th is to be on the Fampoux – Athies road. The companies are to work their forward beginning immediately until they are approximately 300 metres from the railway. Up until 3.00 pm our artillery will bring down destructive fire on the railway then, at 3.00 pm, it is to be captured. 12th is to remain in the Third Position for the time being."[25]

Unfortunately the plan began to unravel at once. The runners sent to take it to 10th and 11th Companies could not find them. This left Weigel with no choice but to bring 12th Company into line and launch forward with only two companies, having amended the objective to the Second Position, one kilometre short of the railway.

Major Miller, commanding 3rd Battalion Bavarian Infantry Regiment 25, was second to arrive at Fresnes. His orders were to extend the attack frontage of Bavarian Infantry Regiment 4 to the north and to advance with Gavrelle on his left to the eastern slopes of the high ground between Fampoux and Point du Jour, prior to assaulting the line of the railway. Miller, as the senior member of the reinforcements, was placed in command of this regimental sized force, command of his own battalion devolving on Hauptmann Michell. Quite how he was meant to exercise command and control over these widely scattered elements is far from clear. Arriving last, Hauptmann Würth of 1st Battalion Bavarian Infantry Regiment 8, reinforced by several machine guns, reached Gavrelle about 12.15 pm and was ordered by Major Hoderlein of Bavarian Infantry Regiment 4 to advance rapidly, linking with 3rd Battalion Bavarian Infantry Regiment 25 on his left, with a view either to occupying or recapturing the railway and the Intermediate Position just west of it.

Of course it was by then far too late in the day for any such operation to hope to succeed. Nevertheless, Würth's party set off along the Gavrelle – Point du Jour road at 12.30 pm until heavy shelling forced him to deviate off the road for the slight cover afforded by the battered communication trench – the *Gavreller Weg*. This of course slowed the movement down drastically. Bringing up the rear was 3rd Company Machine Gun Sharpshooter Battalion 22, led by Reserve Leutnant Brauns. Transported forward from Douai in trucks, Generalmajor von Reck ordered them when they reached Fresnes to catch up with the advancing battalions and provide whatever support they could to the assault. Having passed through Gavrelle, the guns then deployed on a 1,500 metre front and struggled as best they could to close up with the attacking infantry.

In the meantime Weigel's 9th Company had managed to make some progress, reaching the *Point du Jour Riegel* about 1.40 pm. This trench line west of Fampoux was under heavy fire and British troops were already occupying it slightly further north. The situation for Reserve Leutnant Dowe's men was extremely precarious. They had lost touch with 12th Company after they set off and never had any sort of contact with 10th and 11th Companies at all. Had they but known it there was never going to be any help from that quarter. The speed of the British advance and the length of time it took the Bavarians to manoeuvre into position meant that, far from getting forward, British superiority and firepower would force them back in short order to their start line along the Third Position. Although the British attack was losing momentum, by about 3.00 pm the Bavarians who had thus far survived were ejected from the Third Position and the British had taken the *Polenwerk*.

The machine gunners did their best throughout to support the rifle companies, but everything was against them. Their numbers constantly reduced by enemy fire, they continued to fight on, finally with rifles and pistols, until all their ammunition was gone and they were overrun, being captured with the remnants of 3rd Battalion Bavarian Infantry Regiment 4. There were several heroic acts. One machine gun platoon under Offizierstellvertreter Jungk, observing the danger to the *Polenwerk*, rushed forward to try to defend it, but it arrived more or less simultaneously with the British and was also overwhelmed. However, this capture did mark the furthest point reached by the British advance in this sector. Other elements of Bavarian Infantry Regiment 4 may not have been able to get forward, but they could certainly take up blocking positions, did so and brought down heavy fire against every British effort to get further forward.

Around 11.00 am 3rd Battalion Bavarian Infantry Regiment 25 had just pushed on past the southern end of Gavrelle and was heading for the prominent re-entrant on the eastern side of Hill 100, southeast of Point du Jour. This was the stuff of nightmares; under constant artillery fire, they were then gassed as they approached the hill, had to don gas masks rapidly and could only plod forward slowly, not approaching the summit until 1.15 pm, by which time they came under torrents of machine gun fire from British weapons located to the south near the Fampoux – Bailleul track. Casualties mounted with alarming rapidity and the advance stalled. The company commander of 11th Company, Reserve Leutnant Wilking, was killed, Offizierstellvertreter Mohr was missing believed killed,[26] whilst two other company commanders and a platoon commander were wounded. Driven back from crater to crater, the remnants could do nothing to prevent the British occupying the entire length of the *Point du Jour Riegel* by about 2.00 pm.

The whole episode was witnessed by an anonymous member of 2nd Battery Field Artillery Regiment 76, who later wrote a complete account of the day from his perspective:

"When fresh supplies of ammunition arrived about 1.30 pm, the battery resumed its harassing fire. At the same time orders arrived from the observation post to the left rear of the battery to shorten the range by 800 metres. At that we ceased harassing fire and established a new observation post on Point du Jour Hill. We were replenished yet again with ammunition and fired most of it [at targets] on the far side of the hill, over which individual infantrymen were withdrawing. When news arrived and then was confirmed that the arrival of the British on Point du Jour Hill was imminent, we pulled the guns out of their pits, so as to be able to fire them at close range more effectively. A short time later the first of the British appeared on Point du Jour Hill and we fired at them (range 1,400 metres).

"Whilst all this was happening, two companies of our own infantry advanced on Point du Jour Hill and took up positions on its steep eastern slope. Most of them soon flooded back to the rear, together with a few men of the trench garrison, then, when a German howitzer battery in position by Gavrelle landed rounds in their midst, the rest, without exception, rushed to the rear.[27] This meant that there was not one single infantryman in front of the battery, which continued to fire the occasional round at Point du Jour, where individual British soldiers were taking cover in the trenches.

"Suddenly troops, whom we originally took for Germans, appeared on the hill to our left (south). We realised that they were enemy when a machine gun opened rapid fire at the battery. Two guns were swung round at once and fired with good effect at these British soldiers at a range of 500 – 600 metres. We could clearly see the casualties. The British then pulled back and took cover. Because we had fired all but thirty six rounds, the battery commander ordered the abandonment of the battery position. One of the guns fired the remaining rounds at British soldiers advancing once more to our left."[28]

Any lingering hopes of renewing the counter-attack withered away in the machine gun fire and confused shelling; worse, there was little that could be done to stem the tide of the British advance. Reduced to isolated groups, the German troops could do nothing but give ground and attempt to avoid being overrun or outflanked. With little to slow them, the British pushed on towards Point du Jour, which was where Reserve Oberleutnant Ebert of 2nd Battery Bavarian Field Artillery Regiment 23 distinguished himself, calmly laying and firing the last of his guns in the midst of a hail of shrapnel fire, exploding shells and bullets. His efforts and those of the members of his battery who worked to supply ammunition and close protection, enabled Ebert to keep the British at bay until about 2.30 pm, when Hauptmann Martin, commanding 5th Battery personally, managed to get his guns, which he had withdrawn from Gavrelle to Brebières, back into action and add weight to the defensive fire. For the time being this stabilised the situation in this critical sector.

It was around 1.45 pm when Hauptmann Würth, at the head of 1st Battalion Bavarian Infantry Regiment 8, reached the high ground traversed by the *Gavreller Weg* some 1,500 metres southwest of Bailleul and, in the middle of a storm of shrapnel and shell fire, met up with the survivors of Bavarian Infantry Regiments 4 and 25 who were making their way to the rear. In this way he learned about the various setbacks and discovered that what was left of 7th Company Bavarian Infantry Regiment 4, which had been severely mauled during the battle for the railway, had fallen back to a temporary blocking position astride the *Gavreller Weg*. From there they had observed strong columns of British infantry advancing, with cavalry screening their movement, towards 6th Company Bavarian Infantry Regiment 25, manning the Second Position west of Point du Jour and which was now coming under fire.

At more or less the same time the commander of 1st Battery Field Artillery Regiment 76 came by, informing Würth that he had had to destroy his guns because the enemy had closed to within two hundred metres of his position and apparently had already occupied the Second Position. Observing forward, Würth could see groups of British infantry appearing along the crest to his front, so he abandoned any final thoughts of attacking and, instead, sent 1st Company to occupy the battery position containing the destroyed guns of 5th Battery Field Artillery Regiment 600. He then despatched 2nd Company, reinforced by four machine guns under Reserve Leutnant Hausen, to the former position of 2nd Battery Foot Artillery Regiment 68 and directed his 3rd and 4th Companies to pull back to Gavrelle and to go into reserve in the Third Position. It was not much later that the thrust into the centre of the 14th Bavarian Infantry Division sector came to a halt. This had everything to do with the fact that the capture of the Second Position, known to the British as the Point du Jour or Brown Line, marked the limit of the task allotted to the 9th (Scottish) Division that day.[29] This fact did not prevent the Germans from making out subsequently that it was thanks to the heroism of its gunners that this occurred and of course there is no doubt that stout resistance and aggressive leadership by the surviving German artillery did impose some delay on the attackers and cause high casualties.

Oberst Gartmayr, the divisional artillery commander, was under considerable pressure throughout the day. Anticipating serious problems, he had directed that those guns of Bavarian Field Artillery Regiment 23 which had been withdrawn to Brebières for inspection, servicing and repair were to be brought to readiness as a matter of extreme urgency then, when reports began to filter in concerning the losses in guns and advance of the British 4th Division towards the Third Position, he ordered 5th Battery Bavarian Field Artillery Regiment 23 to move forward to the Gavrelle area and to report to Hauptmann Martin, who had been tasked to coordinate all the artillery and surviving infantry and to deploy it to counter the risk to the village itself. Taking control of the situation, Martin intercepted every man attempting to move back to the rear, directing them to reinforce either 3rd or 4th Companies Bavarian Infantry Regiment 8, which were manning the Third Position and providing protection for a revised gun line more to the east. The defences were further strengthened when about eighty men of the divisional mortar company also arrived at about 4.00 pm.

Leutnant F Henigst Bavarian Mortar Company 14[30]

"The heavy enemy fire, which gave the impression increasingly of being directed [by observers], did not stop us arriving as a group at Gavrelle and halting on the southern exit by the cemetery on the Roeux road. Here we noticed that some German guns were still firing, whereas elsewhere we had not come across any sort of German counter action. Gavrelle, which up until a short time previously had been an untouched and heavily populated village, was wreathed in impenetrable red-black brick and tile dust and on fire everywhere. It hardly seemed the sort of place where a regimental headquarters could be based. Then, just before I arrived there, I saw that the barn on the edge of the village and which I had been told housed the regimental command post had been flattened by a direct hit. I gave credence to the reports I had repeatedly received that the regimental command post was already located further to the rear and decided to act on my own initiative.

"The Gavrelle cemetery had been completely ploughed up by enemy shells; the great cross in its centre blown to pieces. Very close to it was a howitzer battery, commanded by Hauptmann Martin, of our divisional Field Artillery Regiment 23. Apparently these were the last of our guns. All the rest were still in their original positions or it had proved impossible to withdraw them along the roads. Nevertheless, some were recovered from in front of our own lines the following night in a daring action led by Reserve Oberleutnant Ebert of Field Artillery Regiment 23. I placed myself under Hauptmann Martin's orders. He knew of no infantry further forward. Deployed in the shelter of the sunken road leading to Roeux, the battery had outstanding views over the hill where *Point du Jour Riegel* ran.[31] Its fire came down with great accuracy and we could see with great clarity how it scattered the Tommies."

Just as 5th Battery Bavarian Field Artillery Regiment 23 arrived in rear of Gavrelle, Hauptmann Martin personally spotted the British appearing on the crest line of Point du Jour Hill. He immediately ordered the battery into action and fire came down quickly, checking forward progress. This put fresh heart into the *ad hoc* groupings of infantrymen whose morale was further reinforced when 4th Battery Field Artillery Regiment 600, redeployed from its position south of Bailleul, went into action from near the windmill 400 metres northeast of Gavrelle. Despite the fact that both positions came under heavy counter battery fire directed by a British spotting aircraft, a high rate of fire was sustained through heroics of ammunition resupply achieved by a light column of a Württemberg regiment. The situation remained fluid, sounds of battle could be heard clearly coming from the south, but valiant attempts to establish the precise situation were only partly successful.

Leutnant F Henigst Bavarian Mortar Company 14[32]

"Hauptmann Martin, however, feared a threat building up on the left flank from Roeux. We could hear the constant sound of small arms fire from there and were under enfilade fire. I sent an officer's patrol under Reserve Leutnants Gumbert and Spies to conduct a reconnaissance in that direction and it returned to report that there were no enemy by the railway platelayer's hut at Roeux, but that the British had pushed forward onto the hill from where they had a clear view of us. Because the only partially developed *Riegel* was apparently in enemy hands there was a real risk of us being rapidly rolled up, since the [Third] Position was unoccupied and the situation was extremely unclear ... "

The deployment of the divisional Field Recruit Depot has already been touched on, as have reservations about its suitability for action in the circumstances but manpower – from any source – was desperately needed forward and thus it had to play a role. It moved into the Third Position about midday and, like many others that day, found itself quite isolated and without contact to the left or right. Following a demanding ten hour march the inexperienced recruits found themselves in an unfamiliar and extremely confusing situation. On arrival at the half wrecked trenches they found themselves being shelled heavily as the British prepared to continue their advance. It was a rude awakening and hard on their nerves. Their commander, Oberleutnant Düsel, was everywhere attempting to provide guidance and leadership, whilst also gathering in survivors from the front and passing machine guns crews to stiffen up the three companies. It was an anxious time until the link up with one of the divisional reserve battalions was finally achieved once the attempted counter-attack had run its course. Fortunately, Düsel was highly experienced and calm under fire. General von Reck placed first of all the divisional Assault Company under his command then the survivors of 3rd Battalion Bavarian Infantry Regiment 4, with the result that, despite further British progress at the *Polenwerk* and down towards Fampoux, it proved possible to hold firmly to the west of Gavrelle.

Throughout the afternoon and early evening Hauptmann Martin had provided ceaseless, courageous leadership, providing guidance, encouragement, clear orders and setting an example to all the defenders in and around Gavrelle. Alarming reports reached him constantly, perhaps none more so than that of Oberleutnant Hartmann, commanding 11th Company Bavarian Infantry Regiment 4, who, having failed to receive orders earlier in the day from his battalion commander, had moved his men into the Third Position. There as the afternoon had worn on he had come under severe pressure from leading elements of the British 4th Division and he was forced to report to Martin that he was badly exposed, lacking all contact with the unit to the south. This came on top of the arrival of a badly shaken Leutnant Stuhlberger, who had had a difficult time forward with his machine guns. Martin rallied them all and buttressed Hartmann's position by despatching his own meagre reserves to cover the exposed flank. By these means, albeit slowly, the crisis was at least partially overcome. There was a lull in the enemy artillery fire towards 6.00 pm, so Hauptmann Martin decided to withdraw his two batteries to slightly less exposed positions, which had been reconnoitred by Hauptmann Fischer, commander of 3rd Battalion Bavarian Field Artillery Regiment 23. These were about three kilometres to the rear, near Mauville Farm, a kilometre north of Fresnes.

Leutnant F Henigst Bavarian Mortar Company 14[33]

"Hauptmann Martin decided to withdraw his battery. Because the teams did not appear, despite having been summoned repeatedly, and the situation was becoming ever more dangerous, I provided half of my men to help pull the guns to the rear and launched forward with the remainder to the *Riegel*. It seemed that the enemy spotted our intention to move the guns to the rear because hardly had the first gun set off than the first fiery greetings arrived. Despite increasing fire, it proved possible to get all the guns back to Fresnes and thus give them the chance of intervening decisively. Heavy snow squalls and small arms fire from all directions made it impossible to see if the *Riegel* Position was in fact occupied by the enemy, which was why we had to storm forward. In fact we found that it was not occupied, but had been badly smashed in places by enemy fire. We ourselves had been engaged with violent artillery fire on the way and also small arms fire to some extent. Despite that we suffered not one single casualty ... Spreading out widely, we occupied the position and I immediately attempted to link up to the left and right. Having gone a considerable distance, at long last I came across some infantry to our left, which meant for the time being at least I had cover out towards Roeux.

"Furthermore, the enemy artillery fire reduced considerably in intensity. It seemed as though either the enemy was content with what had been achieved or that they did not trust themselves to advance any further now that they were beyond the range of their massed artillery ... It is also possible that the effects of the generous ration of alcohol had gradually worn off; men pulling back had told us that all the Tommies were completely drunk.[34] One particularly persistent rumour was that the two British cavalry brigades or regiments were on standby, dismounted, behind Bailleul, waiting for the order to break through. But none appeared that day or during the days that followed ... "

Whilst the German forward defenders were brushed aside and immense efforts were being made to make best use of local reserves, very quickly the German chain of command demonstrated yet again its ability to initiate swift counter-action. Infantry Regiment 31 of 18th Infantry Division had been in billets back in Douai, where the weight of the bombardment had been rattling window panes throughout the night 8/9 April. At 9.20 am it received this radio message from divisional headquarters:

"1. The enemy has thrust into the left flank of 14th Bavarian Infantry Division and has occupied the railway embankment, deploying machine guns there. 14th Bavarian Infantry Division is launching a counter-stroke aimed at preventing the enemy gaining a lodgement at Point du Jour.
"2. Two battalions of the army reserve are to be transported forward by railway, as is Infantry Regiment 31, which is to move immediately to Douai railway station, ready to entrain. Command over all five battalions is assigned to 36 Infantry Brigade, which will simultaneously move in motor vehicles to be briefed in detail by the staff of 14th Bavarian Infantry Division at Brebières.[35]

At about 10.30 am the commander of 36 Infantry Brigade, Oberst Jonas, arrived at Headquarters 8 Bavarian Infantry Brigade in Fresnes to be informed that the three battalions of Infantry Regiment 31, reinforced by two further battalions, were on their way and that their mission was to launch a counter-stroke with the aim of recapturing the First Position, or at least the line of the railway embankment. The briefing was not even complete before a message arrived from 14th Bavarian Infantry Division, watering down the proposal and compromising the prospect for success before the attack was even launched. Instead of five battalions being used, only those of Infantry Regiment 31 would be deployed; crises elsewhere meant that the battalions from 79th Reserve Division and 1st Bavarian Reserve Division respectively were no longer available. Even worse, this attack would not be linked in any way with the counter-strokes already launched by 3rd Battalion Bavarian Infantry Regiment 4 and 3rd Battalion Bavarian Infantry Regiment 25. Instead it was to push forward due west via the *Polenwerk*.

Meanwhile the dynamics of the battle meant that the overall defensive position was deteriorating even more. Despite communication difficulties, enough reports had arrived at 14th Bavarian Infantry Division by 1.30 pm for the staff to assess that the situation in Sector *Eberhard* had become increasingly dangerous, with the enemy firmly established in the Intermediate Position, only two kilometres southwest of Bailleul. Nevertheless, the greatest risk to the integrity of the German position was further south, so it was clear that the counter-attack force, such as it was, would have to be deployed there. It was agreed, therefore, that 36 Infantry Brigade would command the attack of the fresh forces in the southern part of the divisional sector and 8 Bavarian Infantry Brigade the northern operation. 36 Infantry Brigade would also release three companies to the Bavarians to bolster their attacks. These forces were to assemble on the southern edge of Bailleul by the road to Fampoux.

The initial objective remained the Intermediate Position. All the troops were to shake out along the line of the Second Position and the boundary between north and south was set as the line running forward from Point du Jour to Maison Blanche Wood. Any surviving German sub units were to come under command of the respective brigades. This was a somewhat theoretical provision; and in any case, as the situation worsened, the officer from 8 Bavarian Infantry Brigade charged with getting the divisional order out to 36 Infantry Brigade was made aware before he left carrying it that things were coming to a head in both Sector *Eberhard* generally and Point du Jour in particular, so that the greatest haste was essential. If both the brigade and divisional levels of command had only a hazy knowledge of the evolving situation, the reinforcing battalions had none at all. Nevertheless, reacting to their earlier orders, by 11.00 am 1st Battalion and half of 3rd Battalion Infantry Regiment 31were pulling out of Douai and in a little over one hour disembarkation, just west of Biaches-St-Vaast, about eight kilometres from the embankment, was complete. 2nd Battalion and the remainder of 3rd Battalion entrained at midday and were assembled at Biache by 1.45 pm. Meanwhile the regimental staff had been to Brebières and motored from there to Biache (which was being shelled at the time) accompanied by the commander of 36 Infantry Brigade, who issued brief orders, the thrust of which were:

> "The enemy has occupied the railway embankment west of Athies. This embankment is to be retaken during the course of the evening by means of a counter-stroke. The objectiveof the attack is to regain the old K3 Position as far as possible. The regiment is to assemble in rear of the Third Position. Detailed orders will be issued in the *Polenwerk*.[36]

Major Billmann, commanding Infantry Regiment 31, then gave quick oral orders to his three battalion commander: Hauptmann Friedrichs, Major Freiherr von Kittlitz and Reserve Hauptmann Simonsen of 1st, 2nd and 3rd Battalions respectively and each immediately despatched an officer's patrol forward to reconnoitre the route forward and to mark and occupy the assembly area. This was an extremely dangerous task. None of Reserve Leutnants Köster and Münster or Landwehr Leutnant Hildebrandt returned. The first two were killed and Hildebrandt was captured.[37] Regardless of this, the regimental staff pushed forward to the *Polenwerk*, arriving about 3.00 pm. There, in discussion with the local artillery commander, it became clear that although there had been no recent definite news of the British advance, it did appear that at least in places it had reached the Third Position, held only weakly by elements of 14th Bavarian Infantry Division.

This situation had potentially grave consequences so the adjutant, Oberleutnant Herold, was sent back to meet the marching battalions with orders for 3rd Battalion, with 1st Battalion on its right, to advance as fast as possible in the direction of Roeux and to occupy the Third Position. 2nd Battalion was to act in support of the left flank. Whilst this was happening, the regimental commander went forward of the *Polenwerk* himself, taking only two runners with him. Shortly after leaving the field fortification, he saw a line of British infantry advancing on a broad front. Opening rapid fire at a range of 400 metres, this little group served in checking the advance, which had also been observed by 1st and 3rd Battalions approaching the high ground northwest of Fampoux. Shaking out immediately, the companies pushed forward as best they could and succeeded in taking up positions in and around Roeux, where they were joined by the commander who, despite being under constant small arms fire, had managed to avoid injury and capture and eventually make it back by exploiting the inadequate protection of the *Polenweg*, which ran more or less east – west.

At around 7.30 pm, by which time darkness had fallen, 2nd Battalion was ordered to sidestep to the north and close the gap between the 1st Battalion and the Bavarians in the Third Position This proved to be extremely difficult. The area was under fire, it was pitch black, the ground was unknown and there was no information concerning the enemy. Nevertheless, careful reconnaissance and good organisation ensured that, despite all the problems, 2nd Battalion was in the correct area by about 10.00 pm. It then established contact with the Bavarians and, by dawn, had managed to establish several hastily dug in strong points from where they could cover the intervening ground by fire. The actual gap, 1,000 metres across, was too wide to bridge fully. 1st and 3rd Battalions had also dug in as best they could so that, although it had proved to be impossible to carry out the planned attack, the regiment was established on a frontage of approximately 2,300 metres and was in a position to oppose vigorously a renewal of the British advance the following day.

That said, with nine companies strung out in a line, with next to no artillery support initially, it was just as well that no serious attempt was made to renew the advance until the evening of 10 April, by which time the defence had been further strengthened in a number of ways. The German defensive artillery was by then able to contribute to the beating off of these attacks which came in against the area of the *Polenwerk* at 6.30 and 9.15 pm in several waves, but the defending infantry also played a large part in repelling them. When the battle died down, 1st Battalion reported that its three forward companies had fired 30,000 rounds of rifle ammunition and its machine guns, something over 50,000. The bodies of over 700 British soldiers lay out to their front and the defenders were poised, together with reinforcements from Infantry Regiment 85, also of 18th Infantry Division, to fight extremely hard for possession of Roeux.

In the circumstances it was unfortunate that the Infantry Regiment 31 attack failed, all the more so because the Third Position extension, the *Monchy Riegel* south of the Scarpe, was still holding out. The gap which still existed between the Bavarians and Infantry Regiment 31 remained a source of great concern. Oberleutnant Drüsel managed to keep General von Reck fully up to date with the situation and he in turn requested the commander 36 Infantry Brigade, Oberst Jonas, to release any units which could be spared. Despite the fact that his forces were already widely dispersed and the fact that he was under pressure around Roeux, as has been noted, Major Billmann, commanding Infantry Regiment 31, actually extracted his 2nd Battalion out of the line and sent it north. By this time, however, it was after 7.00 pm and pitch dark, so the move was only partially successful. Even with the extra manpower, there were still gaps in the line that night and they were only partly covered with isolated section posts.

It was a night of frantic effort in an attempt to stabilise the lines before dawn on 10 April and to withdraw the fought out regiments north and south of the Scarpe before fresh blows were landed. Infantry Regiment 31 ended up with all three of its battalions in forward positions, each with only one company in reserve. However, during the night the Württemberg 26th Infantry Division began arriving, relieving the remnants of Grenadier Regiment 10 at Roeux, but variations in the depth of the British penetrations meant that Infantry Regiment 31 had to send a number of sections and machine guns in extension of their positions to the south of the Arras – Douai railway line. Recognising the difficulties faced by the regiments engaged, yet another regiment of 18th Infantry Division was called forward. Infantry Regiment 85 had arrived in Flines-les-Raches, some twelve kilometres northeast of Douai, on 8 April. Alerted the following morning, whilst the regimental staff was sent ahead for briefing by 8 Bavarian Infantry Brigade, the battalions marched to Douai, arriving there at 2.00 pm. Divisional orders, not accurate in every detail, but which reflected the extreme urgency, were then received at 4.30 pm.[38]

"1. 14th Bavarian Infantry Division is fighting for Point du Jour Hill, with orders to hold it at all costs.
2. Infantry Regiment 85 and 2nd Battalion Field Artillery Regiment 45 (under command Infantry Regiment 85) is to be deployed with all speed towards Gavrelle via Fresnes. Having occupied the Third Position west of Gavrelle it is to come under command 14th Bavarian Infantry Division.
3.In order to expedite the move of elements of the regiment Motor Vehicle Column 555 is placed at its disposal.
4. Rear Echelon is to remain in Douai.

The route forward along muddy roads was crammed with marching troops and supply columns. As a result progress was slow and even the regimental staff did not reach Fresnes-lèz-Montauban until 7.00 pm. There it was informed, 'The enemy is established on the heights west of Fampoux in the Third Position. Infantry Regiment 31 has launched an attack towards Fampoux.'[39]

It was not until after midnight that 2nd and 3rd Battalions were able to set off for Gavrelle from Fresnes. Passing through the village, they swung north and south, with 2nd Battalion occupying the line of the sunken road towards Oppy and 3rd Battalion that in the direction of Plouvain. Having arrived it was a matter of digging as fast as possible, so as to turn these two sunken lanes into a second line of defence. Despite the fact that accurate placement in the dark was quite impossible, machine guns were deployed either side of the main Gavrelle – St Laurent road and officer-led patrols were despatched to locate the enemy and also friendly forces. Links were established to Infantry Regiment 31 and units of 17th Infantry Division, but it was a dreadful night for men already exhausted from the strenuous march forward as they battled to dig into the clinging mud in the face of the wet, cold conditions and harassing gunfire. 1st Battalion had a somewhat easier time of it, having been retained in brigade reserve around the edge of Fresnes and preparing it for defence. As dawn broke, it became clear that the British were digging in at Point du Jour and were well established in the *Polenwerk* and near to Fampoux.

Field Artillery Regiment 45 also experienced difficulties both on 9 April itself and during the following night. It was well aware that it would become involved in the Arras fighting once the battle began but assumed that, because it was located thirty five kilometres behind the front, it would not be deployed immediately. The crisis caused by the deep penetration soon gave the lie to that assumption; the warning order to begin moving forward finally arriving at 1.30 pm, with the actual redeployment starting about one hour later. One immediate result was the fact that its 2nd Battalion had no possible chance of taking up positions that same afternoon, but every effort was made to overcome the late start and overcrowded routes forward so, by sparing neither man nor horse, it managed to reach Brebières by about 7.00 pm, having covered thirty kilometres in four hours. Negotiating the shelled area and picking routes round wrecked wagons, it finally went into battery positions northeast of Fresnes-lèz-Montauban with most of its observers clustered around Mauville Farm and able, once dawn broke, to add significantly to the fire power on the Gavrelle Roeux front.[40]

For the moment the crisis was over, but the mixing of units and formations led to a confused chain of command, so it was fortunate that the defence was not put to the test seriously until after 14th Bavarian Infantry Division was withdrawn.

Leutnant F Henigst Bavarian Mortar Company 14[41]

"Thanks heavens the enemy were resting on their laurels; we were lucky. Nothing else of significance happened. We did everything we could to improve the position and, in particular, to deepen it. The following day [10 April] we received orders to prepare tank traps and road craters, because reinforcing [enemy] infantry were moving up. Before I could carry this out, orders arrived that all remaining elements of 14th Bavarian Infantry Division were to withdraw. Troops from Württemberg had been rushed forward during the night to occupy the Position. They had only got as far forward as the sunken road running from Gavrelle to Roeux and did not occupy the positions we had taken.

"We, who by a miracle had overcome the shock, could breathe again and pull back, feeling, despite the painful losses, that we had not been entirely beaten. In our various ways we had been able to intervene in a not unimportant way. It was not until much later that we discovered the full significance of our actions, namely when we assisted Hauptmann Martin decisively and helped him save his guns, a feat for which he was awarded the high distinction of the [Knight's Cross of the] Bavarian Max Josef Order. The Mortar Company was also recognised; I received the Iron Cross First Class for my work that day. The news that awaited us in our billets was very depressing. The Bavarian 14th Infantry Division had suffered terrible attrition and had lost almost all the troops deployed in forward locations. Of the men of Mortar Company 14 operating forward, nobody returned. Most were captured after a most gallant defensive action, but many had been killed. The Mortar Company, which had only just recovered from the hard battles at Verdun, had lost the core of its NCOs and several very sound officers. For the time being further deployment was out of the question."

The implied criticism of the 'Troops from Württemberg' is perhaps a little harsh, or at least caused by a misunderstanding of the tasks given to 26th Infantry Division which, before the battle ever began, was tasked with intervening as required in the 11th Infantry Division sector, so its main effort was always going to be placed south of the Scarpe. Nevertheless, recognising the extent of the crisis north of the river, 1st and 3rd Companies of 1st Battalion Grenadier Regiment 119, which was the first unit to arrive, began to dig in on the extreme right of the 21 Infantry Brigade area at around 4.00 am 10 April to secure the gap between Roeux and the crossroads where the Roeux – Gavrelle road crossed the Douai – Arras railway. In addition, 2nd Battalion moved into reserve in a small wood 600 metres northeast of Roeux and 3rd Battalion was held in divisional reserve at Plouvain.[42] Furthermore, Henigst's opinion that, 'we had not been entirely beaten', may well have been common amongst other members of the division, who felt that they had done their duty to the best of their ability in the face of overwhelming odds, but it was not one shared by the army group commander. Reacting later to stinging criticism from Ludendorff, accompanied by a demand for an explanation about what had gone wrong and disregarding any extenuating circumstances, Prince Rupprecht placed the blame on all members of the division from the commander, Generalleutnant Ritter von Rauchenberger, downwards.

Crown Prince Rupprecht of Bavaria, Army Group Commander [43]

"14th Bavarian Infantry Division has clearly failed; both the troops and the commanders. As late as 7 April Headquarters [Sixth] Army stated that 14th Bavarian Infantry Division was, 'still battleworthy in the event of a major assault' and that 11th Infantry Division was 'fully battleworthy'. 14th Bavarian Infantry Division had performed well near Serre during the winter and had had a three week period of rest and recuperation in February. On 9 April it had kept its reserve back in Douai, that is to say up to twenty kilometres behind the front line. In conclusion, it must be stated that certain unfavourable circumstances, beyond the control of Sixth Army, had an influence on the course of events on 9 April, but that the most important reasons for the failure were:

- Insufficient artillery action against the enemy
- The failure to call forward reserves in accordance with orders.
- These two factors amount to serious negligence."

The days following the dramatic events of 9 April were curiously anti-climactic on this section of the front. One of the factors, at least to begin with, was undoubtedly the difficulty faced by the British when they tried to redeploy their guns forward across the shattered battlefield and supply them with ammunition. Major F Graham of 15th (Scottish) Division, writing home, could have been speaking for every single gunner on the Arras front.[44]

"The weather has, of course, been against us. Continual storms of snow, hail and rain do not make it any easier to move guns across country which has undergone a five days' intense bombardment. Albeit, we got 'em up somehow by relays with twelve to fourteen horses in [*sic.*] the guns and the gunners harnessed to the waggons."

On 10 April British troops were observed consolidating their hold and digging in at Point du Jour, Fampoux and the *Polenwerk*. The somewhat chaotic situation of the previous day, when the mixing of units and formations led to confusion regarding the chain of command, eased as the remnants of 14th Bavarian Infantry Division were withdrawn from the battle and, gradually, the gaps in the forward defences were filled as more troops arrived. Not that those arriving were especially enthused at the prospect. Fusilier Regiment 86 complained subsequently that not only were they once more not being deployed to launch an attack, but rather to plug a gap and to hang on day and night under shell fire in damaged trenches, exposed to the cold and the rain. Nevertheless they were desperately needed and spent the whole of the night 9/10 April moving forward through shell fire and, as soon as it became light, repeated attacks from the air. The arrival of the Richthofen Wing overhead during the morning, which led to the speedy shooting down of three British aircraft, came as something of a relief to the hard pressed defenders.[45]

It had been decided to dig a new stop line, the so-called *Fresnes-Riegel*, five kilometres from a point midway between Oppy and Neuvireuil more or less south to a point on the Scarpe, about 500 metres southwest of Biaches-St. Vaast. All troops not required for trench duty were set on this task, which was well on the way to completion by the end of the day. As if an exhausting day of digging after a sleepless night was not enough, as it went dark on 10 April, 1st Battalion Fusilier Regiment 86 advanced to the Second Position to relieve elements of Fusilier Regiment 90 and Bavarian Infantry Regiment 8. This was far from straightforward. Orders for the relief had not reached either of the two regiments involved and neither was prepared to withdraw until the matter was clarified.[46] It was yet another consequence of the muddled command relationships. Later that night 2nd Battalion also relieved 2nd Battalion Infantry Regiment 89 between Bailleul and Gavrelle. It was just as well that relief and reinforcement had been completed, together with improvements to the defences. Throughout 10 April, all the time that some of the British troops had been digging hard, column after column of British infantry were seen moving up then, in the afternoon, these were joined by large numbers of cavalrymen of the British 1 Cavalry Brigade, who had been tasked with seizing the prominent Greenland Hill between Gavrelle and Plouvain.

After a certain amount of British order and counter-order, a number of attempts were made to advance the line by the British 11 and 12 Brigades, but they were all roughly handled by the German defence. Two platoons of 1st Somerset Light Infantry, for example, which attempted to push on from the *Polenwerk* in mid afternoon were wiped out almost instantly by heavy machine gun fire[47] then, when a more serious attack was launched from Fampoux and the high ground to the north about 5.30 pm, heavy German defensive artillery fire, together with concentrated small arms fire, brought the attack to a standstill. Heavy snowfall and the approach of night ruled out a repetition that day. About two kilometres of the German Second Position between Bailleul and Point du Jour had been secured by the British but not much else was achieved. It was proof once more that a break in, even one as deep as that achieved on 9 April, was one thing; exploiting it quite another.

Despite the difficulties on 11 April, the day that Monchy le Preux was captured, the British XVII Corps was ordered to launch a major assault in an attempt to regain momentum north of the Scarpe and create an opportunity for cavalry exploitation. 4th Division was to capture and hold a line running from Plouvain through Greenland Hill to the *Polenwerk*, 34th were to advance to its left once 4th Division had made some progress and 51st (Highland) Division was directed to secure the entire Point du Jour area. Small scale attacks began to be launched once more on what was now the 18th Infantry Division front. In the light of recent experience, Major General Lambton, commander of 4th Division, insisted on a six hour preparatory bombardment, so none of the planned attacks was actually started until the afternoon.[48] The men of Infantry

Regiment 31 were soon feeling the effects of this fire, which began at dawn and rose in intensity throughout the morning until, by shortly before noon, drum fire, as bad as anything they had ever experienced, was hammering down on their inadequate positions.

As noon approached the British assault troops could be seen massing then, behind a curtain of dust and smoke, the British infantry assaulted in several waves from 12.15 pm, advancing with what the defenders described as 'grim courage'.[49] To the east of the *Polenwerk* the attack withered away in the fire of 1st Battalion, but a minor crisis occurred when there was a break in just northwest of Roeux into the 3rd Battalion trenches. This created a gap between the two battalions. The regimental commander, Major Billmann, personally directed his machine gun officer, Leutnant Wendte, to take the final reserve, one platoon of 12th Company, together with every spare man of his staff, and fill it. In response to an earlier call for assistance, 2nd Company Infantry Regiment 85, commanded by Reserve Leutnant Normann, arrived at 1.30 pm and was immediately subordinated to Reserve Hauptmann Simonsen, who was busy organising a counter stroke with every available man of 3rd Battalion.

At 2.45 pm, by which time the British attack was largely neutralised, the reinforced 3rd Battalion Infantry Regiment 31 responded to a series of bugle calls and attacked the isolated pockets of British resistance. Most of these withdrew, though a few prisoners were taken, along with four Lewis guns. By 3.30 pm the old positions had been restored, the British attempt to take Roeux had failed and although there was harassing artillery fire throughout the remainder of the day, these ceased during the evening and there was no attempt to renew the infantry attacks. Infantry Regiment 31, in particular its 3rd Battalion, which was temporarily withdrawn from the line after relief by 3rd Battalion Fusilier Regiment 86 at midnight, had fought well, but at the cost of heavy casualties. Reserve Leutnant Köster had been killed on 9 April, Reserve Leutnants Ulrich and Voigt of 11th Company on 11 April and there were numerous others wounded, together with a proportionately large number of other ranks.

11 April was effectively the final day of the first phase of the battle, the last time when, attempting to exploit the success of 9 April, the British attacks were thrown in with almost reckless disregard of systematic preparation or the situation on the flanks. The stiffening resistance they had encountered – especially at Roeux – and the losses endured made it clear that any further advances on the Arras front would be dependent on careful planning and concentrated artillery fire plans. In other words, within forty eight hours the battle had metamorphosed into a typical Western Front attritional duel, one which would drag on in varying degrees of intensity for several more agonising weeks. Naturally, this change was not obvious to the men engaged in the contact battle, though the early hours of 12 April were notable for the weight of fire being put down by the German artillery, further proof of the defenders' ability to stabilise dangerous situations and rush reinforcements to threatened sectors of the front. For its part the British artillery pounded both the forward areas and the approach routes to the rear, a sure sign of a renewal of the attack, which was confirmed when troops were observed

massing that afternoon for another attempt to capture the chemical works at Roeux and the rising ground towards Gavrelle.

The ensuing battle was a disaster for British arms. To be fair, Lieutenant General Fergusson, commanding XVII Corps, had requested a delay until 13 April so as to allow time for reconnaissance and systematic bombardment, but General Allenby, the army commander, was insistent that pressure be maintained, 'to prevent [the enemy] from consolidating his present position'.[50] A compromise was reached and a start time of 5.30 pm UK time was agreed. It sealed the fate of the men of 9th (Scottish) Division committed to the attack. Everything was against them. The preparations were sketchy and rushed, the British gunnery was wayward, the planned smoke to cover an approach over almost 2,000 metres of open countryside never materialised[51] and the men of the British 4th Division, through whose positions part of the attack was to be launched, were completely unaware of the impeding operation. The defenders of 18th Infantry Division, on the other hand, were more than ready.

In the centre, midway between Gavrelle and Roeux, 10th and 12th Companies Infantry Regiment 31 simply beat back the first rush, though some progress was made up at Gavrelle, where Infantry Regiment 85 came under severe pressure; but heavy fire from 1st Company Infantry Regiment 31 from positions just to the east of the village prevented a further advance. Down to the south, forward of Roeux, Fusilier Regiment 86 watched and waited as 27 Brigade, forced, because of the distances involved, to begin its move forward a full half hour ahead of H Hour, moved towards Fampoux. Inevitably the German artillery responded by pounding the area, splintering the advancing columns and disrupting the movement. 3rd Battalion Fusilier Regiment 86 suffered heavy casualties when the British guns opened up on its trenches, forcing the defenders into cover and enabling the attackers to reach their start line. There, however, their troubles really began. The disruption meant that they never had a chance to keep up with the creeping barrage and as soon as the attack began it was met by a storm of small arms fire.

It was too easy for the fusiliers and, with the blackest of black humour, the word passed along the line of defenders, 'This is range practice with living targets' and 'We are all going to classify today'.[52] The men of 11th Company held their fire until the enemy were at 300 metres and then opened up with rapid fire. None of the attackers got closer than 100 metres. The attack petered out with the whole area littered with dead and wounded men, who had to wait for darkness to fall before they could attempt to make their way to the rear. The fusiliers could not go to their assistance; they were fully occupied evacuating the 150 dead or wounded men in their own lines and repairing damaged defences, though a patrol did go forward, recovered two British machine guns and confirmed that there were British corpses everywhere.

During the following days the weather remained bad. There was rain, sleet and snow and it froze hard every night. Each morning at dawn the defenders, standing to, were confronted by the ghostly sight of countless dead men to their front, their hair rimed with hoar frost. Symbolic of the folly of underestimating the power of the defence to recover from an early setback, they were also a constant reminder of the price in casualties the coming weeks would exact.

Notes

[1] BOH pp 225-226.

[2] Kriegsarchiv Munich B.8.Inf. Brigade *Kampferfahrung bei Arras* dated 14.4.17.

[3] This refers to the so-called *Alberich Bewegung*, the withdrawal to the Hindenburg Line in March 1917.

[4] Kriegsarchiv Munich HS 2020 *Erlebnisbericht – Henigst.*

[5] Moßdorff History Field Artillery Regiment 76 p169

[6] History KB Field Artillery Regiment 23 p 26.

[7] Moßdorff *op. cit.* pp 171-172.

[8] Kriegsarchiv Munich *14. bayer.Inf. Division Tagesmeldung* dated 9.4.1917.

[9] Kriegsarchiv Munich HS 2020 *Erlebnisbericht – Henigst.*

[10] *ibid.*

[11] Behrmann *Die Osterschlacht II* p 103.

[12] Both Leutnant Franz Krembs and Leutnant Wilhelm Heckel are buried in the German cemetery at St Laurent Blangy in the *Kamaradengrab*.

[13] Ewing History Ninth Division p 194.

[14] Götz History KB Infantry Regiment 8 p 28.

[15] Braun History KB Infantry Regiment 25 p 37.

[16] Reserve Leutnants Georg Nabholz and Heinrich Martin are both buried in the *Kamaradengrab* of the German cemetery at St Laurent Blangy.

[17] Behrmann *op. cit.* p 109.

[18] Schoenfelder History Field Artillery Regiment 42 pp 180-181.

[19] Leutnant Siegfried Zapf was killed later that day and is buried in the *Kamaradengrab* of the German cemetery at St Laurent Blangy.

[20] Hauptmann Rudolf Grau and Unterarzt Richard Lurch are both buried in the *Kamaradengrab* of the German cemetery at St Laurent Blangy.

[21] Kriegsarchiv Munich HS 2020 *Erlebnisbericht – Henigst.*

[22] Leutnant Fritz Küffner succumbed to his wounds on 11 April 1917 and is buried in the German cemetery at St Laurent Blangy Block 1 Grave 1142.

[23] Gerok History Field Artillery Regiment 29 p 68.

[24] History KB Field Artillery Regiment 23 p 29.

[25] Behrmann *op. cit.* p 117.

[26] Offizierstellvertreter Mohr has no known grave, but Reserve Leutnant Otto Wilking is buried in the *Kamaradengrab* of the German cemetery at St Laurent Blangy.

[27] This must refer to 5th Battery KB Field Artillery Regiment 23, directed that day by the battalion commander, Hauptmann Martin, personally.

[28] Moßdorff *op. cit.* pp 175-176.

[29] Ewing *op. cit* p 198.

[30] Kriegsarchiv Munich HS 2020 *Erlebnisbericht – Henigst.*

[31] This trench linked the Second position to the Third near Fampoux, running northwest – southeast over the hill north east of Athies.

[32] Kriegsarchiv Munich HS 2020 *Erlebnisbericht – Henigst.*

[33] *ibid.*

[34] This accusation appears in the German literature with monotonous regularity. It is impossible to determine its plausibility, though it seems improbable.

[35] Studt History Infantry Regiment 31 p 183.

[36] *ibid.* p 183. The *Polenwerk*, known to the British as Hyderabad Redoubt, was a field fortification that straddled the Fampoux – Gavrelle road about one thousand metres north of Fampoux.

[37] Köster has no known grave, but Münster is very possibly Reserve Leutnant Eduard Münster, buried in Block X12 Grave 31 of the German cemetery at Hamburg-Ohlsdorf, whither his body must have been repatriated.

[38] Beltz History Infantry Regiment 85 p 97.

[39] *ibid.* p 97.

[40] Bene History Field Artillery Regiment 45 pp 71-72.

[41] Kriegsarchiv Munich HS 2020 *Erlebnisbericht – Henigst.*

[42] Gemmingen History Grenadier Regiment 119 p 195.

[43] Kriegsarchiv Munich HGr Rupprecht Bd 93 Oberkommando Ia/No. 2857 geh. H.Qu. den 21 April 1917.

[44] Stewart The Fifteenth (Scottish) Division p 127.

[45] Studt *op. cit.* p 185.

[46] Jürgensen History Fusilier Regiment 86 p 153.

[47] BOH p 257.

[48] *ibid.* p 269.

[49] Studt *op. cit.* p 186.

[50] BOH p 280.

[51] Ewing *op. cit.* 203-205.

[52] Jürgensen *op. cit.* p 154.

CHAPTER 3

The British Assault South
of the Scarpe

The German defence of the southern sector of Sixth Army was subject to complete change as March turned to April The warning signs concerning the impending offensive had multiplied rapidly during the previous days and weeks and so it was decided to withdraw the Saxon 23rd and 24th Infantry Divisions and to replace them with no fewer than four fresh divisions, subordinated to IX Reserve Corps (Generalleutnant Dieffenbach). From north to south, therefore, the front was held by 11th Infantry Division, commanded by Generalleutnant von Schöler and 17th Reserve Division (Generalmajor von Beczwarzowsky).Then came as a corps reinforcement 18th Reserve Division under command of Generalleutnant von Wundt, recently appointed after his successful command of 51 Reserve Brigade, 26th Reserve Division between Beaumont Hamel and Serre during the Battle of the Somme the previous year. 220th Infantry Division, commanded by Generalmajor von Bassewitz, was deployed in the extreme south, from the Mühlenberg southwest of Chérisy to the boundary with XIV Reserve Corps near Bullecourt, but this division was only peripherally involved in the initial clash of arms.

Once all the divisions were in place along the twenty kilometre front and, in the case of 18th Reserve Division, its forward deployment from a holding area east of Douai was not finally completed until the morning of 7 April, hurried preparations were made to meet the forthcoming attack and IX Reserve Corps was re-designated Group Arras. The increased density of the defence meant that positions could be held in rather greater depth than had been the case before, though real genuine depth, with forces to match, remained unachievable. Across the entire corps frontage, therefore, all the regiments were allocated a sector which they held with one battalion forward, one in support and one in reserve. By this time there was a general appreciation that the ability of the Allies to bring down a massive weight of fire in support of their attacks meant that ambitious moves forward of large scale reserves was likely to be less useful in the short term than to fight the contact battle in the early stages using only local reserves. Events of the first few days after 9 April would put this theory to a severe test.

As a result of the seemingly endless preparatory bombardment, a pall of dust and smoke hung over the entire area. The earth trembled constantly with the impact of the shells, trees were reduced to matchwood, houses and entire villages became mere heaps

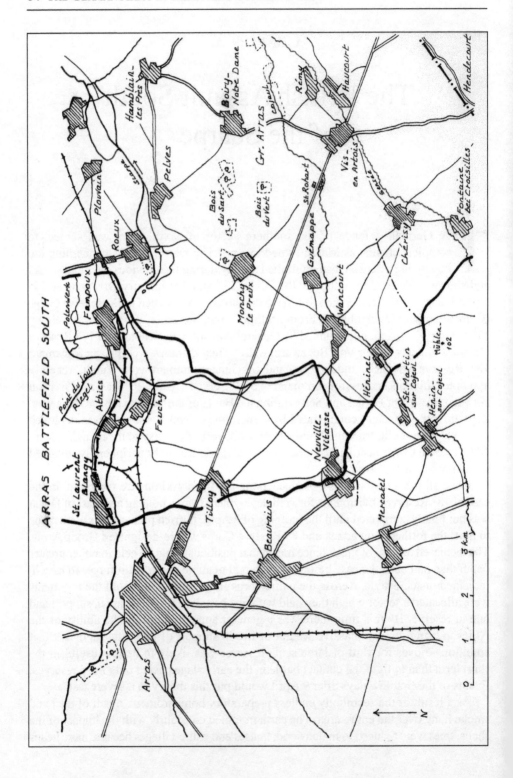

of rubble. If it had not been for the wide availability of reinforced concrete pill boxes and blockhouses, it would have been impossible for the defenders to withstand it. Guided by spotters in aircraft, all the defending batteries were brought under heavy fire, which destroyed or suppressed much of the German artillery. Even those guns still capable of replying were constrained by lack of ammunition and severe resupply problems. Despite all the difficulties, the German sound ranging and flash spotting troops were deployed well forward and succeeded in identifying huge numbers of British batteries.

However there was little that could be done in reply, the work simply serving to show that the defending infantry would be hard pressed to resist the main offensive when it opened; the weight of fire already putting in the shade the worst that had been endured the previous year on the Somme. The bombardment ground on, day after day. Some German batteries were reduced to one serviceable gun, whilst 2nd Battery Reserve Field Artillery Regiment 17, firing in support of 17th Reserve Division, was completely knocked out, having been subjected to 600 rounds of 240mm howitzer fire.[1]

The overall state of the defences did not inspire great confidence. In common with many other sectors of the front, the demands on manpower the previous year and poor winter weather meant that, even before the bombardment opened, the positions left much to be desired. In the north, just south of St Laurent, 11th Infantry Division found itself defending three forward lines of trenches, sited close together, with a fourth rather further away to the east. A Second Position of sorts had been dug about 700 metres further back, then there was a two kilometre gap to the rather sketchy *Monchy Riegel* [Monchy Stop Line] which, nevertheless, was destined to play an important, if brief, role in the battle. The entire area was one great sea of mud. Many trenches had been collapsed by the wet weather and, as a result, most of the approach and communications trenches were no more than knee deep - unusable by day and of only very limited value at night, apart from as a means of maintaining direction in the dark.

Although every effort had been made to keep the front line trench clear, in many places it had proved to be a losing battle. It was not manned continuously, the gaps had been filled with obstacles of various kinds, so the result was a fragmentation of the defence and great difficulty in maintaining contact left and right. East of the St. Sauveur suburb of Arras, Infantry Regiment 51 of 11th Infantry Division was suffering very badly. All links to the forward companies were broken and on 8 April, no report whatever having been received from 11th Company for forty eight hours, the battalion commander, Hauptmann Vahlkampf, ordered a reconnaissance patrol led by Reserve Leutnant Bindseil of 9th Company to go forward and establish the facts. It returned with grim news, 'The position is completely levelled. All the entrances to the mined dugouts have collapsed. Since their arrival on the position during the night 3/4 April they have had no sleep and hardly anything to eat, because very few of the ration carriers are still unwounded. Losses have been severe.'[2]

Orders were then given that 9th and 10th Companies were to organise carrying parties and get both warm and cold rations forward to 11th and 12th Companies during the night

8/9 April. If this was not successful then, instead, the two companies were to relieve the forward companies at day break on 9 April.

Reserve Leutnant Bindseil 9ᵗʰ Company Infantry Regiment 51[3]

"I passed on this order to my company, together with the necessary extra details, and divided it into carrying parties. Landwehr Leutnant Mache with three sections was responsible for moving cold rations forward from the ration dump and the remainder of the company under Leutnant Orlovius was to move forward warm food from the field kitchens as soon as possible. Both squads fulfilled their tasks completely and returned to me almost simultaneously, a little after 5.00 am. Leutnant Mache's group made several trips forward from the ration dump without suffering any losses. The detachment of Leutnant Orlovius could not locate the field kitchens in their normal place at the *Gleisdreieck*[4]. Instead they had to make their way under constant heavy fire through a gassed area to the rest area at Roeux, where the field kitchens had been halted just before the entrance to the village because of the gas.

"At Roeux Leutnant Orlovius, Vizefeldwebel Paul Spoida and Karl Hergert had to report sick with gas poisoning. The entire detachment was also directed to report to the medical officer to be checked for gas poisoning as well. Led by the daring Unteroffizier August Ziegenberg, who had already distinguished himself greatly at Vimy and on the Somme, and Einjährig-Freiwilliger Erich Mocalla, almost all the men ignored this directive, marching forward once more and remarking, 'We are not willing to leave our comrades forward in a mess! If we become ill, we can always report sick later!' With only relatively few losses from the high explosive and gas shells, this squad delivered the entire quantity of rations correctly to the commander of 11ᵗʰ Company. The company commander, Leutnant Ziemann, confirmed to me later in captivity that he was amazed to get back every single ration container full of food."

It was slightly easier for the defenders of the 17ᵗʰ Reserve Division sector, which included the important Neuville Vitasse salient. The main reason was that this was the transitional point to the *Siegfried Stellung* [Hindenburg Line]. The First Position was well constructed, featured an abundance of well made dugouts and the position was completely covered by a wide obstacle belt. Nevertheless, there were still unresolved weaknesses and the so-called *Artillerie Schutzsellung* [artillery protective position] was, on average, only about one metre deep. It had no dugouts and so was unsuitable as a holding place for reserves. The same applied to the incomplete *Monchy Riegel*. Not only did it have no accommodation for reserves, it was badly sited on a forward slope.

It might be thought that the 18ᵗʰ Reserve Division faced fewer problems. It was squarely deployed along a sector which formed part of the *Siegfried Stellung* but, such had been the rush in occupying it, that it was still incomplete in April. The first and second line trenches had been dug deep and provided with shelters and dugouts, but no communications trenches led to the rear and fire steps were lacking almost along the entire length. There was a near total lack of artillery positions or observation and command posts. Telephone links were either missing or unserviceable and all had to be improvised on deployment. The very fact that the 18th Reserve Division was being inserted into the line created an additional set of problems. There was virtually a complete absence of supply dumps, tramways, medical facilities or engineer parks. The only geographically suitable road for major resupply from the rear areas ran from Cantin forward via Estrées, Tortequenne and Sailly-en-Ostrevent, i.e. more or less the line of the modern D135 and D43, but the route was in a terrible state of repair, was barely passable by ammunition columns and completely unusable by motorised ambulances.

The only answer to these and other difficulties, many of which were shared by the 220th Infantry Division, was to go to work with every available man pressed into exhausting service, despite enemy interference and the generally appalling weather. As if that was not problematic enough, it was extremely difficult to place the guns of the corps artillery formations. The lie of the land did not lend itself to covered positions, so the mass of guns had to be concentrated into two small areas: one in a hollow to the east of Tilloy-lez-Moillaines; the other in a large re-entrant north of Wancourt, with all the attendant problems of lack of prepared gun pits, alternative positions or sufficient means of resupply. None of this was good for morale, but the general knowledge that little time remained before the corps would be fully engaged in a desperate fight for survival ensured there was no let up in preparatory work until the nerve-shattering bombardment opened and curtailed most forms of activity or even movement outside the shelters.

The initial British plan as outlined by Lieutenant General Snow, commander VII Corps, was to attack *Telegraphen-Hügel* [Telegraph Hill], south of Tilloy and Neuville Vitasse with two divisions and attempt to force a breakthrough. This would have meant the main effort going against 17th Reserve Division. In the event, he was overruled and, instead, General Allenby, commanding Third Army, insisted that the offensive be opened on as wide a front as possible. In practice this meant launching simultaneous attacks from the Scarpe all the way down to the *Mühlenberg*, located between Héninel and Fontaine-lez-Croisilles. In order to make the following account easier to follow, the initial actions fought within the defending divisional areas will be described separately from north to south.

11th (Silesian) Infantry Division

Grenadier Regiment 10, deployed in the extreme north of the divisional sector, straddled the line of the River Scarpe at St Laurent Blangy. North of the river, the forward defence was entrusted to 2nd and 4th Companies, commanded by Reserve Oberleutnant Filehne and Reserve Leutnant Reuter respectively, whilst, just to the south, the responsibility lay with Reserve Leutnant Schön and Reserve Leutnant Heilmann of 9th and 11th Companies. The lengthy preparatory bombardment south of the Scarpe was every bit as intense and devastating as anything endured by Group Vimy to the north of the river. Dugouts were smashed and pillboxes damaged, as were trenches; and food and drink were in very short supply. The German artillery positions were singled out for particular attention, one such firing in support of Grenadier Regiment 10 was engaged with 750 large calibre shells during the evening of 5 April alone. Small wonder that losses in men and materiel increased alarmingly during the Easter weekend. Meanwhile, pressure on the defenders was maintained by means of a series of Allied probing attacks, which were all driven off, albeit with difficulty. One particular incident occurred at about 2.00 am on 8 April when a raiding force, some hundred men strong, forced its way into the sector held by 10th Company. Landsturmman Richter and Fusilier Lange defended their post with great vigour until both of them fell badly wounded. At that the raiders tried to drag Lange away, but a timely intervention by an assault team from 11th Company, which charged in throwing grenades, both prevented this and succeeded in inflicting casualties on the British troops.[5]

Throughout Easter Day, fire continued to come down. All battery positions and known command posts were gassed and the losses went on mounting; that day saw a further fourteen killed, twenty one wounded and thirty three missing (believed to have been buried alive by the shelling). From 5.30 am on 9 April drum fire came down throughout the sector. At a stroke all means of communication with the rear were cut, including lines painstakingly restored over night. The brigade light signalling station on Hill 102, two kilometres west northwest of Monchy, was knocked out and the troops manning the forward positions were thereafter totally cut off. Hardly a single field gun was still serviceable, so the infantry, huddled into shell holes in the crater field, were left to face the full weight of the attack virtually unsupported. As dawn broke a series of large placards in the Allied front trenches could be read. Couched in perfect grammatical and rhyming German they read: *Den Bayern geben wir Bier und Brot, die Schlesier schlagen wir alle tot!* [We'll give bread and beer to the Bavarians, but kill every last one of the Silesians!]. It was a grim start to the day.

The supporting troops were alerted and began to make their way forwards. In the front line, a desperate hand to hand battle was soon in progress. Despite the fact that they faced overwhelming odds and were in any case badly worn down by weather and bombardment, the forward companies put up a hard fight at close quarters, suffering very high casualties as a result. In addition to large numbers of other ranks, Reserve Leutnant Paul Müller, 2nd Company, was killed, together with Leutnant von Kriegsheim, 11th Company and Reserve Leutnant Bretsch, commander of 3rd Machine Gun Company and Reserve Leutnant Jochimsen, 2nd Company, was severely wounded. Despite all their efforts, such was the weight of the attack that very quickly a deep penetration was made. This occurred primarily in the regimental left forward sector and that of Infantry Regiment 51 to the south, along the line of the railway running from Arras in the direction of the so-called *Gleis* (or *Eisenbahn*) *Dreieck* [Railway Triangle], also known as area *A-Süd* [A South].

At 6.15 am an unteroffizier from 11th Company got a message through to the *Kampftruppenkommandeur* [*KTK* = commander of the forward troops] which read, 'Enemy has broken through in the Infantry Regiment 51 and F10[6] sectors'. At that, every available reserve, primarily from 10th Company commanded by Reserve Leutnant Rudolf Simon, but including carrying parties led by Offizierstellvertreter Loske and engineers from 1st Company Pionier Battalion 6 under Leutnant Kalus, together with a single field gun of Field Artillery Regiment 42, were rushed forward under heavy fire to dig in along the line of the railway embankment running north from the Railway Triangle to the Athies - St Laurent road. By now light signalling had been re-established back to regimental headquarters and news of the impending disaster was quickly relayed to the rear.

Events moved swiftly. Observing the area to the north of the Scarpe, their own forward positions having disappeared under smoke and dust, the regimental commander, Major von Fumetti, together with other members of his staff, saw the light signals going up in the 14th Bavarian Infantry Division sector, showing where the men of Bavarian Infantry Regiment 8 were buckling under the pressure. It was now still only a few minutes after 7.00 am and already the British were pressing up against the newly manned railway embankment. Vainly, attempts were made to direct defensive artillery fire where it would have the greatest effect, but the response from the guns was weak and scattered. The valley of the Scarpe was gassed once more, British gun fire was falling on the railway embankment and, in addition to that, a tank moving along the St Laurent - Athies road was pouring fire the full length of the positions.

It was shortly after this that the Railway Triangle was assaulted and captured, which meant that a British wedge had been established between Grenadier Regiment 10 and Infantry Regiment 51, whose right flank was under distinct threat. It was only the intervention of 7th Battery Field Artillery Regiment 42, which brought constant fire down on the break in, which enabled the defence to hold for a short time longer. Nevertheless, by 10.00 am, the advance had reached to within 200 metres of regimental headquarters, located only 600 metres southeast of that place. It was time to withdraw and, hurriedly, the commander of Grenadier Regiment 10 re-established his headquarters just to the west of Fampoux. Meanwhile the battle for the embankment continued to rage. Having by midday endured no fewer than ten successive waves of attack, outflanked on both sides, their ammunition fired off and yet another attack developing, it was clear that the position was untenable. The senior man on the spot, Major von Rode, gave the order to the survivors to pull back to the Second Position: 1st Battalion to the north of the Scarpe and 3rd Battalion to the south of the river.

It will be recalled that the forward companies of Infantry Regiment 51 were already in desperate straits before the main offensive opened. With a huge effort, food had been got up to the forward positions on 8 April, but all were feeling the effects of the lengthy bombardment. To add to their discomfort there were two mortar-launched gas attacks, first between midnight and 1.00 am on 9 April, then again at 4.00 am. There were few casualties because individual protection was in good order, but the psychological and physical stress of remaining masked up took a further toll on their powers of resistance. The drum fire from 5.30 am claimed more victims so, by the time the British attack came in, the majority of sentries and men in the advanced posts forward of the front line were already dead or wounded. Leaning hard on their protective barrage, the British infantry was in amongst the front line trenches almost before the defence had had time to react.

On the right flank of 12th Company the front line itself was held by a platoon led by Vizefeldwebel Schöpke. It was simply overwhelmed and shot down; barely a man survived. Landwehr Leutnant Tilch and his men, located back in the second trench, managed to resist for a short period. One of his machine guns brought down particularly well directed fire, causing the attackers many casualties. However, enemy progress to the north in the Grenadier Regiment 10 sector meant that a serious threat built up rapidly against the right flank. Decisive action to secure the open flank by Unteroffiziers Sommert and Kudoke stabilised the situation briefly but soon Mills bombs were bursting in rear of the German line and the defence was forced more and more in towards the company commander's pill box. Finally, at about 9.00 am, when grenades were thrown directly into the pill box, followed by a burst of machine gun fire, Tilch surrendered. He later recalled that, 'It was source of great satisfaction to me when a British staff officer said to me during the interrogation in Arras, that he had not expected to encounter any resistance worth the name from the remnants of our regiment and that he was extremely surprised that the trench garrison had resisted so obstinately to the last bullet'.[7]

As an illustration of the feeble German artillery fire during the first assault, 11th Company, just to the south, recorded that despite being engaged in hand to hand fighting, they were only supported by two guns, whose combined fire had no discernible effect on the British troops whatsoever. In an entirely one-sided battle, the forward posts fought until there were only five men left on their feet; then they pulled back to link up with Vizefeldwebel Rösler's platoon, which was down to six men by this time. There could be only one outcome. The second forward platoon commander, Reserve Leutnant Tänzer, fell, severely wounded in the stomach, Vizefeldwebel Rösler went down, having been hit by a shell, which smashed both his legs and the order was given to fall back. The company commander, Leutnant Ziehmann, who was co-located with his third platoon in the second trench, took personal charge and, for a while, the situation stabilised slightly. One by one, however, the machine guns were knocked out or their crews killed. The grenade launcher, commanded by Unteroffizier Paul Schulze, fired off every one of its forty rounds and then fell silent and pressure built up inexorably on the shrinking number of survivors. Numbers told and the remnants of the company surrendered.

This was where the break in occurred. Off to the left the position had suffered rather less damage as a result of the bombardment so, during the early stages of the attack,

Reserve Leutnant Linder's 6th Company put up a stout defence, inflicting many casualties on the attackers. However, as the morning wore on, events took a similar course to that which had obtained to the north. All the time that the two machine guns, commanded by Vizefeldwebel Struzyna, remained in action, supplemented by a third belonging to the neighbouring Fusilier Regiment 38, the defence held. One by one they too fell silent, until only Leutnant Lindner and Gefreiter Tometschek were seen to be left operating the third gun. That too ceased firing and not one single man returned from the forward trench. A follow up rush saw the attackers get to within five metres of the second trench before they were halted by flanking fire from a machine gun directed by Sergeant Schiwek of 2nd Machine Gun Company. The inevitable direct hit on the gun finally put a stop to effective defence, so the senior remaining NCO, Vizefeldewebel Lindner, himself bleeding from a wounded foot, led the sole surviving five men back from crater to crater until they could take up a fresh position in the *Tilloy-Athies Riegel*. It was still only 7.00 am.

Bit by bit the defenders gave more ground until the battle was on to try to hold along the line of the third trench. One of those who came through the ordeal later described what happened:

Reserve Leutnant Schlensog Commander 10th Company Reserve Infantry Regiment 51[8]

"I found myself, together with my third platoon (Offizierstellvertreter Thelaner), providing cover by the battalion command post. Not until 4.00 am did the 9th and 10th Companies return from the front line where they had been delivering rations from Roeux. Although their numbers were reduced and they were tired out, they were in such good spirits that Hauptmann Vahlkampf called out enthusiastically, 'You are really good lads! Every one of you is a hero! If you continue like that, just let the British come!' Hardly had the team laid down in the dugout for a well-earned rest than Hauptmann Vahlkampf, who was in the trenches constantly during these critical days, shouted down, 'Everyone out! The British are attacking!' Immediately everyone rushed up and the trench was manned according to the manual. A patrol despatched forward reported that the enemy had broken into the forward trenches in places and was advancing *en masse*. One patrol sent out to the right to link up with the reserve company of Grenadier Regiment 10, returned to report that the trench was not occupied and that no sentries could be found. Contact to the left with 11th Company was only possible intermittently due to the crazy rate of artillery fire. At that Hauptmann Vahlkampf gave orders that our sector was to be prepared for defence and that barricades were to be erected left and right.

"The British approached our K-4 Trench in dense lines. Due to its commanding position, it offered excellent observation and fields of fire, visibility being limited only by the half light of dawn. Under our well-aimed fire, the British had to pull back repeatedly, despite the fact that they tried to disguise their locations by throwing smoke grenades. When we were later led away we were able to see what heavy casualties our fire had caused. At about 7.00 am the enemy succeeded in outflanking us to the right through the Grenadier Regiment 10 sector and cutting us off from the rear. We were now subjected to a hail of mortar bombs, rifle grenades and small arms fire from three sides. Enemy hand grenades were already flying over the right hand barricade, which was being defended heroically by Offizierstellvertreter Thelaner. The numbers of dead and wounded lying on the floor of the trench rose terribly. I begged Hauptmann Vahlkampf to take cover in the pillbox, at least until another commander was on the spot, but he refused, his words demonstrating his outstanding soldierly spirit, 'Wherever my men are, so must I be! Now we are not just commanders, but fighters!' Taking a rifle in his hand he moved over to join Thelaner at the right hand barricade, where the greatest danger lay.

"The British fire grew ever more in intensity, but we held on, despite a British aircraft joining in, flying very low and dropping hand grenades on us ... By about 9.00 am the British had closed up to the right hand barricade to such an extent that they must have assumed that they could push us back in hand to hand fighting. However, they were repeatedly driven back by well aimed rifle fire, even though our numbers had dwindled to a mere handful, some fifteen strong. Just after 9.00 am the courageous Offizierstellvertreter Paul Thelaner (from Obernigk) was killed by a rifle grenade, as was our revered Hauptmann Vahlkampf, who was by his side. His loss filled us with fury. From start to finish of the battle I was located in the centre of the sector at a point from which I could see all my men easily and they me. The machine gun co-located with the battalion command post brought down effective fire in all directions, but one man of the crew after the other fell dead. When the final man was killed I had the belted bullets extracted and distributed to my men, who were already running short of ammunition.

"It must have been about 11.00 am when that brave Unteroffizier, Max Pabel from Breslau [modern Wroclaw, Poland] ... came up to me and said, 'We have no rifle ammunition left and the bullets from the machine gun belts are also finished!' At that a bullet hit him in the neck and brought his heroic life to an end. Now that we had no ammunition left, further resistance was impossible and to attempt to break out, armed only with bayonets, would have been hopeless. We were completely surrounded and it would have meant certain death for the remainder of my men. Because we had to cease fire, we were at once overwhelmed by the British, who behaved as though they were more interested in robbing us than killing us: watches, rings, Iron Crosses and anything else they considered to be worth stealing were taken with such assurance that it appeared that theft was their primary occupation.

"So we were now prisoners, but we hardly understood why. I had truly believed - and convinced my men of the fact - that Grenadier Regiment 10 would soon recapture their lost position and free up our right flank once more. Even though we had been disappointed in that respect, the belief had enabled us to defend our sector to the last bullet. We took into captivity the proud thought that we had done our duty to the full and that this Easter Monday 1917 would remain a glorious day in the history of our regiment. We felt that we had been undefeated."

This fragmentation of the defensive battlefield also occurred to the south, where the remnants of 10th Company, 9th and 7th Companies, commanded by Reserve Leutnant Bindseil and Leutnant Koziol respectively, clustered together with some engineers around the headquarters of Hauptmann von Tettau, commanding officer 2nd Battalion and *KTK* (South). This was located in the depth K4 trench just north west of Hill 94 [*Beobachtungshügel* = Observatory Hill] and north of Tilloy. Here the enemy penetration was halted for a time and further thrusts to the south into the Fusilier Regiment 38 sector were brought under heavy machine gun fire, directed by Reserve Leutnant Heinrich, commanding 2nd Machine Gun Company. Once more, however, British progress meant that this location was also threatened from the rear. As casualties mounted, Reserve Leutnant Bindseil was shot through the eye and carried unconscious into the medical post. On his release much later from captivity, he produced an account of the day's events.

Reserve Leutnant Bindseil 9th Company Infantry Regiment 51[9]

"As soon as drum fire began to come down, I thought there would be an attack, so I raced up the dugout steps in order to orientate myself on the situation. From my observation post I could see the following picture: our position furthest forward was enveloped by an impenetrable cloud of black smoke, out of which came an endless series of flashes of exploding shells. A short while later, as the artillery barrage moved further forward, lines of infantrymen could be seen advancing slowly. Using my telescope, I could make out the flat helmets of the British. I sent a sentry to warn the 2nd Battalion staff in the dugout, fired flares calling for defensive fire, placed my men in defensive positions and then set about opening calm well-aimed fire, the success of which was quite extraordinary. The leading enemy line suffered heavy casualties, so its men took cover and awaited the arrival of the next three waves. Until that moment they had been moving right across the front at a walk, but now they began to use fire and manoeuvre - first by companies, then by platoons and sections and finally as individuals. As they approached their forward line, they suffered very heavy casualties.

"Finally all movement was halted and little effort was made to conduct a fire fight. Instead they took cover about 200 metres to our front, at which range our small arms fire was murderous. The enemy creeping barrage (there was absolutely no counter-action from our artillery to be seen; the guns had probably been neutralised by gas shells) moved slowly towards and then beyond us, without pausing for long to engage our trenches, so to begin with our casualties from gunfire were fairly light. Having achieved my first objective of preventing the enemy from by-passing us and having heard Reserve Leutnant Heinrich's machine gun open up on the left, I gave the order to the company to adopt its defensive positions; that it to say along the fourth trench from *Ludwigsweg* [Ludwig's Way] to the junction with 10th Company by the 3rd Battalion command post. This was done at the run.

"The situation was now as follows: To my front the enemy was stalled between the third and fourth trenches. To the left the enemy was advancing, whilst the dense marching columns were streaming past Tilloy, leaving it on their right. Because Leutnant Heinrich had no targets to his front, the enemy having been fought to a standstill there, he engaged these columns. Due to the undulating terrain, I could not see what was happening to my right so, taking a section with me, I moved about eighty metres forward along *Ludwigsweg*. Here I made the surprise discovery that a British heavy machine gun was taking up a position about one hundred metres forward of the British line. In a flash the section commander, Unteroffizier August Ziegenberg (from Brieg) and I had shot the crew. Simultaneously, the British line of infantrymen tried to resume their advance but came under flanking fire of such effect from my men that far from running forwards, they took to their heels. A British officer running along the line tried in vain to halt his men, but he was brought down by a bullet and a general enemy withdrawal began, pursued by the heaviest fire we could bring to bear.

"My men were filled with an indescribable feeling of victory. Unteroffizier Ziegenberg came up to me and asked for permission to bring in the machine gun. I agreed but ordered him to wait until I had established the exact situation off to the right. Just as I was turning, I was hit in the head and collapsed (about 6.30 am). I did not regain consciousness until much later, when I had been bandaged up and Landwehr Leutnant Mache was standing next to me. I handed over the company and bade him maintain its honour and keep the British at bay ... the remainder of the story I reconstructed later ... The British tried repeatedly all morning to get forward, but were continually beaten back. Leutnant Mache was wounded and then killed by a shot to the back of his head. Finally, the British abandoned the attempt to capture our position frontally. They had already outflanked the regiment left and right hours earlier and they launched an attack at about midday from all four sides. This caused us very heavy casualties and gradually the small band of unwounded men was forced back to *Umgang II* [communication trench leading east from *KTK* (South)] ... Leutnant Sacher, who succeeded Leutnant Mache,was also killed by a shot to the head. Ammunition began to run out, despite the fact that the pouches of all the dead and wounded had been emptied. Finally, none of the men had any left.

"At 12.30 pm a general assault was launched. The machine gun of 2nd Machine Gun Company fired off two belts of ammunition against the attackers and was then thrown down a well, whilst the crew hurried down into a dugout. Just behind them the first British hand grenades began exploding in the entrance and the remainder of the team had to surrender. In the 3rd Battalion area the sentry had raised the alarm, shouting, 'Defensive fire is being called for on the right!' At that everyone rushed out of the dugouts, but the British had already got rather close, especially in the communication trenches. A battle with hand and rifle grenades broke out at once and the trench was barricaded, to the right at a communications trench; to the left where a one hundred metre length had been totally flattened between the 10th Company and mine. A hard-fought grenade duel took place to the right and the British were driven back. This was where Hauptmann Vahlkampf had been killed by an enemy rifle grenade about 6.30 am ... At about 10.00 am a contact patrol led by Unteroffizier August Ziegenberg was sent to link up with 3rd Battalion. It was retained by Leutnant Seiffen, because he considered the situation to be more serious there than at *Umgang II*. The 3rd Battalion command post was captured about midday because the defenders had run out of ammunition."

Deployed along a frontage which stretched from a point just to the north of the Arras -Cambrai road to near the western exit of Tilloy, the experience of Fusilier Regiment 38 was similar to that of their neighbours to the north though, if anything, their defensive sector was even less suitable for the task than that of Infantry Regiment 51. The winter weather, lack of manpower and enemy interference had all combined to produce an extremely unfavourable situation. Everywhere the walls of trenches had slumped in and, as a result, movement through the knee deep mud was restricted and, in places where the collapses had been total, completely impossible. The net result was that large stretches of trench line were unmanned altogether; the few dismal defended localities dignified by being given the title of an 'Island System', an appellation which convinced nobody during the handover/takeover.

The plain fact was that in its current state the sector was effectively indefensible and the problems were not limited to the forward area. The communication trenches leading to the rear were in an equally poor condition and, which was worse, even where they were partly usable, they only extended back as far as the fourth line. This meant that all movement for whatever reason was confined to the Arras-Cambrai road and only during the hours of darkness. To compound the difficulties, for most of its length in the forward area, this road ran through the 17th Reserve Division sector, so its use had to be negotiated and, furthermore, because of its obvious importance, much of it was under Allied harassing fire. In an attempt to improve matters, the regimental commander ordered that new communications trenches were to be dug so as to ease the movement of supplies forward, but there was no time to achieve this before the offensive began.

If the trenches were poor, the wire obstacle was also in a terrible state. In places it was missing altogether; in others in desperate need of repair. Once again, nothing could be done in the time available and, although there were sufficient dugouts, they were badly placed and no longer corresponded to the change in emphasis towards defence in depth. Command posts were poorly located and there was neither a regimental aid post, or anywhere to locate one. As a temporary measure, Reserve Infantry Regiment 76 to the south agreed to help and the medical officer relocated there. His subsequent work on behalf of both regiments was recognised when he was awarded the Hanseatic Cross by the regiment from Hamburg.

There were only limited stocks of food and water in the forward positions, but quite a large amount of ammunition. This was just as well, because communications were extremely poor. There were no deep dug cable trenches, so the telephones rarely worked. Attempts to employ light signalling met with very little success and only attracted the attention of the British guns. As a result runners had to be used and such were the deficiencies of the trench system that their movement verged on the suicidal. Meanwhile the bombardment grew daily in intensity. It was obvious to Oberstleutnant Burchardi, the commander, that the offensive would not be long delayed, so a superhuman effort was made to get additional supplies of hand grenades forward. Pressing every spare man into service during the night 7/8 April, it was possible to distribute 3,000 grenades to the forward companies, but that was a last gasp effort. Despite all the problems, certain that dawn on 9 April was to see the start of the attack, the forward companies could only wait, having been brought to the highest state of alert.

Unsurprising to relate, when the assault was finally launched, following a period of intense drumfire, 3rd Battalion, occupying the forward positions, was soon involved in a desperate close-range battle, Occupying positions on the right flank, 9th Company, commanded by Reserve Leutnant Joost, put up such a wall of small arms fire, supplemented by the throwing of large numbers of hand grenades, that it succeeded in holding the first wave of attackers. 11th Company, under Reserve Leutnant Gründle, also enjoyed a brief period of success but, once more, an enemy thrust succeeded in penetrating the position and quickly both companies found themselves virtually surrounded and fending off attacks from three sides simultaneously. Tank support was added to the attacking mix and there could be only one result. Their ammunition exhausted, their casualties rising alarmingly, the positions were overwhelmed and overrun. A few survivors managed to withdraw, suffering more casualties from the British artillery fire as they went and, eventually, a handful of men led by Reserve Leutnant Gründler pulled back through Tilloy and reached the *KTK* of the neighbouring 1st Battalion Reserve Infantry Regiment 76. Having reported to Hauptmann Albrecht there, he and his men joined the battle in that sector.

In short order 3rd Battalion Fusilier Regiment 38 had been wiped off the Order of

Battle. Of 10th Company, charged with the defence of Tilloy itself, only seven men returned, one of whom, Vizefeldwebel Rösner, did not get back until the early morning of 10 April, having disguised himself with a British steel helmet and slipping through the British lines in the half light of dawn. 1st Battalion, commanded by Reserve Hauptmann Dziembowski and in the supporting role, had been occupying the K4 trench line. So concentrated had been the bombardment here, however, that the battalion was actually deployed in a crater field. By 7.00 am it was under frontal attack and its right flank in particular was threatened. As was the case elsewhere, initial British attacks were beaten off and some lost ground recovered through swift counter action by 2nd and 4th Companies. Inevitably, however, profiting from ground gained to the north, a strong thrust, supported by machine guns, came in and was only halted temporarily after a huge effort by a team led by Offizierstellvertreter Callies of 4th Company.

As had so often been the case that morning, British pressure grew, German casualties mounted and ammunition began to run low. By mid morning there was no alternative but to withdraw southwards and to link up with Reserve Infantry Regiment 76. The respite so gained was short lived. The isolated small group of men from different units found both its flanks threatened so, by about midday, Hauptmann Albrecht gave orders for a further withdrawal. Having taken up positions in *Ochsenwald* [Ox Wood], 500 metres west of the southern tip of Tilloy, it was at long last possible to re-establish the link with the sub unit to the north. In view of the overall situation, not even this position was tenable for long. By mid afternoon, the remnants of 1st and 3rd Battalions Fusilier Regiment 38 and 1st Battalion Reserve Infantry Regiment 76 had fallen right back to the *Monchy Riegel*, manned by 3rd Battalion Reserve Infantry Regiment 76, where they added their meagre fighting power to the defence. Losses in 1st Battalion Fusilier Regiment 38 were almost as bad as those suffered by its 3rd Battalion. The Machine Gun Company commander, Leutnant Knothe-Bähnisch, and Offizierstellevertreter Herden of 4th Company were both dead, seven other officers were missing and four other wounded. Losses amongst the other ranks were also correspondingly high.

17th Reserve Division
Having suffered intense drum fire for thirty minutes up to 5.30 am there was then a brief pause along the front of 17th Reserve Division. The defenders from Reserve Infantry Regiment 76, and Infantry Regiments 162 and 163 rushed to man their positions when, suddenly, there was a further crashing concentration of fire on the forward areas. Under cover of this latest burst of shelling, a mass of British infantry advanced, supported by tanks, line abreast, with about 150 metres spacing between waves. Flares shot up, urgently requesting defensive fire from the German batteries, but few guns had survived and the fire when it came was desultory and far from effective. As a result, follow up troops carrying all manner of additional ammunition and trench stores were able to close up to the German lines largely unmolested.

Very quickly the forward defenders were in serious trouble. Their small arms fire was sufficient to check the first assault, but their numbers were too few to hold a further concerted attack. The problems caused by incursions further north have already been mentioned. Here there was in addition a break in at the junction between Reserve Infantry Regiment 76, commanded by Major Grützmacher, and Infantry Regiment 162, under Oberstleutnant von Rettberg. As soon as Hill 94, northeast of Tilloy, fell, the fate of the village itself was sealed, as was that of most of the men of 1st Battalion Reserve Infantry Regiment 76. One of those fortunate enough to have been in support when the assault broke over this sector of the front later left a detailed account of the day.

Vizefeldwebel Warnke 1st Company Reserve Infantry Regiment 76[10]

"From the beginning of the month we had been deployed immediately south of Arras in positions in front of the village of Tilloy. All day long the trenches were under very heavy fire. From Good Friday to the morning of Easter Monday it increased to unparalleled strength. The front line was held by 2nd Battalion with 1st Battalion in support. On Easter Monday the British attacked in great masses, supported by many tanks. To our right they broke through and, suddenly, they were in the second and third trenches. The greater part of 2nd Battalion and 2nd, 3rd and 4th Companies were wiped out. 1s Company, which had been furthest to the rear, had to push forward and hold back all those streaming to the rear. That was an appalling journey through the drum fire. We had not been in shell holes for long before we were outflanked and had to pull back to the next available position.

"The enemy followed up vigorously, attempting to drive us out, but were repulsed. The tanks moved up behind slowly, until they got to within twenty metres and began firing at us with machine guns and main armament. We were completely defenceless against them. We had absolutely no artillery support that day, because the Tommies had overrun a large proportion of the guns. Towards evening the enemy broke through again to our right, so the following morning we had to evacuate our position and, some distance to the rear, we scrabbled out a position in shell holes. The 3rd Battalion was also deployed there, but not for long when word arrived that the enemy was already established in a copse to our rear. So once more for 1st Coy it was, 'About turn! Quick march!' - in the direction of the copse.

"In fact there was only a patrol there. It fired at us then withdrew. A new position was prepared at top speed behind the wood. The British followed up in large numbers in skirmishing lines and in column. There was also some cavalry. Towards evening the British launched another attack, but were beaten back with heavy losses. This was repeated several times during the night. Luckily the British artillery did not know where our positions were. The following morning at 5.00 am we were relieved by some Bavarians.[11] We marched for two hours to Biaches but hardly had we arrived than we were stood to once more. It was said that the enemy had broken into Monchy, so we had to march forward again and dig in on a hill top, from which we had superb views.

"The entire landscape was full of lines of infantrymen, artillery deploying in the open as well as ammunition columns and even some cavalry galloping around. Our heavy artillery brought down fire amongst them and not many escaped. It was real manoeuvre warfare. The Tommies did not succeed in getting further forward, so we were able to pull back that evening. We were utterly exhausted and soaked to the skin."

Although casualties in the forward companies were very high, a significant proportion comprised men who were captured when they were outflanked or their positions were overwhelmed. Post-war, those returning from captivity were able to fill in someof the blanks in the story.

Reserve Leutnant Lange 3rd Company Reserve Infantry Regiment 76[12]

"The platoons of 3rd Company were located in the third line (*Lehmgrube,* [Clay Pit] *Artillerieschutzstellung* [Protected Gun Line] and *Wielandschanze* [Wieland Diggings]) at the northern corner of Tilloy lez Mofflaines. Raging artillery fire was coming down on the position then, at about 6.00 am, the British infantry began their assault. By around 9.00 am the first and second lines had been overrun and the enemy was located just to the front of the *Wieland-Schanze*. However, because 3rd Company had just managed in time to occupy their sector, the British came up against obstinate resistance. Meanwhile it was fully daylight. We were standing one behind the other on our staircase. The [shells] were still landing on *Wieland-Schanze*, but not with the previous intensity. Then, suddenly – we could scarcely believe our ears - the drumming stopped as though it had been switched off. 'Everyone out! Here they come! Here they come!' What a relief!

"Initially the harsh daylight hurt our eyes and we staggered, as though drunk, through the trench that had been turned the previous night into a ploughed up furrow. Close by a German machine gun hammered away. The occasional round impacted near to us. The British must already have captured Tilloy ... With three sections and in accordance with orders I occupied a flanking trench which was parallel to the Arras – Cambrai road. Remarkable to relate this trench was almost intact, as was the wire obstacle to its front. A wounded man was lying in front of a dugout and as I jumped over him, I grabbed his rifle. I should be able to do more good with that than with my pistol.

"We had soon occupied the trench and were ready to begin our grim work, but the enemy was nowhere to be seen. The obstacle along the road and the ruins of Tilloy saw to that. Taking a quick decision, I jumped up out of the trench to see what was happening and my men followed me. Then we realised what had happened. The British had broken through the regiment to our right.[13] They were flooding over *Beobachtungs-Hügel* [Hill 94 = Observation Hill] and were swarming towards the *Monchy Riegel*. Wave after wave of them were advancing over the old German positions. That was the most rewarding target we could possibly have wished for. Firing in the open from a standing position, we poured rapid fire at them and forced the Tommies to take cover in shell holes and trenches.

"The cheers of success of our men had barely died away when, suddenly, over our heads and emerging through the mist and powder smoke loomed the great silhouette of a British aircraft, which was flying so low that we could have thrown stones at it. The pilot fired at us and we had to jump down and press ourselves against the wall of the trench. Thank heavens his shooting was so poor that we had no casualties. Once it disappeared and we were able to put our heads up out of the trench once more, we could see the first of the British emerging from the ruins of Tilloy. One Tommy was very close to me behind a wall. He waved and shouted to me 'Come on!' [*sic.*] In reply I sent a bullet drilling into the wall and he did not reappear at that spot.

"We could not halt the British breakthrough of our right hand neighbours. If the British also overran our positions to the south of Tilloy, we should have had it here in the *Wieland-Schanze*, even though we had the *Lehmgrube* to our rear. When I pointed the threatening risk to our company commander, he stated that we should have to await orders from the battalion. Was there, in fact, any link to battalion headquarters, or were we already completely surrounded? I returned to my post and fired and fired until the last bullet had gone down the barrel. A British tank hove into view, but was suddenly cloaked in by black smoke and a sheet of flame shot up from it. Was it a hit by our artillery? All morning we had hardly noticed any activity from our gunners.

"*Sergeanten-Wald* [Sergeant's Wood] to our left was in British hands and the enemy was gathering men there prior to another thrust. A single super-heavy German shell landed in amongst them and did its bloody work. Bits of British soldiers flew in all directions. I turned to my neighbour to demand more ammunition then saw that my men had evacuated the trench. I was totally alone. Probably I had not heard the shouts of my neighbour above the noise of battle. There was no question of staying any longer. I rushed to the rear and rallied my retreating comrades just short of the *Lehmgrube*. A very young lad of the company was just about to jump into the trench when he met his end. Without a sound he rolled over by my feet. It was the fate of a soldier!

"The British followed us into the trench, but we drove them out with hand grenades. They tried to bring a machine gun into action, but well aimed shots dealt with the three machine gunners. If only we could move part of our company back into positions on the dip slope of the *Lehmgrube* from where they could cover the withdrawal of the remainder of the company, and escape from the trap was not out of the question. However, as I managed to cast a glance down into the *Grube*, all I could see was a completely chaotic scene. The remnants of the forward companies were streaming into it from all directions and congregating there. Many attempted to escape from this witches' cauldron to the rear or the side but British machine guns, that we could not see, were maintaining such a weight of fire against the rear edge of the *Grube* that not a man succeeded in passing through it. Just as a man would reach the lip of the *Grube* and attempt to cross it, he would collapse as though hit by a mysterious, unseen, hand and roll back down into the *Lehmgrube*.

"By chance, when I found myself in the rear corner of the *Grube* where men were clustering, wondering how to avoid all the bullets and the exploding hand grenades I met my friend Josef Hachmöller. We had first met on our officers' course and since then had been inseparable ... The British pressed forward in increasing numbers from the *Wieland-Schanze* to the *Grube*. I carried on with my work until a Tommy demanded that I lay down my weapon. I obeyed; there was nothing else for it. The British seemed to be drunk.[14] One British soldier was so drunk he did not seem to know what he was doing. He shot one of the senior soldiers, who had long since laid down his weapon, through the chest at close range, killing him. [But others] offered us their water bottles and gave us cigarettes, saying, 'The war is finished for you.' [*sic.*]"

Operating to the south of Reserve Infantry Regiment 76 and Infantry Regiment 162 and responsible for the Neuville Vitasse salient, one of the British VII Corps' priority objectives, was Infantry Regiment 163. Like all its neighbours, the shelling, which came down on average for twenty hours each day during the past week, had reduced very considerably its ability to resist an attack. If that was not bad enough, every movement in daylight back as far as the *Artillerie-Schutzstellung* was subject to machine gun attack from low flying aircraft. After one or two periods of drum fire, designed to trick the defence into thinking that an assault was about to take place, there was a marked slackening of fire on 8 April, which extended into the night. However, at 5.30 am that all changed.

With one enormous crash drum fire of extraordinary intensity came down. In all directions there was nothing but clouds of smoke and the flash of exploding shells. Such was the volume of noise that it was impossible for the defenders even to distinguish the sound of shells exploding in the immediate vicinity. On the right (northern) flank of Infantry Regiment 163, a fire broke out right forward, cloaking the battlefield with choking smoke and reducing visibility to nothing. Suddenly, out of the smoke, emerged the shape of six tanks, the first that the men of the regiment had ever encountered. Firing as they advanced, they achieved the hoped for shock effect. Unprepared for this type of attack, able to respond only with small arms fire and hand grenades, the forward defence was already melting away when the first masses of infantry, following the tanks, swarmed all over the first two lines of trenches. Those who were not killed were captured and the men of the 56th (London) Division pressed on towards Neuville Vitasse in four great waves.

Simultaneously, supported by a further five tanks, there was another thrust on the right flank. Launched through the sectors of 7th and 8th Companies Infantry Regiment 162, it bore down from the north on 12th Company Infantry Regiment 163 and began to roll up the forward positions. Its commander, Leutnant Pries, did his best to rally his men, but with three tanks probing southwards between the first and second line trenches, the defenders were gradually forced back into the ruins of Neuville, where they were ultimately overwhelmed. Attempting to hold on in the village itself was 11th Company, under Leutnant Jenz, but although he conducted a hard fought action, it lasted only a short time and, by 10.00 am, Neuville had fallen completely to the British attackers. Hardly a single man among the defenders succeeded in regaining the positions to the rear and only a handful were captured. The others had all fallen.

Lacking any sort of information from the front, but acutely aware of the risk of a deep penetration, the *KTK*, Reserve Oberleutnant Westmann, ordered 4th Company to hold the so-called K2 line at all costs, to occupy a communication trench known as *Pionier-Weg* [Engineer Way] and cover towards the north. It was only a temporary measure. By midday, 4th Company had been forced out of the position; the remnants, commanded by Reserve Leutnant Mackenthun, pulling back to the K3 Line, the last line of trenches before the *Artillerie-Schutzstellung* and only about 300 metres west of the *KTK*'s own location. The situation was clearly becoming extremely critical and Westmann contacted the *BTK* [*Bereitschafttruppenkommandeur* = commander of the supports], urgently requesting assistance, the deployment of one platoon in defence of his headquarters. In the event, the *BTK*, Reserve Major Weede, despatched the whole of 10th Company forward, directing that two platoons were to man the *Artillerie-Schutzstellung*, while the third platoon advanced to help Oberleutnant Westmann and his men, who were already engaging British troops. The British in the K2 position were being constantly reinforced, then the headquarters were brought under heavy fire, a British aircraft which had crashed on top of it a few days earlier providing an excellent aiming mark. Gradually the British worked their way forward in a series of rushes, threatening to outflank the position to the north and although the defenders resisted, it was obvious that they could not prevail. Once the attackers were within 200 metres of the blockhouse, Westmann ordered a withdrawal.

His adjutant, Leutnant Reithinger, was severely wounded attempting this and was captured, as was the battalion medical officer, Dr Kümmel, who stayed behind to tend the wounded. Rallying at the *Artillerie-Schutzstellung*, there was a total of about fifty men left capable of mounting a defence, which was quite inadequate, so there was a further short term and partial withdrawal to the *Monchy-Riegel*, which ran from Feuchy south to just west of Wancourt. The defence had been ripped to shreds in this sector and command and control had all but broken down. The only means of communication was by runner and, given the weight of shell fire coming down on the rear areas, it was almost impossible for them to operate and virtually suicidal to try. It took one man six hours to cover 1,600 metres as the crow flies. Sometimes runners had to wait half an hour for the firing to slacken sufficiently for them to rush from one shell hole to another.

Despite the lack of information, it was clear to the commander of 81 Infantry Brigade, located back at Hamblain les Prés, that a serious situation was developing. He immediately despatched his brigade reserve forward. Hauptmann Becker, commanding 2nd Battalion Infantry Regiment 163, and supported by a machine gun section of Reserve Husaren Regiment 6 under Reserve Leutnant Blohm, was directed to move to assembly areas in the Bois du Sart and Bois de Cronières, just to the east of Monchy. It was a wise precaution. By 1.00 pm, Reserve Infantry Regiment 31 to the south having also been forced back to the K3 line, the K2 line was abandoned altogether and there was a real risk of a breakthrough. Every available man, field engineers and those who had been manning the engineer park between Neuville and Wancourt, were pressed into service and the line held - just. The British attackers had also suffered heavily throughout the day[15] and their supporting tanks had ditched or bogged down so, by mid afternoon, they had lost impetus, falling back and taking up positions along a line about 800 metres west of the *Monchy-Riegel*. The attack, with close air support, was renewed at 7.00 and 8.00 pm, but was halted with very heavy losses, largely due to ineffective British artillery fire and the weight of rifle and machine gun fire the defenders were able to bring to bear.

As it went dark, the British continued to press their attack with strong patrols armed with grenades, but there was no comparison with the intensity of the earlier fighting. By around 9.00 pm there was firm contact once more with Reserve Infantry Regiment 31 to the south and the regimental commander ordered a complete withdrawal to the *Monchy-Riegel*, though attempts were to be made to hold onto the *Pionier Park*, 500 hundred metres further forward. Every effort was made during this temporary lull to give effect to the directive, but it proved to be impossible to sustain it in view of continuing British pressure.

18th Reserve Division

This division was moved into the IX Reserve Corps area just before Easter, once it became clear that a major offensive was imminent. It was inserted into the front southeast of Neuville Vitasse between 17th Reserve Division, which sidestepped to the north and 220th Infantry Division, which moved further south east. The midway point of its sector was just forward of Héninel, where No Man's Land was about 1,200 metres wide. In the wrecked village of St. Martin sur Cojeul, about 500 metres forward of the main German lines, Reserve Infantry Regiment 86 assumed responsibility for an outpost position from Infantry Regiment 162, which moved into the line opposite Beaurains.

Unteroffizier Jöhnck 11ᵗʰ Company Reserve Infantry Regiment 86[16]

"After a testing march during the night between Maundy Thursday and Good Friday, 11ᵗʰ Company finally arrived in its battle positions between Wancourt and Héninel. The second and third platoons went and occupied the front line trenches, but the first platoon was allocated a special task. It was to act as an outpost well forward of the main position. About two to three kilometres beyond the frontline trench alongside the River Cojeul was the village of St. Martin.[17] Infantry Regiment 162 had an outpost in this village, which the first platoon was to relieve. We went forward of the front line trench and what difficulties we had! The trees had all been felled and telegraph poles littered the road. Every minute somebody or other got caught up in telegraph wires and had to disentangle themselves carefully. In between were deep shell holes. Weighed down with full packs, it was easy not to spot them and to fall down into them in the darkness. We had driving sleet full in our faces and the road was under artillery fire. The entire area was subject to streams of British machine gun fire so, like it or not, we had to lie flat on the muddy road every few minutes.

"The march may have taken thirty to forty five minutes. Finally we reached our objective. Was not the outpost somewhere in the village? The entire village was one mass of rubble. Not one house was intact, not a stone lay on a stone. In places the road was blocked with rubble. What had happened here? St. Martin had been blown up by the Germans.[18] At the western exits to the village were six double sentry positions, staring hard into the dark night and listening ... the relief took some time, because the instructions for each post were very precise. Twelve of us went on duty ... the remainder crouched amongst the ruins, weapons in hand, ready to go into action at any moment. The complete outpost comprised one officer and three sections and the officer, an unteroffizier and a gefreiter spent the entire night patrolling between the sentry posts.

"There was absolute silence to our front and in the village, so the sound of shells in the air seemed louder, as did the impacts behind us on our front line trenches. Oh, what a long night it was! All our senses were strained to the utmost ... At long last the eastern sky became lighter and the sun announced its arrival. That was the signal to withdraw the sentry posts. Two sections went back to the web of trenches, but the first section had to remain in St. Martin throughout the day. Nobody envied them. The second and third sections went back to the third trench where, after a two hour search, we located our dugout. That was the night before Good Friday 1917. On Good Friday we were able to get some rest for a few hours, but evening came around again all too quickly and the second and third sections had to go forward once again to the St. Martin outpost. Darkness was drawing in and drum fire was coming down all over the network of trenches.

"We had to move through it, pass the forward trench and get to the outpost position! The way forward had not got any easier and we stumbled even more frequently into the shell holes – and they were not small, either. We arrived at St. Martin, where the section which had stayed behind had done its best to man the individual posts. They longed for relief and, as soon as they were, they hurried back to the third trench. So began another long night. There were constant flurries of snow. Silently, the sentries stared into the night. Not a round landed in the village but, to our rear, were the flashes of shell impacts … time crawled by. The night seemed endless. Tired and hungry, the sentries stared towards the enemy. Would it not soon be morning? The clock seemed to go slower than usual. Away to the east a grey dawn was breaking. The third and fourth sections withdrew, delighted to be away from this outpost. We poor souls from second section had to stay here … Food and drink were brought to us before daybreak; an issue of food for the first time in several days. We had pea soup for our midday meal. This had gone cold during the long journey forward, but we consumed the cold soup with glee. It still tasted good and naturally it was forbidden to light fires here. The ration party withdrew. Feeling lonely and abandoned, we stayed here.

"In the centre of the village there were a few walls which had not collapsed entirely. Some planks had been laid across them to provide cover from aerial observation. This space was where the outpost was based and nine men were crammed together like herrings [in a barrel]. Were we really meant to spend the whole day there? Some stones were pushed out. This let in light and served as spy holes for the sentries. In the early morning the artillery fire resumed its former intensity. We abandoned ones wanted to sleep. We managed to do so for a few hours, then that was it. Our limbs were painful and stiff. We could neither lie nor sit up. What agony! Could we risk going outside? It was out of the question. The Tommies would have been at our throats. We stayed as we were half lying or sitting until evening. What a long, long day. Why would the clock not move faster? …

"The day came towards an end. Suddenly! - What had the sentry spotted? British soldiers! A skirmishing line was heading over the rise to the west of St. Martin and bearing down on us. Would it overrun St. Martin? It would be an unequal fight; we had only nine rifles with which to defend the place. A battle would offer no prospect of success. The Tommies reached the crest of the rise … they waved their arms about and began digging in. Slowly darkness fell. With eight men we manned the double sentry posts. How would it go? Would we be prisoners in the morning or still free soldiers? The sentries stared and listened with meticulous attention … Minute followed minute; hour succeeded hour. We were still all alone. No orders reached us. Everything was quiet to our front. When would the British come? We were overcome by complete indifference. Hours stretched out to an eternity.

"By now it was 11.00 pm. We had been holding the village since 6.00 am. Listen! Noises! Footsteps! Where were they coming from? It was our relief!

Lucky us! 12th Company had come to relieve us. We conducted a quick briefing and handed over the sentry posts. We then hurried off. The front line was under heavy shell fire. This was coming from the right, from the direction of Arras. We entered the trench and headed to the rear. From the protection of a dugout in the third line, we hoped to dream the night away. Eating, drinking and smoking were the priority. Our rest period was about to begin – rifle fire from St. Martin. What was happening? This went on for some time then everything was quiet once more.

"The bad news arrived. The British were in the village. The 12th Company platoon had been overrun and captured. We nine men had been really lucky. What was to be done? It was about midnight of the night Easter Saturday to Easter Sunday. It did not look like being a Happy Easter! Orders soon arrived. 'Using eight sections, 3rd Battalion is to recapture St. Martin.' Each company was to find two sections and, at 4.00 am the attack was to be launched ... We did not think that there was much chance of success ... [enemy] drum fire rose to a crescendo. The two assault sections were about to go forward when, suddenly, the fire lifted and the British attacked the 3rd Battalion ... Happy Easter! St. Martin was lost. The enemy were now only 150 metres from the front line trench. Nothing came of the eight section attack. We now knew that we faced days of heavy fighting."

To the south and linking up with Reserve Infantry Regiment 99 of 220th Infantry Division on the northern slopes of the locally dominant *Mühlenberg*, was Reserve Infantry Regiment 84. Whilst 1st and 2nd Battalions, located forward, were enduring the final hours of the hurricane bombardment, interspersed around midnight with large scale probing patrols, members of the 3rd Battalion in billets at Sailly-en-Ostrevent were on tenterhooks, waiting to be called forward.

Offizierstellvertreter William Speck 3rd Battalion Reserve Infantry Regiment 84[19]

"During the night before Easter Day, the roar of the guns, which could be heard clearly coming from the front, increased to such an extent that it rattled the windows in Sailly, a good fifteen kilometres from the front. So it came as no surprise when the alarm call arrived at the companies of the 1st Battalion at about 8.45 am on 9 April. 'Everyone in the billets, prepare to move!' In all honesty, initially the majority were more pleased than downcast."

Whilst the Reserve Infantry Regiment 84 reserves were reacting, Reserve Infantry Regiment 31, defending the sector immediately south of Neuville Vitasse, was subject to a particularly heavy assault. As soon as the British attacks began, its 1st Battalion was involved in hand to hand fighting. The initial assault was beaten back, but as its commander, Oberstleutnant Burmester, observed the action through his telescope from some distance to the rear, the deployment of a number of tanks enabled the British to penetrate into the village itself. Later that morning a renewed infantry assault overwhelmed 1st and 2nd Companies in the front line, the survivors being forced to drop back to the second line trenches, gallantly supported by 1st Machine Gun Company, commanded by Leutnant Holzbrecher. Despite being located right forward along the line of the sunken road between Neuville and Hénin sur Cojeul and threatened with being outflanked on either side, he managed to keep his guns in action until the partial withdrawal was complete. For a while there was the risk of a gap opening to the north, but a vigorous counter-attack mounted by 2nd Battalion succeeded in re-establishing the link with Infantry Regiment 163 and with the use of the 3rd Battalion it was possible - at least temporarily - to stabilise the front and bring effective artillery and machine gun fire to bear on British attempts to deploy cavalry forward south of the Arras - Cambrai road.[20]

All along the front the situation was totally unclear. In the rear all the commanders at various levels could do was to feed forward immediate reserves, attempt to predict future Allied movements and reorganise the forces to meet these potential risks. In the north rumours were circulating that 11th Infantry Division had been comprehensively defeated, that Fampoux had fallen and that the British were advancing rapidly on Roeux. The fact that the German artillery had by now more or less ceased firing added credence to these ideas, especially when the withdrawal to the *Monchy Riegel* caused the abandonment of the guns and other equipment to the west of that line. 2nd Batteries Field Artillery Regiment 20 and Bavarian Field Artillery Regiment 16 had taken heavy casualties in men and weapons that morning and 2 and 9th Batteries Reserve Field Artillery Regiment 17, commanded by Reserve Hauptmann Ebmeier and Reserve Oberleutnant Schönfeld respectively, had had all their guns buried or wrecked by counter-battery fire. Withdrawal of the survivors was the only option, one which was replicated elsewhere along the front, leading to the loss of a large number of guns to the British advance.

Meanwhile frantic efforts were being made to boost artillery fire power just south of the Scarpe. All the British shelling made the passage of information and forward movement extremely difficult and although 1st and 2nd Battalions Field Artillery Regiment 75 and 2nd Battalion Field Artillery Regiment 78 were alerted in the early morning, there were considerable delays before they and 10th Battery Field Artillery Regiment 17 could come into action, in the last case just to the north of Monchy village. The experience of one of the batteries ordered forward to Fampoux is typical of a confused day.

Vizefeldwebel Reinhardt 4th Battery Field Artillery Regiment 75[21]

"Leutnant Driedger rode forward, accompanied by Gefreiter Döring as horse holder, to reconnoitre the fire position, followed by the battery at a walk via Plouvain and Roeux. We could hear the sound of heavy artillery fire and saw in the distance pillars of dirt thrown high in the air and interspersed with clouds of smoke from the explosions. Leutnant Driedger did not return so, as we were approaching Roeux, I received from Leutnant Gossel the task of riding on ahead and linking up forward. I came across Döring, together with both horses, in a clay pit just by Fampoux. He opined that Leutnant Driedger had gone to Group [headquarters]. Following his directions I bumped into some infantrymen in the rear of the village who were heading in the opposite direction. They called out to me that there was nobody further forward and that they had not seen an artillery officer. Small arms fire cracked by very close and, simultaneously, numerous aircraft, swooping very low, with long streamers flying, brought down machine gun fire on every living thing. "Several wounded gunners, whose guns had been destroyed in Fampoux, came crawling up. They were able to inform me that there was no doubt that an officer from [Field Artillery] Regiment 75 lay dead in a hollow in the direction of the enemy, a victim of aircraft machine gun fire. They would have attempted to bring him with them but he had been killed instantly. I could not comprehend it: our revered Leutnant Driedger, the very best of men! I ran fifty metres further and found myself standing by him in a small hollow to the right of the cemetery. He was dead. At the same moment the leading British soldiers appeared. I crawled away on all fours, with our machine gunners providing covering fire from two or three guns located in the cemetery. Back in the clay pit, Döring was still waiting for his leutnant. An infantry officer bawled at us, 'Do not pull back without orders, or I'll shoot!' In extreme haste I reported to him that the entire battalion could find itself blundering, oblivious [of the risk], into the enemy. At that he let us pass. The 4th [Battery] and the riding elements of the regimental and battalion staffs had already ridden through Roeux."

Unfortunately lack of ammunition resupply hampered all attempts to increase the level of fire support to the increasingly hard pressed infantry, a problem shared by the remaining serviceable guns of the original batteries of the IX Reserve Corps' forward divisions. Towards the end of the day the gun lines presented a sorry sight. Some guns, having fired off all their stocks of shells, had been abandoned, others were wrecked or upended, with their dead crews lying round them. The surrounding areas had been ploughed up metres deep by the fire concentrations of the British heavy artillery. Not a single square metre was untouched. Empty brass cartridge cases, shell baskets and live shells littered the entire area. Even where guns were still in action, in many cases they were only served by two gunners, the rest having become casualtes. There was a real fear that a further effort by the British infantry might lead to a breakthrough south of the axis Héninel - Wancourt - Guémappe, so 220th Infantry Division redeployed every gun it could spare to its northern flank and maintained the heaviest weight of fire it could sustain against targets in the 18th Reserve Division sector.

It is difficult to judge how effective this fire support was but, by late evening, the original positions of Reserve Infantry Regiment 84 between Héninel and the *Mühlenberg* were, with the exception of one small group of British infantry holding out in a short section of trench, once more firmly in German hands. The same was true along the frontages of Reserve Infantry Regiment 86 and Reserve Infantry Regiment 31 as far north as the *Lange Gasse* [Long Alley], just to the southeast of Neuville Vitasse. However, the defenders' hold on these trenches was relatively precarious, the more so because units of 17th Reserve Division had been pushed back well to the rear of their original front line, more or less to the line of the *Monchy Riegel*. This developing situation had forced the more northerly regiments of 18th Reserve Division to improvise their own flank protection and it was touch and go for several hours if the resistance they put up would be sufficient to prevent their sector from being rolled up. 1st Battalion Reserve Infantry Regiment 31 played an important role in this action, as did 7th Company, whose well directed small arms fire succeeded in halting, a 'renewed attack by strong British forces'.

As night fell on the battlefield the weather was intensely cold and damp, with patches of slushy snow lying around. There was no rest for survivors of either side as strenuous, if at times vain, efforts were made to reorganise, get ammunition and rations forward and evacuate the wounded. The allied artillery maintained harassing fire on all likely choke points and brought down concentrations of fire on known or suspected defensive positions, whilst the chains of command of both sides worked on future plans and issued the necessary orders. On the German side it was clear that the *Monchy Riegel* offered no sort of basis for a sustained defence and, at 3.30 am on 10 April, 11th Infantry Division ordered Infantry Regiment 51 to withdraw all its remaining troops and to occupy a new line on the high ground about 700 metres west of the Roeux - Monchy road. Here they were to dig in and to link up on the right with 1st Battalion Reserve Infantry Regiment 99, whose line stretched about 600 metres south of the outskirts of Roeux. To the south contact was to be made with elements of Infantry Regiment 162 of 17th Reserve Division. Once more the ability of the German army to recover from an extremely unfavourable, critical position was being demonstrated; the arrival of eight machine guns from Machine Gun Sharp Shooter Detachment 9 underlining the determination to check further offensive progress. There was a minor confusion when counter-orders arrived, directing the recapture of the *Monchy-Riegel*, but by then it was too late. British troops from 37th Division had already overrun the *Riegel*, which underlined the basic correctness of the initial decision to evacuate.[22] As dawn broke, the new trenches were less than one metre deep and were already being subjected to uncomfortably accurate fire from British machine gunners.

In anticipation of the forthcoming offensive, on 7 April 26th Infantry Division, which had just been brought up to full strength and had completed a period of training in the Valenciennes area, was placed on shortened notice to move. Grenadier Regiment 119, for example, located near Denain, received fresh orders during the morning of 9 April, 'Enemy launched an attack this morning from Les Guémappe [*sic*.] and has pushed forward beyond the third German position in places. 26th Infantry Division is placed on full alert to be transported forward for probable deployment along the Scarpe.[23] Given the extreme importance of the high ground around Monchy, it was no surprise that elements of the division were rushed forward by train and truck to bolster the defence on the 11th Infantry Division sector and they were immediately subordinated to 21 Infantry Brigade on arrival. Despite all efforts, it was mid afternoon on 10 April before 1st and 2nd Battalions Grenadier Regiment 119 were completely in position astride the river and thus able to cover the withdrawal of the remnants of the three 11th Division regiments that had been clinging on to an inadequate defence line to the west of Roeux and east of Hill 102.

Leaving 3rd Battalion behind in Plouvain as divisional reserve, the commander then moved forward and established his command post in Roeux. There he was joined by 1st and 2nd Machine Gun Companies, which had marched forward thirty kilometres on foot and they too were immediately deployed. Hour by hour, the defence, though still in a precarious condition, was strengthening and was gradually able to react more effectively to British manoeuvres. At 1.00 pm on 10 April, for example, British troops equipped with bridging materials were seen moving in the valley of the Scarpe and near Fampoux. 2nd Battalion Grenadier Regiment 119 immediately despatched several machine gun teams to a blocking position east of the Roeux - Monchy road where they could bring fire down on the advancing enemy and the artillery began to aim concentrations of fire at possible bridging sites and all groupings of engineers wherever the poor visibility permitted it. The combined efforts of machine guns and artillery succeeded in thwarting bridging operations and, temporarily, to halt a further Allied advance to the east to a standstill.

Naturally all this activity took place under British harassing artillery fire. Luckily for some members of the regiment there were still usable cellars in Roeux which provided protection against shell splinters and small calibre shells. Unfortunately for the civil population, events had moved so fast on this area that many of them were caught up in the British fire and suffered accordingly.

Reserve Leutnant Seyfarth 1st Machine Gun Company Grenadier Regiment 119 [24]

"When the fire eased, we left our cover and were greeted with scenes of misery which we had hardly ever seen, even when we were on the offensive. A seventeen year old girl and her eleven year old sister came running up to me, fell to her knees begging to me and promising, 'I shall pray for you', if I would only rescue her mother from a cellar which had collapsed. When my men got there, they found the entangled bodies of twelve women, together with five seriously wounded women between the ages of twenty and thirty, each of whom had had a foot blown off or had suffered a similar injury. Again and again some old widow or a few children would turn up there. To the left and right buildings were ablaze. It all formed one great shocking image which inspired our men to do everything possible to prevent any such disaster from occurring back in the homeland. That said, it was hats off to our lads. "On no fewer than five occasions four men, at immediate risk to their lives, entered the cellar to rescue the surviving civilians before the next shell landed. The best of them, a Gefreiter, was unfortunately killed yesterday. For the entire night my dugout was crammed with women and children. Once all the attacks had been beaten off by around 7.00 pm, complete calm descended on our sector, so it was possible to move about freely in the open. Assistenzarzt Dr. Stähle took the opportunity to treat the civilians, who made their anger at the British very clear. After that they were all, with one single exception, transported away by ambulance. The exception was a severely wounded woman, with a child. During the day she had lost her mother and two sisters, whilst two other sisters had had their feet blown off. She lay in a neighbouring underground shelter until 12 April when she was once again dug out alive after enemy fire had collapsed it. My field kitchen then drove her to the rear. The Machine Gun Company suffered one man killed in action and twelve wounded, most of them seriously."

The withdrawal of the last remaining defenders of the *Monchy Riegel* and the evacuation of Hill 102 - felt by some to have been carried out prematurely - meant that the next target for the advancing British troops was the dominant village of Monchy le Preux. Targeted throughout 10 April by the British artillery and attacked constantly from the air, it was plain that a serious assault against it would not long be delayed. The British plan was to launch a major assault in a final attempt to exploit the success of 9 April on a broad front. This was the day when Fifth Army made its first attempt on the Bullecourt sector, whilst here the British VI Corps was to launch a major effort against what was thought to be a shattered defence. It was considered vital to maintain the momentum of the offensive, though experience should perhaps have indicated that the defenders would strain every sinew to seal off the semi-breakthrough and strengthen the defence by all possible. In preparation, during the night 10/11 April, Monchy was shelled extremely heavily and reduced to burning ruins. Statements made by captured British soldiers made it clear that a major assault had been planned for early morning of 11 April so, despite the appalling weight of fire coming down all around the village, fresh reinforcements from Bavarian Infantry Regiment 17 were moved forward from their holding positions in the Bois du Sart to the west of Boiry Notre Dame. Hardly had its 1st Battalion taken up their positions along the western edge of Monchy than at 5.50 am red and yellow Very lights were fired along the front from Monchy south to the Arras - Vis en Artois road and the assault on Monchy, supported by tanks, began.

To the north of the village there was an early penetration of the thin line of defenders and the attackers swung south to press on into the village. At this stage the Bavarian Infantry Regiment 17 defensive line was completely intact, though the staff of its 1st Battalion only just evaded capture, taking cover in a copse just north west of Monchy. Within minutes the heights west of Monchy were one seething mass of troops from the British 37th Division, whilst additional marching columns could be seen approaching the front. The Bavarians resisted fiercely, causing large casualties to the attacking troops and beating back several attempts to break through. Eventually, however, numbers told and with the support of the tanks their situation became untenable, despite vigorous close quarter tank hunting by elements of 2nd and 3rd Companies. With British infantry through and behind their trenches, the only sensible decision was taken and the surviving remnants of the forward companies began to slip back in small groups to take up new positions on high ground to the east of the village, where 2nd Battalion was already established. The 3rd Battalion meanwhile occupied a counter penetration position near the Bois de Cronière, north of Boiry.

Despite the success, the attackers did not have it all their own way. Of the six tanks allocated to the attack, four were later stated to have crossed the start line.[25] According to the British Official History, 'All the tanks taking part in it were put out of action, but it is doubtful whether Monchy would have fallen without their aid'.[26] One of the participants later described what happened to one of them which attempted to press forward and by pass Monchy to the south.

Reserve Leutnant Hermann Kohl 3rd Company Bavarian Infantry Regiment 17 [27]

"Four armoured steel monsters came crawling towards the regimental sector: armoured fighting vehicles, tanks, designed to clear the way for the infantry, pushed towards the heart of our frontage. With their light guns and machine guns, they poured fire in all directions. Nearer and nearer they approached. The opposing infantry did nothing. They were waiting for the moment when our positions would be ready to storm. Like impregnable fortresses ... these armoured colossi pushed their way into our midst ... their flanking fire caused panic and claimed one victim after another ... The companies were in complete confusion and fled the field. To my right 4th Company pulled back in one broad line and elements of 3rd Company also disengaged from the enemy. When the panic threatened to spread to my platoon and the crew of its allocated machine gun, I gave strict orders to hold out and forced the machine gunners, who were already in the process of falling back, to about turn. The situation was extremely serious; only 2nd Company to my left, under its daring commander, Leutnant Durein, continued to fight on desperately ...

"We held our line. The fighting vehicle which had driven into the centre of our sector was the scene of mad activity. Rifle and machine gun fire was powerless against the armoured colossus, which was sweating poison from every orifice and was driving our men to desperate fighting. We took the battle to it with bundled hand grenades. There was an ammunition dump in a dugout in the sunken lane and we emptied it completely. Repeatedly groups of our men stormed through the curtains of fire to throw their grenade bundles under its tracks. The boldest among them climbed onto the tank from the rear and sought to exploit air vents and viewing slits, so as to destroy the crew with pistol shots ... Leutnant Durein was wounded early in the fight and evacuated. The defence was now in my hands, but the men had no need of leadership. Each of them went to work as though the outcome of the battle was dependent on he alone. "The battle grew more intense with each passing minute. We ran out of grenades. Should we have to withdraw unsuccessful? Then, suddenly, the monster was disabled. Its track had split and it could no longer manoeuvre. A great cry of *Hurra!* went up and its rate of fire reduced. Had the crew run out of ammunition or courage? They feared the price they would have to pay as several of my men surrounded it with fixed bayonets and left nobody in any doubt about their seething rage. There were a few more shots from the left hand side then the last of the resistance died. We had knocked out the monster."

In the meantime German guns had galloped forward and began to bring down fire at the rapid rate. Unaware that some German defenders were still located forward and south of Monchy. Kohl watched appalled as some of his men were hit by friendly fire and decided that the only sensible thing was to pull back east of Monchy, despite the torrent of fire from both sides and low flying British aircraft, which threatened to make moving in the open suicidal. 'Every man for himself!' he bawled. The survivors then made their way back from shell hole to shell hole until, finally, Kohl and a handful of others reached the relative safety of the hastily occupied positions east of Monchy. Luckily for him and the remainder of 1st Battalion, content with the capture of the village, there was no immediate British follow up, so the defenders used the time to re-establish links left and right and to improve the somewhat inadequate trenches they were occupying. During the afternoon, once reinforcements from Infantry Regiment 121 of 26th Infantry Division arrived, the survivors of 1st Battalion were withdrawn back to Hamblain to rest. As evening fell, 5th, 7th and 8th Companies remained forward, with 6th Company back in reserve in the Bois du Vert, about one kilometre south of the Bois du Sart.[28]

Though the situation in and around Monchy was critical and its loss a severe blow to the integrity of the defence, matters were slightly more favourable north and south of the village. Reserve Leutnant Petersen, commanding 8th Company Infantry Regiment 163 had established his men in very strong self contained defensive positions on the high ground between Monchy and Feuchy, with his left flank about 300 metres from the edge of Monchy. His positions adjoined 3rd Battalion Infantry Regiment 162 and the newly arrived 3rd Battalion Infantry Regiment 125 of 26th Infantry Division under Hauptmann Brandt. Together these forces resisted successfully all attempts by unsupported British infantry to advance, despite the immense weight of artillery fire which came down on the defenders. Almost all attacks were shot to a standstill while still some 400 metres forward of the front line. That said, there were anxious moments of vulnerability, especially when Petersen was forced to redeploy half his company and two machine guns to face towards Monchy and block off any attempt by the British to develop their attack northwards. Two companies of Infantry Regiment 190 were then rushed forward to dig a blocking position in rear of Petersen's men just to the east of the Pelves - Boiry road. The commander 3rd Battalion Infantry Regiment 125 later described his hurried arrival and the hard fighting which followed:

Hauptmann Brandt, Commanding Officer 3rd Battalion Infantry Regiment 125[29]

"A long column of trucks drove up and the battalion crammed into them. Horses and wagons had to be left behind, but as many machine guns, boxes of ammunition and digging tools as could be fitted in were taken. Jolting and rattling we set off into the night. What could have happened at the front to make them need us so urgently? We unloaded in Hamblain at daybreak and marched to Biache on the Scarpe, where we were supposed to receive orders from 11th Infantry Division, but Biache was totally deserted; obviously it had been evacuated in a great hurry. Luckily we were able to get hold of the commander of the transport column and he drove the battalion commander at high speed to Vitry. There we located first of all the staff of 11th Infantry Division, then that of 21 Infantry Brigade. It was there that we discovered that the British had broken through the German positions along the Scarpe and that the battalion was to move to Pelves under command of Infantry Regiment 51 ...

"We reached Pelves in a squall of snow and simultaneously with the arrival of the first British shrapnel, whilst the inhabitants left their homes, moving widely spaced across the fields with their children and their possessions. The village mayor must have rehearsed them well. The first order from Infantry Regiment 51 required the battalion to have advanced south of Monchy and to have occupied the hill two kilometres to the west, closing the gap between Infantry Regiment 162 and the *Monchy Riegel* south of the Cambrai - Arras road. We were in the process of carrying this out when a second order arrived: the battalion was to relieve elements of Infantry Regiment 51 and Reserve Infantry Regiment 99 forward of Pelves. This was carried out at 11.00 pm and work began immediately to develop the position, which had only been roughly outlined. Officers and men worked ceaselessly throughout the night ...

"The right flank of the battalion rested on Roeux lake, south of the Scarpe. Grenadier Regiment 119 was deployed north of the Scarpe ... The *KTK* was established by the Roeux - Monchy road to the west of Pelves. A number of machine guns from Sharpshooter Detachments 13 and 9 remained on the position. Hardly had it become light on 11 April than the British infantry launched forward. Wave after wave advanced over the hill opposite us [Hill 102] to be met by the crack of our hail of rifle and machine gun fire. The British had not been expecting that on their breakthrough front and before long, first as individuals, then in larger groups, they hared back behind the protective hill. Morale in our trenches shot up and the British cavalry could hardly have selected a worse moment than then to attempt to get forward. We could hardly believe our eyes when we saw British squadrons in widely dispersed lines riding towards us from the Arras - Cambrai road. Laughing, our musketiers climbed out of their trenches and, standing in the open as though they were on the ranges back home, prepared to greet this rare target. They did their work thoroughly, as was proved by the number of empty saddles as the horse clattered away ...

"The Tommies now realised that they could not regard the front of 3rd Battalion as broken and soon our lines were subjected to British artillery fire. Under this protection, the British infantry tried a fresh attack. This, too, was halted by our fire but, off to the left of the battalion, the neighbouring regiment had to give up its positions. There the British consolidated and set up machine guns. A British tank also appeared; this was new to us and we looked at it suspiciously. However, our artillery soon knocked it out ... Once more the British attacked us under the cover of a heavy snow shower, but failed again. Night fell and our patrols sent forward found no trace of the enemy to our front - only their stretcher parties at work. We did not interfere with them and soon motorised ambulances were moving within the range of our weapons. The British later thanked us by carrying forward machine guns on stretchers.[30]

"The following day (12 April) was initially extremely quiet and we soon discovered the reason. The British wanted to move their heavy guns forward before daring to resume the dance with us. From about midday they opened up, not only against the battalion, but also against the Olga Grenadiers [Grenadier Regiment 119] in Roeux. Most unfortunately, misdirected fire from our own howitzers also fell on our trenches with pinpoint accuracy, so the order had to be given to the inner flanks of 9th and 12th Companies to withdraw one hundred paces. Nevertheless, they re-entered their trenches like lightning when, at 5.00 pm, the British assaulted once more. Our fire forced the enemy to go to ground some way off, but in one place, making use of dead ground, they approached to within 200 metres. However they were not going to be allowed to stay there overnight. Leutnant Hoß, the liaison officer for 1st Battalion Field Artillery Regiment 65, rushed forward from the battalion command post to the front line, our gallant signallers repaired the telephone lines which had been cut by shrapnel and shell splinters and soon the battery fire was coming down on the concealed objective. As it went dark our patrols established that the enemy had pulled back everywhere.

"Almost simultaneously with the last attack, the British infantry stormed Roeux. This attack was to have been protected by smoke shells, but the machine gunners on our right flank could observe the area behind the wall of smoke and contributed visibly to the beating off of the attack by our sister regiment. An attempt was made to roll us up from Monchy during the night, but the protective sentry posts we had pushed forward - we had still not been able to construct a wire obstacle - were on hand to ensure that the enemy soon gave up the idea."

Off to the south of Monchy, the British tanks, less that knocked out by Kohl's men, still posed a very real threat to the remnants of Infantry Regiments 162 and 163, which found themselves engaged in an unequal battle with them. Fortunately, in the nick of time, an *ad hoc* grouping of guns (4th, 6th and 7th Batteries of Field Artillery Regiment 11), commanded by Reserve Hauptmann Waltfried, galloped forward through the British bombardment, took up positions in the open and, supplementing the fire of Reserve Field Artillery Regiment 17, engaged the tanks over open sights, setting them on fire and knocking them out. One tank, advancing along the Wancourt - Monchy road, was hit first. It tipped on its side and burst into flames. A second tank halted near the crossroads of the Monchy - Wancourt and Arras - Vis en Artois road and began pouring fire at the German lines. Men of 5th Company Infantry Regiment 163, under Leutnant Hansen, rushed forward and destroyed its right hand track with grenades. A gun of 7th Battery Reserve Field Artillery Regiment 17 then scored a direct hit which set its fuel tank on fire. Hansen's men fired at the escaping crew, preventing them from leaving the tank and they were all burned to death.

Eventually mass told and the men of Infantry Regiment 163 were forced back towards Vis en Artois. However, each attempt by British tanks to push on was countered by the German guns, Oberleutnant Kolster of Reserve Field Artillery Regiment 17 distinguishing himself by personally leading forward one gun and an ammunition wagon and knocking out two.[31] Thereafter, each attack by the British infantry towards Vis en Artois and Hancourt was countered by a storm of shells and small arms fire, which halted each of them at very heavy cost. It was considered imperative that the British be prevented from developing their attack from the newly captured village of Monchy. In point of fact the British survivors were totally exhausted after their efforts but, being unaware of the fact, several emergency measures were implemented. Oberstleutnant Stühmke, commanding Infantry Regiment 125, despatched a reserve company forward with orders to establish a blocking position astride the Pelves - Monchy road, whilst Grenadier Regiment 119 moved its reserves forward onto *Ballon-Höhe* [Balloon Hill], immediately southwest of Plouvain.

Meanwhile Hauptmann Ritter von Gum, commanding 2nd Battalion Bavarian Infantry Regiment 17, was ordered by the commander of 17th Reserve Division, Generalmajor von Beczwarzowski, personally to prepare to counter-attack Monchy. However, with the exception of 3rd Battalion Bavarian Infantry Regiment 17 and 2nd Battalion Infantry Regiment 121 located back in Bois du Sart, there were no other German reserves anywhere near at hand and, with stocks of artillery ammunition falling dangerously low, there was little chance of success had the attack been launched immediately. Instead, arriving companies and battalions were moved forward to thicken up the defensive line and plug gaps. Nevertheless, in accordance with standard practise, the attempt had to be made. Pushing forward towards the village, the Bavarians and Württembergers came under a hail of shrapnel fire. Their so-called counter attack was stopped in its tracks some 600 metres short of the village; so weak had it been that it was not even recognised as such by the British defenders. An uneasy quiet descended on the battlefield, but these were extremely anxious hours for 81 Infantry Brigade.

Throughout the remainder of 11 April confusion reigned. Communications between front and rear were non-existent; there was a terrible mingling of units and sub-units which were scattered all over the battlefield. Assuming command of the sector in the late afternoon, Generalleutnant Ritter von Wenninger, commanding Bavarian 3rd Infantry Division, inherited a more or less chaotic situation, though the withdrawal the following night of the remaining elements of 17th Reserve Division saw clarity eventually emerging - though not before 1st Battalion Bavarian Infantry Regiment 17 had relieved the remnants of no fewer than nine companies from a variety of regiments just to the east of Monchy. The priority now was a complete reorganisation of the sector under cover of darkness. In order to make sure that all the isolated pockets of defenders were identified and relieved, he decided that he had to employ all three of his regiments in line. This process was underway when Group Arras decided to alter the divisional boundaries. Somehow, with an immense effort, order was gradually restored and with it the integrity of the defence. There was early recognition of the fact that the previous day represented the last major effort of the British for the time being. There were minor thrusts around Monchy on 12 April, but they were quickly recognised as localised efforts to straighten lines and improve positions and full use was made of the breathing space to bolster the defence and replenish stocks of ammunition and defence stores.

If the past few days had been an extreme strain on the defence in the sectors of 11th Infantry and 17th Reserve Divisions, the situation was much the same for the hard pressed formations of 18th Reserve Division. Although the forward units had held on firmly for some time, on 11 April Reserve Infantry Regiment 86 was pushed back out of the *Artillerie-Schutzstellung* and its other positions forward of Héninel. The crucial factor was the deployment of tanks in support of the attacking infantry. Emerging out of the morning mist that morning, they closed up on the forward positions of 3rd Battalion. An attempt to halt them with a grenade launcher organised by Leutnant Bodmann failed. Firing at high angle, nothing less than a direct hit would have made any difference and this the crew failed to achieve, despite a few near misses. Lacking armour piercing SmK ammunition for the machine guns, the men of 10th, 11th and 12th Companies could only stand and watch as the tanks closed right up to their trenches, began to bring down flanking fire and to roll them up. Attempts were made to engage the tanks with bundled hand grenades but once again this failed to have any effect. There is nothing more disconcerting for dismounted infantry than to be powerless against advancing armour, so soon there was nothing for it but to abandon the front line. To have stayed would have meant isolation and inevitable capture. Offizierstellvertreter Schröder distinguished himself by remaining behind to keep the British infantry at bay while the remainder of the garrison made their way to the rear.[32]

The overall position was untenable, however. The line now ran in such a way as to leave Wancourt and Guémappe forming a large salient with its base back on the Hindenburg Line, where 2nd Battalion Reserve Infantry Regiment 84 was still clinging on under huge pressure. The divisional commander, Generalleutnant von Wundt, not a man given to panicky decisions, spoke at length that afternoon to Oberstleutnant von Thaer, chief of staff Group Arras. As a result orders were given for a withdrawal the following night to a shortened line, running from the Reserve Infantry Regiment 99 position east past Héninel, Wancourt and Guémappe. This was to be a controlled move back to be completed by the morning of 13 April. However, the confirmed loss of Monchy and knowledge of the relative weakness of Reserve Infantry Regiment 84 caused Wundt to accelerate the move. At 11.15 pm he issued the following order:

" 1. Monchy is occupied by the enemy.
2. 35 Reserve Infantry Brigade is to withdraw tonight to the line: Right flank on existing position on the Cambrai - Arras road - Guémappe - Hill 92 - Saddle east of Héninel - Hollow east of *Sachsenweg*. Depth essential. Strong covering parties are to be left in the current positions and the dugouts are to be blown up.
3. 3rd Battalion Infantry Regiment 176 is to be placed at the disposal of Brigade and is to be deployed to act as divisional right flank guard. Contact is to be made and maintained with 220th Infantry Division on the left flank."[33]

The order was to come into effect at 3.00 am, but it was a long time after that before it permeated down to the companies involved. Furthermore, because it came without warning it was difficult for the men of Reserve Infantry Regiment 31 to implement all the requirements. There were no explosives forward on the positions, so all that could be done was to set fire to everything inflammable and throw bundled hand grenades down into the dugouts to wreck the interiors. Despite that, the rest of the order was carried out successfully as dawn approached and without enemy interference until they were once more in defensive positions near Guémappe.[34] Three weak sentry positions were left behind in the old 3rd Battalion trenches, but these were supported by two carefully concealed machine guns commanded by Leutnant Ritzer of 3rd Machine Gun Company. In the former 2nd Battalion sector, Offizierstellvertreter Evert with three machine guns carried out a similar function then, at 6.00 am, their rearguard function complete, his men crammed the entrance to a former chalk mine in the village Wancourt with grenades, munitions, first aid dressings and straw and set it alight just as a mass of British infantrymen was seen to be advancing. Taking up their machine guns they set off hurriedly, pursued by black smoke and repeated explosions as the chalk mine entrance collapsed.

The battalions of Reserve Infantry Regiment 86 had a more awkward time of it. Having been under pressure throughout the previous day, there were still clashes during the night in its forward positions. The British attacked the 5th Company lines at 2.00 am, causing a breach. Attempts to close the gap and recapture the lost trench were abandoned, but not before there had been several casualties, including Leutnant

Seidensticker killed and Leutnant Seiffe of 1st Company severely wounded.[35] The 3rd Battalion, occupying high ground near Wancourt, was threatened with being cut off. The slowly advancing British were kept in check by the throwing of hand grenades, but the situation was critical and not conducive to breaking clean, something which was clearly required when the Brigade order arrived directing the regiment to evacuate Wancourt Hill, the village and Héninel and pull back to the high ground near Chérisy by 4.30 am.

This was quite impossible to implement fully. There was no time to bury the dead, evacuate the worst of the wounded or to blow up abandoned dugouts. Dawn was already breaking when the move began and it was soon spotted by the British. It was a race against time for the companies to pull back through the boggy Cojeul river valley and to scramble up the hills on the far side, their dark forms showing up sharply against the white of the snow, as they offered easy targets to the British artillery. Nevertheless, the majority who set out made it into the cover of the far side of the hill and set about preparing yet another set of positions. Little had been achieved before the first of the attacks was on them. Shortly after 6.00 am they were once more locked in battle with the British, but succeeded in driving them off. Reserve Infantry Regiment 84 also had to fall back in contact. Orders were delayed in reaching the companies and a close quarter battle was actually in progress in places when the time came to pull out. A few men, notably Vizefeldwebel Brandt of 5th Company, who was killed in the process, hurled themselves at the British and so bought some precious time to enable the main bodies to withdraw, leaving only a few sections armed with machine guns to cover the movement to the rear.[36]

So difficult was the move that it was after 11.00 am before the last of the 6th Company men was back in Chérisy. It then proved possible to get the field kitchens forward and the exhausted survivors received their first hot drinks and food for seventy two hours. The new Reserve Infantry Regiment 31 positions were relatively undisturbed that morning, though they were subjected to some desultory random harassing fire from the British guns, which had not yet identified the precise German locations. However, by the afternoon pressure was building once more. This was, after all, a day of major British effort all along the front. Everywhere the regiments of 18th Reserve Division were pressed, but, despite having been in action for three days continuously, they were still able to rally and to defend their positions with considerable success. The following night they were withdrawn back from the battle to well earned rest. On 13 April there were further isolated thrusts, especially against Hill 92 near Wancourt and in other places artillery fire continued to come down with undiminished ferocity. Nevertheless, it was clear to the men on both sides that the opening phase of the battle was now over. Any further progress would require the move forward of heavy guns and further stockpiling of ammunition.

These early days of fighting east of Arras represented a severe setback to the German army. Altogether on an eighteen kilometre front the British had broken in to a depth of up to six kilometres. Seven German divisions had been so worn down that they had to be relieved. Losses to date were calculated at 23,000, 16,000 of whom were missing. 233 guns, ninety eight of them large calibre, had been lost or destroyed, as had innumerable grenade launchers and machine guns, together with a mass of much needed trench stores and equipment.[37] In the days immediately following 9 April an urgent investigation was launched to establish what had gone wrong and what steps should be taken to remedy the deficiencies. Three main factors were identified. These were that some formations had failed in their duty because they had been too worn down when the battle opened and too little use was made of the defensive artillery and the readily available ammunition. This referred specifically to the failure to drench all known British battery positions with gas once the attacks were imminent. The third major problem was that reserves were held too far back and were not in a position to intervene in the earliest stages of the battle.

These were not new revelations, nor were the measures taken to guard against a repetition in future but, for the moment, they were of theoretical importance only. Confronted with the reality of a battle which had to be fought, despite the initial setbacks, all efforts had to be turned towards defeating further British attacks, full in the knowledge that a major French offensive down in the Champagne area was imminent. Logistic staffs strained every sinew to improve the supply situation and operational planners worked long and hard to stabilise the front and to be ready to counter whatever new attacks were about to be launched. Meanwhile, commanders at all levels were acutely aware that individual and unit morale was going to be of the utmost importance in the coming days. Acts of bravery were swiftly acknowledged through the presentation of medals and orders were published praising collective courage and efficiency.

Infantry Regiment 125, for example, deploying its full strength from 11 April, continued to contribute greatly to the integrity of the defence between Monchy and Roeux during the following seventy two hours and although it and the remainder of 26th Infantry Division was to continue to be deployed in the area for several more days, already on 14 April it was the subject of a laudatory divisional order by 11th Infantry Division:

"His Excellency the commanding general of IX Reserve Corps, Commander Group Arras, has charged me to pass on to Infantry Regiment 125 the expression of his recognition of the courageous beating off of the British attacks on 11 and 12 April. I fully concur with his sentiments. Signed von Hofacker"[38]

It is always hard to know if this sort of public praise actually has a dramatic effect on the morale of those named, but it could certainly do no harm and, in view of the weeks of fighting ahead, every single method of encouraging the defenders was worth trying.

Notes

1 Ritter History Infantry Regiment 163 pp 211 - 212.
2 Nollau History Infantry Regiment 51 p 161.
3 *ibid.* pp 161-162.
4 This *Gleisdreieck*, literally 'railway triangle' was located 1,500 metres east of Arras. It was created where the railway line north to Lens branched off from the Arras – Douai railway.
5 Schütz & Hochbaum History Grenadier Regiment 10 p 184.
6 F = Fusilier, i.e. part of 3rd Battalion.
7 Nollau *op. cit.* p 163.
8 *ibid.* pp 166-168.
9 *ibid.* pp 168-170.
10 Gropp *Hanseaten im Kampf* pp 219-220.
11 They were from Bavarian Infantry Regiment 17, 3rd Bavarian Infantry Division.
12 Gropp *op. cit.* pp 220-224.
13 This was Fusilier Regiment 38 of 11th Infantry Division.
14 This accusation appears with monotonous regularity throughout the German literature. It is impossible to judge its probability.
15 According to the BOH p 207, 2/Wiltshire, for example, which was not deployed until 11.38 am (UK time), suffered 342 casualties, excluding 37 suffered earlier that morning.
16 Klähn History Reserve Infantry Regiment 86 pp 198-203.
17 Jöhnck is in error. St Martin may well have been that distance from Héninel/Wancourt, but was more like 500 metres beyond the forward trench of Reserve Infantry Regiment 86.
18 This was one of many such examples of total destruction carried out as part of the *Alberich-Bewegung* [Alberich Movement = the withdrawal to the *Siegfried-Stellung*/Hindenburg Line].
19 Speck History Reserve Infantry Regiment 84 pp 176 - 177.
20 Förster History Reserve Infantry Regiment 31 p 108.
21 Berr History Field Artillery Regiment 75 pp 377-378.
22 Some accounts suggest that original order to pull back was issued in error, but it still seems highly unlikely that any coordinated defence could have been conducted that far forward. See Nollau *op. cit.* p179.
23 Gemmingen History Grenadier Regiment 119 p 195.
24 *ibid.* p 196.
25 Estimates of the number of tanks deployed varies, depending upon the source consulted. The probability is that in the entire Monchy area six went into action.
26 BOH 1917 p 263.
27 Kohl *Kriegserlebnisse* pp 151-154
28 Riegel History Bavarian Infantry Regiment 17 p 51
29 Stühmke History Infantry Regiment 125 pp 159-160.
30 This type of accusation is yet another which tends to appear fairly frequently in the German literature. It is impossible to judge its veracity.
31 Ritter *op. cit.* pp 222-223.
32 Klähn *op. cit.* p 209.
33 Behrmann *Die Osterschlacht* p 103.
34 Förster *op. cit.* p 109.
35 Klähn *op. cit.* p 214.
36 Speck *op. cit.* p 195.
37 GOH p 234.
38 Stühmke *op. cit.* p 161.

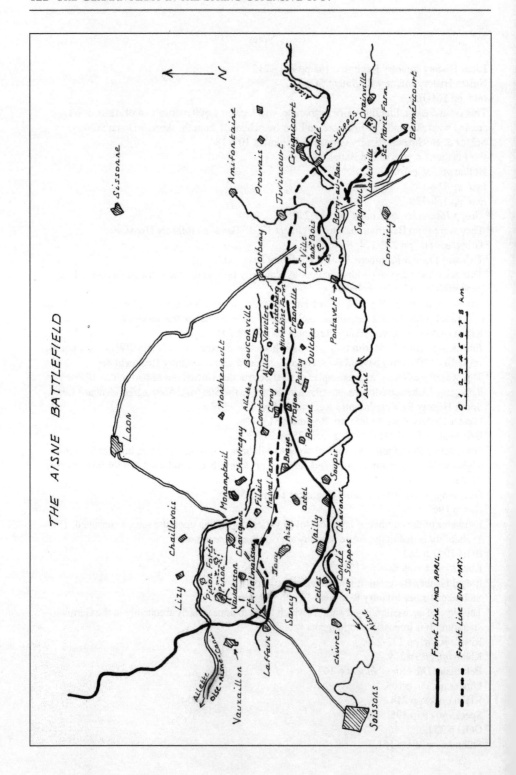

THE AISNE BATTLEFIELD

CHAPTER 4

The French Assault
Along the Aisne

The comprehensive build up to the Nivelle Offensive along the Aisne and in Champagne was impossible to camouflage. As early as February 1917 there was absolutely no doubt at OHL that the French were planning to conduct major operations in the area. Quite apart from other indicators, a French attack directive, which laid out in detail many aspects of the planned artillery battle, was obtained on 15 February. Added to this, as the date of the offensive approached, was the capture of a French sous-lieutenant on 31 March who, in direct contravention of orders, was carrying marked maps, signals instructions and radio codes on his person. At Berry au Bac on 4 April, a sergeant major of 3rd Zouaves was taken prisoner and confirmed the presence of colonial troops, not least because he too had a detailed order of battle with him when he was captured. Then any final doubts at Army Group German Crown Prince about enemy plans must have been dispelled when, on 7 April, a map marked with the planned French deployments along the Aisne front and the objectives to the north was captured near Reims.[1]

In addition, aerial reconnaissance had detected a great increase in airfields and supply dumps to the south of Reims and west as far as Fismes, not to mention the laying of great stretches of railway line for logistic support and to facilitate the use of huge artillery pieces in the area. In response, despite the fact that the attacks were not believed to be imminent, gradually German reserves began to be redeployed and, once it transpired that the French had assembled most of their reserves south of the line Reims - Soissons, it was obvious that Army Group German Crown Prince was facing a major offensive in the near future. The entire Western Front was reorganised and detailed planning and reinforcement for a defence conducted by Third and Seventh Armies was given top priority.[2]

In many respects it was a strange choice of battlefield, especially the western part of it. It featured very awkward terrain, with steep sided valleys, ravines, swampy areas and numerous watercourses. For a breakthrough to succeed, the advancing troops would have to negotiate this sort of ground for a good ten kilometres. The line of the Chemin des Dames, where the bulk of the German defences were located, was naturally strong, as had been proved as far back as September 1914; and the German depth and reserve positions, though not well developed at the beginning of the year, were all in dead ground or reverse slope locations. Thick scrub and unkempt areas of undergrowth all added to the issues to be confronted. For all these reasons it seems almost incredible that General Mangin, for example, commanding the French Sixth Army, directed that all artillery and other operational planning for the assault between Beaulnes and Craonne was to be based on a rate of advance of 100 metres every three minutes.[3] It was, perhaps, yet another manifestation of French overconfidence.

Admittedly he had at his disposal the élite corps; namely I and II Colonial, VI and XX, but over that going it would have been hard to move massed troops at that speed, even if there had been no resistance at all. However, that was not going to be the case and one important reason for this had also been overlooked by the French. The ridge along which the Chemin des Dames runs was dotted, in places virtually honeycombed, with abandoned underground stone quarries. The Caverne du Dragon is well known, but it was simply one of many, all of which offered more or less bomb proof accommodation for supports and reserves, indeed for any troops who could be spared from sentry duty. In places the entire defence was based around the location of these shelters and their use was to prove to be of decisive importance when the attack opened.[4]

For many months the Seventh Army front had been a quiet part of the line. It was weakly held and lacked substantial numbers of heavy guns and air assets. These issues were now addressed as a matter of urgency. As more troops moved in, divisional frontages shrunk and defences, which in many cases had been rather neglected, were improved through constant hard work by the trench garrisons.

Hauptmann Egon von Loebell Footguard Regiment 3 [5]

"The attack was to be directed against Seventh Army, which at that time was known as 'The Sleeping Army'. The positions along the Aisne were always some of the quietest of the entire Western front. The extent of the defensive works left something to be desired. A great deal of time and effort had been devoted to the building of comfortable barracks and similar [constructions]. The gentle, leafy, scenes illustrated and described in the newspapers originated mainly on the Aisne or the Reims district. All over the place we stumbled over beautiful memorials designed to remind us of the World War. The defences themselves, however, had been neglected. The experience gained at Verdun and on the Somme had not been taken into consideration. There were as good as no depth positions or stop lines.

"All these deficiencies had to be tackled by the troops occupying the various sectors, who were themselves mostly worn out. Almost no trench stores were made available; everything had been directed to the active fronts and the *Siegfried Stellung* [Hindenburg Line] and there was a complete lack of labour units. Even though this was the case, the lack of timber, for example, could be made good locally. There were plenty of wooded areas available. Once the aim of the enemy, namely to break through along the Aisne, was spotted - this must have been early February - work went ahead feverishly to fill the gaps. Thank heavens the enemy allowed us sufficient time for this. It is impossible to judge if the offensive was meant to have opened earlier but was disrupted by the withdrawal to the *Siegfried Stellung*.

"In the event there was enough time to move up infantry and artillery. Our own division, 5th Guards Infantry, was redeployed from the St Quentin area. The forward positions could be put into some sort of order, but the depth positions were very imperfectly laid out and, what was worse, the work was under the direction of engineer officers who clearly had little understanding or sympathy with the latest methods of construction and stuck to what they had learned in peacetime."

As early as the beginning of March, Seventh Army had been so reinforced that it had nine ground holding divisions in the front line (up from six in January) between Soissons and Brimont, plus five *Eingreif* divisions behind the line, also an increase of three. To the east, between Suippes and Aubérive on the Third Army front, the three divisions of VII Reserve Corps, which had guarded the thirty five kilometre sector, were supplemented by an additional two, with two more in the *Eingreif* role in depth. This build up continued during the weeks leading up to 16 April, but to have already deployed fourteen divisions, supported by seventy five batteries of heavy howitzers and eighteen super-heavy low trajectory batteries on a one hundred kilometre front represented an extremely tough nut for the French army to crack. By the end of the month, however, three more ground holding divisions had been added to the order of battle and three additional corps headquarters had been deployed to improve command and control. Headquarters First Army was also placed on standby to assume command of a sector of the front once the offensive actually opened and the intervention of the various reserve divisions at the front made the consequent span of command too great to be split solely between Third and Seventh Armies. The French could naturally determine precisely where the blow was to fall, but it seemed clear to the planners at Army Group German Crown Prince that the approximately thirty French divisions which had been identified would permit an assault on a front of up to forty kilometres. Identification and rectification of potential or actual weaknesses in the defensive lines were identified and work went ahead vigorously so as to be at as high a state of readiness as possible before the blow fell.

One planning assumption by the French army, according to the document captured on 15 February, was that final preparations would be relatively undisturbed because the German artillery was likely to remain silent. A decision was taken at OHL vetoing against any such thing and a directive was issued on 19 March once the move back to the Hindenburg Line was complete that, 'As soon as the artillery reinforcement of Seventh Army is complete, systematic counter-battery fire, coupled with local infantry attacks, is to be employed so as to disrupt the enemy offensive and determine their attack plans.'[6] This was duly done and, meanwhile, arrangements were made speedily to redeploy the divisions made available because of the withdrawal to the Hindenburg Line. Ten more were subordinated to the Army Group, which also managed to extract five from quieter sections of the front. The French offensive was now facing no fewer than sixteen divisions in the line between Soupir and Aubérive and fourteen more in various degrees of reserve. Seventh Army and the threatened sector of Third Army could now call on 122 batteries of heavy howitzers and seventy four batteries of heavy low trajectory guns. A clash of massive proportions was looming.

On Good Friday, 6 April, the French bombardment began and fire came down right across the front, reaching well back into the rear areas. Initially, because of the targeting, it was not completely clear if this really was the start of the offensive preparation or merely retaliation for the German shelling of French supply dumps and approach routes. However, from 8 April there could no longer be any doubt. Part of Group Aisne, 5th Bavarian Reserve Division, was located forward right just north of Berry au Bac, which was a key locality in French planning. This was where they intended to launch a massed tank attack on the first day of the offensive, so the bombardment, heavy everywhere, was especially destructive in this area.

Reserve Leutnant Georg Will 3rd Company Bavarian Reserve Infantry Regiment 7[7]

"8 April 1917, Easter Sunday. The enemy are showing signs of life. Their preparations must be complete. They brought our entire positions either side of the Aisne under heavy fire today. My own position was only hit by light calibre, but we were fired on from dawn to dusk. We counted one thousand impacts on a very small frontage ... It looks as though this is the first day of the offensive, of the artillery preparation at least ... I spent the entire day in an open position near the Aisne and behind the trench. I observed, gazed, smoked, planned and weighed everything up. The were plenty of enemy aircraft high up above, but only the occasional one of ours ... I searched the sky through my telescope and spotted our fighter planes extremely high, above the clouds ... One of them attacked a low flying enemy who was observing or directing fire. Suddenly our aircraft dived almost vertically on the unsuspecting Frenchman. After only a few seconds of machine gun fire the enemy went down in a steep glide and landed close behind our lines ...

"9 April, Easter Monday. In the morning the skies were cloudy and it even snowed slightly. We were already hoping that the shelling would ease somewhat and, indeed, during the morning there was all the calm of a holiday. Towards midday, however, when the skies cleared, a storm of hurricane force broke over us, as the enemy fired countless salvoes with perfect precision: heavy and light shells were all mixed in together. Everywhere there were flashes, crashes and the thunderous noises of firing signatures and explosions. Thick smoke settled over the valley of the Aisne, enveloping everything. The air itself was most unpleasant and stank of powder smoke.

"We were caught in a miserable mouse trap. It was an abandoned mortar emplacement, of strong concrete construction to be sure, but with its embrasure open towards the enemy. We were able only to block it roughly ... it was hard for the sentry by the entrance. He had to be able to dash into cover at any moment, but also maintain observation. Because of the depth of the trench a great deal of wood had been used in its construction. As a result, every hit caused shattering, splinters to fly and prolonged heaving and trembling. The enemy paused briefly and immediately heads were raised to inspect the damage, then the storm broke out all over again. During the night only the light guns continued the bombardment, so as to interfere with our clearance and repair work – but what a state our position was in!

"Even by bright moonlight we could hardly orientate ourselves. A huge crater field of devastation met our gaze. Our way was blocked by broken beams and posts, shattered planks and fascines, which were mingled with chunks of concrete blown off the pill boxes. In the centre of the company position the trenches were completely levelled and half the dugouts wrecked. Where concreted and other structures had once stood were now huge craters or broken beams and twisted railway lines pointed up at the sky. The wire obstacle was also badly damaged.

Already by 7 April, the analysis by OHL, based on a combination of the targets being engaged by the French, the simultaneous attack on German observation balloons and examination of captured documents, was that the attempted breakthrough would come north of the Aisne. The main thrust seemed to be aimed at the line Montcornet - Rethel, which meant that the main blow would fall on what were then the sectors of Groups (i.e. corps headquarters) Liebert, Höhn and Eberhardt (later to be designated Groups Liesse, Sissonne and Brimont respectively) These were located more or less astride the junction of Seventh and Third Armies and, therefore, an intrinsically weak point in the defences was being threatened. However, it was obvious that there would also be attacks on the flanks to fix defenders there in position and evidence began to accumulate of further French troop concentrations in western Champagne. It had to be assumed, therefore, that the battle might extend in that direction, even if operations developed as a later phase of the overall offensive. It was still impossible to predict precisely when the offensive would be launched but, according to at least one French prisoner, five days had been allocated for counter-battery fire to wear down the German guns and a further five to smash the infantry positions and barbed wire. This pointed to a mid-April date, one which was increasingly confirmed as the bombardment ground on remorselessly.

The Bavarian Ersatz Division, comprising Bavarian Reserve Infantry Regiments 4, 15 and 18, was defending the sector south of Chevreux. Their experience of the bombardment was typical of that of other formations defending where the French army had massed seven of their best assault divisions, backed by immediate reserves of four more in depth and commanded from left to right on a ten kilometre frontage between Beaulnes and Craonne by XX, II Colonial and I Corps .

Oberstleutnant Vogel 3rd Battalion Bavarian Reserve Infantry Regiment 15 [8]

"The 3rd Battalion of the regiment was deployed at a point expected to be one of the foci of the forthcoming battle, namely the eastern slopes of the notorious Winterberg near Chevreux … The position met none of the requirements of a defensive position in a major battle. However, it was no better for many other units and the same saying applied here as elsewhere, 'It is not the position that matters, but the spirit of the defenders!' The front line comprised a wall of sandbags that had had to be erected in a low lying swampy area where the water table was high. About three hundred metres in rear, on a rise about three to four metres higher than the depression, our second line extended for about five hundred metres left and right of Chevreux. There was then a gap of about five hundred metres to the third line established in a wooded area. Shallow dugouts, not more than five metres deep and sunk into light sandy soil, were only available in the second line.

"That said, our position did have one advantage that must be recognised. The second and third lines were linked by the *Heeringen Tunnel,* which ran north-south. It offered only weak protection in the south where its overhead cover was limited, but this improved further north because the ground sloped upwards. Here were located the *KTK* [*Kampftruppenkommandeur* - commander of the forward troops] and an electricity generator. It also carried all the telephone links to the front and the rear link to the third line. The enemy lines were located about 800 metres away in the marshy Bois de Beau Marais, where dense woods covered from observation all attack preparations. The battalion deployment was 11th Company left forward, 10th Company right forward; 9th Company occupied the second line and 12th Company the third. Two weapons of 3rd Machine Gun Company were installed in the second line and the remainder were held back in reserve at the disposal of the battalion commander. To our right in all these lines was [Bavarian] Reserve Infantry Regiment 4; to the left was our 1st Battalion …

"The enemy bombardment with guns and mortars began at 7.00 am 8 April (Easter Sunday). Our own artillery, which was well placed and deployed in depth, soon began to bring the enemy assault preparations under effective and successful fire. The numerous resulting explosions as enemy ammunition dumps exploded demonstrated to the infantry the outstanding support they could expect from their sister arm. The enemy gun and mortar fire was directed by airborne observers. Throughout almost the entire day up to twenty French aircraft were in the air, whilst about seventeen captive balloons were counted on a very narrow front. Our positions suffered terribly under this heavy artillery and mortar bombardment and the troops had their hands full every night attempting to repair the most essential parts which had been smashed during the day. The sandbagged wall along the front line was blown away. It now comprised a series of water filled craters.

"In consequence the garrison was withdrawn during the night 11/12 into the second position, leaving only listening posts forward by night. The second line was also badly damaged. From time to time the entrances to the dugouts were collapsed, but it was possible to restore them roughly each night to some sort of order. There was insufficient manpower to maintain the third line. The move of rations had to be entrusted to the best and bravest soldiers, who had to negotiate the fire swept rear areas and even then food arrived irregularly or not at all. Despite all of this the morale and spirit of the men remained unbroken so, to the question posed by the battalion to the companies, 'How are your men getting on?', the answer on numerous occasions was, 'They are sheltering in the dugouts and passing the time singing good old soldiers' songs.'

"Once there was nothing left of the front line to destroy, the enemy then concentrated most of their fire on the second line and the rear areas. This meant that the defensive value of the second line, which now formed the main defensive position, suffered greatly. It was only through the deployment of maximum effort each night that some semblance of strength could be restored … It was especially problematic that the *Heeringen Tunnel*, through which all the telephone links ran, was collapsed in several places near the second line. A small stream ran over it at this point, so the result was that water flowed in and one third of it was flooded. There could be no question of restoring this ideal link, so both personnel and communication links had to be moved above ground. This led to constant failures of the latter and endless work at night for the repair crews, whose painstaking work was frequently destroyed once more in the early hours of the morning."

It was inevitable that there were numerous moments of horror as the shelling of the positions increased and, guided from the air, began systematically to wreck shelters, dugouts and strong points. One such incident, typical of many others, occurred in the Cerny area, now defended by 16th Reserve Division; two and a half years back it was the scene of a series of vain and unsuccessful attacks by the British 1st Division in mid-September 1914.

Unteroffizier Fuchs 1st Company Reserve Infantry Regiment 29 [9]

"1st Company suffered a grim loss on 8 April. Gefreiter Lohmar with six brave soldiers of his section had sought cover from the murderous fire in a dugout which was not complete, had no more than a single entrance and was only about one metre deep. Just after 3.00 pm a heavy shell collapsed the dugout. Although desperate attempts were made by various people to dig out those buried, the drum fire coming down on this sector ruled it out. From a neighbouring dugout, which was also not complete, feverish work began to dig a way through to those trapped. By evening sufficient progress had been made to establish that the shell had totally crushed the dugout and that our comrades must have met the death of heroes. It was not possible actually to reach the buried men, because they had been sheltering near the entrance. It had now gone dark, so work was begun once more in the open; we wanted to give them decent soldiers' graves. By about 5.00 pm we had finally dug out one of the buried men. Suddenly fire came down again. A heavy shell landed very close, destroyed the diggings and reburied our comrades. Lohmar and his six comrades still lie deep in the earth in the so-called *Paradieslager* [Paradise Camp].

Almost a week after the bombardment began, General der Infanterie von Boehn came to the conclusion that, regardless of indications that the preparatory period might continue for several more days, in fact there could be a major infantry assault at any time. He despatched an order to all group headquarters ordering, 'Full battle readiness'[10] and, simultaneously he issued a special Order of the Day to all ranks of Seventh Army.[11]

"Soldiers of Seventh Army!

The expected battle has begun. I can no longer pass on my greetings personally to every arm and service. However, I overlook and follow your every deed on an hourly basis, as well as those of our superior commander, the German Crown Prince, the Chief of the General Staff, Field Marshal von Hindenburg and General Ludendorff.

All eyes are on you! Each of you must tell yourself that this is a matter of the honour of the German army and Empire.

Go to it with God for our Kaiser and our Fatherland!

The Army Commander
Signed von Boehn"

As the bombardment ground on, increasing in intensity constantly, minor infantry operations were launched by both sides: by the French to test the defences and seek tactical advantage; by the German defenders in an attempt to disrupt preparations for the offensive. One such battle erupted in the area of the Napoleon Tunnel, which linked the trenches of the First Position on the approach to the Winterberg Plateau, defended at that time by Grenadier Guard Regiment 3 of 5th Guards Infantry Division, the left forward formation of Group Liebert. A junior NCO of 9th Company later provided a flavour of the numerous bitter struggles fought out in the forward areas at that time.

Unteroffizier Schallhorn 9th Company Grenadier Guard Regiment 3 [12]

"On 14 April 1917, after 10th Company had had to be relieved because of the high number of casualties caused by gas, Kernke's platoon of 9th Company occupied the tunnel. Unfortunately, when the French renewed their attacks the following day the first and part of the second trenches were lost. As a result Kernke's platoon in the tunnel found itself caught in a sort of mousetrap between the two trenches. The French placed themselves at the entry and exit of the tunnel and bombarded us with hand grenades and gas bombs to wear us down. However, in this they were to be disappointed. Because they could achieve nothing from this bombardment and we continued to occupy the entrance and exit to the tunnel just as before, they tried to find another way to force us out of the tunnel. A French captain directed a medical orderly from 9th Company who had been captured that same day to shout into the tunnel that we should surrender.

"This demand for our surrender was repeated several times. Neither Kernke, nor the entire platoon, had any thought of doing any such thing. The French then despatched the medical orderly into the tunnel to tell us to surrender. They had no luck with this either. We kept him with us and went on occupying the tunnel. They then tried storming the tunnel and several of them were shot down by the entrance in the first trench. Towards evening the French were ejected by a counter-stroke delivered by 9th Company from the second trench and we were freed from our dangerous position. Vizefeldwebel Kernke deserved the highest praise. He never yielded the tunnel, nor would he ever have done so. I shall never forget those hours in the Napoleon Tunnel. Most of us were suffering from gas poisoning and had to be sent to hospital. However, fourteen days later I was back with the company."

In addition to the problems caused by the bombardment and the need to maintain the trenches as far as possible, during the days prior to 16 April rationing the forward troops and carrying essential supplies up to them was extremely difficult. During the battle of the Somme the previous year it had proved necessary to form a fourth 'platoon' in each rifle company to carry out this function. It was no sinecure. It demanded tough, strong men and the most forceful junior leadership. All along the Chemin des Dames in early April a version of the system had to be revived.

Unteroffizier Fuchs 1st Company Reserve Infantry Regiment 29 [13]

"Rationing the company in amongst all this drum fire was extremely difficult. The field kitchens were moved to the Ailette Valley. From there, once it went dark, food had to be fetched across two hills which were swept with appalling fire, the Chemin des Dames, the *Chivy-Nase* [Chivy Nose, a spur located between Chivy and the Chemin des Dames] and through the *Paradieslager*. [the area forward of *Chivy-Nase* and west of Chivy village] and it was hardly to be wondered at that the men preferred to go without food rather than risk the strenuous effort to collect food through murderous fire. However, on 10 or 11 April, the formation of carrying parties was ordered. These, together with the clerical staff, were housed in the *Colligishöhle* [Colligis Cave]. I was put in charge of our carrying party.

"On 15 April the field kitchens went forward after dark, just as they had every other day. The carrying parties were fed first then they collected food for their comrades. The soup (an all-in stew) was loaded into containers, each with a hollow insulating jacket which was filled with glycerine. These were tightly closed and had two straps to enable them to be carried on your back. Even empty these were heavy and each man had to transport three or four, together with sacks of bread and baskets containing butter, sausages, cigars etc. Once the loads had been distributed amongst the twelve carriers, we set off down the Ailette Valley, which was under fire from large calibre artillery. This was the main route forward and we were forced to traverse it from one shell crater to the next.

"It required constant care to ensure that the group stayed together and that all the men kept coming. This meant that as leader I had to move from front to rear constantly and also lend a hand with the heaviest loads when running through places swept with fire. To add to the misery it was raining. We did not reach the Chemin des Dames until 3.00 am. We were soaked to the skin and drenched in sweat. The fire had eased and, after a short pause, we pushed on with fresh courage to our comrades at the front. Isolated shells were now landing with dull thuds. We soon discovered that they were gas filled so, to add further to the misery, we had to mask up. Everything pointed to the fact that the attack was about to begin; so mustering all our strength we pushed on forward to our hungry comrades. We marched forward now across open ground in a straight line towards the *Paradieslager*. Shortly after 5.00 am we reached our comrades, suffering no casualties. The carriers dropped with exhaustion. Only those with practical experience of such a thing can understand what it means to spend almost twelve hours struggling with heavy loads in bad weather, under fire for hours at a time, rushing from crater to crater.

"The rations were distributed quickly and we set off on our return march. We were caught by French barrage fire on the Chemin des Dames. All we could do was rush from crater to crater along the line of the shot up communication trenches. It took all our efforts and soldierly sense of duty to get to the protection of the *Colligishöhle* as soon as possible, there to regain our strength for the next round trip. We stopped for the first time at Courtecon by the regimental command post. From the observation post there I was able to watch the French attack and see our comrades being led off into captivity. It was a terrible

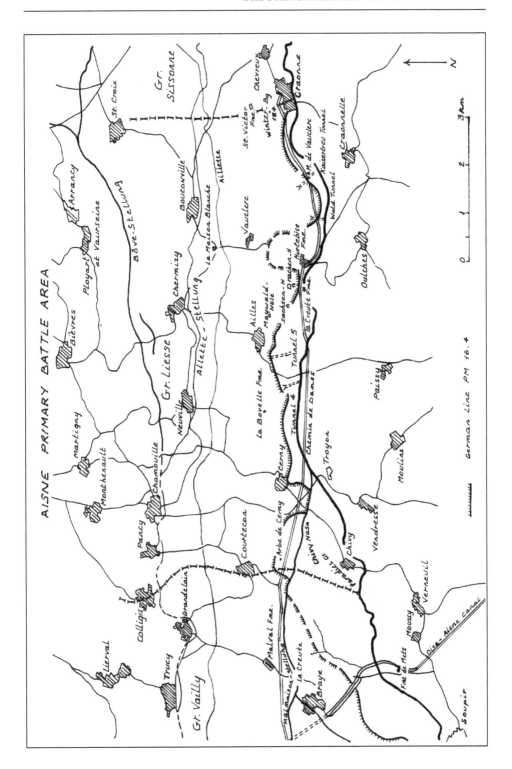

experience! Ailette Valley was once more under heavy fire and we doubled along it. At 9.15 am we reached our final destination, the *Colligishöhle*, again without casualties; the only one of our regimental parties to manage it. For some reason our artillery was not functioning correctly that morning. A battery of field guns near the *Colligishöhle* had not fired a shot until we went by. It was we who alerted them to the attack at the front."

All the preparation on both sides had been leading up to the opening of the massive French offensive, which the Germans were to refer to as the *Doppelschlacht* [Double battle] *Aisne/Champagne*. There was no question of operational surprise; the defenders knew for sure in advance that the date would be 16 April and even the timing was distributed down to the lowest levels in the early hours of 16 April. "The German ambassador in the Hague", stated a Headquarters V Bavarian Reserve Corps message, delivered to regiments by telephone at approximately 3.00 am, "reports that the French attack is due to begin at dawn 16 April. Inform all troops!"[14]

Vizefeldwebel Wagner 9th Company Grenadier Guard Regiment 3 [15]

"Dawn broke on 16 April. From 5.00 am the heaviest artillery and mortar fire of all calibres imaginable had been landing throughout the sector. Tension increased, everybody wished that they would come, because then the fire would have to be lifted forward! After 7.00 am the rate of fire reached its peak and everything was ploughed up. The enemy mixed in gas shells. Our casualties mounted because, at 7.00 am, we had left the Napoleon Tunnel and had deployed left and right along the line of the old front line trench. There we lay, pressed flat, split into pairs and threes, manning the lips of the craters. Because the telephone lines had all gone, communications relied on runners and relay posts, all of whom did their duty fearlessly and faithfully. In this respect Gefreiter Scherer is worthy of special mention, having completed several round trips between the front line and the *KTK*. He seemed to be invulnerable, as did Leutnant Sellschopp, whom all of us in 9th Company revered.

"Towards 7.30 am the attack was launched in our sector. We experienced a brief moment of relief ... but then it was a matter of all hands on deck! There could no longer be any doubt about it, despite the fact that everything was shrouded in morning mist and powder smoke, because the French artillery suddenly lifted beyond us and started bringing down barrage fire behind us ... or was it a creeping barrage to clear the way for the attackers? Machine guns hammered and then we had to bring down and maintain rapid fire to keep the overwhelming numbers of attackers off our backs. Because of the dense clouds of dust and smoke and the racket of battle, it was possible for the enemy to spring a surprise and close right up on the 1st Battalion front line. There, too, all the dugouts were smashed and the greater part of the trench garrison was wounded or dead. All those who could still move or raise themselves up, fought courageously and, initially, the enemy could not get forward.

"From our elevated location we could see quite a long way and we could clearly make out the French reserve columns, in particular off to the right [west] behind the hills around Oulches. We had to do something quickly or the enemy assault troops would be on us in a few moments. There were great gaps in our wire and, as the leading elements closed up to it, we resorted to our hand grenades, which cracked and crashed mercilessly. Gap after gap appeared in the lines of the attackers, confusion reigned and they threw themselves into shell craters. There was no need for orders; every man in my platoon knew what was required ... They lay there, rifles at the ready and fired at the approaching enemy, to begin with not directly to the front, but off to the left and right. This went on for hours.

"After the first attack, there were further thrusts at 11.00 am, then at 1.00, 3.25, 6.00 and 7.55 pm. This just goes to show what a hard day we had. The situation was especially threatening around *Negerdorf* [Niggers' Village = Salient du Jutland].[16] 4th Company Grenadier Guard Regiment 3, which was deployed there, was no longer in contact, so again and again we had to dash down into the re-entrant then, deploying hand grenades, pistols and bayonets, force our way, step by step, along the old first position to clear out enemy who had broken in ... many a fusilier[17] met a hero's death that day. Because of heavy losses some parts of the trenches were not occupied. Sensing the anger I sent my brave runner, Fritschke, to the second trench to report to the company commander. The losses also meant that the enemy had repeatedly occupied and re-occupied places to our left and right and over the hours had also pushed forward to the second trench.

"To our front they came on in endless masses. Our machine guns fired as fast as they could; our rifle barrels never cooled down. Our stocks of ammunition shrank more and more and we had to resort to collecting the grenade sacks and ammunition pouches of the dead and wounded. Our stick grenades saved us repeatedly when the fighting was so close we could not use our rifles. During the afternoon the reduced lines of attackers began to dig in, seeking cover from the murderous defence we were putting up, but even though the slopes to our front were strewn with dead and wounded Frenchmen in their new blue uniforms, fresh waves of attackers arrived to swell the ranks.

"At about 8.00 pm, just as it was going dark, the French launched the sixth major attack of the day! Only someone who experienced that day can appreciate precisely what that means because, in addition, there were endless minor thrusts as every metre of ground was contested all day long. Hardly had the first Frenchman got to his feet than our rifles and machine guns opened up. The enemy hesitated; some began to waver. We then had to summon all our energy and reach for the hand grenades. In no time the stick grenades were exploding and great clouds of smoke rolled along the slopes of the Winterberg. All these bangs and crashes, together with the whirr of splinters, produced a not to be underestimated psychological effect on our opponents. To our front the attack was halted immediately, but what was happening left and right? There weaker machine gun fire and only occasional grenade explosions indicated that the French had succeeded in consolidating in the first trench. 1st Battalion had lost part of *Negerdorf*, but even here the French did not have much success.

"So we stuck it out, hour after hour. Every attack on our elevated positions failed and we carried on firing at the French to our left and right as well as we could. We passed a message back detailing all the losses and, in response, 3rd and 10th Companies were deployed forward, together with 1st and 3rd Companies Footguard Regiment 3. We held on to the front line and the Napoleon Tunnel but, quite apart from all the wounded, we had lost many brave comrades. Of course the enemy had suffered losses which were far heavier. A French deserter who came over to us in the morning and spoke quite good German explained to us that even by that time many of the assault troops gathered in the forward trenches had fallen victim to the destructive fire of our guns. The men refused to attack and had to be forced to do so by officers with revolvers in their hands.[18]

"Towards midnight the carrying group brought us rations about which, in neither their quantity nor their quality, was there much good to say, but who could expect fine food on such a day of major battle? The most important things were something to smoke, mineral water and 'firewater'. It took many mouthfuls of the latter to steady the nerves in this place. The French did not even leave us in peace while we ate. No sooner had the carriers handed over [hot] meals, coffee, bread, preserves and bacon and dropped off a suitable number of bottles of mineral water and schnapps than, all of a sudden, the French artillery brought a huge concentration of fire down on us. All along the horizon were pillars of flame which merged into a sea of fire. It crashed and thundered all round, as though all Hell had broken loose once more. After this torrent of fire, which kept us alert and on our toes for hours, the rest of the night passed off fairly quietly. There were no more attacks in our sector and, in the early dawn, a carrying party from Footguard Regiment 3 brought us bandoliers of ammunition, hand grenades, signal pistols and rapid wire obstacles."

Deployed in the centre of Group Liesse, 19th Reserve Division, manning positions along the Chemin des Dames around Ailles, came under intense and immediate pressure from the élite units of 10th and 15th Colonial Divisions.

Reserve Hauptmann Wilhelm Kellinghusen 4th Company Reserve Infantry Regiment 92 [19]

"On the morning of 16 April, after a ten day artillery bombardment, the longed-for infantry attack began at long last. The previous evening Nivelle had issued his famous order: *L'heure est venu! Confiance! Courage! Vive la France!* [The hour has come! Confidence! Courage! Long live France!]. At 6.50 am there was a sudden hurricane of artillery fire then, at 7.00 am, the waves and columns of French attackers, deeply echeloned, surged towards the Chemin des Dames. It was just like the Russian Brussilov offensive. The positions, trenches and dugouts were long since wrecked. As a result and wherever (unlike us sheltering from the destructive artillery fire in deep caves) they attacked, they encountered very few defenders. Both regiments to the left and right of us, namely Reserve Infantry Regiments 73 and 78, as well as other regiments adjoining them from neighbouring divisions were, apart from a few remnants, pushed right back off the Chemin des Dames. However, our companies held firm for several hours in the second line and in front of the *Creutehöhle*.[20]

"Some especially courageous survivors even managed to cling on in the first line. However, once the thrusts into the neighbouring sectors had occurred, they came under huge pressure on both flanks from the endless flood of French reinforcing waves, became involved in bitter fighting which went on well into the afternoon and eventually had to fall back slowly - officers, NCOs and men breaking through heroically to the third line. Despite all enemy attempts, this line remained firmly in our hands. The French had sent the Moroccan division, one of their best assault divisions, against our division.[21] It comprised nothing but blacks and other Africans. The blacks were equipped with a special weapon, a sort of hatchet with a fifty centimetre handle, which they used to smash the skulls of our wounded. This was definitely a poor idea. Our men were so enraged about it that they subsequently never permitted any black soldier captured with such a weapon to go on living."[22]

As the fighting went on in the depth of the Reserve Infantry Regiment 92 positions, it began to lap around the *Creutehöhle* itself. This rock shelter was situated a short distance more or less due south of the *Drachenhöhle* [Caverne du Dragon] and immediately adjacent to the Chemin des Dames.

Leutnant Oskar Kirchhof Commander 3rd Company Reserve Infantry Regiment 92 [23]

"After the enemy artillery had zeroed in on the *Creutehöhle*, it was impossible for me to retain all the many men there; the wreckage of the cave was now too small. I decided to redeploy the artillery observer and I despatched 4th Company, less Leutnant Norberg's platoon, to the battalion command post in *Sachsenhöhle* [Saxony Cave, located just west of the *Drachenhöhle*]. I kept hold of Norberg because I had learned to value him for his absolute calmness and I tasked him, in the event of an attack, to maintain contact with 1st Company off to the right. At night we had our hands full trying to clear the rubble out of the cave sufficiently to keep the entrance to the front line open. Norberg, at the head of a strong patrol, had established the link to 1ˢᵗ Company, though the trench leading that way was completely smashed. My Vizefeldwebel, Kappmeyer, and Leutnant Grüne made an almost superhuman effort to get forward. There were still two sections of 3ʳᵈ Company in the front line trench and another section armed with a light machine gun in the second line. At 4.00 am I suddenly heard the sound of footsteps descending the stairs. There he was, our dear *Pferdinand*,²⁴ the battalion adjutant, together with Rogge, his runner. They had been round the battalion position once more.

"At 5.00 am Kappmeyer reported to me that the link forward had been re-established. Once I was convinced of this and had also received the reports from the observation post, I laid down briefly for a rest. I can hardly have been there for fifteen minutes when the shout went up, 'Here come the French!' The call was delivered with such urgency that there could be no doubt it was correct. I was up in a flash and everybody poured out. At long last the wearisome waiting was over and now, finally, at long last we could defend ourselves. Norberg rushed off with his platoon, fighting his way to 1ˢᵗ Company. Kappmeyer's platoon and half of Grüne's manned the front line. There was half a platoon under Vizefeldwebel Lemmermann in the second line and two assault groups under Vizefeldwebels Rohde and Bock at my disposal.

"Storming forward towards our positions, deeply echeloned and in several waves, came the French, most of them black. However they could not get a foothold anywhere in the front line of the 3ʳᵈ Company sector. The first of the wounded were already arriving at the cave. The men all fought with boundless doggedness. After a short while came the report, 'Hand grenades needed forward' and straightaway several sacks of them were carried to the front. We soon came to the uplifting realisation that the enemy would beat their heads in vain against our position, thanks to the protection afforded by the cave which, despite all the dreadful shocks and appalling hours endured during the bombardment of the previous days, was still in a defensible condition.

"It was quite another matter for [Reserve Infantry] Regiment 73. Here the enemy soon overran the forward position and threatened to roll us up from the left flank. We spotted the danger immediately and demanded two machine guns from battalion headquarters. Despite extremely heavy fire, my two runners, Steinkamp and Speck, were soon back with the news that the machine guns would be coming. In the meantime, Vizefeldwebels Rohde and Beck had an extremely hard task to perform; namely, together with their assault groups, to keep the enemy, who had been storming forward in strength, off our back. During this heavy fighting the courageous Bock fell. It was a heavy blow for me. Unfortunately he was not the only one. A little later, Leutnant Norberg was also carried down into the cave suffering from a serious stomach wound. He had fought with the greatest daring and determination in order to link up with 1ˢᵗ Company. Here the French had broken in in two places and he had managed twice to throw them back with hand grenades. Suddenly several grenades landed around him. He was badly hit by a fragment and carried to the rear. By now the machine guns had arrived. We despatched them to the left from where they could fire into the enemy flank and soon they were directing lacerating fire at the attacking columns and mowing them down. Through a combination of the timely intervention of the machine gunners and the determined work of the assault groups of Rohde and Bock it was possible for us to keep the enemy in check.

"When I pressed the brave Norberg's hand in grateful thanks and asked him, lying still on his stretcher, how he was, he answered in his courageous way, 'I am fine. Just make sure that forward progress is being made outside'. I pressed his hand once more and left him in the care of the medical orderlies, but he soon closed his faithful eyes one last time.[25] We were all in good spirits. Our main concern was our flanks, but my two two vizefeldwebels, Rohde and Kappmeyer, had barricaded themselves in so well that the enemy were completely neutralised. Meanwhile the enemy artillery had spotted that the attack had stalled completely on our front, so they poured down fire on the front line and against the *Höhle* all over again. The battalion then ordered the evacuation of the front line. Up until that moment it had been impossible for any Frenchman to reach our lines alive. In any case, during the afternoon the enemy attack withered away."

Reserve Hauptmann Wilhelm Kellinghusen 4th Company Reserve Infantry Regiment 92 [26]

"After the death of Norberg, the attacking waves of black soldiers forced their way on the right between the *Sachsenhöhle* and the *Kreutehöhle* over the first line and towards the second and third lines. Here the platoons of Vizefeldwebels Paehr and Wagener from my company, supported by elements of 1st Company and men of the subordinated Mortar Company 219, confronted them and held the position against all assaults. Three separate times the enemy tried to break through in dense columns. Three times they were beaten back with bloody losses and they gave up seeking a breakthrough at this place. Right and left of us the attack soon stalled down in the Ailette Valley. A French attempt to surround the regiment, which was clinging onto its third line positions on the hill, was prevented by the fire of the machine gun nests placed to the rear as far back as the *Keitelriegel*. With courage that was in no way inferior to that shown by their comrades along the Chemin des Dames, they fired ceaselessly into the flanks of the waves and columns of French attackers that were flooding into the Reserve Infantry Regiment 78 and 73 sectors. They fired with such effect that these ended up scattered and isolated in Bauclère Wood. Only shattered remnants and the odd individual made their way forwards as far as the *Keitelriegel* and there they were captured during the course of the day. The machine gun nest up on Hill 376, just to the north of the spur jutting northwards from Hurtebise Farm and commanded by Vizefeldwebel Nennecke, distinguished itself in particular in this task."

As has been mentioned, enormous French pressure against the regiments left and right of Reserve Infantry Regiment 92 swamped the weakened forward defence and initially rapid progress was made by the attackers, despite the heavy losses they were incurring. One result was that many pockets of German soldiers were surrounded swiftly and forced to surrender. Others escaped by the skin of their teeth, including the *KTK* of Reserve Infantry Regiment 78, who just managed to scramble back from his command post to the sunken road west of Ailles as the leading French troops bore down on him.

Hauptmann von Saldern Commanding Officer 1st Battalion Reserve Infantry Regiment 78 [27]

"Together with my staff I had to, 'hop it across the fields' as Hauptmann Bangert … commanding officer 1st Battalion Reserve Infantry Regiment 92 put it. This was because our sole armament was the battalion commander's walking stick. My faithful batman, Zappe, known universally as 'Fritzy', together with my telephonists, was captured. When he was being led off with about twenty other Germans through the Ailette Valley, he realised that German machine guns up on the Chemin des Dames ridge were still firing at parties of Frenchmen which had broken in. By waving his coloured handkerchief he managed to direct the fire of these machine guns at his group then when everyone, including the French, dived into cover, Fritzy hurled himself into a half smashed trench which led to the rear and slipped away. A few hours later he reached me safe and sound.

"By the way, the telephonists also behaved impeccably (they had a dugout to themselves to one side and slightly closer to the enemy than mine). When they realised that they were being overrun - when the French were actually inside the dugout - at the very last minute, they telephoned me, at the risk of being shot out of hand, to inform me that they had been captured. The 'withdrawal' of my staff was also a highly dramatic business. The fact that we were not hit was more of a fluke than anything else, because the French opened fire on us at a range of only fifty metres. Finally we managed to 'disengage from the enemy', thanks to the arrival of a very low flying German aircraft, which drew all the fire and let us get away."

On the eastern end of the 19th Reserve Division front the specialist assault troop of Reserve Infantry Regiment 92, which manned positions astride the Chemin des Dames running west from the *Drachenhöhle*, was on full alert as the opening of the offensive drew close. Although the troop had not been subjected to the weight of fire directed at the forward positions, as it moved forward in support early on 16 April, its commander had ample opportunity to observe the effect of the bombardment on the depth of the German positions, the gun lines and the approach routes.

Leutnant Meißel, assault troop commander Reserve Infantry Regiment 92 [28]

"We had to move through Festieux. The village was utterly destroyed. We were amazed at the precision with which the enemy artillery had fired. Craters had been produced with almost total accuracy on road junctions, bridges and other critical points. Our artillery must have been totally neutralised; hardly a shot was to be heard. Complete ammunition columns were lying about smashed on the ground ... Once we had crossed the marshy valley we worked our way up the slopes to *Boverücken* [Bove Hill]. Here the artillery was digging in its guns once more; in one piece, but lacking ammunition. Ammunition columns were expected at any moment. Ever since 7.00 am urgent calls for destructive or defensive fire had been arriving, but they had been forced to sit idly by. In that respect the 210 mm battery near the cave was in slightly better shape. It was able to fire one shell every half hour.

"On the steep slope on the forward side of the hill, everything was in an appalling state. Shells of every calibre were strewn everywhere in wild profusion with, between them, masked up corpses. The route to the regimental command post was unmistakable, even for those new to the neighbourhood, because so many dead men littered the way. They were mostly young men - runners ... A shaft, emitting a foul stench, led down to the cave where the regimental command post was located. Below ground there was a dangerous press of humanity. Runners, sentries, reliefs and officers pushed their way around. The entire floor space was covered with wounded men. Now and then there was a dull shaking of the earth as a heavy shell impacted on the rocky surface above the cave. In these circumstances, even remaining in the cave was torture. There was a peculiarly feverish atmosphere born of dreadful uncertainty. What was happening out front and what was to made of the confused accounts of the stragglers who had made it to the rear ... ?"

Located at the western end of the Group Liebert [Liesse] sector was 16th Reserve Division, defending the Cerny area. Here the French assault force was particularly concentrated, thrusting forward in mass early on 16 April from the site of the famous sugar refinery. Despite all efforts by the forward troops of Reserve Infantry Regiment 29, some positions were overrun and numerous men were captured, including Leutnant Kahn, one of the platoon commanders.

Reserve Leutnant Süßkind 8th Company Reserve Infantry Regiment 29 [29]

"On 16 April I was in command of 8th Company. Shortly after 6.00 am the enemy attack was spotted and we fired green flares to demand defensive artillery fire. However, there was no response. 8th Company was acting as 2nd Battalion support and was occupying the first line of the Malmaison Position with two platoons. As soon as the attack was observed, Kahl's platoon moved to occupy the southern slope of *Paradieslager* because the enemy appeared over the hill from the direction of the Cerny sugar refinery and, simultaneously, set foot in the front line of Infantry Regiment 68, our neighbouring regiment. In order to prevent Kahn's platoon from being cut off, I withdrew it to the Malmaison Position. Soon, however, the enemy pushed into this position from the left flank and rear. Some enemy sections also launched up from *Paradies Grund* [Paradise Hollow] and occupied the position to our right. This meant that the company was threatened from two sides. Once the machine gun which was deployed in the front line became unserviceable, the company could not withstand the mass of enemy charging forward from the left and covered by machine gun fire, so it pulled back into the reserve position. During this withdrawal two or three sections went into captivity after a two hour battle. The other elements of the company that did not return were doubtless all killed or wounded."

Not all members of 16th Reserve Division were as fortunate. The rapid French advance in places isolated groups of defenders and the majority thus cut off were either killed or captured.

Reserve Leutnant Peters 5th Company Reserve Infantry Regiment 29 [30]

"On 16 April 5th Company was manning the front line trench near Chivy. To the right we linked up with a platoon of 3rd Company, to the left 6th Company. As a result of the ten day bombardment only two dugouts in the company sector were usable, so the entire trench garrison crammed into them because it was essential to protect them and seek shelter from the appalling fire. We too waited the start of the attack, seeing it as a release from the dreadful tension. The day before the attack the company received a 08/15 machine gun, a weapon for which we had been longing for some time. At 6.15 am 16 April the alarm ran along the front line, but we noticed that the enemy to our left were already streaming forward over the hill. The left flank of the company came under attack, but otherwise the enemy did not get into the sector.

"After 5th Company had been observing to its front for about an hour, it readjusted, leaving only a few individuals in sentry positions covering the front and placing the main forces on the left flank, guarding out towards the area between the Troyon crest and the *Chivy-Nase* [Nose]. The *Mainzer Tunnel* over there soon went up in flames and a little later there was a lack of worthwhile targets, because the French had pushed forward through the valley towards the *Chivy Nase*, which they intended to climb. From his own position in depth, the commander of 5th Company could not see very far, so he was unaware about events on the Beaulne Ridge, *Chivy-Nase* or *Paradieslager*. From the very start of the attack the green flares calling for defensive fire were disregarded and there was no German aerial observation.

"5th Company spent the morning convinced that the enemy would enjoy no success, always provided that there was a timely counter-attack. The French troops piled up and the attack stalled. It was essential to be sparing with the ammunition, so the company engaged only targets within easy range and even then with a calm rate of fire and after exact range estimation. It was useful that the company itself was not attacked at all and so could direct its fire at the halted lines of enemy out to its rear. Offizierstellvertreter von Keul, who operated the machine gun, distinguished himself in particular. The enemy observed the 5th Company fire, but rather exaggerated it. A French magazine, *La Vie Aérienne*, described it as an impregnable nest of machine guns, primarily responsible for the failure of the attack. The same magazine also carried an obituary of the airman shot down by 3rd Company. A further French aircraft appeared during the afternoon to direct mortar fire once more on the position.

"At this point the company commander, together with Offizierstellvertreter von Keul, an unteroffizier and several men of 3rd Company, went on a reconnaissance patrol to the right to check if there was still contact with 2nd Company and to see if there was any possibility of conducting a withdrawal, because it was now ever clearer that there was not going to be a counter-attack, that the forward companies were cut off and, lacking ammunition, unable to defend themselves.

"A French patrol approached from the *Chivy-Nase*. While still some distance off they called for our surrender, but departed hastily when two rifle shots were fired at them. Because of the wire obstacle, which criss-crossed a swampy area, the route to 2nd Company was extremely tricky. The trenches were impassable, so it was necessary to move above ground. The enemy pursued us with machine gun fire and we suffered casualties along the way. For a time we obtained some cover in a communication trench leading from *Paradieslager* to 2nd Company. In the meantime Unteroffizier Gangolf carried on to the rear alone and we later discovered that he managed to reach the regimental command post before the ring closed completely.

"We came under extremely heavy enfilade fire from that dominating position when we pushed forward once more towards 2nd Company. From that we were able to deduce that enemy were already occupying the company trenches. Offizierstellvertreter von Keul was seriously wounded. We were in the process of bandaging him up when we spotted the approach of lines of infantry that were following up behind the assault groups and advancing on our section of trench. These moppers-up surrounded us and took us prisoner. As I was led forward, I saw that 5th Company had already been taken away. Our 210 mm howitzers were engaging our company location and we had to pass through this curtain of fire, which was no easy matter, especially as the French, reacting to the overall failure, were in a highly agitated state."

Further to the east, the front between Berry au Bac and la Ville aux Bois was the responsibility of Groups Sissonne and Aisne, with two Bavarian divisions, 5th and 9th Reserve, in the ground holding role and about to be hit by a powerful infantry thrust, supported by a large deployment of French tanks.

Oberst Leupold Bavarian Reserve Infantry Regiment 12 [31]

" Fourteen days before the battle began, 5th Bavarian Reserve Division was deployed in the area of Berry au Bac, north of the Aisne … The French gave us fourteen days in which to establish ourselves. Within this short space of time we produced a defensive work which, defended by courageous men in the early hours of 16 April, confronted the French with resistance they had not anticipated. Bombardment with artillery and mortars began in earnest on 8 April. Within a few days, the forward positions were reduced to a rubble-strewn crater field, whose wire obstacle had been swept away. The garrison - 3rd Battalion and 1st Company from 1st Battalion - did all they could during pauses in the firing to make repairs to the worst of the damage. During the night 15/16 [April] information from higher authority reached Hauptmann Schreyer, the *KTK*, by two separate routes, informing him that he could expect to be attacked by the enemy at dawn on 16th … It was now certain that the appalling physical and mental suffering of the past few days were at an end; suffering which no pen can adequately describe and something which can only be appreciated properly by someone who has experienced such a thing.

"After a heavy, but short, concentration of fire at dawn on the 16th, powerful enemy assault groups launched forward from the *Grabenhorn* towards our positions. Rifle and machine gun fire forced them to ground swiftly; our right hand neighbours from [Bavarian] Ersatz Regiment 3 rendered valuable assistance. In response, the enemy artillery and mortars renewed the bombardment of our first position, Wreathed in smoke, dust and gas, out of which huge fountains of earth were thrown up, it seemed as though all life must have been snuffed out. Then, all of a sudden, a number of tanks rumbled forward, followed closely by large groups of infantry. There must have been five or even ten of them. The blow fell mainly against the left hand side of the position, defended by 10th and 12th Companies and the right flank of our neighbours, [Bavarian] Reserve Infantry Regiment 10.

"Anybody who did not leap to one side in time was crushed. The enemy infantry stormed into the breach and attempted to roll up the right half of the position, using hand grenades and flamethrowers and supported closely by several aircraft, flying at extremely low level, dropping hand grenades and firing machine guns. The battle raged here for hours. The dugouts were filled with numerous French prisoners. A single unteroffizier delivered eighty, including two officers, to Juvincourt. However, the enemy continued to push forward further waves, surrounding and overwhelming small groups. This was how

Oberleutnant Staub, commanding 1st Company, was captured. He, however, refused to accept this or surrender his weapon so, according to his faithful batman, he was killed at short range.[32] The battalion commander, seriously wounded in the chest, also fell into enemy hands.

"In such a situation there could be no question of continuing to fight a coordinated battle. It was virtually every man for himself as small groups held out like rocks in a stormy sea, defending desperately. One such group, sixty three strong and drawn from 9th and 11th Companies, gathered around the battalion medical officer, Oberarzt Dr Volk. Commanded by this courageous man they fought on in la Ville au Bois Wood for another two days until they had fired every last bullet ... 16 April was a day of honour for 1st Battalion. About midday the French launched another powerful attack, preceded by violent concentration of fire. We could hardly believe our eyes when we observed a column of ten to twelve tanks at a range of 600 metres. They followed one another very closely and advanced at the speed of marching infantry along the east bank of the Miette towards the regimental command post.

"At once wild rifle and machine gun fire broke out, swiftly supplemented by the artillery. Five hundred metres in rear could be seen masses of enemy infantry. The column continued to advance despite being under heavy fire from machine guns and quick-firing 37 mm guns. Some tanks were halted; the remainder ended up several hundred metres in rear of the command post, where most were knocked out by two still intact light field guns from a range of a few hundred metres. A mere few escaped to the rear. It was a wonderful sight when there was a direct hit: huge clouds of smoke with the flash of exploding ammunition. This, together with burning fuel, heated the tanks red hot ... Our losses due to the tanks were slight, but the human and material cost to the enemy was substantial There were destroyed tanks everywhere, thirty two of them in and in front of our divisional sector."

Forming part of the artillery group responsible for the defence of the la Ville aux Bois - Berry au Bac sector was Field Artillery Regiment 500. The precise subordination of this regiment is unknown, though like other regiments with numbers in the 400 and 500 series, they were probably formed in late 1916 or 1917 and allocated as independent formations to armies in a reinforcing role as required. It definitely had a coordinating gunnery role during this particular battle. Its 1st Battalion was deployed along the line of the Juvincourt - Guignicourt road and so was in the thick of the fighting. On 19 April its commanding officer wrote home describing the day.

Landwehr Hauptmann Bieberstein 1st Battalion Field Artillery Regiment 500 [33]

"I had hardly closed my eyes when the sentry shouted, 'Defensive fire!' Flares, difficult to make out in the morning mist, were dancing in the sky, but within five minutes our fire was coming down all along the line … An hour later it was reported that our First Position had been overrun and broken through … It was now our task to stop the advancing enemy. I ran to the observation post of one of our batteries that was 200 metres forward of our hill and could clearly see the French massing for a renewed assault. The word was passed at once to my batteries and soon our fire was tearing holes in their ranks. However, they had ample reserves that kept reinforcing them from the rear. Some of our infantry went forward but they were too weak against this massed attack and our reserves were only just being alerted in their camps and bivouac sites. As a result, despite their heavy losses, the French kept pushing slowly forward and we had to keep adjusting our fire several times as the battle developed.

"Suddenly Vizefeldwebel Schürer and an unteroffizier who had been with a forward observation party came running up, completely out of breath and reported to me that they had only just avoided capture because the French thrust up the right hand side of the Miette valley had made considerable progress. At that I ordered the range to be shortened even more and, together with an officer from the staff of Bavarian Reserve Infantry Regiment 12, searched in that direction. This revealed the fact that the enemy were already in our Intermediate Position in places and only about 1,000 metres further forward of us. At that I sent orders to all the battery commanders to act independently. The telephone links were long since destroyed, many of my runners had already been wounded and, furthermore, we were constantly subjected to awful gas shells, forcing us to mask up repeatedly.

"The battery commanders then acted in an exemplary fashion as I could easily see from the trench which ran behind my command post … One brave officer or man after the other fell, but the batteries did their duty. Each of them had 4,000 shells dumped on the gun lines [i.e. 1,000 per gun], so they were able to go on firing for some time … Once more I sent a runner to the rear when I received a report that some thirty tanks were crawling forward along the valley bottom. My orderly officer, Leutnant Lorenz, immediately requested permission to go forward and man a nearby anti tank gun, because we were not sure if the crew had the requisite skill. That turned out to be the case and, once an unteroffizier was killed, Lorenz himself and one other gunner served the gun, knocking out two tanks. The crews of three of them also baled out and some others turned about as shells impacted just in front of them.

"The whole thing had degenerated into close quarter battle. Our infantry could not hold out against the masses; the few still on their feet pulled back. Our hill was already outflanked on the left; to our right ten tanks were already behind us. Of these six had been halted, some of them in flames. Four others were engaged in a duel with our batteries, but were then knocked out too. Altogether I spent two hours expecting to be captured, because no reinforcing infantry arrived, then Leutnant Simm of the 4th Bavarian Battery [Bavarian

Reserve Field Artillery Regiment 5] reported to me that there was none of our infantry left to our front and that he had had to beat off two French officers at his observation post with his revolver. At that I went to the neighbouring infantry command post to ask the major personally how much longer he intended to hold and how many machine guns were still serviceable.

"I discovered that the major and his staff had withdrawn with the infantry and that there was only one usable machine gun left. The gentlemen of the heavy [artillery] group had left at 10.00 am to direct their batteries so there I was with ten infantrymen, eighteen members of my staff and my officers alone on Hill 141, which was also now the front line. I quickly had the machine gun brought into action and assembled my men, interspersed with my officers, in a small communication trench. Initially I could not get my revolver to fire, but later I did aim one shot at a low flying aircraft … machine gun bullets whistled past, shells smashed into the ground to our rear … where my batteries were still engaging tanks. From one came a violent flash of flame, three pillars of fire rose and then it was blown to smithereens just in front of one of my batteries … it was a spectacular scene of battle.

"From midday onwards it was accurate to speak of a battle *for* Hill 141 … As we manned our trench ready to defend it, a low flying enemy aircraft appeared and machine gunned us. I think that in my fury I fired my revolver at it twice; a somewhat piffling action. We could not as much as expose our noses, because we were under permanent enemy machine gun fire and the bullets cracked around our ears, mingling with the delightful musical sound of machine gun ammunition cooking off in the destroyed tanks. Four of them were knocked out behind us, eighteen others in the valley bottom. The Army Communiqué spoke of twenty six or twenty eight. Of these, twenty two fell to our batteries. This was certainly a brilliant result. The batteries fired in raging fury and one [tank] was actually knocked out within a battery position. You can well imagine how exciting it was to watch.

"For two hours the situation was extremely critical then, to our rear on the hill by Aisne Fontaine [*sic.* - Amifontaine], I saw groups of our infantry approaching carefully, apparently seeking out our front line. To indicate where this was and to avoid being caught by friendly fire, we waved our caps and shouted *Hurra!* At that, the brave Rhinelanders of *Regiment Ludendorff* [Fusilier Regiment 39] began to run towards us and arrived on our hill almost without casualties."

Hauptmann von Volckamer 1st Battalion Bavarian Reserve Infantry Regiment 7 [34]

"Huge enemy superiority meant that the front line positions of Reserve Infantry Regiments 7 and 10 were overrun in the first rush. Despite numerous local counter-strokes, by 9.00 am the enemy were established in the *Artillerie-*

Schutzstellung, which ran [southeast] from the hill south of Juvincourt to the Aisne via Mauchamp. The artillery sub-group gave their all, firing in the direct role to beat off the assault; but first 2nd and then 3rd Batteries Bavarian Reserve Field Artillery Regiment 5 were knocked out by enemy fire and French assault troops got as far as the gun lines of 8th Battery. There was hard fighting for the *Artillerie-Schutzstellung*. Oberleutnant Gahr blocked off the valley of the Aisne with the remnants of 11th Company, four machine guns and some sections from the regimental staff. Just after 12.30 pm it was possible to link up once more with 1st Battalion [Bavarian] Reserve Infantry Regiment 7.

"The regimental commander, Oberstleutnant Aschenaur, ordered the battalion to launch a counter-stroke against the *Artillerie-Schutzstellung*, but in fact at that time there were already three companies advancing on it. The battalion commander, Hauptmann Lienhardt, had previously despatched 3rd Company at 11.15 am towards the Aisne valley, so as to come to the aid of the weakened Battlegroup Gahr. At 12.45, reading the situation, he despatched 2nd Company in the direction of Pilone and 4th Company against the southern corner of Foot Artillery Wood. In other words, the regimental order for counter-strokes was already being fufilled on the initiative of Hauptmann Lienhardt. It was just as well, because there was no time to lose. Already at 12.07 pm an observer at the divisional intelligence collection point on Provais Hill, two kilometres north of Guignicourt, had noted the advance of several tanks followed by infantry along the bottom of the Miette Valley and, by 12.20 pm the long barrelled naval guns had already opened fire at seven tanks, accompanied by French assault troops, which were moving along the Aisne Valley. A short time later several armoured vehicles were seen moving on the Pilone road.

"The forward elements of the regiment, which had by then pushed forward onto the northeast slopes of Pilone Hill, could not prevent this and a huge and overwhelmingly violent artillery concentration on their position left them in no doubt that a new storm was imminent. The defenders made ready. As the first of the armoured vehicles arrived at Pilone Hill and thus found themselves under observation from the front line positions, the battle-ready guns of 8th Battery Bavarian Reserve Field Artillery Regiment 5 and 3rd Battery Field Artillery Regiment 57 opened fire and the leading tank burst in flames, hit by 8th Battery over open sights at a range of one hundred metres, just as its tracks were about to flatten the obstacle in front of Strong Point 3.

"This visible success raised the fighting spirits of the weak group of men, encouraging them to face up to the enemy. All inflexibility was set aside as Leutnant Ibach of 8th Battery had his undamaged guns pulled out of their fire positions and deployed in the open to counter the armoured monsters that were pushing forward in three columns by Mauchamp Farm, the Pilone road and the Aisne Depot. His fire knocked out five tanks and 3rd Battery Field Artillery Regiment 57 accounted for another … The red glow of the burning tanks - there were four on Pilone Hill alone - put the wind up those following. They turned away and sought shelter in rear of the protective hill. However there was no security here either.

"Much the same happened to the columns of tanks heading for Bavarian Reserve Infantry Regiment 10 via Mauchamp Farm and Bavarian Reserve Infantry Regiment 12 via the Miette Valley bottom. The sector artillery engaged most of them, but one tank was attacked by the infantry armed with hand grenades. Towards 4.00 pm those tanks still able to manoeuvre were in retreat all along the divisional front, pursued by the foot artillery, a 100mm field gun and the artillery of 9th [Bavarian] Reserve Division, whose assistance had been requested by Bavarian 5th Reserve Division as long ago as midday. About seventy tanks had been launched against the German lines in order to force a breakthrough. Of these, thirty four were scattered over the battlefield, burnt out or destroyed. Only half of them survived.

For his outstanding courage that day, Reserve Leutnant Ibach received the Knight's Cross of the Military Max Joseph Order and, henceforth, like all other such recipients, became Leutnant Ritter von Ibach. The work of the gunners had turned one of the first massed tank attacks of the war into an armoured death charge. Thirty two tanks lay destroyed in the 5th Bavarian Reserve Division sector alone. A post war study concluded, 'By the evening of the first day of battle, of the 132 tanks which had gone into action, fifty seven were reduced to burnt out heaps of twisted metal. Sixty four more had been knocked out and abandoned by their crews and only eleven remained serviceable. The losses amongst their crews - all picked men - amounted to thirty five officers and 147 other ranks.'[35] In amongst all the carnage, one solitary French tank pushed on beyond the *Artillerie Schutzstellung* as far as the regimental aid post of Bavarian Reserve Infantry Regiment 12. There its crew, comprising an officer and two other ranks, leapt out. Posting the men armed with a machine gun at one entrance to the dugout, whilst he covered the other with his pistol, the officer then relieved all present of their weapons and binoculars, informed them that they were his prisoners and then settled down to await the arrival of the French infantry, arranging for the wounds of two other tank commanders to be dressed. Despite a lengthy wait, no Frenchmen arrived; their attack had withered away in the fire of a machine gun courageously operated by Unteroffzier Heintz from a point near the regimental command post. There was nothing for the French tank crew to do but to withdraw, so this they did eventually, managing to make good their escape in the general confusion.[36] Whilst all this tank action was taking place and despite the German success, ground had been lost to the assaulting infantry so, early in the morning, regimental commanders began instituting counter measures on their own initiative, making use of reserves held in the immediate vicinity for the purpose. Taking part in one of these immediate regimental counter-strokes within the 5th Bavarian Reserve Division sector was 3rd Company Bavarian Reserve Infantry Regiment 7, which had spent the past few days whilst in support carrying out endless fatigues, repairing damaged positions and carrying stores forward. Assembled in a forward standby area during the final day of bombardment, it received its call to action early on 16 April, as this diary entry makes clear.

Reserve Leutnant Georg Will 3ʳᵈ Company Bavarian Reserve Infantry Regiment 7 [37]

" We are stood to at 7.00 am. Orders: 'The battalion is to advance at once to the Second Position and there link up with the regiment. If this is not possible the battalion is, without pausing, to launch a counter-stroke against the *Artillerieschutzstellung*.' Good grief! That is certainly food for thought: the first line lost; the enemy in the *Artillerieschutzstellung*! Contrary to expectations, the battalion reaches the Second Position without difficulty. My company is leading, filing along the trench to the left. The 4ᵗʰ and 2ⁿᵈ Companies extend the line to the right, while 1ˢᵗ Company is distributed in rear the full length of the line as a back up. The enemy has observed the move forward of the supports and brings down fire on the Second Position. With absolute precision the heavy shells land on the trench and plough up everything. Huge clods of earth hang together; however, the great blocks which lie around provide cover. But this is not a good place to be; far better to be up front!

"The company is ordered to move forward at once to the regimental command post. It is not without casualties. One heavy shell kills four or five men in one go, amongst them Unteroffizier Beck ...[38] The only reserves are a few junior members of staff, some musicians and runners. Machine guns without crews are available. The artillery in the hollow to our front sends for help. Already the batteries have almost fallen into French hands. At once the half company rushes to their assistance; the other two sections I lead through the park to its western edge, which we occupy. An observer reports, 'Eleven tanks are coming along the road. Others can be seen forward of Foot Artillery Copse.' We can already see these monsters ourselves. But relief follows swiftly. Quick work by our artillery knocks out the tanks one after the other; some bursting into flames. This frightens off the tanks at the rear and they turn about. The attack stalls; the enemy infantry ceases to thrust forward.

"At 5.45 pm this order reaches us: 'Battlegroup Gahr, comprising all the forces located in the park, together with a company of Regiment 90 [Reserve Infantry Regiment 90, part of 54th Infantry Division in corps reserve around Avaux], is to thrust down the Aisne valley to the *Artillerieschutzstellung* whilst 2ⁿᵈ and 4ᵗʰ Companies attack frontally. Advance immediately on receipt of this order.' An addendum arrives. '10ᵗʰ Regiment [Bavarian Reserve Infantry Regiment 10, also of 5ᵗʰ Bavarian Reserve Division] will also begin a counterstroke at 4.00 pm.' The order had been issued long ago; it should already have been carried out. The company strength is very low. From my company there are only two sections available, the ones manning the edge of the park. Of 11ᵗʰ Company, also mentioned in the order, not a single man is present. The Regiment 90 company arrives complete. Two of its platoons are deployed in the *Aisnegraben* [Aisne Trench], the remaining part I lead forwards, parallel to the Aisne.

A machine gun, manned by the very capable Unteroffizier Hirschmann and Infanterist Lippert, renders excellent service during this process. Moving from bound to bound, they position the gun and engage the enemy in the *Aisnewäldchen* [Aisne Copse] to our front. In this way we almost reach the line of our *Artillerieschutzstellung* and dig in. Left we are anchored on the Aisne, Right are the 39th [Fusilier Regiment 39, 50ᵗʰ Infantry Division - an *Eingreif* formation], which had been sent forward in support. Our thrust has brought us forward of the line of tanks. One is about one hundred metres in rear, two are in amongst our lines and several more a short distance further forward. They are all burnt out with their dead crew lying by them. We succeed in capturing a lieutenant and a tank driver and the following day we evacuate a seriously wounded French sergeant. I estimate that at least twenty tanks were destroyed in the 7ᵗʰ and 10ᵗʰ Reserve Infantry Regiment sectors. During the night we searched some of the monsters. From one we salvaged two serviceable machine guns, from a tank which was not burnt out we recovered a load of chocolate, white bread and tinned milk. The armour did not seem to us to be very strong. Our 'K' bullets would have been able to pierce it.[39] The men are now using the tanks for cover."

Immediately west of Bavarian Reserve Infantry Regiment 9 and forming the right forward regiment of Group Sissonne, covering Corbény, was the Bavarian Ersatz Division. Its forward regiments put up strong resistance and there was little progress towards Corbény and although a two kilometre section of the First Position was lost, this was not on the Bavarian Reserve Infantry Regiment 15 front.

Oberstleutnant Vogel 3rd Battalion Bavarian Reserve Infantry Regiment 15 [40]

"At 7.00 am on 15 April enemy artillery and mortar fire of all calibres came down with increased weight, increasing from 3.00 pm to 6.00 pm to drum fire of unsurpassable intensity. Everyone knew, without the need to put the thought into words, that the enemy assault would take place the following day. Nerves were at breaking point. The following night a massive effort was made, regardless of casualties, to improve the positions and re-establish links to the flanks and rear. It served to provided a degree of relief for the soldiers, who had spent the day stuck in enforced idleness in their cramped dugouts as they endured the destructive fire.

"The expected enemy infantry assault began at 7.30 on 16 April all along the front. The French launched forward on our sector from the Bois de Beau

Marais in strong columns. Alerted, our infantrymen rushed up from their dugouts and greeted them with a torrent of rifle and machine gun fire. The fire of the light machine guns was particularly effective. Our machine guns also brought down enfilade fire with devastating effect against the dense waves attacking to our right and left. Our artillery defensive fire, which was called for in good time and responded to promptly by our alert gunners, contributed, whilst the fire of our heavy artillery directed at the French assembly areas prevented reinforcing French troops from getting forward. No Man's Land to our front was dotted with the blue-grey uniforms of the Frenchmen who had fallen in droves. Those who remained pulled back to their start lines.

"The main French attack was beaten off completely. We did not lose one single foot of ground and the French were unable even to establish themselves in No Man's Land. Towards 10.00 am the enemy artillery began bringing heavy fire down, though the trench mortars remained silent. In front of [Bavarian] Reserve Infantry Regiment 4 the enemy attempted towards evening to work their way forward from crater to crater. Our grenade launchers fired rapidly, forcing them out of the craters, whereupon they were shot down by machine gun fire. Quite rightly the battalion looked back with pride at their victorious defence against the French offensive directed at its sector."

In addition to these minor regimental actions. the chain of command was quick to put its prepared plans into action. During the course of the afternoon there was a hasty counter-stroke by Infantry Regiment 53 of 50th Infantry Division, which was deployed in the *Eingreif* role on what became the intercorps boundary between Groups Sissonne and Aisne later that day. Unfortunately it was hastily launched, lacked weight and stalled without getting beyond the lower slopes of Hill 141; but another, organised by 213th Infantry Division at about 5.00 pm from its assembly area in the wooded area south of Goudelancourt-lès-Berrieux, was more successful, arriving in the forward area in time to beat back a renewed French assault.

Vizefeldwebel Striedieck 2nd Company Infantry Regiment 368 [41]

"Just after 9.00 am an order arrived with the companies warning them to prepare to conduct a counter-stroke. 2nd Company withdrew the first platoon from the third position into a nearby wood. There, shielded from aerial observation, assault order was prepared and rations distributed: the well known battle rations with plenty of fat. The field kitchen delivered tea and rum and postcards were passed out so final greetings could be sent home. 11.30 am came; there was feverish expectation. Hauptmann von Reden returned from Division with orders. The battle orderly came running up from the battalion command post, carrying orders, 'The Division is to launch a counter-stroke in the direction of Villers Berg. Start Line as planned along the railway line St Erme - Amifontaine. 1st

Battalion is to advance on the left flank, together with a subordinated section of Field Artillery Regiment 272 … '

"With the exception of a few casualties from 4th Company, the other companies reached the start line unscathed. It was not under fire and the companies deployed. 2nd Company had the honour of forming the first regimental wave. Reserve Leutnant Klessing, the company commander, gave out his orders. 'First platoon will shake out with three paces between each man. Second platoon is also to spread out ten paces in rear. Third platoon, also at ten paces' distance, is to form up by sections, covering off the advancing platoon'. The company dispersed and bayonets were fixed. Unteroffizier Flecke was sent forward to establish a link with Infantry Regiment 149 to our right. Vizefeldwebel Wichmeyer and I took station in front of our platoons. I was eager to see how things would develop and had no negative thoughts. Out in front of our platoons were the four company commanders, where they could overlook the ground over which we were to advance.

"Suddenly, off to our right and level with us, Infantry Regiment 149 was moving. The moment had arrived! The battalion began its assault! Hauptmann von Reden, accompanied by his adjutant, Reserve Leutnant von Otten and his staff, placed himself at the head of his battalion, his riding crop swinging gently. It was 3.00 pm. Our left was anchored on the River Miette, on the far side of which 50th Infantry Division was, like us, also conducting a counter-stroke. We kept each other in sight as far as Damary Farm, then took a short breather in a hollow behind the Second Position. To our front the farm and position were under extremely heavy enemy fire. The artillery was called forward. After a short halt we continued the advance; the enemy fire had slackened a little. South of the Fayaux river, Hauptmann von Reden waved, then used hand signals to indicate a turn to the left, in order not to lose contact with the Miette. My runner and I maintained visual contact with the staff and I passed on the order to turn to the first platoon.

" I did not look round much, so did not really notice the casualties which were beginning to mount up. Heavy enemy fire of all calibres was falling on the gun lines northwest of Juvincourt. We paused once more in low ground to the north of the Juvincourt - Corbény road. During the advance the platoons had already become entangled. The company commander ordered the platoon commanders to maintain the gaps better. A large number of enemy aircraft suddenly appeared over us. Hauptmann von Reden waved to the front vigorously. His shouted, 'Move, Lessing! Don't you want to get forward?', spurred us on and we launched forward, so as to ensure that we in the first wave were the required distance in front. A short time later enemy artillery fire, directed from the air, opened up, falling in the hollow we had just vacated and to which the other companies were moving. All the companies doubled forward as the enemy opened rapid, but ill directed, rifle and machine gun fire from the newly captured positions to the north of the site of the mill near Juvincourt.

"All this time we were suffering numerous casualties. My orderly, Bursche, fell at my side and Hauptmann von Reden was wounded; I saw him collapse right next to the enemy trench, twenty metres to our front. Behind me Reserve Leutnant Klessing shouted, 'I'm hit!' I dashed a few paces to the side and saw that he had been wounded in the lower abdomen. Calling for a medical orderly, I hurried on forwards. Shouting *Hurra!*, we closed up to the enemy. The trumpeters blew for all they were worth. The machine guns followed up in ever longer bounds, because they could hardly fire with groups of infantrymen to their front. The main body of the enemy seemed to be located in the *Artillerieschutzstellung* and in the trenches to the north of the site of the former mill. Keeping close up to neighbouring elements of Infantry Regiment 149, we pushed towards it. 2nd Company broke into the enemy trenches. Any of them who seemed inclined to resist were bayonetted; the main mass of the front line garrison was taken prisoner."

In a follow up to the storming of the position, an intense close quarter battle erupted as the positions were cleared. In one place, gathering together two assault groups and attacking the French with great violence, Vizefeldwebel Striedieck managed to break through to the remains of a Bavarian company that was cut off in an isolated stretch of trench and freed them. Subsequently and quite unusually, Striedieck was awarded the Bavarian Service Cross for his leadership and courage. This contribution to the overall counter-attack was bravely conducted and very successful, but it came at a considerable cost. Of the 1st Battalion, for example, the commanding officer and all four company commanders (Bornholt, Klessing, Klock and Schwartau[42]) became casualties, as did Leutnant Ballerstedt and one hundred and twenty other ranks.

Infantry Regiment 149, which participated alongside Infantry Regiment 368, was actually alerted at 8.15 am. Its preparations followed a similar course, as did its initial advance towards Damary Farm. Once the Berrieux - Damery Farm track had been crossed, there was a brief pause near the Third Position so that the link up with the intimate support artillery could be made. That done, the advance continued more or less southwest. However, reports began to accumulate that the enemy was located rather more to the east than had been originally visualised, so the direction of march was altered towards the southeast and Reserve Infantry Regiment 74, in reserve, was deployed to provide security to the right rear of the advance.

Oberleutnant Steinsieck 10th Company Infantry Regiment 149 [43]

"The company commanders met up with Hauptmann von Schmeling in a huge crater. Following brief orientation on the situation, a new axis of advance was given. It was at that moment that the first heavy shells came down on us - without, by the way, doing very much damage. 'Victory or death, and forwards with God!' These, the final brief words of Hauptmann von Schmeling, acted like an oath on the battle ready warriors, filling them with an almost religiously serious determination. We carried on! There was another short halt by the so-called *Pferdebusch* [Horse Copse], then at long last we were able to launch our attack in the allocated direction. The drummers beat for the attack; the trumpeters' notes rose high and clear. The Frenchmen, who must have been observing us for some time, seemed to have been jerked out of indecision, pouring small arms fire at us.

"This served merely to clarify the situation and showed us where to aim for. 'Forwards' was the word on every lip; up and at the enemy! Today we storm forward! Neither frontal rifle fire, nor enfilade machine gun fire could hold the stormers up for long. The first casualties were soon incurred, disproportionately leaders, all of whom set a good example by leading from the front. But everyone knew what was at stake, knew that most of the Juvincourt area was already in French hands and that the 12th Bavarians [Bavarian Reserve Infantry Regiment 12], under severe pressure, were holding out and awaiting our help.

"There could be no question of the assault stalling here. 'Forwards!' I shouted, and at once Leutnant Doerks leapt up, taking with him fighters from a large radius around him. We were now in really heavy small arms fire and men were going down left and right. Leutnant Fiessel, the courageous commander of 8th Company, lay in a shell hole, shot through the head. Next to him crouched his faithful batman, who later brought him back. Finally, a great weight of enemy defensive artillery fire started coming down, but it landed in rear of my battalion. Enemy tanks rolled out of Juvincourt. Our brave intimate support batteries immediately engaged them over open sights and knocked out a great many. The attack had long since passed Juvincourt Hill off to our left. Wherever we encountered the French they were paralysed with fear, falling to their knees and begging for mercy. We were able to release many isolated Bavarians, who had been pinned in their trenches or foxholes since dawn. Joyfully they joined us and formed a welcome replacement for our numerous fallen comrades."

Altogether more than 1,000 prisoners, including a regimental commander, were taken at bayonet point, together with numerous machine guns, some of which were actually still being fired when they were overrun. Once again casualties were high, with more than one hundred all ranks killed in action. These included Leutnant Fiessel 8th Company, Leutnant Ditz 2nd Machine Gun Company, Leutnant Trilling 1st Company and Fähnrich Schwab 11th Company.[44]

At about midday on 16 April, Headquarters 10th Reserve Division issued a situation report.

"On the right bank of the Aisne, the French pushed forward through the 5th Bavarian Reserve Division sector as far as Guignicourt. Efficient blocking by Fusilier Regiment Steinmetz [Fusilier Regiment 37] of its threatened right flank,

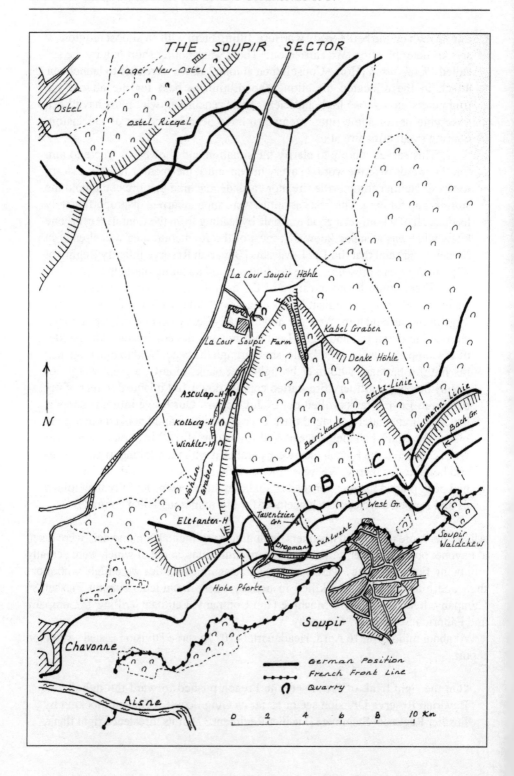

THE SOUPIR SECTOR

Lager Neu-Ostel

Ostel

Ostel Riegel

La Cour Soupir Höhle

La Cour Soupir Farm

Kabel Graben

Denke Höhle

Asculap-H.

Seitz-Linie

Hermann-Linie

Kolberg-H.

Barrikade

Bach Gr.

Winkler-H.

Höhlen Graben

A

B

C

D

West Gr.

Elefanten-H.

Tauentzien Gr.

Dropman Schlucht

Soupir Waldchew

Hohe Pforte

Soupir

Chavonne

German Position

French Front Line

Quarry

Aisne

0   2   4   6   8   10 Km

N

together with counter-strokes launched by 50th Infantry Division, prevented the feared breakthrough in this area. Within the divisional sector there was bitter fighting for Hills 108 and 91. Hill 100 is firmly in our possession. The enemy have partially occupied the third line of our neighbouring division to the left. Further to the left, in Sector E, the enemy even thrust as far as the railway embankment and some elements reached Orainviller Wood. The Guard Ersatz Division is also conducting counter-strokes there."[45]

Higher up the chain of command, the major French thrusts had been confirmed by early morning and, as early as 2.00 pm, First Army, commanded by General der Infanterie Fritz von Below, took some of the weight off both Seventh and Third Armies, assuming command of Group Brimont (formerly Seventh Army) and Groups Reims and Prosnes (formerly Third Army); then, later that same day, the Guard Corps, commanded by General der Infanterie von Quast, formed a new Group Aisne, which took over the front from la Ville aux Bois via Berry au Bac to La Neuville (two kilometres east of Cormicy). These changes, which had been thoroughly thought through and discussed in advance, produced further significant reductions in the length of front for which each headquarters was responsible and permitted much sharper focus on particular French threats during the coming days.[46]

Towards the western end of the French breakthrough sector, elements of three divisions had attacked 183rd Infantry Division around Soupir. The terrain here to the north of the village offered several advantages to the defence. There were ravines, sunken roads and no fewer than six underground quarries in the immediate vicinity: *Elefanten-, Winkler-, Kolberg-, Äsculap-, La Cour Soupir* and *Denk-Höhlen*, five of which ran north in a line between the western end of Soupir and La Cour Soupir Farm. When the battle began, the front line north of Soupir was divided into four subsectors, A-D, each the responsibility of one company of Infantry Regiment 418. From left to right they were manned by 1st, 2nd, 4th and 3rd Companies. 3rd Battalion, in support, was located as follows: 10th Company complete in the *Elefantenhöhle*, two platoon 11th Company in the *Seitzlinie*, with one platoon in the *Denkhöhle*, two platoons of 9th Company in *Soupirhöhle*, with the third in the *Kolberghöhle*. 12th Company was back in the *Ostelriegel*, but the 2nd Machine Gun Company was also underground throughout the bombardment, with two platoons in *Äsculaphöhle* and one each in *Soupirhöhle*, home to Major von Oven's 2nd Battalion command post and *Denkhöhle*, which also housed the 1st Battalion command post under Major Bade.

It can be seen at a glance how much the layout depended on the availability of these huge natural shelters and how valuable it was to have been able to keep the support battalion totally protected during the preparatory bombardment. A complex of trenches linked these features and the fighting raged throughout the 16 April for possession of the various quarries. Much of the day was spent in hand to hand combat and some quarries changed ownership more than once. It was small wonder, therefore, that Infantry Regiment 418 was generally more successful in slowing the advance than were the other regiments on its left and right, both of which were forced back. Infantry Regiment 184 had to withdraw about one and a half kilometres, leaving the French in possession of the whole of the high ground between Bois de la Bovette and Ferme du Metz, adjacent to a lock on the Canal de l'Oise west of Moussy-sur-Aisne.

The battle for Soupir was an extremely bloody affair. Casualties amongst the units of the French 56th Division were extremely high as they attempted to force a way through resolute and well deployed defenders. These descriptions of events of 16 April by men who participated in the battle in sub-sectors B and A immediately north of Soupir help to explain why.

Alfred Beermann 2nd Company Infantry Regiment 418 [47]

"At dawn I had just returned from the sap when the duty unteroffizier raised the alarm, 'The French are attacking!' Because I was still wearing my equipment I was first up top. In the re-entrant the enemy had already overrun the second line and was massing to our front in huge shell craters. This was their undoing because we had a clear view into the craters from our position. With only five riflemen on hand we nevertheless immediately brought down rapid fire. I gave orders only to fire into the craters which were full to overflowing, because it was essential to hit with every shot. Our fire had an extraordinary effect. In no time at all some Frenchmen sought relief in flight. 'Shoot strictly into the craters!' I ordered once again. Because when I was in training I was the best shot in my platoon, I undertook the job of bringing down those of the enemy who were trying to get away. Gefreiter Schulz loaded for me so that there were no pauses. 'None of them will get away!', I shouted and with every hit our confidence grew.

"All of a sudden an aircraft appeared and dropped a bomb to our left. Comrade Eichoff was torn apart and collapsed at my feet, streaming blood. He died in the arms of the medical orderly only seconds later. We went on firing and ever more Frenchmen ran to the rear. There was a lieutenant amongst them. The first shot at him missed, but he was taking bounds which were too long. The second bullet did not hit either; a curse escaped my lips. Finally, with my third shot, I hit him in the head and brought him down as he tried to leap over a shell hole. He collapsed and lay completely still.

"At this point a few Frenchmen attempted to get into our section of trench from the right [west]. Comrade Koschinsky covered us from that direction. He did his job well, so well that we could calmly continue our destructive work. Ignoring murderous machine gun fire, I raised myself up to see if the enemy were creeping up on us. In the same instant a ricochet smashed through the front of my helmet. The bullet was burning hot and I fell back, tearing my helmet off. 'Nothing's happened!' shouted my comrade. The bullet had been deflected upwards and was resting on my head. We carried on shooting. Panic broke out among the French whose dead were already lying one on top of the other. They took to their heels. '*Hurra!* Beaten off!', we shouted, just as a second bullet tore through the cuff of my jacket.

"But what's that? Suddenly French soldiers forced their way into out trench from the rear. I saw a bayonet thrust towards me and saved myself by diving head first into the dugout entrance - captured! The Frenchmen shouted at me to come out. A wounded Frenchman held his rifle to my head and was about to fire. Instantly I twisted away like a slippery eel. The enemy bullet tore open my collar badge. Flight was useless. I was definitely captured. I must have been a dreadful sight. As my comrade Fritz Held later described, my uniform was in ribbons and red with the blood of my fallen comrade. I was white with shock. So I went into French captivity. A few days later I read the army communiqué in a French newspaper. According to it, 'We made progress all along the front. Only around Soupir did we encounter stiff resistance and suffered severe casualties. It was not possible for us to scale the steep slopes. However, we later captured large quantities of guns and mortars.' At that my feelings of depression were lifted. It was my regiment, 2nd Company amongst it, which had fought for Soupir and in particular for the re-entrant, out of which thousands of wounded were carried. Having been a prisoner for twenty eight months, I was the first man to escape from our prisoner of war camp and regain my golden freedom."

Musketier H Siersleben 1st Company Infantry Regiment 418 [48]

"At long last on 16 April, a day I shall never forget, the enemy infantry attack began. With urgent shouts, the few commanders called their handfuls of men together. The weapons were covered with mud, the hands stiff and cramped; nevertheless, here and there came the noise of a machine gun. Hand grenades exploded as we crawled or leapt from shell hole to shell hole, giving ground gradually because we could not fight off the huge superiority in manpower. It was complete and utter chaos! But the enemy hesitated; they had not expected to encounter resistance but then, as though sent from heaven, the reserves got involved and our defence stiffened more or less along the line where our third position ran three days ago [the so-called *Seitz-Linie*]. The enemy attacked repeatedly, but were beaten back in hand to hand fighting. As soon as it began to go dark, we pushed forward and spent the night near Ostel and then in the Malmaison Position.[49] As dawn broke the French attacked again. They were reinforced with flamethrowers but before they could be used they were knocked out with well aimed shots. Enemy aircraft buzzed around like poisonous wasps. Guns firing at short range ploughed up our thin lines yet again then suddenly, anticipated, but still a surprise, another attack came in. Weapons were levelled but some jammed. Hand grenades exploded and soon we were enveloped in thick smoke in which it was barely possible to distinguish friend and foe.

"Our losses were huge, but we were still in possession of the Chemin des Dames. Hand to hand fighting broke out again, during which my pal Neddermann, a Dutch wartime volunteer, was killed, then the French fell back again. It was really strange feeling for us to note that the attackers constantly pulled back, or at least did not push forward energetically. We were permanently filled with fury because enemy artillery fire was constantly being aimed at us. We had now become Battalion Hillebrand [normally commander 12th Company]. Ammunition reached us forward now and then, as did water and food. We felt like going down on our knees to thank our comrades who had forced their way forward in terrible circumstances and then remained with us. It was no different for the 184th and 440th [Infantry Regiments 184 and 440]. Severe losses also forced Infantry Regiment 184 to pull back slowly and to consolidate around Malval Farm.[50] The situation was identical for Infantry Regiment 440, deployed between us and the 184th and also for Field Artillery Regiment 183, all of whose observers had become casualties. 3rd Battery had found it impossible to hold on by the Prinz Heinrich Höhle, and wanted to withdraw, but no teams of horses could be got through. In any case, three of its guns had already been knocked out and the fourth was also later smashed by enemy fire. 7th Battery had to blow up three guns in Grélines hollow[51] and a fourth was dismantled. Of the 90 mm guns of 479 Battery, five had to be blown up to prevent them falling into enemy hands."

Along those parts of the front, such as the Craonne - Cerny sector, where it was obvious that the French had placed their best attacking troops in dense masses, care had been taken to reduce the frontages of the ground holding divisions. 5th Guards Infantry Division, for example, was placed along a sector so narrow that Grenadier Guard Regiment 3 and Infantry Regiment 20 were the only ground holding regiments in the forward sector when the attack fell. In depth, poised to intervene, was 1st Guards Infantry Division, acting as one of the *Eingreif* divisions for Group Liesse, but such was the resistance put up by the Grenadier Guards in particular that the initial response in this area came from the other formation of the division, namely Footguard Regiment 3, held back in support in the depth of the divisional sector. A great deal of thought had been devoted as to how best to deploy this regiment in the event of a major assault, but its actual experience provides ample proof of the adage that no plan survives the first contact with the enemy.

Hauptmann Egon von Loebell Footguard Regiment 3 [52]

"The tank attack was an interesting performance for we spectators. We could clearly see nine of these monsters driving in single file in the area of Ville aux Bois. The pleasure did not last long because they were soon bracketed by our artillery. That halted them and several of them sent up great pillars of flame. It appeared that their fuel had caught fire. It was not long before we received a report, 'The enemy has broken in near Ville aux Bois'. Simultaneously, Brigade informed us that the French had overrun the front line trenches of the *Tauentzien Regiment* [Infantry Regiment 20] and that fighting was still going on for the second trench.[53] It later transpired that [the enemy] had managed to push further forward in the neighbouring division to the right [19th Reserve]. The battalion of Reserve Infantry Regiment 73 to the right of the *Tauentzien Regiment* was completely overrun; the battalion staff either killed or captured. The assaulting French troops pushed forward into the Ailette valley, which was later very unpleasant for us. The sole regiment in the entire corps sector which held its ground was *Regiment Elisabeth* [Grenadier Guard Regiment 3], the only guard regiment deployed forward. We were also able to share the glory in that, after we had been deployed into position near Craonne on the Chemin des Dames, we not only lost no ground, but were also able to free prisoners who had been taken earlier.

"It did not take long for the expected order for a regimental counter-stroke to reach us. For weeks the battalions had been rehearsing the mechanics of this attack. We were to form up in the Ailette Valley and to launch forward from there. Oberstleutnant von Schönstadt gave orders that the Fusiliers [3rd Battalion], the 2nd Battalion, less two companies which had already deployed, together with 2nd and 3rd Machine Gun Companies, commanded by Hauptmann von Wangenheim, were to work their way forward in to the designated area, shake out and launch the counter-stroke. Meanwhile 1st Battalion and 1st Machine Gun Company were to move to covered positions on the northern slope of Bove Hill and remain there at the disposal of the regiment. It worked out quite differently! Most of the telephone links were destroyed. Orders and counter-orders flew backwards and forwards. For example, Brigade despatched elements of 1st Battalion (which was meant to have been kept intact in reserve) forward to Bouconville in the Ailette valley.

"In the end, half of 1st Battalion had to be subordinated to the *Elisabeths*, whose right flank had been endangered by the break in in the *Tauentzien* sector, so that [the enemy] could be rolled up out of the *Tauentzien* second line from their sector. This particular counter-stroke eventually failed due to inadequate artillery support. As the battle developed the remainder of 1st Battalion, together with 1st Machine Gun Company, was despatched to Sector *Elisabeth*. However, most of 1st Machine Gun Company, with four weapons commanded by Leutnant Chamier, ended up with the 73rd [Reserve Infantry Regiment 73]; in other words, with the neighbouring division. Here they played a large part in halting the French counter-attack, but the battalion was totally wiped out.[54] Crossing the crest of Bove Hill was very difficult and thoroughly unpleasant for the companies. This was because the entire German artillery was located on the crest or forward of it and it was the subject of furious French fire when the attempted breakthrough failed. In addition, low flying French aircraft attempted to halt the forward movement with their machine guns.

"Gradually the regiment, less the mortar company, succeeded in gaining the Ailette Valley. Here the battalions found themselves out of the frying pan and into the fire, because the French were bombarding the valley to prevent the movement of reserves. The splintering continued because Oberstleutnant von Peschke, commander of *Regiment Tauentzien*, directed that one company was to be deployed into each of his two battalion sectors, because he was fearful for his Third Position. A further company was to form a blocking position in the sector of the 73rd where, as has been mentioned, the enemy had got a long way forward. 3rd Machine Gun Company under its able, prudent and battle proven commander, Reserve Leutnant Wegener, was despatched to the *Tauentzien* sector, which was the most threatened. In this way, as we had always feared, our wonderful, tough regiment was dispersed and a unified thrust right up to the forward trenches was out of the question. Of course it was only later that we obtained clarity about the situation just described. That afternoon no such overview was possible. Given the situation, how could it be otherwise?"

So much for planning and preparation, but the difficulties of the day did not end there. With the various elements of his regiment scattered far and wide in the sectors of two different divisions, the overall situation unclear, but certainly extremely difficult, the commander received orders that same afternoon for a completely different task; Hauptmann von Loebell once more:[55]

"At 4.30 pm orders reached the staff that our regiment was to relieve Regiment *Tauentzien* during the night; a very 'pleasant' task given the confused battle picture and our complete scattering. At that moment the regimental commander commanded nothing but the Mortar Company, located in reserve back in the camp at Courtrion. Even the assault pioneer company was scattered everywhere forming message relay teams, this being the only practicable method of transmitting orders. In order to obtain at least some clarity about the situation, Leutnant von Schlieben was sent to the *Tauentzien* command post, located up on the Bove Crest near La Bove Chateau. At 7.00 pm the *Herr Oberstleutnant*, Lonicer and I, together with some members of the regimental staff, moved to the new command post. It was good to be able at least to see where we were going but, on the other hand, the fact that our artillery was firing in preparation for the planned attack at 8.00 pm was not exactly favourable because, as ever, the French were not guilty of leaving it unanswered. If we veered off to avoid a battery which was under particularly heavy fire, we simply bumped into another that was firing. The roaring of shells overhead did not add to the appeal either. In this unenviable state we worked our way forward and soon we could see the ruins of La Bove Chateau [located about one kilometre due north of

Bouconville]. A wall running along the edge of the park was our marker; the command post was supposed to be located near its end.

"We came across an appalling sight. A group of ammunition wagons had been destroyed here and the ground was covered with dead horses and next to them, shocked and with their heads hanging down, were wounded horses. Who was going to help them? Who could help them? Perhaps their salvation would be another shell that would put them out of their misery. It was still daylight but, despite that, at a sharp trot - the half starved, exhausted, horses could no longer gallop - columns bringing much needed ammunition approached. The greatest respect is due to these men. Theirs is anything but child's play. These brave drivers bear a far heavier burden than other rear details. It is an especially hateful task.

"We headed for our park wall but, unfortunately, we realised that at the end of the wall, our objective, shell after shell was landing and all of them of the heaviest calibres. We thought it best to take a roundabout route to our objective via the slopes leading down to the Ailette Valley. During this process we became split up and it had gone dark by the time I and some others arrived at the command post. It was an unfinished mined dugout. The entire entrance was crammed with wounded men. To get to the staff I had to climb carefully over them. The space in which they were sitting was so small that it was only just possible to move around. Suddenly there was a shout of, 'Gas!' We masked up quickly and the wounded were protected with covers.

"It was a most unpleasant feeling to be wedged together deep underground and then to be gassed. Luckily it was not too bad; it had been caused by a few gas shells. Because it would have been impossible to accommodate all the members of our staff in the dugout, it was decided to send Arnim to the bivouac site in Maison Rouge Wood. I myself was ordered to go to the camp in Mauregny Wood and to supervise training of the machine gunners. That made sense. There was no way I could control all the machine guns centrally when the companies were so dispersed. Their use would have to be directed by the sector commanders. This meant that the battle was over for me. This went against the grain, but I contented myself with the thought that I had certainly participated in many fights since 1914 and, equally, it was of the greatest importance that the training of the machine gunners went well, in order that the combat strength of the regiment would be enhanced very swiftly once the light machine guns arrived."

Of the numerous *Eingreif* divisions poised to plug potential gaps in the lines and to carryout counter-attacks, 50th Infantry Division, comprising Fusilier Regiment 39 and Infantry Regiments 53 and 158, located in assembly areas between Amifontaine and Prouvais, was on immediate standby to intervene in the critical area around Juvincourt, la Ville aux Bois and Berry au Bac, defended by Bavarian 5th and 9th Reserve

Divisions. The French army clearly regarded it as a vulnerable point and, as has been discussed, they aimed a huge tank attack at the Bavarians where the front line bent away sharply south southeast towards Reims. The German defenders, very much aware of the risk of a breakthrough at this point, had a carefully planned response prepared and ready to be executed. Whilst the bombardment was still coming down, the relevant reserve formations were already moving forward from cover to cover. Fusilier Regiment 39, for example, spent the night 15/16 April bivouacked in woods north of Juvincourt, near to Malmaison. It was to have one of the hardest tasks on 16 April.

Whilst the dense columns of French infantry of V Corps were storming forward and massed tanks were on the move against Berry au Bac, General von Below, commanding First Army, gave the order *Freudenfest* [Festival] that launched his *Eingreif* divisions forward. At that, Regimental commanders reported to Headquarters 50th Infantry Division at Magnivillers Farm, south of Malmaison, at 10.00 am to receive final orders and to begin one of the more successful German counter-actions of the day. There the General Staff Officer, Hauptmann Weise, summarised the situation, 'The enemy has thrust forward along the Pontavert - Corbény road, to the west of Villers Berg and along the Miette Valley'.

The reaction was immediate. By 11.00 am the marching columns were heading south, with reconnaissance teams led by officers out in front to observe the situation for themselves. One hour later Fusilier Regiment 39 received a further report that the French had entered Juvincourt. After a short pause for reorganisation and to shake out the various attack waves, by about 1.40 pm the battalions in line abreast crossed the Amifontaine - Prouvais road and advanced to contact. As 2nd Battalion launched an attack towards *Bahnwald* [Railway Wood = Bois Envain, astride the railway], news arrived that the enemy were in Guignicourt and this was followed closely by an order from 100 Infantry Brigade to ignore the wood and swing the axis of advance round towards Mauchamp Farm, south of Juvincourt, and the eastern slopes of the Miette valley. A despatch rider on horseback galloped forward and just managed to reach the leading elements in time to permit the change to be made.

A few minutes before 3.00 pm 1st and 3rd Battalions had shaken out along the line of the railway when a company commander from Bavarian Reserve Infantry Regiment 10, 5th Bavarian Reserve Division, arrived with information that the enemy were now established on the heights north of the farm. This was then reinforced by an officer of the foot artillery who described their whereabouts in some detail. Four surviving tanks appeared along the road running towards Guignicourt but, within minutes, the German artillery had left them knocked out and blazing. At 3.15 pm Major Wasserfall had given out confirmatory orders. 1st and 3rd Battalions were now to take and hold the *Artillerieschutzstellung*, here known to the French as the Tranchée de Wurtzbourg, then, in a second phase, the advance was to continue to Mauchamp Farm.

No sooner had the troops set off than heavy French artillery fire came down. However, such was the speed of advance that the companies were soon clashing with French infantry advance posts in amongst the cluster of small woods and copses northeast of Mauchamp Farm. It is difficult to be precise about the locations, because the German and French names for the various wooded areas are completely different. What is clear is that the French, who were able to summon reserves and call on the support of another small group of tanks, forced the Fusilier Regiment 39 companies to consolidate and dig in, though elements of 3rd Battalion continued to press forward, coming under heavy machine gun fire as they advanced near Guignicourt, but succeeding in linking up with remnants of Bavarian Reserve Infantry Regiment 7 and the unfortunate cut off gunners of Field Artillery Regiment 500; and completely halting any further French advance in the area.

The brigade reserve under Hauptmann Wolfram arrived and reinforced 3rd Battalion then, shortly after 5.00 pm, the entire regiment moved forward once more. An hour later Hauptmann von Blomberg, commanding 3rd Battalion, reported that his men had crossed the Guignicourt - Juvincourt road, despite being under heavy fire; and shortly before 8.00 pm Hauptmann Kletsche, 1st Battalion commander, reported that parts of his unit were now occupying the *Artillerieschutzstellung*. Already other parts of the regiment had been beating off renewed French attempts to get forward. The few remaining French tanks had been knocked out and, as night fell, a continuous line was established and developed through the night. This decisive counter-attack by Fusilier Regiment 39 halted the French thrust in this area in its tracks and, despite heavy fighting to come, hardly any more progress was made northwards by the French army in this particular sector. The cost to the French army had been high, but Fusilier Regiment 39 had also been hit hard. Its casualties during the attack amounted to three officers and seventy other ranks killed, with eleven officers and 240 other ranks wounded.[56]

Not all the *Eingreif* divisions were fully committed on 16 April, though most of them were at least moved further forward. In depth behind 16th and 19th Reserve Divisions were the regiments of 20th Infantry Division occupying holding areas between Monthenault and Bièvres. One member of an uncommitted rifle company later described how the day unfolded.

Vizefeldwebel Kramer 10th Company Infantry Regiment 77 [57]

"12th Company remained behind in the depth position as battalion reserve while the remainder went forward. It was now a matter of exploiting every piece of woodland, every rise in the ground as cover. Because of balloon observation, we doubled past Chéret, crossed the Bruyères - Monthenault road, moved up hill and down dale through the wooded areas, hurrying along in one great battalion-sized single file. The sun burnt down out of the sky, the first warm sun of spring. Our knapsacks dug into our backs, harder with each passing hour; there was not a single drop of water to be had. If only we were already at our destination. We had not closed our eyes for two days and nights. There was no use worrying about it; we had to get on, even if old wounds were playing up and hurting. We passed Les Carrières Farm and moved along the crest of the hill towards Presles, about seven kilometres south of Laon.

"We constantly moved through woods, right through the undergrowth and brambles. It was fortunate that one of my men who had gone out on one of the nightly patrols from the destroyed and abandoned Bièvres, unconcerned about the falling shells, had managed to plunder a load of biscuits. At least we had something to nibble on from time to time. 'Take cover! Aircraft!' The whole battalion lay flat on the floor of the wood. What was it? A French aircraft dropped out of the clouds, diving like a bloody hawk towards us and opened fire with his machine gun. Over there our dear old captive balloon near Chéret was on fire, blazing as it fell earthwards. A dark mass floated slowly, suspiciously, towards the ground. The occupant had baled out, hanging from his parachute. He was now the target of the French machine gun, but he was not hit and he arrived safely on solid ground. Airmen, our famous fighter pilots, arrived on cue, then disappeared with their French colleagues into the clouds to settle their dispute up there. Good, we were able to continue.

"We changed direction southeast, passing Chaumont Farm on Hill 207 and filed along the wood edge along the road to Colligis, which we reached at 7.00 pm. The fourth platoon of each company remained behind in the *Colligishöhle* to act as a labour force and ration carrying party. We paused briefly. It began to pour with rain as the heavens opened and we pushed on through the centre of the village. There were a few destroyed houses, their windows smashed. It was as though the Wings of Death had fluttered over it. A strange and sinister atmosphere prevailed; it was almost tangible. We pushed on half left from the village, crossing the swampy ground and water meadows between Pancy and Crandelain, with fifty metre intervals between sections. With crater overlapping crater it seemed as though titanic forces had ploughed the ground up. The companies closed up; to our front was the steep crest of Courtecon, which provided cover from view.

"Meanwhile night had fallen and complete groups of wounded crossed our path. 'What's it like up front?' 'Awful, but they can't break through! Give 'em hell, comrades!' Wagons pulled by teams of four or six, heavy laden with ammunition, lurched past, driving forward determinedly through this morass of craters, bog and mud. With six or eight men pushing the spokes, sharp cracks of the whips on the horses' backs, the nags strained, their nostrils flaring, as they pulled hard twice, three times - as though they knew what was at stake, then the wagon was through and they galloped on. We passed Courtecon, which was under heavy fire, to our left then, with our last reserves of energy, we tackled the steep hill. The countless flares, both green and white, helped us to make out our route. It was a wonderful lightshow in the night sky, but we could not devote much attention to it. It lit our way and that was enough.

"We carried on up the hill, stumbling over tree stumps, wire and wooden steps. Thank heavens, we were now at the highest point. We had completed the approach march. Despite balloon observation, despite passing through wild gun fire, the battalion had not lost a single man. What a miracle. Nobody could quite believe it! Now the dance could begin. We should have been deployed straightaway, but the forward trenches were still full of assault troops. We spread ourselves out in sheds that had lost their protective roofs and in a few dugouts. Here we crammed in, wringing wet, covered in mud and in a miserable state. We leaned on our knapsacks and smoked. The artillery battle raged outside. The ground heaved with the impact of heavy shells and mortar bombs and, amidst all the racket, was the sound of hand grenades and the crazed rattle of the machine guns. It was 4.00 am. The order arrived, 'Sort out your assault order!' Carefully, in the dark the heavy wet things were packed, the iron rations stowed away and steel helmets donned.

"Off to battle! - snow, hail, rain and an icy east wind. It suited the night time chaos and the gruesome din of battle all around perfectly. A few hundred metres along the slope and then we disappeared into a trench. The attacks could begin. The first light of dawn glimmered. We worked our way forward through the knee deep mud from crater to crater towards the *Rheinlandgrabenriegel* [Rhineland Trench Stop Line] which we, 10th Company, were to clear. The first casualties [occurred]. Here a man went down, there another, many whom I had known for so long that they had become good friends - 'I cannot give you my hand, but may you be granted eternal life my faithful comrade'.[58] We were soon in the stop line, then, thud! I was hit again - a shell splinter in the left thigh. Hell, not my left leg again! It happened during the last regimental attack in Poland, now yet again?! Into a hole, trousers down and field dressing applied. 'All the best comrade, get well soon, see you in the Homeland!' Five hours I lay under drum fire; for the time being I could do nothing. That same night I was taken to a field hospital and slept the sleep of the dead. Not even the shells the enemy fired near Laon could wake me."

Thus ended this epochal day on the Aisne front. The dislocation of expectations of the French army must have been simply dreadful. They had been told, assured, that they would carry all before them yet, by any objective standard, their gains, measured against the appalling losses they had suffered, were pathetic. The seeds of what were to become known euphemistically as the 'collective indiscipline' of the French army had been well and truly sown.

Army Communiqué 17 April 1917 [59]

"Along the Aisne one of the greatest battles of this colossal war and, therefore, of the history of the world, is underway. Preparation by the French artillery and mortars began on 6 April and continued ceaselessly. Of unprecedented duration, volume and weight, it sought to render our positions ready to be stormed, knock out our batteries and wear down our troops. Early in the morning of 16 April a massive assault was launched on a forty kilometre front from Soupir on the

Aisne to Bétheny, north of Reims. Conducted by strong infantry forces, supplemented by the move forward of reserves, the French, operating deeply echeloned, attempted to break through. During the afternoon the French threw in fresh masses into the battle and fought strong subsidiary attacks against our front between the Oise and Condé sur Aisne. Because of contemporary fire plans that flatten positions and produce great crater fields, rigid linear defence is no longer possible; instead there is a fortified zone organised in depth. As a result the fight for the forward positions ebbs and flows. The aim is to weaken the enemy decisively by inflicting bloody losses, whilst sparing our own, even if materiel is lost in the process. These aims were fully achieved thanks to outstanding leadership and the brilliant courage of the troops. Yesterday the great French attempt at break through with its distant objectives failed totally. The enemy suffered heavy, bloody, losses and we took more than 2,000 prisoners. In the few places where the enemy forced a way into our positions, the battle continues and renewed enemy attacks are expected. The troops are facing the coming heavy fighting with complete confidence."

Notes

[1] Miquel *Le Gâchis des généraux* p 160.
[2] GOH pp 282-284.
[3] *ibid.* pp 307-308.
[4] See the map of the Soupir sector for a clear illustration of the technique.
[5] Loebell *Tagebuch* p 240.
[6] GOH p 285
[7] Meier-Gesees *Vater Wills Kriegstagebuch* pp 140-143.
[8] Dellmensingen *Das Bayernbuch* p 418.
[9] Hillebrand History Reserve Infantry Regiment 29 pp 139-140.
[10] GOH p 290.
[11] Jordan History Reserve Infantry Regiment 81 p 150.
[12] Rosenberg-Lipinsky History Grenadier Guard Regiment 3 pp 436-437.
[13] Hillebrand *op. cit.* pp 140-141.
[14] Guttenberg History Bavarian Reserve Field Artillery Regiment 5 p 112. The story, as circulated subsequently, was that a young German diplomat, who had only recently been posted to the Hague and was thus unknown within the diplomatic community, had overheard a conversation in a coffee house between the British and French military attachés, during which the offensive was discussed.
[15] Rosenberg-Lipinsky *op. cit.* pp 437-439.
[16] To 21st century eyes this is disgracefully racist. However, that was the name given to a spur of land just west of Craonne and it appears as such on contemporary maps. The old German army was extremely racist in outlook, referring, for example, to all French black colonial troops generically as *Senegalneger*. It is of course questionable if it differed much, or even at all, in this respect from the other white belligerents at the time.
[17] 3rd Battalions were known as 'Fusilier' battalions in the old German army, hence the use of the word 'fusiliers' to mean members of it, regardless of their rank.
[18] It is impossible to place a value on this remark, which was written in hindsight when the extent of the subsequent French mutinies was known. It is, nevertheless, feasible.

[19] Kellinghusen *Kriegserinnerungen* pp 594-595

[20] *Creute* is a local dialect name for an underground stone quarry, so the best translation is probably 'Quarry cave.'

[21] Kellinghusen is wrong about this. The Moroccan Division was engaged against Aubérive, well to the east of Reims on 16 April. It was the right flank formation of the French XVII Corps. African troops of II Colonial Corps did attack both 16th and 19th Reserve Divisions, with10[th] Colonial Division carrying out the initial assault on Reserve Infantry Regiment 92.

[22] This appears to be the only mention in the literature of such weapons. It is impossible to judge how much credence to give the story.

[23] Kellinghusen *op. cit.* pp 596-598

[24] This is an unexplained German pun. The man's name must have been Ferdinand and *Pferd* is German for horse. Clearly something linked the two.

[25] Reserve Leutnant Theodor Norberg died on 17 April 1917. He is buried in the German cemetery at Sissonne Block 5 Grave 788.

[26] Kellinghusen *op. cit.* p 598.

[27] Möller History Reserve Infantry Regiment 78 pp 211-212.

[28] Blankenstein History Reserve Infantry Regiment 92 pp 253-254.

[29] Hillebrand *op. cit.* pp 135-136.

[30] *ibid.* pp 138-139.

[31] Dellmensingen *op. cit.* pp 421-422.

[32] Oberleutnant Emil Staub is buried in the *Kamaradengrab* of the German cemetery at Sissonne. The *Volksbund* has wrongly recorded his date of death as 15 April 1917.

[33] Benary *Das Ehrenbuch der deutschen Feldartillerie* pp 457-459

[34] Dellmensingen *op. cit.* p 419.

[35] Guttenberg History Bavarian Reserve Field Artillery Regiment 5 p 124.

[36] Demmler History Bavarian Reserve Infantry Regiment 12 p 221.

[37] Meier-Gesees *op. cit.* pp 148-150.

[38] This is quite possibly Unteroffizier Johann Beck, killed 'near Guignicourt' on 16 April 1917 and buried in the *Kamaradengrab* of the German cemetery at Soupir.

[39] 'K' bullets is shorthand for SmK armour piercing ammunition, issued to the infantry for use in machine guns and rifles.

[40] Dellmensingen *op. cit.* pp 419-420.

[41] Rhein History Infantry Regiment 368 pp100-102.

[42] Reserve Leutnant Wilhelm Schwartau succumbed to his wounds on 18 April and is buried in the German cemetery at Sissonne Block 9 Grave 194.

[43] Selle History Infantry Regiment 149 pp 258-259.

[44] With the exception of Trilling, all those named have known graves. Reserve Leutnant Herbert Fiessel and Reserve Leutnant Heinrich Ditz are buried in the German cemetery at Sissonne Block 9 in Graves 194 and 192 respectively. Offizierstellvertreter (Vizefeldwebel) Michael Schwab is buried in the *Kamaradengrab* of the German cemetery at Cerny-en-Laonnois.

[45] Meißner History Reserve Infantry Regiment 37 p 235.

[46] GOH pp 328-329.

[47] Christian History Infantry Regiment 418 pp 236-237.

[48] *ibid.* pp 234-235.

[49] It is probable that Siersleben was confused about this. He may have been referring to something which happened at a later date. According to both the history of Infantry Regiment 418 pp 38-40 and FOH 2e Pochette Carte 52, the French advance was halted on 16 April two kilometres short of Ostel.

[50] Located about one kilometre northeast of Braye-en-Laonnois. Once again this refers to a date later in the battle. By nightfall on 16 April, the French front line in this sector was still one kilometre south of Braye.

[51] Located about three kilometres northeast of Soupir.

[52] Loebell *op. cit.* pp 250-252.

[53] This message was probably timed at around 7.00 am. According to Doerstling History of Infantry Regiment 20 pp 290-291, although the weak forward garrisons were overrun swiftly, by the time the battle for the second trench was in full swing, isolated shots from members of the regiment cut off right forward could still be heard as late as 7.30 am.

[54] Presumably this refers to a Reserve Infantry Regiment 73 battalion.

[55] Loebell *op. cit.* pp 252-256.

[56] Rudorff History Fusilier Regiment 39 p 130.

[57] Foerster *Wir Kämpfer im Weltkrieg* pp 330-331.

[58] This is a quotation from the German soldiers' lament for a fallen comrade, *Ich hatt' einen Kamaraden* by Ludwig Uhland (1826).

[59] Christian *op. cit.* p38.

CHAPTER 5

The French Assault
in Champagne

A s April opened, it was already quite clear to the German High Command that there was going to be a major offensive launched either side of Reims along a front bounded by approximately Soissons in the west and east to Somme-Py and Ripont. So certain were they that reinforcements on a large scale were despatched to the area, so as to reduce the width of divisional sectors and to place a plentiful supply of reserve divisions well forward behind the main defensive line. Typical of this development was the deployment of 29th Infantry Division to Generalleutnant de Beaulieu's Group Prosnes (XIV Corps) and its insertion south of Nauroy between 14th Reserve Division to its west and 214th Infantry Division to the east. This placement of a fourth ground holding division in the part of the corps sector known as the *Wald-Champagne* [Champagne Forest] made a strong Intermediate Position anchored on a ridge of high ground (the *Langer Rücken*) even more formidable. Here the lines had never moved since they were first established in 1914.

The arrival of 29th Infantry Division meant that Group Prosnes now had four ground holding divisions at its disposal to cover its twenty kilometre frontage, with Saxon 32nd Infantry Division available in the *Eingreif* role. Here again, as on the Aisne, the defenders had several advantage. The terrain was extensively wooded and hilly. At its western end it adjoined the Group Reims sector, which benefitted from possession of the mountainous Berru feature east of Reims, complete with its pre-war French fortifications; whilst its eastern flank rested on the fortified village of Aubérive and the valley of the River Suippes.

Located two to three kilometres north of the German front line was the so-called *Langer Rücken* [Long Ridge], a ridge line seven kilometres in length, along which ran the *Zwischen-Stellung*/R1 Line [Intermediate Position]. *Mont Cornillet* (208 m), one and a half kilometres southeast of Nauroy, was the key terrain in the 29th Division sector then, in a line to the east, came the *Hexensattel* [Witches' Col] and, in the 214th Division sector, successively *Lug ins Land* [Also written as *Luginsland* = Watchtower/Lookout Post] (221 m), *Hochberg* (257 m), Hill 253 and the *Pöhlberg* (236 m). The Saxon 58th Division, which abutted Group Py to the east, held strong positions on the *Marien-Höhe* (183 m) and the *Hindenburg-Höhe* (145 m), with weaker forces forward on the *Fichtelberg* (205 m). The wooded, undulating nature of the

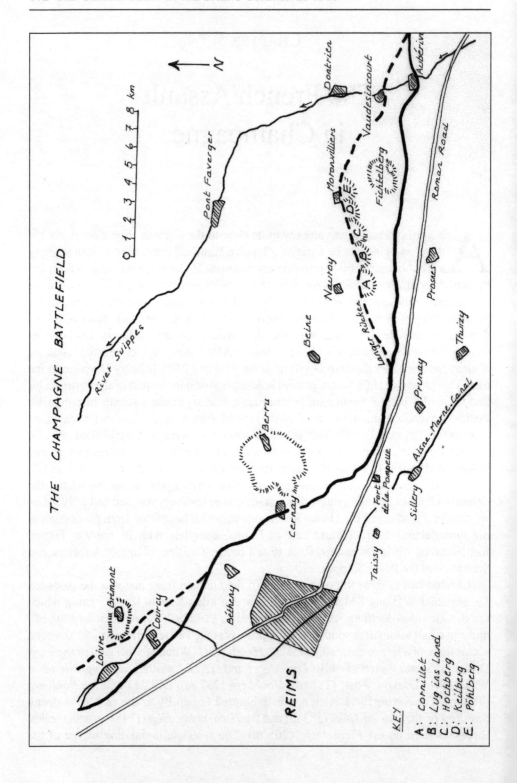

THE CHAMPAGNE BATTLEFIELD

River Suippes

Pont Faverger

Dontrien

Moronvilliers

Vaudesincourt

Aubérive

Fichtelberg

Nauroy

Langer Rücken

Roman Road

Beine

Prosnes

Thuizy

Berru

Prunay

Cernay

Fort de la Pompelle

Aisne-Marne-Canal

Sillery

Taissy

Brimont

Courcy

Loivre

Bétheny

REIMS

KEY

A: Cornillet
B: Lug ins Land
C: Hochberg
D: Keilberg
E: Pöhlberg

terrain provided an abundance of battery positions and numerous covered routes forward for both mounted and marching columns.

All these features and the ground in between were to be heavily disputed in the days and weeks to come. However, when the bombardment opened, the vital *Cornillet* feature was still occupied by Infantry Regiment 159 of 14th Reserve Division, which had been stationed there continuously since 27 December 1916. It was obvious that an offensive was imminent and both sides produced special orders of the day that were passed down to the forward troops. General Freiherr von Soden, who had played a prominent role during the Battle of the Somme the previous year when he commanded 26th Reserve Division, was now commander VII Reserve Corps (Group Reims). His Order of the Day, typical of all of them, was promulgated on 11 April:

> "Comrades of VII Reserve Corps!
> The great decisive battle has begun. Our enemies will attempt, using all the latest equipment, to defeat us.
> They must not succeed!
> We go into battle well prepared. Everything that could be done was done. It is now up to you to stand fast, to trust in your strength, to look the enemy straight in the eye and for each of you in your place to do your duty with good old German faithfulness.
> Then the attack will be broken by the tough resistance of our courageous regiments and, with God's help, victory will be ours." [1]

Orders arrived the same day calling 29th Infantry Division out of reserve and forward into the front line. Its three regiments were each allocated a sector of the front in the order (west to east) Infantry Regiments 112, 142 and 113. This meant that Infantry Regiment 113 had the task of defending the vital *Cornillet* feature.

During the night 12/13 April the regiments of 29th Infantry Division, commanded by Generalmajor von der Heyde, began the process of relief in the line. 2nd Battalion Infantry Regiment 113, which had completed an approach march of forty two kilometres the previous night, was sent in reserve to the *Rheinlager*, a forward bivouac site located in dead ground on the northern side of the *Rhein-Höhe*. This location was four kilometres north northeast of the *Cornillet* feature. For its part, 1st Battalion, leaving one company in the *Rheinlager*, moved forward to occupy the extensive *Cornillet Tunnel* in support of 3rd Battalion, which took over the front line from Infantry Regiment 50 of 214th Infantry Division.

Leutnant Rodenburg Adjutant 3rd Battalion Infantry Regiment 113[2]

> "In bright moonlight the staff met up with guides from Infantry Regiment 50 in a grassy valley. A number of large shell holes indicated that this attractively wooded valley was not entirely peaceful and undisturbed. We moved forward

on foot behind the guides, past our batteries, which were engaging targets from positions on the *Cornillet* and *Lug ins Land*. Near the entrance to the *Cornillet Tunnel* a few shot up wooden huts and shelters showed that, up until a few weeks previously, this had been a peaceful location where fought out divisions could be sent to rest and refit. The sight also led us to fear that further forward more priority had been given to comfort than security against fire. This was not a rosy prospect for veterans of the Western Front, [who had fought on the] Lorette Spur, in Champagne and on the Somme!

"Our guides hurried as they reached the tunnel entrance, because the French brought down a lot of fire on this spot. We hurried too, climbing the gentle rise between *Cornillet* and *Lug ins Land*, prior to disappearing into the main defensive line on the enemy side of the *Cornillet*. It was fairly quiet. Out front there was the occasional concentration of fire and the odd flare went up. Piles of white chalk thrown up bore witness to hasty construction. During recent days a great deal of effort had gone into the construction of mined dugouts. We asked, 'How deep are they and how any entrances do they have?' Up to now only one entrance was finished, but cross frames had already been installed below. 'Mousetraps', we thought.

"The members of a battalion staff from Infantry Regiment 50 were waiting for us at the battalion command post in the main defensive line. They were in a great hurry because they were not moving back into rest, but had to conduct a relief in the line three kilometres to the left. 'What would the position be like?' It had been quiet for a long time, but recently a great deal of work had been done. Casualties from artillery fire had been high. We were soon left on our own; previous reliefs had often been equally brief and our predecessors might well face bigger problems than us. We sorted ourselves out as best we could. Deep beneath the earth was a narrow, cramped space, with barely room to study maps of the position. Most members of the staff could only be accommodated on the steps of the dugout.

"The companies reported that they had taken over successfully. Reserve Leutnant Rasch was on the right with 9th Company. 11th Company with Leutnant Neuhoff was forward left, whilst 12th Company, commanded by Leutnant Gretz, was in the main defensive position. Reserve Leutnant Fuchs had placed his 3rd Machine Gun Company in blockhouses overlooking the main defensive line. The battalion commander, Hauptmann Lange, went forward with a runner to make contact personally with the companies. Just then the first heavy shells began to land on our dugout, making the whole place shake. This soon became drum fire. Hauptmann Lange was seriously wounded as he made his way along the main defensive line and the runner led him back to us with blood streaming down his face.

"A shell had exploded right next to him. We thought - and he was in agreement – that he had lost both eyes. Thinking of his mastery of the piano, he took comfort from the fact that his hands were unharmed. Two runners helped him to the rear, where it proved possible to save his eyes. Deep blue scars on his face remained as a reminder of 14 April 1917."

As the process of relief continued, elements of Infantry Regiment 159 of 14th Reserve Division were amongst the last to move to the rear, when Infantry Regiment 142 took over their positions. They had been under constant bombardment for five days and nights by that point. A member of 9th Company later described the move:[3]

" The night was pitch black, broken only by countless shells exploding, sending bright flashes up into the sky and making the move to the rear sheer Hell. The heavy shelling had taken a severe toll on many comrades, who were badly worn down by the five days of drum fire. Not until we reached our second artillery positions could we allow ourselves to relax a little. Involuntarily, our thoughts turned back once more to the battle area where, off to the south, the black summits of the *Cornillet* and *Hochberg* were silhouetted by the light of flares. We could see them looking like erupting volcanoes as we furtively made our way onwards, half asleep and picking our way carefully.

"Above our heads shells from the long range artillery roared and growled, whilst shrapnel shocked us out of our sleepiness now and then. In the grey light of dawn we came to the *Warschauer Hof* [Warsaw Farm]. Hardly had we put down our weapons and removed our equipment than many men, dog tired and footsore, simply fell to the wet ground. The longing for quiet and rest had quite overwhelmed us. Some were tortured by hunger and thirst. The older warriors just wished for a pipe of tobacco. Bread pouches and knapsacks were searched for pieces of bread and pockets for a few strands of tobacco. It was reassuring to see the old soldiers gathering together their last scraps to hand over to the younger men.

"A whole group offered the last of their tobacco to the commander of 9th Company [Reserve Leutnant Bleimehl], knowing that a pipe of tobacco was to him one of life's essentials. It was impossible to think of the 'Papa' of 9th Company, even in the midst of a totally chaotic situation, without his pipe or a cigar. This selfless mutual support; this comradely relationship between leader and led, make up some of the finest memories of the Great War. It was days such as this, witness to the finest old Germanic faithfulness and the greatest Prussian soldierly characteristics, which put heart into both troops and commanders. Rations had been awaiting our arrival in the *Dessauer Lager* for hours. We gulped it down hastily; we all just wanted to sleep, nothing but sleep."

Infantry Regiment 112 was occupying a front line position at the western end of the 29th Division sector, comprising two 'sacrificial' trenches (K1 and K2) and the main defensive (K3) line, known as the *Hauptriegel*. These were located forward of the

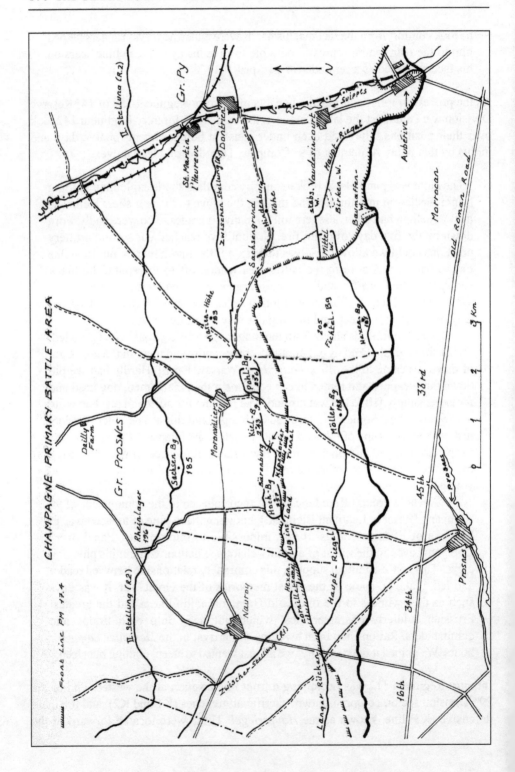

wooded area on the *Langer Rücken* along which ran the *Zwischenstellung* [Intermediate Position or R1 Line]. This in turn was supported by prepared and concealed fall back strong points positions in the woods, all of which led back to the *Hornlager* and *Kaiserlager*. An anonymous member of 3rd Battalion Infantry Regiment 112 later wrote a comprehensive description of both the lead up to the first assault on 17 April and subsequent events.

"At 2.00 am 16 April, when the switch to summer time was made, it was relatively quiet in the front line, but things were far harder for the companies in the *Hauptriegel*, which was being systematically bombarded by the enemy. This was not just a matter of high explosive shells of all calibres which ploughed up the ground and shattered the trenches. The [following] night there were lengthy concentrations of gas shells, that quickly smothered the rear positions and the wooded areas with suffocating fumes. Woe to he who did not mask up in time. He was usually beyond help because the gas had extremely serious effects; in many cases these were fatal. That the firing of gas was a sure sign of enemy offensive intentions became a certainty at 4.00 am when, suddenly, the front line trenches were subject to the massed fire of field guns. The intense showers of fragments, the sheer quantity deployed, would certainly have caused very bloody casualties in these trenches which had no dugouts had the policy not been to keep the manning levels as low as possible."[4]

Whilst trying to shelter from the worst of the shelling, all the ground holding forces were on the highest state of alert, including the Saxon 23rd Infantry Division in the *Eingreif* role for Group Py, which moved to secure crossing points over the Suippes in case a deployment on its western bank became necessary. The bombardment continued in full ferocity then, despite the fact that it was still dark, the forward sentries observed the first waves of French infantry launch forward at 5.15 am. By this time they had been under constant drum fire and gas attack for well over an hour, but, nevertheless, the defenders were alert to what was occurring to their front. Immediately, light signals calling for defensive artillery fire went up but there was a delayed response, which meant in turn that the leading French elements had overrun both the K1 and K2 trenches before shells began landing. In accordance with orders, the trench garrisons fell back, fighting as they went, to the depth positions, which had been sited and dug for all round defence.

"It was still dark and foggy when at 5.15 am red signal flares went up from our neighbouring regiment. We could already make out the dull thuds of hand grenades exploding and the rattle of small arms fire. Our men were on the highest state of alert, their eyes straining to see through the mist and the darkness. Suddenly, looming up in front of the outposts, were dark masses of Frenchmen. In no time they had closed right up and wild hand to hand fighting with spades, rifles and hand grenades broke out. How did the courageous 2 Platoon of 10th Company react to the need to defend against the first rush, despite being outnumbered many times over? Without a thought for their own salvation, they launched themselves forward against the huge assault waves and none asked the reason why, not even if they were hit by splinters from hand grenades in the confused crater field. In the end two thirds of them stayed forever in this advanced place of honour; amongst them three of the best unteroffiziers in the company. Still, *vivere non est necesse!* [It is not necessary to live!][5]

"Their task was superbly carried out. The companies in rear were alerted, time had been gained and the leading enemy elements had been broken up. Not until the enemy had penetrated in the neighbouring regimental sector to the left, 300 metres beyond the line of strong points, 250 metres forward of which outposts of 9th, 10th and 11th Companies were posted, did the fighters pull back step by step towards the strong points. The enemy obviously had decided to push forward between the wood blocks to the line of strong points, to overrun them, followed by the occupation of the *Hauptriegel* if it was insufficiently defended."[6]

There then followed an extremely hard fought battle for the two strong points. Repeatedly, the French soldiers of 16th Infantry Division, VIII Corps, threw themselves forward, but each time they were halted with staggeringly high losses. Around the more westerly *Tietze-Stützpunkt* the attempt was abandoned completely early on and moves were made to try to outflank it and to push on to the main defensive line, the so-called *Hauptriegel*, which followed the crest line east towards the *Cornillet* and *Hochberg* features. This had been anticipated and concreted machine gun posts had been established to prevent any such move. That to the west caused great execution amongst the assault troops and halted them yet again. However, the weapon covering a broad ride through the wooded area between the strong points was damaged and ceased firing.

"In dense masses they pushed on along the approach ways and through the rides in the woods, first being held in front of the strong points, because the enemy columns came under lacerating fire when they were forced to halt temporarily in front of a fairly intact wire obstacle and offered extraordinary targets to the defenders. Ignoring the danger, each man adopted a firing position from where he could bring his weapon to bear with best effect. Some took up positions outside the trenches; others fired standing up as though they were on a practice range, enthusiastically firing bullet after bullet, few of which failed to find a target. Of course the enemy soon realised that in tackling the strong points they were poking at wasps' nests. The one remaining hope was that these obstinately resisting garrisons would fall of their own accord if they thrust further forward on both flanks. To that end they tried to split their attacking line into right and left halves. The existence of rides and blocks of coarse fir trees made the task somewhat easier, because they provided cover from view, but that was the only and not undisputed advantage.

"It had by now become lighter and the days of bombardment had thinned out the trees somewhat, thus offering the German gunners valuable prey. The sound of the chatter of the guns of 3rd Machine Gun Company from the *Tietzestützpunkt* rose in derisive scorn, as dense masses of enemy made repeated vain attempts to push on along the *Bertramweg* to the right. To those who witnessed it, the sight of entire rows of men in long coats falling was truly grim. Those following up absorbed the lesson. They abandoned the advance, took cover in shell holes or behind the heaps of fallen comrades and some pulled back to the rear. The columns appeared to enjoy more success to the left between the *Tietze* - and *Speestützpunkts*, where our weapons were insufficient to be able to deal with the numerical superiority. Despite the fact that some bullets dealt with several men at once, the gaps were immediately filled and the attacking waves bore down on the battalion command post."[7]

Taking immediate advantage, the French infantrymen swarmed forward until they were threatening the trench where the *KTK*, Reserve Hauptmann Bullinger, was located. This was a clear crisis. Summoning every reinforcement within range, Bullinger launched a succession of counter-strokes. With the aid of two companies of 1st Battalion, such was the aggression of this action that not only were the French halted in their tracks, they were actually driven all the way back to the K2 trench. Two hundred of them were taken prisoner and five heavy and eight light machine guns were captured.

"They got to within thirty metres along the communication trench between *Tietzeweg* and *Schampweg*. But no further! In the meantime there was full daylight and it was easier to observe the entire situation. From the two strong points came the happy news that they were firmly in our grasp but that they both urgently needed strong reinforcement. The *KTK*, Reserve Hauptmann Bullinger, began at once to arrange counter-strokes. No task in wartime is harder or more costly than fighting between the walls of trenches where every step demands endurance and is gained only with bloody casualties ... This hard task fell mainly to the assault troops of 9th Company, under Leutnants Mürköster and Scheuring, who had to clear out the enemy forward along the densely occupied *Schampweg* and in the *Bataillongraben* [Battalion trench] to the right. The counter-attack made only slow progress, because the enemy tried everything to hold on to the ground they had gained. Our men were literally swamped with hand and rifle grenades, together with rifle and machine gun fire from a numerically superior enemy who had been equipped with plenty of ammunition.

"No sooner had we delivered the first thrust that launched our counter-strokes than the commander of both troops, Leutnants Mürköster and Scheuring, were severely wounded. Unteroffizier Ladda and his men from 4th Company took over the lead in *Schampweg* and, in a ceaseless action, fought their way forward, traverse by traverse. However, at the half way point the courageous lads of 4th and 9th Companies had to call a halt when they came under fire from two enemy automatic rifles, which had a wide field of fire, making it impossible to move out of cover. Coming to a swift decision, Unteroffizier Ladda on one side and Dreher on the other moved outwards in wide arcs and succeeded in coming up on the flanks of the guns and then knocking them both out with the first, expertly thrown, hand grenade. The assault troop, which had been waiting for this moment, stormed forward again, past the captured weapons ... and onwards, overcoming all problems.

"During the morning contact was established with 11th Company, which had held out with obstinate endurance in the *Speestützpunktgraben*, beating off repeated enemy attacks. With that, the main part of the position was back in German hands. The other half platoon which had come to the battalion command post was also confronted by no easy task. It transpired that not only *Bataillongraben*, but also the stand of trees this side of the *Tietzestützpunkt* were teeming with enemy. This meant that 12th Company, surrounded by the French, was in a critical situation. At all costs it was essential to link up once more and to deliver help swiftly. Fresh assault troops were organised from the company. Volunteers came forward then, starting at *Tietzeweg*, began to overcome the enemy systematically in a bitterly fought close quarter battle. "Our small group was once more facing huge odds but, as before, German attacking spirit served to counter inferiority in numbers. Unteroffizier Armbruster of 4th Company, who was later joined by the superb Vizefeldwebel Reibel[8] and the old, tried and tested, Landsturmman Bender[9] of 11th Company (both of whom were mortally wounded later during the action), conducted a series of heroic actions. The greatest success, however, fell to the four battalion runners of 3rd Battalion. Launching themselves along *Bataillongraben*, they tore into the Frenchmen, oblivious of whether they were in cover or not. Their one aim was to smash into the considerable mass of Frenchmen who still remained there and scatter or destroy them. Incredible though it may seem, that is exactly what happened. The enemy hesitated. They were unable to pull back to their start point, because of a gun manned skilfully by Gefreiter Hauk of 3rd Machine Gun Company, firing from the *Tietzestutzpunkt*.

"Any attempt to pass through its fire would inevitably have had to be paid with the death of those attempting it. In any case these were good soldiers, possessed of plenty of attacking spirit and they did not want to give up. Surely an attempt to overcome the few German defenders there would succeed! This was tried several times, again and again, but each time the Germans fought back

Demolition during the withdrawal to the Hindenburg Line, March 1917.

Vimy.

La Folie Chateau in ruins, Vimy Ridge.

A happy member of Reserve Infantry Regiment 262, having survived the Battle for Vimy Ridge.

Givenchy under shell fire.

German forward position on the *Gießßler Höhe* Vimy Ridge.

Casualty evacuation near Gavrelle.

Canadians searching captured soldiers, Arleux 27 April.

2nd Battalion Infantry Regiment 75 counter-attacking, Oppy, 27 April.

Runners on standby at the BTK in Neuvireuil, April.

A 210 mm heavy howitzer firing from a position in Izel-lès-Equerchin.

Shell hole defence south of the Scarpe, May.

Monchy le Preux from German positions to the east, 23 April.

KTK to the east of Chérisy.

Chérisy.

Hendecourt.

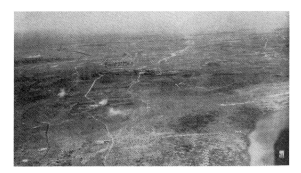

An aerial view of the Bullecourt battlefield.

The wrecked front line trench of the Hindenburg Line near Bullecourt.

KTK located by the Hendecourt-Riencourt track, May.

Riencourt in ruins, May.

Knocked out tank,
Bullecourt,
11 April.

Tank knocked out and captured at
Riencourt, 11 April.

Officers and men of 4th Australian
Division captured at Bullecourt,
11 April.

An assault group of
Grenadier Regiment
123, led by a
flamethrower team,
counter-attacking the
Engländernest,
Bullecourt, 4 May.

Vizefeldwebel Rahn, Machine Gun Company 2nd Battalion Grenadier Regiment 123, with the driver of a tank and his carrier pigeons that he captured at Bullecourt, 3 May.

A member of Grenadier Regiment 9 firing a captured Lewis gun.

Ration carriers from Grenadier Regiment 9, Bullecourt, May.

A ration carrying party of Reserve Infantry Regiment 121 near Bullecourt, late May.

A camouflaged anti tank gun near Berry au Bac.

The Berry au Bac - Guignicourt battlefield, 16 April.

One of the many tanks destroyed during the 'death ride' at Berry au Bac, 16 April.

Wrecked armour littering the Berry au Bac - Guignicourt *Tankstraße*.

The railway embankment at Guignicourt; start line for one of the counter-attacks on 16 April.

The Soupir sector viewed from the French front line.

Men of Footguard Regiment 2 sheltering in the *Maywald Höhle*.

Entrance to the *Sachsen Höhle*.

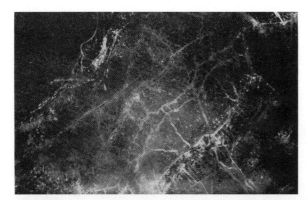

Malval Farm from the air.

French assault on the Chemin des Dames, April.

French colonial troops killed during the assault on the Chemin des Dames.

Messenger dogs on the Chemin des Dames.

An ambulance collecting casualties at Ailles.

A team of mules waiting to load supplies in Chermizy-Ailles.

The Ailette Valley viewed from the Chemin des Dames.

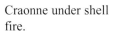

Craonne under shell fire.

An aerial view of the *Winterberg* [Plateau de Californie].

The *Winterberg* under shell fire.

The ruins of Vauclerc.

The *Haupt-Riegel* forward of Mont Cornillet, early April.

A forward sentry post in Champagne.

A well maintained sap head, Champagne.

The view of Mont Cornillet from near the *Rheinlager*.

French defence from shell holes. On Mont Cornillet the two front lines were only a few metres apart.

French casualties on the
Champagne battlefield.

German front line
positions, Champagne.

A French position
after a successful
counter-attack in
Champagne.

Digging a reserve
position, Champagne.

Men of Infantry Regiment 143 working on the R2 Line north of St Martin l'Heureux.

Men of Infantry Regiment 143 await nightfall and relief near Dontrien.

A smashed communication trench leading forward from Beine to *Langer Rücken*.

A light signalling station south of Corbény that was destroyed on 20 April.

A group of men from Infantry Regiment 476 by
the entrance to the Cornillet Tunnel, 20 May.

Regimental command post
Reserve Infantry
Regiment 247 on the
Pöhlberg, May.

Crater field defence south of Nauroy, May.

like devils with bullets and grenades, spreading death and destruction amongst the massed French ranks. Then, Unteroffizier Weißschnur (9ᵗʰ Company) climbed out of the trench and signalled them to raise their hands whilst Gefreiter Neu, Volz, Schanz and Pielhöfer together with, off to one side, Unteroffizier Armbruster and his men, all stood with grenades in their hands ready to throw. There could be no misunderstanding any more. Their will broken, the attackers gave up. They had lost the battle! Slowly a few began to throw down their arms, then more and more. Soon those who had surrendered outnumbered the little band of defenders many times over."[10]

The immediate situation having calmed somewhat, 7ᵗʰ and 8ᵗʰ Companies were withdrawn as a reserve force by 58 Infantry Brigade. They then spent the remainder of the day on various degrees of alert, before being placed at the disposal of Infantry Regiment 113 on *Mont Cornillet* at 6.30 pm. During the night 8ᵗʰ Company was sent forward to plug a gap which had developed between Infantry Regiments 113 and 142 and there they remained for the next forty eight hours. Meanwhile heavy French shelling continued to hammer down throughout the area indiscriminately, causing casualties both to the German defenders and the French prisoners who were being moved to the rear.

"From a distance came the roar of a heavy calibre shell, men had hardly leapt to the stairs of the *KTK* than in that split second there was an almighty crash. Planks of wood and shreds of blue-grey cloth, stained with black powder smoke which had once clothed living beings, were thrown into the air. There was no sign whatsoever of the Frenchmen, but three brave unteroffiziers from 8ᵗʰ Company (Ruland, Zocher and Pulver), who had been with us since the start of war and served us faithfully, lay motionless nearby, having bled to death.[11] In the meantime, all the prisoners, 118 in total, were led away and then, from the cleared wooded areas, four machine guns and seven automatic rifles were recovered. The position was almost completely in our hands now; only from the left flank could be heard the noise of the continuing, bitterly fought, counter strokes. This was the weak point of the sector. Our neighbours [Infantry Regiment 142] had recaptured their front line apart from the *Hauptriegel* … This left a gap through which the enemy pushed strong forces and faced us with the need to recapture the territory with hand grenades … The courageous, combined, efforts of 3ʳᵈ and 1ˢᵗ Battalions meant that finally we needed no longer to fear a serious threat on this flank.

"That was the situation during the evening of 17 April. Reliable patrol reports indicated that the enemy were ensconced in our outpost line and that the *Deckungsgraben* was completely flattened and unusable as a defensive position. At that news the regiment decided to abandon the forward position and hold the *Stützpunkt* Line instead; it had in any case originally been designed as the main defensive position. Reserve Infantry Regiment 16 [14th Reserve Division] had not been attacked and was still occupying its front line, so a new stop line had to be created, together with one to our left hand neighbours. Although Infantry Regiment 112 held on to almost all of its sector on 17 April, the enemy had captured more ground to the east: less in the 29th Infantry Division sector than in that of the adjoining formation [214th Infantry Division], where parts of *Luginsland, Hochberg, Keilberg* and *Pöhlberg* had been lost."[12]

The French had faced a difficult task in assaulting this particular sub-sector. The defence had been well organised and resolute, so the attackers had nothing significant to show for their efforts as night fell. It had been a successful day for the defenders, but some idea of the intensity of the battle is demonstrated by the Infantry Regiment 112 casualty figures: forty one other ranks killed, with a further thirty two missing and 231 wounded.[13]

Occupying the centre of the 29th Infantry Division sector was Infantry Regiment 142, which had assumed responsibility for the area from Infantry Regiment 159 on 14 April. As the companies marched forward, they were already well aware that a battle was raging to their front. As the individual peaks of *Langer Rücken* came into view, it was obvious that the entire length from *Mont Cornillet* to the *Pöhlberg* were under extremely heavy artillery fire. Losses were relatively light during the move forward, but Reserve Leutnant Statsmann, 1st Battalion, was unlucky enough to have been killed by a direct hit by a shell during the approach march.[14] The bombardment had laid waste to the entire area so the various positions - when they finally reached them - had been so badly smashed as to be unrecognisable. That said, at least Infantry Regiment 142 was fresh and work began immediately to try to restore some defensive value to the flattened trenches and wrecked dugouts.

In order to expedite the work, in addition to each company forming a fourth platoon to carry supplies forward - a technique which had proved itself the previous year at Verdun and on the Somme - 120 men were drawn from the whole regiment and turned into a construction company. In the event the short time left before the offensive opened reduced the value of this particular initiative. Already by the evening of 15 April the French suddenly lifted to the rear the bombardment which had been falling on the front line, the *Hauptriegel* and K1 Line, and launched a surprise limited attack at 6.35 pm. On the 1st Battalion front, artillery defensive fire came down swiftly and accurately and broke the thrust up, but 2nd Battalion had a harder time of it. 5th and 6th Companies were occupying the front line. 5th Company was able to halt the attack with small arms fire, but in front of 6th Company, where the response of the artillery had been late and not particularly effective, the French succeeded in breaking into the front line. They were later ejected, leaving behind, captured, three men from the French 85th Infantry Regiment of 15th Infantry Division. As elsewhere along the attack frontage, the intensity of the bombardment increased throughout 16 April then, as it went dark, gas began to be mixed in. Realising at 4.00 am on 17 April that the offensive was imminent,

3rd Battalion, located back in reserve in rear of the Second Position (R2 Line), was brought to full alert.

Despite the fact that the regiment had only been in the line for three days, it was already somewhat worn down. A relatively high water table in this part of the K1 and K2 lines meant that the dugouts only had two to three metres of overhead cover. As a result, almost all of them had been wrecked. With no protection in their shell hole positions, casualties had been high in the forward companies and some of the machine guns were already out of action. Nevertheless, when the French assault waves flooded forward, they were met by a hail of small arms fire. Such was their numerical superiority, however, that the defenders quickly had to turn to their stocks of hand grenades in an attempt to hold them back. Within a few moments of the attack beginning, German artillery fire was coming down on the French jumping off trenches. This reduced their ability to reinforce the attacking waves for a time, but did not affect the masses, which quickly closed up to the German positions and were already thrusting towards the *Stützpunkt* line in places.

It proved to be impossible to hold the attacks along this line, so the surviving defenders pulled back, conducting a fighting withdrawal towards the *Hauptriegel*. This time, when the enemy closed to within 200 metres of this point, a number of German assault groups launched forward, scattered the French columns and bought a valuable, if brief, breathing space. Messages were passed back to the artillery at 7.15 am, informing the gun lines that the French were now established in the *Stützpunkt* Line and a concentration of fire was brought down. Profiting from this, assault groups from 1st and 2nd Battalions stormed forward. One such, led by Unteroffizier Ackermann 1st Company, got into the *Ludendorff Stützpunkt* and captured four machine guns. Teams from 2nd Battalion recaptured the *Tiedestützpunkt* at about 8.30 am and, at the same time, a further push by groups from 1st Battalion recaptured the K2 Line to their immediate front.

Naturally, the French assault troops were not quiescent at the time. Four companies, advancing in column from the southeast, tried to force their way into the *Hauptriegel* and to roll it up. Reacting quickly, Leutnant Bosse moved his 3rd Company to counter the threat and succeeded in holding firm until the assault groups, which had pushed into the K2 line, had withdrawn to the *Hauptriegel* to strengthen the defence there. The situation, nevertheless, continued to give cause for concern until the arrival at 11.30 am of 3rd Battalion, which had force marched forward, placing two of its companies in the R1 Line and pushing the other two forward to the *Hauptriegel*. Its arrival could not have been more timely. By now the enemy were firmly established in the K1 and K2 lines and were bringing forward additional troops constantly. An intervention by the German artillery prevented a French renewal of the attack for the time being.

The bulk of the French force was from the 27th and 85th Infantry Regiments. They were well equipped, especially with rifle grenades, machine guns and automatic rifles. They had made good progress to begin with, but Infantry Regiment 142 fought back hard and decisively; company and platoon commanders repeatedly used their initiative, intervening several times at critical moments during the whole hard-fought day and managing repeatedly to break up repeated attempts by the French to storm forward. Numerous prisoners were captured, as was a considerable quantity of arms and equipment. One of the junior regimental officers later produced a short, but atmospheric, account of the day's confused fighting.

Leutnant Schloß 1ˢᵗ Machine Gun Company Infantry Regiment 142[15]

"It was 5.00 am 17 April 1917 and fine drizzly rain was falling when, suddenly, the French drum fire, which had been coming down for days, lifted to the rear. Simultaneously a violent assault was launched. The attack was on us surprisingly quickly, but we were still equal to it. Up on the *Cornillet*, where the regimental boundary ran, were two blockhouses containing a platoon of our company led by the young Vizefeldwebel Heinrich Widenfohler, who had already the previous year been awarded the Iron Cross First Class for his outstanding leadership. The company commander was located further to the right by a machine gun. Here on the *Cornillet,* to the left of our regimental sector and off to the right where a strong point was a thorn in the eye for our opponents, the fighting was most intense. By the time the machine guns were ready to start their work, the enemy had already climbed the hill to within fifty metres and was attempting to bear left and so roll up the entire sector.

"Its first waves were mown down. They pushed forward fresh forces, a third then a fourth wave, then it became a matter of appalling hand to hand fighting, with an enemy thrusting forward blindly, filled with anger. However, where the three guns were located they made no progress. We mowed them down like ripe corn before the scythe. However, off to the left [east] they had managed to break in, so now we were faced by men in pale blue charging our weapons and our heroic infantry from the rear. The company commander, Leutnant Ziegler, saw that it was pointless to remain up there with just a handful of infantrymen and the ammunition had run out. He moved further to the right [west], where he knew that there was another machine gun.

"From there he covered his arc with the two weapons that he now had at his disposal and protected the withdrawal of his platoon, which was still up on top and fighting with the remnants of the infantry to prevent their position from being surrounded. He also ensured that the regiment was not outflanked on the left. That done, he returned to the Vizefeldwebel's platoon. There was no ammunition there either and the ring had almost been closed. At that point he ordered a withdrawal, because the fighting infantry of the neighbouring regiment had also had to pull back. The odds against had become overwhelmingly high and the tiny heroic band became constantly fewer.

"The machine guns were disassembled rapidly. The Feldwebel took one gun himself and headed down through the crater field. Shells crashed down left and right, an enemy machine gun opened up from the top of the hill and it seemed as though the little band would never get back to their own side. As the small group reached the bottom both guns and their mounts were missing and nobody knew where they were. A Gefreiter, a reservist with a wife and children back home, gave orders that ammunition was to be fetched from where it was stored in a nearby tunnel and that the men were to wait for him there. He was going to locate his gun and see what had happened to the platoon commander. At that he made his way back through the craters and up the hill, the exact same way that we had only just descended.

"He ignored all the shells; his one thought was that the guns must be retrieved. Whilst he was searching for the weapons a daring counter-attack had succeeded in regaining the crest line. Suddenly he came across a gun and, next to it, the young feldwebel, who had been brought down by an enemy shell. He had been faithful unto death; he was the finest man in the company! He returned with the intact gun and then went forward again to fetch the second weapon. Once his platoon was reunited, he made his men available once more and helped to beat off the remainder of the attack. As soon as night fell on this dreadful day, he rushed off with a few other men and brought his dead comrades back to the rear. His reward later was promotion to unteroffizier and the Iron Cross First Class.

"Another platoon, commanded by Reserve Leutnant Riester, was located in the third trench in the centre of the position when the storm broke. Despite the torrent of fire that this platoon laid down forward of our front line trench, the enemy succeeded in breaking in left and right and overrunning the German garrison. The first waves were dealt with in dreadful hand to hand fighting, but ever more stormed forward and our ranks became very thin. Suddenly, from the rear, came the order, 'Evacuate the front line. Hold the Second Position!' and that is precisely what the surviving infantrymen did. An entire regiment's worth of French assault waves dashed forward on a very narrow frontage, but were beaten back and beaten back again.

"The infantrymen stood up in the open by the trenches and fired at the assaulting enemy until they closed up, then brought them down them with hand grenades, Mounted on top of the cover, the machine guns fired until, by 10.00 am, the enemy had to give up, having suffered enormous casualties. That day the regiment fought at odds of three to one against an enemy which had reckoned on a major breakthrough. [Each man] was carrying five days' rations. Quite apart from the huge casualties which we and our artillery had caused, the enemy also left several hundred prisoners in our hands that day."

By evening, the situation on this part of the front was that the French were in possession of everything forward of the K3 line, which was still being defended stubbornly by

Infantry Regiment 142, with the exception of one small pocket of resistance holding out on the left [eastern] flank. Defensive positions, echeloned back in depth, prevented this from being expanded further and junction points with Infantry Regiment 112 to the right and Infantry Regiment 113 on the left had been established and manned. This was significant. Hardly any French meaningful progress had been made and they were forced to dig in along the high water mark of their assault. Similarly, overnight Infantry Regiment 142 so arranged its deployment as to ensure that six companies were manning and improving the defences of the *Hauptriegel* and the other six the R1 Line. The temporary construction company retained its independence and was used wherever the need for repair was greatest. There was still a total of twenty three serviceable machine guns available to the defence, so the overall outcome here was stalemate, with advantage remaining with Infantry Regiment 142.[16]

Infantry Regiment 113, responsible for *Mont Cornillet*, estimated that when the attack began on their front they were also faced with odds of three to one. Three major assault groups, backed by a further three waves of infantry reinforcements, bore down on their forward positions. Here a combination of darkness and snow squalls meant that visibility was so poor than none of the signals to the artillery were seen and the machine guns could only open up at the very last minute. The lightly held forward positions were simply overrun, though the remnants of 11th Company, under Leutnant Neuhoff, held out briefly in places. Unfortunately, most of the German soldiers present were ration carriers who did not have their weapons with them for some reason and the supply of hand grenades soon ran out. The experienced Vizefeldwebel Gerber pointed out the severe risk of encirclement so, just in the nick of time, Neuhoff, who was suffering from the effects of gas inhalation, led his thirty remaining men back to the Cornillet Tunnel where, having reported in, he collapsed at the feet of the regimental commander, Oberstleutnant Kuhlmann.

The companies of 1st Battalion that were on standby were deployed exactly as they had been rehearsed the previous day. Although all the tunnel entrances were under fire they were nevertheless able to deploy swiftly and without heavy casualties. Sad to relate, Offizierstellvertreter Thurner was killed as he was mounting a machine gun above one of the air vents. Nevertheless, as the French arrived, puffing and panting, along the crest of the *Cornillet* they came under heavy fire. During the ensuing confusion, these troops were thrown back off the ridge and back down its southern slopes. Leutnant Neuhoff's little group then inserted itself into a gap between 4th and 3rd Companies but, despite this redeployment, it proved impossible to push the counter-stroke any further forward. The French gains were then sealed off by a heavy curtain of fire to their front. The overall situation would have been perfectly manageable had it not been for the fact that Infantry Regiment 363 of 214th Infantry Division had been pushed back off *Lug Ins Land*. This presented a gap in the *Hexensattel* area which the French, supported by heavy machine gun fire, attempted to exploit. Quickly and supported by two machine guns, 3rd Company under Leutnant Finke moved to counter the threat. Bending back his left flank, he managed to beat off repeated assaults and caused the enemy heavy casualties

Naturally there were casualties, too, among the defenders and gradually virtually all of the personnel located in the Cornillet Tunnel - engineers, gunners, and mortarmen - were thrown into the battle, whilst the three doctors on hand treated no fewer than 160 wounded men in the first thirty six hours of the battle. Just at the point when there were no reserves left and the situation was looking critical, Major von Goeler, commander 2nd Battalion, who had headed forward on his own initiative, arrived. He had been certain that the *Cornillet* had been lost and planned to launch a counter-attack. Fortunately for him and his unit, the artillery fire on the rear areas had slackened somewhat and the battalion arrived at the tunnel totally unscathed. Following a short pause, 5th and 8th Companies were deployed to the left to extend the defensive line, with 7th Company behind in depth. 6th Company then moved to fill a gap which had developed between 2nd and 3rd Companies. Nevertheless, the situation remained extremely precarious.

Leutnant Bürkle Adjutant 1st Battalion Infantry Regiment 113[17]

"The view from the *Cornillet*, especially off to one side in the area of the blockhouses down towards Prosnes, was appalling. Everywhere you looked there were great masses of troops, against which, for the time being, our artillery seemed able to do hardly anything. Later, in fact from the very next day, our guns were better organised and poured plenty of fire down into the Prosnes Valley."

It was now about 10.00 am. Oberstleutnant Kuhlmann ordered Hauptmann Dierich, commanding 1st Battalion, to launch an immediate attack at the Blockhouse Line and the *Hauptriegel*, where some of the guns of 3rd Machine Gun Company were still operating, despite being hampered by the siting and construction of the blockhouses, which meant that they could only engage targets to the front. The result was that the French were able to attack each of them in the flank from the east until, eventually, only one was still in German hands. The counter-attack was launched at 3.00 pm, but on the left fire from *Lug Ins Land* halted it, Reserve Leutnants Funk[18] and Hoffmann, commanding 7th and 8th Companies respectively, both being killed. Here casualties mounted and the effort had to be abandoned, with the assault troops pulling back to their start lines. On the right, however, progress was better initially and one officer and forty five other ranks from the French 13th, 59th and 83rd Regiments of 34th Infantry Division were captured.

Despite this it was not possible to achieve the full aim of the attack, because there were too few troops to extend the attack sufficiently to the west. The regiment had to accept the situation and the front line defences were split between 1st and 2nd Battalions, with the boundary between the two fixed as the southern tip of the *Cornillet* feature.

Numerous French attacks that afternoon were broken up, fighting patrols went forward to deal with pockets of resistance and a few prisoners were captured. French reconnaissance patrols during the following night were all easily beaten off by the defenders' fire. As has been mentioned, two companies from 2ⁿᵈ Battalion Infantry Regiment 112 arrived to reinforce during the early evening. They were sorely needed and immediately deployed. The day's fighting had cost Infantry Regiment 113 dearly. Altogether it had suffered 450 casualties, including Reserve Leutnants Rieder, Thum and Lautz.[19] In addition, a further 250 men were missing, mostly killed or wounded. Subsequently one of the battalion commanders recorded his impressions of the day

Hauptmann von Rundstedt 1ˢᵗ Battalion Infantry Regiment 113[20]

"Most of the mined dugouts had been crushed and the trenches had been transformed into crater fields. The concrete blockhouses for the machine guns were still largely intact, but it was only possible to fire frontally from them, which was a serious disadvantage. Unflinchingly, the French continued to bring down well observed destructive fire until 5.45 am 17 April. Led by strong assault groups, three waves of attackers then launched forward, followed by columns certain of victory; the officers mounted and the men with their rifles slung. Although they were lucky, inasmuch as the German artillery had been withdrawn further back the previous night and could not bring fire down, nevertheless the relatively weak resistance of the remainder of 3ʳᵈ Battalion was sufficient to give the regimental commander, Oberstleutnant Kuhlmann, time to deploy his supports.

"1ˢᵗ Battalion Infantry Regiment 113 poured out of the only slightly damaged entrances to the tunnel, reaching the summit of the *Cornillet* just as the French were about to charge down its northern slope. Well organised and gallantly led, the impetus of the men of Baden threw the stronger enemy back down to the R1 position on the southern slope. Unfortunately, progress was checked by machine gun fire from the left flank. From *Luginsland*, which they had taken in the first charge, the French worked their way against the flank of Infantry Regiment 113, which was also subject to simultaneous mass attack from the east. Swiftly assessing the situation, Leutnant Finke, commanding 3ʳᵈ Company, spotted the danger and established a position against which all attacks withered away. Despite the fact that his firepower was enhanced by a machine gun, the fate of the defence would have been sealed had it not been for the timely arrival of 2ⁿᵈ Battalion. As soon as news of the attack reached the *Rheinlager*, Major Freiherr Göler von Ravensburg put on his steel helmet and declared, 'I am going to recapture the *Cornillet*'. He could hardly have reckoned that it would still be in the hands of the regiment. The battalion was fortunate as it made it way forward then, from about midday, it was able to establish itself, deeply echeloned to the left, and support the threatened flank.

"The regimental commander now wanted to concentrate on regaining the defensive position where 3rd Machine Gun Company was still holding on and the two battalions stormed forward. On the right, especially where 4th Company under Leutnant Melchior was deployed, ground was gained, prisoners and equipment captured. However, the further to the left [east] the higher the casualties mounted because of flanking fire and, which was worse, the French continued to hold the blockhouse line. That was how matters stayed during the coming days. French artillery fire came down ceaselessly on the smashed chalk of the *Cornillet* where the 113th held on in the craters, enduring the worst that the April weather could throw at them. How quickly major battles wear men down physically and spiritually!"

214th Infantry Division, comprising Infantry Regiments 50, 358 and 363 and commanded by Generalmajor von Brauchitsch, occupied a key sector of the front line south of Moronvilliers. From the beginning of April the signs of impending attack were unmistakable. As early as 6 April such was the weight of fire coming down on the K1 Line that it was completely flattened, its protective wire obstacle blown away. The K2 line was not quite so badly damaged, so a decision was taken to evacuate, at least temporarily, the front line. French patrols moved to occupy the space thus abandoned, but no serious attempt was made by them to establish a permanent presence there. It was clear that this sector had been marked out for special attention by the enemy, so its regiments were given priority for the issue of the new lightweight MG 08/15. The scale was only one per company with initially a mere 4,000 rounds of belted ammunition. Nevertheless they would prove to be extremely useful once battle was joined and, in addition, each company was provided with a belt filler and large stocks of loose ammunition, which enabled plentiful quantities of ammunition to be stored adjacent to each weapon.

If this preliminary softening up of the positions seemed severe to the defenders, it was nothing compared with the real bombardment when it began early on 10 April. Suddenly, immense quantities of fire were coming down on all the trenches, approach routes and gun lines, with special attention apparently being paid to observation posts, which were subject to huge numbers of heavy calibre shells directed from the air. The defenders discovered with some alarm that such was the penetrating power of the larger shells that dugouts with eight metres of overhead cover were being smashed repeatedly. Losses mounted and there was some concern that there might be an attack that very day. In response, 3rd Battalion Infantry Regiment 50 was rushed forward from the *Rheinlager* behind the Second Position into support locations along the Intermediate Position - the so-called *Zwischen- or R1 Stellung*.

In the event nothing of the kind happened and the bombardment ground on. Two French spotting aircraft, venturing too close to the *Möllerberg*, were shot down around midday and a strong fighting patrol, presumably sent forward to test the defences, was beaten off with ease. By late that afternoon however, there was another scare. Enemy trenches north of Prosnes were observed to be filling up with troops and field artillery was moving up forward. A forty five minute period of drum fire all along the line at 6.30 pm was followed by a limited assault on the adjoining Infantry Regiment 159 sector. Eventually this spilled over onto the 214th Infantry Division frontage and by 7.30 pm green flares, calling for artillery defensive fire, were being sent up. The French enjoyed little success that day, but kept probing away; the following evening a thrust directed at the boundary between Infantry Regiments 159 and 50 led to ten men of the latter being captured.

In view of the pressure, as has been mentioned already, two regiments of 29th Infantry Division (113 and 142) were inserted into the front line on 14 April and so the defence began to assume its final shape prior to the shock of 17 April. The shuffling of forward units continued so, from being the most westerly of the 214th Infantry Division's regiments, Infantry Regiment 50 was reassigned new positions. After a complicated redeployment, 1st and 2nd Battalions Infantry Regiment 50 were withdrawn from the front line and the regiment was reinserted between Infantry Regiments 363 (which side stepped to the right, i.e. west) and 358, though three companies were withdrawn into reserve: 2nd Company to the *Kipsdorf Tunnel* and 4th Company to the *Wettiner-Lager* in rear of the Second Position. There followed a series of minor readjustments designed to create and locate appropriate regimental. brigade and divisional reserves and to establish relays of runners and signalling stations, in order to ensure that communications would be guaranteed, despite the immense destruction caused by all the shelling.

As has been mentioned, a particular concern was the penetrative power of the larger calibres. In one particularly unlucky instance this happened to the command post of 2nd Battalion Infantry Regiment 50 during the afternoon of 16 April. Landwehr Hauptmann Müller, its commanding officer, was buried alive, lucky to be rescued and had to be evacuated. A machine gun, complete with crew, which were also in the same dugout, was not as fortunate. The gun was lost and all the crew killed. At this critical moment, command devolved on the next most senior officer - Reserve Leutnant Schmidt. Elsewhere, moving in the open was increasingly suicidal. The regimental adjutant, Oberleutnant Rochlitz, had been seriously wounded just after his arrival forward and casualties were mounting in all the companies. News arrived that there had been French attacks in the German Seventh Army sector along the Aisne and that statements from prisoners confirmed that the attack was due to be extended to the Champagne front the following morning.

On full alert, the defenders were subject to endless drum fire through the night 16/17 April then, as dawn approached, intense mortar fire began tearing gaps through the barbed wire obstacles. Profiting from the darkness and clouds of smoke clinging to the ground, the French attacking infantry, 45th and 33rd Divisions, XVII Corps, closed up on the forward German positions and launched forward about 5.45 am. On the Infantry Regiment 50 front the attackers had selected their main break in points with some care. There was some pressure all along the front, but specially organised assault groups concentrated on those points where communication trenches led to the rear. This enabled them to make progress rapidly as far as the K2 and K3 lines and also to cut off the three forward companies. In the event, all were able to break out and get to the rear, but there were serious casualties in both 10th and 12th Companies.

8th and 11th Companies rushed to occupy the K3 line, where they were subject to a torrent of rifle grenades. Reserve Leutnant Munk, commanding 11th Company, was wounded. He was succeeded by Reserve Leutnant Hartwig, who was killed and, by 8.30 am, command was being exercised over what remained by Unteroffizier Schulz. Enemy pressure was intense, so what remained of the defenders were forced at this time to fall back. The problem was French success in thrusting into the defences on narrow fronts in some depth. Meanwhile 9th Company had received information about the French successes and moved on its own initiative to reinforce the K3 Line. Having arrived there through a heavy bombardment, it found itself isolated, under pressure and forced to pull back to the R1 Line, where it rallied and took under command all the surviving personnel of the forward companies.

12th Company Infantry Regiment 363 arrived and, with its aid, an immediate counter-stroke was mounted, led by commander 9th Company. This crashed into a faltering French attack which had almost thrust forward to the R1 Line, despite being checked by the fire of blockhouses, machine guns posts and the occasional section of occupied trench on the southern slopes, throwing it back with losses estimated at fifty killed and wounded, thirty prisoners and the loss of two light machine guns. Once again, however, in a pattern which was repeated all along the line throughout the day, the German attackers found themselves isolated and unsupported. There was no alternative but to withdraw to the R1 Line once again, thus yielding ground of some importance to the French troops. So far most of these counter moves had been small scale and launched without proper fire support. However, a more concentrated effort under the command of Reserve Hauptmann Masur was ordered for 1.00 pm.

Strenuous attempts were made by means of flare signals to indicate the objective to the artillery, but snow squalls and generally reduced visibility meant that either the gun lines could not observe the demands for fire or were in some other way prevented from responding. Once again and unsupported the infantry launched forward. At an agreed signal, elements of 2nd, 5th, 6th and 9th Companies Infantry Regiment 50 rushed the blockhouses along the *Haupt Riegel* forward of the *Hochberg* and *Pöhlberg* positions. This attack did develop a degree of synergy and though some of the French troops defended themselves vigorously with machine gun fire, others hesitated and after an extremely aggressive battle with hand grenades, during which Reserve Leutnant Hildbrand of 2nd Company distinguished himself, the line was secured, though unfortunately at heavy cost, due primarily to the failure of artillery fire to neutralise the French machine guns.

Whilst this attack was unfolding, Infantry Regiment 358 had been given the task of pushing the enemy out of the former German battery positions, but this attack failed completely. Once again there was no supporting gun fire and many of those involved were unable even to get clear of the start line, such was the weight of fire directed at them. Then worse was to come; by mid afternoon the snow storms began to disperse, French spotting aircraft appeared over the battlefield. German troops exposed in forward positions or in isolated groups began to be engaged systematically. Resupply of ammunition, virtually all movement in fact, became impossible and the French launched one attack after another, wearing down the defence. It had been a gallant effort, but one which could not be sustained. As darkness fell, the survivors pulled back yet again to consolidate in the R1 Line. This move was disguised by means of vigorous patrolling activity and the firing of flares well to the south of the R 1 Line.

The day's operations had been exhausting and costly for the men of 214th Infantry Division. Most of the survivors were assembled in the *Kipsdorf Tunnel* on the *Keilberg* where, to general relief, carrying parties managed to get forward during the night 17/18 April with supplies of food and drink. Equally welcome was the arrival of 1st Battalion Infantry Regiment 177 of the Saxon 32nd Infantry Division, the *Eingreif* Division for Group Prosnes. Major Kruspe's men immediately assumed responsibility for this section of the R1 Line and spent the remaining hours of darkness improving the position and preparing to meet a renewal of the French attack. In the event there was no attack in the early morning, but pressure built up and around midday there was a concentrated assault all along the ridge line from the *Hochberg* to the *Pöhlberg*.

Throughout the night 17/18 the other battalions of Infantry Regiment 177 had been gradually making their way forward. Whilst counter action against the *Hochberg* - Hill 253 sector had been split between men of Infantry Regiment 50 under Major Mensur and Major Kruspe's men, the main weight of the counter-attack on the *Pöhlberg* was carried by Infantry Regiment 177. The action was observed by a reporter, who later left an atmospheric, if somewhat overblown, account of events that day.

Kriegsberichterstatter Katsch [21]

"The chain of hills where this battle took place dipped away [south] east of the *Pöhlberg*, via an area of low ground towards the wooded and somewhat lower hill, the so-called *Fichtelberg*. Now, the entire chain did not form one continuous ridge; on the contrary, ravines and depressions ran in all directions between the hills down towards the flatter ground. This meant that it was an extremely difficult battlefield. The rows of craters which represented the positions furthest forward ran up hill and down dale, sometimes overlooking, sometimes overlooked by, the enemy. Often the smoke of the explosions, coupled with dust hanging in the air, rendered observation from the various viewpoints impossible. Furthermore, whenever the telephone links were broken - which was usually the case - it was impossible to keep commanders informed.

"Here, between the *Pöhlberg* and the *Fichtelberg*, the French had attacked successfully on a narrow front, broken in and massed forces had passed through and were surging forward. The Saxon infantrymen were deployed here to restore this dangerous situation. The regiment had been on standby to intervene, but naturally it had to complete a demanding march forward in order to get to the point where its involvement had become necessary. The bulge that the French had driven into our lines threatened the flanks, almost the rear of other sectors. "Without any preparation, lacking knowledge of the ground, the regiment stormed forward in a form of open warfare against the new enemy front line. The lines of infantrymen deployed, only to be met by raging artillery and machine gun fire. Scattering, they gathered together once more in small groups so as to be able to pass through the destructive fire with fewer casualties. Forwards they went, unstoppably, across a valley bottom and through a newly erected wire obstacle. The Frenchies had to yield. A few examples will best serve to illustrate the nature of these battles.

• The enemy put up strong resistance in a copse. One company advanced using fire and movement; the men, sweating profusely, leaping forward from crater to crater. One unteroffizier and a few men managed to get into a shot up sap, but when they tried to move forward, they were met with machine gun fire from the front ... They were only few, immediately suffered casualties and had to dive into cover. The attack threatened to stall, which would have presented huge difficulties for all the assault troops. However the unteroffizier, Forker by name, calmly fired round after round at the crew of the machine gun. Heartened by his example, the remainder of his men tried everything to close up on the machine gun. Finally, led by the unteroffizier, they silenced the gun with hand grenades. This combination of rifle fire and grenades had dealt with the crew and the weapon itself was captured.

• The field artillery, which was tasked to follow up close behind the attack to provide fire support, also had a hard time of it. One gun, for example, lost its gun commander and another gunner. This left only the gun layer, himself severely wounded by a shell splinter, to serve it. The man involved was Gefreiter Kerstan who, despite the pain of his wound, stuck to his gun, well aware that the gunners and their guns were of the first importance to the infantry out forward. A medical NCO attempted to evacuate him to an aid post but he refused until a replacement for him arrived from another gun. At that he collapsed from loss of blood. He was then taken to the aid post and he now bears an Iron Cross First Class on his chest.

• The battery telephonist: he does not have it as bad as the men on the guns, does he? Well the heaviest possible fire was coming down on the battery position as well as on its observation post. The observer had no contact with the guns; all the lines had been cut. The two signallers, Gefreiters Apitz from Dresden and Israel from Herrenhut, were ordered to go out and fix the breaks, so that fire control could be re-established. Off they went through the craters, the cable passing though their hands, sometimes crawling, sometimes dashing forward until they came to a swampy stream. The bridge across it and the entire area were under appalling fire; they should not really have attempted to pass it, but on they went through bog and water, holding the cable in their raised hands. On the far bank they came under lacerating fire. Israel was killed, smashed to pieces by a heavy shell but Apitz, sweating freely, pressed on; he simply had to connect the battery commander with his forward observation officer. Through sheer effort, skill and luck he got through. He could now relax but his comradely feelings exceeded any self-satisfaction and he returned to collect the body of his dead friend. Nobody else would have known where to look for it. As it was, he received a soldier's grave.

"The infantry assault succeeded; despite the fact that the brave lads were almost overwhelmed with the torrents of machine gun fire on the slopes of the *Pöhlberg*; despite the fact that the ground was covered with pockets of enemy resistance, each one of which had to be cleared separately during the attack, and despite all the strong forces which the enemy had thrown forward through the break in point. Despite all that, the objective had been captured as ordered - and held."

During the Group Gerlach operations on the *Hochberg* 17 - 18 April, some of the participants were captured by the French.

Landsturmmann Karl Lüdke 1st Company Infantry Regiment 50[22]

"I belonged to the storm troop which, at 1.00 pm 17 April 1917, had the mission of recapturing the German Third Line [the R1 *Zwischenstellung*], which the French had taken from us during the morning. Arriving on the crest of the Hochberg, we came under machine gun fire from the *Fichtelberg* opposite.[23] We dived into shell holes for cover, but came under fire from our own artillery and were ordered by the feldwebel to drop back to the second section of trench. A short time later there was a hailstorm and, profiting from this, we exploited the moment to rush forward over the summit of the *Hochberg* and, before the storm was over, to begin to dig in on the slope facing the French. Despite very heavy enemy fire, we held on to the position from the afternoon of 17 April until the afternoon of 18 April. There then followed drum fire, which lasted a full six hours and completely buried the section next to mine. That evening, taking advantage of foggy conditions, the French attacked. German field guns fired, but over the heads of the French, who pushed on well beyond our position. I was captured, together with fourteen other comrades. What became of the rest of my battalion I do not know.

"We were escorted by Zouaves back to a large dugout aid post in the lost German Second Line. Here we were literally robbed of everything we possessed by Zouaves who had been held back there in reserve. I never saw my money, watch, ring or knife again. We spent four days in that dugout. From dusk until dawn we had to carry the wounded back through German fire. Motorised trucks, that were driven to within five kilometres of the front, then transported them further. The French suffered heavy casualties; the communication trenches were full of them. Most had suffered head wounds. Nobody thought of giving us any rations, so we searched through knapsacks which were lying all around for iron rations. We had nothing to drink for four days and were totally parched, almost dying of thirst. Forced to work constantly, my strength gave out on the fourth day. As a wounded man was being transported to the rear I collapsed. I signalled to the medical orderlies who were with us and made them understand by saying, *malade, malade*. The only reply was a kick in the guts. All we were granted was rest by day. On 24 April Zouaves escorted us to a holding cage about fifteen kilometres behind the front. 100 prisoners from Infantry Regiments 50, 358 and 363 were already there."

Meanwhile there was a desperate struggle for control of the critical area around the *Kipsdorf Tunnel*, just west of the *Keilberg*. There were repeated French thrusts against the tunnel throughout the day. One particularly heavy one around midday was only beaten off at the cost of heavy casualties amongst the defenders and the personal intervention of Major Kruspe. The fighting continued throughout the afternoon, prior to a final effort by the French being beaten off just short of the tunnel at 7.30 pm.

While the Saxons were restoring the situation on the *Keilberg* and the *Pöhlberg*, a critical situation also developed further west, where a fresh French thrust succeeded in gaining a foothold in the R1 Line between the *Hochberg* and Hill 253, 500 metres to the east. What was left of Reserve Hauptmann Masur's battalion was instantly alerted and formed into three 'companies'. There were dispiritingly few of them. Reserve Leutnant Matuschik commanded fifty men; Schumann and Hill seventy five each. Masur assumed command of all troops on the *Hochberg* and launched his men at the break in point. In one great rush they retook the R1 Line at this point and then established contact with 11th Company Infantry Regiment 177 to the right. Naturally there was a violent French reaction. Following a three hour bombardment with all calibres up to 280 mm, another attempt was made on the R1 Line and yet again the French broke in.

Reacting, the regimental commander placed Reserve Leutnant Schmidt in charge of the only counter-attack force which could be mustered. This comprised forty survivors from Masur's battalion and the last forty men of 10th Company 177. His orders were to throw the enemy back off Hill 263 or at least to seal off the penetration. Schmidt realised immediately that his force was too weak to eject the enemy, so he sealed off the right [eastern] flank of the break in and held it against three attacks the following night. All these effort bought time for a properly constituted attack to be launched at 8.00 am from *Lug ins Land* to *Pöhlberg*. This was successful, though it was far from the end of the story in this heavily disputed area, but it was for the exhausted remnant of 214th Infantry Division. They had by then been in action constantly for ten days and were temporarily finished as a fighting formation. Gratefully, Infantry Regiment 50 handed over its sector to Infantry Regiment 64 and moved back, first into reserve, then to a quiet sector elsewhere.

At the end of March 1917, 58th Infantry Division relieved 212th Infantry Division, assuming responsibility for the front between the *Hexenberg* [Hill 181, just south of the *Fichtelberg*] and Aubérive. Infantry Regiment 106, the right forward regiment, abutted Infantry Regiment 358 of 214th Infantry Division, Reserve Infantry Regiment 103 and was deployed in the centre, with Infantry Regiment 107 located to the south of Aubérive. The layout of the positions mirrored those which obtained elsewhere in Champagne. The First Position, as elsewhere, comprised three main lines of trenches, designated K1, K 2 and K3, but actually forming part of a complete network of saps and communication trenches that formed a dense labyrinth in places. It should have been a reasonably strong layout, but the winter weather had played havoc with the various excavations. In many places trenches had collapsed and were more than knee deep in mud - and that was before the destructive preliminary bombardment had even begun.

Prior to the opening of the offensive, many of these minor trenches were totally flattened or had been abandoned. In general there were sufficient dugouts in all three lines from the trench garrisons, but they did not correspond to the latest thinking, being insufficiently deep or reinforced. The result was that many were crushed or buried. Infantry Regiment 107 was perhaps the worst off in this respect. Far too many of its dugouts were placed in the K1 Line, which meant that there was a constant risk of much of the trench garrison being cut off in the event of a surprise attack.[24] Various attempts were made to improve the situation, but there was too little time and the constant shelling meant that opportunities to work in the open became few and far between. Located in depth about two and a half to four kilometres behind the front line was the R1 Line, comprising a single continuous trench equipped with dugouts and some strong points. A further two kilometres in rear was the R2 Line.

The defence in depth adopted by Reserve Infantry Regiment 103 was typical. Its sector was split in half, with one battalion responsible for each subsector. Both battalions deployed two companies forward, with the remainder back in support. The third battalion served as the regimental reserve. The K1 Line was only occupied by advanced sentry positions and listening posts. The main forces were located back in the K2 Line, with supports back in K3, which is also where battalion command posts were placed. Prior to the bombardment, the German artillery support was judged to be strong but, strangely, Reserve Infantry Regiment 103 commented that infantry-artillery cooperation was not as skilfully handled as it had been on the Somme. The reasons are not made clear and it is possible that this was a judgment made after its sub-units were destroyed or largely neutralised prior to 17 April.

No Man's Land was between 150 and 800 metres wide at this point and although Reserve Infantry Regiment 103 was initially opposed by Russian troops in late March, later raids yielded prisoners from the French 185 Territorial Brigade and Infantry Regiment 207.[25] Regimental Headquarters was in the *Sachsengrund*, a low lying, wooded area just west of the *Hindenburg Höhe* and co-located with large shelters for reserves, most of the divisional artillery, supplies of all kinds and signalling stations. As March turned into April there continued to be feverish activity all along the front. Artillery fire increased and there were numerous gas attacks, both using shells and cylinder gas. One major instance occurred near Aubérive on 29 March, but an alert sentry saw the gas being released, raised the alarm and, despite three major clouds of a chorine/phosgene mix being released, all ranks of Infantry Regiment 107 were masked up in time and suffered only three gas casualties.[26]

It was of course completely clear that the start of the French offensive could not be long delayed; the intelligence indicators were multiplying rapidly and warnings circulated with ever increasing frequency. During the evening of 6 April, XIV Corps [Group Prosnes] sent a flash message to all subordinate commanders: 'This afternoon, enemy aircraft attacked our observation balloons on a wide front.'[27] There could be no clearer signal that artillery preparation was about to begin, so high alert was maintained and, in accordance with the new aggressive counter-battery policy, identified French targets - both gun lines and observation posts - began to be engaged vigorously by the German heavy batteries. There was a limit to what could be achieved, given the overwhelming numerical superiority of the French artillery, so losses mounted and the problems increased day by day.

1st Battalion Infantry Regiment 107, for example, reported during the morning of 11 April that French gunfire, directed from the air, had caused numerous casualties, mostly men crushed in wrecked dugouts or buried alive and followed this that afternoon with a message which read, 'Enemy fire is extremely heavy and is being directed against our wire, K1, K2 and astride the Aubérive - Vaudesincourt road. It seems that the enemy is attempting to isolate Aubérive, so they could be planning a large scale raid or may attempt to capture Aubérive by means of a preliminary operation. Casualties so far have been quite significant. Almost every dugout in the left hand company sector has been smashed.'[28] The situation worsened by the hour. The following day its routine report read, 'C5 and left hand section C4, K1 and K2 impassable. Most of the dugouts have been destroyed. The majority of the garrison is located in craters. *Einsiedelweg*, *Ehrentalweg*, *Masurenweg* and *Kurfürstenweg* have all been destroyed. Heavy enemy destructive fire guided from the air is coming down all over the position. The medium and heavy mortars, which were to have fired in support of the rearranged raid at 10.30 pm, have all been buried. Enemy infantry is firing at our men manning the craters. Our destructive fire must be increased.'[29] The situation for the forward troops was becoming desperate and there were still a further five days of the bombardment to be endured.

It was exactly the same story all along the divisional frontage. One of the hardest aspects for the infantry to accept was the fact that French counter-battery fire had had such a devastating effect on the German artillery that for long periods they were pinned down by French gunfire without seeing any response at all. Infantry Regiment 106 suffered especially severely from French mortar fire, complaining later that, 'Although repeatedly from 10 April and five times on 14 April precise targeting was provided to our artillery and gunfire was requested, not one single round was fired.'[30] Meanwhile the bombardment ground on inexorably. On 11 April, the command post of the *KTK* of Reserve Infantry Regiment 103 was totally destroyed. Hauptmann Israel himself escaped to re-establish command from a dugout on the northern edge of *Mittelwald* [Middle Wood], but company runners, Förster and Seiler (5th), Kießling (6th) and Frenzel (7th), were all buried alive; then the same fate befell Vizefeldwebel Bullert and Gefreiter Süß (8th) as they led a rescue attempt. At that, efforts were abandoned, but, remarkable to relate, two and a half days later Gefreiter Förster, the sole survivor, emerged, having dug his way out unaided.[31]

Air observation and numerous German raids added to the intelligence picture. The last of these raids took place in the early hours of 17 April, when Vizefeldwebel Göthel, 7th Company Infantry Regiment 107, closed right up on the French lines south of Aubérive.[32] It was certain that the opposing forces were from the Moroccan Division, XVII Corps, that had established a reputation as a powerful and effective attacking formation. It was also clear by this stage that the main enemy thrusts would be directed to the west of Aubérive, and against the junction between Infantry Regiment 358 and at the boundary between 1st and 3rd Battalions Infantry Regiment 106. This deduction arose from a study of the final phase of the artillery bombardment. Although the entire area had suffered a severe battering, the emphasis during the night of 16/17 April, the places where the drumfire was at its most intense in this sector was between the *Möllerberg* and the *Hexenberg/Fichtelberg*. All approach routes were gassed repeatedly, while the weight of fire falling on all known and suspected German forward positions reached previously unparalleled proportions.

Suddenly, at 5.45 am, as a total of six French divisions attacked on a fourteen kilometre frontage, the numbed survivors of 58th Infantry Division stood to and attempted to stem the tide of assault troops. Their losses in men and weapons had been severe, so they were forced to gather together in small groups and, making best use of the machine guns that were still serviceable, they did their best, but the outcome was more or less one sided. Profiting from the darkness and snow squalls, attacking in depth on narrow fronts, the German nests of resistance were soon crushed or bypassed. The K1 to K3 Lines were lost rapidly; their garrisons rolled up from the flanks or rear. The crucial *Fichtelberg* position, whose defence had been weakened even further by the removal of a rifle company the previous night to strengthen the front line, was lost in the first rush. The attack was conducted so rapidly that surprise was complete. In many places the trenches were totally empty and the Moroccans just moved in. It would be easy, but unfair, to be over critical of the defence. The men who had endured a solid week of bombardment, who had gone without sleep, hot food or drinks for days, were simply worn down and, with morale at rock bottom, were unable to coordinate their efforts.

Here and there isolated acts of resistance, which in many cases caused the attackers severe casualties, showed how events might have played out had it been possible to relieve the defenders just before the attack was launched or had a network of machine guns, backed by counter-stroke troops, been placed in depth and resolutely manned. As it was, during a day of reverses, French attempts to push on through the *Sachsengrund* and take the *Hindenburg Höhe* and the R1 Line west of Dontrien were thwarted completely by the vigorous leadership of Reserve Leutnant Hottenroth, commanding 2nd Machine Gun Company Infantry Regiment 106, who repeatedly halted all efforts to press in that direction.[33] It was, however, impossible for the *KTK* to build on this. Only very small groups of reserves were immediately available. Whilst deployable in minor reinforcing roles, they were completely unequal to any sort of counter-stroke mission.

In the Reserve Infantry Regiment 103 sector, where the forward sub units had by 17 April been manning the front line for twelve days without relief, the massed assault groups of Moroccan troops were spotted early and the alarm was raised in good time. Unfortunately, calls for artillery defensive fire produce only a negligible response and very quickly the forward troops were engaged in a hand to hand struggle - especially on the right flank, where 5th Company under Reserve Leutnant Meusel was deployed. For a time two machine guns, one heavy and one light, forced the attackers into cover and a battle with hand grenades raged. Unfortunately one of the guns was knocked out by a direct hit, pressure was building and it was necessary to begin falling back. Vigorous defence by 6th Company, supported by machine guns of 7th Company in *Baumaffenwald*, where the Moroccans had gained a foothold, was fairly successful and even succeeded in pushing the attackers back temporarily. However, the thrust in the Infantry Regiment 106 sector when the *Fichtelberg* was captured threatened the entire integrity of the defence. The Reserve Infantry Regiment 103 *KTK* had no alternative from about 7.00 am but to use every available man to shore up the crumbling position and prevent the French assault being developed further to the east.

The regimental commander sent the Assault Pioneer Company forward to reinforce the threatened area and the French continued to push and probe the defences. To the east of *Mittelwald* was a dense web of trenches that saw vicious close quarter see-saw fighting throughout the day as French thrusts made some progress, only to be thrown back once more by desperate counter-actions. Naturally, the position had been laid out to defend against attacks from the south. Furthermore virtually all the trenches had been flattened. Nevertheless, the numerous communications trenches, though badly hit, did at least provide a framework for the defence and were fully exploited. The so-called *Mittelwald Stützpunkt*, located on the northern edge of the wood, was critically important. It was defended by 1st Company, under Reserve Leutnant Fischer and elements of Reserve Leutnant Kettner's 10th Company. It was well served by machine gun posts and also housed the *KTK*, Reserve Hauptmann Israel, who was therefore immediately on hand to lead the defence. Despite every effort by the Moroccans, this strong point stood firm and repelled all attacks mounted against it. This was just as well, because its possession provided a start line for the attempted counter-attack against the *Fichtelberg* when the divisional reserve was launched forward that afternoon.

Infantry Regiment 107, the most easterly of the regiments of Generalleutnant von Gontard's 58th Infantry Division, had a rather different experience. Its forward defenders watched as Reserve Infantry Regiment 103, to the west of its 3rd Battalion, and Infantry Regiment 105 of 30th Infantry Division to the east of 2nd Battalion were subjected to mass attack by the French 24th Division, XII Corps, but it was itself not attacked directly. To begin with the situation was anything but clear but, by about 8.00 am, regimental headquarters was able to pass on the message that the advance had reached the K3 line in the Reserve Infantry Regiment 103 sector. Contact had apparently been lost with that regiment and substantial progress had been made along the line of the Suippes towards Vaudesincourt. This was an uncomfortable situation. The village of Aubérive was now occupying a narrow salient in the French front line, meaning that there was a real threat of it being isolated and captured. About the same time an attack against the south of Aubérive managed to establish a foothold in the K1 Line there.

Orders were issued to 3rd Battalion to pull back to the east along the K1 Line and to reorganise its companies to provide strong flank protection. Now, unknown to the regiment, there were still some parties from Reserve Infantry Regiment 103 holding out forward, so for the time being the commanding officer held back from carrying out this order. To the east Infantry Regiment 105 had managed to conduct an immediate counter-stroke, supported by a platoon of Infantry Regiment 107 under Vizefeldwebel Mühlbach. This had driven back troops of the French 34th Infantry Division and thus reduced the risk to Aubérive from that direction. This did not prevent further French attempts to storm the northeast corner of Aubérives, but obstinate defence by a section of the 2nd Machine Gun Company of Infantry Regiment 107, led by Unteroffizier Köbe, checked every attack.

58th Infantry Division, aware of the vulnerability of Aubérive, gave permission for its evacuation 'if necessary' but, after consultation with the local commander, Reserve Oberleutnant Leskien, the offer was turned down. Aubérive was to be held for the time being as a bastion of the defence.[34] In an attempt to improve the tactical situation further, discussions took place with Infantry Regiment 105 that afternoon with the aim of carrying out a limited counter-attack that evening at 8.30 pm. It proved extremely difficult to coordinate artillery participation and to confirm final details with Infantry Regiment 105. In the event, only 5th Company Infantry Regiment 107 under Reserve Leutnant Schoer and supported by elements of 3rd Company attacked. There was some success. The French were driven out of *Torgauergraben* northeast of Aubérive, but a strong counter-attack, launched in pitch blackness at 10.30 pm, forced Schoer's men back once more, though an officer from the French 105th Regiment was captured. There had been no contact with Infantry Regiment 105 and the men of Infantry Regiment 107 had been too few to be able to hold on to their gains. Nevertheless, despite its precarious position around Aubérive, Infantry Regiment 107, with the exception of 5th Company now forced back into the K2 Line, was still holding right forward. On a day of reverses all along the front, this was no mean achievement.

It must be remembered, of course, that Infantry Regiment 105 had been under immense pressure from the moment that the attacks came in. The initial surge that 30th Infantry Division, as the most westerly formation of XII Corps (Group Py), had to try to counter, produced a penetration as far as the K3 Line near Vaudesincourt, so the first and continuing priority was to counter that. While Infantry Regiment 99 held firm to the east, two companies (10th and 11th) of Infantry Regiment 143, back in reserve positions just south of Dontrien, were called forward to launch a counter attack. As Oberleutnant Lehnung led 10th Company forward, it came under heavy artillery fire and was scattered. 11th Company, led by Leutnant Maerker, threw the French back from their recently captured position and set up a blocking position, which then succeeded in beating off a series of attacks.

So scattered was 10th Company that when it arrived at the *KTK* for orders, Oberleutnant Lehnung had less than a platoon with him. Other elements of the company sought to get forward and eventually fetched up at the command post of Hauptmann Wunderlich of Infantry Regiment 105, who gratefully took them under command as a useful reinforcement. One of the platoon commanders of 10th Company later wrote up his experiences of the day.

Reserve Vizefeldwebel Brauns 10th Company Infantry Regiment 143[35]

"During the early morning of 17 April, there was heavy artillery fire at the front. We still had no clear idea what was happening when we were suddenly stood to at 8.00 am. By around 9.00 am we were marching along a section of railway track via Dontrien, past a battery in action, to the regimental command post of Infantry Regiment 105. From there we were directed to one of the regimental battalion command posts, from where we were to be deployed. We took off our knapsacks and were issued with hand grenades. The company was split into assault groups, thus:

1st GroupLeutnant Kästner and three sections
2nd GroupVizefeldwebel Staufenbiel and two sections
3rd Group Me with two sections
4th GroupKunz with two sections

"Rather hastily, our Oberleutnant [Lehnung] explained the route which we were to follow through completely unknown terrain. Then 1st Group left at once, together with the company commander. He was followed by Staufenbiel, but my men were still being issued with grenades. By the time we were able to set off all contact had been lost. We ran after the others, sweating freely, and suddenly found ourselves in a maze of shot up trenches which was under heavy artillery fire. I could not tell one from the other, so I left my men in a dugout and ran back to a trench junction then forward until there was no trace of any trench. Lying behind a mound of earth I observed a wide flat area that looked as though it had been ploughed up and which was being swept by enemy machine gun fire.

"I simply could not lead my men forward here. I ran back to my group, intending to collect one other man and to return to the battalion command post to request a guide. On the way I bumped into the 4th Group, which was accompanied by an unteroffizier of Infantry Regiment 105, who was supposed to show us the way. We set off once more. A few Saxons were still around; a sergeant ran just in front of me. Suddenly we came under violent attack. Kerr - bammm!! Just to our left a shell landed on the edge of the trench. We were showered with mud and enveloped in thick smoke. The sergeant lay at our feet, bleeding. We just pushed on past him. We finally arrived at the R1 Line, where my group was. The unteroffizier from the 105th said that we should have to push on right through the stop line.

"I gathered my men up and we arrived at the *Görnerweg*, a trench that led to the Aubérive - St Souplet road. We dashed across the road and threw ourselves into an adjoining trench. Where to now? Not even my unteroffizier had a clue. The two trenches soon petered out, but as soon as we emerged we came under a crazy rate of machine gun fire. We were certainly not going to get forward here! We hared back across the road and found Kunz and his group back in the stop line. He had no idea where we were meant to be either. Luckily, Ringert turned up leading a party carrying hand grenades forward. We pushed further left and arrived at the regimental headquarters of Infantry Regiment 99. The commander, our Major Hoffmann, directed us on our way. We hurried on and succeeded in reaching the command post of 2nd Battalion Infantry Regiment 105. Hauptmann Wunderlich explained that we could not get to the right flank from here, because the forward trenches were full of enemy.

"We wanted to carry on, but Hauptmann Wunderlich ordered us to stay with him because he had no reserves left. We were sent forward to come under command of Leutnant Lose, 8th Company. There we came across very few men and those that there were were all down in the dugouts, totally exhausted. By now it was evening and I set about posting my men in sentry positions. Despite their tiredness they had to stay awake all night, so as to give the 105th a chance to recover. There were French attacks to the left and right, but they were all beaten off. Here we stayed, more or less forgotten. There was a lack of bread. All we could find forward was some tinned food. Finally, troops from another unit arrived at 11.30 pm on 20 April to relieve us. Hauptmann Wunderlich thanked us and provided us with a certificate to confirm where we had been during the fighting. We never closed our eyes for three days and nights."

In reserve and in support of 58th Infantry Division was Infantry Regiment 103 of 32nd Infantry Division . When the attacks began on 17 April, the regiment was still several kilometres from the front line. The sound of artillery firing and the bombardment of the Second Position [R2 Line] were the only indicators that a critical situation was unfolding. Arriving there in the late morning, it was greeted with the news that, 'The enemy forced their way under cover of darkness into the positions of Infantry Regiment 106 and Reserve Infantry Regiment 103; the *Fichtelberg* has been lost.' [36] A short time later the battalions received orders from Oberstleutnant Bock von Wülfingen, commander Infantry Regiment 106, for a counter-attack. The attack was to begin at 6.00 pm. 1st Battalion was to launch forward directly from the R1 Line, whilst 2nd and 3rd Battalions conducted flanking attacks. 3rd Battalion, attacking deeply echeloned, was to carry the main weight of the attack.

Inevitably the timings were over optimistic. 2nd Battalion managed to make its way to a start line in *Mittelwald*, which was still being held by elements of Reserve Infantry Regiment 103, but did even begin to arrive there until 6.30 pm. 3rd Battalion, which had had a much longer approach march and which had been harassed all the way by gun fire, was not in position until 9.30 pm. A counter-attack that night was clearly out of the question; indeed Haupmann Reich, commanding 3rd Battalion, had requested and been granted a delay until the morning of 18 April while his unit was still moving forward. However, that was not the end of the story. 1st Battalion, due to attack from the R1 position, was in place in good time. Its companies lined up in the order from east to west of 3rd, 2nd and 1st, with 4th Company in reserve. Eight machine guns were allocated in support of the leading companies and were dispersed along the attack frontage.

It was clear that the most difficult aspect would be the coordination of the converging attacks and, because of the distances involved, it had been decided that when 2nd Battalion was ready to start, several yellow flares would be fired. Most unfortunately, the signal to the German artillery to increase the range was also two yellow flares. At 6.40 pm as 6th Company Infantry Regiment 103 arrived in *Mittelwald*, two heavy German shells landed right on top of their ranks, killing two men and wounding a further seventeen. There was nothing for it but to fire two yellow flares, which 1st Battalion promptly interpreted as the signal to advance. As a result, instead of the *Fichtelberg* being subjected to a violent, converging, attack, the French defenders could concentrate entirely on troops from 1st Battalion advancing across open country.

With great determination, these troops pushed forward approximately 1,500 metres, getting to within 500 metres of the summit of the *Fichtelberg* but, because they were under fire, including heavy machine gun fire from the east throughout the process, they suffered grievously. 3rd Company was especially exposed, losing its company commander, Leutnant Pfundt, killed, together with Offizierstellvertreter Zeidlick and Leutnant Bretschneider of 1st Machine Gun Company, as well as numerous other ranks.

Leutnant Rothe and Fähnrich Weiland were wounded, as were many others.[37] They had, however, not suffered entirely in vain. They recaptured two German heavy artillery batteries (210 mm and 150 mm) and the guns were recovered. The survivors of 1st Battalion dug in along the line they had reached, pushing out listening posts and other patrols to avoid being surprised during the night.

Whilst the fighting continued, orders had gone out in various directions and reinforcements began moving into position. Appreciating the risk to the overall integrity of the defence if 214th Infantry Division failed to hold along the *Lug ins Land - Pöhlberg* front, Generalleutnant de Beaulieu ordered the final uncommitted regiment of 32nd Infantry Division - Infantry Regiment 102 - to move forward to Moronvilliers via Pont Faverger, ready to be deployed. He also sought priority for the use of 5th and 6th Infantry Divisions, which were being moved forward. This was noted but, initially, both remained under command of First Army, whose staff continued to monitor the situation and prepare contingency plans. By mid afternoon, with the *Eingreif* forces closing up to the forward area, there was some concern that the French were about to launch a renewed heavy attack against the R1 Line.

The Army Commander, General der Infanterie Fritz von Below, decided, therefore, to counter the threatened breakthrough on the 214th Infantry Division front by means of, 'a coordinated counter-attack from the front and both flanks'.[38] To that end, he ordered one regiment of each of 34th Infantry Division (Group Reims) and 32nd Infantry Division to be prepared to attack from the west, 5th and 6th Divisions to launch a joint attack from the north and 23rd Infantry Division to advance from the east. In the event the expected major French attack did not materialise, though persistent small scale offensive operations continued throughout the day. There was a noticeable slackening of French effort at the western end of the battlefield, where their VIII Corps, having battered repeatedly at the *Cornillet* and been repulsed each time, called a halt to the attacks. 214th Infantry Division managed to hold on until nightfall, but the losses it had incurred and the intensity of the battle meant that its forward units were effectively fought out. As has been mentioned, Infantry Regiment 177, 32nd Division, assumed responsibility for the critical sector of the front and stabilised the situation.

The *Fichtelberg* counter-attack did not go as planned. Nevertheless, the fact remained that at the end of the first day of battle the French offensive that had been so long in the planning and preparation, had achieved its objectives neither against Groups Prosnes, nor around Aubérive. They had caused the forward defenders serious casualties, but had only managed to capture the approaches to *Langer Rücken* and achieve a minor penetration near *Lug ins Land*; a very poor return indeed, for the investment in men and materiel. On the German side, the disappointing end to the attempt to retake the *Fichtelberg* on 17 April, was not the end of the story. By 5.20 am on 18 April, the leading companies of 2nd and 3rd Battalions Infantry Regiment 103 were in position on their start lines near *Mittelwald*, ready to begin the attack in three waves. However, it was to be a dispiriting and disappointing day, as this comprehensive account by one of the company commanders explains.

Leutnant Otto Besser 7th Company Infantry Regiment 103[39]

"Regimental order during the afternoon [of 17 April]: 'The regiment is to mount a counter-attack and retake the *Fichtelberg*'. Our move forward was slow because the guides did not know the routes. Finally the battalion reached the appointed place, but the attack was postponed. 2nd Battalion stayed in *Bataillonsweg* [Battalion Way], spending the freezing cold night crouched down or lying in the trench. With our teeth chattering, sleep was out of the question. Finally the attack order reached the company commander at 3.00 am and was read by the light of an electric torch. OK, 5.30 am! The platoon commanders were summoned, the situation was explained and the ground was described as well as it could be at night. The objective was defined, together with links left and right and watches were synchronised. 7th Company was divided into three waves. The leading wave, reinforced by strong grenade teams, was led by Vizefeldwebel Schneider and deployed on the right flank. The second was under Leutnant Mühler and the 3rd by the company commander in person. With the wish, 'Break a leg', the platoon commanders were dismissed to go and prepare for the attack.

"5.30 am! The first wave left the trench in accordance with orders, followed closely by the other two. The unknown landscape was lit by a pale moon, as the ghostly lines advanced with 5th Company to the left of 7th Company. To the front, all was still. The German artillery was more or less totally silent. To begin with all went smoothly. We came across a German field battery position, abandoned by its crew, but not occupied by the French. Its surrounding barbed wire was almost intact. Because of the over-extended width of the company sector, the junior commanders had enormous difficulties in trying to keep their platoons together in the dark. The net result was that the three waves fused into one. As for the enemy, we still had no idea where they were.

"The ground began to rise. This had to be the *Fichtelberg*. By the light of the moon we could just make out its outline against the sky. Suddenly there were hand grenade explosions to our right and the rattle of an enemy machine gun. 'Get forward, that is nothing to do with us!' ... The company began to double forward. Soon the rattle of machine guns and the explosion of hand grenades could be heard coming from our right rear. The 7th Company hand grenade team bravely engaged enemy outposts on the right flank. We closed up towards the crest line. Suddenly loud shouts of *Hurra!* could be heard coming from 5th or 6th Companies. They had already reached the enemy trenches. 'Double march!' We had just crossed an intact wire obstacle when enemy machine guns opened up death-dealing streams of fire. Suddenly there was intense small arms fire and volleys of hand grenades. It was impossible to get forward. The lucky ones found cover in shells holes. Enemy fire slackened and the moans and screams of the wounded could be heard.

"Gradually things quietened down, dawn broke so we could see that the enemy trench was less than fifteen metres away and there were other enemy positions to our right rear. We had blundered into a sack and we almost completely surrounded. The small shell hole I was sharing with my faithful batman, Gefreiter Weber, had to be deepened quickly. We did not have a spade, so we dug with our hands and improved our cover. We loosened the earth with a bayonet and worked feverishly with our fingers. A small fir tree to our front provided some cover from view. As it became light we had to stop, warned by the impact of a bullet which threw up particles of chalk. What could we do? We were but few. The close proximity of the enemy ruled out any form of contact with our comrades in adjoining shell holes.

"The enemy began to get active and started to practise their rifle grenade shooting. There were cracks to the left and right but mostly from the rear. I took off my steel helmet, smeared my cap with chalky mud and slowly raised my head out of cover. They were shoulder to shoulder and very close indeed. They were big brown chaps - Moroccans, élite African troops. Suddenly there was intense firing, involving several machine guns. Hand grenades were thrown and orders shouted. They must be coming for us! I readied my revolver and held it firmly, ready to fire. All went quiet then a voice called monotonously, 'Comrades, comrades, do not shoot, come over here!' These cowards, afraid to attack, actually wanted us to desert. We should sooner die honourably as men! Ten or twelve of these brown brutes were already out of their trenches, rifles at the ready with bayonets fixed. They shouted and waved, indicating that they did not actually know how close we were, or exactly where. Ought we to shoot? It did not come to that. All of a sudden a German machine gun opened up at a range of 700 - 800 metres and the Moroccans disappeared even faster than we did as we also took cover from the fire. As I later discovered, a machine gun positioned on our original start line had spotted the enemy.

"Aircraft appeared from all directions. The few feeble rays of sunshine, which had slightly warmed the pitiful remnants of the company as they lay in their shell holes, disappeared. The sky clouded over and it began to snow or rain alternately. We carefully pulled out a ground sheet from our equipment, huddled together in the small hole and covered ourselves with it. The minutes seemed like hours. It rained and rained. The temperature was at freezing point - not exactly what was needed in this particular situation. One man was freezing in a neighbouring shell hole. You could hear him freezing! Slowly we became saturated from beneath. Our right sides were just one mass of mud. Occasionally, with great care, it was possible to stretch our cramped limbs. Half a bar of chocolate, meticulously shared, was our sole nourishment since the previous evening and the contents of a small brandy flask warmed us for a while. Of course the Moroccans did not like the weather either, so things became rather more peaceful.

"Even this day eventually had to end. It was 7.00, then 8.00 pm. We gathered our dulled wits, realising that we had link up with the remainder of the battalion once more; we were certainly not longing for captivity. The rain stopped. Unfortunately this meant that visibility improved and the enemy machine guns began to rattle again. The whole area was tirelessly swept and one machine gun, firing from our half right rear, was especially unpleasant. We soon discovered that the only gap through which we could escape was half left to our rear. It was 9.30 pm. We could see that the enemy trench was still fully manned, with the garrison half in and half out of the trench. Wild grenade throwing was happening to our half left. Suddenly, a figure rose from a shell hole to our right. He was followed by another. We joined them and rushed for the next cover in a hail of machine gun fire. We then orientated ourselves and in the end there were fourteen to sixteen of us.

"By the light of flares we could confirm our direction through this unknown terrain. Taking every precaution to avoid being shot by our own men back on the start line, we eventually arrived on the position of our neighbouring company. There was great joy because we brought longed-for reinforcement to the weak defence. I reported to the battalion commander, Oberleutnant Monse. 'Thank heavens, at least another one!' was his happy reply and he shook my hand vigorously. I had a drink of coffee and brandy with something to eat then stretched out my aching body on a louse ridden bunk in the former dugout of a flash spotting section where battalion headquarters had been established."

While these major actions were being played out, the French High Command was in the process of evaluating progress to date and redeploying its forces. General Nivelle allocated X Corps to Army Group Pétain so that the impetus of operations could be maintained, whilst General Micheler issued fresh orders that Fourth Army was to strive to achieve its previously allocated objectives. In consequence, General Anthoine was given specific orders to renew the assault on *Langer Rücken* and the ridge line to the east on 18 April. He then directed 45th and 33rd Divisions to clear the southern slopes of the crest line, whilst the Moroccan Division captured Aubérive and the area to the west of the village. Only then, with these preliminary operations out of the way, were VIII and XVII Corps to launch a general assault on the R1 Line between 6.00pm and 7.00 pm.

As has been mentioned, the defenders were not content just to wait for the next French move and although the attempted counter-attack on the *Fichtelberg* stalled, then failed, there was more success around the *Lug ins Land - Hochberg* sector, where the attackers had managed to established a foothold as part of the initial moves to capture the crest line. This had occurred after a brief preliminary bombardment and, about midday, the French forced their way into the R1 Line between *Hochberg* and Hill 253. There was an immediate reaction from Infantry Regiment 50, Major Masur took over command of all troops in the *Hochberg* sector then, with three companies (though these totalled a mere 200 men in all), he launched a hasty counter-attack against the break in point. Caught by surprise, the French were ejected in short order and the line was re-established.[40] However, that was not the end of the story. Preparations for the evening attack by XVI Corps continued and the ridge line was subjected to a three hour fire plan involving all calibres up to 280 mm. During the course of this gun fire, a further French thrust led to another break in being achieved, this time by Hill 253.

Few reserves could be found to counter this, but Reserve Leutnant Schmidt was allocated the roughly forty men who remained from the previous counter-attack and the remnants of 10th Company Infantry Regiment 177, also about forty men strong, and ordered to respond. His force was far too weak to carry out an attack but, nevertheless, he managed to seal off the break in and hold it through the following night. Also playing a prominent role in the desperate close quarter fighting for the ridge line was an important element of the divisional reserve, the so-called Group Gerlach. This *ad hoc* formation, which comprised 1st and 2nd Battalions Infantry Regiment 50 (less 1st Company), 9th Company Infantry Regiment 358 and Pionier Company 341 had finally concentrated to the north of the *Sachsen-Lager* in rear of the Second Position [R2 Line] on the evening of 15 April. Here it was reinforced by 2nd Battalion Infantry Regiment 358. From 5.30 am on 16 April, Group Gerlach was on full alert. A special report concerning its contribution to the battle appeared later in the Infantry Regiment 50 history.[41]

"Group Gerlach which comprised nine companies (1st and 2nd Battalions Infantry Regiment 50 (less 2nd Company), 9th Company Infantry Regiment 358 and Pionier Company 341, formed part of the divisional reserve during the battle. When, on 17 April, the enemy forced their way into the position on the *Hochberg*, the Group was subordinated to Oberstleutnant Hay, commander Infantry Regiment 363, then sent to conduct a counter-stroke. At 10.45 am the Group set off, with 4th Company Infantry Regiment 50 and 2nd Battalion Infantry Regiment 358 in reserve. As soon as it reached the R2 [Second] Position, the advancing troops began to suffer badly as a result of enemy artillery fire. The summit of the *Hochberg* was cleared of enemy but, as contact was lost with neighbouring troops to the left and right, the Group was constantly threatened with being outflanked, because the enemy had thrust forward noticeably further on both flanks.

"About 4.00 am on 18 April heavy enemy gun fire began falling on the *Hochberg* and the enemy attempted to break through along the line of a ravine and so encircle Group Gerlach. 9th Company Infantry Regiment 358 and 4th Company Infantry Regiment 50 formed a flank guard and successfully halted an enemy attack about 6.00 am. The risk of being outflanked to the right [west] was temporarily averted, because Group Herbert (Infantry Regiment 363) held the enemy in check on the *Lug ins Land* and Piefke's platoon from 1st Company Infantry Regiment 50 covered the right flank effectively. The risk on the left flank was altogether more serious, because the enemy tried repeatedly to breakthrough from the *Württemberger Weg*. The danger was not reduced until Masur's battalion carried out the successful counter-stroke described above. This gave the garrison on the *Hochberg* a breathing space, enabling them to pull together an altogether more effective defence.

"An aggressive counter-stroke threw the enemy, who attempted to conceal themselves by means of smoke grenades, a good distance back down the hill. In the process 3rd Company Infantry Regiment 50 captured a light machine gun, whilst 1st Company made prisoners of a lieutenant, a sergeant major and three men of a Zouave regiment. Three captured maps, which showed precisely how the attack had been planned, were immediately sent to Brigade. As night fell the general situation forced a withdrawal to the second trench of the R1 Position [*Zwischenstellung*], thus preventing a threatened envelopment under cover of darkness. Once again artillery fire caused heavy casualties. Leutnant Hetscher, commanding 4th Company, was killed and Leutnant Krüger, commander of 3rd Company, was severely wounded. Towards 9.00 pm two companies of 2nd Battalion Infantry Regiment 177 [32nd Infantry Division] under Hauptmann Nietze arrived to reinforce. The Group then held the position until 21 April and prevented the enemy from advancing one single step further. The remains of Group Gerlach were then relieved and returned to the *Wettiner Lager*, where they linked up with the rest of the regiment once more."

In view of the fluidity of the situation and the risk that the ridge to the south of Moronvilliers might be lost, General Fritz von Below once more turned early on 18 April to the question of how his advancing reserve divisions were to be employed. At about 8.00 am, 5th and 6th Infantry Divisions were ordered to push forward from the line Selles - Béthenville, followed that afternoon by a supplementary order, directing them to advance their leading elements as far as the R2 Line between *Warschauer Hof* [Warsaw Farm], northeast of Beine and the Pont Faverger - Moronvilliers road. Simultaneously, Infantry Regiment 145, 34th Infantry Division, located near Epoye, was directed to move south to Beine and 23rd Infantry Division was ordered to deploy east of Moronvilliers, front facing west. Had a French breakthrough occurred, therefore, strong forces would soon be in position to counter the new thrust. All these formations were subordinated to General de Beaulieu (Group Prosnes), who had clear orders to use them all in a three sided pincer movement should the situation have deteriorated.

As the day wore on and the weakness of the original ground holding division became clear, as did the risk of the 58th Infantry Division front collapsing, warning orders were sent out directing the reserve to prepare either to reinforce the ridge line or to counter any attempt by the French to capture the line of the Suippes from the west. In the events the situation as night fell, though still serious, was not critical. The French had indeed launched a major assault on *Langer Rücken*, but the attack on Mont

Cornillet was halted in its tracks by German defensive artillery fire. The situation on the 214th Infantry Division front gave most cause for concern. There was stalemate round *Lug ins Land*, but the fighting for the *Hochberg*/Hill 253 sector had been intense. The French got on to the summit of the former feature, but the defenders managed to hold fast to its northern slopes. Further east, towards the *Keilberg* and *Pöhlberg* features, all attacks were successfully beaten off.

The picture was slightly more mixed to the east. Elements of 58th Division, fighting east and northeast of the *Fichtelberg*, had prevented the French from developing their attacks towards the Suippes, but the strongpoint north of *Mittelwald* was lost, Aubérive was increasingly outflanked and First Army finally ordered its evacuation during the night 18/19 April, despite the fact that 30th Infantry Division had been relatively successful in holding French attacks on the east bank of the Suippes and had re-established firm links with 58th Infantry Division just to the south of Vaudesincourt. Reviewing the day's events with his chief of staff, Generalleutnant de Beaulieu sought the permission of First Army to use the formations subordinated to him for a decisive move against the R1 Line early on 19 April. The aim was to push the French back at least 500 metres down the southern slopes, whilst 23rd Infantry Division renewed the attempt to recapture the *Fichtelberg*. Despite the fact that the situation, though bad, did not amount to a crisis, despite the fact that the operation would leave First Army with no reserves until 7th Reserve Division arrived - and that could not possibly be before 20 April - General von Below assented.

H Hour was set for 8.00 am, the regiments of 5th and 6th Infantry Divisions moved up into assembly areas behind the R2 Line in the 29th and 214th Infantry Division sectors during the early hours. The inter-divisional boundary was the Pont Faverger, *Hochberg* - Prosnes road. The initial objectives for 5th Infantry Division was the *Langer Rücken*, *Mont Cornillet* and *Lug ins Land*; those for 6th Infantry Division, the *Hochberg*, *Keilberg* and *Pöhlberg*. Overnight, the orders for 23rd Infantry Division were changed. It was now to place most of its infantry to the west of St Martin l'Heureux and so secure the eastern flank of the assault. This reduced the forces available to tackle the *Fichtelberg* to one regiment.

In war operations rarely go to plan and such was the case here. Before the German bombardment got into its stride, the French launched a surprise attack against the entire crest line. Once again it had no success against the *Cornillet*, but there was hand to hand fighting further east and the summits of the *Hochberg* and *Pöhlberg* were both lost. That said, as the French attempted to exploit their gains further, they began to butt up against the advancing 5th and 6th Divisions. Despite having to negotiate a great deal of French barrage fire, Generalmajor von Wedel's 5th Division was able to close up by mid morning to the *Langer Rücken* and the *Cornillet*, which were still held by 29th Infantry Division,. There, however, fire from *Lug ins Land* forced a pause until that summit could be stormed at midday. Even then there were still problems, because flanking fire also began to come down from the *Hochberg*.

6th Infantry Division, commanded by Generalleutnant Herhuth von Rohden, had a harder time passing through the French protective artillery fire. It had to fight hard on the northern approaches to the crest line and was drawn too far to the east. This left the *Hochberg* unattacked; it remained a major problem for some time and again caused the attack to stall. 23rd Infantry Division, advancing from the east, made quite reasonable progress against the Moroccan Division, but it too ran into flanking fire - this time from the *Pöhlberg* - once it had gained about 1,000 metres. Fortunately, Group Prosnes had been tracking developments carefully and General de Beaulieu took a decision to order 23rd Infantry Division to swing round to the north and get on top of the *Pöhlberg*, both to prevent further French exploitation and to ease the task of 6th Infantry Division. In the event it was difficult to give substance to this order; the only uncommitted elements of 23rd Infantry Division were too far in rear to be able to react swiftly and, for some unexplained reason, Infantry Regiment 396, echeloned back behind Infantry Regiment 64 in reserve, was not deployed forward at all that day.[42] In the meantime, French pressure intensified all along the front, leading to a further thrust, supported by a new fire plan, at 1.00 pm.

Just how hard the day had been for the regiments of 6th Infantry Division is clear from this account by a member of Infantry Regiment 24, which had the task of taking the *Pöhlberg*.

Regimental Adjutant Infantry Regiment 24[43]

"It was a stimulating military spectacle to see the companies, led calmly and carefully through the dense barrage fire with only moderate casualties, arrive at the [northern] slopes of the *Keilberg* and the *Pöhlberg* and there, though extremely tired, to shake out into their attack formations. Here, by the Moronvilliers - St Martin l'Heureux road, there was shelter because they were in an 'artillery shadow'. Perspiring freely, the companies gathered. It had been hard work, first a long march in saturated clothing, with heavy packs, then they had to pass through the barrage and the maze of shell craters, finally to arrive on the steep slopes ... Soon they were setting off up the slopes, through shot up stands of fir trees, until the leading companies were almost at the summit. Here they came up against heavy machine gun fire and had to take cover in craters. It turned out that two summits, separated by a small flat col, had to be stormed. The orders were to attack the enemy and to drive them initially to the Blockhouse Line, some 500 metres behind the more southerly peak. At this point the reserve companies were deployed to help the leading wave get forward. The enemy were located on and round the southern peak, about 400 metres from us ... to the left of the regiment, there was no sign of 23rd Infantry Division; only by judging where the shrapnel was landing and listening to the machine gun fire was it possible to estimate where the battle line lay.

"Patrols pushed out established that Saxons of Infantry Regiment 177 were located down in a hollow in front of 2nd Battalion and, because it was possible to move about freely on this slope of the hill, it seemed sensible to push the companies forward through the Saxons' sector. Time passed, our artillery ranged in. Communications were established to the rear and the order arrived that, come what may, the attack was to be launched that afternoon. The commanding officers of 2nd Battalion assembled his officers for a conference. The general opinion was that it would be best to delay until dawn the following morning, because of the problem of moving with any speed through this difficult terrain and thus avoiding machine gun fire. In the meantime our gunfire was coming down on the French trenches so accurately that first individuals, then ever more Frenchmen began fleeing to the rear. Hardly had the front line troops spotted this than somebody - not a company commander - gave the order to attack. Bayonets were fixed, drums beat, trumpets blew and with loud shouts of *Hurra!* the companies chaged

"Despite heavy French fire, despite serious casualties, the first position was overrun [allegedly] to shouts of *Hurra! - Hurra! - Hunga! Hunga! - Franzmann partie! - Allemands! - Allemands!* Torrents of hand grenades were hurled at the Frenchmens' heads. All those who did not surrender were put to flight. The 1st, 2nd and 3rd Lines were captured, then we pushed on down the slope. The leading troops, Reserve Leutnant Schmidt amongst them, had just reached the Blockhouse Line when a French counter-stroke went in ... The attack was launched by pushing on straight past the 177th in their trenches, some of whom joined in and just as the companies stormed forward we heard a Saxon [with a thick accent] shout, *Nu, haben denn die Leite ihr Läb'n gornich mehr lieb?* [Crikey, don't these blokes want to live?] ...

"Around 7.00 pm the mountain was in German hands, but a few moments later it had to be evacuated once more and we were pushed back to the French First Position ... We took seventy prisoners from the 11th Regiment from Montauban in Gascony. We attacked a second time and then lost the summit once again. Yet again the 24th had to pull back, ready to return a third time. In the end we occupied the second French line on the reverse slope and improved its defences. The summit itself remained unoccupied. The strenuous fighting had caused heavy casualties, especially amongst the company commanders. Leutnant Lohöfener, commanding 7th Company, was dead, as was the brave, tried and tested Leutnant Schünemann, commander of 5th Company, [44] together with the courageous Reserve Leutnant Glanz. Leutnant Smith, 8th Company, fell in one of the trenches on the far side of the crest."

Hard fighting went on throughout the afternoon until, by about 7.00 pm, it appeared that the Germans had gained, if not the upper hand decisively, certainly an advantage. *Langer Rücken*, *Cornillet* and *Lug ins Land* were more or less strongly held, the front line at the *Hochberg* now ran along its southern slopes. That said, according to Grenadier Regiment 12, 5th Infantry Division, this did not prevent the French bringing down aimed fire constantly against their positions on *Lug ins Land* on the adjoining *Hexensattel*, thus preventing further movement.[45] The German defence had a precarious grip on *Keilberg* and *Pöhlberg* and French attacks southeast of Vaudesinscourt had been beaten off by local reserves. The decision was then made to try to push 5th Infantry Division and one regiment of 34th Infantry Division forward on the western flank that same evening.

Responsible for the attack at the western end of the line, south of Nauroy, was Infantry Regiment 145, 34th Infantry Division. As has been noted, differing rates of advance and enemy resistance had made coordination difficult. Hours passed, the link up with the right hand formation of 5th Infantry Division proved to be elusive, guides got lost and the approach routes were extremely confusing. Nevertheless, pressure mounted to launch forward and eventually, only at 6.30 pm, and not until two companies of 1st Battalion had been inserted between 2nd and 3rd Battalions, could the operation be launched. A white flare was fired and the attack began. It made some ground, but was not particularly successful; typical of much of the rest of the day's fighting, in fact.

Hauptmann von Prondynski Commander 2nd Battalion Infantry Regiment 145 [46]

"On the left flank, 8th Company (commander Reserve Leutnant Müller) was the first to set off. Moving at the double, it quickly arrived at the *Tiede-Stützpunkt*. 5th Company on the right (west) of it, was engaged heavily with hand grenades as soon as it moved out of the trench. The company commander, Leutnant Koch, was killed at once and the company could not get forward. 7th Company, led by Reserve Leutnant Ritter, set off somewhat later from the northern edge of the *Spee-Stützpunkt* and moved to capture its southern edge. Advancing towards the K2 Line, organised into three assault troops, it captured an automatic rifle, but then came under pressure from machine gun fire and hand grenades from the right flank. The company pulled back slowly and fighting all the way to the *Spee-Stützpunkt* and occupied its southern edge.

"6th Company, under its tried and tested commander, Reserve Leutnant Siepmann, launched forward energetically and partly under cover. Despite coming under fire from four machine guns and being subject to a large scale French counter-stroke, it managed to capture both the K1 and K2 trenches to the left as far as *Schampegraben*; to the right, to the boundary with Reserve Infantry Regiment 16. Vizefeldwebel Pribbenow was killed along with several other brave men. Finally, however, a shortage of hand grenades and small arms ammunition, coupled with the loss of his machine gun, forced this company commander to yield his position. On the left flank the brave company commander of 8th Company (Leutnant Müller) was mortally wounded. Vizefeldwebel Rune assumed command and, because 1st and 3rd Battalions were unable to cross the open ground and get as far forward as them, he gave the order to withdraw. Both Vizefeldwebel Rune and Holtschneider were killed here. 6th Company captured four machine guns, but could only recover one of them, because they also had to take the wounded back with them. 8th Company captured three machine guns or automatic rifles. On the way to the rear those carrying them came under artillery fire. They had to drop the weapons and they could not be found later. One wounded and one unwounded prisoner were also brought in."

It is questionable if it was a good idea to persist with the evening attacks at all, given the lateness of the hour and all the problems and losses the day had brought. The assumption has to be that General de Beaulieu wished to ensure that his front line was a complete tactical bound forward of the crest line. 5th Infantry Division may have had a somewhat easier time of it than the 6th. Nevertheless, Infantry Regiment 52 reported that, although the first part of its approach march had been screened by the bad weather, it suffered 'heavy casualties' from the protective bombardment and more when, nearing the foot of the *Cornillet*, it came under small arms fire from *Lug ins Land*. Then, having finally reached the crest, its commander, Major Wenzel, decided that with night falling, lacking proper contact with Infantry Regiment 145 on his right and none whatsoever with Grenadier Regiment 12 on his left, to press on further would be folly. He had no means of communicating with higher headquarters or the guns either, so, on his own responsibility, he cancelled the attack,[47] an action mirrored by Grenadier Regiments 12 and 8 to the east.

Both sides were almost completely fought out after this exhausting first French attempt to break through the *Champagnewald*. Patrols and listening posts were pushed forward and digging went on throughout the night to improve the positions, despite numerous interruptions and minor clashes.

Reserve Leutnant Fischer 6th Company Infantry Regiment 64[48]

"On 19 April 1917 I lay with two men of a machine gun crew on the ploughed up soil of a small hill in Champagne. To our half right was the much disputed *Hochberg*. I was the Orderly Officer of 2nd Battalion and had been ordered to observe because we had been warned of an impending attack that evening. It was about 8.00 pm, the air was heavy, it was misty and morale was low. Out to the front men ran to and fro amongst clouds of smoke. Apart from the continuing bombardment there was little to be seen which could indicate an attack. The atmosphere was foreboding and it was with mixed feelings that we awaited the coming battle. Suddenly, 'Red flares!' the three of us bawled as one. Simultaneously, an appalling weight of deadly accurate fire was coming down on our hill. I sent a man back to Battalion Headquarters to report. He leaped up and dashed off. My thoughts were, 'I hope that you make it'.

"Shell after shell hammered down and we were showered by lumps of chalk of all sizes. Clouds of smoke blew over, cloaking us for several moments. We were unsettled and scrabbled with our bare hands to get down deeper into the chalk. It was not a lot of use, but death was staring us in the face. Now and then we glanced up to our front. There would come a roar, a shell would land and we would duck down rapidly. Out forward in our defensive line we could see figures dashing about then disappearing back into the earth. Whether they were our comrades or Frenchmen we could not tell. The firing continued. To our left I could see German soldiers advancing. Bent over, moving slowly, they crossed the difficult terrain facing death. Some were carrying machine guns over their shoulders. Fire was still coming down on the typical Champagne copses to our rear and our artillery replied. It was a sight I shall never be able to forget. Clouds of white and grey smoke rose from the dark woods and harsh flashes lit up the gaps in between. The fire slackened; men breathed out. Smoke clouds hung in the air and the classic, choking, Champagne dust drifted back to earth. The show was over; the attack beaten off. Some shells still rushed through the air, but most landed way to the rear. We could now be sure of a quiet night."

In fact, Fischer and his men were soon preparing for a line straightening operation the following day, but in one sense he was correct. That night saw the end of the first serious attacks on this front. There would be others later in the month and in early May before the battle moved on but, for now, the defence, though hard pressed first by the lengthy bombardment and then three days of intense, frequently close quarter battle, had prevailed. Just as along the Chemin des Dames, Nivelle's grandiose offensive plans had come to nothing; appalling casualties had produced only the most pitiful gains.

Notes

[1] History Infantry Regiment 159 p 229.
[2] Rundstedt History Infantry Regiment 113 pp159-160.
[3] History Infantry Regiment 159 p 241.
[4] History Infantry Regiment 112 pp 139-140.
[5] This is the second part of a quotation attributed to the Roman general Pompey by Plutarch and refers to an incident in AD 56 when Pompey insisted on sailing for Rome in ships carrying much needed grain, despite the fact that a storm was raging. Plutarch's Greek account was first translated into Latin in the mediaeval period and Pompey's words were rendered as *Navigare necesse est, vivere non est necesse*. [It is necessary to sail; it is not necessary to live.] The quotation was well known in Germany, partly because it was regarded as an unofficial motto of the Hanseatic League and it is to this day carved on the portal of the *Haus der Seefahrt* in Bremen, which is the oldest seamans' charitable institution in the world, having been established in 1545.
[6] Schiel History Infantry Regiment 112 p 140.
[7] *ibid.* pp 140-141.
[8] Vizefeldwebel Ludwig Reibel, who succumbed to his wounds on 18 April, is buried in the German cemetery at La Neuville-en-Tourne-à-Fuy Block 3 Grave 38
[9] Landsturmmann Heinrich Bender is buried in the *Kamaradengrab* of the German cemetery at Berru.

[10] Schiel *op. cit.* pp 141-144.
[11] Of those named, Unteroffiziers Robert Zocher and Ernst Pulver (whose name is wrongly rendered by the *Volksbund* as Pulfer) are buried in the Block 1 of the German cemetery at St Etienne-à-Arnes in Graves 527 and 525 respectively.
[12] Schiel *op. cit.*112 p 145.
[13] *ibid.* p 61.
[14] Reserve Leutnant Friedrich Wilhelm Statsmann is buried in the German cemetery at Aussonce Block 2 Grave 24
[15] Müller-Loebnitz *Die Badener im Weltkrieg* pp 273-274.
[16] Schmidt History Infantry Regiment 142 p 90.
[17] Rundstedt History Infantry Regiment 113 p 164.
[18] Reserve Leutnant Paul Funk is buried in the German cemetery at Sissonne Block 10 Grave 50.
[19] Reserve Leutnant Josef Rieder is buried in the German cemetery at Aussonce Block 2 Grave 72. The body of Reserve Leutnant Heinrich Thum was repatriated later to Germany and he now lies in the military section of the Heidelberg Friedhof Grave 72.
[20] Müller-Loebnitz *op. cit.* pp 275-276.
[21] Hottenroth *Sachsen in Großer Zeit: Band I* pp 287-288.
[22] Vogt History Infantry Regiment 50 pp 171-172.
[23] Lüdke may well have been mistaken about this. The *Fichtelberg* was three kilometres east southeast of the *Hochberg*. It is more probable that the firing came from the *Möllerberg* feature, about 1,500 metres away.
[24] Auenmüller History Infantry Regiment 107 p 325.
[25] Poland History Reserve Infantry Regiment 103 p 91.
[26] Auenmüller *op. cit.* p 328.
[27] *ibid.* p 331.
[28] *ibid.* p 335.
[29] *ibid.* p 336.
[30] Böttger History Infantry Regiment 106 p 158.
[31] Poland *op. cit.* p 93.
[32] Auenmüller *op. cit.* p 342.
[33] Böttger *op. cit.* p 159.
[34] Auenmüller *op. cit.* p 344.
[35] Rust History Infantry Regiment 143 pp 273-274.
[36] Monse History Infantry Regiment 103 p 156.
[37] Of those named, only Leutnant Rudolf Bretschneider has a known grave. He is buried in the German cemetery at La Neuville-en-Tourne-à-Fuy Block 2 Grave 72.
[38] GOH p 338.
[39] Monse *op. cit.* pp 326-328.
[40] Vogt *op. cit.* p 169.
[41] Vogt *op. cit.* p 171.
[42] Fröhling History Infantry Regiment 396 p 41.
[43] Brandis History Infantry Regiment 24 pp 316-317.
[44] Leutnant Edmond Lohöfener and Leutnant Martin Schünemann are buried next to one another in the German cemetery at La Neuville-en-Tourne-à-Fuy Block 4 Graves 65 and 66.
[45] Schönfeldt History Grenadier Regiment 12 pp 120-121.
[46] Isenberg History Infantry Regiment 145 pp 301-302.
[47] Reymann History Infantry Regiment 52 p 119.
[48] History Infantry Regiment 64 p 200.

CHAPTER 6

Bullecourt

For two months, from early February 1917, 27th Infantry Division from Württemberg, which had distinguished itself earlier in the Argonne Forest and during the defence of Guillemont the previous August during the Battle of the Somme, had been involved in the withdrawal from St Pierre Vaast Wood to the *Siegfriedstellung* [Hindenburg Line] and had then acted as a training and demonstration formation near Valenciennes. Its earlier commander, Generalleutnant von Moser, appointed to command XIV Reserve Corps, had just handed over command to Generalleutnant Maur, who had previously been the successful artillery commander of 26th Reserve Division, when orders arrived directing the division to relieve 26th Reserve Division between Bullecourt and Quéant. This sector, coincidentally, was the responsibility of Moser's XIV Reserve Corps, so the close association of the division with its former commander continued as battle was joined.

In common with many other formations, the men of 27th Infantry Division were not particularly impressed with the state of the newly constructed defensive line; their view being that there was no point in having two defensive lines and large amounts of wire if there were no suitable dugouts or if the only signs of the originally planned concrete pillboxes and blockhouses were the outline of their foundations. There was also concern that depth defences were almost totally lacking in their sector. The one positive aspect of taking over this section of the front was that their immediate predecessors had been the formations of 26th Reserve Division, also from Württemberg, which, building on their positive experience of deep dugouts during their long term defence of the Somme front, had lost no time digging deep and digging quickly. In a mere two weeks' of intensive work they had succeeded in creating the dugouts to which the men of 27th Infantry Division ascribed their ability to withstand the extraordinary pressures of the weeks of fighting for Bullecourt.

Naturally the work achieved by 26th Reserve Division was uneven in its effect. Infantry Regiment 124, occupying the centre of the divisional frontage forward of Riencourt, noted a number of deficiencies in the positions it took over from Infantry Regiment 180. Its initial deployment was 1st, 2nd and 3rd Companies of 1st Battalion forward right (west), with 10th 11th and 12th Companies forward left (east). 4th and 9th Companies were held back in support, benefiting from catacombs beneath Riencourt village, but facing the problem that the entrances to the old underground workings were unprotected and vulnerable. 2nd Battalion began the battle in reserve back in

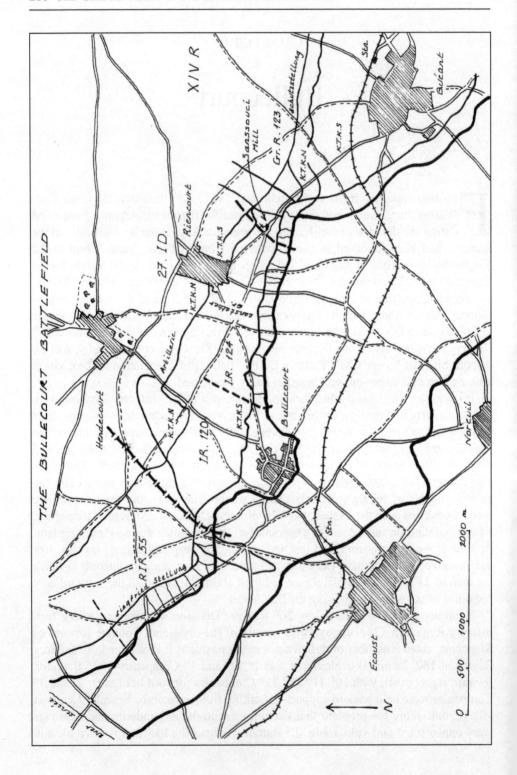

Cagnicourt. The regimental commander would have preferred to have arranged his troops in greater depth, but was constrained by lack of suitable dugouts and there was little time to rectify the situation in any way before the fighting began.

Because the *Siegfriedstellung* was laid out here on a reverse slope, the troops manning the front line could not directly observe active preparations to their front as men and equipment began to be assembled along the line of the Ecoust-St Mein - Quéant railway. Observation posts pushed forward filled the gap to some extent and several patrols went forward to investigate what was happening, though one three man reconnaissance patrol, commanded by Leutnant Reich, failed to return from one such during the night 10/11 April. It was thought that they had bumped into an Australian fighting patrol and been captured. In addition the divisional guns brought down defensive fire in an attempt to hinder Allied preparations but, as was frequently the case, the defence was subject to a far greater weight of British fire than it could itself generate.

Nevertheless the division was lucky in its timing. Taking over the forward positions during Easter weekend, 7-8 April, Generalleutnant Maur assumed responsibility for the sector on 9 April, the very day that battle commenced further north. Luckily for him and his men, the Bullecourt sector was not subject to attack that day or the next, so there was time for orientation and further improvement of the positions to the sound of the thunder of the guns coming from the north. 10 April had seen a major thrust in the direction of Monchy le Preux, but it was not until 11 April that the offensive was extended to include attacks south to the Bullecourt - Quéant sector. In combination with this was a simultaneous attack along the axis St Martin sur Cojeul - Wancourt, which the defenders took to be a serious attempt to breach the *Siegfriedstellung* [Hindenburg Line] on a twelve kilometre front.

The reason for this delay was rooted in the unexpected occupation of the Hindenburg Line by the German army in March 1917. This radical alteration in the tactical situation on the Somme front caused major headaches for the Allied operational planners. The Nivelle offensive by the French army remained on course but the British attacks, intended to divert attention and reinforcements away from the Aisne and Champagne, were compromised badly. Now only Allenby's Third Army was in a position to launch attacks to the east of the Arras area. The German withdrawal from the Bapaume salient meant that Gough's Fifth Army was confronted with an advance across a huge area which had been laid waste and liberally strewn with obstacles and booby traps. This imposed considerable delay, as road and rail links had to be repaired, guns moved forward and logistic support relocated well forward of the original planned locations. Despite these major problems, with British planning based on the capture of Cambrai, if Fifth Army could somehow force a way rapidly through the Hindenburg Line on the Bullecourt - Queánt front, it would contribute significantly to the achievement of Third Army's task overall mission.

So much for the theory of course. On the ground the difficulties appeared virtually insurmountable. If Fifth Army was to make a meaningful contribution, very considerable risks would have to be run. Such were the physical problems imposed by the devastated terrain that few guns could be got forward. First roads and railways required major repair and there was also a lack of sufficient draft horses, especially in view of competing demands by the logisticians who needed greatly increased transport capacity to move ammunition and all the other impedimenta of war into place. Such were the delays that there was neither time to destroy the massive barbed wire entanglements of the Hindenburg Line, nor heavy artillery to carry out the task. Staff checks soon determined that there would be resources sufficient only for an attack on a very narrow frontage, which in turn increased the danger considerably. In view of the failure of attempts to cut the wire, which were confirmed by patrol activity, it was, as ever, a matter of making the best of a bad situation. In this case the plan depended on the ability of a few Mark II training tanks to flatten sufficient gaps in the wire to enable the men of 4th Australian Division to storm the front line positions. Already it can be seen that this was a plan which depended on everything unfolding in a particular way. This is extremely rare in military operations, so it was inherently weak. What made matters much worse, however, was the fact that that the defence of this sector had been entrusted to one of the very best ground holding divisions on the Western Front. 27th Infantry Division, which had learned its business in the hard school of the Argonne Forest, had gone on to demonstrate its exceptional quality in the defence of Guillemont during August 1916, where it had repulsed repeated British attacks for weeks on end. Such was its collective quality that, having been reconstituted and rested, it went on to carry out duty for several months near Valenciennes as a training and demonstration division. Here its main speciality was the defensive battle.[1] As a result, when Infantry Regiment 120, Infantry Regiment 124 and Grenadier Regiment 123, responsible for the Bullecourt, Riencourt and Quéant (north) sub sectors respectively, moved into position, it could hardly have been in a better state of training and readiness for what lay ahead.

When the attack began on 11 April it enjoyed no tactical surprise whatsoever. The original British intention was to launch the assault the previous day. Unfortunately for the attacking troops, it proved to be extremely difficult to get the tanks up to the start line in the dark. As the time for the start of the operation came and went they were still well short of their correct jumping off points. No tanks meant no attack. There was no realistic choice but to postpone the attack by twenty four hours. Given that the plan had been compromised, complete cancellation might have been more appropriate but, such was the urgency of the situation, the decision was taken to hold the Australian infantry forward and to launch the attack the following morning. It was doubly unfortunate that it had proved impossible to prevent strong fighting patrols from 185 Brigade of the British 62nd Division being sent forward in probing attacks against Bullecourt.

Had there been need for proof of the imminent Allied aggressive intentions, these actions would have confirmed them. As it was, British losses of 167 all ranks were incurred (7th Battalion Battalion West Yorkshire Regiment suffering particularly badly)[2]. Nothing at all was achieved and later that day Generalleutnant Heinrich von Maur, commanding 27th Infantry Division, issued an order which stated,

> "This morning the enemy launched an attack in battalion strength against the right flank of Infantry Regiment 120. Our machine gun fire caused it heavy casualties. Between 5.00 and 6.00 am strong skirmishing lines, followed by columns of men, moved behind the railway embankment opposite [Sector] C North. The railway embankment is still occupied by substantial enemy forces … It must be assumed that there will be enemy attacks against [Sectors] A [Bullecourt] and C [Riencourt]."[3]

Under normal circumstances the response to this knowledge would have been to rush reinforcements to the threatened sector. On this occasion, pressure of events further north ruled this out. The only other German forces anywhere near at hand, namely two battalions from 2nd Guards Reserve Division, were engaged on the improvement of trench connecting the Cagnicourt - Hendicourt road with Vis en Artois. In the absence of outside help, Maur, a noted gunner, issued specific instructions for the use of his artillery assets and close infantry-artillery cooperation.

> " The artillery is to maintain deliberate harassing fire, day and night, on the sectors of the railway occupied by the enemy, together with embankments, sunken roads and trench lines. In addition, concentrations of destructive fire by all calibres are to be brought down on these targets at precisely [coordinated] times. The programme for these shoots is to be reported prior to their start, so that the infantry can be appropriately informed. Plans are to be drawn up to gas those batteries which can be most damaging to us as soon as heavy enemy fire starts coming down. The proposal is to be presented by 6.00 pm … Both the infantry and the artillery are to take all steps to ensure that swift and frictionless cooperation is achieved [between them]."[4]

The following night, regardless of intense shelling and the drenching with phosgene gas of Bullecourt and Riencourt, all the regiments of 27th Infantry Division pushed forward patrols and listening posts. In its after action report, Infantry Regiment 124 later recorded the night's events.

> "At 2.00 am, patrols which had been sent forward beyond the barbed wire obstacle detected loud engine noise. Little notice was taken of this because it was assumed that the British [sic.] were moving stores forward by lorry. Throughout the night Riencourt and Bullecourt were subject to heavy artillery fire, but initially there was very little shelling of the position itself. Because it appeared likely that there would be an attack, the companies maintained a high state of alert."[5]

Their own observations, coupled with the earlier warning from divisional headquarters, meant that the forward companies were on full alert when sentries reported at 4.30 am that parties were working on the wire obstacle. There was an immediate stand-to then, when at 4.45 am the noise of engines increased to a roar, there was a general realisation that a major attack with tank support was about to begin. Some subsequent reports speak of a somewhat chaotic situation on the Allied side, but the German accounts all comment that the situation they confronted was a tank attack with up to five waves of infantry following up. Not only that, but it was tank fire that drove in the patrols and listening posts back to their front line trenches and that low flying aircraft that gave horn signals provided close support for the attackers.[6] Whatever the precise state of affairs, it is fairly evident, however, that some sort of early warning had been given to the German guns because, according to the Australian Official Historian,[7] at 5.23 am [4.23 am Allied time] 4 Australian Brigade was shelled in its forming up place. A green flare went up from Bullecourt at 5.35 am (though this may have been an unrelated coincidence) then, within the next five minutes, green and yellow flares were also being fired from Bullecourt.

The attack was meant to have begun with the tanks crossing the start line at 5.30 am, then the plan was for a brief, but intense, period of drum fire followed by an infantry assault at 5.45 am by the 4th Australian Division, supported by eleven tanks. These were intended to spearhead the attack and, in the case of four tanks, to advance in the unfortunate gap which vagaries of the terrain imposed between the two attacking brigades. 4 Australian Brigade attacked on the right with two battalions leading (14th and 16th) and two more in support (13th and 15th). On the left was 12 Australian Brigade, with 46th Battalion leading, 48th Battalion following up and 47th Battalion in support. For the second day running the tanks, upon which so much of the plan depended, failed to perform as expected. By 5.30 am only four were actually in position - three in front of 4 Australian Brigade and a fourth on the right flank of 12 Australian Brigade.

Of the three with 4 Australian Brigade, two were stationary when the infantry passed them and the third veered away to the right for some reason. In consequence, 14th and 16th Battalions had to force their way through the German wire without support and suffered heavily in consequence. One tank did manage to break through the wire prior to the arrival on the German front line of 13th and 15th Battalions, but it is evident that the staggered arrival times of the tanks meant that much of the shock effect they were should have generated was lost. In the confusion 12 Australian Brigade waited then, with uncoordinated tank movements and friendly force clashes adding to the problems, the battalions eventually set off at 6.15 am. These staggered starts and normal splitting into assaulting waves probably explain why the German defenders counted five separate lines of infantry bearing down on them. The net result, with tanks breaking down, sheering away or arriving late, was that once more the Australians of 12 Brigade found themselves trying to break into the German front line unsupported. From the German perspective, as soon as it became clear that a full scale attack was underway, flares went up all along the line calling for defensive artillery fire. The guns were certainly ready to respond. However, when the fire came down, 'it was much too weak for the width of Sector C'.[8]

It must be assumed that the Australian view was quite different as the German artillery directed large quantities of shells at them and the trench garrisons, fighting for their lives, poured small arms fire at the assault waves and threw hundreds of hand grenades to break up the attacks launched by the Australian troops. However, such was the determination and dash of the Australians that there was soon a break in to the southeast of Riencourt-lez-Cagnicourt, along the front line of sub-sector C1, defended by 1st Company Infantry Regiment 124, under the command of Leutnant Adolf Mohr. By this time on average each defender had already fired seventy rounds.[9] The attackers broke in and, for some time, the threat of the attack being further developed was acute. However the Infantry Regiment 124 reserves located back in the village of Riencourt and the *Artillerie-Schutzstellung* were launched forward and succeeded in halting the advance from positions lining the sunken road leading southeast from the village. Despite this spirited resistance, such was the intensity of the battle here and the pressure exerted by the assaulting troops that the defenders were quickly overrun. A great many defenders were killed or wounded, whilst a hasty counter-attack, led by Mohr along V1 [Communication Trench 1] failed and Mohr was killed during a battle with hand grenades.[10] Following that failure the remaining thirty survivors were forced to pull back into the trenches in the depth of the position.

The defenders of sub sectors C2 and C3 also came under considerable pressure, but despite being subject to torrents of fire from three tanks, which drove up and down the line of their trenches, engaging everything in range, they succeeded in holding on to their positions. One of the tanks became stuck in the barbed wire in subsector C3 and was swiftly knocked out by a machine gun firing SmK armour piercing bullets from close range and a grenade launcher from a range of 450 metres which - to a combination of general amazement and relief - scored four hits.[11] Simultaneously another attack built up against sub sectors C4 and C5, where Leutnants Moll and Nestle of 10th and 11th Companies respectively were in charge of the defence. Here,

"Several tanks advanced and drove backwards and forwards in front of the barbed wire. Everything within range was shot down. It was impossible to remain in the beaten zone of the tanks, from each of which six machine guns raked the parapet of the first trench, causing heavy casualties to 10th and 11th Companies. Unprotected, the men could only hold on in the trench, not knowing when the monsters would claim them. From here it was impossible to attack the tanks from the trench, but here too a tank was hit by a grenade launcher which split a track and halted it. The crew baled out and attempted to clamber into another tank. They were brought under machine gun fire. Later the abandoned tank was engaged by the artillery."[12]

Despite the fact that a large proportion of the tanks was knocked out, mainly by direct gun fire from the artillery, the forward elements of 10th and 11th Companies were soon forced to abandon even the Second Line trenches. Grenadier Regiment 123, located east of Infantry Regiment 124, did not face anything like the type of attack to which Infantry Regiment 124 was subject, nevertheless found that two tanks were advancing towards it. Seizing the initiative, Reserve Leutnant Gotthold Schabel, the commander of 3rd Machine Gun Company, rushed forward with the crew of one of his guns, took up a hasty fire position and personally fired at a tank at a range of approximately150 metres. That was close enough to be effective, especially against the side of a Mark II tank. Having fired 1,200 armour piercing rounds, he pierced it seventy seven times. Three bullets passed through the fuel tank and set it on fire.[13] In acknowledgement of his courage, he was awarded the Knight's Cross of the Royal Württemberg Military Service Order on 24 May 1917.

Causing the attack to stall was one thing, driving out the troops which had broken in or destroying them was a sterner test altogether. Luckily the commander of 53 Infantry Brigade, Oberst von der Osten, had anticipated such an eventuality and he had already prepared a counter-attack plan and discussed it with his regimental commanders. As early as 8.15 am Osten had issued orders to the reserve companies of Infantry Regiment 124 to launch a frontal attack to restore the front line and to specialist storm groups of Infantry Regiment 120 and Grenadier Regiment 123 to roll up the left and right flanks of the penetration, so as to eliminate it and restore the original front line.[14] In addition, machine guns deployed to previously reconnoitred positions were to prevent the Australians from escaping to the rear. In a matter of a few minutes these counter-measures, some of which had already been launched without specific orders by the highly trained regiments, were underway and the crisis was soon past, though there was still hard fighting ahead. Within Infantry Regiment 124, the *KTK* was so confident of the ability of the company commanders to interpret his instructions correctly that his actual order was reduced to, 'Counter-stroke by 9th and 5th Companies along the line of *Calwergraben*, by 7th Company from the *Artillerie-Schutzstellung* in the direction of Sanssouci Mill and by 6th and 8th Companies via [Communication Trench] V6. All assault groups to set out at 9.00 am.'[15]

Naturally there was a great deal of close quarter fighting of absolutely murderous intensity, but once the convergent attacks began to gain momentum, the initiative swung quite rapidly towards the defence and by midday the fighting was largely over. The Australians, who could not be reinforced because the defence dominated No Man's Land with fire and who were equipped with only the weapons and ammunition they had been able to carry forward, soon began to run short of munitions, especially hand grenades. Furthermore, the fact that they were having to yield ground constantly made it extremely difficult to recover and redistribute the ammunition of their dead and wounded comrades. Despite all their problems, such was the spirit of the attacking Australians that they fought on until they were completely surrounded, squeezed into a very small area and ran out of ammunition. A relative handful attempted to break through the German cordon and get back to their start line, but hardly any made it back. It was broad daylight and, as has been mentioned, the entire width of No Man's Land was covered by German artillery and machine gun fire.

While this mopping up action proceeded, follow up waves came under sustained artillery bombardment, not only from the guns of 27th Infantry Division, but also those of the adjoining 220th Infantry Division and 2nd Guards Infantry Division, which superimposed their fire on the defensive fire zones forward of Bullecourt and prevented further threats to the divisional frontage from developing in any significant way. An entirely predictable heavy price was being paid for the decision to attack on a very narrow front. Had the tanks been able to perform as intended, it seems that the Australian troops would have found it easier to gain a lodgement and might have been able to develop their attack with more success. Even allowing for the fact that German after action reports would have been seeking excuses for the perceived setback, for which the presence of tanks provided a convenient cause, nevertheless it does appear that in some places the presence of tanks had a definite influence on the battle, though, as has been mentioned, the shock effect of the appearance of armour was relatively short lived.

A combination of machine gun fire, grenade launchers and artillery proved to be very effective in the anti-tank role. Most of the tanks fell victim to artillery fire, not only from specially designated anti-tank guns, but also the heavy artillery and normal field guns, some of which were galloped forward by their batteries into positions where they could fire directly at the armour. There is considerable debate about the numbers that advanced and how many were destroyed, or broke down. Altogether, of the eleven[16] tanks which went into action, four or five were knocked out or broke down forward of the German front line and two others within it. The remainder survived to turn away and make their escape from the torrent of fire directed at them. As night fell on the Bullecourt battlefield, 27th Infantry Division could reflect on a truly extraordinary defensive success. Seldom could one division claim to have thrown back an attack with such high losses. To knock out so many tanks, even if they were training models, and to capture over fifty machine guns on one day was a real rarity on the Western Front. Consequently there was considerable satisfaction amongst the defenders about the outcome of the day.

Once the battles of 11 April had subsided, the German chain of command reacted in two quite different ways. Generalleutnant von Maur of 27th Infantry Division issued an order[17] in which he stated, entirely accurately, that 4th Australian Division had suffered a serious defeat. '4 and 12 Australian Infantry Brigades have been totally wiped out.' It then went on to list the prisoners and equipment captured. In total, according to initial figures, this involved twenty seven officers and 1,137 other ranks.[18] Two aircraft had been shot down and fifty three machine guns (mostly Lewis guns) captured, together with quantities of ammunition. Nine of the tanks that went into the attack were destroyed, seven of them either inside or very near to the German lines.

The order also included a reminder that if a unit could prove it had destroyed a tank, then in accordance with regulations, there was an entitlement to a reward of 500 marks.

On the same day, however, another order[19] was issued. Specifically, 53 Infantry Brigade was required to report, 'The reasons why the British [*sic.*] were able to achieve success during the initial attack'. The collection, processing and dissemination of lessons learned was always accorded a high priority by the German army and emphasis was placed on complete honesty and objectivity. In his response, which was based on returns from all his surviving battalion and company commanders Major Reinhold Lägeler, commander of Infantry Regiment 124, highlighted three major contributory reasons for the initial break in, which had led in turn to regimental losses of 188 killed and more than 200 wounded, *viz:*

- The sector was held too weakly. Based on Somme experience, six companies with an average bayonet strength of only 110 were required to hold two lines of defence, both between 1,800 and 1,900 metres in length; worse, each company had only two platoons in the front line. Had the attack been preceded by a lengthy bombardment this dispersal would have been suitable. In the event it was completely inappropriate to meet an attack launched, 'without artillery preparation worth the name' and conducted with great aggression.

- The artillery defensive fire zones were too wide and there was a general lack of experience in dealing with a tank attack. The tanks closed right up on the forward trenches and engaged them with flanking fire. The individual was 'powerless to confront these monsters'.

- The inherited defensive position was poorly laid out. In places the wire was seventy to eighty metres forward of the front line trench. Furthermore, there was dead ground on the right flank [i.e. forward of the 1st Company sub sector] where one of the break ins occurred.

Lägeler's report,[20] together with those of the other two regiments, was processed by 53 Infantry Brigade and a combined paper was sent to 27th Infantry Division for its consideration and action. One thing which emerges clearly is the fact that although Allied accounts suggest that the contribution of the tanks was negligible, even derisory, the German opinion was totally different. Infantry Regiment 120 later emphasised specifically that the break in on the Infantry Regiment 124 sector occurred because, 'the Australian troops exploited the momentary confusion and uncertainty which seized the fighting troops when the tanks appeared'.[21] Furthermore, there was universal agreement that the allocation of only one man to almost two and a half metres of defensive frontage was far too little. Immediate steps were taken to try to remedy this problem, but such was the pressure on manpower generated by constant Allied offensive action along the Arras front that the division found it extremely difficult to introduce any significant improvements.

Despite not inconsiderable losses, 11 April has to be judged a significant defensive success. After the initial break in, the defence recovered swiftly and decisively, carrying out that morning what one Australian officer allegedly described to his captors as a, 'splendid action' [*sic.*].[22] One peculiarity from the German perspective, however, was the fact that although 27th Infantry Division was under incessant heavy attack on 11 April, the neighbouring divisions were not involved at all. In fact, as has been mentioned, the selection of the narrow front against Bullecourt simply came about because General Gough's British Fifth Army was unable to devote greater resources to the operation and it was felt that breaking through the two lines of defence at Bullecourt would be a simpler proposition than an attack around Quéant, which would have involved assaulting defences roughly twice as strong.[23]

Very soon congratulations were coming in from the entire chain of command from the corps commander to Supreme Army Headquarters. The defeat of the Australian forces forward of Bullecourt and Riencourt provided an auspicious start to his time in command for Generalleutnant von Maur and represented the first really significant piece of good news for the defence since the Arras offensive opened. The failure of the tanks and the concomitant demonstration of their vulnerability in the face of determined defence was also a welcome development. Maur was awarded an immediate Pour le Mérite, as was Generalleutnant von Moser, the previous commander and now the commander of XIV Reserve corps with responsibility for the entire Quéant sector. Moser, unsurprising to relate, was highly delighted with the outcome of the fighting.

Generalleutnant Otto von Moser Commander XIV Reserve Corps [24]

"Full of pride and joy, I drove to 27th Infantry Division and stayed for some time as I learned what an outstanding day of honour Bullecourt 11 April had become for my dear old division. The first demonstration of this was the numerous prisoners who filled the garden and courtyard of divisional headquarters: some twenty eight officers, 1,140 other ranks with fifty three machine guns. Amongst them were many young, slim men. Both officers and men were clean shaven, proving that this division had been moved swiftly out of reserve and deployed specifically to carry out this operation … I was thus able to pass to the divisional commander, its general staff officer and the whole of 27th Division my heartiest congratulations and thanks. I despatched a report of the day's events to the King of Württemberg by telegram and also passed the information to the commander of XIII Corps, General von Watter.

"Congratulations also arrived at my headquarters. General der Infanterie Fritz von Below sent heartiest congratulations, as did General von Kuhl in the name of Crown Prince Rupprecht. From the Army Group up to Supreme Army Headquarters there were three reasons to be especially delighted at the brilliant halting of the enemy attack at Bullecourt. [These were] first, because a successful break in or breakthrough by the enemy on the XIV Reserve Corps front would have been strategically very problematic. It would have given the enemy access to the rear of the entire Arras front; second, because after the striking misfortune of 9 and 10 April east of Arras, this marvellous success with all its attendant captures had a marked positive effect on the sunken morale along the Western Front and in the Homeland and third, because it simultaneously drastically reduced the continuing nightmare of the tank threat on commanders and troops alike and also raised confidence in the efficacy of our means of defence."

In the wake of the setback of 11 April, the Bullecourt sector became relatively quiet once more, though Allied artillery fire continued to exact a severe toll on the defenders during the next three weeks. The corps commander, General Moser, who was always looking for ways to take the fight to the enemy, was not content to have his troops sit passively and wait for the next attack. Apart from any other consideration, the battle on the remainder of the Arras front raged on, so any means of distracting the British had merit. For the attack on 11 April, 4th Australian and the British 62nd Divisions were concentrated along a six kilometre front, leaving 1st Australian Division to cover an eleven kilometre sector from Quéant south. The severe losses suffered by 4th Australian Division had led to 1st Australian Division taking over another one kilometre section, meaning that its front line troops were now stretched very thinly.

Moser's formations, having detected that the British lines south of Bullecourt and Quéant were only lightly held, meant that on 13 April he placed a formal request for the use of 3rd Guards Infantry Division, together with the cooperation of the adjoining Group Cambrai, be allowed to launch a limited assault in association with 2nd Guards Reserve Division on the general line Lagnicourt - Hermies. The limit of exploitation was to be four kilometres. Anxious to support any viable offensive action, both army and army group gave immediate permission, not only for the subordination of 3rd Guards Infantry Division, but also 38th Infantry Division and 4th Ersatz Division. Moser, naturally, was delighted to have four divisions available in support of his plan. So urgent was the matter that Moser himself drew up the operations plan and order, leaving his general staff officer to concentrate on all the logistic and service support matters.

By early morning on 14 April the paperwork was complete, printed and distributed. Operation *Sturmbock* [Battering Ram] was scheduled to begin at 4.00 am on 15 April. Already, during the evening of 13 April, the general staff officers of all four divisions had arrived for an orders group then, later, during the afternoon of 14 April, Generaloberst Freiherr von Falkenhausen, still commanding Sixth Army at that stage, received a full briefing from Moser. The aims of the attack were :

" To interrupt completely the further advance of enemy infantry and artillery and in the process to capture or destroy as many men and as much materiel, especially guns, as possible.

• To reduce the offensive power of the enemy along the XIV Reserve Corps front, as well as that of the adjacent Group Arras, to such an extent that time would be bought to improve the defences.

• To show the enemy that German infantry was in no way cowed; on the contrary it was well able to attack."[25]

When the various divisions had further worked on the orders, the outline versions arrived typically with the forward regiments at about 8.00 am 14 April. This provided very little time for preparation and, which was worse, final adjustments did not finally reach battalions until late that evening. A mass of troops had to be moved forward through a very constricted area and, after considerable regrouping, there were inevitable delays. In the case of Reserve Infantry Regiment 91, attacking on the right towards Noreuil from just north of Quéant, this meant that leading elements were fifty minutes late over the start line, which in turn led to a loss of impetus and synergy.[26] Nevertheless, good progress was made initially, as it was also by Reserve Infantry Regiment 15, attacking in the centre of the division. One of the 1st Battalion company commanders, who was wounded during the attack, later provided a detailed account of the day from his hospital bed.

Leutnant Petersen 1st Battalion Reserve Infantry Regiment 15 [27]

"I am sorry from the bottom of my heart to have to leave the proud 1st Battalion so soon. I have never felt so quickly at home with any other unit. Now I am keeping my promise to provide a report about the battle. I set off promptly at 4.00 am, because 4th Company did as well. Against battalion orders, I formed three waves and this proved itself to be a good method, because the company drifted too far to the right during the advance. I reacted immediately by placing the second platoon to the left, next to the first platoon. Later the company swung left once more because the Quéant - Lagnicourt road curved to the south. At that the third platoon filled in the gap to 4th Company. A little later the first shots rang out. Thereafter we double marched forward. Suddenly, a machine gun opened up and brought the movement to a halt. It appeared to be located about seventy metres away. At any rate I had a hand grenade passed to me and attempted a throw, because I can achieve forty five metres. Scared by the explosion, although they were not hit, the British abandoned their gun. With a dash forward we reached the sunken Lagnicourt - Bullecourt road. We captured three machine guns and took ten prisoners. Four guns were taken just west of Lagnicourt.

"The sentries were overrun, but only 100 metres away the outpost line, protected by wire, was being defended. Every time one of us raised his head, we were fired at with rifles and machine guns. I had everyone lie down in cover then, when I shouted, 'Fire!' they popped up and directed a volley at the enemy. Over time, this became unpleasant for the enemy and, suddenly, about two hundred Tommies took to their heels. They were pursued by fire and fell like flies .. It was a perfect hare shoot. I received my knee wound during the follow up, but by then the company had captured fourteen guns, five machine guns, an officer, a feldwebel [company sergeant major] and twenty men."

2nd Company also advanced successfully and pushed right up to a cluster of guns in a hollow next to the road to Vaulx. There were no fewer than seventeen, belonging to1 and 2 Australian Field Artillery Brigades. Most were dug in facing Bullecourt, but some were pointing towards Quéant. For some reason this assault group lacked explosives or a means of detonation, so all they could do was to smash up the sights and remove the breech blocks, where the Australian gunners had not already succeeded in doing do.[28]In any case, once the Australians returned after the Australian 9th and 20th Battalions had counter-attacked, the damage was swiftly rectified. 3rd Battalion had intended to advance in conjunction with the Lehr Infanterie Regiment on its left. Unfortunately, that regiment was delayed, so it was forced to advance alone and look to its own flank protection.

Vizefeldwebel Ebeling 9th Company Reserve Infantry Regiment 15 [29]

During the night 14/15 9th Company was deployed, the first platoon under Vizefeldwebel Hasselbeck and my second platoon forward. The third platoon, commanded by Leutnant Niemeyer, was in depth. About 1.00 am, just as I was about to get my head down, the call came, 'Platoon commanders to the company commander!' We knew for certain now that the rumours of an imminent attack were about to come to fruition … At 4.00 am we were to lunge towards our beautiful former rest and recreation centre! We hurried back, not forgetting to drain our last bottle of beer. At 3.30 am the platoons started to make their way carefully through the wire. By 3.50 am all was ready. Hauptmann von Widekind hurried along the front of our forward companies: 10th right, 9th left, giving out final instructions. Surprise was critical. We were to rush forward silently, break in to Lagnicourt in one bound and push on through it. Our 9th Company was to capture Hill 103 [modern Hill 101, just southeast of the village], push on through the village itself to the gun lines and then dig in on the heights beyond until the order arrived to withdraw.

"We advanced in complete silence, overran sentry posts and machine gun nests as our unstoppable forward motion carried us to the sunken road Lagnicourt - Doignies by Hill 103. Here we captured some prisoners, but not without losses ourselves. This was where the outstanding, proven, Unteroffizier Nolte-Kuhlmann fell. It became light. As we pushed on we came under machine gun from the Lagnicourt - Beaumetz road. 'Dig in on the hill and link up with 10ᵗʰ Company!' My platoon was on the right flank among the remains of houses by the Beaumetz exit of Lagnicourt. Meanwhile 12ᵗʰ Company assumed the flank protection role. There was nothing to be seen of the division to our left. We were hanging in the air! ... From the village came the sound of the engineers blowing up guns."

Hauptmann von Widekind, Commanding Officer 3rd Battalion Reserve Infantry Regiment 15 [30]

"Once information arrived that the Lehr Infanterie Regiment was not ready for battle, Rackelmann's 12ᵗʰ Company received the order at 4.15 am to echelon left to cover the [open] flank. 11ᵗʰ Company had already been ordered not to push on beyond the northeast corner of Lagnicourt. At 5.30 am, 10ᵗʰ Company was able to report that Lagnicout was in the hands of the battalion and that positions and gun lines were unoccupied! There was no further advance along the heights south of the village because the left hand company did not reach the southern edge until 6.30 am, apparently because of stiff resistance. At 6.45 am, 12ᵗʰ Company reported that it had contact on both flanks and was digging in on Hill 103. 9ᵗʰ Company was located between 12ᵗʰ and 10ᵗʰ Companies. All of them had encountered only light opposition in the village, had hauled individual British [*sic.*] soldiers out of bed and had driven off a machine gun firing from beneath a roof tile.

"In amongst all this, patrols and groups of engineers moved ceaselessly through the village, rendering dug in guns unusable and capturing equipment. Everywhere there were calls for engineers with their explosives and everywhere sighting mechanisms were being smashed. One daring patrol from 10ᵗʰ Company pushed on along the sunken road from Lagnicourt to Morchies to within one kilometre of Morchies. However, enemy artillery fire started coming down from 6.15 am and, on the right, a move to the rear began at 6.45am. Apparently strong enemy pressure was building up from the north. The Lehr Infanterie Regiment off to the left were held up by machine gun fire about 1,000 metres to the rear. This meant that the enemy infantry was able to take up positions in the sunken road north of Morchies and to take the companies under fire from a flank. One machine gun firing from the sunken road towards Beaumetz was especially unpleasant. As the right flank of the battalion gradually became exposed the companies pulled back, one after the other, to the *Siegfried-Stellung*, protected by 12ᵗʰ Company acting as rearguard."

It is not hard to discover what had gone wrong for the Lehr Infanterie Regiment. The operation was planned in great haste and it took time to transmit the necessary orders forward. On the basis of a warning order, 3ʳᵈ Guards Infantry Division directed that the Lehr Infanterie Regiment was to advance on the right flank, with the Fusilier Guard Regiment to its left. Despite the fact that the attack was scheduled to begin at 4.00 am on 15 April, detailed divisional orders did not reach the regiment until 8.45 pm on 14 April, then more time was lost getting them to the battalions, which were some four to five kilometres from regimental headquarters. If that was bad, a supplementary order from Brigade did not reach the front line until 5.20 am. As it was there was no time for reconnaissance and guides supplied by Reserve Infantry Regiment 15 became disorientated or fell victim to harassing fire. From that moment the difficulties simply multiplied. There was no sign of any engineers or explosives, there were delays in distributing hand grenades and problems negotiating the barbed wire. Eventually 1st Battalion Lehr Infanterie Regiment set off forty five minutes late, by which time it was getting light, surprise had been lost and, as a result, the outcome for the regiment fell well short of what had been hoped for.[31]

Further south, the Fusilier Guards made only a relatively minor contribution. In contrast to the Lehr Infanterie Regiment, its forward elements were able to set off at the correct time, but such was the need for flank protection that the number of troops available to advance was relatively limited. Reasonable progress was made to begin with. Some outposts and machine gun positions were reduced; the occupants were either captured or shot down but gradually resistance increased and casualties to machine gun fire began to mount, until there was no point in trying to get further forward. At that the lines of attacking guardsmen dug in at the furthest point of their advance, still only 2,000 metres beyond the start line. From there attempts were made to thrust forward with strong fighting patrols, but these too were halted well short of the planned line between Lagnicourt and Louverval. There they dug in and held out until late afternoon, finally returning to their starting position, some seventeen hours after they had left it.

Its 1st Company had an unusual experience. Advancing in the dark, they found themselves as it became light occupying a dip in the ground between the occupied Australian trenches. The occupants had kept quiet as they had pressed forward but, as time passed, unable to regain their lines and fearful of being attacked from the rear, a large group of Australians surrendered. When the surviving German soldiers returned to their own lines, soaked to the skin, they bought in one officer and forty two other ranks as prisoners. Nevertheless, the price paid had been high. Two officers, Reserve Leutnants Plewka[32] and Mallmann were killed and a third, Reserve Leutnant Hachtmann, died of wounds two days later.[33] 103 other ranks were killed, 205 all ranks were wounded and a further fifty were missing.[34]

On the extreme left of the German assault, Infantry Regiment 96, 38th Infantry Division, also participated, attacking somewhat ineffectively towards the area held by the 10th Australian Battalion just to the north of Louverval. One of its platoon commanders was wounded but survived the day. Evacuated, he later wrote an interesting letter home from his hospital bed in Cambrai. The compressed timetable for the attack comes through very strongly.

Leutnant Barg 3rd Machine Gun Company Infantry Regiment 96 [35]

"At 8.00 pm (14 April) I received an order to report by 11.00 pm that every man had a full water bottle, personal assault order equipment, steel helmet and gas mask. I thought, 'Ah, they are expecting an attack and we have been earmarked for a possible counter-stroke'. My runner got to work on the weapons. By 11.00 pm all was ready and the report had been made. There was no question of sleep under these circumstances; everybody thought that something was going to happen that night ... My batman obtained a steel helmet for me (I only had a field cap with the red stripe), iron rations and a water bottle. About midnight a runner came into my dugout, summoning me to the company commander. I wondered if it was something important or if he just wanted a social call ...

"There was considerable hustle and bustle in the battalion command post where I reported to the company commander. He greeted me with the words, 'We are attacking'. I then sat and took down the attack order. Three divisions were to attack at 4.00 am to relieve pressure on the troops fighting around Arras. I was allocated six machine guns and was to storm forward with the first wave of infantry. We were to set off [for the start line] at 2.45 am. I was wished good luck, returned to my dugout, called the gun commanders together and gave them the necessary orders. I placed the attack order together with a map in my right hand jacket pocket where I found both of them later after I had been wounded, ripped by a ricochet. The same happened to my wallet - but I must not anticipate. Leaving letters, sketches etc in the dugout, I took only essentials with me.

"At 2.00 am I put on my steel helmet and equipment and hung my knapsack and gas mask around me. I was consequently barely recognisable as an officer. I then set off with my batman, without a thought about what the coming hours might bring. Silently we passed through the wire in single file and advanced several hundred metres further on. The infantry was already lined up in two waves and I inserted my machine guns amongst the 3rd Battalion. I was the only machine gun officer present. My company commander remained with the staff. There was still much to organise and I had no opportunity to relax right up until 4.00 am. Like a wraith I crept along the line of riflemen, each one with steel helmet and equipment and sacks of hand grenades hanging from his shoulders. I took two with me myself, but lost them later. The Tommies did not seem to have noticed anything, for no rounds were fired. I felt as though I was taking part in an exercise at night. Lacking a watch, as I did, I had no idea what time it was. I did not really need one because, as one, the assault line moved forward and, simultaneously, our guns brought down a crashing concentration on the enemy position. Because there were only a few hundred metres between [the lines], the shells roared just over our heads. Thank heavens, none fell short. We had had absolutely no idea that there was to be this concentration of fire. We felt that it served only to warn the enemy, and to cause them hardly any damage, because most of the shells landed beyond them.

"Calmly the lines advanced. The Tommies still did not notice anything until we reached a flat topped hill where we must have been silhouetted against the horizon. All of a sudden an utter torrent of machine gun fire came from the left, right and front. Everyone lay flat on the ground and there were isolated cries for help. As soon as one of our sections tried to advance it came under such a weight of fire that it was forced straight back into cover. One of my machine guns had already been hit by a ricochet and was unusable. Three others suffered the same fate, but the others courageously fired on. It was an extraordinary sensation to be pinned down under machine gun fire. Off to the right and left somebody was crying out and, because we were effectively lying on a presentation platter, we expected a bullet at any moment Gradually it became light and we lay where we were because the infantry could not get forward.

"In order to orientate myself I raced across a road under heavy fire, but my steel helmet stayed put. I dived into a short section of trench containing a dead musketier. The 2nd Battalion advanced in the open to reinforce. During this time there were too many individual deeds for me to be able to mention them all. A machine gun of 2nd Machine Gun Coy was rushed forward through raging fire to the section of trench where I was, took up a fire position and fired like mad at the British [*sic*.]. I simply do not understand how nothing happened to these lads. The British also brought up reinforcements, which came under heavy fire. Because things were getting crowded in my trench and I wanted to get further right to a machine gun, I decided to take the risk. To get there I had to run across fifty metres of open ground. Just before I reached the gun I was aiming for, I saw a leutnant from 2nd Machine Gun Company. I had just shouted, 'Good Morning!' to him and was about to dive into a hole, when I felt a blow and realised that I had been wounded. That was Sunday 15 April, about 8.00 am.

"My legs buckled under me and I collapsed. My men pulled me into a hole where I took off my helmet and knapsack and my wound was examined. All I could see was a large hole, streaming blood, in the right hand side of my lower abdomen. One man said, 'There is no point bandaging that, Herr Leutnant!' I was expecting to lose consciousness or just expire, but I remained fully in possession of my senses and ordered someone to bind me up. My field dressing was insufficient but, luckily, a medical unteroffizier appeared and dressed my wounds as best he could … Unfortunately I could not take part in the rest of the assault, but my company captured a machine gun and took a lot of prisoners. The army communiqué for 15 April reported a thrust towards Boursies and Lagnicourt. I was there."

Against all the odds Barg was carried to the rear in a groundsheet, then evacuated and operated on successfully. He was more fortunate than most and had much to thank his men for. It is difficult to assess the extent to which *Sturmbock* achieved its aim of taking pressure of the Arras front. The British counted it, 'a costly failure'.[36] However, on balance it was probably good for German morale, despite the fact that losses in some regiments were felt to be disproportionate. Reserve Infantry Regiment 77, for example, suffered two officers and thirty six other ranks killed, twelve officers and 191 other ranks wounded, with 276 missing: a total of 522 all ranks. Despite the destruction of twenty five guns and the capture of 102 prisoners and numerous machine guns, the regiment was left with mixed feelings.

Reserve Leutnant Günther Reserve Infantry Regiment 77 [37]

"Sunday 15 April 1917, the day of Lagnicourt, was one of the saddest for the history of my regiment. My battalion suffered heavy losses, but we had no idea about that when we climbed out of our trenches. We made rapid progress forward because nobody had seen us. When the British [*sic*.] discovered us, rapid machine gun fire was opened from numerous different locations. We could still see nothing. We knew that the British Lewis guns had very poor sights but, nevertheless, the racket speeded our footsteps. We had still not fired a shot; for the time being all we did was run. I could not see anything, but I could hear that the bullets were coming from short range. During a short breather I spotted a machine gun nest on a rise half right. We had to get past it. It was a wonderful, uplifting feeling for me to be able to lead my platoon in a genuine attack. I watched as some individuals fell. To my right and left I watched grooves being formed in the ground [by bullets] as the earth was kicked upwards. What luck that the bullets in the air left no traces! Suddenly I felt a blow on my left foot and tumbled down into a shell hole, which was luckily very close. The battle continued over me - further forwards!"

Günther's opinion was, however, not universally shared. Another participant left a far more upbeat version of events.

Unteroffizier Dietze 1st Company Reserve Infantry Regiment 15 [38]

"Thanks to the foresight and prudence of our commanders, the allocated tasks were completed in their entirety. The wells in Lagnicourt were blown up and about two hundred prisoners were captured. The Germans had once again demonstrated their superiority in open warfare! Everyone was proud to have participated in such a brilliant success, proud of having played their part, proud of their officers. We really achieved something! The thing that stuck in the throats was the need to withdraw. It manifested itself in anger at our left hand neighbours, whose late appearance caused our hasty withdrawal. We received the battalion order of 18 April with enthusiasm when it was read out to us. Stories about 15 April circulated for a long time afterwards; many amusing incidents had contributed to it. A lot of teasing went on, contributing to the fun."

The battalion order which had enthused Dietze and his comrades read in part:

"Thanks to the exemplary, manly way 3rd and 4th Companies advanced the enemy was completely surprised. The other companies rushed to join them and the entire battalion, complete with six courageous machine gun crews, brought down a rate of fire which will long remain in the memory of the enemy. In that way, soldiers, you pressed the elusive luck of war into your service. You overran thirty one guns, of which twelve were destroyed and took five of the machine guns which were brought back.[39] In addition you captured a quarter of all the prisoners. Thanks to your ability and the training given by the company commanders, losses in the assault were slight ... No guards battalion could have attacked more skilfully or courageously ..."

Successful or not, the operation certainly acted as a wake-up call to the British army. Thereafter work went ahead at breakneck speed to improve its defences in this sector. The experience of the Australians, having been caught napping with their gun lines rather exposed, led to considerably more emphasis on advance posts pushed forward of the main positions and a great increase in patrol activity and, consequently, clashes by night in No Man's Land. In places, success had been complete. Wehrmann Ringe of Reserve Infantry Regiment 77 summed the situation up neatly: 'The British [sic.] seemed not to have been expecting our morning visit. We surprised them while they were still asleep and when they met us were still only half dressed. One Tommy ran through our lines. In his hurry he had only been able to put on one boot. Despite the seriousness of the situation, we laughed heartily at that.'[40]

One immediate consequence of the attack was that on the severely pressed 27th Infantry Division front there was near calm throughout 15 April but, when 16 April dawned a fine spring day with clear skies and sunshine, although there was no repetition of the attack on Bullecourt, nevertheless artillery fire of all calibres up to 240 mm began to land with increasing intensity all across the sector. These concentrations lasted for hours at a time, convincing the defenders that a renewed attack was simply a matter of time. In reaction and also following analysis of the events of 11 April, Grenadier Regiment 123 was inserted into the line between Infantry Regiments 120 and 124 and the right hand formation of 2nd Guards Reserve Division closed the gap to Infantry Regiment 124. The net effect was to narrow the frontages each regiment was required to cover and to increase the depth of the defences. In general the regiments now defended with four companies in the front line, two in close support in the second line trenches, with two companies in reserve close by, along the line of the *Artillerie-Schutzstellung*.

Even the 'resting' battalions were held in reserve no more than four to five kilometres in rear. Not that there was much rest to be had. Those not involved with repairing and improving the forward defences were deployed nightly to dig depth positions. Some *Musketen* companies were placed under command at this time, adding the fire power of their light machine guns to the overall defensive effort. Meanwhile, although the main emphasis of the battle shifted north to the northern section of the IX Reserve Corps front, it was evident that Bullecourt - Riencourt - Quéant would not be long spared, an impression which gained weight daily as the artillery continued its systematic bombardment, guided by aerial observers, overhead enemy aircraft patrolled constantly, attacking opportunity targets well to the rear with machine guns and bombs. The German artillery, now somewhat recovered from the mauling it had received earlier, undertook extensive programmes of harassing and destructive fire, which concentrated as dawn broke each morning on likely enemy assembly areas and start lines.

Time passed, April turned into May and there were unmistakable signs that the attack was about to be renewed against Bullecourt. The implications of a further assault began to dominate the thinking of the German chain of command. There was, for example, a great increase in enemy air activity, with attacks by groups of twelve to fifteen aircraft a constant fact of life. Yet another reorganisation of the front produced a further increase in the strength of the front line garrisons. Though it was impossible to predict the likely outcome of this front loading of the defensive force, it did at least demonstrate that everything possible was being done to prepare for an attack and in any case there would not be long to wait. By the night of 2/3 it quite clear to all that the attack would begin the following morning. It was to be the start of a major effort on a twenty two kilometre front by (from north to south) the British First, Third and Fifth Armies. The Bullecourt - Quéant sector was to be the responsibility of I Anzac Corps. There were differences of opinion between the army commanders regarding the time that the offensive should begin. In the end an uneasy compromise was reached and, finally, 4.45 am German time was chosen. At that time it was still dark, a factor which suited the Canadians in the extreme north and, to a lesser extent, the Anzacs in the south.

The British Official Historian later claimed[41] that it was this choice that compromised the attacks but, as has already been mentioned, the entire enterprise had been so telegraphed that the German defenders had done all in their power to prepare and were already on the highest state of alert when the blow fell. Sure enough, at 4.30 am 3 May, just as 27th Infantry Division was about to bring down destructive fire on enemy assembly areas, extraordinarily heavy Allied artillery fire began crashing down on the forward positions. After an estimated mere ten minutes of this drum fire, a massive infantry assault was launched across the full length of the divisional frontage and, simultaneously, eight tanks[42] lumbered into view forward of Bullecourt in support of the British 62nd Division attack, whilst the 2nd Australian Division, with 5 Brigade right and 6 Brigade left, eschewing the support of tanks, in which they no longer had any confidence, left set off in a direct line for Riencourt. Very quickly Infantry

Regiment 124, ably assisted by elements of Reserve Infantry Regiment 91and numerous machine guns from positions to the north of Quéant, shot the 5 Brigade assault to a standstill. Much of the wire in their sector was uncut, there had been some bunching and then, in the dark and confusion, an order was given to pull back. Something akin to a rout occurred and numerous Australians on this flank - the Australian Official Historian mentions a figure of 400 unwounded men - rushed back about 1,000 metres to the safety of the sunken road running between Quéant and Bullecourt.[43] The troops who remained in contact, however, caused very considerable difficulties to the forward companies of Infantry Regiment 124.

According to several German sources, the experience of 11 April meant that the tanks did not succeed in producing a shock effect on the defence. The infantry attack, however, enjoyed more success. On the extreme right flank of 27th Infantry Division, to the northwest of Bullecourt, there was a break in which was eliminated only after bitter hand to hand fighting; whilst to the east of the village the Australians established a firm foothold in the forward trenches of Grenadier Regiment 123. Furthermore (and in contrast to the situation on 11 April) it was possible to get reinforcements forward, first by exploiting a conveniently placed depression in the ground and later along a communications trench dug specifically for the purpose.

The centre of the regimental sector, though threatened, was never captured, but there were problems on both flanks. The contribution of the tanks had been a definite disappointment. Those that were not knocked out by guns in the anti-tank role or forced to turn away, were subject to ferocious attack by the machine gunners; on this occasion plentifully equipped with SmK armour-piercing ammunition. Vizefeldwebel Rahn, commander of a machine gun platoon of Grenadier Regiment 123, personally rushed up to one despite being wounded. He destroyed it and captured its driver, whom he escorted to regimental headquarters, complete with his basket of carrier pigeons.[44]

On the Infantry Regiment 124 regiment front, one of the heaviest assaults was delivered by 6 Australian Brigade to the southwest of Riencourt. This sub sector was defended by 9th and 10th Companies in the front line. It had suffered especially heavily during the preliminary bombardment and the final drum fire in the thirty minutes leading up to the assault had been particularly effective. The trenches and dugouts, such as there were, were largely flattened or destroyed, as was most of the wire obstacle. Worse, a high proportion of the trench garrison had been caught in the gunfire and many were already dead, wounded, or buried alive when the assault came smashing in. Within a very short time these two companies had been overrun though, fortunately for the integrity of the defence, off to their left 11th and 12th Companies of 3rd Battalion and 3rd and 4th of 1st Battalion had managed to hold firm. Immediately next to the break in, decisive action by Unteroffizier Pfeiffer prevented the breach from being widened to the east, whilst the Australian thrust along *Canstatter Graben*, a communication trench leading towards Riencourt, was nipped smartly in the bud by an immediate hasty counter-attack by men of 5th Company.

Whilst reinforcements came tumbling into the breach, to the immediate front masses of Australian troops, who had taken cover there, maintained a heavy fire fight with the forward companies. This very much limited the freedom of action of the defence as the day wore on. A further problem soon manifested itself. The fighting was at close quarter and intense, so supplies of hand grenades dwindled alarmingly. To make matters worse, three forward dumps of them had been destroyed by shelling prior to the attack and resupply was severely constrained by the weight of fire coming down on the rear areas. Men of 2nd Company gathered up all that could be obtained easily and got them forward, but the shortage was to have a negative impact on the ability of the defenders to counter-attack. As far as possible the German guns attempted to seal off the break in point to prevent further Australian troops from getting forward, but this enjoyed only limited success.

The defenders did their best, but the problems kept multiplying. Enemy machine gun and light mortar teams pushed on beyond the Grenadier Regiment 123 positions, established themselves in a section of sunken road there and began to bring down enfilade fire along the Infantry Regiment 124 trenches. Losses began to mount, 2nd Company was deployed forward to assist and 6th Company moved to take over its positions in the *Artillerie-Schutzstellung*. Meanwhile the Australians continued to make gradual progress. Counter action was required urgently so, at about 9.20 am, the first major effort was made by Infantry Regiment 124 and Grenadier Regiment 123 to pinch out the breach by rolling it up to the right and left respectively, whilst the 27th Infantry Division storm group, commanded by Reserve Oberleutnant Bauer and rushed forward by truck, attempted to make progress along the *Canstatter Graben.* Unlike the situation on 11 April, however, this time no significant progress could be made. It was felt that the Australians, learning from their previous experience, had brought very large numbers of rifle grenades with them. This kept Bauer's men in particular at bay by preventing them from getting within hand grenade throwing range.

The situation for the teams trying to roll up the breach was equally difficult. The positions had been so smashed up by gun fire that it was impossible to move under the protection of trenches and the defenders were forced to rush from shell hole to shell hole, which splintered the teams and wrecked their momentum. There were some small successes, largely as a result of individual bravery or dash. Unteroffizer Pfeilsticker and two others recaptured a MG 08 belonging to 3rd Machine Gun Company and here and there some slight progress was achieved. In an attempt to break the stalemate, two companies from Infantry Regiment 120 were deployed forward from Riencourt, arriving loaded up with extra ammunition and grenades. It was all to no avail. The Australian infantry began to dig in only 150 metres forward of the remnants of the wire obstacle, which virtually ruled out the use of defensive artillery fire because of the proximity of friendly troops.

Two more companies of Infantry Regiment 120 were deployed and, at 7.05 pm, a further attempt was made to counter-attack inwards, with Oberleutnant Bauer commanding what was left of the divisional storm group and 4th and 6th Companies Infantry Regiment 124. This time more ground was gained and a section of the forward position was recaptured. Nevertheless, Australian counter action won the disputed trench back. This failure was highly depressing, especially because Bauer was seriously wounded during the course of the action and one of the most experienced and battle hardened commanders, Vizefeldwebel Hinderer, was killed.[45] Although fighting went on late into the evening, after eighteen hours of continuous battle the attempt to regain the lost trenches was abandoned for the time being. However, General Maur was not willing to accept the situation and, at 10.00 pm, orders arrived for a counter-attack to be mounted during the morning of 4 May.

"Today, thanks to the courage of its infantry and the outstanding support of the artillery, four heavy enemy assaults have been beaten off with bloody losses. The enemy have succeeded in breaking into sub sectors B4 and C1 and have established themselves there.

• The first task is to ensure by all possible means that the enemy who have broken in neither expand their position or manage to get reinforcements, ammunition or rations forward to the *Engländernest*. After that the nest is to be eliminated.
• The infantry is to barricade itself in, not only from the flanks, but also from the rear. The artillery is to maintain barrage fire throughout the night forward of the break in point, so as to prevent the enemy from crossing the fire zone.
• The infantry brigade commander is tasked with the systematic clearance of the *Engländernest*. The divisional storm troop is placed at his disposal. The commander of an infantry support battery and a flamethrower commander will report to him later today. To the extent possible all the artillery is to be moved up in support.
• Every effort is to be made, even before tomorrow morning, to destroy the enemy by rolling them up from all sides.
• The two battalions in group reserve back in Villers [Plouich] have been placed at the disposal of the division. If the brigade commander wishes to plan on using them, he is to pass a request to me.

Signed: von Maur."[46]

Oberst von der Osten, commanding 53 Infantry Brigade, did indeed accept Maur's offer and directed that teams from Grenadier Regiment 123 and Infantry Regiment 124, preceded by flamethrowers, were to advance along the line of the forward trench, thus cutting off the attackers.

At 1.00 am 1st Battalion Reserve Infantry Regiment 15 arrived from its rest billets in Hancourt to reinforce and were held in readiness between Riencourt and Cagnicourt then, following a short but heavy fire plan, the attack began at 4.15 am. To begin with progress was quite reasonable and the twin thrusts made approximately 250 metres.

However, as the flamethrowers approached the site of the original break in, resistance stiffened. In addition the Australian troops were also dispersed in various shell holes, which made it difficult to focus the attacks and, once more, widespread use of rifle grenades proved to be an effective way of holding back the German teams at a relatively safe distance. Gradually the reinforcements were drawn into the battle as it developed. One of the participants left a detailed description which is doubly interesting, because it must be typical of many such situations all along the front at that time.

Vizefeldwebel Dietze 1st Company Reserve Infantry Regiment 15 [47]

" Dawn broke on a misty morning with visibility about 200 metres. As it became light, the enemy began to bring down systematic counter-battery fire. Small whizz-bangs and heavy shells roared overhead. As so often the enemy were profligate with their ammunition. Off to our left a destroyed battery position stood, quiet and abandoned. Only craters, trampled earth, wooden beams and wire bore witness to the fact that gunners had been deployed there once. From about 7.00 am, one hundred metres from us, every minute two heavy and two medium calibre 'dugout crushers' landed, together with four shrapnel rounds. We could not quite believe it at first, then we got used to it and enjoyed watching the beauty of columns of earth being thrown up … We went forward about 1.00 pm. The communication trench was deep, but for the final hundred metres before the front line it was flattened into a low depression. It was under a crazy rate of fire and to this very day I am amazed that we passed through it unscathed.

"The trench forward was in good condition, almost undamaged and supplied with deep dugouts. We moved to the right and the picture altered somewhat: dead men! Friend and foe lay peacefully together: British grenades - by the box!; Lewis gun drums - piles of them! Helmets, webbing, rifles, all lay in complete confusion. It was as though a British trench had been captured. Every hundred metres there were tanks in the barbed wire, destroyed by artillery and machine gun fire. Large metal fragments of tanks knocked out by direct hits lay all round … the fighting must have been bitter; for the entire area was strewn with corpses. For the time being there was no firing. We were in the correct place. Some of the Grenadiers [from Grenadier Regiment 123] were down in a dugout. An unteroffizier gave me a briefing.

" 'The Tommies got the trench back repeatedly, but they were heaved out again each time. About six to seven traverses further on six men are manning a sandbag barricade. The Tommies are twenty metres beyond that …' I left two men of Unteroffizier Carl Heumann's section in the dugout and, together with the Grenadier unteroffizier, led the other six to the barricade. There were a few pieces of timber from a dugout with some earth thrown in behind them, a few sandbags and a bit of barbed wire - and this was supposed to be a 'barricade'!

Its garrison disappeared, breathing sighs of relief ... It was allegedly a witches' cauldron but, for the time being, was strangely quiet ... I gave Unteroffizier B. this order, 'If things get lively, send a runner immediately! Otherwise, stick to your post!' I strolled back to the dugout, absorbing my surroundings.

"The silent witnesses to the fighting brought home to me how heroically we ill equipped Germans had to fight to counteract the numerical and material superiority of the enemy ... We had to count out our small arms ammunition; the British stuff lay around by the sack. We used to hang three hand grenades to our belts where they hindered us or were lost every time we dashed forward. There were crates of British ones everywhere! As for the difference in availability of machine guns ... At 1.00 pm [sic.] the sentry bawled 'The British are attacking the barricade!' I rushed up out of cover and sure enough a real battle with hand grenades was taking place there and there were other dull explosions in between. 'Everyone out! The British are attacking!'

"Together with the dugout sentry I headed for the next traverse and was met by the panic-stricken barricade guards, with the exception of one reservist who was hanging on. Unteroffizier Heumann arrived and we ran towards the barricade, but did not get far because rifle grenades and shrapnel rounds were landing everywhere. We took up positions along a parapet and shot at the Tommies, who, firing, had sprung up from the earth like mushrooms. I counted at least five to seven rifle grenadiers alone. Before each shot, they lay down in the trench then the round was fired. We took aim at where they disappeared and as soon as a flat helmet appeared, we fired several bullets. We had some success and soon only isolated grenades were coming from over there. I looked through my telescope and the former German trenches were teeming with flat helmets. From the low ground to our front helmet upon helmet advanced in a great brown snake ... From our side came not one single shot.

"I then spotted other Tommies lying down at another place. Then, suddenly, six or eight rifle grenades flew up. Describing elegant arcs in the air, they then landed - horrors! - right on us. One of us lay where he was, two others staggered to the rear groaning. Some of our weapons were smashed and then the next shower landed. Another of us fell. We were down to four: Heumann, Gefreiter Ahnefeld, the reservist and me. We were powerless, our grenades would only reach the next traverse, whereas the rifle grenades could be launched comfortably from one hundred metres. The casualties we caused the Tommies made no difference, because they were coming forward in masses. Behind us the trenches were sealed off by mortars and artillery. We were caught in a mouse trap. From our front and flanks came rifle - and hand grenades; behind us a defensive barrage. Only those who have experienced similar danger can have the slightest idea how we felt.

"Remarkably, there was no sign of the others. Before the next salvo, we rushed back to the dugout. Offizierstellvertreter Tosaute stood on the steps and behind him was the remainder of the platoon, one and a half sections. 'Where are the Tommies? [asked someone] as Tosaute fired a red flare past me. Furious, I bawled. 'Get out and look for yourselves … !' My three faithful comrades had occupied a parapet and were firing rapidly. That was the only sound that could steady the nerves. I soon joined in. Suddenly a machine gun began firing from a trench to our rear and we held our breath. Tosaute launched up from the dugout, daringly leapt out of cover, then disappeared once more, but the machine gun stopped. The Tommies were through the barricade, the rifle grenadiers moved ever closer and began zeroing in once more. The rifle grenades were now coming from our half left. How had they got there? …

"We began to run short of ammunition. Unmoved, the brave Heumann and his two faithful companions continued to fire calmly from behind the parapet, which rather showed me up as I was getting flustered. Down came the rifle grenades once more. Splinters flew everywhere, some clattering against the steel helmets … we looked anxiously at the trench to our rear. Then a shot split my index fingers and tore off my middle finger. Handkerchief applied! Carry on! … our lungs were full of dust and powder smoke. The sun beat down and now and then I felt that I was being overcome with sleep. Gefreiter Ahnefeld was killed, I lost my helmet. Heumann had a stoppage. The reservist fiddled with the bolt [of his weapon]. What a hopeless situation!

"We could hold on no longer! The Tommies were only three traverses away and were hurling loads of egg-shaped hand grenades, of which, luckily, only a few exploded … We threw the last of the grenades and pulled back, but fate took a hand beyond the second traverse. An unseen force threw me in the air, something heavy hit the right hand side of my chest. I saw the reservist thrown against the side of the trench then landed on Heumann who was lying there, groaning terribly. I lost consciousness, but was awakened by bangs and crashes. Blood was pouring out of my mouth and nose, my uniform jacket was ripped, the front soaked with blood. My chest hurt. Heumann groaned. I spoke to him, I wanted to help him, even though I could not stand myself. He writhed in agony. The ground all around him was red with blood. Ahnefeld was dead, I could do nothing for Heumann. The Tommies were close so, by summoning all my reserves of strength, I tried to crawl away and save myself … I shall not describe the scenes I saw, they were too simply too dreadful …

"Late that afternoon I arrived at a section of *Musketen* [light machine gunners]. Their leader pointed his revolver at me and said, 'Are you trying to avoid the front?!'. I gasped for air and told him carefully that there were none of his men further forward … My time at the front was finished … Heumann died in captivity. I shall never forget the men who came out from under cover. Most of them stayed there. Sadly I do not know their names. I am writing these few lines in memory of Heumann and Ahnefeld."

As the day wore on, the battle lost impetus but, at around 4.00pm, a further Australian attack, which presumably included the battle which Dietze described, forced a route through the German positions and launched forward in the direction of Riencourt. This could have been an absolutely critical moment, had it not been for the presence of the ever-reliable men of Reserve Infantry Regiment 15. Although used earlier in the day, to their chagrin piecemeal, to reinforce the various counter-attacks, their few uncommitted men were now optimally placed to help scupper the latest threat to Riencourt.

Leutnant Petersen 1st Battalion Reserve Infantry Regiment 15 [48]

"At 6.15 pm the order arrived, 'Third Platoon 2nd Company Reserve Infantry Regiment 15 is to move immediately to reinforce the other two platoons of the company which are locked in battle with the British [*sic.*] troops attacking Riencourt'. The British tried repeatedly, bayonets fixed, to take Riencourt by storm but, thanks to 2nd Company and its tireless leaders, they did not succeed. The battle raged on until after midnight, but all attempts to capture Riencourt failed. The day cost many casualties: 1st, 2nd and 3rd Companies suffered considerably. Leutnant Lindau was wounded and the outstanding Offizierstellvertreter Tosaute was killed. I led the survivors of the company back to the *Wotan Stellung*, where they were able to snatch some rest. 4th Company got away with it best; they were still in the *Wotan Stellung*."

The reprieve so gained was only temporary. A resumption of the assault by the Australians saw them recapture their positions and they remained determined to close up on Riencourt. In this they were once again unsuccessful so, by the end of the second day of battle, one of the first day objectives remained out of reach. Furthermore, every subsequent attempt to get forward was met by a torrent of defensive fire, though maintaining the defence was becoming harder by the hour. At 8.30 pm Reserve Leutnant Gundermann, commander 12th Company Infantry Regiment 124, was killed by a burst of machine gun fire while rallying his men. Despite this setback a further resumption of the counter-attack was ordered. There was a short counter-bombardment and the attack was launched. A hasty, improvised night attack of this type is always fraught with difficulties and this was no exception. After sporadic violent clashes in the dark, by 2.00 am 5 May, this was halted by the Australians, despite the fact that a combined force of Grenadier Regiment 123 and Infantry Regiment 124 had actually forced a way forward as far as the original front line. It was, however, too weak to hold forward and had to withdraw once more. Dawn on 5 May saw the Australians still in possession of a significant section of the front line. In order to take some of the pressure of the defenders, Headquarters 27th Infantry Division arranged for a counter-attack, preceded by a heavy bombardment, to be launched at 10.30 am with the aim of restoring the breach in the lines completely.

"The attempt to clear out the *Engländernest* with the assistance of flamethrowers has still not led to complete success … it is now crucial that the infantrymen barricade themselves in securely so that the enemy are prevented from expanding [their gains].

• During the morning of 5 May the *Engländernest* is to be cleared systematically. The operation will be directed by a commander designated by 53 Infantry Brigade. All participating units will be subordinated to him.
• In outline, the operation is to be conducted as follows:

a. The Mortar Company is to deploy forward as many weapons as possible during the night and the grenade launchers of the regiments are to be concentrated and subordinated to it. The task of the mortars and grenade launchers is to bring fire down on the sunken road and enemy occupied trenches.
b. Infantry Support Battery 8 is to deploy during the night to a position northwest of Riencourt. Its mission is to support the infantry by taking on especially dangerous point targets and to bring enfilade fire down on the sunken road.
c. After dawn on 5 May the mortars and intimate support batteries are to range in. Following that there is to be fire for effect at designated times and places.
d. Once all is ready, assault groups armed with hand grenades are to close in on the British [*sic.*] from all sides. The thus far undeployed element of the divisional storm troop, together with selected men from the regiments, will be made available to the commander, who, if he requires it, can request flamethrower support.
e. The divisional artillery is the bring down barrage fire during the night and up to one hour after the start of the operation on the enemy side of the *Engländernest.*

Signed von Maur" [49]

Despite careful preparation, the renewed attack with flamethrower support did not succeed either, but by that time it was not just a matter of rolling up a few captured trenches. The Australians had had time to create a complex defensive zone some two to three hundred metres deep. Participation in this attack and another the following day with the assistance of the Lehr Infanterie Regiment was the very last act of the survivors of the worn down 27th Infantry Division. It was clear that the fighting power of the division was, for the time being, exhausted, so during the evening of 6 May the remainder of the Lehr Infanterie Regiment moved forward to carry out a relief. Coming on top of a lengthy tour of duty forward, this second battle with its heavy casualties had completely worn out the division.[50] Reflecting on the recent battles, Infantry

Regiment 120 commented: 'For three long days, from 3 - 5 May, the division - and the regiment in particular - were confronted by an enemy many times stronger in a battle, that in its intensity was fully the equal of the murderous days of battle at Guillemont from 18 - 21 August 1916. Attack followed attack, counter-strokes threw the enemy out of their break in points repeatedly and the regimental reserve companies even went to the aid of neighbouring troops ... To the very last minute it was a classic example of military virtue and German manliness.'[51]

The final withdrawal after four weeks in the line took place during the early hours of 7 May, leaving the continuing operations to the formations of 3rd Guards Infantry Division. An extreme example of the cost of the tour to the Württembergers was the experience of 4th Company Grenadier Regiment 123. Having lost its company commander, Landwehr Leutnant Hencke, during the first day in the line, by the time it was relieved he had been joined by twenty four men killed, fifty two wounded and nine missing. From a fighting strength of only one hundred and ten, this represented a loss rate of a staggering ninety percent.[52]

Because of the earlier commitment of elements of 3rd Guards Infantry Division, the desire to launch a major counter-attack against the Australians as quickly as possible was thwarted by the need to relieve those formations which had already been in action for up to forty eight hours and to complete all the necessary reorganisation which the assumption of command over a sector brought with it. There was to have been an Operation Colberg[53] on 9 May in yet another attempt to eliminate the Australian salient. The plan was for 1st Battalion Grenadier Regiment 9 and 3rd Battalion Fusilier Guard Regiment, following a short but intense bombardment, to attack frontally, left and right respectively, while 1st Battalion Lehr Infanterie-Regiment rolled up the position from the east and storm troops made available by the Army attacked from the west. The friction of war meant that a twenty four hour postponement was ordered then, as the start time approached, the entire plan was first shelved, then scrapped, to be replaced by another, 'Operation Potsdam', scheduled for 15 May.

Eventually a report filtered down that the reason for the change was that the Australians had been strengthening their newly-won positions vigorously and it was felt by corps headquarters that nothing short of a full-blown regimental counter-attack could possibly hold out the prospect of success. As preparations went ahead, the front was far from quiet. The battalions manning the forward positions suffered in particular from the incessant artillery fire, which meant that there was a constant need to try to repair and maintain the defences, whilst there were almost nightly battles for the outpost line, the various sap heads and the places where only trench barricades separated the two sides.

Fähnrich von Obernitz Fusilier Guard Regiment[54]

"Even the march forward to the positions on 14 May [*sic.*][55] was terrible. We first came under low trajectory enemy gun fire in Cagnicourt,where we were being issued with grenades. The situation was unpleasant but all passed off well.

We were faced with a crater field four kilometres deep, which was under heavy fire. It was a terrible experience! Roaring and exploding, shells of every calibre slammed into the ground all around us as the company moved forward in a snake, one behind the other. Sometimes we ran, at other times we moved slowly through this hellish hurricane and here we suffered our first casualties. We then arrived on the position; no, in fact all that could be seen were the remaining traces of the former trenches. At long last, hours later, we reached the front line, 300 metres west of Bullecourt.

"Here we found that there were dugouts: well constructed and deep. A great feeling of relief came over us. The British would not be able to dislodge us from here! It would be a pleasure to give battle in this place, despite the inhuman artillery fire, because there were dugouts available where we could take a nap and escape from the battle for a few moments. The British attacked tirelessly. They brought down drum fire day and night, only lifting it to the rear when they were about to attack and then only for a short period, because each battle never lasted for more than one and a half hours. In dense waves the British [*sic.*] would work their way forward to our barbed wire obstacle that gun fire had reduced to an utter tangle of wooden and metal stakes and twisted wire. A combination of our rifle, machine gun and artillery defensive fire then stalled them forward of this obstacle.

"Huge losses and faltering courage would force them to turn tail. If a wave managed to get into our wire, nobody ever returned; there the Tommies remained, dead or wounded, hanging on the wire. Despite all the fire, we managed to recover about one hundred of them altogether and move them to the dressing station. Captured British soldiers gave us useful insights into the state of the British army and their homeland. It was then that we heard about the appalling effect our Zeppelin raids had had on London and the industrial towns. There was no opportunity to sleep. We would take a short pause in a dugout, then re-emerge. The longer we stayed in the position, the hotter the battle and the more the British pressed us.

"For the first three days everything went well. The sun shone and the oppressive clouds of gas and smoke soon dispersed. The British exploited the fine weather to photograph our positions in exact detail from low flying aircraft, so they knew the position of every dugout and machine gun post. The drum fire directed at these points was especially bad and it took real skill, artistry and speed to be able to exit the dugouts. If everything had not gone so well and if the men had not performed so brilliantly, we should have had the British in our trenches before we had had time to react. This did actually happen once but, after a sharp fight, man against man with revolvers and grenades, we managed to bring down every man who had penetrated.

"Our anger grew as our nervous energy was worn down. Shortly after we had beaten off an attack about noon on the fourth day that we had been holding the position, the British engaged our shelters with 300 mm shells fitted with delay fuzes: the so-called dugout smashers. We survived four such shells unscathed. The period of waiting was dreadful then, howling and roaring they came down, slamming into the ground like thunderclaps before exploding with an appalling crash down at the level of the dugouts. Each time our dugout rocked like a ship at sea. Another shell was on the way. An unteroffizier shouted, 'That's on target!', then a whirl of impressions hit me in split seconds. There was an appalling crash. The lights went out. Everything was thrown into confusion. There was another explosion, then another. My head was wedged under a bunk. There were shouts and curses; all our heads were spinning. There was a lurch to the rear and my aching head was freed once more.

"A rekindled light revealed a dreadful scene! The shell had smashed through the centre of the dugout ceiling, had exploded and set off five boxes of hand grenades and light mortar rounds. The sight before me was terrible. As though paralysed I stood for a moment, hardly able to comprehend what was before my eyes. There was a dreadful jumble of men, body parts, splintered logs, smashed weapons and torn clothing. Was everyone dead? No, two were still alive; three, then another. Two of them got to their feet and then, like the wind, the three of us set about clearing up. Wading through blood we laid the dead near the staircase which, luckily, was almost intact, and stacked up the scattered limbs. This one shell had killed eight men and wounded another twenty one; it was awful! The atmosphere, thick with carbon monoxide from the explosion, was almost unbearable.

"There were four of us left. The sentries could not be relieved and had to stay where they were until reinforcements could arrive that evening. When it went dark, we buried the dead in a shell hole where they were uncovered and then reburied by enemy fire. Twelve reinforcements arrived so, instead of thirty two men, there were only fifteen. By now we had six days behind us, some harder than others. To that must be added six nights without sleep: twelve times twelve hours of dreadful experiences! We could not have gone on much longer; our nerves were at breaking point. On 15 [May] we were relieved by our 3rd Battalion. Only somebody who has experienced it can possibly imagine what it means to be tied down to a tiny space, some few hundred metres square and there to endure days and nights of attritional drum fire, whilst still summoning up the strength, though physically exhausted, to repel countless enemy attacks.

A critical shortage of secure dugouts posed considerable problems and the net result was a steady stream of casualties. Maximum use was made of the Riencourt catacombs to provide shelter and rest in complete safety, but for the most part the defensive garrisons on both sides had to hold on, despite the deficiencies of their exposed positions. In order to give Operation Potsdam the best chance of success, Reserve Infantry Regiment 91 assumed responsibility for the Lehr Infanterie-Regiment sector to enable preparations to take place behind the lines.

The basic plan was similar to the counter-attacks which had been tried previously. It could be argued that this demonstrated a lack of imagination on behalf of the planners but, in reality, the geography dictated what could be done. Two battalions of Lehr Infanterie-Regiment were to attack frontally, while storm troops from the Fusilier Guards, Reserve Infantry Regiment 91 and Storm Battalion 6 allocated by the Army itself, were given responsibility for the flanks. Harassing fire was to give way to systematic bombardment designed to smash up the Australian defences from midday 14 May and this was to increase to drum fire, with gas shoots on all known battery positions shortly before the start time of 5.00 am 15 May. Naturally this activity did not go unanswered as the Allied artillery, with more or less limitless access to ammunition, responded with ferocity, making all movement within and forward of the German rear areas extremely hazardous.

The Lehr Infanterie-Regiment deployed with 2nd Battalion right and 3rd Battalion left. The right flank was anchored on the sunken road running from Hendecourt - Bullecourt; the left on the track running southwest from Riencourt. Each battalion had two companies in a first wave, with the remainder following up a short tactical bound behind the leading elements. As the start time approached, 5th, 6th, 12th and 10th Companies lined up along the first trench of the Hindenburg Line, with 7th, 8th, 11th and 9th approximately where the second line had run. Major Herold, the regimental commander, also allocated one platoon of 1st Battalion to each of the assault battalions as immediate reserves, but held the remainder back under his command. As the battalions completed final preparations and the storm troops prepared to advance from Bullecourt (Storm Battalion 6 and Fusilier Guards) and Sector C (Reserve Infantry Regiment 91), for some reason the Allied artillery remained silent. The attackers could not decide if this was because the gas shoots had been effective or if the Allies were watching and waiting for the attack to go in.

The bombardment rose to a crescendo and problems began at once. On the right it was coming down immediately to the front of the start line, whilst 12th Company were already taking casualties from shells falling short. Setting off in the dark of the pre-dawn and prior to the actual assault time, there was a further problem when some 5th Company men clashed in error with the neighbouring Reserve Infantry Regiment 213. Hand grenades were thrown, providing a perfect alarm call for the waiting Australian troops.[56] The worst fears of the waiting infantry were realised when, just before zero hour, the sound of machine guns could be heard all along the Australian main defensive line. Despite that setback, the entire line moved forward at the appointed hour. Poor visibility and the cratered ground made it almost impossible to maintain a coherent advance. Very quickly the second wave merged with the first in places and the attack degenerated into a series of uneven minor thrusts which played straight into the hands of the defence.

In any case the days since the Australians had taken this bite out of the lines had not been wasted. Work had gone ahead swiftly to improve the defences and there was even a fully concreted machine gun stand facing 6th Company. Regardless of the fragments flying around and the curtain of shrapnel put down by the German artillery in front of the lines of infantry, this weapon continued to be operated calmly and to take a considerable toll on the attackers. Once more as the range closed, widespread use of rifle grenades by the Australians gave the defence a considerable edge during the close quarter battle, especially because the firers were dispersed for the most part in a crater field position, which provided ample opportunity to fire at the assault troops from the flanks and, at times, even from the rear. The approaches to the sunken road, which ran from Bullecourt to Riencourt, posed particular problems. Largely untouched by the bombardment, its numerous defenders so swept the ground to their front that the first and second waves here (5th and 7th Companies respectively) could not get forward at all. Every attempt to advance was shot to a standstill.

Things were not a whole lot better for the men of 2nd Battalion. 6th and 8th Companies did manage to push forward, but were fairly swiftly halted and forced into cover, 8th Company having already lost its commander, Reserve Leutnant Hoffmann back on the start line.[57] 3rd Battalion had the best of the advance. Reserve Leutnant Hawlitschka led men of 12th Company into the first trench of the Hindenburg Line and followed this success by personally knocking out a machine gun post with hand grenades. Unfortunately this was an isolated success. With both his flanks in the air and the area to his rear swept by fire, there was no possibility of reinforcement or replenishment of ammunition so, eventually, Hawlitschka and his surviving men were forced to withdraw, racing from shell hole to shell hole, until they were able to regain their start line after it went dark. Even then it proved to be impossible to evacuate the wounded so that one of his platoon commanders, Reserve Leutnant Herzog, and a good many other men were taken prisoner later.

On the left flank the other companies of 3rd Battalion enjoyed mixed success. Reserve Leutnant Stephan managed to work his way forward at the head of 10th Company as far as the wire obstacle between the first and second lines of the Hindenburg Line, but was severely wounded in the process and died a short time later. 9th Company, which formed part of the second wave, drifted somewhat to the left when it came under enfilade machine gun fire. Having, nevertheless, pushed on as far as the second line, Reserve Leutnant Struve attempted to lead a team rolling up the Australian position to the right [west], but was killed during a battle with grenades. All the while the Australians rushed reinforcements and resupply forward and, in truth, though the day was hard fought, at no time was the defence in anything other than full control of the situation. Some 10th Company men did manage to pull back through the Reserve Infantry Regiment 91 sector, but the majority of the survivors of this failed attack were forced to spend the entire day under a hot sun in the cover of one of the numerous shell holes, where they were subject to showers of rifle grenades, constant gun fire and bursts from machine guns whenever they attempted to move.

One man, who spent the entire day in this manner, left a vivid, if somewhat breathless, description of the experience of the main attack.

Sergeant Kreibohm 10th Company Lehr Infanterie-Regiment [58]

"Dawn was already breaking when, at one minute to 5.00 am, Leutnant Stephan, next to us, shouted, 'With God's help! Let's go!' We gripped our rifles tightly and leapt up out of cover. We were immediately met by an appalling torrent of fire. Ghostly grey figures rose up out of the trench then ran and staggered from shell hole to shell hole. It seemed to be impossible to pass through this hail of bullets. All around was the racket of the artillery battle. Rounds howling [overhead]; shells bursting. We pushed on forwards, sometimes blown over by the air pressure; soon showered with clods of earth. Again and again we hauled ourselves up, every man for himself, because we could hardly make out our neighbours. Those who fell or were wounded remained where they went down. Appalling machine gun fire, mostly from half left. It was as though an attempt was being made to chop our legs off. Swathed in clouds of smoke and covered in earth we had soon advanced 150 metres. Six or eight Tommies came towards us, their hands held high. They too were caught up in the machine gun fire and rushed down into a large shell hole to my immediate left.

"Suddenly I felt a blow on my left hand side. I spun round and leapt into a hole. I did not know what it was so I looked carefully. I had taken a ricochet in the left arm and was hit in the chest. My jacket was in ribbons. Somewhat rattled, I checked and realised that a bullet had gone straight through my pay book and prayer book in my breast pocket. My identity disc was bent out of shape, but the main force of the split bullet had been taken by a small metal figure in my pocket which my sister had given me when I went off to war. It was not until I set off that I put it in my breast pocket; normally I carried it in my trouser pocket. It had stopped the bullet completely and all I had was a small bruise near my heart.

"The attack seemed to have stalled. I could see nobody to my front. They had got further forward on the right, but the Tommies were still securely holding their position, even though we were within thirty metres of them. I dug myself in deeper, so deep that only a direct hit would have got me. I thought that the Tommies were still next to me in the crater. Gradually it became day and all I could see behind and in front were corpses, though wounded men were still moaning and groaning. I could only, with the greatest of care, lift my head a little and despite that there was an immediate burst of very accurate machine gun fire ... To my half right, huddled in a crater, were Roth and Henke, two men of my section. I was not able to speak to them but made myself understood by tearing out a page from my note book, writing on it, wrapping it in a piece of clay and throwing it to them. They replied the same way.

"Despite the fact that we were so close to the enemy that we received no artillery or mortar fire, nevertheless these were very uncomfortable hours. The Tommies stood in their trench smoking and I must say they were a very upstanding lot. They did not fire at the wounded as they attempted to get back to the rear. In the same way ambulances were able to drive backwards and forwards between Cagnicourt and Riencourt in broad daylight. Towards evening someone near me began groaning, I thought it must be the Tommies, but questions and responses determined that it was Leutnant Stephan. He said that he was seriously wounded, with bullets in his hip and shoulder. The Tommies had bandaged him up but now they were no longer there. He had remained unconscious until now and he questioned me about the battle situation. I tried to make it clear to him how unfortunate it had all been and promised that if I possibly could I would arrange for him to be evacuated.

"I agreed with Roth and Hocke what we should try to do. The Tommies, I assume the same ones who had treated Stephan, kept a very sharp lookout. As soon as I tried a test by raising my steel helmet on a spade firing began, followed by rifle grenades, which landed very near. It became darker and gunfire started once more. Red, green and yellow flares went up. It looked as though we were about to be engaged by our own artillery. Leutnant Stephan called out again. I summoned my courage and gripped the edge of the hole with both hands ready to go over to Leutnant Stephan when a rifle grenade landed next to me. I felt a blow to the right hand side of my head as though I had been hit by a brick. Half dazed, I threw myself back down in my hole and felt the blood running warm from my head. It really was streaming down, In a few seconds my hand and jacket were soaked.

"I gathered my thoughts and tried to decide what to do when I saw the Tommies, silhouetted against the horizon as they climbed out of their trench to gather us all in. I yelled to Leutnant Stephan and Roth that I could do no more to help them then set off to the rear. I crept from hole to hole with the speed of a weasel because I was still under fire from a flank. Blood was streaming from my ear as well now. When I realised that I could not be very far from the sunken road I leapt up and raced to the sentry, shouting, 'The Tommies are coming! The Tommies are coming!' 'Where are they? You're mad!' I was helped down into a dugout in the sunken road and was bandaged up by the 9th Company medical orderly. I described to him where I had left Leutnant Stephan. Having checked the exact details with me, he set off at once with two stretcher bearers. I felt weak from loss of blood.

"Later I moved off down the evacuation route, which led me to the catacombs under Riencourt, where the regimental medical officer, Dr Puth, carried out his onerous duties. I told him that Leutnant Stephan would soon be arriving, because Henke, who was also here, stated that he had called out to the stretcherbearers to confirm where he was lying. Fusilier Roth had been shot again in the back as he was being evacuated. Unfortunately I found out afterwards that Leutnant Stephan and the stretcher bearers had been taken in by the Tommies and that he had succumbed to his wounds in captivity."[59]

So much for the fate of those of the Lehr Infanterie-Regiment, which bore the main brunt of the attack. The situation was little better for those entrusted with attacking in from the flanks as this description, also by a member of 3rd Guards Infantry Division demonstrates.

Fähnrich von Obernitz Fusilier Guard Regiment[60]
"During the night 14/15 [May] we moved to Villers [-lez-Cagnicourt] on the Cambrai – Arras road. The rest we had been allowed, which was only until the evening of 15 [May], was interrupted by bombs and enemy aircraft machine gunning us. I was writing a letter when a machine gun bullet came through a window and tore into the centre of the letter. On average the companies had lost fifty to sixty men, so each was down to a strength of only forty to fifty. That evening we went forward once more, following the same hellish route we had traversed twice before. Just as it went dark we found ourselves back at the front, having already lost a complete section to a direct hit. This time we were located on the western exit of Bullecourt, an absolute Hell! There were British to our front; British to our left in the ruins of the village and British half left of us [all Australians, of course].

"I was placed in charge of the assault troop and, just after I arrived, was ordered to clear the British out of the left half of the village. I set out with twenty four men and returned with six. A constant hail of shrapnel burst just overhead. The mission was accomplished. We cleared the sector we had been allocated shell hole by shell hole, killing fourteen British soldiers and destroying four machine guns. I was very proud that the clearance of the left half of the village was mentioned briefly in the Army Communiqué. The British artillery fire had increased in power and strength to such an extent that it was almost beyond any man to withstand it. The British wanted to occupy the whole of Bullecourt so that they could roll up our position from there, but they did not manage it.

"Our huge losses forced us to throw in every available man to this place and there was a chaotic mixing of [men of] 1st, 2nd, 4th, 5th, 7th, 9th and 12th Companies. The only officers left were Hauptmann von Dewitz and Leutnant Eisenträger. All the others were dead or wounded. We stuck out this chaotic situation for three days. There was nothing to drink; our tongues stuck to our gums and we gasped for breath. An order was rushed to us that we were to clear through the entire village of Bullecourt during the night 17/18 [May]. We were to set out at 3.00 am. We summoned what was left of our remaining strength and looked forward to it. Senses dulled, we waited for the start time. On the stroke of 3.00 am we set off one behind the other, but the stroke of 3.00 am was also the moment when the British unleashed a crazy rate of drum fire. What could it be? Had the British found out what we were doing? Were they themselves about to attack?

"Instantly there was almighty confusion as everyone rushed in all directions. Hauptmann von Dewitz, who tried in vain to restore order, went down, shot through the stomach and was dragged away by his men. It was so pitch black you could not see your hand in front of your face. It was impossible to orientate ourselves. Parched and aching with hunger, we all staggered from one crater to another. I saw one section disappear into a dugout. Madness! It meant certain capture! They had to be made to come out! I had no sooner got in behind them than I heard English voices – but they faded away again; they had not noticed the entrance in the darkness. It was high time they moved! With the last of my strength I succeeded in pushing them out one at a time.

"I set off myself, stumbling over dead and wounded men. I then fell into a water-filled crater and had no idea which way was forward and which led to the rear. Gasping, I moved forward clutching two hand grenades when, suddenly, I heard a British word of command just in front of me. Ducking down, I hurled myself into a crater full of rain water and kept absolutely still. All around me whistled bullets from a machine gun which, judging from the voices of the crew, could only have been six or seven paces away from me. Had they spotted me? My courage almost failed me. It seemed that I should either be killed or captured. I lay in the water for half an hour, then I tried to creep away. My very first movement brought four hand grenades flying towards me, but I had to get out of it.

"After another fifteen minutes I tried again, really quietly and this time I was a further crater away, then another and yet another. I then realised that I was safely away and I pressed on, always heading away from the machine gun. One and a half hours later, I came across a German post where I was orientated at long last then, half an hour later, I came across my batman, Fusilier Guard Mertens, who was waiting for me and who had spent the whole time trying to find me. The two of us made our way through the terrible gunfire to the rear. As I was stumbling along, a shell splinter tore my gas mask off my belt, which I found most amusing.

"I believe that my thoughts were in total confusion after these dreadful weeks. The sights and impressions were really too much for one barely eighteen years old. My physical appearance was equally chaotic. My trousers hung in shreds. One boot had been torn right open on barbed wire and the sleeves had been ripped off my jacket. As day dawned I got clear of the position at long last and moved to Hendecourt [-lez-Cagnicourt]. My first objective was a mineral water dump. I poured down litres of the cool liquid until I felt my strength returning. Much refreshed, I headed off with my batman for Villers [-lez-Cagnicourt], where I was to experience a rare pleasure.

"Spring had sprung. Everything was cloaked in fresh green colours and fruit trees were in bloom. I stood and stared in wonder. We had just spent three weeks in a tree-less, grass-less desert of clay and had no idea it had happened."

The total failure of this attempt to restore the original front line in the Bullecourt area came as a great disappointment to the chain of command. Every effort had been made to give the operation the greatest chance of success, but the spirited performance put up by the Australians had thwarted every attempt to get forward, even though the effort had completely exhausted the weary defenders. Generalleutnant von Moser, who had observed the attack from a good vantage point, summarised the day from his perspective that evening.

Generalleutnant Otto von Moser Diary Entry 15 May 1917 [61]

"During last night and this morning thirty one batteries fired about 60,000 high explosive and gas shells at the *Engländernest*. 5.00 am found me up the church tower at Oisy, which provided long views. This was the time when Operation Potsdam was launched. Despite all the courage shown by the troops, it did not succeed. Since 9 May the enemy had not only vastly reinforced their artillery, but also deployed ever more machine guns and grenade launchers in the *Nest*. Our dugouts had been 'turned round' and so our assault troops were greeted with torrents of machine gun fire. As a result the losses of the Lehr Infanterie-Regiment were heavy; naturally those of the British [sic.] deployed in this 'hell' were too. Prisoners described the appalling scenes there, but also spoke of the constant resupply of men and materiel. "According to statements by captured officers, Bullecourt has cost them two or three of their best divisions - this due to the dogged determination of the British commanders to hold on at all costs to at least this dismal section of the position, the only gain of the battles of 11 May. Other aspects of the prisoners' statements were worthy of note. Gone was the previous overconfidence found in the wake of 9 and 10 May [*sic*. April] east of Arras, 'In fourteen days we shall be in Douai!' They openly admit to war weariness. Their admiration of German bravery is unreserved and they are amazed to be treated so correctly. The extent to which they have been deceived and lied to is clear because many of them believed that they would be shot out of hand …

"Once we did not succeed in recapturing the *Engländernest* east of Bullecourt, we had to take a decision whether or not to hold on to Bullecourt itself. It was reduced to a complete heap of ruins, but we were in firm control of it. However it formed a sharp salient and it would cost us a high toll in casualties to remain there and we could not do so indefinitely anyway. I requested permission from higher authority to evacuate it and it was granted."

Essentially this marked the end of the main battle for Bullecourt, but this did not mean a complete end to the fighting in this area. Another formation from Württemberg, 26th Reserve Division, arrived to relieve 3rd Guards Division, who had endured a very hard tour of duty. This relief when it finally arrived, was nothing short of essential.

Oberleutnant von Drewitz-Krebs, commander 6th Company Fusilier Guard Regiment [62]

"16 May 1917. Once I had gone round the position yet again with Rittmeister von Hoffmann, I finally managed to get some sleep during the morning. Just as we had been informed the previous day, we were to be relieved this evening by Württembergers (Reserve Infantry Regiment 121). The entire length of the trench was completely ploughed up again by shells during the night. It was almost impossible to pick a route through the position; all movement was made extremely difficult and costly by the constant British shelling. All was well with the sentries, however. The British in the village kept quiet initially; apparently confining themselves to the eastern part. It was a different story to the front. Enemy snipers were very active along the railway embankment and patrols sought to close up to the barbed wire obstacle. Some British soldiers paid with their lives for this. During the afternoon the morning drizzle turned into heavy rain. The Lehr Infantry Regiment, whose own attack had not gained more ground, was itself attacked again by the British ...

"Meanwhile a Württemberg advance party arrived ... They intend to cover this area only with patrols and to shift the main defensive line back to the second trench on the northern edge of the village. I begin preparations for the move out and arrange for the stocks of iron rations dumped in the dugout to be distributed. The Württembergers took some of the signal flares with them. The engineers and the explosives are nowhere to be seen, so the planned demolition of the dugouts cannot be carried out. It continues to rain stair rods, the night is pitch black and the enemy artillery fire on the rear areas constantly increases in strength.

"Ascension Day. 17 May 1917. I am sitting with Rittmeister von Hoffmann in the dugout and waiting for 3.00 am. I shall despatch the machine guns somewhat earlier, starting with the heavy ones. The last of the wounded on the position were taken to the rear during the afternoon and evening and the same applied to captured equipment, ammunition, weapons etc. I have directed that, at 3.00 am, the entire trench garrison is to turn to the right and march back to Villers [lez Cagnicourt], via sectors A3 and the left half of A2. The last of the light machine guns will set off ten minutes earlier. Bringing up the rear of the 6th will be a Vizefeldwebel, charged with rearguard duty. If necessary the way will be lit be means of flares fired from signal pistols.

"It is 3.00 am. There is no sign of the Württembergers. 1st Company has already come past our dugout, as must everyone from the eastern sectors. Eisenträger and Hoffmann have already gone. I am still trying with an engineer unteroffizier to prepare all the hand grenades, so as to blow up the dugout. All the papers which we are not taking have been burnt. Suddenly some men came tumbling into the dugout, 'Quick, quick, the British are behind us!' I calmed down the mass of people and called for quiet, so that nothing untoward could happen. Apparently the British had picked up some signs of our withdrawal. I got myself ready, then the pull out of 6th Company began. Outside we were greeted by heavy artillery and machine gun fire. Numerous flares went up, forcing us to duck down repeatedly. Even in their light it was hard to negotiate the cratered footpath which ran through our position.

"Closed up tightly together the single file of men carried on. To our rear no more flares went up, but torrents of machine gun fire passed over our heads. Men were slipping and stumbling on the slippery uneven path. Suddenly I felt a cracking blow on my right shoulder. A machine gun bullet had passed through it. My right arm went limp, I fell to the ground, but was immediately helped back to my feet by Engel, my faithful batman, and soon reached a dugout in A2 occupied by Württembergers. After I had been bandaged up and had had a short rest, I followed my men to the assembly area at Villers. Looking dreadful, my ripped jacket covered in clay and blood, I arrived during the morning, to be greeted joyfully by what was left of my ninety eight brave men."

During the following days there was still sporadic fighting in the Bullecourt - Quéant sector, but it was essentially localised, aiming merely for improvement in positions and minor tactical advantage, because the evacuation, or capture, of Bullecourt village marked the end of the Battle of Arras. For both sides it had been an extraordinarily sanguinary affair, with gigantic losses and huge expenditure of ammunition. The small Bullecourt salient had indeed been eliminated at the end of a month of intense fighting, but the fact that thereby the lot of the Australians holding the line to the east of the ruined Bullecourt had been rendered slightly easier was a poor return for all the sacrifice. The shortened line that the German defenders had pulled back to north of the village was every bit as strong as the original had been before battle was joined and, in any case, given that the original objective had been a full scale breakthrough, in the final analysis this battle ended or, rather, ground to a halt, as a pyrrhic victory on points for the defence.

Notes

[1] Deutelmoser History 27th Infantry Division p 55.

[2] BOH p 363.

[3] HStA Stuttgart M411 Bd 909 Infantry Regiment 124 Anlagen Apr 17 27. Inf. Div. Ia Nr. 1060 op. vom 10.4.17.

[4] *ibid.*

[5] HStA Stuttgart M411 Bd 909 Infantry Regiment 124 Anlagen Apr 17 *BERICHT Über den Angriff der Engländer gegen den Abschnitt C (I.R. 124 im Verbande der 27. I.D.) östlich Bullecourt am 11.4.17.* p2.

[6] Wolters History Infantry Regiment 124 pp 66-67.

[7] AOH pp 291-292

[8] HStA Stuttgart M411 Bd 909 Infantry Regiment 124 Anlagen Apr 17 *BERICHT* p2.

[9] *ibid.* p3.

[10] Lt Mohr's body was recovered later and he is buried in the German cemetery at Rumaucourt Block 1 Grave 12.

[11] Infantry Regiment 124 *'BERICHT'* p 3.

[12] *ibid.* p 5.

[13] Moser *Die Württemberger im Weltkriege* Stuttgart 1928 p 566.

[14] HStA Stuttgart M411 Bd 695 Grenadier Regiment 123 Anlagen Apr 17 *Bericht über die Tätigkeit des Regts. am 11.April 1917.*

[15] Infantry Regiment 124 *'BERICHT'* p 6.

[16] This is the figure given by Keech *Bullecourt* pp 47-52. At least two German sources provide different figures. Moser *Die Württemberger im Weltkriege* p 464 states that of twelve involved, nine were knocked out. Deutelmoser *Die 27. Infanterie-Division im Weltkrieg* p 56 also mentions twelve, describes one being knocked out by machine gun fire, another disabled by a grenade launcher, seven being destroyed by artillery fire and only three escaping. To add to the confusion, a map in Moser p 563 displays the routes of only nine tanks. Whatever the exact truth, it is the case that the tanks did not achieve what they were meant to do, most were knocked out or broke down and the Australian infantry suffered because of it. However, in some cases they had a very damaging, if temporary, effect on the German infantry subject to their fire.

[17] HStA Stuttgart M411 Bd 909 Infantry Regiment 124 Anlagen Apr 17 27. Inf. Div. Ia Nr. 1093 op. vom 12.4.17.

[18] This figure was later refined by the Germans to 28 officers and 1,142 other ranks. See Deutelmoser *op. cit.* p 57. The most accurate Australian figure is 1,182. See Pedersen and Roberts *Anzacs on the Western Front* AWM 2012 p 140.

[19] HStA Stuttgart M411 Bd 909 Infantry Regiment 124 Anlagen Apr 17 27. Inf. Div. Ia Nr. 1200.

[20] HStA Stuttgart M411 Bd 909 Infantry Regiment 124 Anlagen Apr 17. *Kampferfahrung beim Angriff der Engländer bei Bullecourt am 11.4.17.*

[21] Simon History Infantry Regiment 120 p 66.

[22] Bechtle History Grenadier Regiment 123 p 95.

[23] BOH pp 357-358.

[24] Moser *Feldzugs-aufzeichnungen* pp 266-267.

[25] *ibid.* p 269.

[26] Kümmel History Reserve Infantry Regiment 91 p 271.

[27] Forstner History Reserve Infantry Regiment 15 p 38.

[28] This incident is confirmed in the BOH p 375, which includes the comment that it was, 'astonishing that so little damage should have been done to the batteries'.

[29] Forstner *op. cit.* p 39.

[30] *ibid.* pp 39-40.

[31] Mülmann History Lehr Infanterie Regiment pp 378-379.

[32] Reserve Leutnant Gustav Plewka is buried in the German cemetery Bouchain Block 1 Grave 155.

[33] Reserve Leutnant Siegfried Hachtmann is buried in the German cemetery Bouchain Block 1 Grave 101.

[34] Schulenburg-Wolfsburg History Fusilier Guard Regiment pp 163-164.

[35] Foerster *Wir Kämpfer im Weltkrieg* pp 325-328

[36] BOH p 375.

[37] Wohlenberg History Reserve Infantry Regiment 77 pp 275-276.

[38] Forstner *op. cit.* p 46.

[39] The British accounts admit to only five guns destroyed by the raiders and one knocked out by shellfire. The others were soon back in action once their breechblocks and sighting mechanisms had been replaced. BOH p 375

[40] Wohlenberg *op. cit.* p 272.

[41] BOH pp 430 - 433

[42] The figure given on p 421 of the AOH is ten.

[43] AOH pp 434-435.

[44] Bechtle *op. cit.* p 98.

[45] Deutelmoser *op. cit.* p 59.

[46] HStA Stuttgart M411 Bd 910 Infantry Regiment 124 Anlagen May 17 *27. Inf. Div. Divisions-Befehl* vom 3.5.17.

[47] Forstner *op. cit.* pp 57-59.

[48] *ibid.* p 57.

[49] HStA Stuttgart M411 Bd 910 Infantry Regiment 124 Anlagen May 17 *27. Inf. Div.1a Nr. 1484 op. geheim. Divisions-Befehl zur Wegnahme des Engländernests im Komp-Abschnitt C1* vom 5.5.17.

[50] Deutelmoser *op. cit.* p 61.

[51] Simon History Infantry Regiment 120 p 68.

[52] Bechtle *op. cit.* p 98.

[53] The code name was presumably derived from the title of the third regiment of the division; namely *Das Colbergsche Grenadier-Regiment Graf Gneisenau (2. Pommersches) Nr. 9.*

[54] Schulenburg-Wolfsburg History Fusilier Guard Regiment pp 171-174.

[55] This must be a misprint for 10 or 11 May.

[56] In its after action report Reserve Infantry Regiment 213 makes little reference to this clash, restricting comment (quoted in Tiessen History Reserve Infantry Regiment 213 p 492) to, 'Although the Storm Battalion had success, the attack conducted by the L.-I.-R. was quickly spotted, brought under heavy fire and partly beaten off', thus absolving itself of any possible blame for the incident.

[57] Reserve Leutnant Erich Hoffmann is buried at the German cemetery Rumaucourt Block 1 Grave 560. Reserve Leutnant Wilhelm Knolle, also killed the same day, is also buried in Block 1 Grave 1107. The other officer of Lehr Infanterie-Regiment killed that day, Leutnant Struve, has no known grave.

[58] Müllmann History Lehr Infanterie-Regiment pp 390-392.

[59] It is possible that this officer is the Leutnant Friedrich Stephan who died on 30 May 1917 and is buried in the German cemetery at Cannock Chase Block 17 Row 11 Grave 246.

[60] Schulenburg-Wolfsburg History Fusilier Guard Regiment pp 174-176.

[61] Moser *op. cit.* pp 277-278.

[62] Eisenhart-Rothe *Ehrenbuch der Garde* pp 402 - 403.

CHAPTER 7

Attrition and Stagnation
East of Arras

I t will be recalled that the investigation into the failure of the defence north and
south of the Scarpe during the opening phase of the battle highlighted, in addition
to the worn down nature of the ground holding divisions, mistakes made by the
artillery, which neither engaged the British preparations, nor gassed their batteries
when the attack was imminent. Added to this was the placement of reserves too far to
the rear, so they were unable to intervene in a timely manner when the blow fell. There
were all manner of reasons and explanations for this but, in the final analysis, it was
clear that more could and should have been done by the German gunners. As for the
problem of the reserves, there was considerable irritation at Army Group Crown Prince
Rupprecht that their redeployment forward - originally directed on 6 April - had been
carried out too slowly or even delayed altogether. In slight mitigation it might be said
that the Army Group did not emphasise sufficiently the extreme urgency of the situation
and insist on immediate reaction. Be that as it may, the fact remains that the German
guns did not do all that was expected of them and the *Eingreif* divisions were not where
they were needed when the blow fell.

Once the offensive began, Sixth Army was left in no doubt about the need to be far
more pro-active in the use of its reserves and, from 10 April, there was a dramatic
improvement in this respect. Ominously for the further development of the British
plans, the Army Group swiftly ordered Sixth Army to make immediate use of the seven
divisions at its disposal, created at once another reserve of three divisions under its
command and set about concentrating behind the Arras front nine more divisions from
elsewhere within its sector of responsibility. Added to this, prompt work by the artillery
staff led to rapid replacement of the batteries which had been lost in the initial surge
and a considerable increase in the number of heavy batteries, including the crucial 210
mm howitzers, devastating weapons that were always placed where the danger was
most acute.

Of course all these measures amounted to bolting the stable door after the horse
was gone. The fact remained that the British Army had scored some notable successes.
Vimy Ridge had gone, captured by the Canadian Corps, who now enjoyed wide and
dominating views over the Douai plain. To recapture it would have placed far too great
a demand on scarce resources at a difficult time, so it was never attempted. Instead

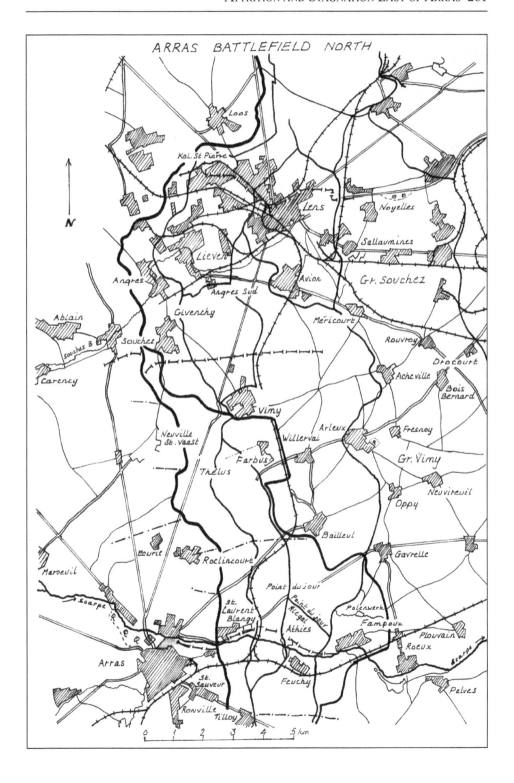

ARRAS BATTLEFIELD NORTH

there was recourse to the only possible reaction in the circumstances; the main defensive line was pulled back to the planned and partly prepared Third Position. By 13 April, therefore, the German front line ran south from Lens to Gavrelle, via Avion, Méricourt, Acheville, Arleux and Oppy. Stay behind parties imposed delay on British follow up forces and, in any case, such was the ruined state of the ground east of the ridge that moving the guns forward was a major and long drawn out operation. Without plentiful fire support there could not be a fresh general attack. All this meant that, with the exception of continued fighting for Croisilles, south of the Scarpe, from 13 - 15 April, an uneasy relative calm prevailed across much of the battlefield.

These battles caused the attackers additional serious casualties and German counter-action led to a thrust to the line Lagnicourt - Hermies on 15 April and the recapture of Wancourt on the 16th. However, that same day the British opened a new and heavy bombardment on German positions from Arleux to the Scarpe and others to the south. Eventually the entire front from Lens to Quéant was being shelled with increasing severity, right through until 21 April, when fire was concentrated more on the flanks. Although there was no major action from the British infantry, nevertheless it was quite clear that a fresh assault astride the Scarpe was being prepared and counter-actions were instituted. This time, however, the German heavy guns and howitzers engaged targets behind the British front line vigorously and also managed to shell several minor British probing attacks to a standstill in short order. Passive measures taken, apart from making emergency repairs and modest improvements to the front line crater field positions, were to put a great deal of effort into the development of communications trenches and stop lines further to the east. This included advanced planning and some preparation of a fallback position running south from Lille to Quéant via Douai.

Because the defensive battle was about to be conducted in a new way tactically, it is important to note the underlying philosophy. Oberst Loßberg, who had been despatched to Sixth Army as chief of staff to see what could be rescued from the disaster of 9 April, was an expert in the defensive battle, having honed his skills in the autumn 1915 battles in Champagne and then again on the Somme in 1916. He insisted on an end to the rigid defence of readily identifiable fortified points or trench lines but, at the same time, he did not advocate a universal application of elastic defence; his contention being that if front line troops were given carte blanche to abandon particular areas as soon as the pressure built up, it would be difficult, if not impossible, to induce them to counter-attack with vigour. Instead he reorganised the entire Arras front into a deeply deployed, defensive zone with *Eingreif* formations placed and primed for counter-action as appropriate. It was a technique defined by Loßberg as *offensive Abwehr* [offensive/active defence].

Oberst Fritz von Loßberg Chief of Staff Sixth Army[1]

"From 14 April onwards I was out and about all day long organising the future offensive defence. I received the full agreement of commanders at all levels.

The underlying principle of this was that major British attacks were to be defended against by means of German counter-attacks. Within the Army Group I arranged for almost all divisions that had been involved in the enemy attacks on 9 April and which had suffered heavy casualties to be relieved by 20 April by fresh divisions. The divisions that had been relieved became reserves, some subordinate to the Army Group, others to OHL ... The positions that were evacuated during the night 12/13 April were not totally abandoned, but occupied by only token forces - mostly officers' patrols equipped with plenty of machine guns. These were required to deceive the enemy as to the strength of the old positions then, when a major enemy attack developed, they were to withdraw in front of the rolling barrage in accordance with an overall plan and pull back to our new position.

"There was to be no construction of full scale defences along the new position. Instead the infantry was to occupy existing craters, surrounding these with camouflaged wire defences. All the other positions held by the infantry in depth were similarly disguised. The artillery also constructed no fixed positions. Instead they were placed in folds in the ground, selecting places so that the guns could be manhandled forward and be able to fire over open sights at the British infantry advancing behind the enemy's rolling barrage. Then, as soon as this barrage had passed our infantry, deeply echeloned, were to launch counter-attacks supported by the heaviest fire our artillery could produce."

After 21 April the renewed assault was expected daily, because the British troops had pushed forward to the German lines and also increased the strength of their artillery noticeably. That afternoon there was a thrust directed at Oppy, but it was repulsed; then, the following day, the bombardment, mainly of high explosive shells, but with considerable quantities of gas in the mix, intensified all the way from Lens to Bullecourt. By this stage of the war, phosgene had largely supplanted chlorine as the chemical filling of choice. Its effects could be deadly and almost beyond the ability of existing gas masks to cope.

Reserve Assistenzarzt Dr Wunderlich 3rd Battalion Infantry Regiment 88[2]

"The fifty two gas casualties I have treated during today have exhibited every degree of phosgene poisoning. Nine gas casualties died, despite treatment, within the first six hours after exposure. Fifteen of the casualties must be categorised as serious. Of them a high proportion will die. At the aid post oxygen was provided to ease breathing and injections were administered to counteract coughing fits. These measures eased their life-threatening condition to some extent. Twenty eight of the casualties are classified as slightly gassed. However, it must be assumed that these too will be affected by dangerous subsequent illnesses and about twenty five of them are likely to be out of action for a lengthy period. It must also be assumed that as a result of the delayed effect of gas poisoning there will be an increased number of men with lung disease amongst the companies at the centre of the gas attack. These late developing conditions are certain to become even more frequent the longer these companies are subject to severe physical stress and exposure to the bad weather. It is to be expected that during the coming days men will report sick to the medical officer with lung complaints."

By 6.00 am on 23 April the bombardment, preparing for what the British later referred to as the Second Battle of the Scarpe, had reached drum fire proportions and was followed by an assault on a thirty kilometre front, though the intensity varied from place to place. Méricourt, Acheville and Arleux were not much affected, but serious battles broke out around Lens, Avion, Oppy, Gavrelle, Roeux and Guémappe. There was a minor crisis between the last two named places when the attackers broke in to the German forward positions, but they were ejected by means of a series of vigorous counter-strokes that same afternoon. Elsewhere, despite the odd minor success, the defence prevailed all along the line and gains were extremely small.

Although the British main effort went in further south, First Army launched sharp diversionary attacks in the Lens-Avion sector, defended at that time by 80th Reserve Division under Generalmajor Körner and Generalmajor von Wichmann's 56th Infantry Division. The most northerly of these, virtually to the east of Lens itself, was countered relatively easily by Fusilier Regiment 35 and Infantry Regiment 88, but the main thrust, which went in against the inter-divisional boundary, was a more serious prospect. All the regiments were well aware that a renewal of the offensive was imminent, so each conducted vigorous patrol programmes, despite the weight of fire that had been directed at them. When the bombardment eased at about 3.30 am on 23 April, Fusilier Regiment 35 put into action a planned raid. During the thirty minutes to 4.00 am, the German artillery pounded the opposing positions with 4,000 shells, then large fighting patrols went forward. That under Leutnant Wolff 9th Company penetrated as far as Liévin, destroying several dugouts with satchel charges and returning at 4.30 am without any casualties.

Vizefeldwebel Wiesler of 10th Company was less fortunate. At 3.15 am a large calibre shell collapsed the entrance to a dugout where two of his sections were waiting. It took an hour to dig them free, by which time it was too late to carry out his intended mission. 12th Company despatched a patrol under Leutnant Mai, which, having advanced, bumped into a strong British force in an assembly area where it was waiting to storm forward. There was an immediate reaction. Mai was mortally wounded, another man was killed. One unteroffizier and one man were missing and another wounded. Although the information was expensively bought, the survivors were at least able to confirm the imminence of an attack and the direction from which it was to be launched.

As a result, when the attack came in, the defence was on full alert so, although there was a break in, it was followed by immediate counter action, during which Reserve Leutnant Schröder 12th Company and Gefreiter Kosiolek 11th Company distinguished themselves, each being awarded the Iron Cross First Class.

Reserve Leutnant Kurt Schröder 12th Company Fusilier Regiment 35[3]

"It was the night 22/23 April. Reserve Leutnant Mai carried out a fighting patrol with an assault group drawn from 12th Company. Unfortunately, he came into contact with an enemy attack that was forming up, was mortally wounded and died later in hospital. The entire time up to this the sector was under the heaviest imaginable large calibre enemy shelling. At dawn, I was just returning from outpost duty when, from the left and right, came the sound of firing. Flares went up calling for defensive fire against the enemy who were attacking on all sides. In order to get to the bottom of what was happening - because there was no slackening in the rate of fire - I rushed off to the right, taking a vizefeldwebel and a fähnrich with me. There, not fifty metres away, were British steel helmets! 'Fähnrich, you do your damndest to make certain that the hand grenades keep coming! You, feldwebel, guard me from the left and rear.'

"Tack, tack, tack! The British had already brought a machine gun into action. Dropping to the ground, I wormed my way forward into grenade throwing range. I suddenly bumped into a tommy, who was barely five metres away. Astonished, for an instant we both froze. He then threw a grenade that landed between my legs and I hurled one too. We spun round, raced off and hit the ground. The British grenade went off after three seconds and mine not until five seconds had passed. The danger was over and I was unscathed. I looked out briefly, but my jolly opponent had vanished. I was now within thirty metres of them. Tack, tack, tack went the machine gun once more. That had to go! I pulled the ignition cord then threw the grenade. It landed about three metres too far to the right, but the range was good. I needed to throw better. Here I could be throwing for an Iron Cross First Class! The second was more accurate then the third and fourth landed close together. They were spot on. Protected by the explosions, I rushed forward two traverses. Hello, the machine gun had disappeared!

"Suddenly I was aware of a fusilier with an armful of grenades standing next to me. Right, up and at them! Throw after throw was on target. Success gave me strength. Further and further I went along the trench, with hand grenades clearing the way from traverse to traverse. All of a sudden a tommy leapt up out of the trench and raced for the rear, then two, three - a whole gang of them … *Hurra!* we had won! The tommies were in full retreat; over there I could now see German helmets The trench was completely cleared! Taken from the right and the left, they could no longer hold on. Now it was a matter of following up rapidly. *Hurra!* More and more grenades were hurled at the retreating foe. Twenty one, twenty two, twenty three ... blam, smoke ...Two British soldiers fell dead, then another, then three together ..."

According to prisoner statements, three British companies had attacked. Two machine guns and a signalling lamp were recovered from No Man's Land.

Further to the south the British 63rd (Royal Naval) Division, XIII Corps, had been tasked to attack Gavrelle, which was defended by Fusilier Regiment 90 of Generalmajor von Gabain's 17th Infantry Division. Here the shelling had been so severe and the casualties in the ground holding 2nd Battalion so considerable that the regimental commander, Oberst von Hahnke, was forced to order its relief by 1st Battalion. Its commanding officer, Hauptmann von Plessen, decided to defend with three companies (1st, 2nd and 3rd) forward to the west of Gavrelle, with his 4th Company in reserve and manning the *Gavrelle-Riegel* [Gavrelle Stop Line], just to the east of the village. The guns of 1st Machine Gun Company were distributed evenly amongst the companies, but the defence was not in a good state overall. This battalion had never been there before and was unfamiliar with the ground and, worse, 2nd and 3rd Companies in particular had suffered heavily from the bombardment during the march forward, taking numerous casualties before the fighting even began.

The assault here, preceded by forty five minutes of drum fire, began at 6.15 am when the men of Hood, Nelson and Drake battalions stormed forward astride the Bailleul - Gavrelle and St Laurent Blangy - Gavrelle roads. At once the German artillery opened up and there was a mass of small arms fire from the forward trenches. However, despite some confusion amongst the attacking units, such was the weight of the thrust that the forward trenches of 2nd and 3rd Companies were soon overrun and the Fusiliers' second trench followed soon after. The machine guns fought on long and hard, but eventually their crews too were killed and the guns knocked out. One of the platoon commanders was the only survivor of the crews in support of the forward companies.

Reserve Leutnant Billig 1st Machine Gun Company Fusilier Regiment 90[4]

"We could also see through the powder smoke shadowy figures looming up along the Bailleul - Gavrelle road. The gun was swung round and fired at the rapid rate at anything which could be identified ... Gefreiter Krohn of 2nd Company was hit in the head by a shell splinter and collapsed on the ground, streaming blood. Kiesbüge bandaged him up, but could not save him. Fire on! Jam! Then a short burst - Rrrack - Damn it! The belt is jammed, the ammunition has been badly belted. Reload! - another jam and then a few more. After that it was somewhat better. Suddenly there was a shout. 'Over there! Are they ours, or British soldiers?' Telescope to eye. Sure enough, approaching Gavrelle, half right rear, were the British! The gun was heaved onto the parados. This was an excellent target for continuous fire, because more and more groups appeared.

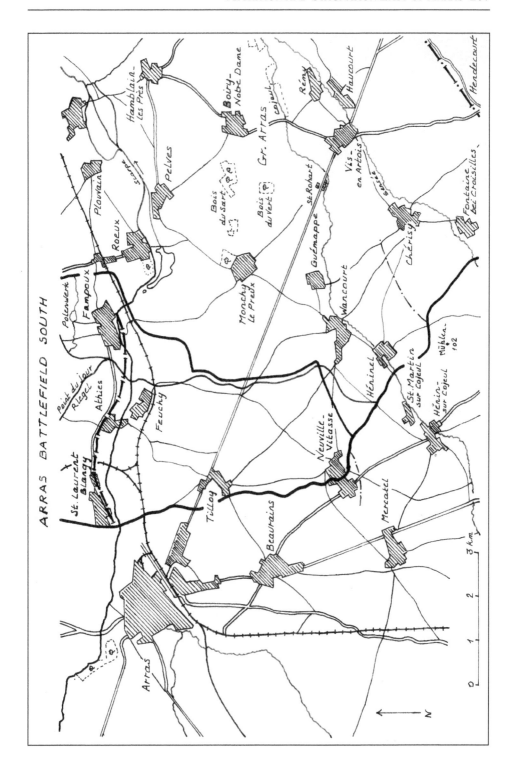

How that gun fired. It was a pleasure to hear it rattling out its savage music. The British took cover and began working their way forward in bounds ... News passed from man to man confirmed that the enemy was closing in along the trench from the right. Unteroffizier Markus and some men from 2nd Company moved to counter them. In the meantime the sun had risen and visibility improved. We could now see the impacts of our own shells coming down on the ruins of Gavrelle. Was it all over?

"To the right, somewhere near the Bailleul - Gavrelle road, the enemy had set up a machine gun which was pouring fire at the trench. We could not direct a stream of our own bullets at it, because we could not locate it precisely ... A quick glance to the south revealed that the dip slope was teeming with troops, all of whom were advancing on Gavrelle. So they were through there as well! All we could do now was hold on as long as possible until our own counter-stroke provided a breathing space. Once more the gun was moved, this time so that it could fire to the south and we began to shoot at the dense lines of infantry at a range of 800 metres. We then began to come under attack from the rear, from Gavrelle itself, as they tried to eliminate our vicious wasp's nest. Once more we shifted the gun and fired at the [new threat]. This worked and the enemy were halted. However, with renewed courage, those half right sprang forward again. The gun was moved and poured fire at them too. Simultaneously, they launched forward from the left, out of the 3rd Company position. There were enemy in all directions! We quickly sent men with hand grenades against them. Closing in from three sides, the ring drew tighter. Only from the front was there no enemy action. It was now 7.00 am. The dreadful thought now entered our minds: there was no way out. With clenched fists and gritted teeth, our hearts beating fit to burst, we were consumed by one single thought: 'You have got to hold on! Think of your comrades, of your duty! ... '

"In the last quarter of an hour 3,000 bullets have travelled down the barrel. One and half belts, the last of the ammunition, is all that is left and it is badly belted, muddy and covered with muck. Our counterstroke will not bring us relief, that is clear. Once again will triumphed and rifles were manned. None of it was any good. More and more of them closed in. Hand grenades! Ignition cords were pulled and they were thrown. Not one exploded. How could that be? Final actions now. The working parts [of the machine gun] were removed and hurled away into the filth. Thank heavens, at least that worked. The weapon was now unusable and could be of no use to the enemy. The ring was now complete and the British sought a final decision with the bayonet ..."

Leutnant Steinmüller, commanding 1st Company Fusilier Regiment in reserve, had not stood idly by watching events unroll. As the attack developed he redeployed his forces, paying particular attention to the need to block the advance to the north. Recognising the importance of the knoll topped by a windmill just to the northeast of Gavrelle, he made sure that it was manned by machine guns with plenty of ammunition. This point of resistance, stoutly manned by a team under Unteroffizier Scheur, played a large part in disrupting every attempt to develop the attack north between Gavrelle and Oppy, a fact fully acknowledged by the compiler of the British Official History, who made the point that the defenders attached far greater significance to this minor hill than the village itself.[5] Typical of the determination shown here was an action by Fusilier Otto Eggert who, at a critical moment, charged forward alone and took out a British machine gun and its crew, scattering the men and capturing the gun. His Iron Cross First Class was well earned. Nevertheless all this effort, including determined action by a crew equipped with a captured Russian machine gun at the southwest corner of the village, could not prevent the loss of the village right up to its eastern limit.

The *KTK*, Hauptmann von Plessen, had intended to fight the battle quite differently. 7th Company had been allocated to him as a first reserve and he had placed it in a quarry in the eastern end of Gavrelle. He meant to deploy it once the attack was launched and sent the first of several messages to its commander while the final drum fire was actually falling. Unfortunately for him, neither that runner, nor any of the others who followed at intervals, managed to survive to carry the orders. It was not until 7.00 am, by which time the British attackers had closed right up to the quarry, that a message got through. By then shell fire had partially collapsed the quarry, exiting it was awkward and the survivors from 7th Company could do no more than man the *Gavrelle Riegel*. That, however, was sufficient to hold up any attempt by the Royal Naval Division to push on eastwards for the time being. During the day there were several German counter-strokes, but all failed and the British attack was renewed at about 5.30 pm between Oppy and Fontaine les Croiselles. The defence of Gavrelle had been costly. 2nd and 3rd Companies suffered a great many casualties. Those not killed were almost all captured or missing, including Leutnants Rübsamen (commanding 3rd Company), Franke, Hannemann, Nesbach, Billig and Michaelis.[6]

Grenadier Regiment 89, 17th Infantry Division, was responsible for counter-action against the Royal Naval Division. One of the participants left a harrowing description of the hopeless attempt to retake Gavrelle and the surrounding area.

Gefreiter Hüls 2nd Company Grenadier Regiment 89[7]

"The enemy had captured a piece of dominating high ground, together with the villages of Roeux and Gavrelle. We were required to conduct a counter-attack. What? By day and in perfect sunshine? We simply could not get that idea into our heads. We followed the road as far as Fresnes [-lez-Montauban]. It was a beautiful spring day, with outstanding visibility. I thought that it would be a miracle if our assault were to succeed. It was neither a pleasant, nor an encouraging, feeling, but we had to obey. Deployed and widely spaced we moved forward across the fields without stopping. Despite all the fire, we had no casualties. Although the high ground to our front meant that the enemy could not see us directly, we were, nevertheless, under observation from numerous balloons. Arriving at the hill we halted, were told to remove our equipment and dig in. We signallers had no spades. We were able to make use of a section of old communication trench for cover, but soon realised that the Tommies had ranged in on this trench. Blam! Blam! We were up to our ears in muck and shell splinters. Soon the other comrades were also under fire. It was fortunate that so many of the shells were duds, though the enemy also fired a lot of tear gas. No sooner had most of the men dug in than we had to advance once more. Again we took a short breather in an existing trench; I was so tired that I immediately fell asleep.

"The area was totally desolate - nothing but crater after crater filled with bodies and pieces of equipment. It was a battlefield just like the Somme. We now passed the crest. Our objective was Hill 71 [approximately 1,000 metres south of Gavrelle]. We had hardly gone more than a few paces before we began to take casualties. We were in the midst of machine gun fire and could go no further. We dived down into cover at once, everyone dropping to the ground exactly where he was. We were alongside Leutnant Graf [Count] Moltke in a place where attempts had been made to start to dig a trench. We tried to get down deeper. Machine gun bullets cracked and whizzed overhead. Battle had been joined good and proper. The enemy had spotted our intended attack, was shooting at us and, soon, very accurately. Wheesh - Blam! A really heavy shell flew overhead and exploded. We could not hear a thing in all the racket. There was no chance of progressing, even the company commander could see that. The terrain was flat, offering very little cover.

"Patrols were despatched to try to link up with 2nd Battalion. The bombardment continued, shell after shell, all of the heaviest calibres, whilst bullets whistled so close overhead that we could not risk glancing out. It was an awful feeling. We would have loved to have been able to fire ourselves, but it would have been useless; first, because we could not locate the enemy and, second, the distance was too great for accurate shooting. Jammed in together we lay in this shallow trench. Nobody was able to move, because enemy aircraft were circling overhead and watching carefully. It was a thoroughly unpleasant situation. I was pleased, therefore, to be tasked with taking a report to the battalion, though where the headquarters was nobody knew precisely. It was somewhere near *Ballonhalle* in Fresnes.

"Hansen went with me. Rushing back in short bounds, we successfully got back across the crest. Now we were at least safe from machine gun bullets. Of course shells kept landing right and left but we were now more or less indifferent to them, even to drum fire. In addition, as old soldiers we could judge the trajectory of the shells instinctively and then, if need be, throw ourselves down and let the splinters fly over us. We found 3rd Battalion, deployed here in reserve. Leutnant Pötzsh also tasked us with taking a report

from him to 3ʳᵈ Battalion, but we had to carry out our own task first. We began
to search for battalion headquarters. Some thought it was in one place, others
elsewhere. Finally, we headed for the brick dust covered ruin that was Fresnes.
Could there still be human beings here? Some engineers were lying by the
village, caught by a direct hit. Two men had been decapitated and a third
disembowelled. Many were seriously wounded and one man had lost a hand.
It was an appalling scene, in total contrast to the beautiful sunshine and the
joyful singing of the larks above … "

Just to the south, in the sector of 18ᵗʰ Infantry Division, the battalions of Infantry
Regiment 161 found themselves engaged north and south of the Vitry – Roeux railway
line on 23 April. The battle for the *Mühlenhügel* [Mill Hill], between Roeux and
Plouvain, was especially hard fought.

Gefreiter Schmitz 12ᵗʰ Company Infantry Regiment 161[8]

"There was no time to think. Continuous machine gun and rifle fire announced
the approach of the battle. Tucked away behind the pathetic remains of walls
we waited for the enemy; the fighting was raging white hot. Roaring over the
heads of the defenders was an arched roof of defensive shells; whilst behind
them could be seen a dark wall of smoke coming from crashing and bursting
shells, intended to hinder the forward movement of reserves. From right in front
of the ruins of the former station and to its left came the ear splitting rattle of
small arms fire, interspersed with the dull thuds of our own artillery that was
bringing down fire to the front and on the enemy batteries. No information was
getting through from the front. Nobody knew what the situation there was. The
wounded were all in a hurry to disappear to the rear and out of this hell, so there
was no time for detailed questions and answers.

"At that moment a tank was clearly seen approaching from the north. It
was observed jolting along, stopping to fire and crawling forward once more.
A second, then a third hove into the view of the defenders of the station. Men
from the forward companies appeared. Offizierstellvetreter Bedorf halted them
and used them to reinforce his position.[9] Leutnant Weiß (12ᵗʰ Company),
cigarette in mouth and pistol in hand, gathered up everyone he could find.
Standing in the middle of the rubble-strewn road as shot and shell whizzed by
he gave orders and fired to prevent [further movement to the rear]. Now the
first of the British could be seen behind the tank. We were grateful that we had
a target at long last. A rapid rate of fire came from the ruins into the open area.
But already rounds fired from the rear were hitting the walls.

"Where were they coming from? Suddenly plate-like helmets appeared
along the railway embankment. Lanky figures sprang up and, in an attempt to
cut off the defenders, rushed towards the protection of a long wall that was part

of a shot up factory. Offizierstellvertreter Bedorf took in the situation at once and reorganised the defence in attics and on roofs, so as to counter the outflanking manoeuvre. He himself, together with Unteroffizier Degen and Gefreiter Schmitz, fired from the attic of the house on the corner against the western entrance, whilst other comrades opened up on the approaching enemy from hastily smashed loopholes. The shell craters were full of them but for the time being they were reluctant to close up on this pocket of resistance without reinforcement.

"From Fampoux advanced lines of infantrymen, small groups and entire companies, whilst in the former German communication trenches could be seen helmet after helmet, like the links in a long chain, and lines of German prisoners headed for Fampoux, where British cavalry was on stand-by to go into action and individual despatch riders scurried about through the cratered landscape. In amongst them could be seen the strikes of German shells. Off to the right in a dip in the ground tanks roared about, sending shells from the rear into pockets of resistance which were still holding out. Off to the north dense waves were pushing eastwards through the sector of our neighbours and disappearing over the hill, behind which Gavrelle was located.

"One tank crawled up to the house where Offizierstellvertreter Bedorf and his faithful companions were fighting the battle. A dozen shots pumped through the firing slits of this great monster into its interior and all the Tommies leapt into shell holes, but merely provided targets which were defenceless from above. Bedorf showed off his shooting prowess and had bagged a dozen in no time at all, spurring the others to attempt to imitate him. In this way a handful of unshockable individuals, operating in a focussed manner, managed to check and cause severe damage to a superior opponent. But what was happening off to the right? Had it been possible to neutralise the British who had pushed into the factory?

"Soon Offizierstellvertreter Bedorf was receiving definite information that he was now threatened from the left as well. With a heavy heart he had to yield his position in order to preserve his force for later use. The withdrawal was from ruin to ruin and, apparently, was not noticed by the enemy. However, the Scots had already occupied the edge of the cutting to the east of the station and were engaging every man who tried to get to the rear with a hail of machine gun fire. Bullets also began to come from the village itself and we began to run a life and death gauntlet. Leaping past dead and wounded comrades, we dashed like lightning from crater to crater. 'Breakthrough' was the watchword. Forward meant freedom, death threatened from the flank whilst from the rear the prospect of wearisome years of captivity gave wings to our feet and drove us to superhuman efforts.

"It seemed as though we were going to succeed. Those racing to the rear could already hear our machine guns operating in the Second position, when, suddenly, our way was barred by a thick hedge and there were no nearby craters to offer protection. Bedorf and Schmitz were now on their own. Unteroffizier Degen had disappeared and the other comrades had fallen dead or wounded along the way. What now? 'Fritz, come here!' [*sic.*]. Four Scotsmen appeared and others were lying down aiming at us. Should we hurl ourselves at them with our rifles? That would have meant certain, pointless death. 'Drop your equipment!' Suppressing his fury, Offizierstellvertreter Bedorf threw his equipment and rifle away … It was all over."

The *KTK*, Hauptmann Seiler, whose headquarters had been established in Roeux itself, had been able to follow events as the German defenders pulled back, fighting crater by crater, towards the Plouvain - Gavrelle road, where they linked up with elements of 2ⁿᵈ Battalion Grenadier Regiment 89, 17ᵗʰ Infantry Division. His position was becoming dangerously exposed and, furthermore, it was essential that he set an immediate counter-stroke in action. Runners having failed to get through, he decided that he had no choice but to head in person for *Ballon-Höhe*, a kilometre to the east, where his reserve 5ᵗʰ Company, commanded by Reserve Leutnant Henrichs, was sheltering in a gravel pit.

Hauptmann Seiler 1ˢᵗ Battalion Infantry Regiment 161[10]

"What a way that was! It took only twenty minutes, but those twenty minutes were under raging drum fire, through a wall of steel, dust and gas. There were heavy shells, light shells, shell bursts, and all sorts of fuzes that we had to avoid. As it was our tiny band, comprising only ten men, formed a skirmishing line and headed up *Ballonhöhe* [Balloon Hill], expecting at any moment to come under fire from our own reserves. With all the constant crashing and roaring of shells and through the powder smoke and gas, it was actually impossible to see or hear if we were being shot at. We drew closer, but still could see nobody … The Second Position, no more than a knee deep trench, was empty. We entered the gravel pit and there we found a small number of men – about eight sections with two machine guns - all crammed into the limited cover. All around them trees were crashing down, gravel, chunks of wood and clods of clay flew in all directions.

"Immediate action was needed. According to the one report that had got through from the wounded Offizierstellvertreter Türkow (3ʳᵈ Company), waves of enemy assault troops could emerge from the village at any moment. The trench, barely knee deep, had to be occupied and machine guns placed in overwatch positions. This all occurred but the British did not come. Nothing could be seen but the small white clouds of the shrapnel rounds and the impact of heavy shells. The village itself was completely quiet. I weighed up all the possibilities in my mind. What was happening? Where on earth were they? Already a good half hour had gone by since the report arrived. Would it be possible to retake the village? If so, how? Henrich's company had been placed to guarantee security and, according to the regulations, could not be deployed in a counter-attack. This, then, was my train of thought.

"All of a sudden a white flare rose slowly and majestically into the sky from beyond the village, hanging like a shining star in the air before it went out. That was the signal that German troops were still holding our forward of the village, battered by enemy storm waves like rocks in the surf. 'Every section is to go into all-round defence.' Frequently I had preached and practised this principle of defensive operations around Brugge [Bruges] during recent weeks. 'Hold on! Fire a white flare! All the time I still have one man left you can rely on the two of us counter-attacking!' I had given my word; now there could be no holding back.

"Security? Two sections and two machine guns would have to suffice. Everyone else would come with me, but where exactly? I decide to advance to the south of the station with my right flank covered by the left flank of 4th Company, which would give me protection. If we were successful then we should achieve a continuous line between the railway embankment and the church. The left flank as far as the park on the Scarpe [Roeux Park] would have to rely on the courage of the junior members of the battalion staff and the 2nd Company.[11] Leutnant Henrich set off, followed slowly by his men – about two platoons in strength. We linked up, so as to make sure that the direction was towards the ordered objective and to round up and bring forward anybody who might be hanging back. Three or four enemy aircraft appeared. They flew directly over the advancing company and fired at it, before turning and circling over us, ignoring our shots and remaining there until 5th Company disappeared into the village."

Further south the British subjected Guémappe to heavy attack, forcing Bavarian Infantry Regiment 18, 3rd Bavarian Infantry Division, out of it and the line was pushed a few hundred metres along the Arras - Cambrai road, but this was poor return for the extremely high British casualties incurred. In describing the loss of Guémappe later, the Bavarians made a number of interesting points. The first was that although the shelling was of extraordinary intensity, 'at first the casualties in the frontline were quite manageable because the unconnected, independent pockets of resistance offered a very poor target'.[12] Although they added that there were still heavy casualties in the rear areas, this observation provides clear proof of how Loßberg's initiative filtered down rapidly and bore early fruit on the battlefield.

The Bavarian 3rd Division had, of course, already been in the line for several days before this attack and the men were somewhat worn down. Nevertheless, they fought hard to retain Guémappe, even after it was outflanked deeply both north and south, launching repeated counter-attacks, all of which failed due mainly to the British protective barrage. Leutnant Geißler, adjutant 1st Battalion Bavarian Infantry Regiment 18, received the Knight's Cross of the Military Max Josef Order for his heroics during the street fighting after his commanding officer, Hauptmann Risser, was killed.[13] By the end of the day, 1st Battalion was reduced to ninety all ranks, having lost three officers and 257 men captured, twenty killed in action and twenty six wounded and the situation of Bavarian Infantry Regiment 17 was little better, having been called forward from reserve to bolster the counter-attacks from the east.

Reserve Leutnant Hermann Kohl Bavarian Infantry Regiment 17[14]

"Extremely heavy enemy artillery fire came down on the entire line from 5.30 pm. As the commander of the first assault wave, I was at that moment about fifty metres beyond the start line. It was out of the question to think any more about advancing. The men vanished into shell holes and buried their heads in the ground. An appalling storm of steel hammered down on us. Thousands of shrapnel pots spewed their awful contents over us. The rattle of shrapnel balls on the steel helmets sounded like the noise of hail hitting a window pane. The sight to the front was spectacular. Fountain after fountain [was thrown up], both large and small, whilst in between them endless clouds of white and yellow smoke were being blown about. Our troops lay apathetically in their holes. Every individual was simply waiting to die. Half left the attack of the 9th [Grenadier Regiment 9] was making some slight progress ... The 17th suffered extraordinarily high casualties. Thirty three officers and men were killed, 131 were wounded and 158 were missing. Of the officers, Adjutant Mayerhofer and Leutnant Körzinger were killed.[15] Leutnants Benz, Wich, Laudan, Kölbel and Groh were wounded and Leutnant Günther was gassed."

In actual fact Grenadier Regiment 9 only made modest progress at the cost of serious casualties. They later ascribed even that slight success to the heroics of their direct support battery from 1st Battalion Guards Field Artillery Regiment 5, which operated precisely as laid down by Loßberg.

Major Mackensen Guards Field Artillery Regiment 5[16]

"We shall never forget the sight as 2nd Battery, spaced just as if it was on the parade square, galloped forward, going into action far in front of all the other batteries on the gun lines and immediately in rear of the attacking grenadiers. Already, as they were unharnessing, a great concentration of fire came down on them, enveloping in smoke all the ammunition wagons which were driving up and showering them with dirt. For several minutes nothing could be seen of them. Together with the regimental staff of Grenadier Regiment 9 we believed that there would be nothing left of this magnificent battery, but not a hair of a head, neither of man nor horse, was touched. Truly, the world belongs to the brave!"

The London Times, reporting later on the events of 23 April, stated, 'In some locations masses of prisoners were pleased to surrender. In other places, especially around Guémappe, the Bavarians fought bravely. Although many prisoners were taken south of the Cojeul River, to the north of it the men of 3rd Bavarian Infantry Division fought very well. It was extremely difficult to get forward there.'[17] Crown Prince Rupprecht lavished congratulations on Sixth Army for its performance, singling out Oberst Fritz von Loßberg, its replacement chief of staff, who had masterminded the change in tactics, for particular praise.

Although Gavrelle was the only village north of the Scarpe attacked on 24 April, there were further efforts south of the river down as far as Bullecourt. These enjoyed very little success, not even along the Arras-Cambrai road, despite the fact that the attack was renewed at 4.30 am on 25 April and repeated on 26 and 27 April. On each occasion the defence came out on top; the attempts to breakthrough failing with serious losses. Despite these repeated failures after the initial success of 9 April, the German chain of command was convinced that there would be further battles to come and so it proved. Given that they calculated that the reserves they had on hand would be sufficient to guarantee all necessary reliefs until at least mid-June, Army Group Rupprecht was quietly confident that its formations would be able to hold whatever was thrown at them. It was just as well. On 29 April, the British began their fourth major effort of the battle, the focus having now shifted to north of the river. A bombardment began to come down on 26 April, directed primarily at the Arleux Loop, Fresnoy and Oppy. This increased dramatically on 27 April, a day on which Lens and Roeux were subject to intense gas attack. The following morning, the third major British assault on a frontage from Lens to Riencourt was launched. Wave after wave of attacks went in, but they all, with very few exceptions, failed. Such was the weight of defensive artillery fire that many assaults, especially those on the flanks, were shot to a standstill. The British did gain a foothold in Oppy, only to be ejected once more, but the smoking ruins of Arleux, attacked by the Canadians, were the only tangible gains of the day. General von Below had now assumed command of Sixth Army, so the rough handling of the assault by no fewer than three British divisions of Third Army astride the Scarpe meant that his period in command got off to an excellent start.

The verdict of the Canadian official historian was that poor British tactics were mainly to blame, in that the plan of attack and the choice of arbitrary phase lines in particular meant that insufficient or no account at all had been taken of the move by the German defence to the occupation of reverse slopes and other covered localities.[18] The British 34th Division near Roeux and the 2nd at Oppy paid an especially high price. At Arleux-en-Gohelle, it was a different matter. This village was the objective of 2 Canadian Brigade, 1st Canadian Division, with 1 Canadian Brigade in support and flank protection on the left of the main attack by one battalion from 2nd Canadian Division. The village was held by Fusilier Regiment 73, 111th Infantry Division and it was captured at a cost of approximately 1,000 Canadian casualties by 6.00 am.

The German defenders were impressed by the imaginative use of covered approaches and the weight and accuracy of the bombardment, not only of the village itself, but also all the areas likely to be traversed by counter attack forces. It was far from a one-sided affair, but once the Canadian 8th Battalion, having attacked at 4.25 am and taken a great many casualties from machine gun fire, had broken through the forward defences of 3rd Battalion Fusilier Regiment 73 in the 9th Company sector and had pushed on through the village, the integrity of the defence was totally compromised. 10th Canadian Battalion had also pushed past the northern edge of Arleux and was established along the road to Fresnoy. This meant that the fusiliers were exposed to attack from the rear, so large numbers of them, feeling that further resistance was hopeless, surrendered. There were some small exceptions to this overall pattern. One small group, under Leutnant Hauerstein and supported by a machine gun, commanded by Unteroffizier Borbe, put up determined resistance for some time until, having fired off their ammunition and kept the approaching Canadians at bay by throwing hundreds of grenades, a handful of them succeeded in getting away and rallying back at Fresnoy. By the end of the battle a mere forty all ranks of 3rd Battalion Fusilier Regiment 73 had escaped from Arleux.

Leutnant Hauerstein 10th Company Fusilier Regiment 73[19]

"When the drum fire began we were still at night routine. Half the company were manning their fire positions. Immediately, the remainder rushed out of their dugouts and went to their places. Mine was in the sap. So began the battle of 28 April which, according to later newspaper reports, was one of the hardest and costliest for the enemy. Vimy Ridge looked as though it was lit by electricity as thousands of flashes came from it in an unceasing stream. Salvo after salvo of shells smashed down in rolling drum fire. Despite the hellish racket, the sound of close quarter battle could be heard clearly coming from a point to the north of our right flank. Red flares were being fired to the left and right. Because I could see nothing of the enemy, I fired a few white ones. Vizefeldwebel Dittmer, who had been forward on patrol with four men, came running back to the sap. Almost simultaneously, I saw a mass of troops off to the right of the sap, heading east. I now began to fire red flares. Those manning the sap - one unteroffizier and eleven men - opened fire at the enemy, supported by a gun of 2nd Machine Gun Company.

"We carried on firing until we were threatened with outflanking to our right. I then withdrew all the men back to the end of the sap and began firing to the north once more, still supported by the machine gun. We fired until masses of the enemy forced their way into the sap and, simultaneously, threatened once more to outflank us to our right. I ordered a further small withdrawal. Unteroffizier Ahrend distinguished himself especially by throwing hand grenades into the sap that was filled with British [*sic.*] soldiers and causing them heavy casualties. We paused and opened fire again. Unteroffizier Borbe managed to get his gun, which had been damaged, back into action.

" This was so clearly successful that the masses of enemy were split up and our men threw themselves at them to shouts of *Hurra!* However, in order to avert the risk of being encircled, I directed a further withdrawal to a trench fifty metres to the rear, intending to set up some sort of strong point. During the subsequent defence I was supported by men of 11th Company and the survivors of 1 Platoon of our company, led by Unteroffizier Christmann. Some unteroffiziers, who were over forty five years old and whom we had received as replacements in December 1916, hauled as many hand grenades as they could out of the dugouts for us to throw. Gefreiter Hesselfeld shot a British [*sic.*] soldier with a Lewis gun who was closing in from the left. We went into all round defence until we had fired all the machine gun ammunition and thrown three hundred hand grenades.

"In order to avoid capture I decided to break through with my men. The machine gun crew had one box of bullets left. This they fired at the enemy to the east, which cleared the breakthrough point and made it possible for almost all my men to force their way out. We came under rifle and machine gun fire from the hedge in front of Arleux and had hand grenades thrown at us. The seven man crew of a British [*sic.*] machine gun crew was killed with rifle fire and hand grenades by Gefreiters Hesselfeld and Kruse, assisted by Fusiliers Peter and Heinemann. A group of the enemy approaching from the north hesitated when they suddenly saw us, possibly thinking that we were carrying out a counter-stroke. They turned tail and raced towards the hill to the north as fast as they could. Despite heavy barrage fire to the east of Arleux, that action made it possible for us to break through. The next day, still fully equipped for battle, Fuslier Hoffmeister arrived, having spent the night hidden beneath some planks in Arleux. He had managed to run back in the early morning, leaping over several trenches occupied by the enemy, who were taking cover from our artillery fire."

1,500 metres to the southeast, Oppy was defended by the Hanseatic Infantry Regiment 75. This regiment was temporarily under the command of 1st Guards Reserve Division. It had previously not been as heavily engaged as the other formations of its parent 17th Infantry Division, which had been pulled back to Cambrai to rest and absorb reinforcements. Because of the recent move to deep zonal defence, 1st Battalion Infantry Regiment 75 with its commander, Hauptmann Krull, as the *KTK*, found itself responsible for a sector 1,000 metres wide, including the village of Oppy. 3rd Battalion under Major Hergt was in support, with 2nd Battalion, commanded by Hauptmann Caspari, back in divisional reserve at Izel-lez-Equerchin. The consequence of this was that a concentrated thrust by the British 2nd Division at 5.50 am on 28 April succeeded in fighting through Oppy extremely rapidly. Counter-strokes launched later in the day by first 3rd Battalion, then 2nd, once it had been released by 1st Guards Reserve Division, succeeded in retaking the village. There were three lines of defences here. To the west of Oppy, K1 and K2, which were in reality crater positions, were held from north to south by 2nd, 3rd and 4th Companies, with 1st Company manning a K3 line about 400 metres to the rear and 10th Company located in reserve in the village.

Gefreiter Winter Fusilier Regiment 73[20]

"The hardest assault was directed at 2nd Company, which was covering the right [northern] flank. It is true that the platoon on the extreme right held out. The company commander, Leutnant Baer, and two machineguns were co-located here. Within the other two platoons, the sections nearest the platoon commanders resisted the longest. But gradually the enemy pressed the sections harder, tore ever larger holes in the defence and finally streamed through to the chateau grounds behind the trenches. 3rd Company in the centre stood its ground. In fact it succeeded in winning back one hundred metres of the 2nd Company's position. This reduced the width of the break in to 200 metres for a time, though the company sector was then no less than 600 metres wide and had to be defended to the north, west and east. 4th Company was on the right. Because machine guns were hammering away to its right and from the rear, the British ended up in a confused huddle in front of its centre. However, a massed charge pushed through on a section frontage.

"Once about 150 men had passed through the gap it was closed once more, but the position of the company soon became critical when the enemy broke through the neighbouring regiment. Now they were pressing on from the sides and also occupying trenches and the general area to the rear. Some might have thought at that point of throwing down their weapons, but fresh courageous deeds overcame this tendency. The bravest set an example and others followed. Very quickly they adapted to the new situation. The company was down to a strength of four sections. One blocked off the regimental sector to the left, one moved forward towards the enemy who were occupying shell holes, one section kept the enemy to the rear under fire, whilst the company commander placed the fourth in a fallback position, as protection against being overwhelmed. This is how 4th Company defended itself against the enemy.

"The village itself and the chateau grounds were the responsibility of 10th Company, whose members were distributed amongst cellars and dugouts. Already by 4.00 am the company commander had his men on full alert and ready ... but hardly had the drum fire begun, with destructive and harassing fire hammering down on roofs and dugouts, than the Tommies suddenly appeared, pushing ahead, despite their own fire This ruled out coordinated action by the company. It was straight into close quarter fighting: section against section, man against man. An attempt by the company commander, Leutnant Goering, aided by a grenade launcher, to force his way forward into the open ground in the centre of the village and the walled chateau grounds failed at once. He was carried, severely wounded, into a dugout and succumbed to his wounds within an hour.[21] The company had to pull back to the edge of the village. But there it held on, a performance that was decisive in terms of how the day ended."

It was still only 6.00 am. The area to the south of the village began to fill with British troops and other thrusts developed against the village. By now, however, German defensive artillery fire was coming down heavily, surviving defenders were maintaining a high rate of small arms fire and the attack faltered somewhat. That said, elements of Infantry Regiment 75 were under severe pressure and the southern flank was hanging in the air. Hauptmann Krull, the *KTK*, together with his staff intervened personally, rallying the survivors of 2nd, 9th and 10th Company and preventing a further thrust to the east of Oppy. Fighting continued for some considerable time without a fundamental change in the situation, then German counter-attacking forces began to intervene around 9.00 am. As soon as the attack opened, the regimental commander moved the remaining companies of 2nd Battalion forward in support and, by 7.00 am, divisional headquarters had released 3rd Battalion back to regimental command. It took these companies two hours to get forward due to the weight of the British protective barrage, but eventually they were in position to wrest Oppy back from the attackers. From about 8.00am to 9.00am, individual German sections and platoons attempted during the course of numerous small scale actions to push the attackers back. There were small local successes, but the attacks lacked weight and momentum and no significant progress was made. However, at the cost of rising casualties and a huge expenditure of ammunition, the overall situation was stabilised and, at about 10.00 am, Hauptmann Caspari, commander 2nd Battalion, was in position near Neuvireuil with five companies, a light mortar platoon and 2nd Machine Gun Company ready to despatch three companies under Oberleutnant Kaegler against Oppy, with his 6th and 8th Companies attacking slightly to the south. The weapons of the machine gun company were deployed across the full width of the attack frontage. The German guns opened up and the counter-attack launched forward.

Oberleutnant Flach Infantry Regiment 75[22]

"In fits and starts, metre by metre, we won back the small dwellings, courtyards and gardens. We rushed across the Arleux - Oppy - Gavrelle road and, once our grenade launchers and small arms had delivered death dealing blows against the enemy lines, closed in on the chateau grounds from two sides. The companies of 2nd and 3rd Battalions deployed here broke in over five walls and through hedges left and right then, in the course of a bloody struggle, mopped up the entire park crater by crater. Soon the machine guns and grenade launchers we had lost earlier were back in our hands. Simultaneously, 6th and 8th

Companies, operating south of the park and village, captured several strong British pockets of resistance and forced their way victoriously forward into our original front line.

"There was great rejoicing all over the devastated battlefield when we were able at last to free our hard pressed comrades of 3rd and 4th Companies from their precarious positions. For six hours solid they had stuck it out in the frontline, pressed on all sides, fearing the worst, but waiting and hoping for the best; all the while fighting to preserve their freedom. The greetings exchanged by two friends who had been separated by a world tour could not have been more sincere than those between the men who had been given up as lost and their rescuers."

From about one kilometre to the south of Gavrelle, then as far as the Scarpe, the German reinforced 208th Infantry Division was responsible for the defence. In this case and similar to the experience of Infantry Regiment 75, Infantry Regiment 65, part of 185th Infantry Division, had not been involved in earlier fighting so, when other formations of that division were deployed elsewhere, it was rushed forward into front line action when it became necessary to relieve Infantry Regiment 161 during the evening of 27 April. Together with its right hand neighbours to the north, Reserve Infantry Regiment 65, it fought off the British 34th Division, whilst Infantry Regiments 185 and 25 were in action against the 37th Division. Responsible for the defence of Roeux village was 1st Battalion Infantry Regiment 65, commanded by Hauptmann Schwerdtfeger, who was the designated *KTK*. The *BTK* [commander of the supports], Hauptmann Piedmont, commanding 2nd Battalion, was located on *Ballonhöhe* [Balloon Hill], just southwest of Plouvain and 3rd Battalion was back in divisional reserve.

Barely had the 1st Battalion taken up its positions than the usual heavy bombardment began, followed by a determined infantry assault. 4th Company, located between Roeux village and the station, spotted this development early; the *KTK* was just able to warn regimental headquarters before the telephone line was destroyed. Infantry Regiment 161's machine guns were still in position, so the attackers were met initially by a storm of small arms fire. Unfortunately the defensive artillery fire arrived late and fell too short, so almost immediately there was hand to hand fighting, during which the veteran Landwehr Leutnant Stolz, commanding 4th Company at the age of forty two, was unfortunate enough to be killed by a bayonet thrust through the chest.[23] Just to the north, Reserve Infantry Regiment 65 came under considerable pressure but was not attacked with the same narrow front intensity as Infantry Regiment 65. Furthermore, it had been in position for several days and was well organised and deployed. None of its positions was taken, though on the extreme left a section of trench that had temporarily been manned by Infantry Regiment 65 was lost. A very aggressive immediate counter-stroke by 1st Company Reserve Infantry Regiment 65, reinforced by one platoon of 5th Company under Feldwebelleutnant Carsjens, regained the lost position and caused heavy British casualties, including the capture of 200 prisoners.[24]

Despite hard fighting from house to house, the determined British infantry nevertheless broke right through Roeux and clashed with elements of 2nd Battalion and Reserve Infantry Regiment 65, before ending up in approximately half battalion strength on the western edge of *Ballon-Höhe*. At this point, while the British were under heavy fire from 7th Company Reserve Infantry Regiment 65 and part of that regiment's machine gun company and holding off immediate counterstrokes organised by the *BTK* Infantry Regiment 65, orders arrived at 3rd Battalion Infantry Regiment 65, back in reserve near Biaches-St Vaast, at 6.30 am. 'The British have broken through at Roeux. The battalion is to advance immediately with its left flank anchored on the Scarpe and recapture the village.'[25] There then followed an extremely vigorous, if costly, counter attack. The main weight was provided by 3rd Battalion, but as the advance closed in on Roeux village, 2nd Battalion men joined in, followed later by the survivors of 1st Battalion. The fighting was heavy, impetus was lost as troops had to be sent to cover flanking threats and the leading companies began to run out of small arms ammunition and hand grenades. Heroics by the drivers of some of the machine gun wagons saw resupply brought right up to the eastern edge of Roeux amidst heavy fire and, eventually, not only was the entire village retaken by about midday, but in places the attack was pressed right up to the British front line. It is debatable if this exploitation was worthwhile. It cost numerous casualties, including the leader of the regimental assault troop, Reserve Leutnant Häsele and Leutnant Frank, commanding 12th Company.[26]

Whilst the situation at Roeux was being restored, a dangerous British thrust had developed south of Gavrelle. Here, profiting from early morning fog, smoke from the bombardment and covered approaches, 3rd Battalion Infantry Regiment 25 manning a section of the *Gavrelle Riegel* was overrun by the British, who despite enduring heavy casualties from machine guns located along the *Fresnes Riegel*, 1,500 metres to the east, surged forward in dense groups. One by one these guns fell silent as their crews were killed or wounded, though Reserve Leutnant Berten, who had lost two fingers, continued for some time to fire one of the weapons by himself, using only his unwounded hand.[27] At the same time, 2nd Battalion Infantry Regiment 25 spotted a force of British soldiers in approximately battalion strength advancing along the Gavrelle - Fresnes-lez-Montauban road and brought it under heavy fire. According to the regiment, Gun 6, commanded by Gefreiter Kopetzke 2nd Machine Gun Company, put down such a devastating weight of fire that, their retreat barred, they were forced to a man to surrender. The British Official Historian, though stating that this claim was an exaggeration, conceded that this unit, identified as '2/R. Marines', did in fact 'lose a very large number of prisoners'.[28]

Elsewhere on this sector the British enjoyed somewhat greater success. One half battalion thrust coming along a wide re-entrant from the southwest actually dislodged a battalion staff and the defenders from *Ballon-Wäldchen* [Balloon Copse], one kilometre west of Fresnes. It took until midday for a converging counter-attack with a unit of 1st Guards Reserve Division advancing from the north and 1st Battalion Infantry

Regiment 25 from the south to restore the situation. The adjacent Infantry Regiment 185 observed most of the action from a flank. It had itself been attacked at 5.30 am and there had been a break in at the junction between 2nd and 8th Companies. There was an immediate counter-stroke by 4th Company, which was in support, but it was only partially successful because some British troops had already advanced towards the rear of the Infantry Regiment 185 position. Over the next few hours the regiment partly resolved the situation from its own resources, restoring sections of its original line - but at a high cost. Infantry Regiment 65 was able to relieve its 9th and 12th Companies in the *Fresnes Riegel* then, together with a machine gun platoon and half of 11th Company, launched forward at 12.40 pm. Because it was broad daylight, British artillery fire took a heavy toll, much of the impetus drained away and it took the survivors until evening to get anywhere near their objective and, even then, in places the attack stalled 500 metres short of the former front line.[29] To round off an unsatisfactory day, the whole area was subject to a major gas attack at 8.00 pm.

On 30 April there was thrust to the east of Monchy then, on 1 May, Lens was attacked. Each of these relatively minor operations failed but then, during the night 2/3 May, the entire front from Lens to Quéant came under heavy fire, swelling during the early morning until, at 5.30 am, there was a major assault from Acheville down to Quéant. There were initial break ins at Fresnoy, Oppy, Roeux, Chérisy and Bullecourt. Immediate counter-strokes were set in motion by the defence and, during a day of bitter fighting, Oppy changed hands five times. Fresnoy was captured by the Canadians and there were minor gains near Bullecourt in fighting which dragged on into 5 May and beyond.

This latest major attack turned out to be the final large scale British offensive of the battle of Arras. Some days earlier it had already become clear to Sir Douglas Haig that Nivelle's removal from command following the failure of his Aisne-Champagne offensive and the first stirrings of disaffection amongst the troops could not be long delayed. His thoughts were turning to a switch of the British effort north to Flanders, yet he persisted with a fresh attack by First, Third and Fifth Armies on a frontage of almost twenty five kilometres. The operation could have been called off at the last minute, but all the preparations had been made, there was still a possibility that the French, who at that point were still fighting along the Aisne, might rally if the British were successful, pressure had to be maintained on the German defence and all previous experience had shown that attacks on a broad front had more chance of success than limited ones. So the decision to go ahead was confirmed and the formations committed paid a very heavy price.

The two northernmost formations of Group Vimy, 15th Reserve Division and 1st Guards Reserve Division, were responsible for Fresnoy and Oppy respectively. 1 Canadian Infantry Brigade made short work of the defence of Fresnoy by the somewhat worn down Reserve Infantry Regiment 25 of 15th Reserve Division, which had only been in position for twenty four hours, then beat off a series of counter-strokes, which cost Reserve Infantry Regiment 17 no fewer than 650 casualties in a matter of hours.

The attack frontage extended either side of the village, covering not only the Reserve Infantry Regiment 69 to the north, but also affecting the left forward company of Grenadier Guard Regiment 5, 4th Guards Infantry Division to the north. Here, following a short sharp action, men of 2nd Canadian Division were ejected, leaving behind one officer and twelve other ranks, together with a Lewis gun.[30]

It was known that Reserve Infantry Regiment 69 had been driven back and that this loss of ground meant that there was a threat to the left flank of Grenadier Guard Regiment 5 but, with all telephone lines destroyed, the first accurate information did not reach the *KTK* until a small patrol of volunteers from 8th Company succeeded in passing through intense shellfire to deliver the message, though Grenadier Bierwagen was killed in the process.[31] Subsequently, 3rd Battalion, accompanied by 3rd Machine Gun Company, became involved in counter-attacks during the afternoon, but although tenuous contact was made with Reserve Infantry Regiment 69 and an attack in five waves was conducted from 3.15 pm, the furthest point any group reached (before the arrival of strong Canadian reinforcements at 5.30 pm put a stop to the operation) was the cross roads near the northern tip of Fresnoy Wood, about 500 metres short of the centre of the village. There the German troops dug in and held on anxiously throughout the following night. The capture of Fresnoy was one of the very few success stories of 3 May.

The situation at Oppy and Gavrelle was rather different. 1st Guards Reserve Division had been subordinated to Group Vimy on 23 April in the *Eingreif* role. Reserve Infantry Regiment 64 had indeed been deployed to counter-attack Gavrelle on 25 April and had suffered heavily in the process. As a result, it was too weakened to go into the ground holding role when 17th Infantry Division had to be relieved. Consequently Reserve Infantry Regiment 64 was withdrawn to rest and recuperate. In order to shorten regimental frontages and generally thicken up the defence Reserve Infantry Regiment 28, 185th Infantry Division, was moved into the centre of the divisional sector on 1 May. This meant that when the attack began on 3 May, 2nd Guards Reserve Regiment was defending Oppy, 1st Guards Reserve Regiment Gavrelle and Reserve Infantry Regiment 28 the high ground in between the two.

At the same time the guns firing in support of the division were reinforced further by a special group based on Field Artillery Regiment 94. The existing subgroups (south, centre and north) of the organic artillery, Guards Reserve Field Artillery Regiment 1, were retained, each of them disposing of three field gun and two light howitzer batteries.[32] The new arrivals made a substantial difference to the fire support available and, even before their deployment, the re-entrant between Izel-lez-Equerchin and Neuvireuil had been described as, 'crammed with batteries'.[33] During the night 2/3 May all these guns fired destructive missions against likely forming up places and brought down devastating defensive fire as soon as the men of British 2nd and 31st Divisions of XIII Corps left their trenches. The actual British attack was preceded, as it was elsewhere, by a short, sharp bombardment. Mauville Farm, one thousand metres north of Fresnes-lez-Montauban, was subject to a storm of gas shells and Vitry was hammered by both heavy guns and field batteries firing shrapnel.

Despite the trenches of 1st Guards Reserve Regiment around Gavrelle being heavily shelled, the forward companies had no trouble, in association with the artillery, in beating off the British frontal assault. Minor penetrations on either flank were countered immediately by supports and were driven off easily, as was a further attempt on 7th Company at 7.00 am, which was ejected by means of a vigorous counter stroke led by the company commander, Leutnant Strenger, himself. Unfortunately he died instantly from a gunshot wound as he reached the front line trench at the head of his men.[34] Altogether, during an anxious day for the defence, three separate assaults were held or thrown back by means of counter-strokes. 9th Company on the right flank was threatened more than once with encirclement, especially during the afternoon, when there was a determined British thrust towards Gavrelle windmill. The company commander, Leutnant Wischowatty, was reported as killed at one point, but it transpired that he had 'only' been buried alive. Having been dug out he was able to resume his duties.[35]

As the morning wore on the defence was increasingly in control of the battlefield. The *KTK* was able to observe reserves massing in the forward British trench and direct his trench mortars onto them. Advancing columns moving forward of Bailleul were spotted and brought under heavy artillery fire. Further attempts to press home the attack on Gavrelle were abandoned, the British withdrew from their front line trenches and the lodgement gained near Gavrelle windmill was evacuated in the early afternoon, German patrols reoccupying the area at about 2.00 pm. There was to begin with slightly more British success against the Reserve Infantry Regiment 28 sector. The regiment noted that as a result of the final drum fire, which included smoke and gas fire missions, a combination of those fumes, dust and smoke from exploding shells and the morning mist, meant that visibility on this part of the front was effectively zero when the attack began. In consequence, the attackers were able to close right up to the forward trenches and overrun them in the first rush, though hand to hand fighting went on for some time in certain places.

At the boundary between 1st and 3rd Companies about 200 British infantrymen managed to push through to the third line trench. At that point they were taken under fire by machine guns under the direct control of Reserve Leutnant Löltgen, commanding 3rd Company, and a counter-stroke by Reserve Leutnant Gissels, leading the weak remnants of 2nd Company, stabilised the situation long enough for the regiment to launch forward 11th and 12th Companies in a concentrated counter stroke at 5.40 am and to call forward the remainder of 3rd Battalion in support to the *Fresnes Riegel*.[36] By 7.00 am the forward trenches were back in German hands and the British had pulled back, leaving behind more than one hundred prisoners and several Lewis guns. Pockets of 1st Battalion soldiers who had either been holding out in the front line or who had temporarily been prisoners of the British were thereby reunited with the remainder of the regiment.

The overall situation remained relatively calm, though some isolated battles did continue for most of the morning. However, there were no further noteworthy infantry assaults, so quite soon, about mid-morning, companies of Reserve Infantry Regiment 28 were being detached to assist in the heavier fighting for Oppy and Fresnoy 2nd Battalion complete was subordinated to 2nd Guards Reserve Regiment as early as 7.10 am, moving in support to the artillery hollow north west of Neuvireul. Once there, despite the fact that Oppy was disputed fiercely and attack and counter-attack gained and lost the village more than once that day, the greater priority was Fresnoy, where the Canadians had a firm grip. At 12.45 pm 5th and 8th Companies launched forward in the direction of Fresnoy Park, but they enjoyed no more success than had Reserve Infantry Regiments 17 and 5 and later Grenadier Guards Regiment 5.

Making no progress, the commanding officer, Hauptmann Brauer, withdrew his men to the so-called *Nouvroy Riegel* and prepared to take part in a more general counter-attack, but the idea did not come to fruition. South of Oppy the fighting settled down to a desultory long range fire fight with small arms. There was a final British effort against the northern edge of Oppy just before nightfall. That failed with further bloody losses and the fighting died away. 2nd Guards Reserve Regiment was extremely worn down after the intensity of the fighting, so at 9.30 pm 7th and 8th Companies 1st Guards Reserve Regiment moved to take over sections of the front line and positions in Oppy Park and there they remained until they were relieved forty eight hours later.

Down on the front forward of Chérisy and Fontaine-lez-Croisilles, the regiments of 220th Infantry Division, which had been holding the line ever since the battle opened, were finally relieved by 49th Reserve Division at the beginning of May. Up until a few weeks previously this division had been fighting on the Eastern Front, so this deployment represented a distinct change of scene and battle intensity. It was deployed between 199th Infantry Division to the north and 27th Infantry Division, which was responsible for the Bullecourt - Quéant sector to the south. Reserve Infantry Regiment 226 was on the right flank, with Reserve Infantry Regiment 225 in the centre and Reserve Infantry Regiment 228 on the left.

Reserve Infantry Regiment 226, relieving Infantry Regiment 190, began its move forward during the evening of 1 May, having been issued with extra hand grenades in Dury. Even the relief was far from straightforward. To begin with, artillery preparation for the next round of attacks had already begun, so the closer the battalion got to the front, the worse the harassing fire and the more the casualties mounted. It had been arranged that the advancing units would be met by guides to lead them forward onto the positions. Unfortunately, the rendezvous was next to a German battery position that was under heavy fire. There was no sign of the guides, the companies could not risk remaining there for long, so they were forced to try to pick their way forward across craters, old barbed wire and collapsed trenches. Slipping and sliding in deep mud, forced repeatedly to take cover from the shell fire, they eventually made it, tired out and disorientated.

Luckily, at least for some members of the regiment, they were moving into a part of the *Siegfried Stellung* [Hindenburg Line], which had survived, if not intact, certainly better than most other places on the Arras front. The company commander 7th Company later described what he found on arrival in one of the left forward positions.

"We were now located in a deep, mined dugout of the *Siegfried Stellung*. About twenty five wide steps led down into the depths, where a tunnel ran along parallel to the trench. Rough bunks had been built along the side of the passageway and, in places, rooms for particular purposes had been constructed off to the side. In this case the dugout held the complete [2nd] Battalion; that is to say the staff, all the company commanders and two platoons of each company. The trench above that formed the second line was very deep, so it was easy to move along it without being seen. It was only possible to fire or observe by climbing onto the fire step, which was half to three quarters of a metre above [the floor of the trench]. We had to be able to fight either to the front or the rear, because our position had been partially rolled up from the right. This meant that a section of trench on the right flank, which had originally been intended as a communication trench, had now become part of the front line. This was a relatively shallow trench that did not everywhere provide cover from view. The accommodation here was in strong concreted blockhouses, which thus far had withstood all the shelling."[37]

Reserve Infantry Regiment 226 assumed responsibility for the Fontaine sector on 1 May and, that very day, had to beat off a probing attack. British shell fire went on increasing and the signs multiplied that there would soon be a resumption of the offensive. On 2 May heavy calibre guns concentrated mainly on counter-battery fire, so the German gunners suffered, but not exclusively; the front line infantry also came under numerous fire concentrations so that by that evening the sectors of 2nd and 9th Companies were virtually flattened and many of the dugouts were destroyed or buried. Naturally by this stage of the battle it was not all one way traffic and the German artillery succeeded during that evening in causing a temporary reduction in the weight of British fire. Given that there were in any case several distinct gas shoots overnight 2/3 May, this slight respite was extremely welcome for the defending troops.

From about 4.00 am, however, drum fire, supplemented by mortars firing large quantities of incendiary rounds and gas filled bombs, was making life extremely difficult for the forward defenders. Quite apart from the danger of being exposed to shells and splinters during this final bombardment, the entire area was cloaked with clouds of dust, powder smoke and gas, making it impossible to see more than a few metres, despite the fact that dawn had broken by the time the attack began. With all the telephone lines cut and the light signalling stations damaged or destroyed, the outcome of the battle would once again be determined by the actions of individuals and isolated groups of defenders.

When the attacks came in, for once there was a good response from the artillery defending the Fontaine sector and the initial British thrusts were severely blunted. Only in a few places did small groups break in and they were dealt with or ejected by local assault groups who made free use of hand grenades to recover lost sections of trench. As visibility improved, Reserve Infantry Regiment 226 suddenly realised that the attack was being supported by a pair of tanks, not that either was able to contribute much. In one case the tank had barely moved forward of the British front line before it bogged down. Luckily for its crew it was more or less completely hull down to the German front line and with little more than the top few centimetres to aim at it was not possible to destroy it. The second tank succeeded in advancing right up to the positions of 4th Company, but was unable to prevent the well protected trench garrison from bringing down withering fire against the British infantry. In the meantime, Offizierstellvertreter Klann managed to get two machine guns into position near the tank and to engage it with *SmK* armour piercing ammunition. As a result it was forced to cease fire and turn away, finally coming to a halt, possibly having broken down, close to the British lines southwest of Chérisy.

Assaulting Fontaine from the northwest, the British took very serious casualties along the line of the *Mecklenburg-Schweriner Weg*, a former communication trench running almost north towards Chérisy. Repeated attacks were beaten off then, even when there was a temporary break in, Reserve Leutnants Planert and Schmeil at the head of 2nd Company and part of 3rd Company threw the attackers out, capturing three officers, eighty other ranks and five Lewis guns in the process. However, though the British could not make much of an impression on the 49th Reserve Division lines, the same was not true further north in the 199th Infantry Division sector. To the northeast of Chérisy at the junction between Infantry Regiment 114 and Infantry Regiment 357, there was a serious penetration and, with 2nd Battalion Infantry Regiment 114 pressed right back to Chérisy, there was a real threat to the right flank of 49th Reserve Division. For a time the situation was critical.

Reserve Leutnant Vogel 11th Company Infantry Regiment 114[38]

"In the first glimmer of dawn, prior to 4.30 am, Unteroffizier Schirrmeister of 5th Company, who was out on patrol, spotted the enemy preparations but, before he could return, drum fire suddenly came down from guns along the entire horizon, followed by German return defensive fire as green flares went up along the front. Within minutes the entire ruined landscape was cloaked with dense smoke and dust. After between fifteen minutes and half an hour, the fire lifted abruptly from our positions, lingered for some minutes on the village of Chérisy, located 300 - 500 metres in rear, then moved to *Visier Höhe* on the far side of the Sensée, hammering down mighty blows on the positions of the support battalion on the rearward slope.

"To the front, emerging from the darkness, the smoke and flame came shadowy lines of infantrymen. Those of the trench garrison still able to fight - and they had lacked protective dugouts that might have protected them during the bombardment - began to pour fire at the enemy with every available weapon ... Out on the regimental right flank north of the road to Guémappe, which was manned by two platoons of 6th Company, the battle situation appeared threatening to the defence from the very beginning of the attack. Here, hardly had the defenders begun to fend off the frontal attack, than they found themselves under attack from the flank. It was not clear if the British had already pushed so deep into the Infantry Regiment 357 sector that they were already established to the rear of Infantry Regiment 114, or if, taking advantage of the relative lack of fire power in the area between the regiments, they had exploited this weak part of the defence.

"In addition the loss of the fire of the two heavy machine guns deployed on the right flank due to the deaths or wounding of their crews meant that it was simple for the British, armed with bayonets, hand grenades and machine guns, to turn a flanking threat into one from the rear. This had all come about due to the heavy losses suffered by this company during the drumfire. It was simply unequal to the task that confronted it. Surrounded, it had no choice but to lay down its weapons. Those who resisted were bayonetted. Its brave commander, Reserve Leutnant Ackermann, already lay dead on the parapet, killed by a hand grenade.[39]

3rd Battalion Reserve Infantry Regiment 225 was located back in reserve at Dury when the British attack was launched at 5.45 am. Having been stood to it was moved forward at 8.00 am to the *Schmidthöhle* [Smith's Cave][40] where it was placed under command of Reserve Infantry Regiment 226 and received this order:

"Reserve-Infantry-Regiment 226. 3 May 1917, 8.30 am

I. The enemy have forced their way into Chérisy and have advanced to a point about 200 metres east of Chérisy.
II. The right flank of Reserve Infantry Regiment 226, located about 200 metres south of Chérisy, as well as the reserves located in the valley of the Sensée and in the narrow gauge railway cutting, are seriously threatened.
III. 3rd Battalion Reserve Infantry Regiment 225 is to advance via the Chalk Pit in the direction of the eastern exit of Chérisy and is to eject the enemy who have broken in by means of a thrust from south to north, pushing the enemy's right flank all the way back through the village of Chérisy. The same orders have been issued to the regimental reserve (two companies) with machine guns. The commander, Rittmeister von Buddenbrock, is located in the Chalk Pit.

Signed: Hart"[41]

On receipt of the order, the battalion, well dispersed, set off immediately, with the commanding officer's orders group well to the fore so that all the company commanders would have the opportunity to orientate themselves before the main body arrived in the forward assembly area. Fortunately, the British protective barrage was successfully negotiated without casualties and, having arrived on the summit of the hill two kilometres east of Chérisy, it was established that the right flank of Reserve Infantry Regiment 226 was co-located with the headquarters of its 1st Battalion in the chalk pit. To the left there was no sign of the left flank of Infantry Regiment 114, 199th Infantry Division. In other words there was a gap of more than two kilometres. Scattered groups of Infantry Regiment 114, amounting altogether to about two platoons in strength, were also gathering to the northeast of the chalk pit. It also became clear that the British had taken up positions to the east of Sensée river and were in Chérisy in some strength.

To add to the potential difficulties, reinforcements could be seen advancing to Chérisy from the west. However, they were being engaged by the German artillery, as was Chérisy itself. Urgent action had to be taken, so the commanding officer issued this order:

"11th Company is to advance with its right flank directed at the centre of Chérisy and is to seek to link up with Reserve Infantry Regiment 226. 9th Company is to provide right flank protection on a three hundred metre frontage in a line north to the northwest until the arrival of 12th Company, which is then to assume the task. Thereafter, 11th Company is to take position between 9th and 10th Companies. For the time being there is to be no advance forward of the cross tracks located two kilometres east of Chérisy.[42] The main attack will not start until contact has been made with Infantry Regiment 114. The sections of 3rd Machine Gun Company will be distributed evenly to the companies. Two companies of Reserve Infantry Regiment 226 will participate in the attack from the chalk pit."[43]

In point of fact events began to move swiftly, so there was no time for all the manoeuvrings outlined in the orders. The weight of the German shelling began to take its toll on the leading British elements. By 11.45 am, the British began pulling back hastily from the eastern bank of the Sensée, being pursued all the way by machine gun fire. Exploiting the consequent confusion, the assault on Chérisy was launched at once. There was sharp resistance and hand to hand fighting once a way had been forced into the village but, by 12.50 pm, not only had Chérisy been recaptured, so had the original German front line. This success was partly due to the aggression of the 3rd Battalion companies which, newly arrived from the Eastern Front and going into action in the west for the first time, had a point to prove, but equal credit has to go to the German guns, which provided extremely accurately directed fire, keeping the retreating British troops on the move and completely preventing any reinforcements joining in the battle from the west.

The vigorous action would certainly have met with the approval of Commander, Group Arras (IX Reserve Corps), Generalleutnant Dieffenbach, who, concerned that earlier in the battle counter-attacks were not being driven home sufficiently strongly, issued the following directive on 23 April: 'I wish to re-emphasise that the battle is to be conducted for the trenches the furthest forward. Counter-strokes in cases where portions of the defensive positions have been lost are not to aim simply at securing intermediate lines, but are to be pushed forward as far as the previous front line.'[44] The link up to Infantry Regiment 114 to the right was finally achieved at 2.00 pm. Two of its platoons had indeed joined in the attack on the village. Other elements extended the attacking frontage to the north and two companies of Reserve Infantry Regiment 225 had also attacked to the south.

Reserve Leutnant Vogel 11th Company Infantry Regiment 114[45]

"In response to my question concerning the counter-stroke posed to 10th Company Reserve Infantry Regiment 225, I received the assurance 'We are taking part'. The German artillery carried on firing ... Then it was time. The desire of the companies to push on forward could no longer be restrained. Without any particular attempt at winning the firefight, the commanders of 11th and 12th Companies bawled at the top of the voices above the racket of enemy machine gun fire, 'On your feet, double march! 'The assault waves rushed up the hill, the British guns roared and rattled madly, but most of their fire was too high. Here and there a brave comrade did go down and some bullets cracked and ricocheted round our heads ...With gritted teeth we pressed on in bounds ... Then with one final rush and a wild *Hurra!* - the best I ever heard - we leapt up at the sandbag barricades of the machine gun positions broke in and through the position. Anybody still shooting got a bayonet in the guts ...

"The great battle was all over about 1.00 pm; the entire regimental sector had been recaptured. There was absolutely no sign of the enemy. Anybody who had wanted could have gone for a wander along the line of the trench. Because 11th and 12th Companies were very weakened - 11th Company was down to barely three sections - 10th Company Reserve Infantry Regiment 225 occupied the 180 metre section of the regimental position north of the road towards Guémappe. Simultaneously, Infantry Regiment 357 had restored the situation. The divisional frontage was secure once more. At nightfall the enemy attacked once more, only to be beaten back with serious losses after hard fighting and another counter-stroke. The regiment captured 230 prisoners, including three officers, and recovered twenty eight machine guns. The enemy losses were incalculably high. According to prisoner statements by the evening of 3 May the companies of 12th [Battalion] Middlesex Regiment were reduced to under fifty men each. Our own casualties were correspondingly high. On 3 May alone we suffered ninety four killed, including three officers, 233 wounded (five of them officers) and seventy eight missing."

Naturally, the British reacted at once to the recapture of Chérisy. Fire for effect was brought down on the old German front line from 1.00 pm to 2.30 pm and then again from 7.30 pm to 8.45 pm, at which time another British attack was launched. However, it was almost entirely broken up by the defensive artillery, only a few isolated sections came closer than 150 metres from the position and those few that did get into the forward trenches were soon ejected with hand grenades.

Although 3rd Battalion Reserve Infantry Regiment 225 had the hardest day, 2nd Battalion, back in its original location and holding the line, beat off several minor attacks and raids and also engaged enemy aircraft to good effect. At 7.35 am one spotting aircraft operating at 100 metres altitude was shot down by a machine gun operated by Gefreiter Berns then, when at 8.25 am two more arrived overhead, they were immediately driven off, with one seen diving steeply back towards the British front line with a dead engine. Apart from the shot down aircraft, which generated prize money, Reserve Infantry Regiment 225 captured large quantities of a wide variety of equipment and even a homing pigeon, which was delivered to the divisional pigeon loft later. The regiment suffered fairly minor casualties, though 3rd Battalion recorded fifteen killed in action and fifty five wounded but, in addition to the 180 prisoners taken, a rough count within the area fought over that day established that the British had lost at least 800 men killed, to say nothing of the unknown numbers caught by defensive fire to the west of Chérisy.

It was a minor disaster for British arms; their official historian reduced to stating in respect of Chérisy in particular that, 'The Germans made clever use of ground, but most of their counter-attacks would have been held by troops who could really use their rifles',[46] hardly a ringing endorsement of the fighting ability of those engaged. Be that as it may, the overall fact of the matter is that the major renewal of the British offensive on 3 May 17 was an almost complete failure. All sorts of reasons were subsequently adduced in explanation. The full moon silhouetted the attackers because the assaults went in before dawn, the start lines and axes of advance were inadequately marked, many of the assault troops were near exhaustion and the standard of training was extremely poor in some instances. There may well be some truth in all of this, but it is also a fact that Loßberg had by this stage transformed the defensive effort by means of his new tactics, through considerable reinforcement of the German heavy artillery and the replacement of worn out ground holding divisions with fresh troops. All this put fresh heart in the defence, which was conducted with the utmost ruthless aggression. The British attack was anticipated, German gunfire disrupted final preparations and, when the attacks were launched, defensive fire came down rapidly, heavily and accurately. From that point the reverse was as good as inevitable.

Crown Prince Rupprecht of Bavaria: Diary Entry 5 May 17[47]

"A wounded officer informed me that during the latest battle for Chérisy the British simply fled in the face of the German counter-attack. According to universal reports from the front it appears that, with the exception of the Canadians and Australians, acclaimed on all sides for their courage and skilful use of ground, the British troops are no longer as hard to beat as they once were."

In the aftermath of these battles the front became relatively quiet once more. The artillery battle continued unabated, however, with concentrations being directed almost randomly at different areas. Infantry operations, however, were sporadic. During the night 6/7 May there was fighting near Avion then, the following day, a battle took place at Quéant, with others on 7 May at Roeux and between Croisilles and Bullecourt on 8 May, a day when a German counter-attack wrested Fresnoy back off the British. Of all the minor conquests made by the British army, the capture of Fresnoy was the gain that the German defence most wished to reverse. Its elevated position on a spur meant that it offered the British army extremely good observation over a large length of the German lines. 5th Bavarian Infantry Division was warned for the task, released from Sixth Army reserve and began to move forward under command of Group Vimy on 5 May.

Whilst Bavarian Infantry Regiments 7, 19 and 21 were moving into position, the German artillery, considerably reinforced for the purpose, began the softening up process. This was to be a full blown counter-attack, methodically prepared and conducted. On 7 May seventeen field artillery batteries fired 42,000 shells at Fresnoy, this was added to by 17,000 rounds from 17 heavy batteries and every other battery within range superimposed their fire, so that a total of over 100,000 shells rained down on the village and its immediate surrounding area. During the night 7/8 May every known British battery position was gassed; 27,500 'Green Cross' [phosgene filled] shells being used.[48]The three regiments were deployed in line with Bavarian Infantry Regiment 19 in the north advancing with its right flank on the Bois Bernard - Arleux-en-Gohelle road. Bavarian Infantry Regiment 19 was deployed in the centre, with objective the village itself and the wooded area, now shattered, immediately south of it. Then came Bavarian Infantry Regiment 7 on the left flank.

The attack went in at 5.00 am. The weather was cold and rainy, the battlefield one great muddy crater field, which made all movement extremely difficult and caused the advancing troops to lose the barrage in places. Each regiment advanced two up with one battalion in reserve. The leading battalions had two companies each in the front line with one in support and one in reserve. This made it easier to maintain the momentum of the attack when pockets of resistance were encountered. In the south Bavarian Infantry Regiment 7 made reasonable progress, despite coming under heavy machine gun fire from a flank that temporarily held up the advance whilst casualties mounted. Reserve Leutnants Hirsch, Schad and Laubmann were killed[49] and Reserve Leutnant Friedrich seriously wounded. Seizing the initiative, the commander of 4th Company, Reserve Leutnant Christian Popp, moved round to a flank and, displaying extraordinary determination and courage, rolled up an entire British battalion [1st Battalion East Surrey Regiment] from the side and rear. Large numbers raced for the rear, but 200 other ranks, four officers and six machine guns were captured by Popp's men. Popp himself was immediately awarded the Knight's Cross of the Military Max Joseph Order, the highest honour available to an officer of his rank in the Bavarian army.

Bavarian Infantry Regiment 19 ran into difficulties from a British strongpoint well equipped with Lewis gunners and located about 200 metres east of the wood just to the north of Fresnoy. Their movement stalled but, fortunately, Bavarian Infantry Regiment 21 made more progress to the north, exposing the British left flank and permitting an intermingled group of men from all the companies of 1st Battalion to manoeuvre on the open flank, close to within grenade throwing range, break through into the park and advance rapidly to a point about 200 metres beyond its western edge, where they consolidated and beat off with machine gun fire later attempts at hasty counter-attacks by the British. Reserve Leutnant Taeffner, commanding 3rd Company, was killed at this point.[50] On their left, men of 8th Company, supported by flamethrower teams, cleared through the village, mopping up as they went and capturing thirty five prisoners. At 7.55 am, regimental headquarters received a report despatched as early as 6.45 am, '1st Battalion has reached the western edge of Fresnoy. Advance posts have been pushed forward and contact has been established with [Bavarian] Infantry Regiment 21.'[51]

It is an interesting aside and a reflection of how the experience of the war varied greatly from formation to formation that, in recounting the day's events from the perspective of Bavarian Infantry Regiment 21, its historian noted that when the companies assembled on their start lines, for all the newer members of the regiment this was to be their first major attack of the war and, for the handful of men who had served with it since mobilisation, the first since October 1914, when they were operating in Lorraine.[52] When the assaulting companies set off in a series of waves, it was still dark enough to provide some cover from view but, having worked their way forward a short distance, 8th Company suddenly came under heavy fire and there were casualties at once. Their commander, Reserve Leutnant Hoffmann, who was well to the fore, rallied his men and led them in a charge which overwhelmed the pocket of resistance, but it cost him his life.[53] Other companies following up pressed the attack home, exploiting out well to the west of Fresnoy, but once more a company commander, this time Reserve Leutnant Karl Gollwitzer of 7th Company, was killed along with numerous members of his company.[54] Finally, all resistance overcome, the regiment reorganised. Such were the muddy conditions that cleaning weapons and ammunition to get them back into working order took far longer than the assault itself. Several awards for bravery were won, but the cost of this relatively brief battle were high, with a disproportionate number of junior commanders killed or wounded. In addition to those already named, Offizierstellvertreter Seidl, 3rd Company was killed and three other 1st Battalion officers were wounded. From the 2nd Battalion fatal casualties also included Offizestellvertreters Mosandl (7th Company) and Wilhelm (8th Company), along with Vizefeldwebel Amberg (2nd Machine Gun Company) and Fahnenjunker Sprengler (8th Company). Five other junior commanders were wounded.

3rd Battalion escaped with fewer casualties, but Reserve Leutnants Winter and Reis of 11th and 12th Companies respectively were also killed.[55]

All was more or less quiet for the infantry on 9 and 10 May, apart from a weak attempt to counter-attack Fresnoy during the early hours of 9 May. The problem was that this delay was too long for a hasty counter-attack to have had a good chance of success, but too soon to mount a successful deliberate counter-attack. Despite this setback, British artillery fire continued to be directed in quantity against the rear areas, stretching back as far as Douai. There were further battles on 11 May with skirmishes west and south of Lens and astride the Scarpe. 9th Reserve Division, which by this stage had been in the line for nearly two weeks, was heavily involved in the defence of Pelves throughout this period.

Oberleutnant Löwe 1st Company Reserve Infantry Regiment 19 Diary Entry 13 May 1917[56]

"Yesterday was a hard day. We came under drum fire five times. It all started at 6.45 pm. The storm died down about 10.00 pm then began all over again. At that moment I was actually in a shell hole near my dugout. Shells and shrapnel rounds were bursting all around and over me. I then worked my way forward, moving from shell hole to shell hole. Eventually I reached our defensive line and dived into a hole. I then sent word to the left and right informing everyone that I was there. I lit up a cigarette and awaited developments. A little later my Leutnant Prahm arrived. We lay in wait together. Suddenly, off to the right, the signal calling for defensive fire went up. It was reported subsequently that the enemy trenches were tightly packed with personnel. A few groups did leave their trenches but scuttled back to them when we opened up with machine guns and artillery fire. I stayed forward until 2.30 am then returned."

Once again artillery stopped most of the British attacks, but there was some success near Roeux. A further major effort, especially south of the river, failed late in the afternoon of 12 May, shot to a standstill by a combination of artillery and machine gun fire.

Leutnant Mersi 3rd Machine Gun Company Infantry Regiment 395[57]

"On the whole 12 May passed off quietly but, at 4.00 pm, there began the usual deluge by all calibres of shell. After that had passed over, causing relatively few casualties, we, namely Hauptmann Hohlfeld, Leutnant Pfeiffer, Leutnant Ehlers and I, met under a groundsheet that had been stretched over the trench. Because of the circumstances I shall never forget our little chat. Almost as though he had had a premonition of what was about to happen, Hauptmann Hohlfeld in his jovial, conversational way said, 'Wouldn't it be just wonderful to be on the receiving end of a *Heimatschüßchen* [German equivalent of a 'Blighty one'], then to be evacuated unconscious to a hospital to be lying on white sheets and to be awakened by the gentle strokes of the hands of a nurse?' Just as Hohlfeld was describing a nurse's tender hands, a group of British gunners let fly, spraying our trench with a hail of shells. We leapt up as a shell landed on the edge of the trench and Leutnant Ehlers collapsed with concussion.

"The drum fire lasted a few minutes then came a shout, 'Here they come!' ... and indeed they did. Two men manning my gun furthest to the right lay dead, shot through the head. One of them was still clutching the butt with his hands. I laid him to one side and opened fire. An entire belt went through without a single jam. It was as though the little machine knew that it had to save the situation. Sure enough the attack was halted fifty metres short of our line. Half right I could see the flashes of a machine gun being fired from a shell hole. We engaged in a duel and moments later, both weapons fell silent. He sent a bullet into my left shoulder and I hit him so hard that he was sent flying backwards. The attack was beaten off and the enemy must have suffered enormous casualties.

The German counted these battles the fifth phase of the campaign, which ended with the British in possession of the station and village of Roeux but little else to show for their efforts. The fighting persisted for another week, bringing further success for the Australians at Bullecourt, the loss of Roeux on 15 May when the British 4th Division attacked 4th Ersatz Division. However, it was partly recaptured on 16 May when 38th Infantry Division, released from Sixth Army reserve, conducted Operation Erfurt. The German artillery brought down heavy preparatory fire on Roeux and the station complex to the north for almost twenty four hours, then the counterattack, spearheaded by Infantry Regiment 94 on the right (objective Roeux Station) and Infantry Regiment 95, aiming for the village itself, attacked at dawn. Timings were critical. A heavy concentration was to crash down at 4.30 am, with the assault companies moving off their start lines at 4.39 am. From 4.40 am the rolling barrage was planned to lift 100 metres per minute and drum fire to come down on Roeux Station at 4.46 am. The plan was for the British positions to be rushed immediately after this, so as to give the defenders no chance of being able to react before the leading elements were upon them. Inevitably things did not proceed so smoothly. There were losses moving forward onto the start line, which caused delays. As a result 2nd Battalion Infantry Regiment 94 did not even arrive there until 4.00 am. Nevertheless, its leading companies were able to advance with the remainder of the first assault wave at the appointed time.

Despite the prompt arrival of British defensive fire and a hail of small arms fire, 1st and 2nd Battalions overran the first British trenches within three minutes. There was then a protracted battle for the second line, before approximately 100 British survivors pulled out hastily, under constant heavy German fire, from which very few escaped. The fighting continued at varying degrees of intensity throughout the day and into the following night. Eventually Infantry Regiment 94 had to withdraw from its positions furthest forward, owing to British pressure and the fact that the formations had been unable to get very far forward on either flank. This was a particular problem to the south, where the Infantry Regiment 95 attack on Roeux was a costly failure. Infantry Regiment 94 had given its utmost and had been relatively successful. Nevertheless, with thirteen officer casualties, forty other ranks killed, together with 263 wounded and no fewer than 232 missing, this had been a severely trying day for the regiment.[58] Despite this, it remained in the line until the end of May and saw very little additional fighting.

The story of what happened at Roeux is swiftly told. Infantry Regiment 95 also stepped off at 4.40 am to take not only the village, but Roeux Park to the west of it. The bombardment had been just as heavy, but the ruins of the village offered better protection for the defenders and the entire area was full of machine guns. Leading companies clashed at once and there was severe close quarter fighting throughout the day. Then, as German losses mounted, so the scale and strength of the British hasty counter attacks increased until the remnants of Infantry Regiment 95, under great pressure, were forced to withdraw from the last of their forward positions at 9.00 pm. Their losses must have been enormous, though the regimental history merely mentions that they were 'heavy'. One of the survivors attempted to put the best gloss on the events of the day as he summed up the battle. Reading between the lines, a mixture of bombast and wishful thinking, it is clear that this was a serious setback both for the regiment and its parent division; which in no way detracts from the courage of the men involved.

Reserve Leutnant Kohlstock Infantry Regiment 95[59]

"'The 16 May 1917 showed once more not only the old and so frequently proven offensive spirit of the Thuringians, but also their deeply rooted faithfulness and great sacrificial courage.' These were words used in the divisional Order of the Day, issued by General Schultheiß, commander 38th Infantry Division, as he expressed his thanks to the troops who had taken part. The Army Commander had ordered the attack on Roeux and deployed 38th Infantry Division to conduct this hard battle, because other German major attacks, with distant objectives, on other fronts were due to take place shortly afterwards. In order to divert substantial enemy forces away from the planned operational areas and to force them to move them to the Scarpe sector, Roeux had to be subjected to a surprise attack. The mission was a hard one, but it was carried out with honour. The operational objective was achieved!"

On 17 May part of Bullecourt was evacuated and there were three assaults directed at Gavrelle. None of these succeeded and there was another reverse at Monchy on 19 May. Although some action continued on into June on the Arras front, the sixth and final notable assault went in on 20 May after drum fire had been directed all along its length from Acheville to Quéant. The width of the bombardment may have been intended to deceive the defence, because infantry attacks were restricted to the line from Monchy to Bullecourt. These assaults were repeated at least five times and fighting went on right up until midnight. There were no British gains but, in places, the defence had been so reduced and intermingled by the end of the day that the defenders were withdrawn to the Second Position to reorganise.

With that the main battle may have been effectively over, but during the next few days there were numerous deadly incidents and low level clashes, which could be extremely damaging to those directly involved. One such occurred to 3rd Battalion Reserve Infantry Regiment 84, which had just moved into front line with 10th, 9th and 12th Companies forward of Chérisy when, at 4.00 am 27 May, a concentrated gas attack, probably delivered by Livens Projectors, took place. 10th Company was hardest hit, with forty two men killed. 9th Company and 3rd Machine Gun Company lost three men each. In addition fifteen men were wounded and ninety seven gassed. As a result of this, possibly a 'Chinese' attack (i.e. diversionary attack, with no infantry assault), the battalion suffered no fewer than 160 casualties. 10th Company had to be withdrawn and 11th Company took its place. The appalling effectiveness of phosgene gas had been demonstrated all too clearly, as this lengthy, but graphic, account illustrates.

Leutnant Weidemann 11th Company Reserve Infantry Regiment 84[60]

"During the fighting the front line had been pushed back to the northern edge of Chérisy, where the road to Héninel led off. The fighting around Chérisy had been very hard, with the British storming up to and through Chérisy. However, courageous German soldiers had re-established the original front line and the heavy artillery finished off the Tommies, who were cut off in the valley of the Sensée. All this we of Reserve Infantry Regiment 84 observed as we moved forward from Dury and traversed the ravine in front of Chérisy, which was strewn with British bodies, heading for *KTK-Wäldchen* [Commander of the Forward Troops Copse] and deploying to support positions near the great *Schmidthöhle* [Smith's Cave].

"Others roaming the battlefields had already established, by examining the dead British soldiers, that several regiments (said to have been six) had attempted to force a break through at Chérisy. The small topographical maps found on the corporals, which were marked with the exact day's objective, indicated that the Tommies had once again badly miscalculated. From the cap badges I can recall the King's Royal Rifle [Corps], the Sussex and Essex Regiments and some other regimental insignia. The break through failed to materialise because, as has been mentioned, the front line was re-established and the cut off troops shot to pieces with murderously heavy artillery fire.

"The front line now ran immediately to the west of the village of Chérisy, manned by two platoons of 10th Company. The first platoon was located north of the fork where the roads from Chérisy to Héninel and Wancourt led off. The second platoon was to the south. The third platoon was deployed in the sunken road which ran towards *KTK Wäldchen* and Fontaine les Croisilles at the southern exit of Chérisy, so here the front line stepped back somewhat. *KTK Wäldchen*, which rather resembled parkland dotted with large trees, was where the commanding officer 3rd Battalion Reserve Infantry Regiment 84 was located. The position was quiet. It was a breathing space after the Easter battle.

"Whilst in the line, the first platoon shot up an [enemy] patrol led by an officer. The officer was killed, a corporal wounded and a lance corporal severely wounded. The lance corporal was totally disorientated by the explosion of the hand grenades. He constantly asked for a doctor and said, 'Where is my gaske?' [*sic*] , i.e. 'Where is my gas mask?' I remember the word 'gaske' very clearly. Possibly a gas attack had been planned for that morning and had only been postponed because of the presence of these three. Eventually surprise attacks with concentrations of phosgene-filled projectiles began. The first warnings of them arrived in a routine order received when we were once more back in the support position east of the River Sensée near Chérisy.

"However, the warning did not reach us until 26 May, a few hours before we were due to go forward. We were on highest alert, therefore, and the troops were cautious as they moved forward. Nobody visualised the form the attack would take, assuming that the placement and operation of the gas projectiles would be a lengthy matter. However the British laid them out in a honeycomb pattern and fired them electrically, so the simultaneous launch and explosion of this mass of projectiles came as a violent shock and produced a very dense gas cloud. During the night 26/27 May the company entered the position between 11.00 pm and 1.00 am. When the gas attack came at about 4.30 am, the sentries were being changed for the second or third time.

"Every former front line soldier will recall the nights when reliefs took place – the tiredness after the approach march, organising the dugouts, or standing getting chilled after working up a sweat on the way forward. It is entirely possible that not every man was at the highest state of gas alert ... I had begun my duties as deputy commander of the third platoon and was making my way through its sector. A few light artillery shells landed then there was an almighty explosion. We all heard it and just had time to wonder if the Tommies had suffered an accidental explosion of ammunition before the air began to whistle, groan and roar above our heads. Our front line instincts took over and we knew that a hellish load of shells was coming down on us. A flare went up as the shells burst, but they were not as loud as we expected; resembling more the dull crack of fireworks.

"However, the series of detonations betrayed the number of rounds involved. By the light of the flare I could see the trench enveloped in a great grey mass and had just time to shout 'Gas' as everyone reached for their gas masks. Everywhere seemed silent. The density of the gas dampened the sound, though I could hear the sound of shells, which forced us to the ground or to take cover in the bunkers. I held my breath until my mask was properly fitted, then gulped in a deep breath. I had almost given up hope of breathing oxygen again, but felt a sense of freedom under my mask. Within moments, men came rushing up to me. I could not tell if they were friend or foe or if an attack was about to be launched. They were actually comrades, who had either forgotten to mask up, or were panicking beneath them, From under my own mask I bawled, 'Just get forward!' grabbed them by the arm and pointed out the direction, but they were like drowning men … they had had it.

"I rushed through the third platoon position and down the sap where the sentry post equipped with the Lewis gun was located. The two comrades there had decided that there was no need to mask up because the wall of gas was behind them. They stood there calmly waiting for the Tommies, but they did not come. They obviously wanted to avoid getting involved in this mess. The two forward platoons were initially not so endangered by the gas and many of them took their masks off again after a short while. There was a tendency to assume that rapid collapse would follow breathing in the gas, or at least that its effect would be obvious, but this gas was treacherous. Only a very small quantity was needed to cause death or severe poisoning. Removal too soon of the gas mask carried with it the danger that gas clinging to clothing would be breathed in and these quantities were sufficient to attack internal organs and cause death.

"To begin with that morning there was virtually no wind. Very slowly the gas rolled downhill towards the *KTK* but did not quite reach it. The God of War then seemed to be displeased by the unknightly, murderous attack and as day broke the wind began to blow the gas back towards the Tommies. This meant that the front line was once again covered by much diluted gas which was largely unnoticed but, nevertheless, still in sufficient concentration to deliver an additional dose to most of the men stationed there. They had all long before unmasked and were overjoyed at having survived. In fact there was greater concern for the men who had had to move to the rear, severely gassed. They were the soldiers of the third platoon, who had remained in the deep mined dugouts. The gas had descended into them in such quantity that the candles were all extinguished! Many sleeping men had been unable to find their masks quickly and the sudden, unexpected events led to terrible confusion in the darkness.

"It was only these comrades gasping for breath or suffering from severe headaches who made their way to the rear and sought out the dressing station to report sick. Only gradually did everyone else begin to feel unwell and to suffer headaches. I stayed at my post for another two hours and then was so far gone that I could only get to the *KTK* dugout slowly and with difficulty. The scene that confronted me was appalling. Initially the sight of so many comrades choking and gasping for breath was dreadful but, as I became more ill myself, my feelings of sympathy were replaced by those of powerlessness and indifference. There the poor men lay, facing a dreadful death. Thick mucus laden foam spilled from their mouths. Again and again they coughed to free themselves of it.

"It was essential however, to try to remain calm and not to think about death, which was reaping a rich harvest here; to try also to avoid the sympathetic glances of the comrades who were unaffected, so as not to lose the total determination to resist death. Despite serious warnings, some comrades tried to make their way to the *Schmidthöhle*, but not all of them made it. They were found later lying along the way. Then the stretcher bearers came along to evacuate the living to the rear. It was a hard carry along the valley of the Sensée the *Schmidthöhle*. The next morning the ambulances arrived and brought us to the casualty clearing station at Tortequenne.

"Our faces were blue; our blood apparently completely poisoned. At the dressing station I was bled to improve the aeration of my lungs.[61] All we gas casualties were together in one ward, and most fought a hopeless fight against death. A further consequence of the illness was a very serious infection of the lungs, which only cleared slowly and often infected other organs. The company cyclist who visited me in hospital told me of fifty four deaths in 10th Company alone. I have already mentioned that a contrary wind which got up at dawn blew the gas back at the British and I heard later that the Tommies had to transport gassed men to the rear throughout the day, just like us. This revenge eased my own fate and my thoughts about the many faithful fallen!'"

Counter-battery and harassing fire continued to come on the German positions and rear areas down right into June. There were infantry assaults at Bullecourt on 21, 22, 24 and 27 May and Monchy on 30 May and 2 June, but they brought the British troops no gains. By now the focus had shifted north to Ypres and the Messines Ridge, where the opening of that battle with the explosion of a series of huge mines south of Ypres in the early hours of 7 June effectively brought the long drawn out and costly Battle of Arras to an end. What had been achieved? The British had penetrated the German positions to a depth generally of about five to six kilometres (in places eight) on a twenty eight kilometre front. Vimy Ridge had been captured and the right hand end of the *Siegfried Stellung* [Hindenburg Line] was lost. The German front line now ran from Loos to Fontaine les Croisilles via Lens, Avion, Fresnoy, Roeux and Chérisy. It had also been pushed back to the east of Bullecourt. The great success of 9 April had led to the capture of a great many German prisoners and the losses of large numbers of guns. Altogether, German losses to the end of May totalled more than 85,000.

That said, the outcome for the British army was anything but rosy. Its daily loss rate was the highest of the entire war, its numerous hastily and inadequately trained battle casualty replacements had shown themselves in many cases to be of dubious utility and the later attacks were not pushed with anything like the determination shown on 9 April. It had striven for a breakthrough between Douai and Cambrai and had come nowhere near to achieving it. Yet again the techniques to achieve break through, as opposed to break in, proved to be beyond its capabilities. The ground it had captured was completely worthless and of no strategic importance whatsoever, though possession of Vimy Ridge proved to be useful over the coming eighteen months. In addition it had paid a high price for aiding its French allies, being forced to continue the battle long after it had run its natural course. At the final count British losses were somewhere in the order of 170,000, approximately twice those of the defence.[62]

The German successful defence was a vindication of Loßberg's new defensive techniques, which would continue to be effective in 1917 right up until the battles of the Menin Road Ridge the following September. The infantry had developed further its use of crater field defence, pioneered the previous year on the Somme and used to great effect later in Flanders, together with defence in depth and bold use of *Eingreif* troops. The artillery had learned the critical importance of counter-battery fire and to take every opportunity to disrupt attack preparations. These were all valuable experiences, which would inform the defence east of Ypres in the forthcoming four month campaign in Flanders.

Notes

[1] Loßberg *Meine Tätigkeit im Weltkriege* pp 287-288.
[2] Rogge History Infantry Regiment 88 p 347.
[3] History Fusilier Regiment 35 pp 232-233
[4] Behrmann *Die Osterschlacht bei Arras II. Teil* pp129-130.
[5] BOH 399.
[6] Of those named, only Leutnant Karl Michaelis has a known grave. He is buried in the *Kamaradengrab* of the German cemetery at Neuville St Vaast.
[7] Zipfel History Grenadier Regiment 89 pp 307-309.
[8] Behrmann *op. cit.* pp144-145.
[9] Offizerstellvertreter Anton Bedorf died later in British captivity on 16 November 1918. He is buried at the German cemetery at Cannock Chase Block 14 Row 2 Grave 52.
[10] Behrmann *op. cit.* pp146-147.
[11] This was a considerable risk. 2nd Company was down to forty riflemen at the time. Behrmann p 148.
[12] Ritter History Bavarian Infantry Regiment 18 p 175.
[13] Hauptmann Hermann Risser is buried in the *Kamaradengrab* of the German cemetery at St Laurent Blangy.
[14] Kohl *Mit Hurra in den Tod!* p 160.
[15] Leutnant Wilhelm Mayerhofer and Reserve Leutnant Heinrich Körzinger are buried in the German cemetery at Neuville St Vaast in Block 19 Grave 1167 and Block 18 Grave 1230 respectively.
[16] Hansch History Grenadier Regiment 9 p 368.
[17] Riegel History Bavarian Infantry Regiment 17 p 53.
[18] COH p 270.

[19] Voigt History Fusilier Regiment 73 pp 486-487.

[20] Zipfel History Infantry Regiment 75 pp 273-276.

[21] Reserve Leutnant Armin Goering is buried in the German cemetery at St Laurent Blangy Block 2 Grave 516.

[22] Zipfel *op. cit.* p 282.

[23] Leutnant Heinrich Stolz is buried in the German cemetery at Billy-Berclau Block 4 Grave 217.

[24] Liedgens History Reserve Infantry Regiment 65 p 62.

[25] Piedmont History Infantry Regiment 65 p 225.

[26] Leutnant Kurt Frank is buried in the German cemetery at Billy-Berclau Block 4 Grave 218.

[27] Krüger History Infantry Regiment 25 p 123.

[28] BOH p 425.

[29] Mücke History Infantry Regiment 185 pp 50-51.

[30] Stosch History Grenadier Guard Regiment 5 p 381.

[31] Grenadier Erich Bierwagen is buried in the Gemran cemetery at Carvin Block 5 Grave 578.

[32] Kutzleben History Guards Reserve Field Artillery Regiment 1 p 155.

[33] *ibid.* p 154.

[34] Brederlow History 1st Guards Reserve Regiment p 243.

[35] *ibid.* p 244.

[36] Peters History Reserve Infantry Regiment 28 pp 136-137.

[37] Rohkohl History Reserve Infantry Regiment 226 pp 22-23.

[38] Müller-Loebnitz *Die Badener im Weltkrieg* p 261.

[39] Reserve Leutnant Ernst Ackermann is buried in the *Kamaradengrab* of the German cemetery at Neuville St Vaast.

[40] This was a major underground working pressed into service by the defence, which was located on the eastern slope of the hill, known as *Visier Höhe,* midway between Vis-en-Artois and Hendicourt-lez-Cagnicourt.

[41] History Reserve Infantry Regiment 225 p 237.

[42] In fact the cross tracks were located more like 1,500 metres from Chérisy.

[43] History Reserve Infantry Regiment 225 pp 237-238.

[44] History Infantry Regiment 114 p 355.

[45] Müller-Loebnitz *op. cit.* pp 266-267.

[46] BOH p 454.

[47] Rupprecht *In Treue Fest: Zweiter Band* p 161

[48] Schaidler History Bavarian Infantry Regiment 7 p 42.

[49] Leutnants Max Hirsch, Anton Schad and Hans Laubmann are all buried in the German cemetery at Carvin Block 5 Graves 737,738 and 814.

[50] Reserve Leutnant Johann Taeffner is buried in the German cemetery at Carvin Block 5 Grave 755.

[51] Jäger History Bavarian Infantry Regiment 19 p 291.

[52] Reber History Bavarian Infantry Regiment 21 p 183.

[53] Reserve Leutnant Richard Hoffmann is buried in the German cemetery at Carvin Block 5 Grave 736.

[54] Reserve Leutnant Karl Gollwitzer is buried in the *Kamaradengrab* of the German cemetery at St Laurent-Blangy. The *Volksbund* has incorrectly recorded the date of his death as 9 May 1917.

[55] Four of those named have known graves. Vizefelwebel Werner Seidl and Vizefeldwebel Wilhelm Amberg are both buried in the German cemetery at St Laurent Blangy in the *Kamaradengrab* and Block 3 Grave 827 respectively. Vizefeldwebel Johann Mosandl and Leutnant Rudolf Winter are buried in the German cemetery at Carvin in Block 5 Graves 734 and 754.

[56] Schwenke History Reserve Infantry Regiment 19 pp 225-226.

[57] Dessau History Infantry Regiment 395 pp 77-78.

[58] Hartmann History Infantry Regiment 94 pp 215-216.

[59] Buttmann History Infantry Regiment 95 p 228.

[60] Speck History Reserve Infantry Regiment 84 pp 209-212.

[61] There was and remains no specific treatment for phosgene poisoning. However it was known that patients suffering from left heart failure, which often produces a frothy pinkish fluid that fills the lungs, sometimes benefited from venesection to lower blood volume. It is possible, therefore, that in this desperate, life or death situation a doctor was attempting to use the technique in the hope that it might at least produce some symptomatic relief in his patient.

[62] BOH pp 556-561 As usual the British official historian used all manner of accounting tricks in an attempt to boost the German casualty figures and minimise those suffered by the British army. Nevertheless, the fact remains that Loßberg's change of tactics and overall control of the battle enabled the defence to be conducted in manner which was sparing of German army manpower. For once there was a very clear disparity between the casualties suffered by the attacking side and those of the defenders.

CHAPTER 8

Flogging a Dead Horse:
Stalemate and Mutiny on the
Aisne/Champagne Battlefield

During the evening of 17 April, then throughout the following night, fighting continued for the high ground to the north of Vailly, on the right flank of Seventh Army. In places this caused the German army substantial casualties. It was clear that the French were trying their best to pinch out the German salient between Sancy and Vailly. Repeated attacks went in against 25th Landwehr and 185th Infantry Divisions. This led to their wresting Chavonne from 185th Infantry Division and forcing its formations to withdraw to a stop line which ran to the west of Braye but, around midnight, this too was penetrated. The situation was rapidly becoming critical for all the forces in this area and a quick decision had to be made. There were insufficient uncommitted forces on hand to attempt to throw the French thrust back sufficiently far to be effective. Having carried out a swift appreciation and accompanying staff checks, Headquarters Seventh Army then directed Group Vailly to withdraw 25th Landwehr Division, together with 222nd and 183rd Infantry Divisions, to fallback positions, running from Lassaux to Fort de la Malmaison and then further along the line of the Chemin des Dames. 183rd Infantry Division, supported by elements of the 45th Reserve Division in the *Eingreif* role, conducted a difficult rearwards movement in contact all the way back to its sector north of Braye.

The intensity of the battle around Soupir had been such that it is no exaggeration to speak of the shattered remnants of Infantry Regiments 184, 193 and 418 pulling back to the Malmaison position, where elements of 45th Reserve Division had already taken up position. In the case of Infantry Regiment 418, they fell back through 1st Battalion Reserve Infantry Regiment 211 and rallied slightly further to the rear at the so-called *Lager Neu Württemberg*. Despite all they had endured, this was still not relief. As an interim measure, the divisional survivors were regrouped with men from Infantry Regiment 193 to form a composite battalion. It is tribute to their staying power that by midday 18 May they were ready to be redeployed forward. Shortly afterwards a gap in the new front line was identified and they were sent to fill it. There they endured yet another day of heavy shelling, which cost yet more casualties, though fortunately

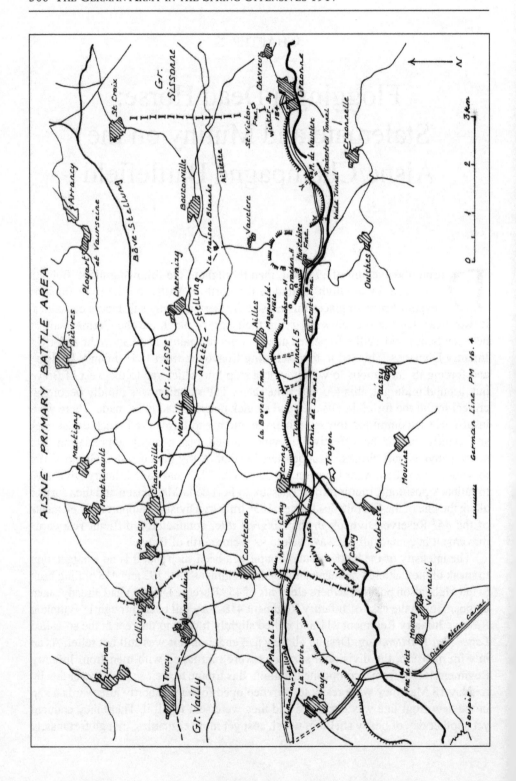

the weight of fire eased a little during 19 April and, at 11.00 pm that day, a battalion of Reserve Infantry Regiment 211 arrived to take over. When they finally arrived back at *Lager Neu Württemberg* they could only muster the equivalent of two companies. 1st to 9th Companies formed one and 10th to 12th the other. The casualties had been nothing short of catastrophic.

Musketier H Siersleben 1st Company Infantry Regiment 418[1]

"At long last during the night of 19 April came the order, 'The 418th is to move to the rear!' But we were still not out of danger, because the march to reserve was every bit as dreadful as holding on in the face of the enemy. We then suddenly realised what heroics our runners and carrying parties had achieved, quietly fulfilling what they regarded as their primary responsibility, namely to supply their comrades forward with the essentials they required. We gathered at Vorges then, after a hard march on foot, arrived on 23 or 24 April in Toulis, where transport was waiting."

The story for the other formations of 183rd Infantry Division was broadly similar, except that in the case of Infantry Regiment 184 only one company (12th) moved briefly into reserve near Malval Farm after withdrawal and it was soon sent forward once more after repeated French probing attacks had taken a further toll of casualties from 9th and 10th Companies (11th Company was already down to a handful of survivors). The remainder went straight into the line and stayed there until 20 April, with some elements remaining in place until they were relieved by 3rd Battalion Reserve Infantry Regiment 67. When it was finally withdrawn the regiment could only muster fifteen officers and 550 men, some of whom had been wounded but had refused to be evacuated.[2] The other two divisions delayed their moves until the morning of 18 April, then pulled back without enemy interference.

The German defence now found itself in a strange situation. As far as the senior levels of command were concerned, it was beyond any doubt that so far their forces had enjoyed success. The French offensive had been held and the threatened breakthrough had come to nothing. At unit level this view was not generally shared or even understood. Ground had been lost almost everywhere along the line and casualties had been very high. The ground holding divisions were almost all fought out and required urgent relief. The chosen expedient was to move the former *Eingreif* divisions into this role, despite the fact they had also generally suffered serious casualties. Furthermore, in most cases it was not possible to move the relieved divisions straight back into rest because several had to be retained in reserve or temporarily as *Eingreif* formations until fresh forces could be moved forward.

Along the Aisne front, 17 and 18 April brought only a minor series of local attacks, none of which achieved anything of significance. 16th Reserve Division, which had been heavily engaged since the start of the offensive, beat off an attack directed against the sugar refinery at Cerny; the Bavarian Ersatz Division, one against Chevreux. Near Ailles 19th Reserve Division, heavily engaged ever since the beginning of the battle, succeeded in pushing back the French well beyond the Chemin des Dames, almost recovering their former Third Line. It was a different story for Generalleutnant Freiherr von Watter's 54th Infantry Division, which launched a full counter-attack, aimed at recapturing the *Artillerie-Schutzstellung*, between the River Aisne and Juvincourt. It came up against strong French resistance, which it was unable to break down.

5th Guards Reserve Division had also been hard pressed by the initial attacks. Although the ground they yielded was minimal, the forward companies had suffered from considerable attrition and there had to be a significant amount of internal divisional redeployment to ensure that key places such as the mouths of the *Wald Tunnel* and *Kaisertreu Tunnel*, both located immediately south of the Chemin des Dames and to the east of Hurtebise Farm, did not fall into French hands. One such reinforcement was of Infantry Regiment 20 by the Fusilier [3rd] Battalion, Footguard Regiment 3.

Leutnant Deesler Machine Gun Company 3rd Battalion Footguard Regiment 3[3]

"On 16 April the Fusilier Battalion was ordered to move forward to the position of Infantry Regiment 20. Because the company commander, Reserve Leutnant Wegener, had gone on ahead to check out the route, I led the company forward from the regimental command post at La Bove Chateau [1,500 metres north of Bouconville]. We advanced with fifty metre spacing between each man along a cable trench as far as Bouconville, but we came under an enormous weight of fire because the ground was overlooked by a large number of observation balloons. Despite this I succeeded, at the cost of only one man slightly wounded in the forehead, to arrive at the *Kaisertreu Tunnel* by about 5.00 pm. I remained in this tunnel until the morning of the 18th. At midday that same day I assumed command of the four machine guns at the *Wald Tunnel*. Two of the guns were deployed at the tunnel entrance and one at each of the other exits. Because of lack of clarity about the overall situation, the only factor of importance was to defend the tunnel entrances. The French tried to force a way into our position towards evening on 18 April, but were driven off by machine gun fire and the use of hand grenades. Mahlke's gun [crew] distinguished itself because, although it suffered frequent stoppages, all were cleared speedily. Despite coming under heavy fire from rifle grenades and mortars, the crew stuck to their posts and maintained constant rapid fire against the enemy who were surging forward.

"The French attacked twice during the day on 19 April. During the afternoon the assault began at 5.00 pm. The enemy were attempting to seize the right hand entrance but, thanks to Mahlke's gun and bold grenade throwers, they were thwarted. Due to the fact that the location of the machine gun was now known precisely, it came under heavy fire from rifle grenades, which wounded some of the crew. As a result, Mahlke brought the gun over to the left hand entrance, where it was taken over by Gefreiter Fuchs, because its previous commander had just been wounded. Both Krüger's and Fuchs's guns performed exceptionally well, being operated coolly and courageously. During the attack, because the asbestos covering on Krüger's gun had come loose, he had to change barrels during the actual attack. This was done with great rapidity despite all the fire. These two guns fired extremely well. There were almost no stoppages. Despite the fact that the battle lasted for three hours and the men were totally worn out, the French did not succeed in getting forward."

East of Reims, it will be recalled, the ridge line south of Moronvilliers was once more the scene of fierce battles throughout 18 April. During the morning, the French artillery brought down heavy fire all the way from the *Cornillet* to the *Pöhlberg*. The German 58th Infantry Division had no success in an attack aimed at the *Fichtelberg* then, later in the day, the French attacked the 214th and 58th Infantry Division sectors. On the *Keilberg* and *Pöhlberg* the defenders held on, but some ground was lost on the *Hochberg* and 30th Infantry Division was unable to dislodge the French from the eastern sector of Aubérive, which forced a tactical withdrawal at that place. The attempted counter-attacks launched by Group Prosnes on 19 April were generally unsuccessful, to the annoyance and disappointment of General Ludendorff.

General der Infanterie and First Quartermaster General Erich Ludendorff[*]

"In the meantime the attacks in Champagne had begun. They were directed at the high ground around Moronvilliers. One division failed and we lost the decisive heights. As the French attempted to descend the northern slopes they were engaged by our artillery and halted. Unfortunately, as I later discovered in discussions with the regimental commanders of one of the divisions involved, our *Eingreif* divisions were sent into action over hastily, so we failed to regain the high ground on 19 April. Its loss was painful, because it provided observation to the north far into our territory but, for the time being, we had to make the best of it and the climax of the April battles was over."

In truth the setback must have owed at least as much to the fact that the French had had time not only to improve their captured positions, but also to redeploy and regroup their artillery, whose intervention was decisive. It also proved to be beyond the capability of the German artillery to provide a preliminary bombardment of sufficient weight and there were subsequently suggestions that a surprise pre-dawn attack might have enjoyed greater success. That is of course mere speculation and it glosses over the extreme difficulty experienced by the *Eingreif* troops as they moved forward onto their start lines. Elsewhere, the French moved to occupy the evacuated ground around Vailly and Celles and pressed hard against Fort de la Malmaison.

Along the Aisne there were numerous probing attacks against the Chemin des Dames. In most places these were beaten off, but 16th Reserve Division was forced out of the ruins of the Cerny sugar refinery. The French, however, were driven off relatively easily by elements of 2nd and 5th Guards Infantry Divisions as they attempted to storm the *Winterberg* [Plateau de Californie], northwest of Craonne. The regiment which carried the heaviest load on the *Winterberg* and which incurred total casualties of no fewer than nine officers and 1,000 other ranks during their tour of duty there was Grenadier Guard Regiment 3, the so-called Elisabeth Regiment.[5] The morning of 18 April passed off fairly peacefully, though squalls of snow made observation difficult then, towards 5.00 pm, French attacks were beaten off all along the divisional sector. It was a different matter the following afternoon when, after a protracted period of drum fire, there was a partial break in near Hurtebise Farm and the Guards' right flank was threatened.

Vizefeldwebel Bertram 11th Company Grenadier Guard Regiment 3[6]

"Suddenly a shout went up, 'The French are attacking. Everybody out!' Leutnant Reif was first off the mark. Never have I seen the irrepressible Unteroffizier Räbiger in such high spirits. His calmness and sense of humour quickly spread to everyone else. There were the French coming towards us, struggling hard to negotiate the ploughed up and softened sticky clay soil. There then followed a classic infantry defence; a more thorough one is hard to imagine. The leading elements certainly never returned. The attack bled to death between the first and second line of the *Winterberg* trench system. Leutnant Reif, Unteroffizier Räbiger and Unteroffizier Plöthner were the heroes of the day."

There was also hard fighting for the regimental left flank positions, located at the eastern end of the *Winterberg*, more or less due north of Craonne. Here the front line trench, the so-called *Hoeder Linie*, ran parallel to and immediately south of the Chemin des Dames. The second trench of the First Position, the *Williard Linie*, also paralleled the Chemin des Dames, but slightly to the north of it, cutting straight through the *Winterberg* from east to west. Following drum fire that lasted all day and wrought havoc with both positions and trench garrison, a French assault took part of the *Williard Linie*, which was then the scene of a vicious close quarter battle until Grenadier Guard Regiment 3 wrested it back and held it once more. It was a small victory, but of decisive importance.

Leutnant Dannemeyer 8th Company Grenadier Guard Regiment 3[7]

"My platoon, which was already somewhat under strength, was allocated the left hand sector. Leutnant Böhm was deployed in the right hand company sector.

Two mined dugouts, each with two entrances, were at my disposal. The two dugouts were about fifty to sixty metres apart. From the early hours, harassing fire began to come down, increasing in weight constantly and swelling to drum fire. It was barely possible to maintain sentries at the dugout entrances and out of the question in the trenches themselves. I already had two wounded men on my hands and it was quite impossible to maintain a link with the dugout on the left. The trench outside was completely flattened then, of all appalling luck, the left hand entrance was collapsed completely, so there was only one entrance available. We gathered on the steps, ready to rush out at any moment when the artillery fire lifted. Then, unfortunately, the final exit was also destroyed and we attempted to dig it out. Whilst this work was going on, I had the impression that the enemy barrage had been lifted further to the rear. The moment had arrived when we needed to be manning the trench. We worked feverishly to clear the way. At long last we managed it. Together with my twelve men I raced up. It was not before time. We had hardly made it into the trench before French hand grenades were being thrown over the parapet and into it.

"That confirmed to me that the French, skilfully exploiting their artillery fire, had made use of a communication trench eighty metres to the left of our position to force their way into the *Williard Linie*, were already rolling it up and had overrun the left hand dugout containing the other two sections of my platoon. I had to barricade the trench at once to prevent the enemy from rolling it up further. I then directed two men to act as grenade throwers and a further four to keep them supplied [with grenades]. The remainder lay on the remains of the parapet, rifles at the ready. With excellent fields of fire half left they were able to bring effective flanking fire to bear on the enemy in the communication trench. Our heavy machine gun did the same to great effect. All these actions had to take place faster than the time taken to write about them, because it must be borne in mind that the French were not sitting on their hands. Their grenades were already falling in the trench and causing casualties.

"We were, however, well aware of our responsibilities. If the French got established in the *Williard Linie*, that amounted to the capture of the *Winterberg*, because then there would be observation over the entire rear area. I had already made that crystal clear to my men that very morning. They were all aware what was at stake. It was our task not only to stop the enemy but also to eject them once more from the *Williard Linie*. Meanwhile my grenade throwers were going about their work calmly and systematically. In particular we soon realised that my range estimator, Riemenschneider, who could throw thirty to forty metres, was causing the French assault troop heavy casualties. One very unpleasant feature was a French aircraft, flying above us at twenty metres and dropping small bombs. Because of the noise of battle we did not realise at first where they were coming from. The sound of its engine could not be heard above the racket. Once it had delivered its load, it flew off.

"I could see that the flanking fire of my men, together with that the of the machine gun, was increasingly causing French movement along the communication trench to stutter. My grenade team was also apparently operating successfully, because the French assault group was gradually giving ground. It was time for me to launch a counter-stroke, despite the fact that because of casualties I was down to eight men. However, only a few determined men are needed in order to roll up a trench. So as to make the counter-stroke effective, it was essential to get the reserve *Franzers*[8] located on the dip slope to launch a frontal attack simultaneously. I tried to bring this about by waving to them, but could not make myself understood. At that moment a very good idea occurred to me. My range estimator had to blow the signal to charge with all his might. This was a very unusual thing in trench warfare, but the effect was fantastic. The *Franzers* leapt up over the parapet with bayonets fixed and counter-attacked. We were filled with a feeling of superiority and were encouraged to be almost reckless in our behaviour. We leapt up, raced over to the trench and fired down into it. Unfortunately this brought tragedy, in that not only my estimator, Riemenschneider, but also two other men were killed.

"The recaptured trench was a terrible sight. Dead and wounded Frenchmen lay there in it, almost touching. It was an indication of how effective my grenade throwers had been. My greatest concern now was to establish exactly what had happened to the men in my left hand dugout. I rushed over and found that both entrances had been collapsed. The survivors had just cleared a small route out of one of them and came to meet me. They were in a state I shall never forget. There were dead and wounded lying on the steps. The survivors had a crazed look and some had had their clothing blown off. Only one man escaped totally unscathed. He explained to me that artillery fire had collapsed both entrances but no sooner had his comrades partially cleared one of them than Frenchmen in the trench above had thrown grenades into the dugout. Every man on the steps was killed or wounded. He had saved himself only because he had crawled into the furthest corner of the dugout, laid flat on the ground and covered himself with damp blankets. That way he avoided the concussion and the ensuing clouds of gas."

The pronounced salient gained by the French on 16 April in the Hurtebise Farm sector was a particular problem. 1st Battalion Footguard Regiment 1, part of the *Eingreif* force and reinforced by a company of Infantry Regiment 20, 5th Guards Infantry Division (originally placed there for flank protection purposes) was deployed forward to the eastern flank of 19th Reserve Division in order to prevent further French progress to the north.

The Infantry Regiment 20 men performed extremely well, so much so that the regimental commander received this letter the following week.

"1ˢᵗ Battalion
Footguard Regiment 126 April 1917

On the 17ᵗʰ of his month the 1ˢᵗ Battalion was deployed to the former sector of
Reserve Infantry Regiment 73 south of Vauclerc. The only friendly forces
encountered as the battalion advanced to contact with the enemy was 9ᵗʰ
Company Infantry Regiment Graf Tauentzien (20), which was occupying the
northern slope of Point 156.5 northeast of Hurtebise.

A brief situational orientation revealed that the courageous action of this
company had prevented a French breakthrough in the direction of Vauclerc.
Their resolute performance had inflicted heavy casualties on the enemy and had
halted all forward movement so firmly that the enemy dared not risk pressing
on into the trackless, densely wooded area.

The performance of the company was exemplary and I regard it as my duty
formally to report the fact.

von Stephani
Major and Battalion Commander"[9]

The same day there was a change in command arrangements. Group Sissone,
previously commanded by XV Bavarian Reserve Corps, was taken over by General
Kommando z.b.V. 65 under Generalleutnant Graf von Schmettow.[10]

20 April saw further action at Cerny as a counter-attack mounted by Reserve
Infantry Regiment 68 and Infantry Regiment 92 of 16ᵗʰ Reserve Division and 20ᵗʰ
Infantry Division respectively, took possession of the ruined sugar refinery once more.
Elsewhere the day was marked by further French local attacks, with emphasis on the
area to the north of Braye, the *Winterberg* and to the west of Juvincourt. There were
also attempts by the French to improve their positions near Moronvilliers and Brimont.
Vast amounts of mainly field artillery ammunition were expended but they produced
little in the way of success. One of the reasons for the easing up of the overall weight
of fire was a realisation by the French High Command that stocks of heavy shells were
being expended at an unsustainable rate.

General Micheler, commanding the French Reserve Army Group and a man who
had always been sceptical about the viability of the Aisne/Champagne battle, sent a
signal to his army commanders as early as 21 April concerning the quantity of shells
available for the period 22-25 April. 'The allocations made available by the *général en
chef* have been reduced drastically. It is essential to reduce consumption to the absolute
minimum.' Then, on 23 April, by which time he was already scheming against Nivelle,
he followed this up with an order suspending all firing by super heavy artillery until
further notice.[11] Of course shells were by then being stockpiled for a further general
assault at the end of the month, but it is difficult not to draw the conclusion that
Micheler's lack of faith in the entire offensive was at least to some extent beginning to

influence his military judgement and decisions. The pattern of activity involving limited local thrusts then continued for several days. Additional attacks were mounted near Hurtebise Farm and Cerny, with a sharp action contested near the tunnels east of Hurtebise Farm on 24 April, but none of them led to any significant change in the overall situation. Having been involved in heavy fighting for several days, 5th Guards Infantry Division was in urgent need of relief and 2nd Guards Infantry Division, comprising Grenadier Guard Regiments 1, 2 and 4, were ordered forward. The final three kilometres of the march between Bouconville and the front line were especially difficult.

Gefreiter Barget 1st Company Grenadier Guard Regiment 1[12]

"The entire length of the Chemin des Dames ridge to our front was lit by illuminating flares and the flashes of shells exploding. The bursting of massive shells, interspersed with *Ratsch-Bumms* [whizz-bangs], split the night. Some fell at a distance, others closer, awakening the sixth sense of the old campaigner and making him aware once again of the language of the major battlefront ... The [route] became disgusting with corpses lining the road, virtually side by side! Carefully we squelched past them, lifting our feet over their outstretched limbs. Harnesses still hung in disorder on dismembered dead horses. Wheels, half wagons and limbers lay strewn about ... We passed a giant shell hole which filled the whole road. Three quarters full of water, it contained dead horses, still in harness ... A duckboard track which moved and shook led off into a wood ... it was not the place for a comfortable stroll, because it attracted French artillery fire, called down whenever it was in use. Yet woe betide any poor *Feldgrau* who attempted to leave it; a treacherous bog lay in wait. It was bottomless, slowly sucking men down and the chances of rescue were slight.

"The wood seemed to amplify every detonation; broken branches and uprooted trees lay around in one great mass. With stretched nerves we continued along the duckboards, listening hard for where the next shell would land ... if only we knew how far we still had to go! Two men pushed past, carrying a wounded man in a groundsheet. 'Hallo comrade, how far to the front?' 'You're nearly there', they grunted and pushed on. The duckboard track was no place for a chat. Suddenly, out of the darkness of the night, came a salvo of shells so close overhead that we could almost feel the air pressure of them. Four or five exploded all round us. We were splattered with filth, branches flew in all directions and a head-sized clod of earth whizzed past us. Nobody stood around. Ducking low, we pushed on ... We saw a flash of light through the darkness. It was what we were aiming for. It was a huge hole driven far into the hillside: the *Kaisertreu Tunnel*. In we went. Lying along the sides, wrapped in their greatcoats, were the sleeping forms of our *Feldgrau* comrades of Footguard Regiment 3. They had done their duty here forward and were sleeping the sleep of the dead as they awaited relief."

Almost at once the Footguards began to fall back but the relief, a time of considerable vulnerability to defending troops, was not to allowed to proceed smoothly and undisturbed. In the midst of the complex redeployment and hand over formalities, the area was once more subject to a determined French assault.

Leutnant Deesler Machine Gun Company 3rd Battalion Footguard Regiment 3[13]

"We were to be relieved on 24 April. The French must have got wind of the relief because, at 5.30 am, they attacked. Some of our men had already withdrawn and some were still in the tunnel, which was jam packed. The first of the wounded to arrive there were from the Alexanders [Grenadier Guard Regiment 1, 2nd Guards Infantry Division], who had only just arrived on the position and were in a somewhat confused state. Reserve Leutnant Roepking and I were the only officers of the regiment still present. Leutnant Roepking set about getting the interior of the tunnel organised and ensuring the supply of ammunition. I had total responsibility for the trenches outside. The situation was extremely serious. It was still dark and the French attempted to outflank us to the left [east]. The right hand machine gun could not bring much fire to bear, due to a poor field of fire. This placed an even greater load on the three by the left hand entrance. Twice changes in the situation forced a redeployment of the guns. Because fairly large numbers of the French attacked frontally, I went and occupied a shell hole forward of the left hand communication trench and threw stick and egg-shaped grenades up to eighty [*sic.*][14] metres.

"When I spotted the enemy moving back in bounds, I returned to the trenches and brought down flanking fire to the right, using the rifle of Unteroffizier Neunzig, whom I had despatched to fetch water and ammunition. Unteroffizier Krüger was wounded right at the start of the action and the courageous Fusilier Dänner fell, mortally wounded through the lung.[15] For a time I operated the grenade launcher and kept a general grip of everything from the right to the left flank. One particular problem was the way the Alexanders were deployed. The main contribution to the failure of the attack was that of the machine guns. When the attack was finally beaten off, I was able to place the relieving machine guns of the Alexanders in position. Together with the remainder of men who were due to be relieved, I then returned to the *Kaisertreu Tunnel* and reported in to my company commander."

Meanwhile, despite the plethora of local actions, intelligence indicators began to accumulate that a major renewal of the French offensive on a scale similar to 16 April was feasible, but unlikely in the short term. Analysis of prisoner interrogation reports confirmed the impression. On 21 April Army Group German Crown Prince reported to OHL that, of the sixty eight assault divisions known to have been massed for the offensive, thirty eight had been in action, six of the original assault divisions had been

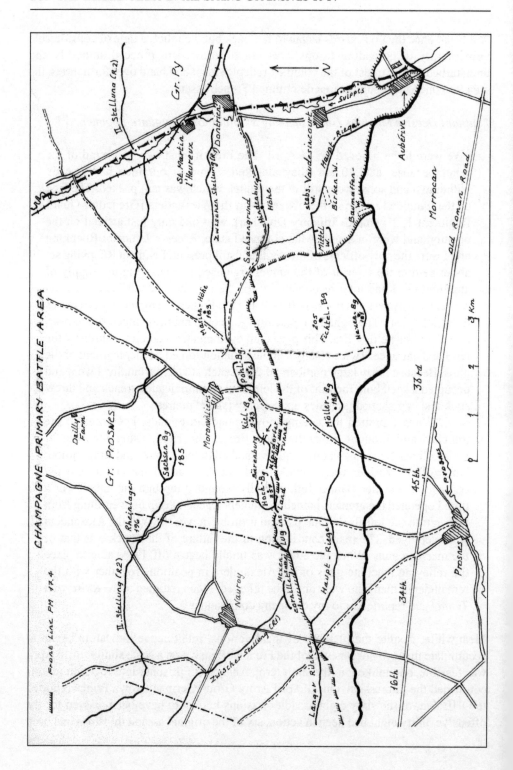

relieved by fresh troops and that a further fourteen, according to French prisoners, were in need of relief.[16] However, even if another assault on a total frontage of forty five kilometres could be ruled out, it was also evident that smaller operations on narrow fronts were a distinct possibility. In an attempt to forestall such a policy, Army Group German Crown Prince issued orders that all points along the battlefront that could be used as jumping off points for this type of attack were to be captured. In addition, First Army was still faced with the task of recapturing the *Artillerie-Schutzstellung* between Guignicourt and Juvincourt and the heights from *Langer Rücken* to the *Pöhlberg* still needed to be taken from, or at least denied to, the French. Vigorous action was taken to enable both First and Seventh Armies to relieve fought out divisions and additional manpower was allocated, such that the armies had five and seven spare divisions under command to act as reserves or *Eingreif* formations.

Throughout these difficult days, pressure was building up on Nivelle, who could see that his plans were unravelling day after day and, with them, his own credibility, as the government, the French people and his own soldiers lost faith in his ability to deliver on his promises. He was still unwilling to admit that he was presiding over a major failure, so there was nothing for it but for a continuation along the road already travelled. Orders were issued for a resumption of the attacks at Moronvilliers, Brimont, astride the Aisne, and the full length of the Chemin des Dames. It was accepted that the timetable had been thrown out by German counter-action, but that breakthrough was still possible to contemplate. Planning went ahead for a resumption of the main offensive at the beginning of May, with artillery preparation commencing two to three days before that.

Although this timetable was generally adhered to, Seventh Army, despite being on the highest state of alert, was not subject to infantry attack. From 4.00 am 30 April there was an increase in the weight of fire from Vauxaillon to Lassaux then all along the Chemin des Dames as far as Cerny, which was hit especially hard. There were also several sustained concentrations of fire at Hurtebise Farm, Craonne and Juvincourt. However, careful observation of the French positions and approach routes made it clear during the morning that there was no need for the continuing state of alert and it was reduced. The situation was quite different on the Champagne front and Fourth Army was attacked in some strength east of Reims.

The weather was fine but clouds of powder smoke cloaked the German positions throughout the morning of 30 April. The air was full of shells and the hills of Champagne echoed to the sounds of countless thousands of explosions. All the German batteries north of the *Cornillet - Pöhlberg* ridge were drenched with gas then, that afternoon, six fresh divisions launched forward. The German 14th Reserve Division opposite the French right flank held the attack in the forward battle zone, then threw it back and the same happened in the sector of the 29th Infantry Division.

2nd Battalion Infantry Regiment 112, 29th Infantry Division, having been in regimental reserve initially, was placed in the front line south of Beine on 21 April. There then followed several days of shelling etc then came the long expected attack.

Hauptmann Söding 2nd Battalion Infantry Regiment 112[17]

"During the afternoon of 29 April the bombardment of the position increased to such an extent that it was certain that we could expect to be attacked that evening. Reports from the front line confirmed that enemy assault troops were preparing for action. By means of light signals we were able to arrange for destructive fire to be brought down incredibly quickly on the trenches that were full of enemy. This was done so effectively that those opposite lost the will to attack that day. The following morning, our gallant artillery brought down defensive fire that wrecked every enemy attempt to attack. That night a second battalion staff arrived. It was due to relieve us the coming evening, but this meant that we were uncomfortably cramped in the dugout. We still had no idea how valuable this increase in our strength was to be later.

"From 10.00 am, the enemy artillery resumed its destructive concert, its melody soon rising to drum fire. The so-called *Bataillonsgraben* [Battalion Trench] ran past the battalion dugout and two sentries were posted nearby. When, at about 11.00 am, I went to check the sentries, I found them lying in a pool of their own blood and saw a line of French infantrymen to our front and in the trench, a mere thirty paces away. I later discovered that after a sudden lifting of their artillery fire the enemy had rushed the strong points, only to be beaten back with serious casualties after hand to hand fighting.[18] However, strong parties – later said by prisoners to have been two companies – thrust between the strong points and towards battalion headquarters.

"Like lightning the garrison of the dugout was alerted and rushed out. Suddenly a thunderous roar came from the staircase. Had the enemy already reached the command post and dropped a charge in? God be praised, no! It later transpired that when my poor batman was rushing out, he caught the firing cord of a hand grenade on his belt on a nail. [The subsequent explosion] blew him to pieces. Everyone who was fit and able scrambled over him, came up and engaged the enemy at point blank range with rifle and machine gun fire. They arrived in the nick of time. Only a small group of us was available, but everyone took up post: commanders, adjutants, orderly officers, artillery liaison officer, batmen, runners, cooks and the remainder of the sentries and, although greatly outnumbered, all fought with weapons and hand grenades against the enemy.

"By this time runners who had stormed along the trench were already returning with a captured machine gun and eight prisoners whom they had discovered in a dugout. There was a quick signal and all the blue jackets rushed back through their own artillery fire to the rear where their main defensive line was manned. This first visible success caused doubled the confidence of the brave garrison. In addition to their normal equipment the enemy had large quantities of rifle grenades with them and they tried to force us back by firing showers of them at us. They also brought us under an unpleasant weight of fire from the rear, using machine guns which had previously pushed on past us. Massed enemy artillery fire cut us off from the rear and greatly hindered the move forward of reinforcements from the main position. Above our heads, several enemy aircraft circled, supporting the attackers with machine gun fire. The noise of battle was ear splitting.

"The determined conduct of the garrison meant that the enemy advance was not only brought to a halt, but also completely prevented from pressing further forward. Our heavy fire disguised our small numbers and, suddenly, after half an hour, we saw first a few, then several Frenchmen running back and taking cover in shell holes. Soon there was a general withdrawal and our riflemen had first class targets to aim at. Simultaneously, several assault groups from the reserve companies rushed forward from the main position then pushed on forcefully and daringly along the trenches using grenades. Soon the Frenchmen flooding to the rear, pursued by the fire of the brave garrison of the dugout, came under flanking fire from the strong points and suffered dreadful losses. Large numbers of them were killed by their own artillery,[19] which took aim at the retreating masses, so very few of the attackers could have reached their start line once more.

"Unfortunately our losses were also very bad. From the little band, six men were killed and one officer and twelve men were wounded, some of them seriously. The battlefield was a scene of complete chaos, but all members of the staff were filled with feelings of pride and satisfaction. With a light heart I was able to despatch a report to the rear, stating that the position had been held intact. That evening we were relieved and headed for a well deserved rest. It was the early morning of 1 May when we left the destruction of the battle zone and gradually made our way into the rear area. The spring sun shone down, the first green leaves were decorating the trees and the birds were singing. Nature had donned its wedding dress for us. We felt at peace inside and gave thanks to the Almighty, who had once more saved us from the greatest danger and granted us victory."

Leutnant Schloß 1st Machine Gun Company Infantry Regiment 142[20]

"Ever since the unsuccessful attack on 17 [April], the position had been kept under the heaviest possible fire and everyone was aware that the enemy would return once again. Everything was ready when, just before 2.00 pm 30 April the dance began again. Yet again the enemy had miscalculated badly. That day our infantry and the machine guns beat back the enemy who had attacked our sector in divisional strength. Our men had been subject to ceaseless very heavy bombardment then, on the eleventh day, they came under direct attack again – but did not yield a single metre of ground. Wherever they broke in, they were driven away again with hand grenades. We also had a terrible effect that day.

Cut down like cornstalks before the scythe, the attacking waves went down to our fire. Ever more waves stormed forward and were cut down in their turn. Off to the left a gun was put out of action early in the battle by a direct hit, but part of its crew pushed through the heavy artillery barrage to bring valuable ammunition forward, whilst the remainder carried hand grenades to their fighting comrades and helped their hard pressed comrades by throwing grenades and forcing the enemy back to their start lines."

The regimental historian was later full of praise for Schloß. 'Several of the machine guns were destroyed by the drum fire', he wrote, 'the others were outstanding, especially Gun *'König'* [King], under the direct control of Leutnant Schloß, which brought down enfilade fire on the enemy who were attacking the *Hindenburg* Strong point.'[21] Some progress was made north of the *Hochberg*, but counterstrokes, first by Infantry Regiment 135 and then by elements of Leib Grenadier Regiment 8, 5th Infantry Division and Infantry Regiment 370 of 33rd Infantry and 10th Ersatz Divisions respectively, against the line *Hexensattel - Lug ins Land* quickly restored the situation. A bold and skilfully executed night operation by 33rd Infantry Division was launched at 10.00 pm. Infantry Regiment 135, having fought its way forward using mainly hand grenades, captured fifteen prisoners, together with a great deal of other materiel.[22]

The following morning saw two companies of Infantry Regiment 370 under command of the support battalion of Leib Grenadier Regiment 8 begin the assault on the northern slopes of the *Hochberg*. This was far from straightforward. The area was under constant heavy French fire, so the attackers had to advance with shrapnel bursting overhead and shells throwing up pillars of dirt and dust all the way. The crest itself was disputed. Having been thrown back, the French recaptured it at 3.00 pm, but were driven off, this time decisively, at 4.00 pm. Reserve Leutnant Ziegenfuß, having distinguished himself, was killed at this point and other casualties were high.[23] Within the first thirty six hours of their commitment, Infantry Regiment 370 lost twenty six men killed and a further sixty six wounded.[24]

The latest thrust did see the French capturing the northern side of the *Keilberg*, but by means of deploying what remained of the local reserves, they were pushed right back off the *Pöhlberg* and made no impression whatsoever on the positions further east towards Vaudesincourt.

Offizierstellvertreter Kägeler 7th Company Infantry Regiment 24[25]

"My platoon was in forward position near the aid post when it received the order to counter-attack. Moving through the 3rd Battalion sector, we arrived at the 2nd Company sector where we came across a mixture of men from 2nd and 3rd Companies. I enquired of Reserve Leutnant Tietze what the situation was and he replied, 'The lost position must be recaptured'. All around were shot up stands of fir trees, so it was impossible to know where the French were. I replied,

'Not without sending a patrol forward first, however'. Leutnant Tietze asked, 'Will you carry out the patrol?' - 'Yes, if no one else is available.' I set off with Unteroffizire Wiese. It was a very strange patrol, conducted in broad daylight. We came under fire from the machine guns of Infantry Regiment 396, but managed to identify ourselves by waving. We went on further through the empty trenches.

"There was not a single shot from the enemy. After 200 metres we came across a machine gunner by a machine gun firing position. It was a man from 1st Company, in his death throes with a fractured skull. We quickly grabbed the ammunition and the gun and hurried back, feeling that an attack here would be successful. Accompanied by all the available manpower we headed forward once more. I took my platoon along the trench to the place where the machine gun had been. As we advanced in to the next traverse we came across a large group of Frenchmen. We were only two paces apart. All I can remember is talking to a German speaking Frenchmen and demanding his surrender. As far as I could see the others were very drunk. Whilst the discussion was going on, I had my platoon deploy out to the right, with the intention of capturing the Frenchmen. All of a sudden firing began from all directions and I met my fate. Seriously wounded, I spun round and went a few steps before collapsing. Despite being seriously wounded I came to and made my own way back to the aid post about 11.00 am. From there I was transported to the rear as a hopeless case."

In fact, though his war was over, Kägeler survived and his initiative enabled his men to occupy and defend the lost trench. Elsewhere a desperate attempt was made by the very last reserves of Infantry Regiment 24, 6th Infantry Division, which, after several days of intense fighting amounted to a mere fifty eight men of the combined 5th and 8th Companies, to retake the *Keilberg*. There was time to arrange some signals with the supporting artillery, then the small group launched forward from the R2 line. French barrage fire was hammering down on the approaches to the *Keilberg* and it seemed that it would be impossible to penetrate it. However, widely spread out, the advance resumed and, as if by a miracle, the French fire ceased and they were soon all through, collecting up additional manpower in the shape of members of the Divisional Recruit Company who were manning some trenches.

Deploying his force into two attacking waves, the commander waved his stick and fire support came crashing down on the French who could be clearly seen digging in on the *Keilberg*, one lucky shell sending a machine gun spinning in to the air. The attack was pressed and the French were forced to pull back. However it proved to be impossible to eject them from the crest line so, when Infantry Regiment 369, 10th Ersatz Division, arrived that night to relieve them, they had to take up unfavourable positions on the partially recaptured northern slopes. Once again a huge French assault backed up by the expenditure of vast quantities of shells had failed; a weak attempt to renew the attack that same evening achieving nothing either. There followed a period of relative calm on this front, thought the battle continued elsewhere.

Relief, however, came too late for many men of Infantry Regiment 64. For a complete week, the focus of much of their defensive duties had been centred and focussed on the *Kipsdorf Tunnel* on the western slope of the *Keilberg*. It was an all too familiar story. The French, having recognised the importance of the various underground mined out features, had brought up large quantities of heavy howitzers, of the type used to pound Fort Douaumont at Verdun the previous year. Directed by aerial observers, these giant shells eventually smashed through the overhead cover, wrecking air shafts and blocking entrances. With a large number of men cut off in the tunnel, the defence was sufficiently weakened for the French to succeed in pressing home their attacks and securing the area finally on 29 April. The remaining units of Infantry Regiment 64 then effectively dashed themselves to pieces during the next forty eight hours in a hopeless attempt to retake the lost ground and bring succour to the men suffering in the blackness of the *Kipsdorf Tunnel*.

Reserve Leutnant Fischer 6th Company Infantry Regiment 64[26]

"The French attacks of 29 and 30 April had been successful and the *Kipsdorf Tunnel* was lost. Both tunnel entrances had been collapsed by heavy artillery to such an extent that they were effectively unusable. French soldiers were posted at the entrances, ready to shoot down any man who managed to force his way out through the tangle of wrecked wooden supports, wire and piles of earth. Despite this, two men - Röthling and Fischer - did manage to crawl out of an entrance and escape unscathed. It was their report which led on 1 May to the mounting of counter-strokes. It was all in vain. The tunnel remained lost and the garrison, almost all wounded or sick with gas poisoning, were forced to surrender."

In fact, by the time the situation at the tunnel was completely clarified, Infantry Regiment 64 was simply too weak to mount another attack. However, it along with the other regiments of 6th Division was due to be relieved during the night 1/2 May and elements of Infantry Regiment 371 were already on hand for that purpose. Barely feasible though the undertaking would be, it was decided that a final attempt was to be made by these fresh troops to retake the tunnel. Whilst its 1st Battalion remained back in reserve, 2nd Battalion was deployed forward to reinforce the weak defence of the cratered northern approaches to the *Bärenburg* and *Keilberg*, losing numerous casualties, including its commander, Hauptmann Nichterlein, who was buried alive and had to be evacuated, badly injured. Responsibility for the actual attack devolved on 3rd Company. Orders were issued that morning to attempt to rescue the two trapped companies of Infantry Regiment 64 and to capture the *Bärenberg*.

Only the desperate situation could possibly have justified the operation. There was barely time for the companies to move into position for a start time of 4.00 pm and none at all for reconnaissance. Only the sketchiest arrangements could be made with the artillery and the preparatory fire, when it eventually came down, was totally inadequate, serving only to alert the French, who by now were well dug in on the heights and bringing down torrents of defensive fire. Nevertheless, the gallant attempt was made. The Infantry Regiment 371 men moved forward over Hill 200 to the north of the *Bärenburg*, but there they were hit by such a storm of fire that they could not even advance as far as the German front line and had to take cover as best they could in the craters that covered the hilltop. Even to get this forlorn hope that far forward had cost a large number of casualties, including all three company commanders; then the following night 1st Battalion in its reserve position was hit by a heavy concentration of gun fire, one direct hit by a shell killing its commander, Hauptmann Meyer and the two other officers of his staff. It was an inauspicious start to a long tour of duty at one of the main foci of the battle.[27]

On the Aisne front, concentrated bombardment of Cerny, Hurtebise Farm and on the *Winterberg* left little doubt as to where the next blows were going to fall, so the defence was redeployed accordingly. This was far from straightforward. To the north of the Chemin des Dames it was difficult to arrange defence in depth, whilst the Ailette Valley was kept under such intense artillery fire that it became almost impassable. Nevertheless, an attack during the evening of 3 May between Fort de la Malmaison and Braye was held successfully by 44th and 45th Reserve Divisions. Artillery fire, much of it directed from the air, had been coming down throughout the afternoon. The German artillery replied and the carrying parties of the forward regiments suffered heavily as a result. An infantry attack then took place at about 8.00 pm and immediately broke into the trenches of 1st Battalion Reserve Infantry Regiment 208, 44th Reserve Division which was the left forward unit of the division. About two hundred metres of trench was then rolled up in an easterly direction, which took it across the inter-divisional boundary and into the forward trench of 1st Battalion Reserve Infantry Regiment 212, the right forward formation of 45th Reserve Division. An immediate counter-stroke launched from the support trench of Reserve Infantry Regiment 212 regained the lost ground and caused the French attackers severe casualties.

Leutnant Ingelbach 1st Company Reserve Infantry Regiment 212[28]

"During 3 May 1917 the positions of 45th and 44th Reserve Divisions lay under heavy drum fire, which had in fact begun in the early hours of 1 May, but reached a peak of intensity at the fork in the road Chevregny-Braye during the evening of 3 May.[29] 1st Company Reserve Infantry Regiment 212, deployed out on the regimental right flank, had the task of defending this fork in the road that marked the junction with 44th Reserve Division. Together with my platoon I was on the extreme right of the company, acting as the Junction Point reserve.

Protected by the heavy drum fire and under cover of the ploughed up ground and broken terrain, the French, in about two company strength [probably about 300 men], had smashed into the neighbouring Reserve Infantry Regiment 208 half battalion sector. From there they had rolled up about one hundred metres of the company front line. I established this fact when I, concerned about the situation as it went dark, rushed forward, accompanied by my runner Krause and was greeted by French light machine gun fire.

"At once I reported the facts to my company commander, Leutnant Focke, then was ordered to launch an immediate counter-stroke. Because my 'magnificent' platoon numbered in addition to myself only two unteroffiziers, ten men and a machine gun, a frontal attack was out of the question. Leaving Unteroffizier Jahnke and five others behind, together with the machine gun, I took only Unteroffizier Kreß, my two runners and three others with me. Loaded down with hand grenades we leapt half left from crater to crater; the French rifle fire indicating exactly how far the enemy had rolled up our front line. We arrived at an unoccupied section of our forward trench and made contact with our third platoon to the left. They had no idea that off to the right of them were Frenchmen who were busy preparing the trench for defence under the cover of darkness.

"I tasked the platoon commander of our third platoon with following us up and occupying the trench as we rolled it up. I then advanced with my six men against the enemy flank. My first grenade landed in a crater containing six Frenchmen, my second hit the previously mentioned light machine gun. Exploiting the ensuing confusion quickly we pushed onwards, working exclusively with grenades. Two men had the task of shooting down fleeing Frenchmen. Within ten minutes we had established a link with Reserve Infantry Regiment 208. To this regiment fell the task, temporarily under my command, of reoccupying this sector once more. It stretched about the width of two companies. The entire affair was achieved without spilling a drop of German blood. Numerous Frenchmen were killed and they left behind as prisoners one unwounded and several wounded men, together with the light machine gun and a load of other small arms. We resumed our old position and duties as Junction Point reserve, enjoying from about 2.00 am the white wine that our battalion commander, Oberleutnant Brandt, had sent forward. This successful and extremely lucky night action brought two comrades the immediate award of fourteen days' home leave"

Probing attacks against 14th Reserve Division north of Prunay were also held. French artillery fire of all calibres increased during the afternoon until prior to the launch of the attack uninterrupted fire fell for two hours against the two forward lines of Infantry Regiment 159, followed by several low level clashes.

Reserve Leutnant Schürmann 2nd Company Infantry Regiment 159[30]

"A sap led forward from the left flank of the regimental sector as far as the *Betrambarrikade*. Whenever attacks were launched to the left, the *Barrikade* was always also attacked because it threatened the French left flank. Leutnant Otte and a few of his men were defending it. During every attack they came under a hellish weight of artillery and mortar fire, added to which were any shells from our guns that dropped short. I was on duty on the K1 Line in rear of the *Barrikade*, which was also under extremely heavy fire by guns of all calibres. I had about five men with me and we took cover as best we could in miserable fox holes dug into the trench walls. There were no dugouts. I had good observation from my firestep over the ground to the front and the *Barrikade* itself. Suddenly white flares went up. Leutnant Otte called for defensive fire from the artillery and the French attacked.

"Together with my five men I ran forward along the sap, which in fact comprised nothing but shell holes. All soldiers are familiar with this business of rushing forward. We raced on blindly, stumbling, getting to our feet once more and continuing on. As soon as I reached the *Barrikade*, Leutnant Otte told me, with much satisfaction, 'The Frenchmen have been beaten off!' He was as calm as ever. On two other occasions that evening I hared forward to the *Barrikade* on seeing white flares; on the final occasion entirely on my own. Quite what I should have done had the French forced their way in, I cannot say. All I did know was that I simply could not leave Leutnant Otte and his men to struggle on alone. Later I heard the full story of the fight for the *Barrikade* from those who had fought for it. 'It was not so bad. After all we had a platoon in support behind us!' They were oblivious to the fact that this comprised no more than a few individuals.

"The company commander 2nd Company, Reserve Leutnant Bornemann, in whose sector the *Barrikade* was located, had no knowledge of its fate and, as was his wont, he decided to satisfy himself personally and retake the *Barrikade* if the French had established themselves within it. I was standing in the trench observing to the front when I heard a noise behind me. Reserve Leutnant Bornemann with an assault troop was storming forward, with Bornemann out in front. His face was marked by toughness and wild determination. They threw themselves down in the trench for a few moments to get their breath back. I exchanged few words with Bornemann, then he hurled himself forward, together with his men. Bornemann was later killed flying.[31] I was a platoon commander in his company and throughout the entire war I never met a calmer or braver officer than Bornemann. Leutnant Otte was also the very model of a calm, courageous, front line soldier. He was killed serving with the regiment during the final days of the war.[32]

"When I later moved to a position on the left flank of the company, I was joined by Gefreiter Cosanne, a calm and absolutely reliable man. Despite the heaviest fire, he joined me up on the fire step. Shells were landing to our front and rear and several landed very close to us in the trench itself. We leaned on the wall of the trench and stared to our front, a grenade in each hand. We should certainly have not been able to hold an enemy attack, but we would have done our duty. A shell landed, not two metres from me, hurling a small tree into the trench. The endless fire of the day had set my nerves on edge, despite the fact that I still looked calm and I said to Cosanne, 'Should we move a bit more to the right?' To this he replied, 'Well *Herr Leutnant*, they are firing there as well!' He was absolutely calm when he said it, just as though he was at home one evening, sitting on a bench outside his house. I was deeply impressed by him."

There was extremely heavy fighting on 4 and 5 May. The Ailette Valley was gassed continuously during the afternoon of 4 May and throughout the following night. Reserve Infantry Regiment 205, 44th Reserve Division, defending the area around Royère Farm, immediately south of Filain, found itself extremely hard pressed. The entire area was cloaked in gas, dust and smoke and all links to the rear, with the exception of one light signalling station, were broken. Sensing that an attack was imminent, its commander, Major Barack, as well as the other regimental commanders, sent an increasingly urgent series of message back to 87 Reserve Infantry Brigade: 'Drum fire on our position. Urgently request aerial observation and destructive fire.' This simply elicited from brigade, 'No concentrations observed'. A telephone line having been repaired at 9.35 am, Reserve Infantry Regiment 206 was able to pass a message, 'Very heavy drum fire on 208 and 205; also on left flank of 206' then, at 10.20 am, 1st Battalion Reserve Infantry Regiment 206 managed also to get a light signal message back. 'Enemy trenches full. Destructive fire.'[33]

Unfortunately these fragmentary messages left brigade with only a hazy overview of the situation and in any case the final one arrived too late to be of any use. At 10.15 am the French bombardment lifted and the front line trenches were simply overrun. Much the same happened in the second line, where the attackers were swarming over the various posts before the defenders had time to react. The supports from 2nd Battalion, located round Royère Farm itself, were just able to man their positions in time to put up a defence, but nothing could be done to prevent deep outflanking movements on either side. Desperate battles went on all day, but by nightfall the situation was more or less in crisis, Major Barack informing brigade at 8.45 pm, 'No reserves have arrived as yet. If they do not get here soon, it will be impossible to hold the gardener's hut and steep slope' [both in close proximity to the farm].

If that was not enough for 87 Reserve Infantry Brigade to deal with, Reserve Infantry Regiment 208, the left forward divisional formation, reported at the same time, 'Enemy established in the Third Line and on the crest line to the north ... The regiment has been virtually wiped out ... [signed von König]'. Luckily the previous day's efforts had temporarily exhausted the French and there were no more probing attacks during the night. At midnight a battalion and four assorted platoons did get forward to Reserve Infantry Regiment 205, but they were insufficient to do more than some limited clearance around the farm and had no chance of conducting counter attacks - either at 5.30 am, when all was still confusion or later, when at 8.35, Major Gaertner, the *KTK*, received a message from Reserve Infantry Regiment 205 stating, 'Division demands the recapture without fail of the first and second lines at midday'.

This was crying for the moon and Gaertner immediately replied, '1st and 3rd Battalions together muster a total of only one and half companies. The ordered attack will only be possible if the specialist sector assault group is made available. In any case the French are still in control of the 2nd Battalion sector and which is full of machine gun nests that provide enfilade fire over the entire rear area. Furthermore, there is another machine gun post behind our left flank which is also bringing down enfilade fire.' The attack was scrapped and the survivors were just able to hold further French attacks that afternoon and on into the evening. It had been a period of heroic defence. The crucial Royère Farm held - but only just. Elsewhere counter actions had limited success, though the French made no more significant advances. 2 Ersatz Brigade arrived that night to assume command of the sector and, after a brief period of reserve duty just behind the front, 44th Reserve Division was withdrawn from the battle, its remnants transported to Metz for a brief rest. The final word on Gaertner's performance came later from his regimental commander.

Major Barack Commander Reserve Infantry Regiment 205[34]

"In general there is plenty of talk about the appalling battles along the Chemin de Dames. Throughout the entire Army Group, however, the sole topic is the heroic defence of Royère Farm. Without Major Gaertner this would have been lost. In essence it was entirely thanks to his exemplary performance and bearing that the farmstead could be held. He is the Hero of the Day."

Further to the east on 3 May, drum fire came down for hours on end on the positions of 2nd Guards Division around Hurtebise Farm and those of Generalmajor Ziethen's 28th Reserve Division on the *Winterberg*, causing large numbers of casualties. When the attack came in that evening against Hurtebise Farm, Grenadier Guard Regiment 1 (Kaiser Franz) put in a quick counter-stroke against the French attackers and drove them out once more. Up on the *Winterberg* it was different story. The shelling had set on fire the entrance to the tunnel used by the defenders to house reserves forward and it was rendered impassable. Stored ammunition began to explode, all the ventilation shafts were blocked and the entire place was filled with poisonous fumes. The expression 'a living Hell' is a much overused cliché, but it is hard to think of any other way of describing the situation in the *Winterberg Tunnel*. A small group managed at once to get out and away despite the drumfire, but almost all of the remainder trapped inside and who were not killed on the spot, succumbed to suffocation and dehydration, or were driven mad and suicidal. Only a tiny handful was still alive when engineers dug back into the tunnel six days later. By then it had become the mass grave of two complete companies of Reserve Infantry Regiment 111. One of the survivors later described his shattering experience.

Musketier Karl Fißer 11th Company Reserve Infantry Regiment 111[35]

"It was 4 May 1917 … probably between 11.00 am and midday. We were not paying much attention to the artillery fire, because we were used to bombardments like this. Because 11th Company was back in reserve, I visited some friends then we went on further to a place near the radio room. While we were chatting and warming a cup of coffee over a tallow candle, something unbelievable happened. An appalling detonation hit us like a shock. What could have happened? Other detonations followed. We tried to get forward, but were met by clouds of black smoke and gas. Northern Exit 3 had been collapsed and Exit 4 was full of gas and smoke, We pulled back and began erecting a barricade from knapsacks and coats, We took off our jackets and added them to the heap but we were unable to halt the spread of these poisonous fumes.

"A heavy shell had scored a direct hit on the reserve ammunition that was stockpiled by the entrance. Subsequent detonations drove clouds of gas toward us; the ventilation shaft increasing the effect as it drew in air towards the rear … We built a sandbagged barricade in rear of the shaft in the hope that the gas would be drawn up it and we could be rescued. However, we went on hearing shells explode and it transpired later that the shaft was blocked up. We were cut off from the outside world and the air in the tunnel, which was higher here, was in any case of very poor quality … Time passed and breathing became difficult … We tried [and failed] to dig a ventilation shaft … We realised that the oxygen in the air had been almost used up; lights went out and matches only flickered. The heat was unbearable. We began to feel thirsty … we lost all hope [of rescue].

"Many were near physical and mental collapse. Lying on the ground, they were tortured by thirst and the great heat … Everyone was utterly depressed. It was dreadful … I could hear someone telling his rosary … I shall never forget the death of my comrades. One was calling for his wife, another for his parents and siblings. I, too, was emotionally shattered and I mentally took my leave of all I held dear. The struggle for life or death was slow and dreadful … Everyone was calling for water, but it was in vain. Death laughed at its harvest and Death stood guard on the barricade, so nobody could escape. How long we were trapped I cannot say; three or four days? … Dull shots rang out in the darkness of this tomb. Someone raved about rescue, others for water. It had become a place of final partings and death. One comrade lay on the ground next to me and croaked with a breaking voice for someone to load his pistol for him … I called back and felt my way over to him. He handed me a 08 pistol and, summoning the last of my strength, I cocked it and handed it back to him. There was a short pause, as though he was taking leave of all that was dear to him. There was a loud bang in this living tomb, then he gave out a death rattle - he had found release ...

"I thought that I too could soon find peace. I searched for and found the weapon. I said my farewells, placed the weapon against my heart - the barrel felt cold - and raised my right hand further. When I awoke I was flat on the floor. I had been prevented by a fainting fit from taking that last step ... Near madness, I searched for water, but the empty bottles mocked me. I managed to kneel, made a cup of my hands and drank my own urine ... I crawled on further, bumped unto a mound of sand and lay on it to cool my body a little. I also found a pocket torch and tried to switch it on. It took all my strength and then the light hurt my eyes, but what I saw were terrible scenes. My dead, naked comrades lay in cramped positions and with outstretched arms. I did not want to see any more and switched the torch off again ... and lost consciousness, for how long I do not know.

"I was still lying on my small heap then, though I did not trust my ears - perhaps Death was playing games with me - I heard words. Help! I did not know where it was coming from. I was still engulfed by darkness, but the sound was closer. I turned and lifted my head a little, something flashed in my eyes and I shut them. Could that be light? Was it rescue? I tried with the last of my strength to shout out then I heard them. 'Keep calm, comrade, we are on our way!' They leaned over me, my rescuers, and gave me water. Water! I could not believe it. Was I going to be saved? Once more they had to leave me, then they came and rescued me in a groundsheet. Cold air blew over me and then there was more water. The rescuers said. 'Today is the sixth day since the collapse!' Two other comrades were rescued with me ...

"The doctor told me that less than half a day longer and it would have been too late ... I was told that the interior of the tunnel was a tragic sight. All the other comrades had ended their misery by shooting themselves or cutting their arteries. There were just three of us left."

The disaster at the tunnel at 11.45 am 4 May, meant that most of 3rd Battalion Reserve Infantry Regiment 111 was out of the battle before the infantry assault even began, which left the right flank of the regiment dangerously exposed. However, they were not the only ones to suffer. The entire *Winterberg* had been under fire for seventy two hours and losses mounted throughout the regiment. Following a slight slackening of the bombardment during the night 3/4 May, the following morning from 10.00 am fire was intense once more. Every effort was made to obtain additional reinforcements; so the remnants 5th and 6th Companies Reserve Infantry Regiment 111 were ordered forward to thicken up the defences. Such was the weight of fire coming down that only four sections of 5th Company with three machine guns got on to the heights and there was no sign whatsoever of external reinforcements. The net result was that the right flank sub-units were far too weak to hold the French assault during the afternoon of 4 May, most of the *Winterberg* was lost and numerous defenders, most of them wounded, were captured.

Vizefeldwebel Henn 1st Company Reserve Infantry Regiment 111[36]

"At 4.00 pm on 4 May the French stormed our positions in overwhelming strength. Despite the fact that our comrades fought obstinately we were simply unequal to their superiority in numbers. We lost from our ranks a great many comrades killed and wounded, though six men were able to make their escape from the French along a subsidiary trench. The remainder, most of them wounded, went into captivity. The company commander, Reserve Leutnant Koch, who had participated in every battle the regiment had fought, was outstanding during the heavy fighting. But he, too, was overwhelmed and captured.

"A German shell that landed amongst us as we were being transported to the rear blew many comrades apart, most of them having been with the regiment since the start [of the war]. Leutnant Koch, in his comradely way, had led the company for almost three years with courage, energy, kindness and fairness. Now he had to accept his lot as a prisoner of the French. A French officer asked us if we had been willing to have gone on fighting like that for so long. We all agreed and added, 'right to the last man'. He called us mad men. The following day we were permitted to lay to rest in a mass grave all of our comrades who had died during the move to the rear. Sanitätsunteroffizier Mauer, 1st Company, conducted the burial. Honour their memory!"

There was another major thrust by no fewer than four French divisions against the sector from Berméricourt to Berry au Bac, but decisive counter-actions by 4th Infantry, Guards Ersatz and 54th Infantry Divisions, supported by enfilade artillery fire from Brimont, meant that French attackers never penetrated beyond the forward edge of the battle zone. Infantry Regiment 84, 54th Infantry Division was involved in a particularly hard fought battle for possession of Hill 100 near Pignicourt and one company of 1st Battalion was extremely lucky not share the fate of the remainder of the battalion.

Oberleutnant Klinkenberg Commander 2nd Company Infantry Regiment 84[37]

"Between 23 April and 3 May at night we deepened our trenches considerably and extended the dugouts. We had no casualties at all during those days because enemy artillery fire came down mainly in the Suippes Valley and Orainville Wood off to our left. Our actual trenches were barely affected at all. During the night 3/4 May, 1st Battalion was to have relieved 3rd Battalion, which was manning the front line. During the evening of 2 May, Reserve Leutnant

Jürgensen arrived on the 9th Company positions with an advance party comprising several section commanders. He informed me that 9th Company guides would report to 2nd Company at 10.00 pm 3 May. So, at 10.00 pm, we were ready to march off from our trench, having been relieved by a company of Reserve Infantry Regiment 27.

"However, the 9th Company guides did not appear. The other companies left for the front at about 11.00 pm. Because by 2.00 am the guides had still not turned up, a regimental order was issued postponing the relief for twenty four hours. The reason was that it was then too late, because the companies after relief had to be able to cross the Suippes Valley before it became light. We settled down as best we could in the *Franke-Werk* [a field fortification], thinking that we should be able to spend the day catching up with sleep. Things were to turn out differently! The heaviest fire imaginable came down during the early hours of 4 May on the front line, the *Hochwald* [High Wood] and the *Franke-Werk*. Evidently something was happening forward. There were repeated calls for defensive artillery fire, but the flares could only be seen dimly because of all the dense fumes. I learnt from the regimental command post that 1st, 3rd and 4th Companies had been overrun and that Hill 100 was threatened by the enemy.

"Simultaneously, I was ordered to move with my company immediately to Hill 134 and to report in to Hauptmann Hofmeister in *Hochwald*. By now it was about 9.00 am and *Hochwald* was under extremely heavy fire. We watched from the *Franke-Werk* how heavy shells shattered and uprooted the trees. That was where we were supposed to report; that would be a tricky little situation. I came to the conclusion that in these circumstances there would not be much left of my company. I discovered later that my opinion was shared by the gentlemen of the artillery who observed our advance through their tripod binoculars.

"We set off. The platoons were in single file with forty metre spacing. I and my runners were located in front of the centre platoon … We arrived at the *Hochwald* having suffered only three lightly wounded casualties. I should not have been surprised to get there with only three survivors! We had been miraculously lucky. In order to secure Hill 100, we occupied a trench to the left of *Hochwald* that was barely knee deep. To the right was deployed a composite company made up of the fourth [carrying party] platoons of each company. Our trenches offered hardly any cover from view, let alone protection from artillery fire, so we developed them at night. By day nobody could move. We were on the receiving end of a great deal of fire, including gas shells, every day. For six days we occupied these positions on full alert until we were relieved at 6.00 am 10 May by Infantry Regiment 187."

For the men of 3rd Battalion, who had only just moved back into support having been relieved, it was also an exhausting day as they were deployed to counter the French assault.

Reserve Leutnant von Lindelhof Commander 11th Company Infantry Regiment 84[38]

"[We had finally been relieved at 4.00am 4 May]. During our march to the rear, we were constantly subject to constant gas shelling, so we arrived at the *Franke-Stellung* worn out and demoralised. There we were issued with ammunition and iron rations and three sections of reinforcements were allocated to the company. I was just about to lie down on a rough wire netting bed when I was summoned by the regimental commander [Oberst Schultz]. I was swiftly briefed that the enemy had captured the front line and was ordered to lead the company forward to Hill 100, where I should be subordinated to the *KTK*, Hauptmann Hofmeister. We set off at once. My two runners were wounded by shell splinters. Towards midday we arrived at the *KTK*.

"I doubted the chances for success of a counter-attack; the enemy had had five to six hours to occupy the position and set up machine guns. In addition, the ground that we should have to cross was totally devoid of cover. The communications trenches had been flattened, so it would be impossible to launch a surprise attack. Taking a few men, I tried to move forward, but we were greeted by an enormous weight of machine gun fire and it was impossible to advance further. We should have to wait for darkness. "Hauptmann Hofmeister agreed to this. As soon as it began to go dark the enemy brought down such a bombardment and fired so much gas that for the time being we were stuck. About 10.00 pm the weight of fire eased somewhat and, with the aid of my energetic platoon commanders, I assembled the company, which had been scattered by all the firing. Repeatedly, we were subject to heavy concentrations of fire. All the gas and shelling had caused a considerable number of casualties.

"During our advance we suddenly came under heavy machine gun fire and had to take cover immediately. I found myself in a section of trench together with members of 12th Company.[39] I soon found the company commander, Leutnant Fasch. He had no contact to the left or right, so I extended his line to the right. We quickly linked up various craters, so we soon had a continuous position once more. To the left we established contact with 6th Company under Leutnant Saucke so, by the early hours of the morning, I was able to provide Hauptmann Hofmeister with a sketch that showed the line we had occupied. Day had barely dawned when a fresh attack, preceded by a bombardment, began. The machine guns were placed up on the rims of the craters and began to rattle out their grim music. Shortly before our line the French turned around and fled, only to return some hours later when a few tanks also put in an appearance. Leutnant Wamser was killed during this last attack. We were standing together in the trench when a rifle shot from the flank hit him in the heart and he died almost at once. Shouting, 'Ow!' he collapsed dead in my arms. He was a dear comrade, an excellent soldier, a man who knew no fear. Beloved by his men, they carried his body to the rear, despite all the heavy artillery fire ... several other comrades of 11th Company also found a grave up on Hill 100."

There was also another attempt at storming the *Cornillet* and *Hochberg* that day, but once more it failed - this despite the fact that it was quite clear that the French were now concentrating their artillery fire on ever narrower segments of the line. Fortunately for the defence, the fought out 5th and 6th Infantry Divisions had been relieved in the nick of time by 33rd Infantry and 10th Ersatz Divisions respectively, so the assault went in against fresh formations, albeit they contained units which had already suffered severe casualties on 1 May in an attempt to counter-attack the French held crest line. 10th Ersatz occupied the crucial *Pöhlberg - Keilberg* sector with Infantry Regiment 369 on the *Pöhlberg*, Infantry Regiment 370 in the centre between the hills and Infantry Regiment 371 responsible for the *Keilberg*. The assumption on the German side was that the French concept of operations was to tear out parts of the overall defensive positions and so threaten the entire length with collapse. So much for the theory; first the French infantry had to make a sustained impact on the defenders. On 4 May they largely failed to do so.

That said, there was great concern that French air superiority was leading directly to increased attrition of men and equipment. Infantry Regiment 369 reported that on one single day in early May, of the thirty five heavy guns and howitzers in support of Group Prosnes, no fewer than seventeen were knocked out by systematically directed heavy artillery fire and, most unusually, it went on to blame strikes within the German aircraft industry for the shortage of friendly aircraft.[40] Be that as it may, the nervous tension and physical strain of holding on in a crater field position under incessant aimed fire took a considerable toll on the defenders. Choking from the dust and smoke of countless shell bursts up on the crest line, the defenders were tortured with thirst and because every drop of liquid had to be carried forward during the hours of darkness, it was almost impossible to solve the problem, especially as the same applied to the carriage of rations, ammunition and defence stores.

On 5 May the attacks were concentrated between Braye and Brimont. Heavy fire came down from the early hours of the morning and, because it was a calm day with little or no wind, very soon the German positions were enveloped in dense clouds of smoke, gas and dust. Taking advantage of the consequent battlefield obscuration, there was a series of attacks on narrow fronts at 9.00 am. These developed into isolated battles that in some cases lasted all day. By evening the French were in possession of all of the *Winterberg*, the German defenders had been pushed back at Ailles and Hurtebise Farm and, to the north of Reims, 223rd Infantry Division lost part of its forward positions. The situation could have been much worse. Time and again effective counter-strokes were mounted by the *Eingreif* formations, every single one of which was in action at some point.

Elements of 1st Guards Infantry Division were deployed east of Cerny and around

Hurtebise Farm at that time, with Footguard Regiment 2 basing its defence on the *Drachenhöhle* [Caverne du Dragon] and associated underground stone quarries. That the French made no more progress in that area on 5 May was due in particular to the heroism of a member of 3ʳᵈ Machine Gun Company, Gefreiter Ptock, who had already distinguished himself in the battle between 21 and 28 April and had been awarded the Iron Cross 2ⁿᵈ Class. His company commander later described his actions.

Leutnant von Petersdorff 3ʳᵈ Machine Gun Company Footguard Regiment 2[41]

"5 May was a major day of battle. At 10.00 am, after hours of drum fire, the enemy launched forward in dense assault waves against our sector. All of our machine guns were buried or out of action for other reasons. Before our reserves had been able to exit the [*Drachen*] *Höhle* the French had already occupied all the exits and were throwing hand grenades down the shafts. The only reserve machine gun that was able at this most critical of moments not only to clear an exit, but also to halt the French who were swarming forward into the Ailette Valley and cause them severe casaulties, was that of Gefreiter Ptock. The French machine guns responded and fired at Ptock, but he, calm as ever amidst the hail of steel, changed his shot out barrel and fired box after box of ammunition until the French attack was halted and no further assault waves were following up.

"Suddenly a bullet hit his gun and knocked it out and he himself was wounded in the hand by a splinter. Coming to a quick decision, Ptock grabbed a rifle which was lying nearby and was about to fight his way out, weapon in hand, when, with his second rush, he found himself in a crater, together with a perfectly serviceable light machine gun and several boxes of ammunition. He immediately engaged the Frenchmen, who were advancing, bolt upright, in the open. The effect of this well aimed curtain of fire at close range was annihilating; it broke the impetus of the attack completely. Even those enemy detachments that were pressing forward from the Ailette Valley towards the Bove crest line faltered when they realised that their comrades were not following up. By then there was no going back. They scattered aimlessly and those who did not fall into our hands were captured in the neighbouring sector of Foot Guard Regiment 4.

"All those isolated Frenchmen caught in the desolate crater field who attempted to crawl back, were shot down by Ptock. He then turned his attention to the exits to the *Drachenhöhle* still occupied by the French and, in conjunction Leutnant Gehrholz, who led the mortar company boldly, swept the Frenchmen back. Our reserves were then able to exit the *Höhle* and launch a counter-stroke which drove the French back to their start line with heavy casualties Gefreiter Ptock played a leading role in the glory of this massive day of battle. After we had been relieved and were back in the *Bangertlager* he was feted by his comrades. His company commander gave up his camp bed for him and, until his wounds healed, he was excused all duties. A few days later, during a divisional parade before the Crown Prince, Ptock received the Iron Cross 1st Class from His Imperial Highness. He had been decorated twice in quick succession and thoroughly merited it."

Though the cost in casualties to the defence was very high that day, for the French army it was enormous. Almost unimaginable quantities of shells had been used, all fresh formations within range had been deployed and yet there was not the slightest sign of a breakthrough, not even where minor gains had been made. An effort on this scale was not repeated along the Aisne for months subsequently, but the ground holding divisions were subject to incessant, wearying artillery fire and from time to time minor operations took place. The loss of the *Winterberg* at the eastern extremity of the Chemin des Dames position was keenly felt. The first attempt to recapture it by formations of Group Liesse occurred as early as 6 May. A properly constituted counter-attack succeeded in reaching the flat summit, but then the French countered The operation degenerated into a confused close quarter struggle, with a somewhat inconclusive end. At its conclusion the flat plateau became No Man's Land dominated by the artillery of both sides, with the French holding the southern slopes whilst the Germans clung to the northern side.

On both 7 and 9 May there was further fighting on the *Winterberg*, though the overall situation remained unaltered. On 9 May repeated attacks near Ste. Marie Farm, located between La Neuville and Orainville, were beaten off completely. There was then a quiet period until 16 May when 211th Infantry Division and 33rd Reserve Division launched limited attacks designed to straighten and strengthen their positions to the northeast of Lassaux. Following a change of command of Group Prosnes, when III Corps, commanded by Generalleutnant Freiherr von Lüttwitz, relieved XIV Corps, the French army launched yet another attempt to seize and hold the entire crest line south of Moronvilliers on 20 May. There was a heavy bombardment lasting several hours then during the afternoon an infantry assault on a front from the *Cornillet* to the *Pöhlberg* was launched.

This critical sector had been taken over by the recently formed 242nd Infantry Division from Württemberg. Comprising two new regiments, Infantry Regiments 475 and 476, it was leavened by the presence of the experienced Infantry Regiment 127. Infantry Regiment 476 was responsible for the *Cornillet*, Infantry Regiment 475 for *Langer Rücken* and Infantry Regiment 127 for the always vulnerable *Hexensattel - Lug ins Land - Hochberg* sector. On 20 May a furious French attack preceded by an intense and lengthy bombardment by heavy and super heavy howitzers, led to the near total destruction of the tunnel network beneath Mont Cornillet. The casualties of Infantry Regiment 476 were extremely high and the position was lost.

"Field Hospital 25 May 1917

Dear Parents,

Now I am, thank heavens, in a position to tell you what happened to our regiment on the *Cornillet*. We arrived there on 15 May and occupied quarters in a real mine in the chalk hill, ten to seventeen metres underground. It comprised three long galleries and one transverse, linking passage. There were three entrances, together with air shafts and ventilation pipes. But what a state it was in! Piles of faeces lay all round the entrances, left by our predecessors who had been trapped by fire inside for weeks on end, Within it was all manner of rubbish, broken weapons and general detritus. There were twenty corpses in one side gallery, all poisoned by carbon monoxide and everywhere there was a superabundance of fleas and lice. 'Right lads', said our battalion commander, Major Wintterlin, 'The first job is to muck out!'[42] That is exactly what we did and things improved. However life was difficult. Day and night heavy fire, directed by circling aerial observers, crashed down on our hill. Food and ammunition had to be brought forward kilometres by our carrying parties, who always took casualties, because there was absolutely no cover until the entrances to the mined tunnels …

Up until 20 May it was more or less bearable, but then things became dreadful. Super heavy shells hammered down ceaselessly on our hill, interspersed with gas. We masked up and gazed anxiously at the lamps that the tunnel commandant, Hauptmann Süß, had caused to be placed on the ground. When shells and mortar bombs explode, they produce carbon monoxide. This creeps along at ground level. It is odourless, penetrates gas masks and is a killer. It is much deadlier than poison gas, against which the masks offer protection and which can be smelled instantly. However, the lamps detect it; they are extinguished. About 8.00 am there was an enormous crash. The airshaft next to the battalion command post was penetrated, the entrance to it almost collapsed, together with a large section of the tunnel system, which meant that the ration store was cut off.

The officers of the staff, together with the mining engineer, followed the transverse gallery to 3rd Company; but hardly had they reached that place than a heavy shell impacted on the other airshaft, burying them all, including our battalion commander and [Hauptmann] Graf [Count] Rambaldi. Hauptmann Süß rallied us and we began at once to dig. After lengthy work, we uncovered Graf Rambaldi and Dr Nagel treated him. However, things continued to deteriorate. The third gallery was full of carbon monoxide, so we sealed it off. The entrances began to collapse. We worked to clear them, but breathing became increasingly difficult and the lamps went out. It must have been about 4.00 pm when Hauptmann Süß ordered, 'Anyone who wishes to leave should get out now'.

I found a small hole at the entrance to the first gallery and crawled out. It was like a thunderstorm outside, with continuous explosions and the whirr of fragments. I rushed from crater to crater, but I must have inhaled too much carbon monoxide and I collapsed, unconscious. When I came to I found myself in hospital. How I got there I have no idea. Apparently stretcher bearers from Infantry Regiment 475 collected me. Hauptmann Süß died in the tunnel. He stayed like the captain of a sinking ship."[43]

The loss of the tunnel complex and the many reserves located within it, meant that there was little to stop the French attack and indeed the commander of the neighbouring Infantry Regiment 127, Oberst Schwab, was able to observe the critical situation unfolding from a position high on the *Pionierberg* [Engineer Hill], just northwest of Nauroy. He immediately summoned his 2nd Battalion, which was in reserve and then, on its arrival, ordered it to conduct a counterstroke in the direction of the *Cornillet* feature (the French having already reached the foot of its northern slopes), there to halt any further advance and prevent the left flank of Infantry Regiment 475 being rolled up. Due to the amount of artillery fire coming down, the commander of 6th Company, Reserve Leutnant Brauchle,[44] was killed during the move to the start line.

Despite this setback, Hauptmann von Hartlieb pressed forward, supported by two sections of 2nd Machine Gun Company. Promised reinforcement by a battalion of Infantry Regiment 476 did not materialise. Nevertheless, during a battle of sharp intensity at close quarters, the French were driven out of the woods on the west side of the *Cornillet*. The battalion consolidated and the Infantry Regiment 127 men dug in along the base of the hill. It was felt subsequently that a better coordinated attack might have wrested the entire hill back from the French, but it was not to be and the cost was high. In addition to Leutnant Brauchle, the adjutant 2nd Battalion, Leutnant Stadler, was killed,[45] as was Reserve Leutnant Schuster[46]. Eight other officers were wounded. Nevertheless, despite lacking all normal defences and being virtually cut off forward, the battalion remained in the line until it was relieved by Reserve Infantry Regiment 13 during the night 22/23 May[47].

If the fighting had been hard for Infantry Regiment 127, the losses for Infantry Regiment 476 were catastrophic. The regiment had deployed to the *Cornillet* with sixty four officers, 2,419 other ranks and twenty eight machine guns. By the evening of 20 May they had lost forty two officers and 1,170 other ranks, most of them in the tunnel complex, where those who had not been killed by the concussion of the massive 380mm shells which penetrated the air shafts died in hundreds, asphyxiated by carbon monoxide. A French report produced later described the most appalling scenes in the complex when it was re-entered. In places corpses were piled five deep. One intersection was totally blocked by the bodies of over one hundred fully equipped men, who had suffocated *en masse* as they attempted to escape the deadly fumes.[48]

More generally along the line of the heights south of Moronvilliers there was initial success as the German front line positions on the northern slopes were driven in. However, the French attackers now found themselves at the mercy of the German gunners, who had excellent observation and the range of each place to a metre. Furthermore, reserve formations of the ground holding divisions, namely 33rd Infantry Division, 10th Ersatz and 23rd Infantry Division, joined by elements of 54th Reserve Division launched counter-strokes, though these enjoyed only mixed success. As soon as the situation became clear, those elements of 54th Reserve Division not already deployed forward, namely Reserve Infantry Regiment 246 and 3rd Battalion Reserve Infantry Regiment 247, were ordered to move with all speed, the Reserve Infantry Regiment 247 men being rushed up to the R1 line in trucks. There followed a renewal of the French thrust at 6.45 pm, after another period of drum fire. 2nd Battalion Reserve Infantry Regiment 247 was ordered to launch a counter-stroke at 6.45 pm. This was followed at 7.30 pm by orders to 1st Battalion attack towards the *Cornillet*. 'Enemy has thrust through the *Cornillet* and is advancing on Nauroy. 1st Battalion Reserve Infantry Regiment 247 is to launch an immediate counter-stroke against the French right flank - direction *Cornillet*.'[49] A somewhat confused situation became more so after darkness fell. A false report arrived at 2nd Battalion that 1st Battalion had been totally destroyed, then it was itself ordered by Infantry Regiment 130, 33rd Infantry Division, to turn and attack the *Hochberg*. It was not until dawn broke that the situation became clearer. The French had occupied the *Bärenburg*, between *Hochberg* and *Keilberg* and had pushed on past the eastern summit of the *Hochberg*, but had been held at the foot of its northern slope and there the positions remained until units of Reserve Infantry Regiment 235, 51st Reserve Division, arrived to relieve them in the early hours of 24 May.

Meanwhile, at 8.10 pm 20 May, 43 Ersatz Brigade 10th Ersatz Division, to which Reserve Infantry Regiment 248 had been subordinated, directed that '1st Battalion Reserve Infantry Regiment 248 [was] immediately to launch a counter-attack against the saddle between the *Keilberg* and the *Pöhlberg*'[50]. The battalion did its best, making full use of natural cover to pass through French defensive artillery fire, but the attack stalled in heavy machine gun fire just short of the French lines, where Reserve Leutnant Josef Grießer[51] was killed at the head of 3rd Company, apparently only thirty paces from the French front line trench.[52] At the eastern end of the ridge, the French were forced back off the *Pöhlberg* and *Marienhöhe*, but they remained in possession of the section from the *Cornillet* to the *Keilberg*.

Following its relief of 33rd Infantry Division, there was more fighting by 51st Reserve Division to defend positions north of the *Hochberg* and *Keilberg*. This was far from easy, given the state of the ground, as this report made by one of the regimental commanders to 102 Reserve Infantry Brigade just after his handover/takeover was complete makes clear. It provides a vivid snapshot of the conditions in this heavily disputed sector after six weeks of fighting.

Oberstleutnant Freiherr von Edelsheim Commander Reserve Infantry Regiment 234[53]

"The sector was taken over at 5.00 am today. The front line comprises craters that are not connected. To the right there is contact with Infantry Regiment 98. To the left our position stretches only as far as *Keilwäldchen* [Wedge Copse]. There is a gap to the left of that. In between there has been no development of the positions. The R1 Position is a non-continuous (in places it is only marked out) trench line on a forward slope. It is only sixty centimetres to one metre in depth, with the occasional section of wire to its front. The reverse slope part of the R1 Position comprises three pockets of resistance, with no communication between them. The entries on the map are not correct. The position has only a few incomplete dugouts.

"The R2 Position does not exist at all, forcing the reserves to bivouac in the midst of enemy artillery fire. There are no communication trenches leading forward. There are no means of contact forward of battalion headquarters, so there is no communication whatsoever with the front line. The telephone system depends entirely on single wire [earth return] links, despite repeated demands by the relieved regiment for supplies of twin core cable. The forward light signalling station has been destroyed by shell fire. The trench tramway has been wrecked, is out of action and must be reconstructed.

"The engineer park lacks even the most essential stores. There are no heavy timber supports at all. There is a daily requirement for 120 sections of light timber framing, but it only has twenty sets available. The holdings of material for the construction of obstacles is insufficient and there is a complete lack of chicken wire needed to produce cover from aerial observation.

"Stocks of small arms ammunition on the positions are lacking. There is an immediate requirement for 200,000 rounds of rifle ammunition and 100,000 for the machine guns. There are no water points and a lack of latrines. There is no means of contacting the artillery. The telephone links for the artillery liaison officer have been shot up and do not work. There are no liaison officers from the heavy artillery.

"Despite the fact that the positions are incomplete, the four engineer companies have been withdrawn from the sector. There are no transport mules. Almost no trench stores have been handed over. The total extent was two serviceable light machine guns, one incapable of being fired, and eight grenade launchers."

The only thing that Edelsheim omitted to mention was the fact that from the summit of the *Keilberg* the French could overlook the entire position, so movement by day was impossible and all activity had to be crammed into the relatively few hours of darkness in late May. The French infantry may not have launched attacks but harassing fire took a constant toll of the defenders, as did mistakes made by the German gunners.

The dearth of proper links between the two arms came into sharp focus when, in response to a call for defensive fire on 26 May by Reserve Infantry Regiment 235, shells dropped short and it was not possible to correct the error. The cost was ten men killed, including Leutnant Gipper[54], and ten others wounded. One unnamed member of 2nd Company recorded, 'We looked on with secret horror every time that defensive fire was called for, because it never arrived without causing us numerous casualties.'[55] As a stop gap, 13th Infantry Division, in Group Prosnes reserve, was called forward in case it was required, but the forces deployed on the main positions were able to deal with the French probes from within their own resources and fortunately their offensives efforts had died away almost entirely by this point. On 27 May there was a further German attempt at the *Keilberg* and *Pöhlberg* to force the French to pull back down the southern slopes. There was savage close quarter fighting but, after a lengthy struggle, the French retained their observation points on the crest line. The day began with a large scale artillery exchange, developing into a bombardment. Then formations of 54th Reserve Division attacked the *Pöhlberg* and Reserve Infantry Regiment 234, with Reserve Infantry Regiment 236 to its right, assaulted the *Keilberg*. Caught out by this surprise attack, one group of French defenders leapt up out of their trenches and surrendered, Reserve Infantry Regiment 236 taking one sergeant, one corporal and sixteen other ranks prisoner.[56] 5th and 9th Companies Reserve Infantry Regiment 236 did attempt to exploit this success, but had to abandon it when the Reserve Infantry Regiment 234 attack stalled under heavy machine gun fire from the *Bärenburg*. A few half hearted efforts and one more serious counter-attacks were launched by the French, but these were beaten off and the sector fell quiet once more.

Along the Chemin des Dames, back on 20 May, elements of 1st Bavarian Infantry Division counter-attacked between the *Drachenhöhle* and *Sachsenhöhle* and took several sections of the French front line near Hurtebise Farm. 1st Battalion Bavarian Infantry Regiment 2, for example, attacked the so-called *Bergnase*, northwest of the farm, at 8.20 am on an 800 metre front and pushed the line back 400 metres, which improved its defensive position considerably. Unfortunately this same attack cost the life of one of the most experienced, courageous and valued members of the battalion - Oberleutnant Otto Ritter von Rompf, killed by a mortar bomb just as he was observing from the entrance to a dugout. He had been awarded the Knight's Cross of the Military Max Josef Order for bravery on Vimy Ridge following a mine explosion in March 1916.[57]

Fighting flared up again from 22 to 25 May around Hurtebise Farm and as far as Corbény. On 22 May 2nd Guards Infantry (manning the *Winterberg* sector) and 8th Infantry Divisions were both heavily attacked, but succeeded in maintaining their positions; only southeast of Chevreux was any ground lost. 2nd Bavarian Infantry Division, the Guards' neighbours to the west, were ordered to stand by to reinforce or counter-attack if required. 2nd Battalion Bavarian Infantry Regiment 12 was actually stood to in full battle order ready to force march forward when the order arrived standing them down. The Grenadier Guards had prevailed.[58]

The 2nd Bavarian Division, which had beaten off several attempts the previous day, mainly with artillery defensive fire, tried a limited and not especially successful attack themselves during the morning of 23 May then, almost in response, there was yet another French infantry assault at 9.30 pm, mainly directed against Bavarian Infantry Regiment 15. It was beaten off with ease.[59] During the following night 10th Infantry Division also came under attack, but its formations yielded no ground at all to the French. During the night 24/25 May 206th Infantry Division launched an attack of its own to the south of Pargny. Attacking on a six company front, their positions were pushed forward and four officers and 503 other ranks were captured.

The performance of Infantry Regiment 359 in this operation, when it successfully stormed the quarry at Pargny and captured the bulk of the prisoners, was all the more praiseworthy because a rogue German artillery gun had been mistakenly shelling its 3rd Battalion positions and causing considerable casualties. Almost incredible to relate, it took several days to identify the offending gun and put an end to the sufferings of the Brandenburgers.[60] The fact that the division had succeeded in pushing the French back from all the positions they had gained on this part of the northern slopes of the Chemin des Dames on 5 May gained it recognition at the highest level and specific mention in the OHL communiqué.

It can be seen clearly that there was no longer any real coherence to events along the Aisne or in Champagne. In complete contrast to the battles of April and the beginning of May, the campaign had degenerated into series of isolated actions of only local significance. It is hard to overstate the profound psychological effect the failure of the offensive had on the morale of the French army and more broadly the entire country. Everybody, whether directly or only indirectly involved, had been given to understand that this time victory was certain and assured. Swift breakthrough would be followed by the pursuit of a routed German army. The war would be over and the bloodletting would cease. Not only was this not the case, if the German casualties had been severe, those on the French side were appalling - 130,000 between 16 and 23 April alone. Of course Nivelle, hailed in advance as the architect of victory and far too eager to trumpet the certainty of breakthrough and success, paid the price once the staunch German defence blunted, then stalled, his attacks. His very last chance of avoiding the sack came and went with the failure of the renewed assault on 4-5 May. That left his position untenable and he was finally removed from command on 15 May; not, however, before attempting to place the blame on the shoulders of his subordinates.

He had no serious hope of averting his fall; he was personally intimately associated with every aspect of the planning and operational process. Had it succeeded, he would have received the credit. As it was he could not shake himself free of the blame and he had to go, being replaced by General Pétain, who found himself plunged into mastering rock bottom army morale and a near total loss of confidence. The writing had been on the wall from the beginning of May, with several divisions attacking on 4 and 5 May with barely concealed reluctance. It was small wonder. Casualties had risen to 140,000 in the four armies engaged. The first confirmed instance of a refusal to move into the trenches prior to an attack occurred near Prosnes on 29 April and affected the French 20th Infantry Regiment.[61] As the month of May progressed, the problems multiplied until indiscipline began to appear more widely, first of all amongst reserve formations, then it spread rapidly to affect close support and frontline units. Left wing extremists were involved in spreading disaffection and encouraging resentment amongst the soldiers, who were only too willing to compare and contrast their hard lot, the danger, poor medical care, appalling rations and virtually non-existent leave arrangements, with the life of comfort enjoyed by workers in the war industries who were in receipt of unprecedentedly high wages.

A Fourth Army Report on the morale of its troops stated, 'The men have said that they would be willing to defend the trenches, but that they would refuse to attack because it is pointless butchery.'[62] Outright mutinies broke out. Although direct attacks on officers were rare, there was in general great reluctance to obey orders and in many cases an absolute refusal to renew the attacks, or even to move forward into the line. In some units Soviet-style 'Soldiers' Councils' were elected and red flags appeared; whilst in others, hotheads called for a march on Paris and tried in various ways to foment revolution, though with very little real success. One typical example occurred on 2 June when up to 500 men of the 310th Infantry Regiment, 170th Division, refused orders to march forward from Coeuvres west of Soissons. The mutineers piled their weapons, dropped their equipment and gathered for mass meetings. All entreaties by their officers were ignored. Their commander, Colonel Dussange, an experienced soldier and respected figure, mingled personally among the soldiers, speaking calmly and begging them to be sensible

He fared no better than his other officers. The men had set out on the road of disobedience and would not be swayed. At 3.00 pm, they formed up and began marching towards Paris. Word had reached them that loyal regiments were waiting to intercept them in the Forest of Compiègne, so they set off southwards, initially towards Villers-Cotterets, instead. Dussange made one final effort to halt them. Standing prominently at the southern exit of the village, he is said to have shouted,

> "Men, Frenchmen, Soldiers! Be sensible! Halt! Turn around! You are heading on a path which will lead to the ruin and destruction of France ... Listen to your old Colonel!"[63]

It did no good. Dussange stood his ground courageously, tears streaming down his face at the humiliation, but he himself was not harmed. The advancing column split round him and some of his soldiers even saluted as they went past. The last flickers of discipline faded shortly afterwards and the words of the *Internationale* were heard being sung as they disappeared in to the distance.

In the event swift counter-measures proved effective. Picked, reliable officers and NCOs, dressed in soldiers' uniforms, intercepted the mutineers, group by group. Pretending to show them to where there were stocks of food and drink, they splintered the formed body and the military police were able to halt them, disarm them and arrest ringleaders. Even though this case was of medium seriousness, compared with, for example, 217th Infantry Regiment (2,500 mutineers) and 221st Infantry Regiment (1,400 mutineers),[64] nevertheless subsequent trials of the thirty one ringleaders led to the very high number of seventeen death sentences being handed down.[65] Of these, however, only one, that of Joseph Ruffier, an agricultural labourer from the small village of Lachassagne in the Rhône Department, south of Villefranche sur Saône, was actually carried out. He was executed by firing squad at Saint Pierre Aigle, Aisne, on 6 July 1917, one of only twenty seven soldiers shot for the 1917 mutinies, though one other man committed suicide and another escaped before sentence could be carried out.[66]

As a mark of how widespread the disaffection was, in response to a question posed in early June by President Poincaré, Paul Painlevé, at that time French Minister of War, allegedly stated in the wake of recent events that there was a day when there were only two divisions available between Soissons and Paris which he could trust entirely.[67] It was a time of extraordinary danger both for France and the Allies as a whole. Decisive governmental action and wise reforms introduced by Pétain overcame the crisis in a matter of weeks, but it was an extremely worrying time.

Despite the fact that the mutinies were hushed up as far as possible and every effort was made to keep word of the problems from the German army, inevitably information began to trickle out and reach the German High Command. One source of intelligence was analysis of prisoner of war interrogation reports and, as the crisis dragged on, questioning on this subject became very much more focussed. As a result a clear impression of the extent of indiscipline, mutiny and revolutionary agitation was obtained. That said, care was taken not to give too much credence to the reports or to overstate the situation, but there was no doubt as May turned into June that war weariness, coupled with distrust of the French army high command and overall direction of the war was widespread.

As ever it is one thing to have intelligence on a subject and quite another to be able to take advantage of it. During a six week period, OHL had rotated no fewer than seventy divisions into the front line along the Western Front. They were all to a greater or lesser extent worn down, there were no completely fresh formations and the British, having continued to press hard and sacrificially east of Arras, were about to begin major operations in Flanders. Furthermore, both the field and foot artillery was still committed to action on both army group fronts and expenditure of ammunition continued to be prodigious. There simply was no possibility of creating the size of fully supported attacking force necessary to make an impact on the French army and to exploit this opportunity. In any case, it was obvious that the French were still fighting hard defensively.

It may well be that there was, nevertheless, a certain embarrassment in the upper echelons of the German army that exploitation of the situation was beyond them, so they sought to produce excuses later.

General Erich Ludendorff[68]

" The French offensive had been smashed in an extraordinarily bloody fashion
… and the mood of France was subdued. In July the Minister of War admitted
the offensive had failed with such high casualties that it could never be repeated.
The [defeat] was so great that the morale of the army began to suffer and
mutinies broke out. However, information about them was scanty and only
gradually came to our attention. Only later did we have a clear picture."[69]

Regardless of exactly how truthful Ludendorff was being, it is undeniable that the
transition from operational defence to offence is extremely difficult to achieve at the
best of times. To have attempted any such thing on a battlefield already torn by weeks
of fighting, without time to put in place all the necessary infrastructure and supply
dumps, would have been foolhardy in the extreme, so it was never attempted and the
French army survived to fight again. Other German commentators also tended to play
down this aspect of the events of Spring 1917, preferring instead to concentrate on the
obvious fact that this massive joint offensive had completely missed its objective and,
apart from some initial success, was a complete and utter expensive failure.

Generalfeldmarschall von Hindenburg[70]

"From the very earliest days the offensive was an unqualified French defeat.
This bloody reverse caused the bitterest disappointment to both the French
commanders and the men they led. The battles around Arras, Soissons and
Reims raged for weeks. [The fighting] produced only one single difference at
the tactical level when compared with Somme the previous year and I do not
wish to forget to mention it. This was the fact that, after the first few days, the
enemy never achieved a single notable success then, at the end of only a few
weeks, all over their battlefields, they sank back, exhausted, into trench warfare
once more. In other words, our defensive procedures proved themselves
brilliantly!"

Ludendorff summed up the battles along the Aisne and Champagne by stating,
'Through extreme effort we had won a great victory and demonstrated that our training
was superior to that of the enemy'.[71] That view was widely shared throughout the army,
whose members drew on the confidence and strength the experience had generated as
they faced new battles during the coming months. One key factor was that the quality
of command and leadership at divisional level and below was still extremely high that
spring, despite the rapid expansion of the number of divisions and high losses. Another
extremely important matter was the introduction of large number of independent
machine gun detachments into the Field Army, together with increased availability of
the 08/15 machine gun, which boosted company level fire power dramatically and

made possible the new active defence in depth pioneered by Loßberg and adopted at once throughout the army.

Of course the huge increases in Allied artillery and mortars were partly responsible for increased dispersion on the battlefield and the need to move away from rigidly defended trench lines, but it was the defensive genius of Loßberg that gave shape and coherence to the new methodology and that, coupled with dynamic leadership and high quality infantry, which continued to pose great problems for the Allies right up until the advent of sophisticated fire plans and the refinement of 'bite and hold' tactics during the latter part of the Third Battle of Ypres. Naturally, it can also be argued that by this point the continuing drain on German manpower resources was having the effect of diluting the quality of the fighting troops and that this in turn, coupled with yet more increases in Allied firepower, meant that by the end of the year the defensive ability of the German army was not what it had once been.

In the immediate wake of the so-called 'Double Battle Aisne/Champagne' there was no complacency in the German army. The usual post action critical analysis, which threw up various points for attention, was undertaken rapidly and conscientiously. It was determined, for example, that one disadvantage of defence in depth, with its lightly held zone forward of the main line of resistance, was that the enemy were able to close up to the German positions effectively unopposed and to launch attacks from short range. This reduced the ability of the German artillery to cause high casualties to the leading waves because of the proximity of friendly forces, whilst the increased areas to be covered in depth by gun fire meant that gaps were inevitable. This in turn provided follow up troops with potential routes forward and meant that they were not subject to an optimal degree of attrition as they closed up to the forward positions.

There were also problems over the use of reserves and *Eingreif* formations. Their positioning and consequent response times were critical. They had to be shielded as far as possible from harassing fire but, if they were ordered forward too soon, they risked running into heavy enemy barrage fire; too late and it was then virtually impossible to fulfil the aim of active defence, namely to restore fully the original front lines and thus ensure that as much terrain as possible remained in German hands. Despite the greatest care with planning, issuing of orders in advance and checking routes forward, the procedure remained an inexact science and demanded much of those troops assigned to the task. Nevertheless, overall it did minimise casualties amongst the defenders and, given that manpower was becoming ever scarcer and the fact that it was impossible for the German army to match Allied firepower weapon for weapon, it is hard to see how anything other tactical approach could have been adopted. Qualified success it may have been, but active defence bought the German army time at the operational level.

During the spring of 1917, the German army had been put under the greatest imaginable strain. At Arras, along the Chemin des Dames and in Champagne the men of Army Groups Crown Prince Rupprecht and German Crown Prince had buckled, given ground, but held the attempted Allied breakthroughs, despite being outnumbered and outgunned. It was a defensive test of the severest type and they had prevailed, albeit at enormous cost. If they or their commanders thought that they had earned a respite, they were soon to be disabused when the opening of the Battle of Messines on 7 June set off yet another battle of attrition, one which would bring both the German and the British army close to the breaking point suffered by the French when all their dreams and hopes had disappeared in the chalk dust and mud to the south.

Notes

[1] Christian History Infantry Regiment 418 p 235.
[2] Soldan History Infantry Regiment 184 pp 50-51.
[3] Loebell *Mit dem 3. Garde Regiment* pp 258-259.
[4] Ludendorff *Meine Kriegserinnerungen* pp 337-338.
[5] Rosenberg-Lipinsky History Grenadier Guard Regiment 3 p 458.
[6] *ibid.* p 452.
[7] *ibid.* pp 452-454.
[8] The *Franzers* referred to were members of Grenadier Guard Regiment 2 'Kaiser Franz'.
[9] Doerstling History Infantry Regiment 20 p 294.
[10] z.b.V. = *zu besonderer Verwendung* [for special purposes]. Essentially this was a standby corps headquarters available for use as and where required.
[11] FOH p 718.
[12] Bose History Grenadier Guard Regiment 1 pp 300-302.
[13] Loebell *op. cit.* pp 259-260.
[14] The original text definitely states '80' metres, though this is improbably far. Possibly it is a misprint for '50' metres, a range achievable by a good thrower armed with stick grenades.
[15] Fusilier Adam Dänner, whose date of death is given by the *Volksbund* as 26 April 1917, is buried in the German cemetery at Sissonne Block 9 Grave 397.
[16] GOH p 351.
[17] Müller-Loebnitz *Die Badener im Weltkrieg* pp 271-272.
[18] An original footnote reads, 'The strong point in the battalion sector was manned by 7th Company Infantry Regiment 112, under the command of Reserve Leutnant Busch, who once again displayed the same energetic and courageous leadership as he had previously and was to do later. A few days later he received the Iron Cross First Class in fully merited recognition of his outstanding behaviour'. See also Schiel History Infantry Regiment 112 p 64, which states that Busch and his men in the *Tietzestützpunkt* had faced odds of ten to one, but had prevailed.
[19] It is impossible to comment on the accuracy of this assertion. It is, however, equally possible that the Frenchmen simply ran into their own defensive fire.
[20] Müller-Loebnitz *op. cit.* p 274.
[21] Schmidt History Infantry Regiment 142 p 92.
[22] Machenhauer History Infantry Regiment 98 p 55.
[23] Reserve Leutnant Eduard Ziegenfuß is buried in the German cemetery at Berru Block 3 Grave 527.
[24] Tebing History Infantry Regiment 370 pp 203-204.
[25] Brandis History Infantry Regiment 24 pp 332-333.
[26] History Infantry Regiment 64 p 212.
[27] Gebert History Infantry Regiment 371 pp 57-58.
[28] Makoben History Reserve Infantry Regiment 212 pp 341-342.

[29] Reserve Infantry Regiment 208 estimated that during the afternoon of 1 May 17 *alone*, no fewer than 13,000 field gun shells and 1,700 of heavier calibres had landed on the regimental positions. Small wonder after three days of such a bombardment that there was some French success on 3 May. See Haleck History Reserve Infantry Regiment 208 p 69.

[30] History Infantry Regiment 159 pp 254-255.

[31] Reserve Leutnant Wilhelm Bornemann was killed in action over Haplincourt, near Bapaume, on 15 July 1918. He is buried in the CWGC Rocquiny-Equancourt Road Cemetery at Manancourt. Plot 10, Row B, Grave 32.

[32] Reserve Leutnant Wilhelm Otte was mortally wounded near Sedan on 7 November 1918 and died of his wounds in captivity on 15 November 1918. The location of his burial is unknown.

[33] Appel History Reserve Infantry Regiment 205 pp 187-190.

[34] *ibid.* p 193.

[35] Bachelin History Reserve Infantry Regiment 111 pp 327-330.

[36] *ibid.* pp 334-335.

[37] Hülsemann History Infantry Regiment 84 2. Band pp 203-204

[38] *ibid.* p 212.

[39] An original annotation in the text suggests that these men were in fact from 9th Company.

[40] Schuster History Infantry Regiment 369 p 39.

[41] Rothe *Das Ehrenbuch der Garde II. Band* pp 389-390.

[42] Major Georg Wintterlin was one of those who died on Mont Cornillet on 20 May1917. He is buried in the German cemetery at Warmériville Block 3 Grave 4.

[43] Kabisch *Das Volksbuch vom Weltkrieg* pp 181-182.

[44] Reserve Leutnant Wilhelm Brauchle is buried in the German cemetery at Aussonce Block 2 Grave 483.

[45] Leutnant Heinrich Stadler, whose date of death is given as 23 May 1917, is buried in the German cemetery at Warmériville Block 1 Grave 687.

[46] Reserve Leutnant Ewald Schuster is buried in the German cemetery at Aussonce Block 2 Grave 6.

[47] Schwab History Infantry Regiment 127 p 97.

[48] Moser *Die Württemberger im Weltkrieg* pp 588-589.

[49] Herkenrath History Reserve Infantry Regiment 247 p 119.

[50] Reinhardt History 54th Reserve Division p 106.

[51] Reserve Leutnant Josef Grießer is buried in the German cemetery at La Neuville-en-Tourne-à-Fuy Block 4 Grave 380.

[52] Reinhardt History Reserve Infantry Regiment 248 p 119.

[53] Knieling History Reserve Infantry Regiment 234 pp 308-309.

[54] Leutnant August Gipper, killed at the age of thirty seven, is buried in the German cemetery at Aussonce Block1 Grave 77.

[55] Hennig History Reserve Infantry Regiment 235 p 146.

[56] Mayer History Reserve Infantry Regiment 236 p 277.

[57] Staubwasser History Bavarian Infantry Regiment 2 p 42. Reserve Oberleutnant Otto Ritter von Rompf is buried in the German Cemetery at Laon 'Champ de Manoeuvre' Block 2 Grave 111.

[58] History Bavarian Infantry Regiment 12 p 106.

[59] Haupt History Bavarian Infantry Regiment 15 p 58.

[60] Delbanco History Infantry Regiment 359 p 50.

[61] Rolland *La Grève des Tranchées* p 37.

[62] Miquel *Le gâchis des généraux* p174.

[63] Ettighoffer *Eine Armee meutert* p 273.

[64] Rolland *op. cit.* p 411.

[65] *ibid.* p 411.

[66] *ibid.* p 381.

[67] GOH p 423.

[68] Ludendorff *op.cit.* p 338.

[69] Writing in *Der Weltkrieg Band II* pp 98-100, General von Kuhl later claimed that it was not until the end of June - far too late to have been of use - that clarity was obtained by German intelligence about the extent of the internal problems of the French army. This date seems to provide an all-too-convenient let out clause but, to be fair to him, Kuhl also makes the point that even had the information been available a month earlier, the German army, having been fighting hard for two months by then, would have been in no position to go over to the offensive in any case.

[70] Hindenburg *Aus meinem Leben* p 193.

[71] Ludendorff *op.cit.* p 338.

Appendix I

German – British Comparison of Ranks

Generalfeldmarschall	Field Marshal
Generaloberst	Colonel General N.B. The holder of this rank was at least an army Commander.
General der Infanterie General der Kavallerie	General of Infantry} General General of Cavalry} General N.B. The holder of any of these last two ranks was at least a corps commander and might have been an army commander.
Generalleutnant	Lieutenant General. N.B. The holder of this rank could be the commander of a formation ranging in size from a brigade to a corps. From 1732 onwards Prussian officers of the rank of Generalleutnant or higher, who had sufficient seniority, were referred to as '*Exzellenz*' [Excellency].
Generalmajor	Major General
Oberst	Colonel
Oberstleutnant	Lieutenant Colonel
Major	Major
Hauptmann	Captain
Rittmeister	Captain (mounted unit such as cavalry, horse artillery or transport). It was also retained by officers of this senority serving with the German Flying Corps
Oberleutnant	Lieutenant
Leutnant	Second Lieutenant
Feldwebelleutnant	Sergeant Major Lieutenant
Offizierstellvertreter	Officer Deputy

	N.B. This was an appointment, rather than a substantive rank.
Feldwebel	Sergeant Major
Wachtmeister	Sergeant Major (mounted unit)
Vizefeldwebel	Staff Sergeant
Vizewachtmeister	Staff Sergeant (mounted unit)
Sergeant	Sergeant
Unteroffizier	Corporal
Korporal	Corporal (Bavarian units)
Gefreiter	Lance Corporal

Musketier	}
Grenadier	}
Garde-Füsilier	}
Füsilier	}
Schütze	}
Infanterist	}
Jäger	} N.B. These ranks all equate to Private Soldier
Wehrmann	} (infantry). The differences in nomenclature are
Landsturmmann	} due to tradition, the type of unit involved, or the
	} class of conscript to which the individual
	} belonged.
Soldat	}
Ersatz-Reservist	}

Kriegsfreiwilliger	Wartime Volunteer. This equates to Private Soldier.

Kanonier	Gunner}
Pionier	Sapper}
Fahrer	Driver} N.B. These ranks all equate to Private Soldier.
Hornist	Trumpeter}
Tambour	Drummer}

Medical Personnel

Oberstabsarzt	Major (or higher)
Stabsarzt	Captain
Oberarzt	Lieutenant
Assistenzarzt	Second Lieutenant

N.B. These individuals were also referred to by their appointments; for example, *Bataillonsarzt* or *Regimentsarzt* [Battalion or Regimental Medical Officer]. Such usage, which varied in the different contingents which made up the German army, is no indicator of rank.

Sanitäter   Medical Assistant} N.B. These two ranks both
Krankenträger   Stretcherbearer} equate to Private Soldier.

Frequently the prefix *'Sanitäts-'* appears in front of a normal NCO rank, such as Gefreiter or Unteroffizier. This simply indicates that a man of that particular seniority was part of the medical services.

Appendix II

Selective Biographical Notes

German

Generalleutnant Martin Châles de Beaulieu (1857 - 1945) Commander XIV Corps. General de Beaulieu joined Grenadier Guard Regiment 2 (Kaiser Franz) as a fahnenjunker in 1877. A talented regimental officer, he was selected for the General Staff and his career progressed smoothly, though as an oberstleutnant and chief of staff, he was involved in a serious falling out in German South West Africa with the local commander, Generalleutnant Lothar von Trotha when he disagreed fundamentally with Trotha's policy of brutality towards the indigenous people. Despite being severely reprimanded by Trotha and given an adverse report, he survived and, as a generalmajor, was appointed commander of 12th Infantry Division in Silesia in 1913. His division fought in the west in 1914 as part of VI Corps then continued to serve in the Argonne. He led his division during the 1915 winter battles in Champagne. Promoted to generalleutnant, he commanded XIV Corps from August 1916 until September 1917 when he was transferred to the army reserve. He tendered his resignation and left the army, loaded with honours and awards (including the Pour le Mérite) and was granted the honorary rank of General der Infanterie in January 1918.

Generalmajor Wilhelm Julius Max Hans von Beczwarzowsky (1862 - 1932) 17th Reserve Division. General von Beczwarzowsky was of noble descent and the son of a soldier; his father was killed in November 1870 as commanding officer 1st Battalion Infantry Regiment 31 at the Battle of Beaumont during the Franco Prussian War. In 1881 he joined Grenadier Regiment 2 in Stettin (modern Szczecin) as a fahnenjunker and was commissioned as a sekondeleutnant the following year. Five years later he was posted to Infantry Regiment 76 in Hamburg and also carried out regimental duty subsequently with Infantry Regiments 72 and 96. He was then involved in the creation of Infantry Regiment 153 in Altenburg, where he distinguished himself by becoming the champion rifle shot of the entire corps. He was a major and commanding officer in Infantry Regiment 153 then, in November 1913, was posted to Stettin as an oberstleutnant and second in command of Fusilier Regiment 34. Promoted oberst in 1915, he was appointed commander of Leib Grenadier Regiment 109; then in April 1916 he succeeded Generalleutnant von Wichmann as commander 81 Infantry Brigade, in which capacity and as acting divisional commander, he fought in the Battle of Arras. In December 1917 he was relieved and went on to command 88th Infantry Division for the remainder of the war. He had two sons, Rolf and Walter, both of whom were killed during the conflict.

General der Infanterie Fritz Wilhelm Theodor Carl von Below (1853 - 1918) First Army. General von Below was a distinguished soldier who began his career as a sekondeleutnant in Footguard Regiment 1. Selected for the Great General Staff, he served in various appointments until his appointment as commander 1st Guards Infantry Division in 1908. In September 1912 he was promoted to general der infanterie and assumed command of XXI Corps in Saarbrücken. In 1914 his corps fought in Lorraine in the centre of Sixth Army, commanded by Crown Prince Rupprecht of Bavaria, and then in October, during the so-called 'Race to the Sea', it was transferred to the Arras area as part of Second Army under Generaloberst von Bülow. Despatched to East Prussia at the beginning of 1915, it was under command of Tenth Army in the winter battles. In April 1915, Below was succeeded in command by General von Hutier and returned to the Western Front to assume command of Second Army, commanding it until mid July 1916 on the Somme, when a reorganisation meant that he was now responsible for the battles north of the Somme as Commander First Army. The following month he was awarded the oak leaf to his Pour le Mérite and he continued to operate in the north until the conclusion of the *Alberich* withdrawal in March 1917. At that moment the entire First Army headquarters was moved to the Aisne front, where it was heavily involved in holding the attacks of the French Fifth Army. In June 1918 he was given command of Ninth Army, but he was already a sick man. He was relieved of his duties in August 1918 and finally retired at the end of the war. He died a short time later of a lung infection and was buried in Berlin in the *Invalidenfriedhof*.

General der Infanterie Max Ferdinand Karl von Boehn (1850 - 1921) Seventh Army. General Boehn came from a distinguished military family. His father, uncle and younger brother all became senior generals in their turn. He entered the army in 1867 as a three-year volunteer and fahnenjunker with Footguard Regiment 3 in Hanover. He was commissioned as a sekondeleutnant in March 1869 and was posted the following year to Infantry Regiment 76 in Hamburg. He fought in several actions of the Franco-Prussian War with this regiment, was wounded in the arm and received the Iron Cross Second Class and the Mecklenburg Military Service Cross Second Class for his performance. Several years of regimental duty interspersed with external appointments followed then, in 1889, having served as a company commander with Grenadier Guard Regiment 1 (Kaiser Alexander) in Berlin, he was promoted major and made adjutant of 1st Guards Infantry Division, also in Berlin. He carried out other appointments with the Guards before returning to Infantry Regiment 76 as an oberstleutnant and battalion commander in 1897, remaining there as its commander when he was promoted oberst in 1899. His career continued to prosper and he was promoted Generalmajor in 1901 and sent to command 9 Infantry Brigade in Frankfurt an der Oder in 1901. Promotion to generalleutnant followed in April 1905, when he took over 18th Infantry Division in Flensburg. He was promoted general der infanterie in December 1909 and assumed the role of fortress commander at Ulm. The King of Württemberg awarded him the Grand Cross of the Order of Frederick in 1911 and he was pensioned off in September 1912.

On the outbreak of war, he was recalled out of retirement to command IX Reserve Corps. To begin with the corps was engaged in anti-invasion duties in Schleswig Holstein, but by late August 1914 had been despatched to Belgium, where it was heavily and controversially involved in the sacking and burning of Louvain. It later redeployed to the Roye-Noyon sector and participated in the battles around Soissons in January 1915. In late 1915 his corps was redeployed once more to Sixth Army for the autumn battles in Artois, remaining there until it carried out a tour of duty on the Somme in mid July 1916. Service on the Somme and Flanders then alternated until, in February 1917, Boehn was appointed commander of Armeegruppe C and the following month of Seventh Army. In the battles along the Chemin des Dames, Boehn received the Oak Leaf to his Pour le Mérite, awarded the previous year on the Somme. In December 1917 Boehn marked fifty years service, for which the Kaiser decorated him with the Grand Cross of the Order of the Red Eagle with Oak Leaves and Swords. Raised to Generaloberst in March 1918, his army was involved in the German offensive and then in May he commanded the attack across the Chemin des Dames, during which his army advanced sixty kilometres; he was made a Knight of the Order of the Black Eagle. He briefly commanded an army group in Artois from August to October 1918 then reverted to command of what was left of Seventh Army up until the Armistice. He left the army in January 1919 and spent his brief retirement in Berlin.

Generalleutnant Karl Dieffenbach (1859 - 1936) IX Reserve Corps General Dieffenbach entered the army in 1879 as an *avantageur* (officer cadet) with Infantry Regiment 69 in Trier and was commissioned the following year. After early regimental service he was selected for the General Staff in 1893 as a hauptmann. In 1896 he was made a company commander in Fusilier Regiment 35 in Brandenburg an der Havel and, two years later, was back on the General Staff where, in 1899, he was promoted major. In 1901 he was given command of a battalion in Infantry Regiment 30 in Saarlouis. This was followed by a tour of duty in Upper Silesia, where he ran a battle school and was promoted oberstleutnant. Only two years later, he was made an oberst and given command of Grenadier Regiment 6 in Posen then, four years after that, as a generalmajor, he went to command 28 Infantry Brigade in Düsseldorf. On the outbreak of war, he was given command of 22nd Infantry Division, XI Corps and he led it on the Eastern Front until the end of 1916, when he was posted briefly to command VII Corps. In March 1917, as part of a policy to give senior commands to younger officers, he was sent to take over IX Reserve Corps. In early April 1917 his command was re-designated Group Arras and it was in that capacity that he directed the Arras battle on the southern flank of Sixth Army and was awarded the Pour le Mérite. He and his corps were subordinated to Fourth Army as Group Wijtschate from June 1917 during the

Battle of Messines and he spent the next few months at Ypres, before moving his headquarters south to Artois in January 1918 for the start of the German offensives. Thereafter he was involved in fighting around the Scarpe, Armentières (under Sixth Army) then, after a period of positional warfare in Artois, IX Reserve Corps moved to First Army near Reims and finished the war subordinated to Fifth Army. Loaded with honours, Dieffenbach then applied to retire, leaving the army in May 1919 with the honorary rank of general der infanterie.

General der Infanterie Karl Ritter von Fasbender (1852 - 1933) I Bavarian Reserve Corps. Having studied law briefly at the University of Würzburg, General von Fasbender joined Bavarian Infantry Regiment 9 in 1872 as a one year volunteer. Deemed suitable officer material, after training he was commissioned as a sekondeleutnant in November 1875. A gifted officer, he completed General Staff training and, after a period as adjutant of a military district in Kaiserslautern, he was posted to the Railway Department of the General Staff in Berlin, where only the most able members of the élite Great General Staff staff worked. In 1891 he returned to Bavarian Infantry Regiment 9 as a company commander and then did a four year tour of duty at the *Kriegsakademie*, where he was an instructor and was promoted to major. In September 1897 he was posted to Ingolstadt as a battalion commander in Bavarian Infantry Regiment 10. The following year he was appointed to command Bavarian Jäger Battalion 1 in Freising and was promoted oberstleutnant in 1900. In 1902, after an appointment running a school of musketry in Lechfeld, he was promoted oberst in 1903 and given command of Bavarian Infantry Regiment 3 in Augsburg. This was followed swiftly by command of Bavarian 9 Infantry Brigade in Nuremberg in the rank of generalmajor. Two subsequent staff appointments led to promotion to generalleutnant and appointment as commander Bavarian 4th Infantry Division in Würzburg. In 1912 he retired with the honorary rank of general der infanterie, but was recalled to duty in August 1914 to command I Bavarian Reserve Corps For his leadership during the fighting around Vimy and Notre Dame de Lorette in October 1914, he received the Knight's Cross of the Military Max Josef Order, an honour which was upgraded to the Commander's Cross after his successful command during the 1915 battles in Artois and from August - September 1916 at Combles on the Somme. During the following spring, despite the fact that Vimy Ridge was captured by the Canadians and there were reverses on the corps front, on the personal recommendation of Crown Prince Rupprecht, his knighthood was raised to that of the Grand Cross of the Max Josef Order, one of only five awarded during the entire war. He commanded his corps in the offensives of 1918 and later the Nineteenth Army, finally leaving the army shortly after the Armistice was signed.

General Arthur von Gabain (1860 - 1939) 17th Infantry Infantry Division. General Gabain was of Huguenot descent. His father, a hauptmann, was killed during the 1866 Austro-Prussian War. He was educated as a cadet and was commissioned as a sekondeleutnant into Infantry Regiment 45 in Insterburg in 1878. In 1886 he was attached to Infantry Regiment 28 in Koblenz. He then alternated regimental duty with a tour as an instructor and in 1889 was posted briefly to Grenadier Regiment 5 in Danzig (modern Gdansk) and from there to the *Kriegsakademie* as a student. In 1899 he was serving as a company commander in Infantry Regiment 17, then was posted as a major in 1902 to Infantry Regiment 144 at Metz. A year later he became a battalion commander to its 3rd Battalion in Diedenhofen (modern Thionville). After a subsequent tour commanding a school in Danzig, he was promoted oberst in 1911 and assumed command of Infantry Regiment 87. Shortly before the outbreak of war, in May 1914, he was promoted to generalmajor and sent to Brandenburg an der Havel to command 12 Infantry Brigade. This brigade, part of 6th Infantry Division, marched to war in Belgium with III Corps. He fought at Mons and Villers Cotterets then, after the Battle of the Ourq, the retreat from the Marne and the Battle of the Aisne and positional warfare, he moved to Artois and led his men in the 1915 battles in Artois. His brigade was then deployed to Serbia but, having suffered a crush injury to his lower left leg, he had to relinquish command of 12 Brigade at the beginning of 1916. After several months of treatment and with the experience of the temporary command of 5th Division the previous year, he was appointed commander 103rd Infantry Division in September 1916. He led this formation with distinction on the Somme, moved down to the Champagne for rest and reconstitution and was redeployed to Verdun in early 1917. From there he was selected to command 17th Infantry Division, which he again did with distinction, both at Arras (though he could not prevent the loss of Gavrelle) and later that year at Ypres, where he was awarded the Pour le Mérite. Promoted generalleutnant in March 1918, his division fought in the offensives that spring then, in July 1918, he was given command of XXIII Reserve Corps briefly, before it was disbanded. He then commanded X Reserve Corps during the final battles. Post war he served on in various staff appointments, finally retiring in September 1920 with the honorary rank of general der infanterie.

Generalmajor Hermann Heinrich Sigismund von der Heyde (1857 - 1942) 29th Infantry Division. General von der Heyde had an unusually wide-ranging pre-war career. In 1880 he was a fähnrich in Infantry Regiment 84 and was commissioned as a sekondeleutnant the following year. He remained at regimental duty for some years, finally reaching the rank of hauptmann in 1892. From 1895 - 1900 he served variously in the 2nd and 3rd Marine Battalions, before being posted to East Asia Infantry Regiment 3 in 1901, where he became a battalion commander and temporary major. In this role, he participated in the defeat of the Boxer Rebellion. In 1902, on promotion to substantive major, he was posted to command 2nd Battalion East Asia Infantry Regiment 2 in Tientsin. This posting was short lived, because he returned the same year to Infantry Regiment 142 in Mülhausen (modern Mulhouse). However, he clearly enjoyed overseas service, because he volunteered for a three year tour of duty in German South West Africa (modern Namibia), where he served as a battalion commander in Field Regiment 1 and fought in several actions. At the end of his tour of duty, he was posted to command 2nd Battalion Infantry Regiment 48 in Küstrin then, in 1909, he moved to the staff of Infantry Regiment 22 in Gleiwitz, where he was promoted to oberstleutnant. Having been made an oberst in 1911, he took command of King's Infantry Regiment 145 in Metz. Just prior to the war he was given command of 24 Infantry Brigade in Neisse as a generalmajor. He led his brigade efficiently and well and, in August 1916, moved to command 29th Infantry Division (until 6 August 1918) on the Somme, in Champagne in the spring of 1917 and then at Verdun later that year. In 1918 he was deployed north to Flanders and also fought that summer between the Marne and the Vesle.

Oberst Fritz von Loßberg (1868 – 1942) Oberst von Loßberg was a key figure in the German army throughout the First World War, rising from the rank of oberstleutnant to generalleutnant and finally becoming a general der infanterie in the Reichswehr after the war. His exceptional talents were first recognised whilst he was serving at Supreme Army Headquarters in 1915, when he briefed the Kaiser in person about the crisis in Third Army at the beginning of the Autumn Battle in Champagne. That same day he found himself posted with immediate effect as chief of staff to that army. This was a considerable honour for a newly promoted oberst and, for the next three years, he was despatched from army to army to handle one crisis after another. Possessed of the ability to reduce major operational problems to their essentials, he repeatedly brought to bear clarity of thought, dynamism and bold decision making. Although nominally working as the adviser to a series of senior field commanders, in fact, armed with the full power of command he always demanded (and was granted) by his superiors, he *de facto* assumed command positions. It was, for example, Loßberg, personally, who directed the defensive battles against the British army on the Somme, at Arras and Passchendaele. He had a very strong constitution and an extraordinary capacity for hard work and long hours. He caught up with sleep by dozing in chairs at odd moments or during his daily car journeys to the front and, at times of crisis, never spent more than four hours per day in bed. He received numerous honours and awards, including the Pour le Mérite and Oak Leaf to it, from all the contingents of the German army.

Generalleutnant Freiherr von Lüttwitz (1859 – 1942) commander 20th Infantry Division. General von Lüttwitz, who was commissioned into Fusilier Regiment 38 of the Prussian army in 1878, is best known for his military and political activities after the war ended when he was responsible as Reichswehr commander in Berlin for putting down the *Spartakus* uprising and later took a prominent part in the failed putsch of March 1920. During the war he held a number of key appointments, including chief of staff to Fourth Army, Fifth Army and Army Group German Crown Prince. Following the end of the Autumn Battle of Champagne, he was given command of X Corps and, from November 1916 until the end of the war, he commanded III Corps. Having won the Iron Cross Second and First Class in 1914, he was awarded the Pour le Mérite in August 1916 and the Oak Leaf to it in March 1918. General von Lüttwitz, like many other senior officers, did not attempt to disguise his opposition to the terms of the Treaty of Versailles and was dismissed from his appointment by Reichswehrminister Gustav Noske on 11 March 1920. Thirty six hours later he marched on the centre of Berlin at the head of a brigade of marines and appropriated Noske's position. The putsch attracted no significant support and Lüttwitz had to escape a few days later to Hungary, not returning to Germany until an amnesty was declared in 1925. He then lived quietly in Breslau (modern Wroclaw) until his death.

Generalmajor Arnold Ritter von Möhl (1867 - 1944) 16th Bavarian Infantry Division. On leaving school, General von Möhl joined Bavarian Infantry Regiment 6 in 1884 as a fahnenjunker. For a year, from early 1885, as a fähnrich, he was trained to be an officer in Munich, finally being commissioned as a sekondeleutnant in early 1887. He spent a brief period with Bavarian Chevauleger Regiment 6, before alternating regimental duty with Bavarian Infantry Regiment 19, General Staff training and a short tour of duty with the Bavarian Airship Detachment. After a period as adjutant 6 Bavarian Infantry Brigade in Landau in the Pfalz, in 1898, he served in the Bavarian Central Staff, was promoted hauptmann and served for a period of time at Fortress Ingolstadt. After spending 1903-4 as a company commander in Bavarian Infantry Regiment 1, he went to Bavarian 4th Infantry Division as Ia (chief of staff), was promoted major and returned as an instructor to the *Kriegsakademie*. In 1909 he became a battalion commander in Bavarian Infantry Regiment 6, then a year later was chief of staff III Bavarian Corps. He became an oberstleutnant in 1911 and in March 1913 was sent to head the Bavarian *Kriegsakademie*, where he was promoted oberst. At the outbreak of war, Möhl was commanding Bavarian Infantry Regiment 6, leading it in the battles in Lorraine and remained in the area during the following winter. He became chief of staff of Bavarian I Corps in March 1915 and was promoted generalmajor the following month. From September 1916 to January 1917, he commanded 12 Bavarian Infantry Brigade, 6th Bavarian Infantry Division and was then appointed commander Bavarian 16th Infantry Division in time for the Battle of Arras. He went on to lead the division during the Third Battle of Ypres and at Cambrai, took part in the offensives of 1918 and ended the war in Flanders. Ennobled in March 1918 and awarded the Pour le Mérite in October 1918, as well as numerous other honours and awards, Möhl served on for a time post war, filling several senior Bavarian appointments and being promoted general der infanterie in 1922, before retiring to go into politics in late 1924.

General der Infanterie Ferdinand von Quast (1850 - 1939) Guard Corps. General von Quast was descended from an ancient noble family from Anhalt. In 1870 he joined Grenadier Guard Regiment 2 (Kaiser Franz), with which he fought during the Franco Prussian War. He was commissioned as a sekondeleutnant in January 1871 and received the Iron Cross Second Class for his performance in battle. He became a hauptmann and company commander in his regiment in 1887 then, in 1894, he became a battalion commander in Footguard Regiment 2. He was posted to Grenadier Guard Regiment 1

(Kaiser Alexander) as an oberstleutnant in 1901 then, two years later, on promotion to oberst, returned to command Grenadier Guard Regiment 2 until May 1907, when he was promoted generalmajor and given command of 39 Infantry Brigade in Hanover. Within a year he returned to Berlin to command 3 Guards Infantry Brigade prior to moving to Potsdam to take over 2ⁿᵈ Guards Infantry Division. In July 1910 he was moved to Danzig to command 36ᵗʰ Infantry Division. Promotion to generalleutnant followed in September and he was immediately appointed to command 6ᵗʰ Infantry Division in Brandenburg an der Havel. He took over IX Corps in Altona, Hamburg in March 1913 and deployed to war with it. After the Battle of Tirlemont in August 1914 he was made a general der infanterie. For his service on the Somme in 1916 he was awarded the Pour le Mérite. In January 1917 he was posted to the Reims area to command the Guard Corps which, under the title 'Group Aisne', he commanded with distinction during the spring 1917 battles; he was appointed commander Sixth Army the following September. In April 1918, early in the German offensives, Quast received the Oak Leaf to his Pour le Mérite and he finished the war back in the *Hermannstellung*. His period in command over, Quast carried out one or two post war function, but tendered his resignation once the Treaty of Versailles was signed and left the army in July 1919.

Generalleutnant Otto Ritter von Rauchenberger (1864 - 1942) 14ᵗʰ Bavarian Infantry Division. General von Rauchenberger joined the Bavarian Leib-Infanterie Regiment as a one year volunteer in 1882. Within a month he was accepted as an offizier-aspirant, went on to officer training in Munich and was commissioned as a sekondeleunant in 1885. He was at regimental duty in various capacities until 1894, when he was posted as a student to the *Kriegsakademie* to train as a staff officer. He graduated and went to the General Staff as a hauptmann, first working in the central staff and then in the Ministry of War at Munich until spring 1901. He then spent fifteen months as a company commander with Bavarian Infantry Regiment 1, before returning to staff duties, including, after promotion to major, a period with the Prussian Great General Staff in Berlin. In October 1907 he became a battalion commander in Bavarian Infantry Regiment 21. Promoted oberstleutnant while on the staff in 1908, he was posted a second time to the Great General Staff and, having been promoted oberst, took command of Bavarian Infantry Regiment 21 in Fürth in October 1911. In 1913 he moved directly to command 1 Bavarian Infantry Brigade and was promoted generalmajor in early 1914. On the outbreak of war, he fought in Lorraine with 1ˢᵗ Bavarian Infantry Division and was wounded on 20 August. Recovered from his wounds, in March 1915 he was given command of Bavarian 20 Infantry Brigade, 10ᵗʰ Bavarian Infantry Division in Artois; after a spell of positional warfare, he took part in the autumn battles in Artois. For two periods of 1915 he was given temporary command of Bavarian 2ⁿᵈ Infantry Division, so was an obvious choice for command of the newly raised 14ᵗʰ Bavarian Infantry Division in summer 1916, with which he fought at Verdun and on the Somme in late 1916. Promoted generalleutnant in January 1917, he received much of the blame for the set back at Point du Jour in April 1917, but his division then fought with distinction later in the year on the Eastern Front, where he was awarded the Pour le Mérite near Riga in September and was also made a Knight of the Military Max Josef Order. Back in the west, Rauchenberger performed well during the spring offensives and was appointed to command 6th Bavarian Infantry Division in May 1918. He also distinguished himself in the defensive battles between St Quentin and Cambrai in autumn that year, for which he was awarded the Oak Leaf to his Pour le Mérite in October 1918. After the war he briefly commanded II Bavarian Corps in Würzburg, but soon tendered his resignation, which was accepted in June 1919 and he left the army. He then became an author of books on military subjects and, on Tannenberg Day 1939, became an honorary general der infanterie.

Generalleutnant Roderich Felix August von Schoeler (1862 - 1935) 11th Infantry Division. General von Schoeler joined Footguard Regiment 4 as a fähnrich in 1879. That autumn he was commissioned as a sekondleutnant, becoming a senior lieutenant after several years at regimental duty in 1888. From October 1890 to July 1893 Schoeler studied at the Prussian *Kriegsakademie*, returning afterwards to his regiment as a company commander. In 1899 he was posted to the Ministry of War, where he was promoted major and remained until early 1905, when he assumed command of 3rd Battalion Grenadier Regiment 89 in Schwerin. The following year he became an oberstleutnant and then was posed to Berlin as a district commander in 1907, in which capacity he was promoted oberst in September 1909. The following January he left to command Footguard Regiment 2 until September 1912 when, on promotion to generalmajor, he took command of 2 Guards Infantry Brigade, but only briefly; he was back in the Ministry of War by July 1913. At the outbreak of war he was made General Intendant of the Field Army and carried out these duties until April 1916, when he was posted to the Eastern Front as commander 20th Infantry Division and promoted to generalleutnant in June of that year. Once more this period of command was short, as he was recalled to become Deputy Minister of War. However, in December 1916 he was posted as commander 11th Infantry Division, a role he carried out during the Battle of Arras. Despite the severe casualties suffered by his division in April 1917, the following month he was given command of VIII Corps. That autumn he was deployed to the Armeeabteilung B down by the Swiss border, but the following year he came under command of Seventh Army, leading attacks in the Aisne - Oise area. By June his corps had been redeployed north to Noyon and, after several successful, if limited, attacks, he was awarded the Pour le Mérite in June. He participated in the final battles of the war in the Antwerp - Meuse position and moved his formations back to Germany after the Armistice. Post war he served briefly in Kassel, commanding Reichswehr Group Command 2, but he resigned in September 1920 and left the army in the rank of general der infanterie.

General der Infanterie Franz Ludwig Freiherr von Soden (1856 - 1945) VII Reserve Corps. General von Soden joined the élite Württemberg formation, Grenadier Regiment 119, as a one year volunteer in 1873. The following January he became a fahnenjunker and was commissioned as a sekondeleutnant in February 1875. From 1880 - 1883 he studied at the Prussian *Kriegsakademie,* then he went as a senior lieutenant to Grenadier Regiment 123 in October 1883, but as early as July the following year he was recalled and from 1 May 1886 he was posted to the Great General Staff in Berlin, where he was promoted hauptmann in 1888. He then spent two years on the staff of X Corps and 19th Infantry Division, before spending the period September 1891 - April 1893 as a company commander with Grenadier Regiment 119. He was then appointed successively Ia (chief of staff) to 26th Infantry Division and XIII (Royal Württemberg) Corps. He then took command of 1st Battalion Infantry Regiment 83 in Kassel in 1898. He became an oberstleutnant in April 1900 and was posted as chief of staff to X Corps until February 1903, when he was appointed commander Infantry Regiment 125. He remained in that appointment until May 1906, when he became commander 51 Infantry Brigade and was promoted generalmajor that September. In January 1910 he was promoted generalleutnant and commander 26th Infantry Division until retirement in March 1911. Recalled at the outbreak of war, he was given command of 26th Reserve Division, part of XIV Reserve Corps. After fighting in the Vosges, the corps was moved north to the Somme, where it remained for the next two years and played a significant part in the Battle of the Somme in the summer and autumn of 1916. Soden led his division with great distinction and energy, despite his sixty years. His reinforced division famously smashed the attacks of the British VIII and X Corps on 1 July 1916. Soden was promoted general der infanterie and given command of VII Reserve Corps in Champagne. This was another successful period of command and Soden received the Pour le Mérite in July 1917. From August to November 1917 he commanded XI Corps, then was posted to V Reserve Corps, where he was simultaneously in overall command of Meuse Group (East) at Verdun. He remained in that area until the Armistice, leaving the army in January 1919. Post war he wrote several books about formations of the Army of Württemberg.

Generalmajor Carl Franz Hermann von Wichmann (1860 - 1922) 56th Infantry Division. General von Wichmann was the son of a Prussian general der kavallerie, who joined Infantry Regiment 26 as a fähnrich in 1880. He became a sekondeleutnant in 1881 and then served at regimental duty until 1889, when he was posted to be adjutant 50 Infantry Brigade for four years. He was then promoted hauptmann and went to Grenadier Regiment 7 as a company commander. This was followed by four years as adjutant Headquarters V Corps. In April 1903 he returned to regimental duty as a battalion commander with Grenadier Regiment 1 in Königsberg (modern Kaliningrad), where he was promoted oberstleutnant in 1907. He then spent three years on the staff of Infantry Regiment 51 in Breslau (modern Wroclaw), before commanding Fusilier Regiment 34 in Stettin (modern Szczecin) from March 1911 to July 1913. He then transferred to the Imperial Navy, where he was Inspector of the Marine Infantry and then commandant of Kiel, where he was promoted generalmajor. He spent the first three months of the war commanding the Marine Infantry Brigade, but returned to the

Prussian army in December 1914 and was given command of 81 Infantry Brigade, 17th Reserve Division, which was deployed near Roye in the south of the Somme region. After a year in that sector and participation in battles to the south near Soissons in 1915, he found himself moved north into Artois and commanded Operation Hamburg, an assault on the *Gießler Höhe*, just north of Vimy Ridge, on 21 February 1916. This successful assault was intended as a diversion for the opening of the Verdun offensive; but it also gained useful ground and places of observation for the German army. Following this operation, Wichmann was given command of, first, 44th Reserve Division then, in June 1916, 56th Infantry Division at Verdun. His 1916 period of command earned him the Order of the Red Eagle Second Class with Oak Leaves and Swords and he was promoted generalleutnant at the end of the year in time for the Battle of Arras. He remained in command of 56th Infantry Division until July 1918 and then left the army at his own request in October 1918.

Generalleutnant Theodor Karl Wilhelm von Wundt (1858 - 1929) 18th Reserve Division. General von Wundt had the same first name as his father, who was a generalleutnant and Minister of War in Württemberg. In 1875 he joined Infantry Regiment 125 in Stuttgart as a one year volunteer. The following year he became a fähnrich and in 1877 was commissioned as a sekondeleutnant. After further regimental duty, he attended the Prussian *Kriegsakademie* in Berlin for three years from October 1881. In 1888 he became adjutant of 52 Infantry Brigade in Ludwigsburg then, after a tour of duty with Infantry Regiment 122 in Gmünd, in 1891 he was seconded to the Great General Staff for a year in Berlin. Having been promoted hauptmann, he then became a company commander in Infantry Regiment 125. After this he was posted for a tour of duty with the Great General Staff and was promoted major in December 1897. The following year he was sent to the staff of 36th Infantry Division in Danzig then, in early 1900, he was appointed to be a battalion commander with Infantry Regiment 122. This was followed by another period of command in 1903 - 1904 with Infantry Regiment 120 in Ulm. At the end of that tour he was promoted oberstleutnant and moved to the staff of Grenadier Regiment 123. He was knighted by the King of Württemberg in February 1906; the following October he took command of Infantry Regiment 124 and was promoted oberst. In March 1911 he relinquished command of the regiment and was appointed commander 59 Infantry Brigade in Metz and promoted generalmajor. His career appeared to be over when he handed over command in March 1913 and he was placed on the retired list with the honorary rank of generalleutnant. On the outbreak of war, he was recalled to duty and given command of 51 Reserve Infantry Brigade, 26th Reserve Division. For two years from September 1914 he served on the Somme in the sector running from Serre to Ovillers on the Albert-Bapaume road. After the success of this period of command, he was appointed commander of 18th Reserve Division, leading it during the Battle of Arras, in positional warfare in Artois and on the Flanders front. He retired in October 1917 and was awarded the Order of the Red Eagle Second Class with Swords for his service as a divisional commander. General von Wundt was an enthusiastic and highly accomplished mountaineer with numerous first ascents to his credit, especially in the Dolomites, but also in the Alps and the Tatra Mountains. He and his English wife, Maud Walters, climbed the Matterhorn during their honeymoon in 1894. He was a pioneering mountain photographer who also wrote books, novels and plays with a mountaineering theme, but they were not conspicuously successful.

French

General François Paul Anthoine (1860 - 1944) Fourth Army. General Anthoine was commissioned into the artillery as a sous-lieutenant 1881, was promoted lieutenant in 1883 and captain in 1889, having served in Tonkin from 1885 - 1887. By 1908 he was a colonel and he worked in the central staff from 1911, becoming a brigadier general in 1913. Once war broke out he was promoted rapidly. Initially he served as chief of staff of Second Army under General de Castelnau, but he was given command of 20th Infantry Division in October 1914 and served in that capacity for one year before becoming commander of X Corps in September 1915. In March 1917, just prior to the Nivelle Offensive, he was given command of Fourth Army, followed by that of First Army in mid June 1917. He led this army during the Third Battle of Ypres and was made chief of staff of all the armies of the north and northeast in December 1917. He served in that capacity until July 1918, when he was sacked (some authorities state he was made a scapegoat) for reverses during the Third Battle of the Aisne. He was made inspector of rear area works and carried out several other relatively mundane duties until he was retired in 1921.

General Joseph Alfred Micheler (1861 - 1931) French Reserve Army Group. General Micheler entered St Cyr in October 1880 and was commissioned as a sous-lieutenant in 1882; he was promoted lieutenant in 1886, captain in 1891, major in 1901 and lieutenant colonel in 1909. In 1912 he was promoted colonel and began the war as chief of staff VI Corps. He was promoted brigadier general in October 1914 and moved in January 1915 to be chief of staff First Army. The following August he became commander 53rd Infantry Division and in March 1916 commander XXXVIII Corps. Only ten days later he was placed in command of Tenth Army and led it during the Battle of the Somme. His meteoric rise continued when, prior to the Battle of the Aisne in spring 1917, he was placed at the head of the Reserve Army Group, poised to exploit the expected breakthrough. Micheler had grave doubts about the viability of the Nivelle Offensive and conspired against Nivelle, especially when the offensive faltered. He survived subsequent attempts to lay part of the blame for the failure of the offensive on him, but he did revert to army command at the head of Fifth Army. In June 1918 General Micheler was sacked, along with General Duchêne, commander Sixth Army, when the two of them failed to follow Pétain's instructions to defend in depth along the Aisne and their armies were swept all the way to the Marne by a massive German assault. He played no further part in the war. Micheler's honours included the Croix de Guerre with three palms and he was made a Commander of the Legion of Honour in 1916.

Bibliography

Unpublished Sources

Hauptstaatsarchiv Stuttgart

M411 Bd 695 Grenadier Regiment 123 Anlagen Apr 17 *Bericht über die Tätigkeit des Regts. am 11. April 1917.*

M411 Bd 909 Infantry Regiment 124 Anlagen Apr 17 *27. Inf. Div. Ia Nr. 1060 op. vom 10.4.17.*

M411 Bd 909 Infantry Regiment 124 Anlagen Apr 17 *BERICHT Über den Angriff der Engländer gegen den Abschnitt C (I.R. 124 im Verbande der 27. I.D.) östlich Bullecourt am 11.4.17.* p 2.

M411 Bd 910 Infantry Regiment 124 Anlagen May 17 *27. Inf. Div. Divisions-Befehl vom 3.5.17.*

M411 Bd 910 Infantry Regiment 124 Anlagen May 17 *27. Inf. Div.1a Nr. 1484 op. geheim. Divisions-Befehl zur Wegnahme des Engländernests im Komp-Abschnitt C1 vom 5.5.17.*

M411 Bd 909 Infantry Regiment 124 Anlagen Apr 17 27. Inf. Div. Ia Nr. 1093 op. *vom 12.4.17.*

M411 Bd 909 Infantry Regiment 124 Anlagen Apr 17 27. Inf. Div. Ia Nr. 1200.

M411 Bd 909 Infantry Regiment 124 Anlagen Apr 17. *Kampferfahrung beim Angriff der Engländer bei Bullecourt am 11.4.17.*

Kriegsarchiv Munich

HGr Rupprecht Bd 122 *AOK 6 No 239 7/4 Beurteilung der Lage.*

HGr. Rupprecht Bd. 93 *A.O.K. 6 541 11/4 gruppe vimy meldet an heeresgruppe kr Rupprecht – voraussichtliche verluste in den kaempfen vom 9/4 17.*

HGr Rupprecht Bd 93 B.8. Inf. Brigade an die K.B.14. Infant. Division Nr. 1060/I *Betreff: Kampferfahrungen Bei Arras* 14.4.17.

HGr Rupprecht Bd 93 Oberkommando Ia/No. 2857 geh. H.Qu. den 21 April 1917 an OHL.

A.O.K. 6 Bd 433 A.O.K. 6. B. Nr. 8950 1.4.17.

A.O.K. 6 Bd 433 A.O.K. 6. B. Nr. 8961 2.4.17.

1 R. Korps *Betreff: Vorbereitungen für die Abwehrschlacht* General-Kommando I.

16. Inf. Div. Bd. 4 Bayer 16. Infanterie-Division Ia,. No. 1767 *Wochenbericht für die Zeit vom 29. März 1917 – 5. April 1917* Division.St.Qu., den 5. April 17.

Bayer. Res. Korps Abteilung Ia No. 13 720 K.H.Qu., 21.3.1917.

1 Res Division Bd 20 79. RESERVE-DIVISION *Nachrichtenblatt vom 6.4.1917* D.St.Qu., den 7.4.1917.

1. Res. Div. Bd 21 *Divisionsbefehle 9.4.17.*

1 Res Division Bd 21 14. bayer.Inf.Division *Tagesmeldung vom 9.4.1917* 9.4.1917

1 R.I.B. Bd 37 General-Kommando I. Bayer.Res.Korps Abteilung Chef No. 14 326 K.H.Qu., 31.3.1917.

1 R.I.B. Bd 30: Bayer.Res.Inf.Regt. Nr. 3 *Gefechtsbericht über die Kämpfe am 9. und 10. April 1917.*

OP 38887 1 Res.Inf.Brigade Nr. 9340 *Gefechtsbericht über die Ereignisse am 9., 10. und 11. April 1917.* Brig.St.Qu., 6.6.17.

R.I.R. 3 Bd. 3 Nr 5154 Bayer.Res.Inf.Regt. Nr. 3 6.4.1917 5.30 abds.

Pi. Btl. 17 Bd 7 Gruppe Vimy Abt Ia /Art No. 14 553 K.H.Qu., den 3.4.17.

R.Pi.Kp. 1 Bd. 5 Gruppe Vimy Korpstagesbefehl H.Qu., Ostersonntag 1917.

HS 2020 *Erlebnisbericht: Oberleutnant Henigst* 20.7.1926

Published Works (German: author known)

Appel Dr. Friedrich *Das Reserve-Infanterie-Regt. Nr. 205 im Weltkrieg* Berlin 1937

Auenmüller Oberst a.D. Leo *Das Kgl. Sächs. 8 Infanterie-Regiment 'Prinz Johann Georg' Nr. 107 während des Weltkrieges 1914-1918* Desden 1928

Bachelin Major a.D. Eduard *Das Reserve-Infanterie-Regiment Nr. 111 im Weltkrieg 1914 bis 1918* Karlsruhe 1930

Bechtle Hauptmann d.R. Richard *Die Ulmer Grenadiere an der Westfront: Geschichte des Grenadier-Regiments König Karl (5. Württ.) Nr. 123 im Weltkrieg 1914 - 1918* Stuttgart 1920

Behrmann Franz & Brandt Archivrat Walther *Die Osterschlacht bei Arras 1917 I. & II. Teil* Oldenburg 1929

Beltz Major a.D. Oskar *Das Infanterie-Regiment Herzog von Holstein (Holst.) Nr. 85 im Weltkriege* Heide i. Holst. 1925

Benary Oberstleutnant a.D *Das Ehrenbuch der Deutschen Feldartillerie* Berlin 1933

Bene Leutnant d.Res a.D. Otto *Das Lauenburgische Feldartillerie-Regiment Nr. 45* Oldenburg 1923

Berr Hauptmann der Reichswehr Günther *Das Königlich-Preußische Mansfelder Feldartillerie-Regiment Nr. 75 im Weltkriege 1914/18* Gräfenhainichen 1934

Blankenstein Oberleutnant a.D. Archivrat Dr. *Geschichte des Reserve-Infanterie-Regiments Nr. 92 im Weltkriege 1914-1918* Osnabrück 1934

Bose Königl. Preuß. Major a.D. Thilo von *Das Kaiser Alexander Garde-Grenadier-Regiment Nr. 1 im Weltkriege 1914-1918* Zeulenroda 1932

Bossert Hauptmann Hans *Wir 143er. Das 4. Unter-Elsässische Infanterie-Regiment Nr. 143 im Frieden und im Weltkrieg Band I* Berlin 1935

Böttger Hptm Karl, Schönberg Oberst a.D. Kurt v., Wülsingen Generalmajor a.D. Georg Bock v. & Melzer Oblt. Walter *Das Kgl. Sächs. 7. Infanterie-Regiment 'König Georg' Nr. 106* Dresden 1927

Brandis Hauptmann a.D. Cordt v. *Die vom Douaumont: Das Ruppiner Regiment 24 im Weltkrieg* Berlin 1930

Braun Major a.D. Heinrich *Das K.B. 25. Infanterie-Regiment* Munich 1926

Brederlow Generalmajor a.D. Tido von *Geschichte des 1. Garde-Reserve-Regiments* Berlin 1929

Buttmann Major a.D. *Kriegsgeschichte des Königlich Preußischen 6. Thüringischen Infanterie-Regiments Nr. 95 1914-1918* Zeulenroda 1935

Christian Leutnant d. Res. Karl *Das Heldenbuch vom Infanterie-Regiment 418* Frankfurt am Main 1935

Delbanco Paul *Das Infanterie-Regiment Nr. 359* Oldenburg 1922

Dellmensingen Königl. Bayer. General der Artillerie z.D. & Feeser Generalmajor a.D. Friedrichfranz *Das Bayernbuch vom Weltkriege 1914-1918 II. Band* Stuttgart 1930

Demmler Major a.D. Ernst, Wucher Oberstleutnant a.D. Karl Ritter von & Leupold Generalmajor a.D. Ludwig *Das K.B. Reserve-Infanterie-Regiment 12* Munich 1934

Deutelmoser Major a.D. Adolf *Die 27. Infanterie-Division im Weltkrieg 1914-18* Stuttgart 1925

Dieterich Generalleutnant a.D. *Die 79. Reserve-Division in der Schlacht auf der Vimy-Höhe/April 1917* Magdeburg 1917

Doerstling Oberstleutnant a.D. *Kriegsgeschichte des Königlich Preußischen Infanterie-Regiments Graf Tauentzien v. Wittenberg (3. Brandenb.) Nr. 20* Zeulenroda 1933

Eisenhart Rothe General der Infanterie a.D. Ernst v. & Lezius Kgl. Preuß. Leutnant d. Ldw. I a.D. *Das Ehrenbuch der Garde: Die preußische Garde im Weltkriege 1914-1919 II. Band* Berlin und Stuttgart

Ettighoffer P.C. *Eine Armee meutert: Frankreichs Schicksalstunde 1917* Gütersloh 1937

Fischer Hauptmann d.R. *Das Reserve-Infanterie-Regiment Nr. 262 1914-1918* Zeulenroda 1936

Foerster Oberstleutnant a.D. Wolfgang & Greiner Hauptmann a.D. Helmuth *Wir Kämpfer im Weltkrieg: Selbstzeugnisse deutscher Frontsoldaten* Berlin 1935

Förster Sigismund von *Das Reserve-Infanterie-Regiment Nr. 31* Oldenburg 1921

Forstner Major a.D. Kurt Freiherr von *Das Königlich-Preußische Reserve-Infanterie-Regiment Nr. 15 2. Band* Zeulenroda 1931

Freund Leutnant d.R. a.D. Hans *Geschichte des Infanterie-Regiments Prinz Carl (4. Großh. Hess.) Nr. 118 im Weltkrieg* Groß-Gerau 1930

Fröhling Adolf *Infanterie-Regiment Nr. 396* Zeulenroda 1931

Gebert Oberleutnant d.R. Oberstudienrat Dr. W. *Geschichte des Infanterie-Regiments Nr. 371, sowie der Brigade-Ersatz-Bataillone Nr. 44, 76, 83* Gotha

Gemmingen-Guttenberg-Fürfeld Oberst Freiherr v. *Das Grenadier-Regiment Königen Olga (1. Württ.) Nr. 119 im Weltkrieg 1914-1918* Stuttgart 1927

Gerok Hauptmann *Das 2.württ. Feldartillerie-Reg. Nr 29 'Prinzregent Luitpold von Bayern' im Weltkrieg 1914-1918* Stuttgart 1921

Gerth Leutnant d. Res. Max *Geschichte des Infanterie-Regiments 395* 1933

Götz Major a.D. August *Das K.B. 8. Infanterie-Regiment Großherzog Friedrich II. von Baden* Munich 1926

Gropp Offizier-Stellvertreter Hugo *Hanseaten im Kampf: Erlebnisse bei dem Res.-Inf.-Rgt. 76 im Weltkriege 1914/18* Hamburg 1934

Guttenberg Hptm. d.L. a.D. Dr Erich Frh. v. & Meyer-Erlach Hptm d.R. a.D. Dr Georg *Das Königlich Bayerische Reserve-Feldartillerie-Regiment Nr. 5* Munich 1938

Haleck Oberleutnant Fritz *Das Reserve-Infanterie-Regiment Nr. 208* Oldenburg 1922

Hansch Oberleutnant Johannes & Weidling Leutnant Dr. Fritz *Das Colbergsche Grenadier-Regiment Graf Gneisenau (2. Pommersches) Nr. 9 im Weltkriege 1914-1918* Oldenburg 1929

Hartmann Hauptmann Alexander von *Das Infanterie-Regiment Großherzog von Sachsen (5. Thüringisches) Nr 94 im Weltkrieg* Berlin 1921

Haupt Oberleutnant a.D. Dr. Karl *Das K.B. 15. Infanterie-Regiment 'König Friedrich August von Sachsen'* Munich 1922

Heinicke Lt. d.Res. a.D. Karl & Bethge Lt. d.Res. a.D. Bruno *Das Reserve-Infanterie-Regiment Nr. 263 in Ost und West* Oldenburg 1926

Hennig Leutnant d. Res. Otto *Das Reserve-Infanterie-Regiment Nr. 235 im Weltkriege* Oldenburg 1931

Herkenrath Oberleutnant d. Res. a.D. Dr. August *Das Württembergische Reserve-Inf.-Regiment Nr. 247 im Weltkrieg 1914-1918* Stuttgart 1923

Hillebrand Leutnant d. Res. & Krauß Leutnant d. Res. *Königlich Preußisches Reserve-Infanterie-Regiment Nr. 29 im Weltkriege 1914/1918* Berlin 1933

Hindenburg Generalfeldmarschall von *Aus meinem Leben* Leipzig 1934

Hottenroth Oberst a.D. Johann Edmund *Sachsen in großer Zeit: Gemeinverständliche sächsische Kriegsgeschichte und vaterländisches Gedenkwerk des Weltkrieges Band I* Leipzig 1920

Hülsemann Oberstleutnant a.D *Geschichte des Infanterie-Regiments von Manstein (Schleswigsches) Nr. 84 1914-1918*

Hüttmann Oberst Adolf &Krüger Oberleutnant a.D. Friedrich Wilhelm *Das Infanterie-Regiment von Lützow (1.Rhein.) Nr. 25 im Weltkriege 1914 - 1918* Berlin 1929

Isenberg Major a.D. *Das Königs-Infanterie-Regiment (6. Lothring.) Nr. 145 im Großen Kriege 1914-1918 Band I.* Berlin 1922

Jäger Oberstleutnant a.D. Hans *Das K.B. 19. Infanterie-Regiment König Viktor Emanuel III. von Italien* Munich 1930

Jordan Generalmajor a.D. von, Marcard Oberst a.D. von & Drüner Major d.R. a.D. Dr. Hans *Das Reserve-Infanterie-Regiment Nr. 81 im Weltkrieg* Osnabrück 1933

Jürgensen Leutnant d.R. Dr. Wilhelm *Das Füsilier-Regiment 'Königin' Nr. 86 im Weltkriege* Oldenburg 1925

Kabisch Ernst *Das Volksbuch vom Weltkrieg* Stuttgart 1931

Kellinghusen Hauptmann d. Res. *Kriegserinnerungen* Bergedorf 1933

Klähn Leutnant d. Res. Friedrich *Geschichte des Reserve-Infanterie-Regiments Nr. 86 im Weltkriege* Oldenburg 1925

Knieling Lutz & Bölsche Arnold *Reserve Infantry Regiment 234: Ein Querschnitt durch Deutschlands Schicksalringen* Zeulenroda 1931

Kohl Leutnant d. Res. a.D. Hermann *Mit Hurra in den Tod! Kriegserlebnisse eines Frontsoldaten* Stuttgart 1932

Kuhl General d. Inf. a.D. Hermann von *Der Weltkrieg 1914-1918 Band II* Berlin 1929

Kümmel Leutnant d. Res. a.D. Adolf *Res. Inf. Regt.Nr. 91 im Weltkriege 1914-1918* Oldenburg 1926

Liedgens Hauptmann d.R. a.D. Landgerichtsdirektor Karl *Das Reserve Infanterie Regiment 65 im Weltkrieg 1914-1918* Cologne 1938

Loebell Hauptmann Egon von *Mit dem 3. Garde-Regiment z.F. im Weltkriege 1914/8: Tagebuch des Hauptmann v. Loebell* Berlin 1920

Loßberg General der Infanterie Fritz v. *Meine Tätigkeit im Weltkriege 1914-1918* Berlin 1939

Ludendorff Erich *Meine Kriegserinnerungen 1914-1918* Berlin 1919

Machenhauer Oberst a.D. *Das Metzer Infanterie-Regiment Nr. 98* Oldenburg 1923

Makoben Ernst *Geschichte des Reserve-Infanterie-Regiments Nr. 212 im Weltkriege 1914 - 1918* Oldenburg 1933

Mayer Hauptmann d.L. Arthur & Görtz Kriegsfreiwilliger Joseph *Das Reserve-Infanterie-Regiment Nr. 236 im Weltkriege* Zeulenroda 1937

Meier-Gesees Karl *Vater Wills Kriegstagebuch* Bayreuth 1931

Meißner Leutnant d.R & Zezulle Oberleutnant *Das Königlich Preußische Reserve-Infanterie-Rgt. Nr. 37 im Weltkriege 1914/1918* Berlin 1933

Möller Hanns *Königlich Preußisches Reserve-Infanterie-Regiment Nr. 78 im Weltkrieg 1914/1918* Berlin 1937

Monse Hauptmann a.D. Rudolf *Das 4. Kgl. Sächs. Infanterie-Regiment Nr. 103* Dresden 1930

Moser General Otto von *Feldzugs-aufzeichnungen als Brigade-Divisionskommandeur und als kommandierender General 1914-1918* Stuttgart 1923

Moser Generalleutnant Otto von *Die Württemberger im Weltkriege* Stuttgart 1928

Moßdorf Major a.D. Werner & Gallwitz Hauptmann Werner v. *Geschichte des 5. Badischen Feldartillerieregiments Nr. 76 1914 - 1918* Berlin 1930

Mücke Kgl. Preuß. Rittmeister a.D. *Das Großherzoglich Badische Infanterie-Regiment Nr. 185* Oldenburg 1922

Müller-Loebnitz Oberstleutnant a.D. Wilhelm *Die Badener im Weltkrieg 1914/1918* Karlsruhe 1935

Mülmann Oberst a.D. v. & Mohs Oberleutnant a.D. *Geschichte des Lehr-Infanterie-Regiments und seiner Stammformationen* Zeulenroda 1935

Nollau Oberstleutnant a.D. Herbert *Geschichte des Königlich Preußischen 4. Niederschlesischen Infanterie-Regiments Nr. 51* Berlin 1931

Peters Leutnant d.R. a.D. Erich *Das Reserve-Infanterie-Regiment Nr. 28 im Weltkrieg 1914-1918* Berlin 1927

Piedmont Major a.D. Claus, Pieper Leutnant a.D Hugo & Krall Oberstleutnant a.D. Paul *Geschichte des 5. Rheinischen Infanterie-Regiments Nr. 65 während des Weltkrieges 1914-1918* Oldenburg 1927

Poland Hauptmann a.D. Franz Theodor *Das Kgl. Sächs. Reserve-Infanterie-Regiment Nr. 103* Dresden 1922

Reber Generalmajor a.D. Karl *Das K.B. 21. Infanterie-Regiment Großherzog Friedrich Franz IV. von Mecklenburg-Schwerin* Munich 1929

Reinhardt Generalleutnant a.D. Ernst *Das Württembergische Reserve-Inf.-Regiment Nr. 248 im Weltkrieg 1914-1918* Stuttgart 1924

Reinhardt Generalleutnant a.D. Ernst *Die 54. (Württembergische) Reserve Division im Weltkriege 1914-18* Stuttgart 1934

Reymann Major a.D. Martin *Das Infanterie-Regiment von Alvensleben (6. Brandenbg.) Nr. 52 im Weltkriege 1914/1918* Berlin 1923

Rhein Major a.D. Ernst, Schünemann Oberleutnant d.R. a.D. Wilhelm & Mankopff Oberst a.D. Albrecht *Geschichte des Infanterie-Regiments Nr. 368 und der Brigade-Ersatz-Bataillone Nr. 37, 38, 39 und 40 während des Weltkrieges 1914-1918* Hannover 1930

Riegel Hauptmann a.D. Johann *Das K.B. 17. Infanterie-Regiment Orff* Munich 1927

Ritter Major a.D. Dr. phil. Albrecht *Das K.B. 18. Infanterie-Regiment Prinz Ludwig Ferdinand* Munich 1926

Ritter Oberstleutnant Holger a.D. *Geschichte des Schleswig-Holsteinischen Infanterie-Regiments Nr. 163* Hamburg 1926

Rogge Oberst a.D. Walter *Das Köngl. Preuß. 2. Nassauische Infanterie-Regiment Nr. 88* Berlin 1936

Rohkohl Leutnant d.R. Pastor Lic. theol. Walter *Reserve-Infanterie-Regiment 226: Teil II.* Oldenburg 1926

Rosenberg-Lipinsky Hauptmann Hans-Oskar von *Das Königin Elisabeth Garde-Grenadier-Regiment im Weltkriege 1914-1918* Zeulenroda 1935

Rudorff Oberstleutnant a.D. Franz v. *Das Füsilier-Regiment General Ludendorff (Niederrheinisches) Nr. 39 im Weltkriege 1914-1918* Berlin 1925

Rundstedt Major a.D. Udo von *Das 5. badische Infanterie-Regiment Nr. 113 im Weltkriege 1914-18* Ratzeburg i. Lbg. 1933

Rupprecht Kronprinz von Bayern *In Treue Fest: Mein Kriegstagebuch Zweiter Band* Munich

Rust Mittelschullehrer Fritz *Wir 143er. Das 4. Unter-Elsässische Infanterie-Regiment Nr. 143 im Frieden und im Weltkrieg Band II* Berlin 1938

Schaidler Hauptmann a.D. Otto *Das K.B. 7. Infanterie-Regiment Prinz Leopold* Munich 1922

Schiel Oberleutnant Otto *Das 4. Badische Infanterie-Regiment 'Prinz Wilhelm' Nr. 112 im Weltkrieg* Oldenburg 1927

Schmidt Oberstleutnant a.D. Walther *Das 7. Badische Infanterie-Regiment Nr. 142 im Weltkrieg 1914/18* Freiburg im Breisgau 1927

Schoenfelder Generalmajor a.D. *Das 2. Schlesische Feldartillerie-Regiment Nr. 42* Berlin 1938

Schönfeldt Kgl. Preuß. Major a.D. Ernst von *Das Grenadier-Regiment Prinz Karl von Preußen (2. Brandenburgisches) Nr. 12 im Weltkrieg* Berlin 1924

Schulenburg-Wolfsburg Generalmajor a.D. Graf v.d. *Geschichte des Garde-Füsilier-Regiments* Oldenburg 1926

Schuster Oberst a.D. Hans *Geschichte des Infanterie-Regiments Nr. 369* Oldenburg 1928

Schütz Generalmajor a.D. v. & Hochbaum Leutnant *Das Grenadier-Regiment König Friedrich Wilhelm II (1. Schles.) Nr. 10* Oldenburg 1924

Schwab Oberstleutnant A & Schreyer Hauptmann A *Das neunte württembergische Infanterie-Regiment Nr. 127 im Weltkrieg 1914-1918* Stuttgart 1920

Schwenke Oberstleutnant a.D. Alexander *Geschichte des Reserve-Infanterie-Regiments Nr.19 im Weltkriege 1914-1918* Oldenburg 1926

Selle Oberst a.D. Hans von & Gründel Oberstleutnant a.D. Walter *Das 6. Westpreußische Infanterie-Regiment Nr. 149 im Weltkriege* Berlin 1929

Sievers Leutnant d.R. Adolf *R.I.R. 93 Geschichte eines Regiments im Weltkrieg* Wilster in Holstein 1934

Simon Oberst a.D. *Das Infanterie-Regiment 'Kaiser Wilhelm, König von Preußen' (2. Württemb.) Nr. 120 im Weltkrieg 1914-1918* Stuttgart 1922

Soldan George *Das Infanterie-Regiment Nr. 184* Oldenburg 1920

Speck Justizinspektor William *Das Königlich Preußische Reserve-Infanterie-Regiment 84* Zeulenroda 1937

Staubwasser Generalmajor a.D. Otto *Das K.B. 2. Infanterie-Regiment Kronprinz* Munich 1924

Stosch Oberstleutnant a.D. Albrecht von *Das Garde-Grenadier-Regiment Nr. 5 1897 - 1918* Berlin 1925

Studt Hauptmann d.R. a.D. Dr. Bernhard *Infanterie-Regiment Graf Bose (1.Thüringisches) Nr. 31 im Weltkriege 1914-1918* Berlin 1926

Stühmke General *Das Infanterie-Regiment 'Kaiser Friedrich, König von Preußen' (7. Württ.) Nr. 125 im Weltkrieg 1914-1918* Stuttgart 1923

Sydow Hauptmann a.D. v. *Das Infanterie-Regiment Hamburg (2. Hanseatisches) Nr. 76 im Weltkrieg 1914/18* Oldenburg 1922

Tiessen Studienrat Max *Königlich Preußisches Reserve-Infanterie-Regiment 213: Geschichte eines Flandernregiments* Glückstadt 1937

Trebing Oberleutnant d.R. a.D. Emil *Geschichte des Infanterie-Regiments Nr. 370 und seiner Stammbataillone der Brigade-Ersatz-Bataillone 28, 43 und 79* Berlin 1929

Vogt Oberleutnant a.D & Otto Leutnant d.Res. Dr. *3. Niederschlesisches Infanterie-Regiment Nr. 50 1914-1920* Berlin 1930

Voigt Oblt. d. Res. Hans *Geschichte des Füsilier-Regiments Generalfeldmarschall Prinz Albrecht von Preußen (Hann.) Nr. 73* Berlin 1938

Wohlenberg Oberleutnant d.R. a.D. Rektor Alfred *das Res.-Inf.-Regt. Nr. 77 im Weltkriege 1914-18* Hildesheim 1931

Zipfel Hauptmann a.D. Archivrat Dr. Ernst *Geschichte des Großherzoglich Mecklenburgischen Grenadier-Regiments Nr. 89* Schwerin 1932

Zipfel und Albrecht Archiväte Dr. *Geschichte des Infanterie-Regiments Bremen (1. Hanseatisches) Nr. 75* Bremen 1934

Published Works (German: author unknown)

Reichskriegsministerium *Der Weltkrieg 1914 bis 1918 Zwölfter Band Die Kriegführung im Frühjahr 1917* Berlin 1939 [GOH]

Mitglieder des Vereins der Offiziere, Sanitätsoffiziere und Beamten *Das K.B. 12. Infanterie-Regiment Prinz Arnulf* Munich 1929

Offizieren des Regiments *Das K.B. 14. Infanterie-Regiment Hartmann* Munich 1931

Das Füsilier-Regiment Prinz Heinrich von Preußen (Brandenburgisches) Nr. 35 im Weltkriege Berlin 1929

Das K.B. 23. Feldartillerie-Regiment Munich 1923

Feldzugsteilnehmer *Geschichte des Infanterie-Regiments Generalfeldmarschall Prinz Friedrich Karl von Preußen (8. Brandenburg.) Nr. 64 während des Krieges 1914/18* Berlin 1929

Verein der Offiziere *Geschichte des 6. Badischen Infanterie-Regiments Kaiser Friedrich III. Nr.114 im Weltkrieg 1914 bis 1918* Zeulenroda 1932

Offizierskameradschaft *Das 8. Lothringische Infanterie-Regiment Nr. 159 im Frieden und im Weltkrieg* Berlin 1935

Mitkämpfer *Geschichte des 4. Hannoverschen Infanterie-Regiments Nr. 164 und seines Stammtruppenteils des 2. Königlich Hannoverschen Regiments* Kassel 1932

Regiments-Vereinigung R.I.R. 225 *Kriegsgeschichte des Reserve-Infanterie-Regiments 225 nach Aufzeichnungen aus dem Felde* Görlitz 1928
Reserve Infantry Regiment 261 *Nachrichtenblätter Nr 41* Berlin Jan-Mar 1930; *Nr 45* Berlin Jan-Mar 1931; *Nr. 49* Berlin Jan - Mar 1932

Published Works (English)
Bean CEW *Official History of Australia in the War of 1914-18: Vol IV The AIF in France 1917* Sydney 1933 [AOH]
Ewing John MC *The History of the Ninth (Scottish) Division 1914 - 1919* London 1921
Falls Captain Cyril *Official History of the War: Military Operations France and Belgium, 1917: The German Retreat to the Hindenburg Line and the Battles of Arras* London 1940 [BOH]
Hayes Geoffrey, Iarocco Andrew & Bechthold Mike (Eds) *Vimy Ridge: A Canadian Reassessment* Waterloo Ontario 2007
Jones HA *The War in the Air: Being the Story of the part played in the Great War by the Royal Air Force Vol. III* Oxford 1931
Keech Graham *Bullecourt* Barnsley 1999
Nicholson Colonel GWL *Official History of the Canadian Army in the First World War* Ottawa 1962 [COH]
Pedersen Peter & Roberts Chris *Anzacs on the Western Front* Australian War Memorial 2012
Stewart Lieut-Colonel J & Buchan John *The Fifteenth (Scottish) Division 1914-1919* Edinburgh & London 1926

Published Works (French)
Ministère de la Guerre *Les Armées Françaises dans la Grande Guerre Tome V Premier Volume + Annexes et Cartes* Paris 1931 [FOH]
Miquel Pierre *Le gâchis des généraux: Les erreurs de commandant pendant la guerre de 14-18* Paris 2001
Rolland Denis *La Grève des Tranchées: Les mutineries de 1917* Paris 2005

Index

Vorges, 307

Waltfried, Hauptmann, 116
Wancourt, 33, 87, 102–103, 108, 116–
19, 219, 262, 299
Wangenheim, Hauptmann von, 161
Wasserfall, Maj, 164
Watter, Gen Lt Freiherr von, 227, 308
Wedel, Gen Maj von, 210
Weigel, Hauptmann, 64–5
Weise, Hauptmann, 164
Wenninger, Gen Lt Ritter von, 117
Wenzel, Maj, 214
Wichmann, Gen Maj, 264, 361
Widekind, Hauptmann von, 230–1
Wiener, Neustadt, vi
Willerval, 15, 18–19
Williard Linie, 310–11

Winklerhöhle, 157
Winnterlin, Maj, 336
Winterberg (Plateau de Californie), 128,
130, 136, 310–11, 313, 323, 327, 329–
30, 335, 340
Wolfram, Hauptmann, 165
Wülfingen, Oberstleutnant Bock von,
203
Wunderlich, Hauptmann, 201
Wundt, Gen Lt von, 83, 118, 362
Würth, Hauptmann, 65, 67

Ypres, 301–302, 345

Zickner Hauptmann 22–3
Ziethen, Gen Maj, 327
Zouave Valley, 5